The EAGLE Companion

An Advanced User's Guide

Mitchell Duncan

an Elektor Publication

LEARN | DESIGN | SHARE

This is an Elektor Publication. Elektor is the media brand of
Elektor International Media BV
78 York Street
London W1H 1DP, UK
Phone: (+44) (0)20 7692 8344

First published in the United Kingdom 2015

British Library Cataloguing in Publication Data
Catalogue record for this book is available from the British Library

ISBN 978-1-907920-42-4

Prepress production: Jack Jamar Graphic Design | Maastricht
Printed in the Netherlands by Wilco Printing & Binding | Amersfoort

This book is dedicated to the memory of my brother James.

7 April 2014

Acknowledgments

Firstly, I would like to thank my dear wife Sadhana, who supported my second foray into the world of EAGLE.
Some of my friends and colleagues deserve special thanks for their support and encouragement in this project. These people are: Dr Rob Curtis who prompted my initial undertaking into documenting EAGLE for a wider audience; Alexander Guelfenburg who provided some insight into German-English translations of CadSoft documentation; Richard Hammerl of CadSoft, who answered my many technical questions about the operation of EAGLE V7.0 and Robert Astridge, who provided assistance with proofreading of this book as it progressed.

Mitchell Duncan
February, 2015

Table of Contents

Chapter 1 • An overview of EAGLE Software

Introduction

This book; the 'EAGLE Advanced User Guide' provides the experienced EAGLE user with insight into using some of the more advanced features of EAGLE software. It is not a guide to teach the reader the basic concepts of EAGLE, nor does it discuss the 'how to' of the EAGLE interface and the simpler operations and commands of the software. That is the purpose of the author's previous title 'EAGLE V6.0 Getting Started Guide'.

This book is intended as an enduring document covering the more advanced modules, commands, and functions which make up EAGLE. It is hoped that this book will sit on the desk or the bookshelf of the EAGLE user, and provide a quick, succinct reference to assist with more complex applications and uses of EAGLE – an 'EAGLE User's Companion', if you like.

Any book of this type can not, by its nature, be exhaustive. This is principally due to the fact that EAGLE software is continually evolving as CadSoftincorporates, as part of their normal software development cycle, increased functionality within the application.

At the time of writing, the material in this book covers version 7 of the EAGLE software suite.

What is EAGLE?

EAGLE stands for "Easily Applicable Graphical Layout Editor "; a professional-grade Computer Aided Design (CAD) software package for the design and drafting of electronic circuit schematics; and the design and fabrication of Printed Circuit Boards (PCBs).

EAGLE is a cross-platform application that can be used on Windows, Linux or Mac operating systems, with minimal differences. It uses the default language of the operating system, but can be configured to use other languages including; German, English, Hungarian, and simplified Chinese.

EAGLE allows the user to create schematic and PCB drawings and then output all the required files required to enable a fabricator to manufacture PCBs to the required specifications and tolerances.

The reader should refer to the company's websites for more information at:
www.CadSoftusa.com (English version) or www.CadSoft.de (German version).

Chapter 2 • The EAGLE User Interface

The EAGLE Control Panel

When EAGLE starts and opens the Control Panel (see Figure 2-1), which is the main focus for the high level operations of EAGLE. It is EAGLE's control center, and brings together the management functionality of EAGLE into a single, unified interface.

The Control Panel's presentation is similar to a file manager utility, in that it presents 'panes' to allow the manipulation of files via a familiar 'tree –like' display structure. In general, the right hand panel displays a description, or more details, about the item selected in the left hand pane.

Once the user has selected an item in the left hand pane, that item can be manipulated through a set of menus. For example, a context menu is opened by Right-Clicking, with the mouse, on an entry in the tree view. This allows the user to, depending on the object, carry out a variety of actions (rename, copy, print, open, create new etc.).

The left pane tree structure provides a quick overview of the libraries, Design Rules, User Language programs, Script files, CAM jobs and Projects.

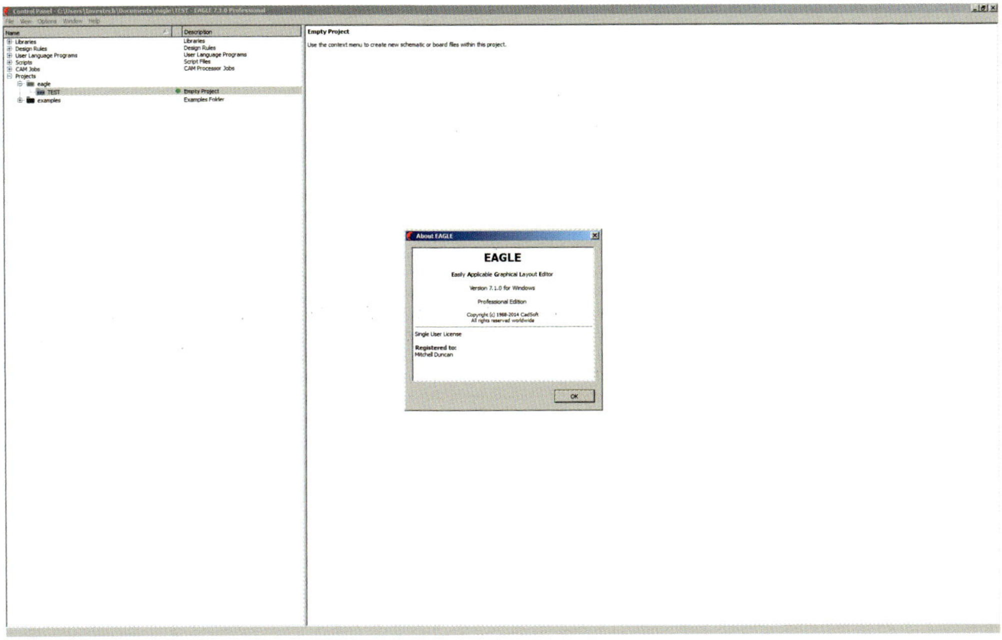

Figure 2-1: EAGLE Control Panel

Library Summary

A Library is a file which contains detailed information and specifications about devices which are available for use in both the Schematic and the PCB Layout Editor modules of EAGLE.

The user can quickly display the contents of a library by expanding any branch within the 'Libraries' tree. By doing this, the user can obtain a quick overview of the available devices within a particular library. Libraries can also be manipulated and edited using commands from within EAGLE.

If the user expands the Libraries entry in the left hand pane of the Control Panel, the user can view the available libraries. In the Description field the user will see a brief description of the contents (as in Figure 2-2). If a library is selected, the user will see more extensive information about the library in the right hand pane of the Control Panel.

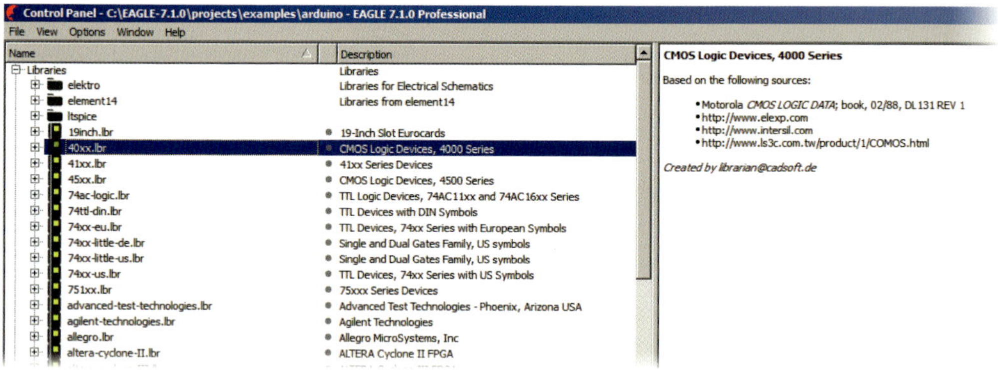

Figure 2-2: Libraries with description

Further, if the user then expands a library entry, the contents will be displayed together with a short description of each element. Devices and Packages are marked with a small icon; as in the left hand pane of Figure 2-3.

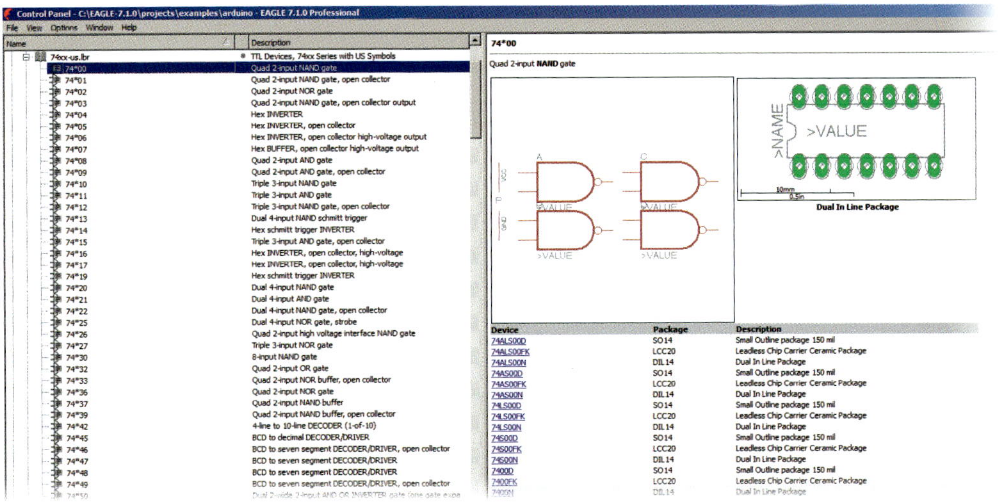

Figure 2-3: Libraries' Devices and packages

If one selects, for example, a Device; the description of the Device and a graphical representation of it appears in the right hand pane. The available Package and technology variants are also listed.

If one clicks onto one of the Package versions, the Package preview shown in the right hand pane will also change accordingly (see Figure 2-4).

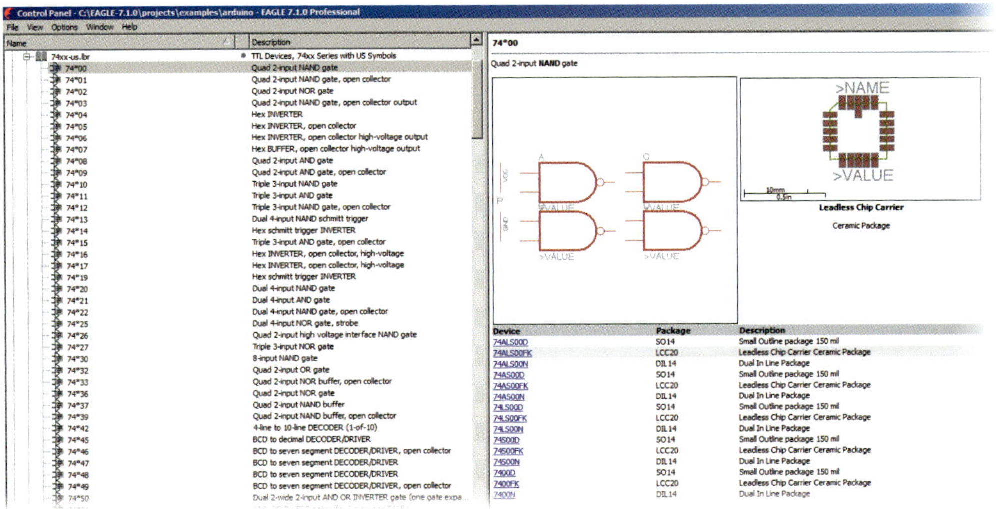

Figure 2-4: Libraries' alternative Device packages

Design Rules

Design Rules are the guidelines which control and determine the output from the system which produce the PC Board design.

A number of parameters can be set to govern the current project. If no data has been provided for the Design Rules (DRC command), EAGLE will itself provide parameters that will be saved in the 'default.dru' file. Further, custom Design Rules can be specified in EAGLE for specific project requirements. These can be saved as data sets in specially named files (**.dru*) and can be seen in the *Design Rules* branch of the tree view (as in Figure 2-5).

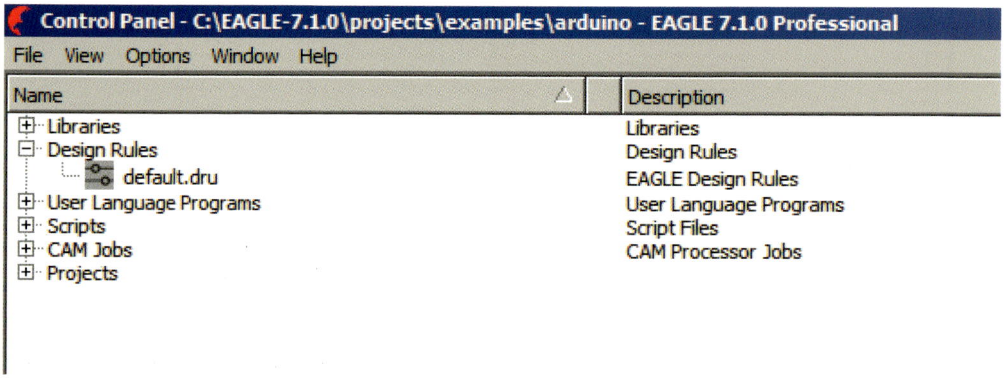

Figure 2-5: Design Rules files

User Language Programs and Scripts

One of the most powerful aspects of EAGLE is its capability to use commands to drive its functionality, behavior and performance. This is done by combining EAGLE commands into User Language programs and Scripts.

The left hand pane of the Control Panel contains entries which show the contents of the User Language programs and Scripts directories. These contain various User Language programs (**.ulp*), script files (**.scr*). By selecting one of these files in the Control Panel, a full description of the file is displayed in the right hand pane.

A Script file is a text file that contains a list of EAGLE commands. These commands draw from the basic EAGLE command set and could be entered from the Command Line in any window. When used within a script file these commands are not pre-checked for syntactic or other errors. When executed the file is run step-by-step, automatically and errors are flagged at runtime.

A User Language program is a text file that contains C-like program instruction code that can access the whole EAGLE command syntax and the data structure, as well as external files. As with script files, errors in a ULP file are flagged at runtime. Of course, one can also write an ULP that creates a script file.

The use of commands, User Language programs and Scripts will be discussed later and comprehensively within this book.

CAM Jobs

The CAM jobs 'tree' contains files which define how the CAM (Computer Aided Manufacturing) Processor generates its output data. These files typically match the output to the production environment, and machines, used by the PCB manufacturer to fabricate your boards.

Projects

The Projects entry is the main entry under the EAGLE Control Panel tree for managing the various stages and elements of a working job.

Under the *Projects* entry various folders are displayed.

A project usually comprises a folder (directory) representing the project's name and its configuration file (named *eagle.epf)*. The project folder usually contains all files belonging to that project e.g. schematic and board file, special library files, script files and etc.

The location of project files is specified in the path setup, within the menu configuration at: *Options ▷ Directories ▷ Projects*.

The project to be edited may be selected in the Projects branch by a single mouse click (**Left-Click**).

A Project may be opened in one of the following ways:

- Open or close a project by double-clicking (2x **Left-Click**) on the entry in the tree view;
- clicking (**Left-Click**) on the entry in the tree view and then pressing the SPACE BAR or ENTER key;
- by using the project marker in the column to the right of the project's name (in the left hand pane of the Control Panel). This marker is a small 'ball' and is colored either grey or green. This marker allows the user to open and close projects. It behaves as follows:
  - Clicking on a grey marker to open a project. The marker is changed to green.
  - Clicking on a green marker closes the current project. Clicking on another grey marker closes the current project and opens the selected new project after closing the old one. This allows the user to quickly switch from one project to another (see Figure 2-6.)

When a project is closed the currently opened Editor Window's settings will be stored in the corresponding project file(in *eagle.epf*), provided that the option *Automatically save project file* is set in the *Options ▷ Backup* menu.

If the project file was created by another EAGLE version than that currently in use, EAGLE will prompt the user for permission to overwrite the file.

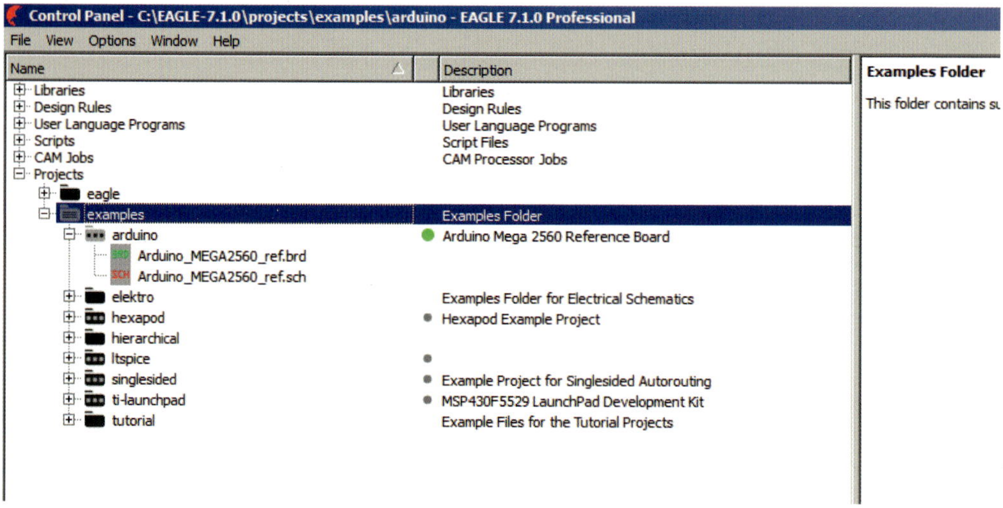

Figure 2-6: managing projects

A new project may be created by **Right-Clicking** onto a folder entry in this branch. A context menu opens, as in Figure 2-7, which permits new files and directories to be created and the individual projects to be managed.

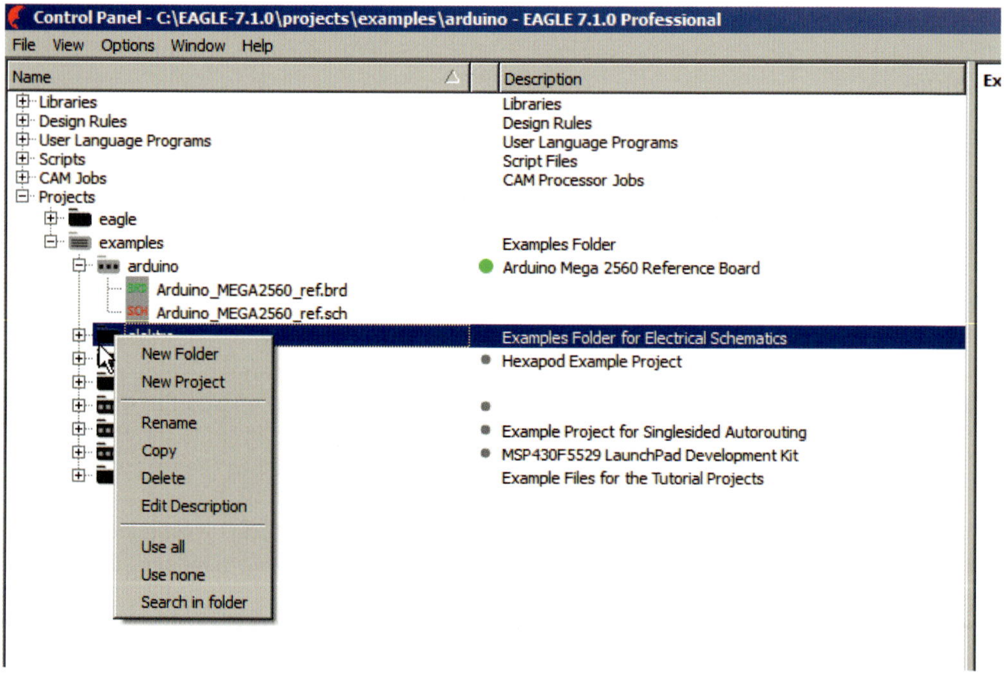

Figure 2-7: Projects management context menu

If the *New ▷ Project* option is selected, then a new folder is created which requires a unique project title to be nominated. After completing this, the project file *eagle.epf* will also then be created automatically

The context menu (displayed in Figure 2-7) also contains the *Edit Description* option. A description of the project can be entered here, which is then displayed in the *Description* box, located in the rightmost column of the left pane of the Control Panel.

A description for schematic and board files may also be created. This is done within the respective editor windows.

A 'preview' of a schematic or board drawing, can be seen simply by clicking on the name of the drawing to be displayed. An example of this can be seen in Figure 2-8, showing the preview of the Aruduino Mega 2560 Reference Design schematic in the right hand pane of the Control Panel.

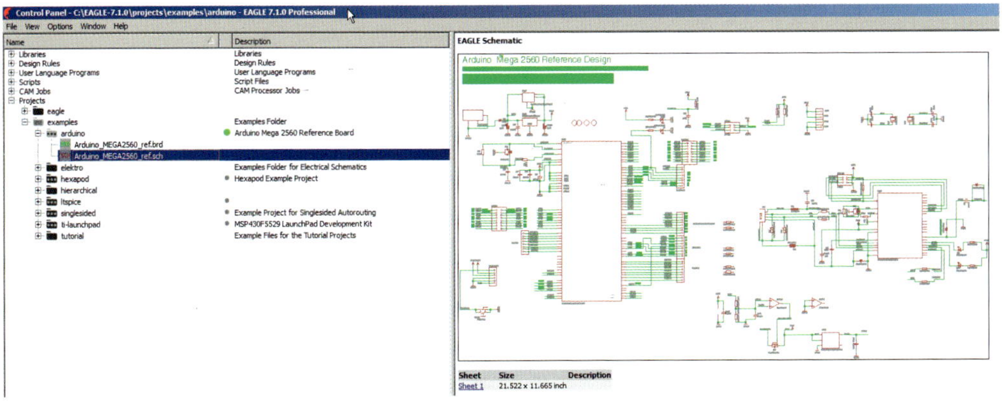

Figure 2-8: Control Panel schematic preview

Menu Bar

The Control Panel Menu Bar (see Figure 2-9) permits various actions to be executed, and settings made, through drop-down menus. These are explained below.

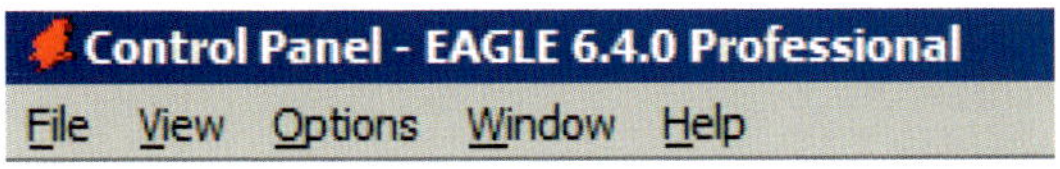

Figure 2-9: Control Panel menu bar

File Menu

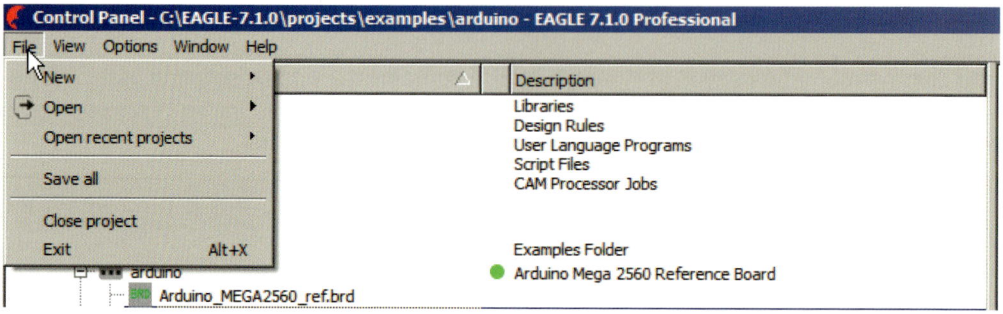

Figure 2-10: Control Panel File menu

The first, left-most item on the Menu Bar is the File Menu. The *File* menu, shown in Figure 2-10 , contains the following items:

New

This menu item allows the user to create a new: Project, Schematic, Board (layout), Library, CAM job, and ULP, script or text files.

The *Project* option creates a new project; initially consisting of a new directory containing the following files:

- schematic diagram and layout;
- project-specific libraries, script files, User Language programs, documentation files etc.
- the *eagle.epf*, file for retaining project-specific settings.

Open

The Open menu item opens an existing file of the types mentioned for the New item above.

Open recent projects

This item lists recently used projects and allows the user to select from them for opening.

Save all

This item forces all changed files to be saved. The current settings for the project are saved in the file *eagle.epf*, and overrides the option setting of: *Automatically save project file* in the menu *Options/Backup*. User-specific settings are saved in the file *eaglerc.usr* (in Windows) or *.eaglerc* (in Linux/Mac).

Close project

This item closes the Project and saves all files and project-specific settings (in the *eagle.epf* file of the current project directory).

Exit

This item terminates the EAGLE program. When EAGLE is started again, the last program status is restored, i.e. the windows and other working environment parameters appear unchanged. If there was no project previously open or loaded, then EAGLE opens at the Control Panel upon re-opening.

The user can also exit EAGLE using the *Alt-X* keystroke shortcut. The current status is also saved when the user leaves EAGLE from within any program in this way. (This can be disabled from the Options ▷ User interface menu if the user deactivates the Pulldown menu option of the Editor windows.)

Opening & Creating Files

There are several ways of opening drawing and library files in EAGLE.

The user can open a particular type of file by using the required menu path, as follows:

File ▷ Open (▷ directory) ▷ Project ▷ *Project Filename*	opens a Project
File ▷ Open ▷ Schematic ▷ select *Schematic Filename*	opens a Schematic drawing
File ▷ Open ▷ Board ▷ select *Board Layout Filename*	opens a Board Layout drawing
File ▷ Open ▷ CAM Job ▷ select *CAM Job Filename*	opens a CAM Job
File ▷ Open ▷ ULP --------------------------------------->	opens a User Language Program File
File ▷ Open ▷ Script --------------------------------------->	opens a command script File
File ▷ Open ▷ Text --------------------------------------->	opens a text file

Alternatively, the user may simply double-click (2x **Left-Click**) onto the required file name in the tree view of EAGLE Control Panel.

If the user wants to create a new file , they would use a similar menu path as above, but use File ▷ New ▷ XXXX ▷ YYYYYname.

For example, to create a new schematic, the user would action:

File ▷ New ▷ Schematic. This will open a schematic with the name untitled.sch in the current project directory.

The user may want to create a schematic diagram straight away in a new project. This done by: **Right-Click** on the Projects entry of the tree view, and select the *New project* option from the context menu. The new project receives a name. Then Right-Click on this entry and select New ▷ Schematic from the context menu. A new schematic opens in this project directory.

NOTE: When actioning the methods above which use a menu to open a file, EAGLE asks the user if they also want to open the complementary drawing i.e. when opening a schematic drawing, EAGLE will ask if the user wants to open the associated layout drawing.

View Menu

The View Menu (see Figure 2-11) allows the user to access different aspects of the tree structure.

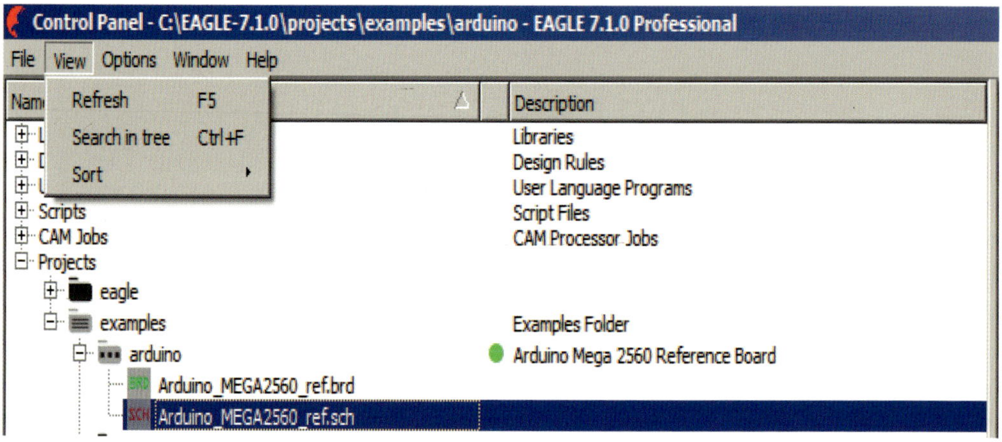

Figure 2-11: Control Panel View menu

Refresh

This simply refreshes the contents of the tree. It can be used, should any changes have been made that do not appear.

Search in Tree

This allows the user to conduct a text search of the complete directory tree. A search bar is opened at the foot of the window. Close the search bar by **Left-Click** on the  icon.

Sort

Sorts the contents of the tree view by *name* or by *file type*.

Options Menu

The Options Menu (see Figure 2-12) is the main location for configuring the behavior and characteristics of the EAGLE interface.

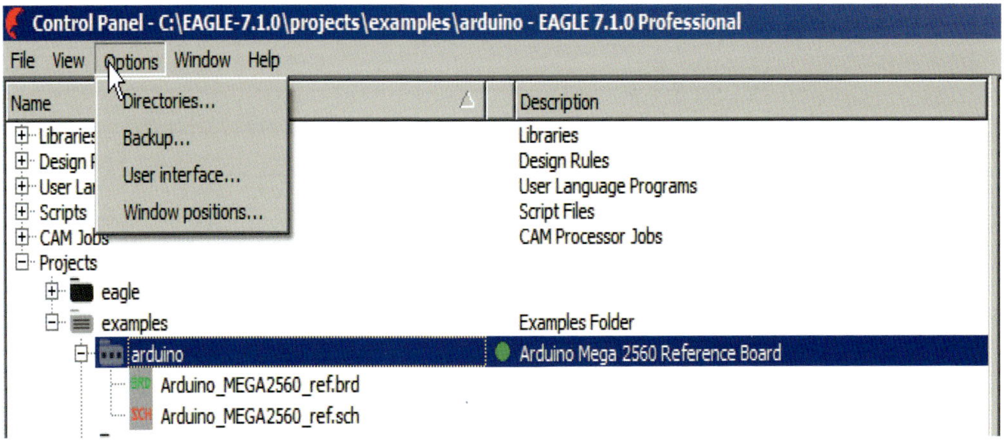

Figure 2-12: Control Panel Options menu

Directories

Selection of the *'Directories'* item from the Options menu opens the Directories dialog box (as in Figure 2-13). This shows the paths for particular modules and sub-programs which comprise EAGLE.

The user is able to change and add to these directories to suit their particular development environment. The user should note:

- More than one path may be entered for each the Directory entry;
- Paths are delineated by ';' (semicolons) in the Windows version and ':' (colon) in the Linux and Mac versions of EAGLE;

It should also be noted from the earlier description of the Control Panel; the *Projects* directory contains subdirectories, each of which represents a particular project.

The *Projects* directory is also the default directory for the Text Editor.

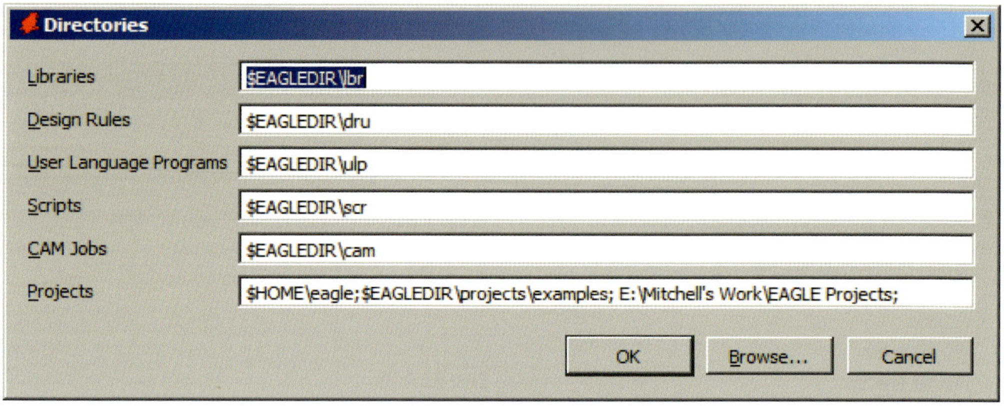

Figure 2-13: Directories from the Options menu

The paths are set up by default upon installation of EAGLE, and begin with *'$EAGLEDIR'.* The user can add to, or modify, these settings by typing the information directly into the corresponding box; or selecting the desired directory by clicking the *Browse* button.

The metadirectory *'$HOME'* may also be used. It is the home directory under Linux or as defined under Windows (by setting the environment variable using the SET command).

SPECIAL NOTES:
If the software was installed from external media (i.e. a CD/DVD drive) the $HOME variable will be set by default to that drive. New projects cannot be written to that drive ! So, the user should begin the installation by copying the files to an appropriate HDD or explicitly re-naming that part of the *Projects* path.
$HOME should ***not*** be set to the root directory of a disc drive.
(If the HOME variable is not setup, then Windows EAGLE will nominate the *Application Data* directory.)

Backup

EAGLE automatically creates a backup copy of files when they are saved. These backup files are named with a specific file extension or ending as follows: Schematic filenames are appended with *s#x*; board files with *b#x*, and library files with *l#x*.

The numbering of the # and x denote the level of backup. *x* can vary from 1 to 9 (where the filename containing *x* = 1 denotes the most recent backup) and the limit being determined by the setting in the Backup Dialog (as seen in Figure 2-14).

Figure 2-14: Backup dialog from the Options menu

An automatic backup function is provided by EAGLE to allow same to be scheduled. The time interval can be between 1 and 60 minutes (with a default of 5 minutes). The backup files have endings determined by the rules stated above.

The user can work on these backup files independently by simply renaming them and giving them usual file endings of *brd*, *sch*, *lbr* for their respective file type.

The user may elect to have the project automatically saved, when closing the current project, or leaving the program, by clicking on the *Automatically save project file* option.

User Interface

The User Interface dialog (in Figure 2-15) allows the Schematic Diagram, PCB Layout, and Library Editor's windows appearance to be adjusted to match the user preferences. This dialog can also be accessed from within the individual Editor windows.

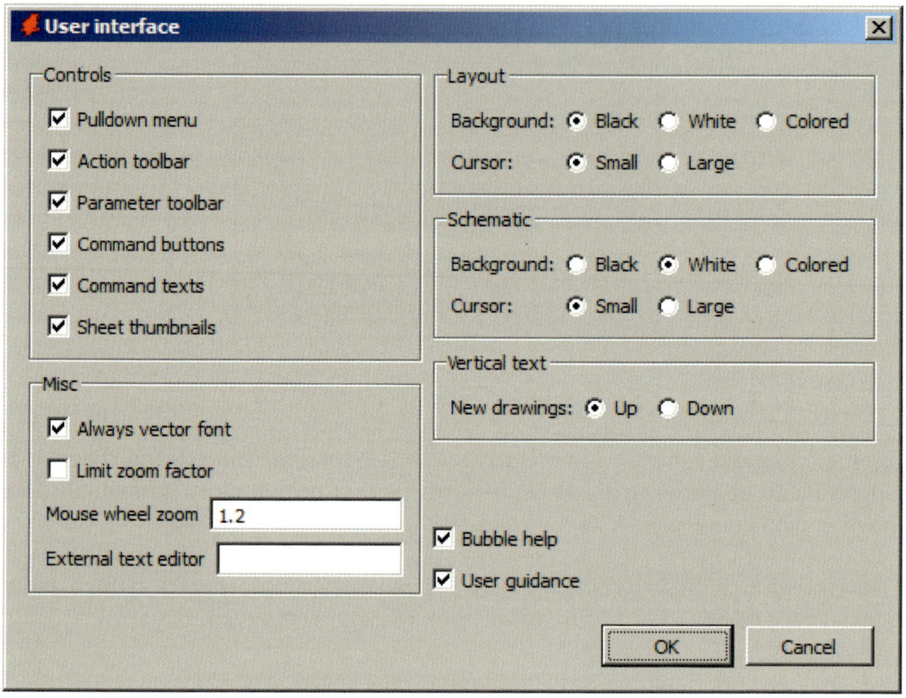

Figure 2-15: user interface dialog from the Options menu

Controls box

Of particular note is the *Controls* box. It is here one can specify which objects are to be displayed in the editor window. This allows the user to maximize the free area available for drawing. However, if all the *Controls* are deactivated, only the command line will remain for command entry.

Miscellaneous

Selecting the option *Always vector font* shows and prints texts with the built-in vector font, independently from the originally used font. This guarantees that the output with a printer or the CAM Processor is exactly the same as shown in the editor window. Fonts other than vector font depend on the target systems' settings and cannot be controlled by EAGLE. The output of non-vector fonts may differ from the editor's view and can lead to some fatal errors, particularly when including text in a board's copper areas.

When the *User Interface* dialog is opened from within an Editor window (e.g. the PCB Layout Editor), an additional item: *'Persistent in this drawing'* is offered under the *'Always vector font'* option. Setting this option causes EAGLE to save the *Always vector font* setting in the current drawing file. This will ensure that the layout will be shown with vector font at another user's computer (for example, at a board fabrication house).

Selecting *'Limit zoom factor'* limits the maximum size a drawing can be 'zoomed 'in an editor window. At maximum zoom level, the width of the drawing is about one Millimeter (approx. 40 mil). If this option is switched off, the screen zoom can continue until the 0.003125 Micron grid becomes visible.

If the user is working with a wheel mouse for scrolling, they can zoom in and out by turning the mouse wheel. The option '*Mouse wheel* zoom' determines the zoom factor for each 'step' of the mouse rotation. The value 0 for this option switches this function off.

The '*External text editor'* field option allows the user to specify an alternative to the built-in EAGLE text editor. Further details on this can be found in the help function in the section: *Editor windows/Text editor.*

The user is able to specify the color of the background for the Layout and Schematic Editors. The background color may be: black, white or Colored. Configuration of the background color is described later in the book.

The cursor type in the Layout and Schematic Editors can be displayed as either a small or large cross-hairs configuration.

The section Vertical text determines whether text should be readable from the right hand side upwards (Up) or from the left hand side downwards (Down) in your drawings.

The check box for *Help,* switches on or off the popup texts for the command icons (*Bubble help*) and the help texts for the commands in the status line, at the lower left hand corner of the window (*User guidance*).

If *User guidance* is checked, additional information about the selected object (e.g. net or signal name, net class, device's name and value etc.), or further options relating to the currently active command, is displayed.

Window Positions

The Windows Positions item (in Figure 2-16) allows the user to determine whether the system should preserve (and save) the size and position of the currently open Editor windows. Future files will be opened with the stored position and size parameters.

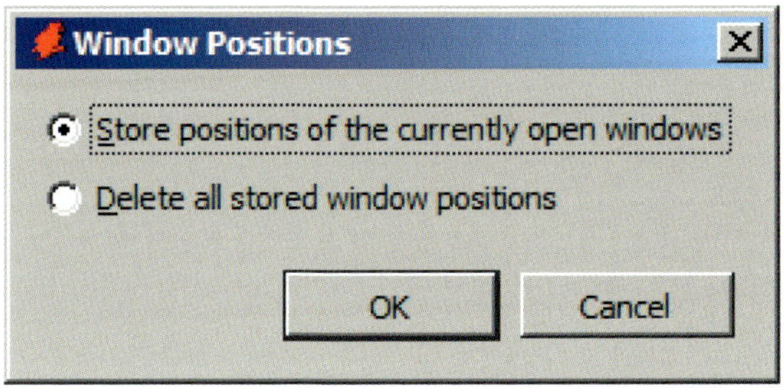

Figure 2-16: preserving Editor window positions

If the *'Delete all stored positions'* button is selected, EAGLE automatically determines the location of an Editor window and uses a fixed size for it, by default.

Window Menu

The *Window Menu* (shown in Figure 2-17) displays the currently open windows within EAGLE. The user may use the menu to choose the window to be displayed in the foreground. Alternatively, the user may use an Alt key combination. This uses the Alt key together with the number given at the right hand end of the line descriptor in the menu. For example, using Alt+1 would bring the Arduino Mega schematic to the foreground.

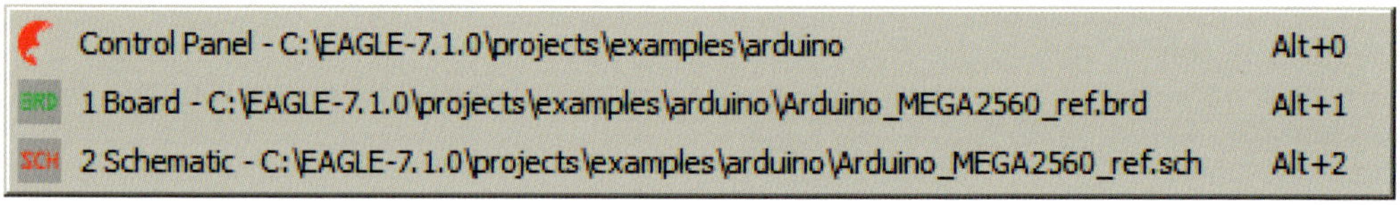

Figure 2-17: Window menu

Using the *Alt+0 key* combination anywhere in the program will bring the Control Panel into the foreground.
NOTE: The functionality of Alt+window-number is ***not*** supported in Mac OS X version; it is only supported under Windows and Linux.

Help Menu

The help menu for EAGLE is shown in Figure 2-18.

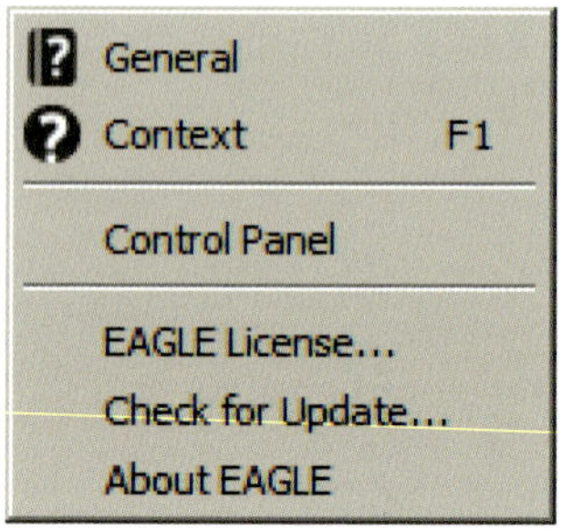

Figure 2-18: Help menu

General and Context Help

The *Help* menu allows the user to access general help functionality within EAGLE as well as context-sensitive help. The latter is also available, at any time, by pressing the F1 key.

Editor Help
This option allows direct access to the HELP file information on the EAGLE Control Panel for the currently open Editor module (i.e. whether Schematic, PCB Layout or Text Editor). The content of the menu option changes accordingly.

EAGLE License
The EAGLE License option is used when registering or upgrading the application. The registration dialog (shown in Figure 2-19) is called automatically when the user start EAGLE the first time.

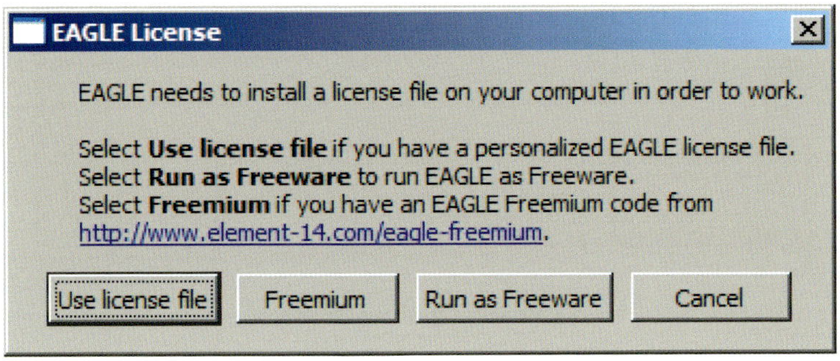

Figure 2-19: EAGLE License dialog

To register an upgrade, this option must be started from the *Help* menu after installation. The user should then enter the necessary information in the dialog. All editor windows must be closed before initiating this option.

Check for Update
EAGLE checks, by default, the status of updates for the target system on the CadSoftweb server. When an update is available the user will be informed by a message window, but it is not automatically downloaded. The check looks like that shown in Figure 2-20.

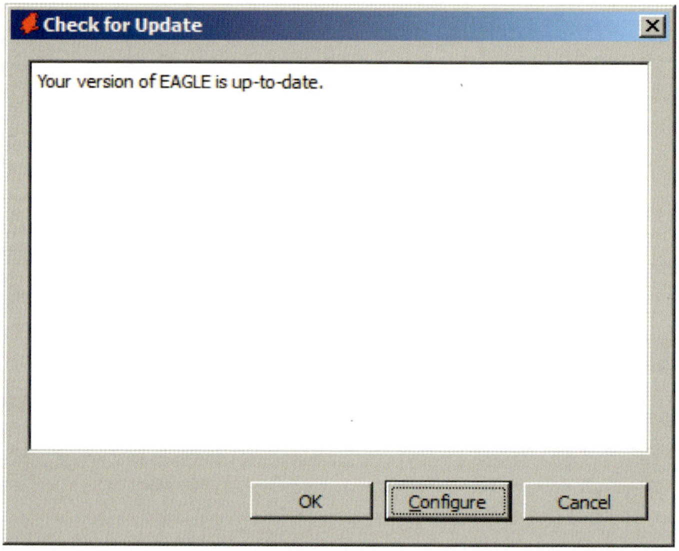

Figure 2-20: EAGLE Update dialog

If the user clicks on the Configure button, EAGLE opens the Configuration dialog (as in Figure 2-21). Here the user may direct EAGLE to check for updates daily, weekly, or never. If using a Proxy server, then the user needs to supply its name. The latest beta version of EAGLE can be downloaded if the check box is activated.

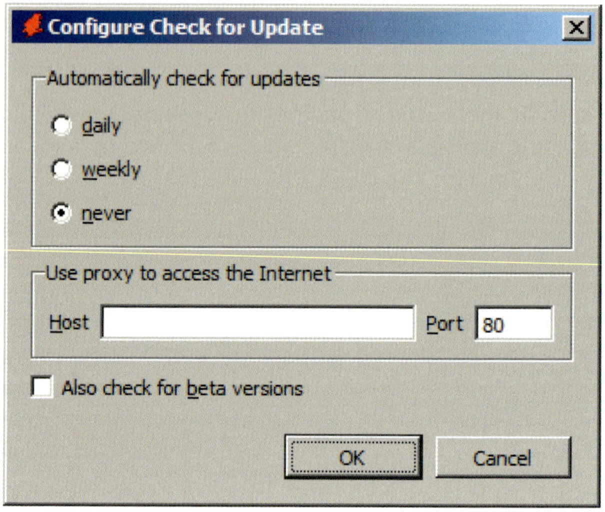

Figure 2-21: Update Configuration dialog

About EAGLE

The information displayed with this option should be used when making support requests to CadSoft.

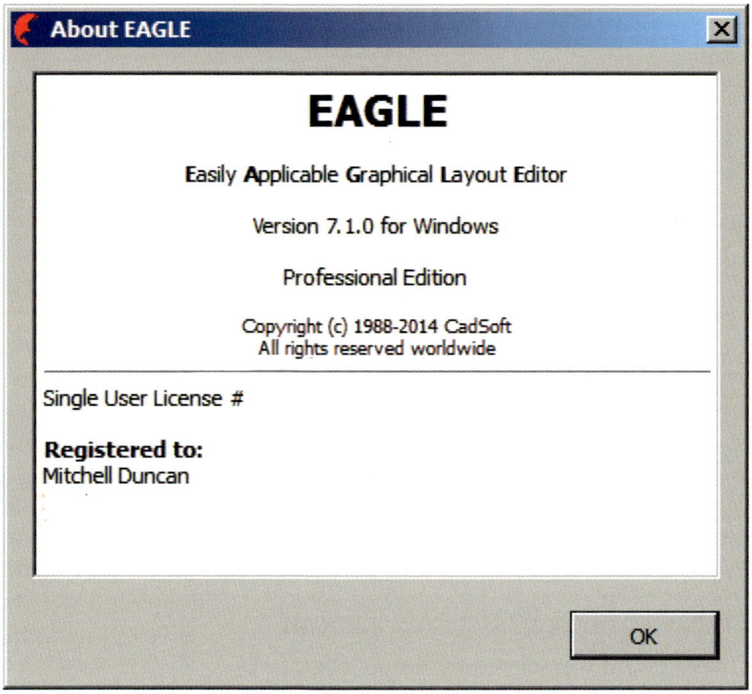

Figure 2-22: License information display

The Schematic Editor Window

In order to operate EAGLE effectively, the user needs to have a working knowledge of the various menus, toolbars and the icons which activate commands. These are outlined in this, and subsequent sections of this chapter.

As discussed previously, the Schematic Editor window (as shown in Figure 2-23) opens when an existing schematic drawing is opened or the user creates a new one.

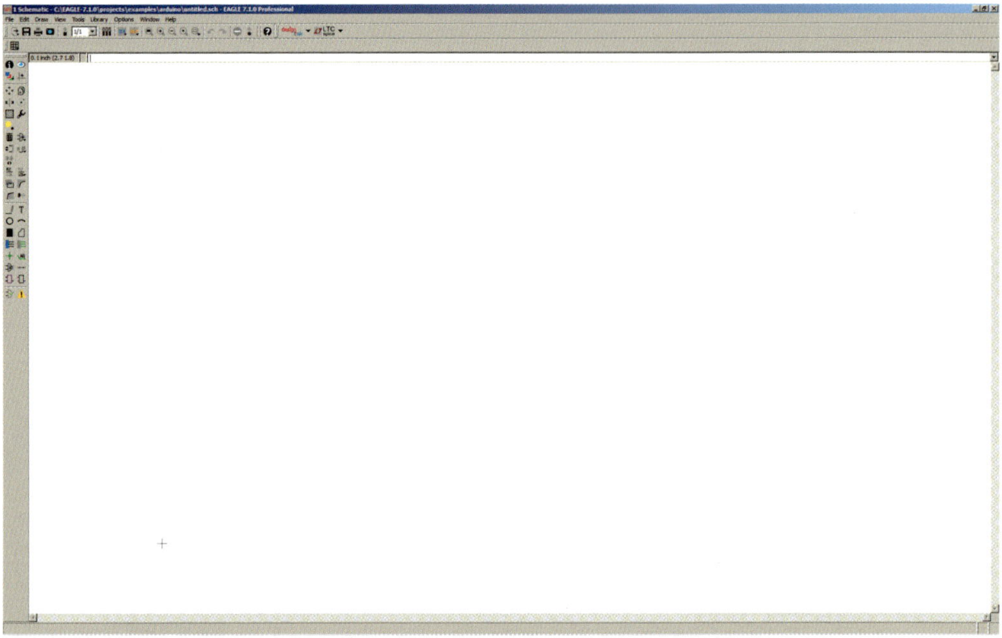

Figure 2-23: Schematic Editor window

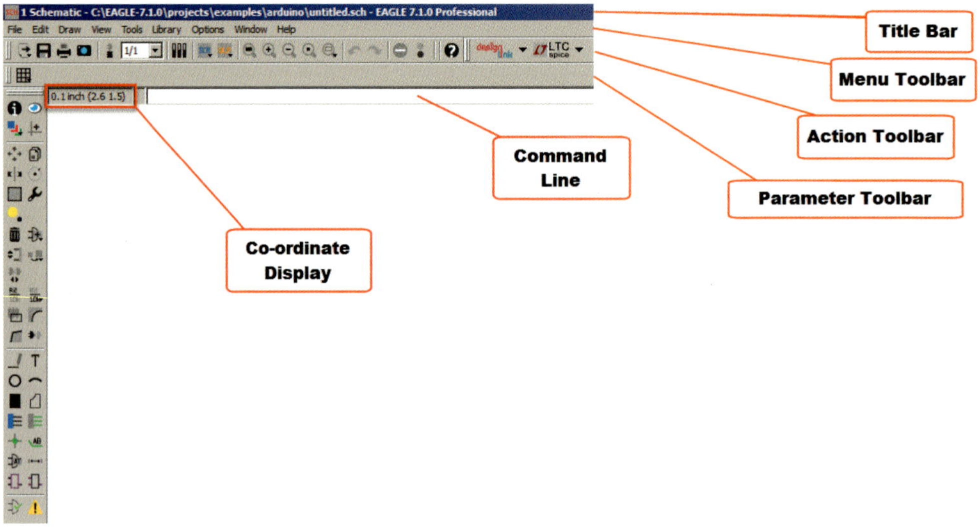

Figure 2-24: Schematic Editor window elements

Figure 2-24 depicts a section of the Schematic Editor Window. In it there are a number of elements which comprise the window itself. The main group of these are: Title Bar; Menu Toolbar; Action Toolbar; Parameter Toolbar; Command Toolbar; Command Line and the co-ordinate Display.
These will be discussed individually later, below.

The Title Bar

The Title Bar displays the currently open file and its path, together with the version of EAGLE being used.

The Menu Toolbar

The **Menu Toolbar** (as in Figure 2-25) contains text entries which act as the 'headers' for access to dropdown menus. These menus are described in detail later in this book.

Figure 2-25: Schematic Editor menu toolbar

The Action Toolbar

The **Schematic Editor Action Toolbar** (shown in Figure 2-26) comprises a number of icons. These icons will be discussed briefly, and also be treated in greater detail later.

Figure 2-26: Schematic Editor action toolbar

The leftmost group of icons (as in Figure 2-27) in the Action Toolbar is related to file operations. From left to right these icons signify commands to: Open file, Save file, Print file, invoke the CAM Processor and Generate (create) or Switch to (open) the corresponding board file (BOARD command).

Figure 2-27: File operation icons

The next icon (Figure 2-28) allows the user to load, remove, or create a new schematic sheet in the current drawing. The icon which follows it (in Figure 2-29), the USE Library icon allows the user to access and attach (USE) component libraries.

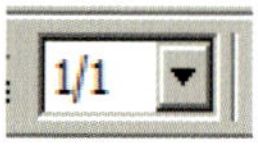

Figure 2-28: Sheet operation icon

Figure 2-29: Library USE icon

The external functionality to EAGLE can be executed by means of Script Files or User Language Programs. These are started using the icons shown in Figure 2-30.

Figure 2-30: Script and User Language Program execution

Manipulation of the display in the Editor window area is done using the Window action icons (Figure 2-31). These represent the action of (from left to right): Zoom to fit, Zoom in, Zoom out, Redraw and Zoom select respectively.

Figure 2-31: Window display actions

More details of these operations are given later in the book.

Figure 2-32: UNDO - REDO command icons

These command icons in Figure 2-32 allow the user to cancel previous commands and to re-execute previously cancelled commands. These command icons preserve their consistency between the Schematic and PCB layout drawing comprising the current open project. This means that: if one is working with a pair of schematic and layout drawings, the UNDO/REDO commands display, in the status bar (at the bottom, left hand part of the screen), which command was undone/redone and whether the command was originally executed in the board or in the schematic editor.

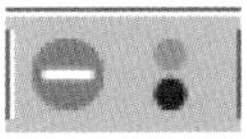

Figure 2-33: command STOP - GO icons

The icons shown in Figure 2-33 allow the user to terminate execution of an EAGLE command or to start the execution of an active EAGLE command, allowing further parameters to be entered.

Figure 2-34: HELP command icon

Figure 2-34 shows the HELP function icon which invokes the built in help functionality of EAGLE. This displays the help window and allows the user access to more information about an EAGLE command.

The Command Toolbar of the Schematic Editor

The Command Toolbar exists in both the Schematic and the PCB Layout Editors, down the left hand side of the window. The icons in the toolbar for the Schematics Editor is illustrated in Figure 2-35; with the corresponding command name or function shown, and associated with the relevant icon.

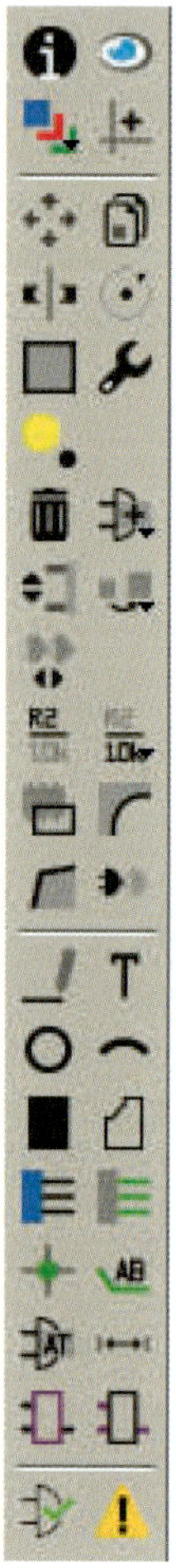

The INFO Command displays the properties of the selected object. The name of the object may also be used as a parameter in the command line. Some of the properties of the selected object can be altered in this dialog.

The SHOW Command highlights the object selected with the mouse Left-Click. In case of objects that consist of more than one part, like elements with several gates or nets that spread over several sheets, the window will highlight all elements.

The DISPLAY command allows the user to select and deselect the layers to be displayed in the current drawing.

MARK Command allows the user to define the new origin for the coordinate display, relative to the drawing Datum point. Relative coordinates (R x-value y-value) and polar values (P radius angle) are shown in addition to absolute coordinates in the coordinate display box.

The MOVE Command allows the user to move and rotate any visible object or Group.

The COPY Command permits the copying of devices, components, Nets, Busses and Groups.

MIRROR Command transforms an object into its horizontal mirror image equivalent.

The ROTATE Command allows the use to rotate the orientation of an element or group, by 90 degrees.

Figure 2-35 — Schematic Editor command toolbar

The GROUP Command allows for a selection of devices to be associated and managed together, such that they may be manipulated using subsequent commands.

CHANGE Command enables the user to alter the Properties of the current drawing; or of an object. (See the INFO Command).

PASTE Command inserts objects from the clipboard buffer into the drawing

DELETE Command allows deletion of a visible device or group.

ADD Command permits adding/inserting device elements from a pre-selected Library.

PINSWAP Command swaps two nets connected to equivalent pins of a Device, that have the same defined Swap-level.

REPLACE Command replaces a device or component with another from any Library.

GATESWAP Command Swaps two equivalent Gates of a Device that have the same defined Swaplevel.

NAME Command allows the user to create or change the name of Devices, Nets or Buses.

VALUE Command allows the user to create or change the value of devices.

SMASH Command separates the name, value and any attribute texts from a Device, allowing them to be manipulated individually.

MITER Command allows the user to round off or bevel the joints of Wires, Nets, Buses and Polygon contours.

SPLIT Command inserts an angle joint into a Wire or Net.

INVOKE Command allows the user to fetch & add individual Symbols (Gates) from Devices that consist of more than one Symbol (Gate). The command also allows the fetching and adding of a Gate from a Device which is located on another sheet.

The WIRE Command is used to draw a line (WIRE is used to define electrical connections in the Layout Editor).

The TEXT Command is used to place text within the drawing.

CIRCLE Command is used to draw a circular line within a drawing.

ARC Command is used to draw an arc, or partial circle, within a drawing

RECT is used to draw a closed rectangle within a drawing.

POLYGON is used to draw a closed polygon within a drawing. In copper areas these may be any shape.

The NET Command is used to draw a Net (electrical connection) within a drawing.

BUS is used to draw a Bus line which is not an electrical signal. A Bus simply aggregates Nets for the purposes of the drawing's readability.

JUNCTION Command is used to logically (and electrically) join two Nets.

The LABEL Command allows the user to place the Name of a Bus or Net, as text, onto the drawing.

ATTRIBUTE Command allows the user to add or edit the attributes of a device or component.

The DIMENSION Command may be used to draw dimension lines and parameters in the drawing.

The MODULE Command allows the user to add or create schematic Modules.

The PORT Command allows the user to add or create schematic module Ports

This Command (ERC) performs an Electrical Rule Check and a consistency check for schematic and board (if it already exists).

ERRORS Command displays errors found by the ERC.

Schematic Editor Menu Toolbar Sub-menus

As shown in Figure 2-25 the menu toolbar contains a number of sub-menus which provides access to many of the functions of EAGLE. These sub- menus are: File, Edit, Draw, View Tools, Library Options, Window and Help.

However, the sub menus Library, Options, Window and Help are essentially the same as those described as for the EAGLE Control Panel. The reader should refer to that section for their description. The outline of the remaining sub-menus follows.

The reader should also note that there may exist equivalent 'shortcut' key combinations for some of the Commands. These are shown on the right of the Command in the sub-menu. For example, the shortcut key combination 'Ctrl+S' invokes the SAVE Command.

The File Sub-menu

The File sub menu for the Schematic Editor provides the following functions. Some of these Commands are available from the Action Toolbar.

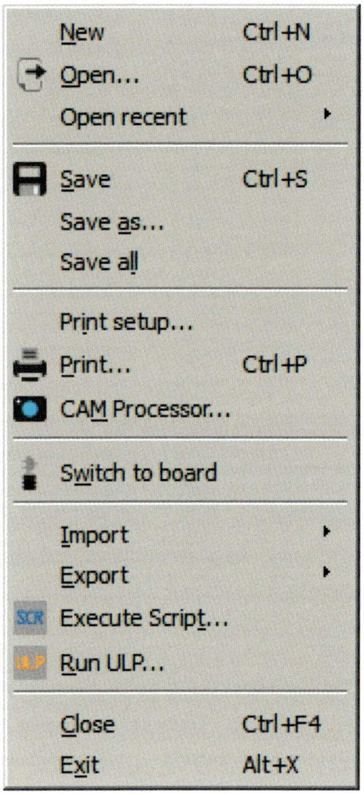

opens a new Schematic file

allows the user to open an existing Schematic file

displays a list of previously opened Schematic files

saves the currently open schematic file

allows the user to save the current Schematic file to a new destination
saves all currently open schematic files

displays the print configuration window for the default printer

prints the current window to the default printer

sends the current Schematic file to the CAM processor

Switches to the currently open PC board window. If the board does not exist, EAGLE will ask if it can create it.

imports a schematic file

exports a part of your schematic for further processing

opens and executes an EAGLE script file.

runs a User Language Program

Closes the current Schematic Editor window

exits the EAGLE application

The Edit Sub-menu

The Edit Menu for the Schematic Editor provides the following functions. Most of these functions are also available from the Command Toolbar.

Undo	Ctrl+Z	Reverses (undoes) the most recent action
Redo	Ctrl+Y	repeats the most recent action
Undo/Redo list...		displays a list of the most recent actions
Stop command		cancels or stops the current action
Add...		allows the user to add a device from a selected library
Change...		allows the user to change attributes of the selected drawing element
Copy		copies the selected drawing element
Delete		deletes the selected drawing element
Gateswap		allows the user to swap components (gates) within a schematic, in the same package
Group		provides a method of selecting and manipulating multiple objects together
Invoke		selects a component from a device (package), already in use, and place it in the schematic
Mirror		transforms the selected object into its mirror image about the vertical axis
Miter		removes the edge off a corner or adds a section to a wire; as a straight or a curved segment
Move		moves an object within a drawing
Name		allows the user to edit the name of an item (object).
Paste		copies the contents of the clipboard to the current drawing
Pinswap		allows the user to swap pins within the same symbol (device)
Replace...		replace a part with a different device
Rotate		used to change the orientation of an object
Smash		separates text parameters from the selected object
Split		separates a wire into segments for manipulation
Value...		assigns a text value to an element
Global attributes...		
Net classes...		
Assembly variants...		
Description...		

The Draw Sub-menu

The Draw sub-menu for the Schematic Editor provides the following functions. Most of these functions are also available from the Command Toolbar.

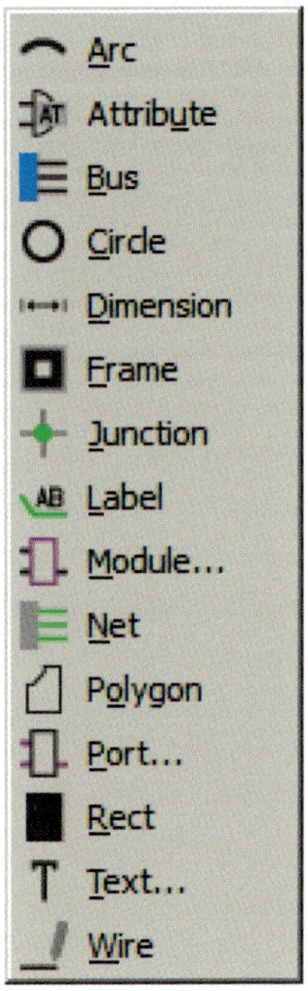

draws an arc of variable diameter, width, and length

allows the user to specify a name and a value for a part

allows the user to draw bus connections onto the Bus layer of a schematic diagram

creates a circle with defined parameters

allows the user to add dimensioning to a drawing

creates a frame with numbered columns and rows in the drawing

draws a connection dot at the intersection of interconnecting (signal) nets

allows for the addition of text "labels' to a schematic drawing

allows the user to add a Module to a schematic drawing

allows individual connections (nets) to be drawn onto a schematic drawing

allows the user to draw a polygon shape in a drawing

allows the user to add a Port to a Module

allows the user to add a rectangle shape to a drawing

used to add free-form text to a library element or drawing

used to add wires (tracks) to a drawing

The View Sub-menu

The View sub-menu for the Schematic Editor provides the following functions:

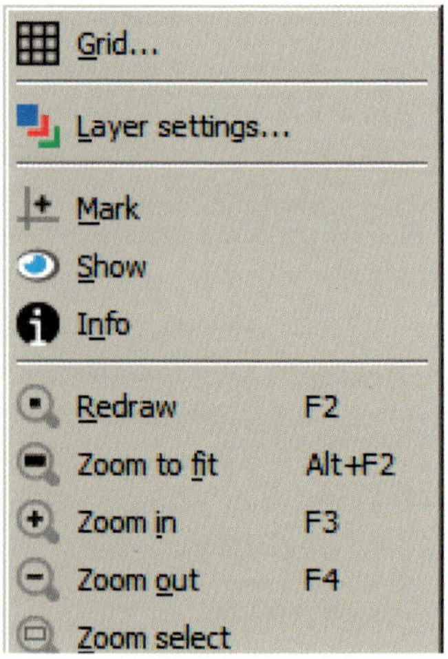

displays the dialog box to allow configuration of the grid pitch & style

displays the dialog box to allow configuration & manipulation of drawing layers

defines a point on the drawing which serves as a mouse coordinate datum

highlights an object and displays its details

displays an object's properties in a dialog box and allows its modification

re-draws the current window/screen

adjusts the drawing to show it full size in your screen

doubles the size of the drawing within your screen

halves the size of the drawing within your screen

allows the user to select an area of the drawing to enlarge

Layout Editor

The Layout Editor window (as shown in Figure 2-36) opens when an existing PCB Layout drawing is opened, or the user creates a new one.
The Editor Window has almost the same layout as the Schematic Window, incorporating elements including: Title Bar; Menu Toolbar; Action Toolbar; Parameter Toolbar; Command Toolbar and Command Line. These elements are almost identical in functionality to those in the Schematic Editor and will not be discussed here. However, details of the Command Toolbar are given below.

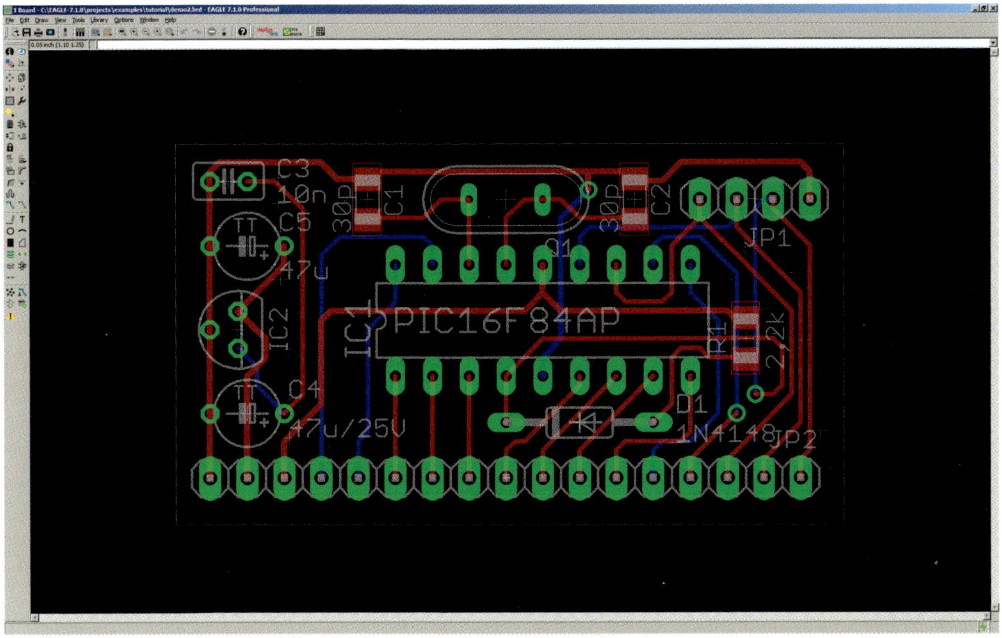

Figure 2-36: Layout Editor window

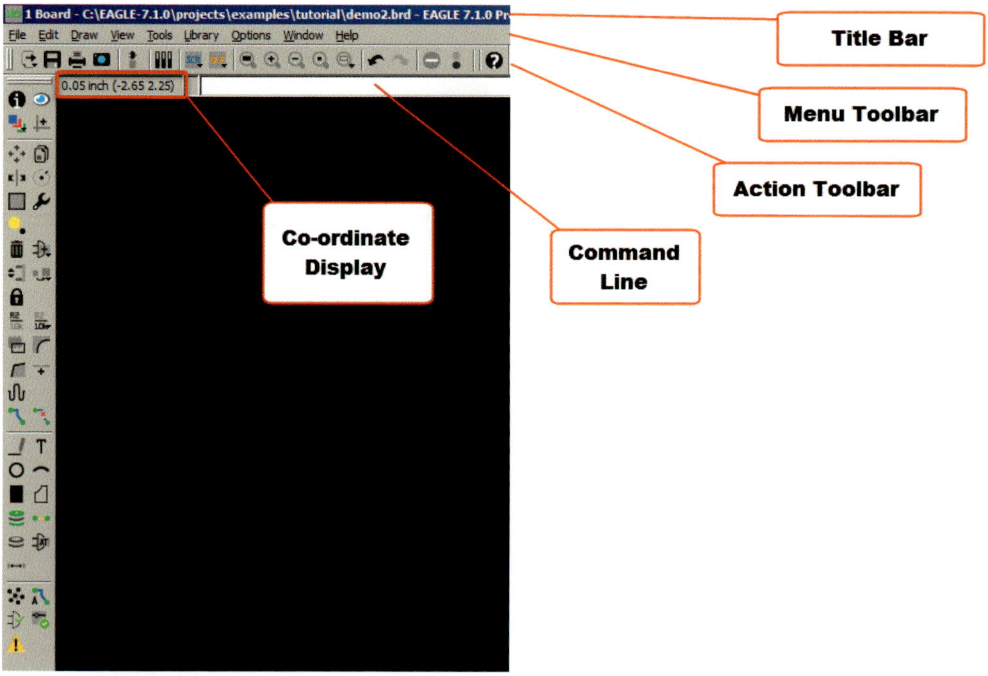

Figure 2-37: Layout Editor window elements

The Command Toolbar of The Layout Editor

The Command Toolbar exists in the PCB Layout Editor, and is displayed down the left hand side of the window. The icons in the toolbars for the Layout Editor are illustrated in Figure 2-38.

However, since there are common Commands which have the same analogous functionality as in the Schematic Editor, *this section will only highlight the Commands which are unique to the Layout Editor*.

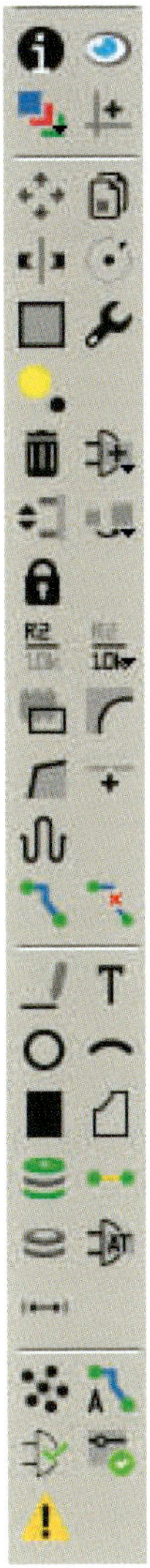

The LOCK Command Locks the position and orientation of a component on the board. A locked component is unable to be moved or duplicated with the CUT and PASTE commands.

The OPTIMIZE Command joins wire segments in a signal layer which lie in one straight line.

The MEANDER Command draw meanders in a copper track in order to balance the length of signal paths. This is especially useful for the balancing of Differential Pairs of signal tracks

The Route Command allows the user to route the board signals manually; where the Airwires are converted to wires as the process progresses.

RIPUP converts routed wires (tracks) into unrouted signals (airwires). It also changes the display of filled (calculated) polygons to outline view.

VIA places a plated-through hole (VIA) at the cursor location.

The SIGNAL Command allows the user to manually create a signal (Airwire) if the Forward&Back Annotation is disabled.

HOLE defines the position and size of a plain (not plated-through) mounting hole in the PCB.

The RATSNEST Command is used to refresh and calculate the shortest Airwires possible and the real mode (filled) display of polygons on the layout.

AUTO starts the Autorouter layout function within the Editor.

The DRC Command allows the user to define the board Design Rules and perform a Design Rule Check.

Displays errors found by DRC and ERC.

Figure 2-38: Layout Editor command toolbar

Layout Editor Menu Toolbar

As with the Schematic Editor, the Layout Editor includes a menu toolbar containing a number of sub-menus which provide access to functions of EAGLE. These sub-menus also include: File, Edit, Draw, View Tools, Library Options, Window and Help.
Similarly, the sub menus: Library Options, Window and Help provide analogous functionality to the same as those described as for the Schematic Editor.
The reader should also note that there may exist equivalent 'shortcut' key combinations for some of the Commands in a menu.

The File Sub-menu

The PCB Layout Editor File Menu functions are:

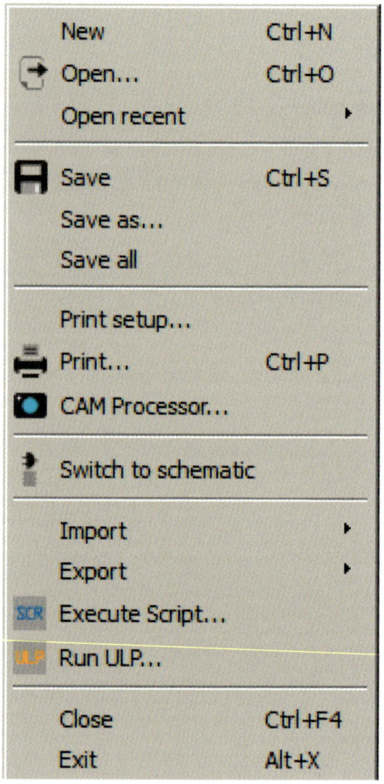

opens a new PCB layout file
allows the user to open an existing PCB layout file
displays a list of previously opened PCB layout files

saves the currently open PCB layout file
allows the user to save the current PCB layout file to a new destination
saves all currently open PCB layout files

displays the print configuration window for the default printer
prints the current window to the default printer
sends the current PCB layout file to the CAM processor

switches to the corresponding PC schematic window

imports a PCB layout file
exports a part of your PCB layout for further processing
opens and executes an EAGLE script file.
runs a User Language Program

Closes the current PCB layout Editor window
exits the EAGLE application

The Edit Sub-menu

The Edit Menu for the PCB Layout Editor provides the following functions:

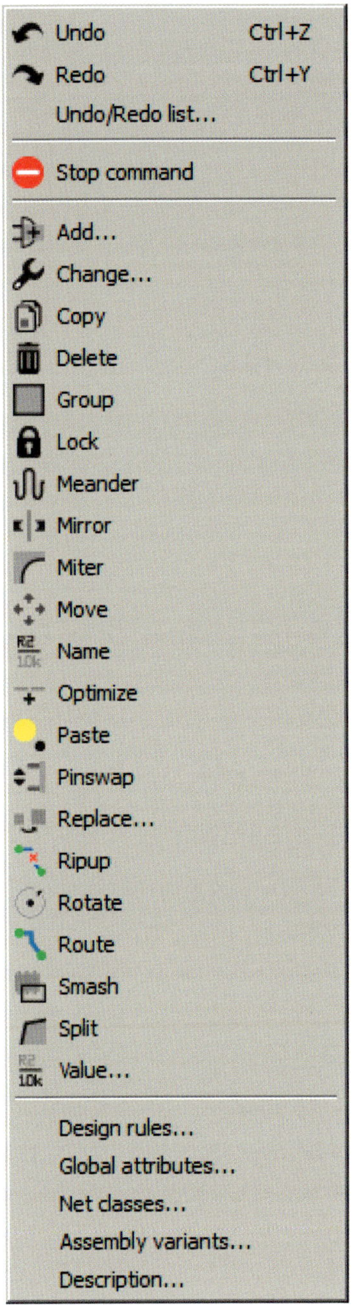

Reverses (undoes) the most recent action

repeats the most recent action

displays a list of the most recent actions

cancels or stops the current action

allows the user to add a device from a selected library

allows the user to change attributes of the selected drawing element

copies the selected drawing element

deletes the selected drawing element

combines elements into a group to allow subsequent command manipulation

locks the position and orientation of a part in the board

used to balance the lengths of wires which form a differential pair of tracks in a layout

rotates the selected object about the vertical axis

removes the edge off a corner or adds a section to a wire; as a straight or a curved segment

moves an object within a drawing

used to display and edit the name of an object

joins wire segments which lie in one straight line

copies the contents of the clipboard or file to the current layout

allows the user to swap pins within the same symbol (device)

allows the user to replace a part with a different, compatible device

changes routed wires (tracks) into "airwires" (unrouted connections)

used to change the orientation of an object

activates the manual router allowing conversion of airwires into real wires

separates text parameters from the selected object

separates a wire into segments for manipulation

assigns a text value to an element

The Draw Sub-menu

The PCB Layout Editor Draw sub-menu provides:

Arc	draws an arc of variable diameter, width, and length
Attribute	allows the user to specify a name and a value for a part
Circle	creates a circle with defined parameters
Dimension	allows the user to add dimensioning to a drawing
Frame	creates a frame with numbered columns and rows in the drawing
Hole	adds a drill hole to a drawing
Polygon	allows the user to draw a polygon shape in a drawing
Rect	allows the user to add a rectangle shape to a drawing
Signal	used to define signals or connections between packages or objects
Text...	used to add free-form text to a library element or drawing
Via	adds a via hole to change a signal track to another layer
Wire	used to add wires (tracks) to a drawing

The View Sub-menu

The View sub-menu for the PCB Layout Editor is the same as for the Schematic Editor, that is:

Grid...		displays the dialog box to allow configuration of the grid pitch & style
Layer settings...		displays the dialog box to allow configuration & manipulation of drawing layers
Mark		defines a point on the drawing which serves as a mouse coordinate datum
Show		highlights an object and displays its details
Info		displays an object's properties in a dialog box and allows its modification
Redraw	F2	re-draws the current window/screen
Zoom to fit	Alt+F2	adjusts the drawing to show it full size in your screen
Zoom in	F3	doubles the size of the drawing within your screen
Zoom out	F4	halves the size of the drawing within your screen
Zoom select		allows the user to select an area of the drawing to enlarge

The Library Editor Window

The Library Editor window opens upon opening and loading a library. It can also be opened directly from the Control Panel File Menu by using the following menu operations:
File ▷ Open ▷ Library; or using Library ▷ Open from within a Schematic or Layout drawing. The Library Editor Window shown in Figure 2-39 will open.

The Library Editor allows the user complete control over objects and their fundamental elements, which may be used in the Schematic and Layout modules of EAGLE. Libraries, in turn, may also be manipulated by commands given within EAGLE.

The Library Editor module may be used to create, edit or delete objects and may be used independently of the Schematic Editor.

A library need not contain only real Components. Examples include: Ground or Supply symbols; drawing Frames; and mounting holes or hardware. These could be stored as Devices in a library.

A library normally contains three different object types: Packages, Symbols and Devices.

- A Package is a Device's housing, and is used in the Layout Editor (on the board).

- The Symbol contains a graphical representation of the Device as used in the schematic.

- The Device represents the link between one or more Symbol(s) and a Package. It is within a Device that the connection between a pin of a Symbol and the referring pad(s) of the Package are also defined.

  A Device set is also named if the component exists in more than one Package and/or technology variant.

  A Component is also defined as a Device.

There are also libraries that only contain Packages and can only be used in the Layout Editor.

The Library Editor Toolbars

As with the Schematic Editor, and the Layout Editor; the Library Editor Window also incorporates a menu toolbar which contains a number of sub-menus. These sub- menus include: File, Edit, Draw, View, Library, Options, Window and Help.

Similarly, the sub-menus: File, View, Options, Window and Help provide analogous functionality to the same as those described as for the Schematic and Layout Editors.

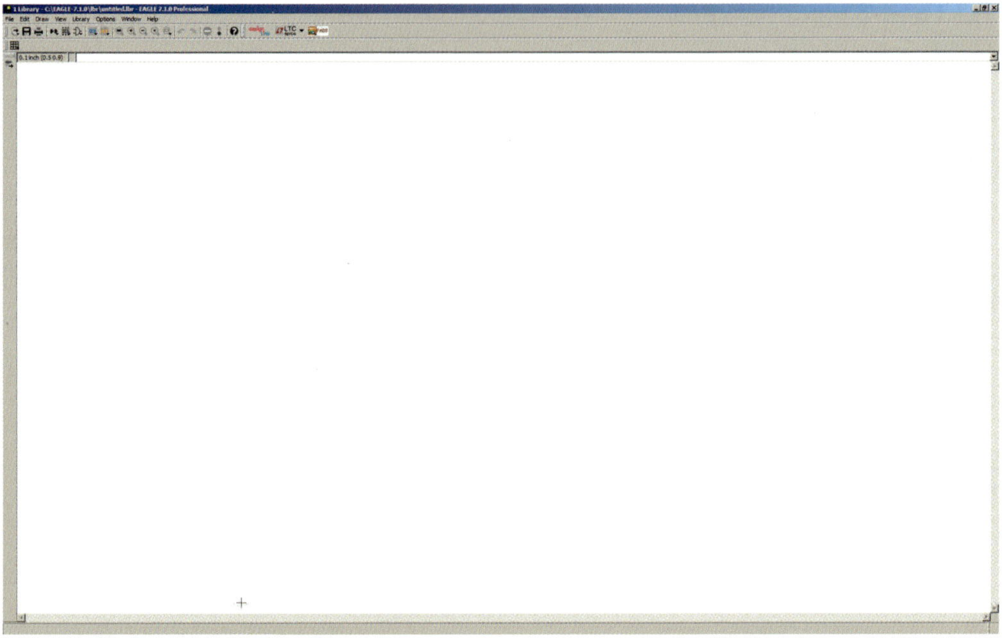

Figure 2-39: Library Editor window

Library Sub-menu

The Library Sub-menu holds the Commands for management of a component library and includes the following functions: Description, Device Package, Symbol, Remove, Rename and Update.

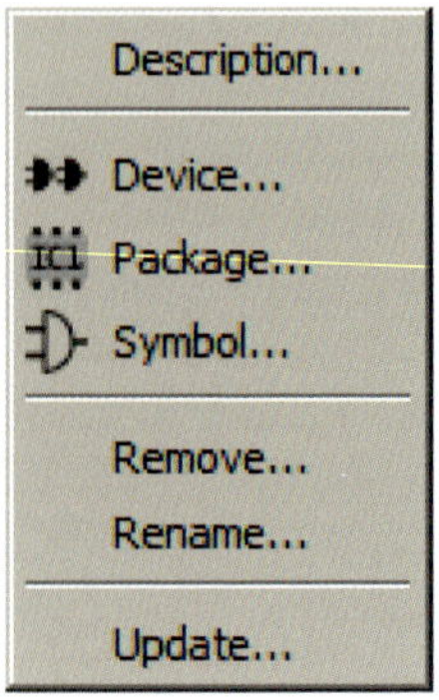

Allows for creation and editing of the Library's description

Used to create or edit a Device in the Library

Used to create or edit a Package in the Library

Used to create or edit a Symbol in the Library

Removes an object from a library

Renames an object within a library

Allows the transfer/update of objects from other libraries

There are a number of Commands that are important for manipulating components from the Library Editor Window. A description of these follows:

 This command icon is used to open the object editing dialog shown in Figure 2-40. This dialog allows the user to readily create or edit a Device, Package or Symbol in the Library.

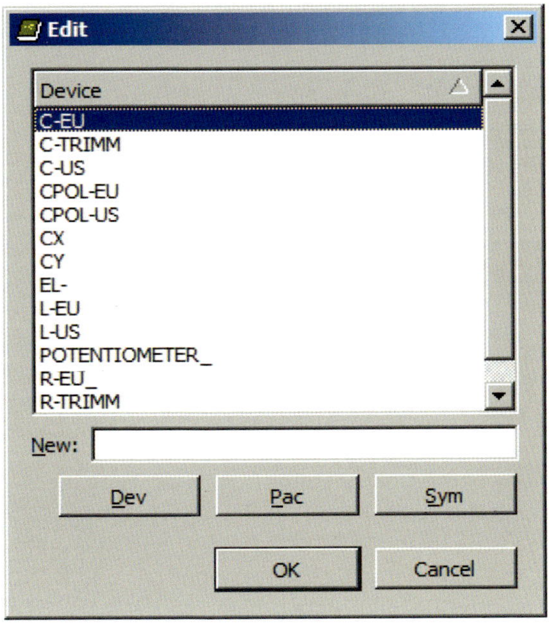

Figure 2-40: Object Editing dialog

Similarly, the Command icons shown in the Action Toolbar (see Figure 2-41) provide quick access to some of the identical commands that exist in the Library Sub-menu and the above Dialog box.

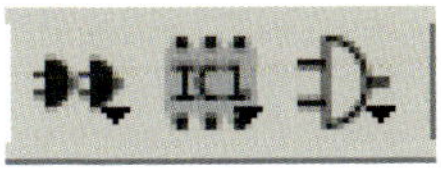

Figure 2-41: Object Editing command icons

The Package Editing Mode

The Package Editing mode of the Library Editor is invoked using the Package icon  in the Action Toolbar or through the 'Pac' button in the object editing dialog, as shown in Figure 2-40. It is used to create or edit the packaging (or container) of a component/device.

The Package Editing mode opens with a Command Toolbar down the left hand side of the window. The Command icons available in the command toolbar are equivalent to the identical icons of the Schematic or Layout Editor. However, there is an additional Command icon in this Toolbar:

 SMD Command allows the user to Place an SMD pad into the drawing. Invoking the command opens the parameter bar shown in Figure 2-42. These control the Size, Roundness (shape) and Angle (rotational positioning) of the pad.

Figure 2-42: SMD Pad parameter bar

The Symbol Editing Mode

The Symbol Editing mode of the Library Editor is invoked using the Symbol icon  in the Action Toolbar or through the 'Sym' button in the object editing dialog, as in Figure 2-40 Defining a Symbol means defining a part of a Device; it is that graphic element which can be placed individually in a schematic. Examples might be: one NAND gate of a 74L00 and the two power pins could be defined as two types of Symbols, representing the Device; another might be a resistor, a Device containing only one Symbol, could represent the complete resistor.

The Symbol Editing mode opens with a Command Toolbar down the left hand side of the window. The Command icons available in the command toolbar are equivalent to the identical icons of the Schematic or Layout Editor. There is an additional Command icon:

 PIN Command allows the user to Place pins and adjust the pin parameters (name, direction, function, length, visible, Swaplevel) in the parameter toolbar (as shown in Figure 2-43).

Figure 2-43: PIN parameter bar

The Device Editing mode

The Device Editing mode of the Library Editor is invoked using the Device icon  in the Action Toolbar or through the 'Dev' button in the object editing dialog, as shown in Figure 2-40. It is used to create or edit the Device or component entity.

In EAGLE, Components are defined as Devices. In the Device Editing mode, the process of defining a Device is executed by establishing the relationship between, and the values of, a number of elements.
These include the following:

- which Package variant is used
- which Symbol(s) is/are used (called Gate within the Device)
- which names are provided for the Gates (e.g. A, B)
- which technologies are available (e.g. 74L00, 74LS00, 74HCT00)
- if the Device should have additional user-definable attributes
- if there are equivalent Gates which can be interchanged (Swaplevel)
- how the Gate behaves when added to a schematic (Addlevel)
- the prefix for the component name (if a prefix is used)
- if the value of the component can be changed or if the value should be fixed to the Device name
- which pins relate to the pads of the Package (CONNECT command)
- whether a description for this component should be stored in the library

The Device Editor Window is shown in Figure 2-44 with the properties of the gates of a 7400 (Quad 2-input NAND gate) Device illustrated.

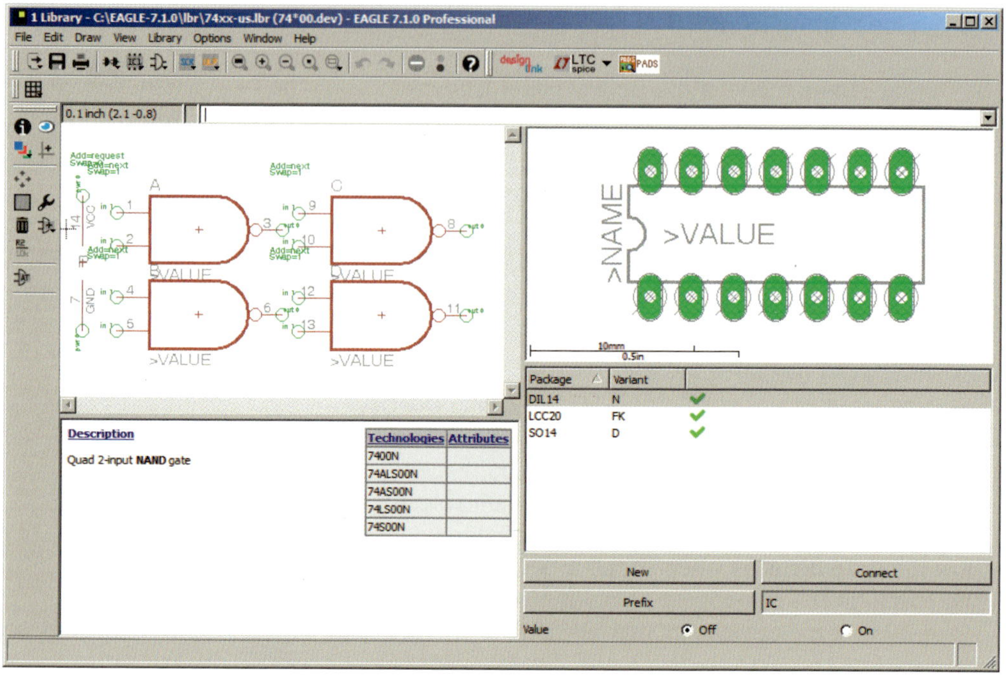

Figure 2-44: Device Editor window

A complete discussion of the use of the Library Editor is given elsewhere in this book.

The CAM Processor Window

The CAM processor module is that which generates the data required for manufacturing of a printed circuit board. The type of data output by the CAM processor is defined in a 'Job' file. The CAM processor comes supplied with a number of de facto industry standard files. These include: *excellon.cam*; *gerb274x-4layer.cam*; *gerb274x.cam*; *gerber.cam*.
Output from the CAM processor is sent to a pre-defined device driver; some are already included with the EAGLE software. These drivers may be plotters, printers, milling machines, drilling machines or PCB fabrication units. The drivers are defined in the file *eagle.def*, which can be edited with any text editor.

Starting the CAM Processor

The CAM processor can be opened in a number of different ways. These are:

- directly from the Layout or Schematic Editor window with the CAM Processor icon  in the action toolbar;

- from the Schematic or Layout Menu Toolbar using: File ▷ CAM Processor;
- from the Control Panel by clicking on one of the Job file entries in the Tree View's CAM Jobs branch.

Using the first two alternatives will require the user to subsequently open the CAM Job required for the processing of output data.

Using the last alternative, the selected CAM Job will be loaded automatically. It then remains for the user to load the schematic or board from which CAM Processor manufacturing data will be produced.

The active CAM processor window appears as shown in Figure 2-45 with a board file *demo3.brd* open using the Job file *gerb274x.cam*.

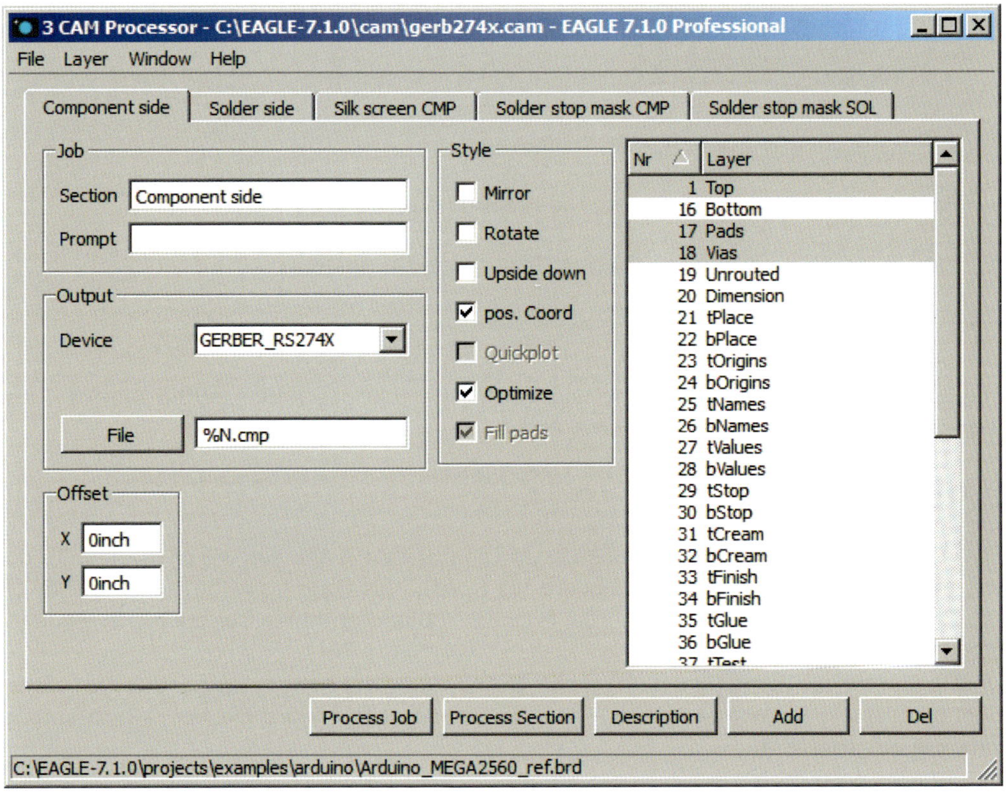

Figure 2-45: CAM Processor window

Loading or Creating Job Files

Before producing any manufacturing data, the user must specify the work which will be performed and on what design. This is specified in the CAM Job File.

A job defines the sequence of several output steps in an automatic data creation task. This sequence can be saved in a Jobfile. The user can, for example, use a job to generate individual files containing the Gerber data for several PCB layers. One such Jobfile is supplied with EAGLE (gerb274x-4layer.cam)

A job may be loaded from the Menu Toolbar of the CAM Processor by performing;
File ▷ Open ▷ Job and then selecting the required CAM Job file.

The user may also create a new job by starting CAM processor and not loading an existing Job file. The process to create a Job is as follows:

1. **Left-Click** on the 

button to add a new section.

2. Setup the parameters within the dialog.

3. Repeat steps 1 and 2. if to create the required number of Sections

4. Save the Job to a Job file by File ▷ Save ▷ Job from the menu.

The 

button allows the user to enter a text description of the Job file. This description will be shown in the Control Panel.

Loading Board Files

The next step is to specify the actual circuit (board) that is the subject of the job. To do this the user must open the EAGLE board file (.brd). This done from the Menu Toolbar of the CAM Processor by performing; File ▷ Open ▷ Board and then selecting the required board file.
Once open, the file name (and path) will be displayed on the bottom left hand corner of the CAM processor window (see Figure 2-45). This, then, is the board file from which output data will be generated.

Setting Output Parameters

Figure 2-45 shows 5 'tabs' within the dialog box. These tabs each contain different 'Sections' of the job process. In this illustration the Sections are: Component Side; Solder Side; Silk Screen CMP; Solder stop mask CMP and Solder stop mask SOL. Within each dialog Section the user is able to configure individual parameters in order to control the CAM process.

Starting Output

To instruct the CAM processor to execute the currently loaded job, the user simply, Left-Clicks on the [Process Job] button.

The user may also obtain output for a single section by **Left-Click** on the [Process Section] button.

The Text Editor Window

EAGLE contains a simple Text Editor which may be used to edit script files, User Language programs or any other text file.
The Text Editor is opened when either a script file or User Language program is opened (say from the Control Panel). When opened, the Text Editor appears as in Figure 2-46.

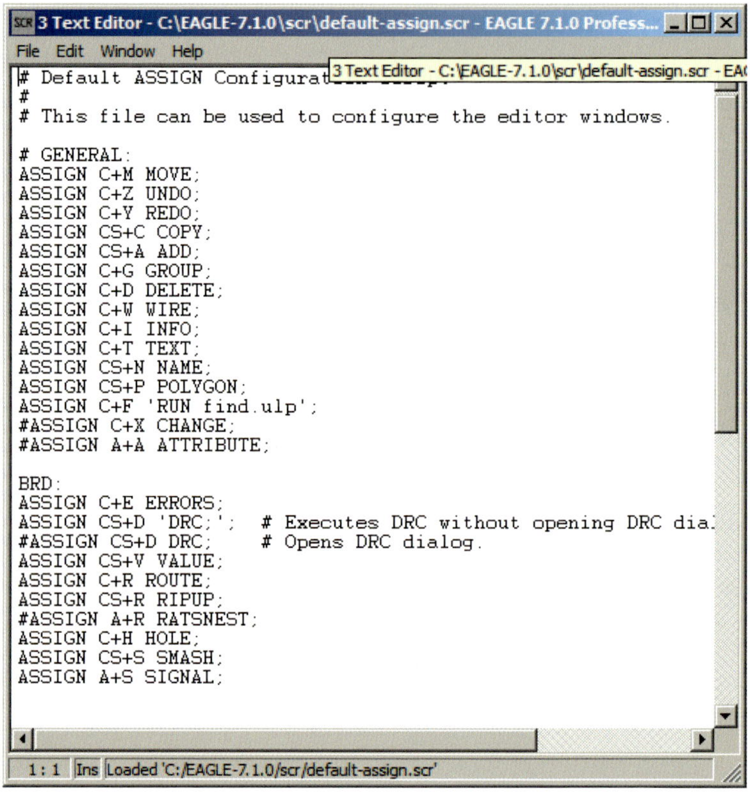

Figure 2-46: Text Editor window

The Text Editor has a Menu Toolbar which contains a set of menus. These menus combine the usual selection of standard operations of a text editor, including file, editing (e.g. copy, cut, paste, search and replace etc.), printing and formatting operations.

EAGLE also allows the user to use their own text editor. This can be configured from the Control Panel or an Editor's window using the Options ▷ User Interface menu selection.

Chapter 3 • Working with EAGLE

Command Input Alternatives and Navigating Around EAGLE

Icons for Commands

Within each Window of EAGLE there are many graphical icons. Icons appear in menus and toolbars; and typically represent, and may substitute, an EAGLE Command (which could be entered via the Command Line). Many of EAGLE's Command icons are shown in the 'Toolbar' sections outlined earlier in this book.

The first action in using an icon is to activate the corresponding command. These may be:

Left-Click on an icon and the user will typically invoke the corresponding Command.

The next action for a Command is usually displayed in the Status Bar at the bottom, left hand corner of the Window display.

Right-Click on an icon, or a component, and EAGLE typically activates the associated Context Menu.

Use of Mouse Buttons & Wheel

Left Mouse Button

The left mouse button is generally used to select, draw or place objects.

Mouse Wheel

The user may zoom in and out on a drawing, whilst inside an editor window, by scrolling the mouse wheel. The mouse wheel usually doubles as a Center Mouse Button. The option setting 'Mouse wheel zoom' determines the zoom factor for each 'step' of the mouse rotation. (refer to the Options User Interface)

Center Mouse Button

Using the center mouse button changes the current layer of, or mirrors, the object currently attached to the mouse cursor during an active command.

Table 3-1 lists the commands' functionality and response when used with the center mouse button:

Mirror Part	Change Active Layer
ADD	ARC
COPY	CIRCLE
INVOKE (mirror gate)	LABEL
MOVE (mirror object or group)	POLYGON
PASTE (mirror group)	RECT
	ROUTE
	SMD
	TEXT
	WIRE

Table 3-1: Command actions for center mouse button

The center mouse button may also be used to Click&Drag a drawing i.e. it will pan the drawing within the editor window.

Right Mouse Button

The right mouse button is mostly used to select a group, rotate objects attached to the mouse cursor, change wire bend styles and several other command specific functions.

If an object is selected with the right mouse button, then a context-specific menu is displayed. The menu contains commands which may be used, and that apply to this object.

If a group has been selected and there is currently a command active that can be applied to a group, then using the right mouse button will invoke a context-specific menu that will contain an entry for this group.

Table 3-2 lists the command with which the user may use the Right Mouse Button, together with the command action response to this.

Command	Right Mouse Action Response
'Change' Commands	
ARC	change direction of arc
BUS	change wire bend
CHANGE	apply change to group
NET	change wire bend
POLYGON	change wire bend
ROUTE	change wire bend
SPLIT	change wire bend
WIRE	change wire bend
'Rotate' Commands	
ADD	rotate part
INVOKE	rotate gate
LABEL	rotate label
PAD	rotate pad
PASTE	rotate group
PIN	rotate pin
ROTATE	rotate group
SMD	rotate SMD
TEXT	rotate text
MOVE	rotate object
'Group' Commands	
DELETE	delete group
GROUP	close polygon
MIRROR	mirror group
MOVE	select group
RIPUP	ripup group

Table 3-2: Command actions for Right Mouse Button

Selecting objects in densely populated areas

When the user tries to select an object at a position where several objects are placed close together, a four way arrow and the question;

Select highlighted object? (left=yes, right=next, ESC=cancel)

will be displayed, indicating that the user may now choose one of the following:

Right-Click will switch to the next object;
Left-Click will select the highlighted object;
Esc will cancel the selection procedure.

If the original selection was done with the right mouse button, a context specific popup menu will be displayed. This menu applies to the first selected object, and contains Next as the first entry. Repeatedly Left-Clicking on this entry will cycle through the objects within the selection radius.

The selection radius may be defined using the command SET Select_Factor select_radius.

Function Keys

Apart from the numerous icons embedded in the various menus and toolbars, EAGLE utilizes function keys as another shortcut for executing commands.
EAGLE is provided with a default set of function keys, which are assigned pre-defined commands. These default function key assignments are shown in Table 3-3.

Key Assignment	Command /Action
Alt + Backspace	undo action
Shift ⇧ + Alt + Backspace	re-do action
F2	redraw window content
Alt + F2	zoom to fit
F3	zoom in with factor 2 (double)
F4	zoom out with factor 0.5 (halve)
F5	center drawing at cursor position
F6	display/hide grid lines
F7	activate the MOVE command
F8	activate SPLIT command
F9	undo the previous action
F10	re-do the previous action

Table 3-3: EAGLE default function key assignments

The function key may be any key, not already utilized by the operating system, including: F1 – F12, Backspace, 0 – 9, A – Z. The modifier keys are: Ctrl Shift ⇧ and Alt . This means that any command, or sequence of commands, may be assigned to a function key by using the ASSIGN command.

The use of Alt + 0 ... 9 (number key) is a function also supported within EAGLE. It allows the user to choose a window to be displayed from those that are open

(e.g. Alt +1 selects window 1).

The combination Alt +0 can be used anywhere in the program to bring the Control Panel into the foreground.
(Note: This functionality is only supported in the Windows and the Linux versions of EAGLE.)

Keyboard and Mouse Combinations

The *modifier* keys (Alt, Ctrl and Shift) are used to modify the behavior of certain mouse actions. Note that depending on which operating system or window manager the user uses, some of these keys (in combination with mouse events) may not function correctly, or at all.

Alt Alt Modifier Key

Pressing the Alt key within a schematic or board drawing, switches the application to the alternate GRID. (Configuration of the Alternate GRID is defined elsewhere). This can typically be a finer grid than the default one. The alternate grid remains active while the Alt key is held down.

This functionality allows the user, for example, to perform fine positioning of an object in a dense area where the normal grid might be too coarse.

Ctrl Ctrl Modifier Key

Ctrl + **Left-Click** controls special functionality of individual commands, like selecting an object at its origin with the MOVE command.

Ctrl + **Right-Click** for commands that support wire bend styles (e.g. WIRE), this key/button combination toggles between corresponding wire bend styles (as displayed in the parameter toolbar).

For commands that support a group action, this key/button combination must be used when selecting the group (otherwise a context menu for the selected object would be opened).

Note: In Mac OS X the ⌘ (Cmd) key has to be used instead of the Ctrl key.

Modifier Key

\+ **Right-Click** reverses the progression of selection of the wire bend styles (for those commands that support wire bend styles).

\+ 

is the only command key sequence that allows the user to manipulate an object at a higher level of abstraction. This can be applied to: a polygon, a component in a schematic with multiple Gates; a Net or a Bus.
This concept is best explained by way of examples, for a user:

If the user activates  (DELETE) and then:

i. **Left-Click** onto a polygon, the vertex clicked on will be deleted. This will continue to work until three vertices are left. After that, the whole polygon will be deleted. If the user actions:

\+  + **Left-Click** the whole polygon will be deleted immediately.

ii. **Left-Click** onto a gate of a component with multiple gates in the schematic, the selected gate will be deleted.

If the user actions 

\+  **+ Left-Click** the whole component is removed; with all its gates.

iii. **Left-Click** (left clicks) onto a net, the selected part of the net will be deleted.

\+  + **Left-Click** erases the whole net segment. The same is valid for buses.

There are other commands that can be used with **Shift**, that have nothing to do with higher levels of abstraction. These are:

Shift + adds a group to a group

Shift + unlocks the component in a Schematic drawing

Shift + starts the WIRE in the same width as the already existing wire in a PCB Layout drawing

Esc Escape Key

The Escape key is used to cancel the current activity of an active command. The activity is cancelled without canceling the entire command. A subsequent press of the Esc key will act upon the command. For example, if the MOVE command is active, using the Escape key will drop the object that is currently attached to the cursor and another object can be selected.

Cursor-Up/ Cursor Down

The cursor up and cursor down keys can be used for:

- to scroll through the command history in the command line of an editor window;
- to select an item up or down a menu.

Basic Screen Functions

The user is able to control the mode of display within an Editor by using some basic screen commands. The quickest method utilizes the command icons shown in Figure 3-1.

Figure 3-1: Window display actions

These icons represent different modes of the WINDOW command and are, left to right:

- Fit drawing into the screen (WINDOW FIT)

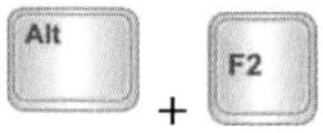

- zoom in by a factor of 2

- zoom out by a factor of 2

- redraw the screen (WINDOW)

- select a new window area.

Context Menus

EAGLE provides the user with a shortcut to some commands by using Context Menus. These menus are both object- and context-specific in that they display the range of options available when the operator **Right-Clicks** with the mouse anywhere within a Window.

If the user **Right-Clicks** on an object, EAGLE displays a Context command menu overlaying the object (see Figure 3-2). The user may then select the next command to be executed by **Left-Clicking** on the appropriate menu icon. The user may further display and edit the object's properties by clicking onto the Properties entry.

The context menu contains all commands that can be executed with the selected object. Some of them can be even changed directly by **Left-Clicking** in the Properties window. The Properties dialog will be opened.

Invoking a Context menu on some Toolbar Command Icons will display a list of prior (historical) 'values' from which the user may select. This is available from the ADD, REPLACE and VALUE command within the Schematic and Layout editors.

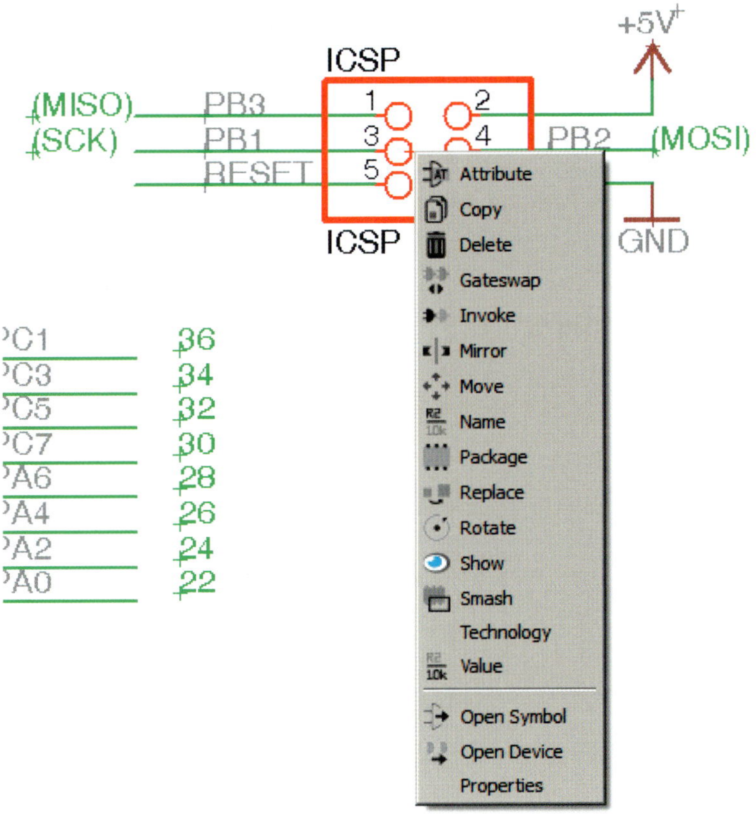

Figure 3-2: Device context menu in a Schematic drawing

Drag & Drop

EAGLE supports the action of 'Drag&Drop'.

The user may, for example, copy, move or create links to files using this technique. It may be used between different programs. For instance files that are 'pulled' from the Control Panel tree structure, into an editor Window are opened and started automatically.

Similarly, User Language programs or script files that are pulled with the aid of the mouse out of the Control Panel, and into an editor window, are also opened automatically in the text editor.

Drag & Drop may also be used from within the Library Manager.
The user may add a new device to a Schematic drawing directly from a Device entry in the library's directory content tree. If a Schematic Editor window is simultaneously open, the user may **Left-Click** on the Device in the library tree, and then drag it with the mouse and drop it into the Schematic drawing.

Similarly, if the user is working with the Layout Editor, Drag & Drop will only operate with Packages. If more than one Package version is available, the ADD dialog will open automatically, so that the required Package can be selected.

Managing Grids and Units

Setting up the grid values of EAGLE is important, since all actions performed by the application are based on a datum and grid measurements which, in turn, determine the spatial relationship between all objects within drawings.

EAGLE performs its internal calculations using a basic grid size (spacing) of 1/10,000 mm (0.1 micron). Any multiple of this value can be set as the working grid spacing. The fundamental unit may be set to either of the following: microns, mils, inches and mm. This base unit is set using the GRID command and applies to all values.

Grid sizes and units should be configured prior to the commencement of any schematic or board layout. The reason for this is that all dimensions on an object are defined relative to that object's origin; and these are established in its library definition. Therefore, schematics should always be drawn on a grid of 0.1 inches (2.54 mm) since the libraries are defined this way. The grid for board layouts should be determined by the components used and by the complexity of the board.

The Grid dialog (as in Figure 3-3) is invoked by **Left-Click** .

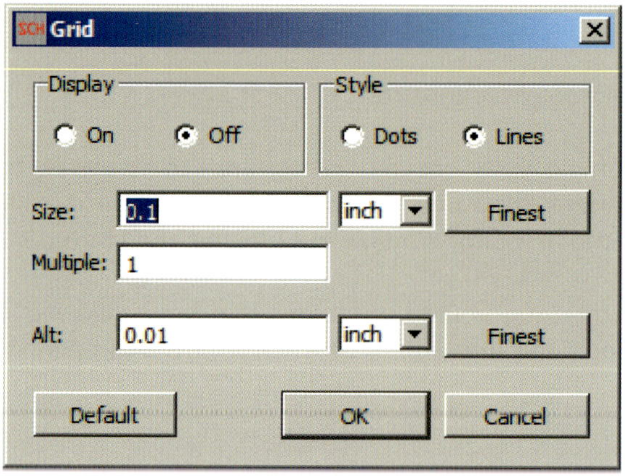

Figure 3-3: GRID dialog

The parameters which may be set in this dialog are:

Display: These options simply switch the grid display on or off.

Style: specifies the way the grid is displayed; as either dots or lines.

Size: Sets the current grid size in decimal whole and fractions of the units chosen in the combo box.

Multiple: The Multiple option indicates how many grid lines are displayed. e.g. if the value 5 is entered at Multiple, every fifth line will be displayed.

Alt : allows the user to set an alternative grid which can be activated by pressing the Alt key during an active command. This can be very useful for placing parts in a dense layout or arranging labels in a schematic drawing.

Finest: sets the finest grid that is possible.

Default: selects the editor's standard grid.

Grid settings can be configured at:

Options ▷ Set ▷ Misc ▷ Min. visible grid size -
sets the limit on zooming, below which the grid will not be displayed.

Options ▷ Set ▷ Colors -
The required color may be selected by clicking the colored button of the respective palette (depends on the background color) in the menu.

Table 3-4 and Table 3-5 give conversions between bases of measurement and some commonly used values of grids in Millimeters, Inches & Mils.

Millimeters (mm)	Inches (inches)	Mils (mils)
1mm	0.03937 inch	39.37mils
25.4mm	1 inch	1000 mils
0.0254mm	0.001 inch	1 mil

Table 3-4: conversion between millimeters, inches & mils

Inches (inches)	Mils (mils)	Millimeters (mm)
0.008	8	0.2032
0.010	10	0.2540
0.012	12	0.3048
0.016	16	0.4064
0.024	24	0.6096
0.032	32	0.8128
0.040	40	1.0160
0.050	50	1.2700
0.100	100	2.5400

Table 3-5: commonly used values in millimeters, inches & mils

The Concept of Layers in EAGLE Drawings

EAGLE provides the user with a methodology for constructing drawings in a planar architecture by using the concept of layers.

Each drawing, whether Schematic or PCB Layout, may contain elements or objects which are placed in different planes (or layers). These layers do not necessarily represent a physical arrangement, but they do correspond to a logical plane, within which all similarly designated objects are constrained. A physical example of the Layers concept, in the PCB Layout Editor, is the use of the Layers named 'Top' and 'Bottom' to designate the 'component' and 'solder' sides respectively of a double-sided printed circuit board.

Further, layers are used in combination to derive a valid, useful output to the manufacturing process. For example, the combination of Top, Pad, and Via layers is used to generate masks for etching the component side of the printed circuit board. Similarly, the combination of Bottom, Pad, and Via layers is used to generate masks for the solder side of the board. The Pad layer contains the through holes for the component connections and the Via layer contains the via holes to transport a signal track to another layer. The name and purpose of EAGLE's layers are given in Table 4-4 and Table 4-5.

The presentation of Layers is controlled using the Layer Settings icon in the Command Toolbar. **Left-Click** will invoke the Display command dialog shown in Figure 3-4 .

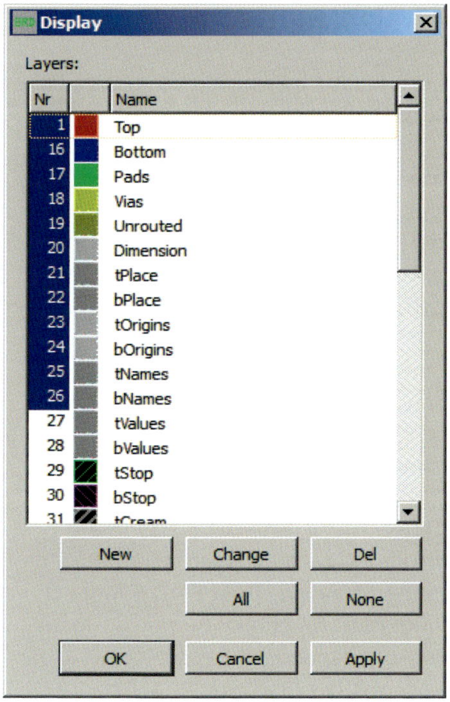

Figure 3-4: Display Dialog

The layers marked by a colored highlight, in the 'Nr' column, are currently displayed in the open drawing. The activation of any layer may be switched on or off by Left-Clicking on the layer number (in the 'Nr' column).
The buttons in this dialog perform as follows:

- The All and None buttons switch on or off selection of all layers.

- Apply immediately reflects the changes in layer selection, in the editor window.

- New allows the user to create a new layer (above layer number 100).

- Delete allows the user to remove layers (provided the layer does not contain objects).

Forward&Back Annotation

Forward&Back Annotation is a means by which a schematic file and its associated board file are logically linked, to ensure their consistency.

When a PCB layout is created (using the BOARD command 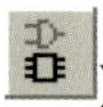) the consistency is established between the schematic and board drawings. Every action performed on the schematic diagram is immediately reflected in the layout drawing. For example, if a new Device is added to the schematic, the device will appear in the layout drawing; similarly if a net is added to the schematic, the corresponding signal lines are simultaneously drawn in the layout.

Particular operations are only allowed in the schematic drawing; for example the placement or deletion of signals. (The Layout Editor automatically prevents the command action and issues an appropriate warning.)

To maintain consistency between the schematic and board drawings of the same project, the user needs to have both drawing files loaded and open simultaneously. If they are not, and a change is made to either drawing, then EAGLE loses the consistency between them and the Forward&Back Annotation functionality can no longer work. Figure 3-5 shows a schematic window after the corresponding Layout drawing has been closed. When both files are opened, EAGLE performs the Electrical Rule Check (ERC) to ensure consistency. If this process finds errors, the ERC opens an Error window containing appropriate messages about the respective drawings.

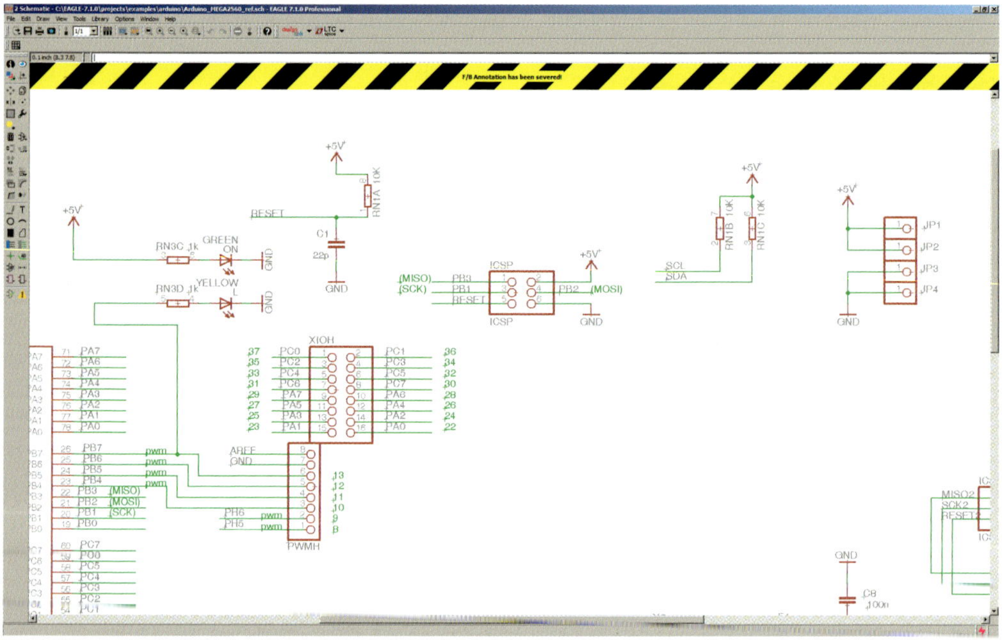

Figure 3-5: Forward&Back annotation

Configuring EAGLE

EAGLE provides the user with the ability to configure the application for his or her own particular requirements. Configuration may be performed for EAGLE - wide usage, or for focus on individual users and/or projects.

EAGLE stores the required configuration settings in different places (files) within the application. These are as follows:

eagle.scr the file which stores basic program settings that apply to all users and each new project;
eagle.epf project-specific configuration settings are held in this file;

eaglerc in Windows this file is named *eaglerc.usr* and in Linux it is in *~/.eaglerc.* In any case it stores personal user preference settings.

Configuration values that are drawing-specific are stored directly within the drawing file itself. For example, a board layout may have unique Design Rules, special layer colors, and newly defined layers or the grid settings – all will be stored directly in the layout file. This functionality also applies to schematic diagram and library files.

The *eagle.scr* File

eagle.scr is a script file which is automatically executed when an editor window is opened or when a new schematic diagram, board or library file is created (except when a project file already exists).

EAGLE looks first in the current project directory for *eagle.scr*. If it is not found then it is sought in the path/directory named in the Scripts entry in the Options ▷ Directories dialog. This file can contain all those commands that are to be carried out whenever an editor window (other than the Text Editor) is opened.

```
# This file can be used to configure the editor windows.
Assign A+F3 'Window 4;';
Assign A+F4 'Window 0.25;';
Assign A+F7 'Grid mm;';
Assign A+F8 'Grid inch;';
Menu '[designlink22.png] Search and order {\
General : Run designlink–order.ulp –general; |\
Schematic : Run designlink–order.ulp; \
}';
BRD:
#Menu Add Change Copy Delete Display Grid Group Move \
#Name Quit Rect Route Script Show Signal Split \
#Text Value Via Window ';' Wire Write Edit;
Grid inch 0.05 on;
Grid alt inch 0.01;
Set Pad_names on;
Set Width_menu 0.008 0.01 0.016;
Set Drill_menu 0.024 0.032 0.040;
Set Size_menu 0.05 0.07 0.12;
Set Used_layers 1 16 17 18 19 20 21 22 23 24 25 26 \
27 28 39 40 41 42 43 44 45;
Change width 0.01;
Change drill 0.024;
Change size 0.07;
SCH:
Grid Default;
Change Width 0.006;
#Menu Add Bus Change Copy Delete Display Gateswap \
#Grid Group Invoke Junction Label Move Name Net \
#Pinswap Quit Script Show Split Value Window ';' \
#Wire Write Edit;
LBR:
#Menu Close Export Open Script Write ';' Edit;
DEV:
Grid Default;
#Menu Add Change Copy Connect Delete Display Export \
#Grid Move Name Package Prefix Quit Script Show \
#Value Window ';' Write Edit;
SYM:
Display all;
Grid Default On;
Change Width 0.010;
#Menu Arc Change Copy Delete Display Export \
#Grid Group Move Name Paste Pin Quit Script \
#Show Split Text Value Window ';' Wire Write Edit;
PAC:
Grid Default On;
Grid Alt inch 0.005;
Change Width 0.005;
Change Size 0.050;
Change Smd 0.039 0.039;
#Menu Add Change Copy Delete Display Grid Group \
#Move Name Pad Quit Script Show Smd Split Text \
#Window ';' Wire Write Edit;
```

Figure 3-6 gives an example of an eagle.scr file.

It can be seen in this example that:

- Commands which are defined before the first label (normally BRD:) are recognized and executed for all Editor windows.

- A comment in a script file is commenced with '#'.

- The *SCH*, *BRD* and *LBR* labels indicate those segments of the file that are only to be executed if the Schematic, Layout or Library Editor window, respectively, is opened.

- The *DEV*, *SYM* and *PAC* labels indicate those segments of the file that are only to be executed if the Device, Symbol or Package editor mode, respectively, is activated.

Editor windows which are opened automatically due to project file specifications do not necessarily invoke the *eagle.scr* file. These windows will need to be closed and re-opened in order to adopt the settings of this startup script. (Alternatively, the user may simply read the eagle.*scr file* through the SCRIPT command).

The eaglerc File

The *eaglerc* file contains information about the following:

- SET command (Options/Set menu)
- ASSIGN command (function key assignments)
- User Interface
- Currently loaded project (path)

The *eaglerc* file stores user-specific configuration data in the certain locations. EAGLE looks for the configuration file in these locations in the sequence given below, and executes them (if they exist).

Under the Windows environment...
This file is stored in the user's home directory:
If there is no *home* environment variable set, the following Windows registry entry is used:
HKEY_CURRENT_USER\Software\Microsoft\Windows\Current-Version\Explorer\Shell Folders\AppData

The eaglerc file is sought in the following directories:
<prgdir>*/eaglerc*
$HOME/eaglerc.usr

Under the Linux and Mac environments...
User-specific configuration data is stored in~/*.eaglerc.*
The *eaglerc* file is sought in the following directories:
<prgdir>/eaglerc
/etc/eaglerc
$HOME/.eaglerc

NOTE: *These files* ***should not*** *be edited.*
Some users may need to work with different EAGLE release versions for different projects. If so, then it is possible to start EAGLE with the command line option *U;* which can be used to define the location of the *eaglerc* file, and to differentiate the functionality of versions and workspaces. It is possible, therefore, to use this as an initial configuration file, say for example, in a network environment.

EAGLE Project File

When a new project is created (for example, from the Control Panel Menu File ▷ New ▷ Project) a directory is created in the Projects branch of the tree view. Further, the *eagle.epf* configuration file (Project File) is automatically created in that project directory.

The Project File stores the following information about a project:

1. changes to object properties that are made with the CHANGE command during editing;

2. the contents of the *Width*, *Diameter*, and *Size* menus;

3. the libraries in use for this project;

4. the position and contents of the active windows at the time the program is closed.

   (This assumes that the *Automatically save project file* option under *Options* ▷ *Backup* in the Control Panel is active. This state will be recreated the next time the program starts.)

Configuration Menus & Commands

Most of the options within EAGLE are set by means of the Options menus within the individual EAGLE editor window.
The Control Panel allows settings to be configured for *Directories*, file *Backup* and the visual appearance of the editor window (*User interface and Windows Positions*). These options are described in the earlier section of the book titled; 'Options Menu'.

The Options Menu

Using the *Options* ▷ *User interface* settings it is possible to select the icon-based menu or a configurable text menu, the latter being one of the most powerful methods of configuring EAGLE. Specifically, it is possible to construct custom menus, comprising a hierarchical structure of text items and associated icons, by using the MENU command within a script file.

The User interface dialog is shown in Figure 3-7

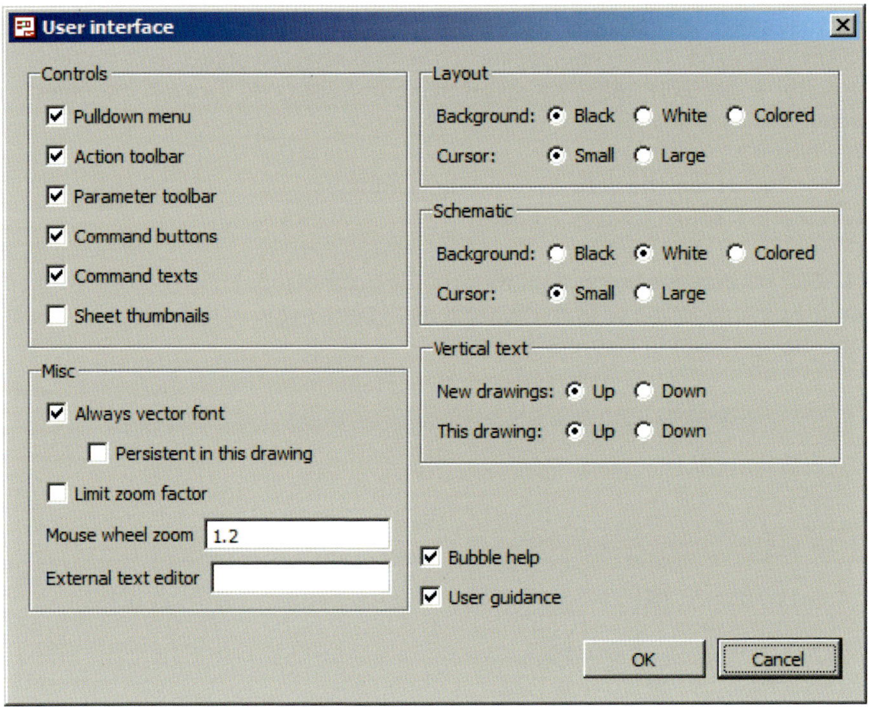

Figure 3-7: User interface dialog

The *Options* menu in the editor windows of schematic diagrams, layouts and libraries, contains two other entries: the *Assign* and *Set* items.

The ASSIGN command alters and displays the assignment of the function keys. This was discussed previously in the section titled:

Selecting objects in densely populated areas

When the user tries to select an object at a position where several objects are placed close together, a four way arrow and the question;

Select highlighted object? (left=yes, right=next, ESC=cancel)

will be displayed, indicating that the user may now choose one of the following:

Right-Click will switch to the next object;

Left-Click will select the highlighted object;

will cancel the selection procedure.

If the original selection was done with the right mouse button, a context specific popup menu will be displayed. This menu applies to the first selected object, and contains Next as the first entry. Repeatedly Left-Clicking on this entry will cycle through the objects within the selection radius.

The selection radius may be defined using the command:
`SET Select_Factor select_radius command.`

Overall EAGLE parameters are altered with the SET command. These can be invoked using SET from the command line or from the Options ▷ Set... menu option. In either case, these invoke the dialog shown in Figure 3-8.

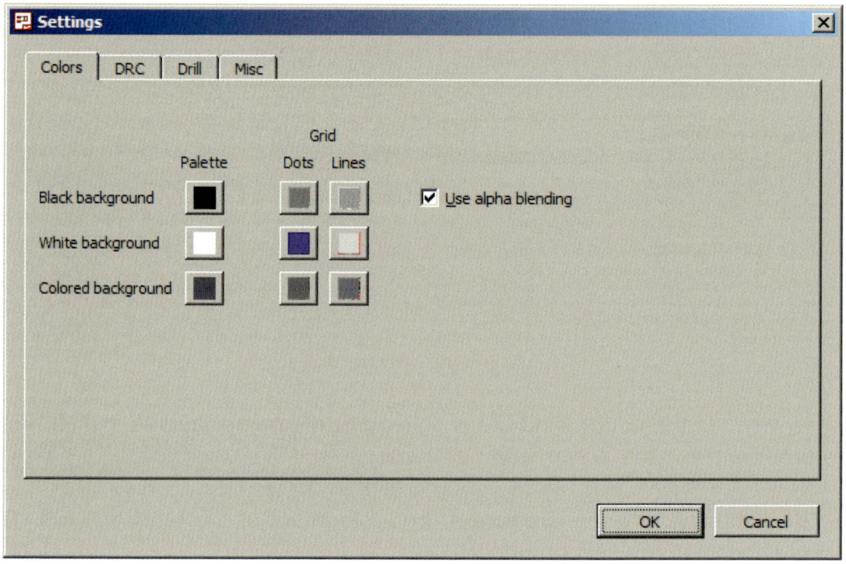

Figure 3-8: Options Settings dialog

Setting Colors

The first tab in the Options Settings Dialog is the *Colors* tab. This allows the user to set colors for the layers and background of a drawing as well as for its grid lines or dots. EAGLE offers three color palettes. These are for black, white and colored backgrounds. **Left-Clicking** on any of these 3 palette icons activates the Color Palette Configuration Dialog of Figure 3-9.

It can be seen that each palette allows a maximum of 64 color entries, which can be configured to any RGB or Alpha channel value. This can be seen in the 'grid' of color boxes in the Color dialog.

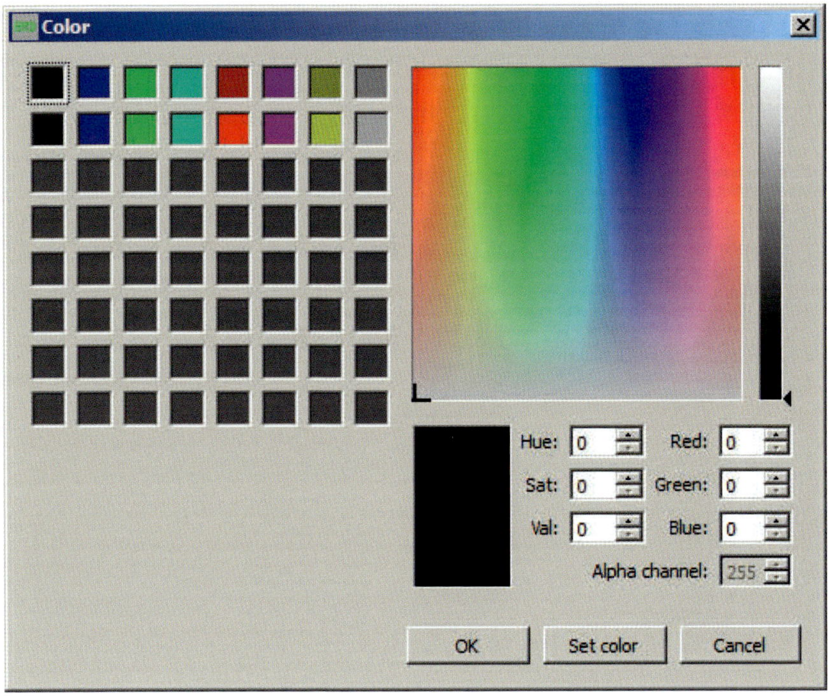

Figure 3-9: Color palette configuration dialog

By default EAGLE uses the first 16 values (entries 0..15) in the palette; eight colors followed by a further eight 'so-called' highlight colors. The first entry of the palette determines the background color. However, in the white palette, the background color is locked, since printed output is normally made on white paper. A color of the palette at position *x* can be given the corresponding highlight color at position *x*+8.

The user may define a new color by selecting an undesignated box in the matrix and then adjust the color in two ways:

i. using the color selection area and the saturation bar to the right of the matrix;

ii. entering values for *Red, Green, Blue , Hue, Sat, Val* and Alpha channel directly into the numbered data windows.

The *Alpha channel* determines the transparency of the color. (The value 0 means the color is totally transparent (invisible), the maximum value 255 means the color is opaque). For printouts the value of the alpha channel should be set to 255 for each color. The alpha value is ignored when using a black background.
Older versions of EAGLE did not use the current technique of mixing colors using an OR function. To turn off the newer functionality, uncheck the *Use alpha blending* check box.

Setting Drills

The Drill tab (in Figure 3-10) of the Settings Dialog allows the user to add, edit and delete drill specifications. This allows a number to represent a size for use in the layout drawings.

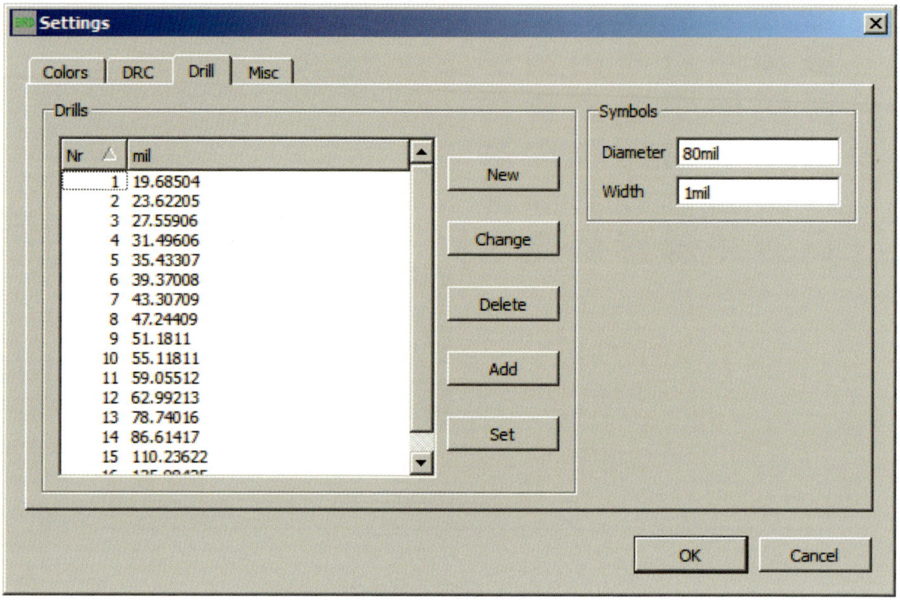

Figure 3-10: Drill configuration dialog

Miscellaneous Settings

The user may configure a number of other options of EAGLE by selecting the *Misc* tab of the *Settings* window (as shown in Figure 3-11). This allows the configuration (on or off) by a series of check boxes, or by the entering of values.

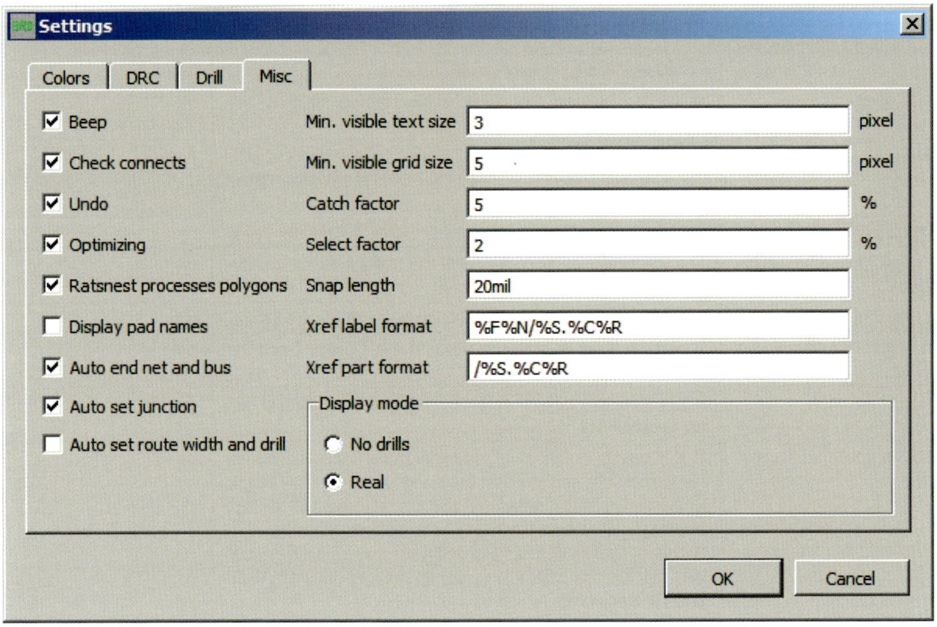

Figure 3-11: Miscellaneous Settings dialog

The Miscellaneous Settings Options are explained in Table 3-6:

Option	Control / Action	Default
Beep	Switches on/off the confirmation beep.	on
Check connects	Activates the package check while placing parts in the schematic.	on
Undo	Switches on/off the undo/redo buffer of the current editor window. This also applies to a consistent schematic/layout pair.	on
Optimizing	Enables the automatic removal of bends in straight lines.	on
Ratsnest processes polygons	The contents of polygons will be calculated with the RATSNEST command.	on
Display pad names	Pad names are displayed in the Layout or Package Editor.	off
Auto end net and bus	If placing a net on a pin or a bus the net drops from the mouse cursor.	on
Auto set junction	A junction will be set automatically when ending a net on another net.	on
Auto set route width and drill	If this option is ON: the FollowmeRouter uses the values for wire width and via drill diameter given by the Design Rules or the net classes for the tracks, and will be set automatically when the user clicks on a signal wire. If this option is OFF: EAGLE will take the value the user has set for the width. e.g. using the previous CHANGE WIDTH command.	on
Min. visible text size	Only text with size ≥ the set minimum size is displayed.	3 pixels
Min. visible grid size	Only Grid lines/dots ≥ the set minimum size is displayed.	5 pixels
Catch factor	A mouse click can reach objects within the set radius. (given in % of the height of the current drawing window). Setting the value to 0 will switch this limitation off.	5%
Select factor	Within this radius EAGLE offers objects for selection (given in % of the height of the current drawing window).	2%
Snap length	Defines the radius of the magneticpads function of pads and SMDs. If the user are laying tracks with the ROUTE command and approach a pad or a SMD beyond the given value (i.e. the dynamically calculated airwire becomes shorter than the given radius) the wire will be snapped to the pads/SMDs center.	20 mil
Display mode	Pads/vias are shown with a drill hole (real) or without it (No drills).	real

Table 3-6: Miscellaneous Settings Options

Importing and Exporting Data within EAGLE

EAGLE supports a number of methods for the import and export of data. These include the use of:

i. The *File* ▷ *Import* and *File* ▷ *Export* menu selections;

ii. The export command for exporting

iii. Script files for importing

iv. EAGLE User Language programs for import and export.

Importing Data

The user may import data using the *File* ▷ *Import* menu selection to import to either a Schematic or Layout drawing. These menus are shown in Figure 3-12 and Figure 3-13 respectively.

When invoked, the File/Import menu offers the alternatives of importing:

a. an EAGLE drawing;
b. a PCAD/ Altium/Protel file;
c. a Bitmap file;
d. a Netlist (Layout Editor only);
e. an Ultiboard file (Layout Editor only).

Importing an EAGLE drawing is self-explanatory.

Importing a PCAD/ Altium/Protel file uses the ACCELASCII data format. It is this format which can be imported into EAGLE. Further information can be displayed when the user selects this function and **Left-Click** on Help...within the dialog box.

Using the Bitmap file selection, an image may be imported into EAGLE. This import may then be used as a template to *re-draw* the desired target drawing in the Schematic or Layout editors. Further information is displayed when the user selects this option.

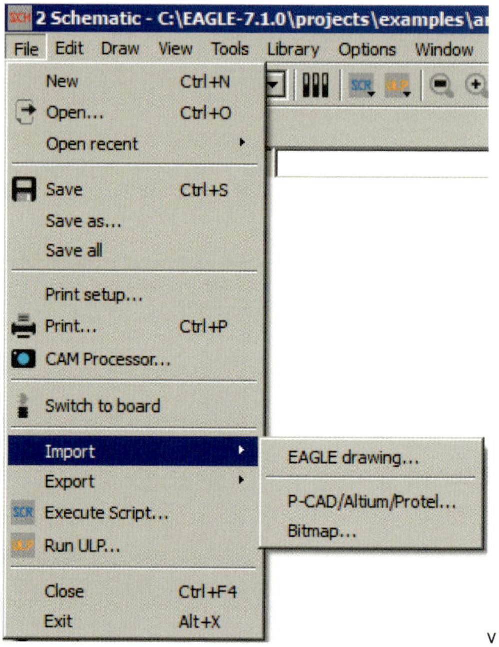

Figure 3-12: File Import menu for Schematic drawing

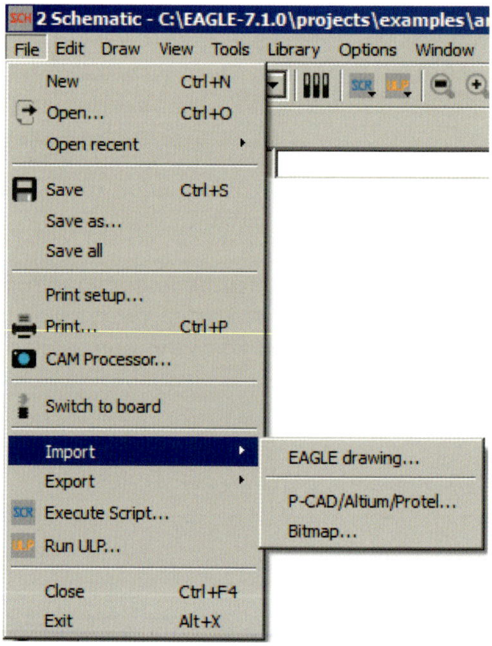

Figure 3-13: File Import menu for Layout drawing

Within a Layout Drawing, the user may import a netlist from another format using this option of the import menu. When selected, the dialog shown in Figure 3-14 will be displayed. (This is in fact the User Language Program; *netlist-converter.ulp*).

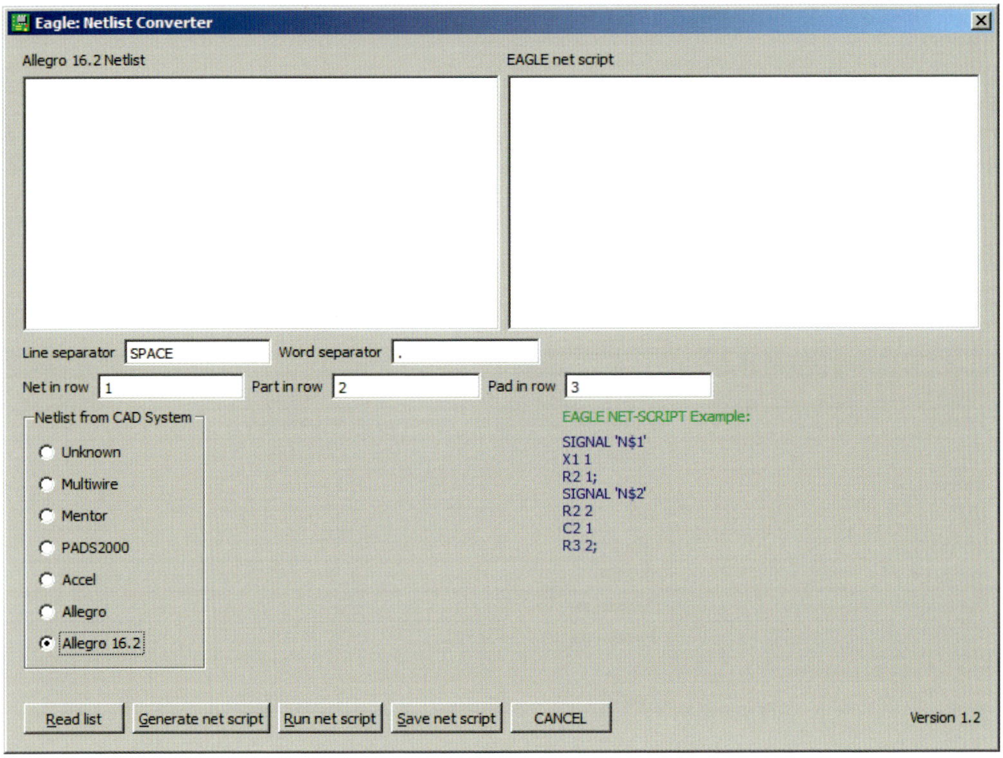

Figure 3-14: netlist converter dialog

EAGLE can import from a number of formats, as listed in the 'Netlist from CAD System' list in the lower left hand side of the dialog. The user imports the netlist from the source format and may then generate a net script. This script may then be used in creating a new layout. Users may also import files which employ the Ultiboard PCB Design Data File format. This is a proprietary format used by the National Instruments' Electronics Workbench range of products.

Exporting Data

The user may import data using the *File ▷ Export* menu selection to import to either a Schematic or Layout drawing. These menus are shown in Figure 3-15 and Figure 3-16 respectively.

When invoked, the File/Export menu offers the alternatives for exporting, as given in Table 3-7.

Schematic	PCB Layout	Library
Netlist	Netlist	Script
Partlist	Partlist	Directory
Pinlist	Pinlist	Image
Image	Image	
DXF	DXF	
Libraries	Libraries	
NetScript	DIF4.0	
BOM	Fabmaster	
	Hyperlynx	
	IPC	
	Unidat	

Table 3-7: File Export alternatives for drawing types

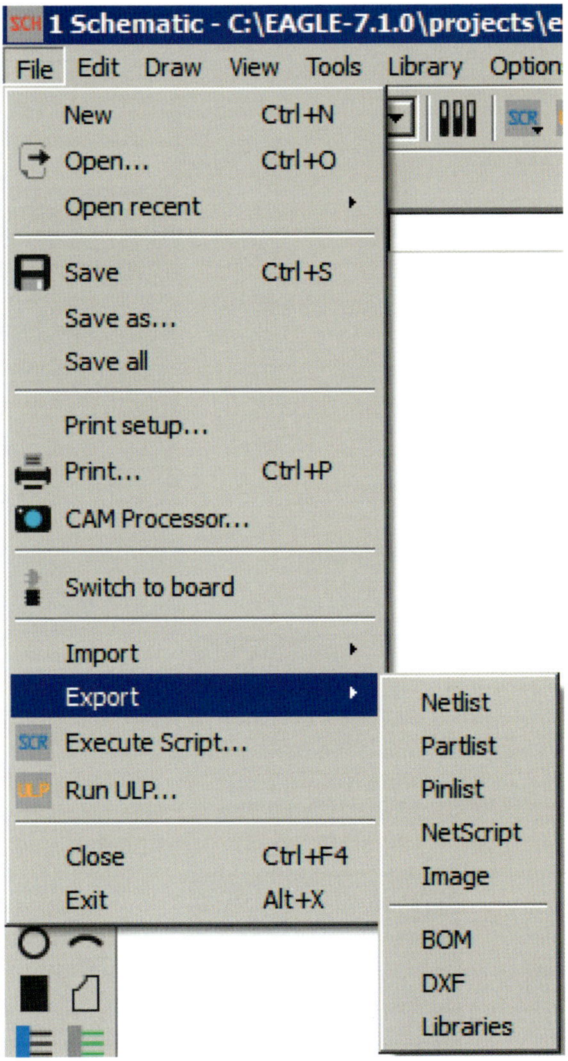

Figure 3-15: File Export menu for Schematic drawing

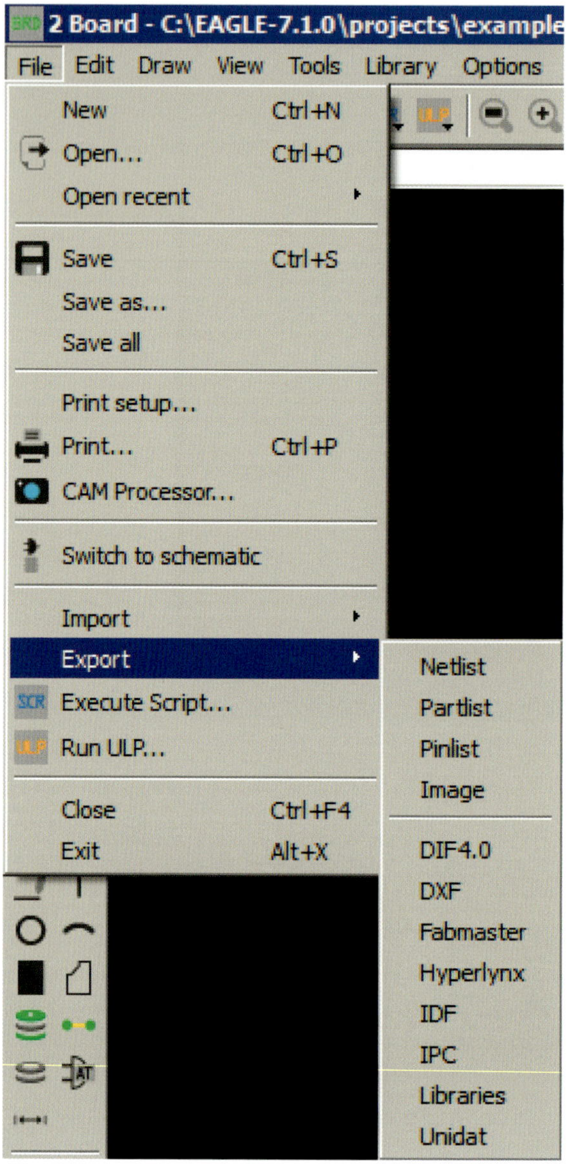

Figure 3-16 File Export menu for Layout drawing

The function of these options is as follows:

Netlist
Outputs a netlist, for the currently loaded drawing, in an EAGLE-specific format. The user may also use several User Language programs that allow the user to export various net list formats. (Refer to CadSoft's Download area at www.CadSoftusa.com/download.htm).

Partlist
Outputs a component list for the current drawing.

Pinlist
Outputs a pin/pad list for the current drawing, also listing the connected nets.

Image
This option allows the user to generate files in the following graphic formats:

- bmp Windows Bitmap file
- png Portable Network Graphics file
- pbm Portable Bitmap file
- pgm Portable Grayscale Bitmap file
- ppm Portable Pixelmap file
- tif Tag Image file
- xbm X Bitmap file
- xpm X Pixmap file

Selecting this option opens the Export Image Dialog, shown in Figure 3-17 .

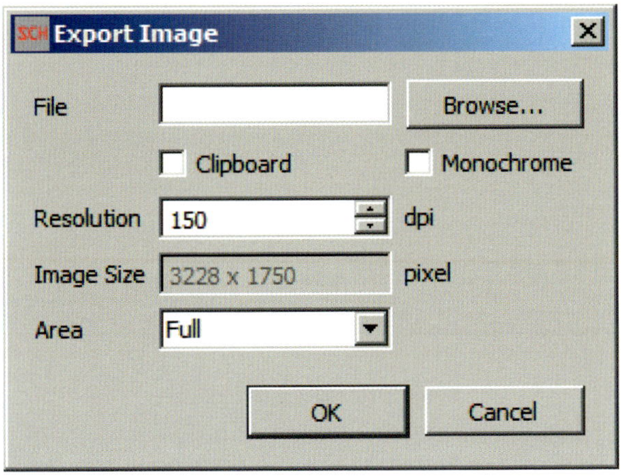

Figure 3-17: Export Image dialog

This Dialog allows the user to enter the path and name of the target file. The user should click the Browse button, select the output path, and type in the graphic file name with its extension. NOTE: The file extension determines the graphic file type.

If the user wishes to generate a black and white image, activate the *Monochrome* checkbox.

To make the image available via the system's clipboard, check the *Clipboard* checkbox.

The final *Resolution* of the output graphic can be set in dots per inch. The resulting *Image Size* will be shown in the lowest field in pixel dimensions.

The *Area* field allows a selection of *Full* or *Window*; *Full* prints the whole drawing, whereas *Window* prints the visible part of the drawing currently in the Editor window.

DXF

This option runs the User Language Program; *dxf.ulp* and opens the Dialog shown in Figure 3-18.

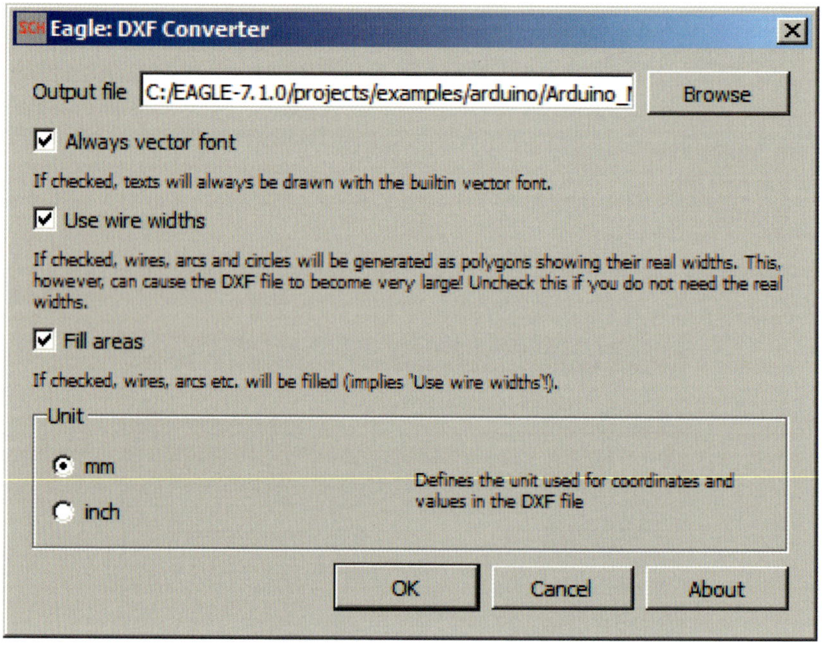

Figure 3-18: DXF Converter dialog

This allows the user to specify a target file for the drawing in the dxf format.

Script

This allows the user to export the currently loaded library in the form of a script file. This script can be edited with any text editor in order to generate, for example, a user defined library; or to copy parts of one library into another.

Further, the modified script file can be imported into a new or existing library using the EAGLE SCRIPT command. (In order to avoid loss of precision the grid unit in the script file is set to Millimeters.)

Directory

Allows the user to export a list of the contents (Devices, Symbols, and Packages) of the currently loaded library.

Libraries

Allows the user to create library files with all the devices and packages that are used in the current project. This option opens the Dialog shown in Figure 3-19.

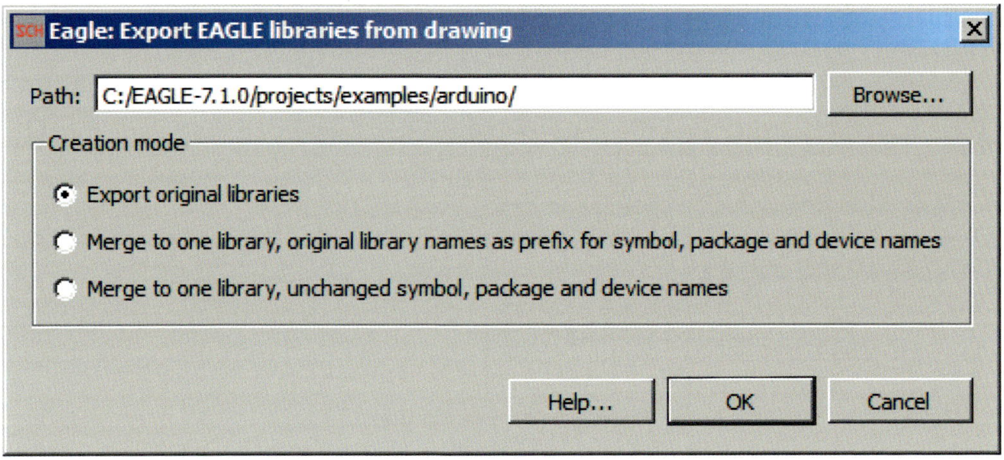

Figure 3-19: Libraries Export dialog

The user must specify the path where the library files shall be stored in the dialog window.

(**WARNING!** – *Care should be taken **not to overwrite** the system libraries.*)

This option allows the user to extract all library definitions from schematic and board drawings and make them available for further editing or usage within personal libraries. This function is realized by running the User Language Program *explbrs.ulp*.

Netscript

This option generates and exports a netlist of the currently loaded schematic in the form of a script file. The resultant netscript can then be imported into a board file with the help of the SCRIPT command. This could be used to detect possible differences between the netlists of a schematic and layout pair, and may be used to find errors, say, if the board and schematic had lost consistency.

BOM

This option runs the User Language Program *bom.ulp*, and opens the Dialog shown in Figure 3-20. This creates a Bill of Materials for the schematic drawing currently open.

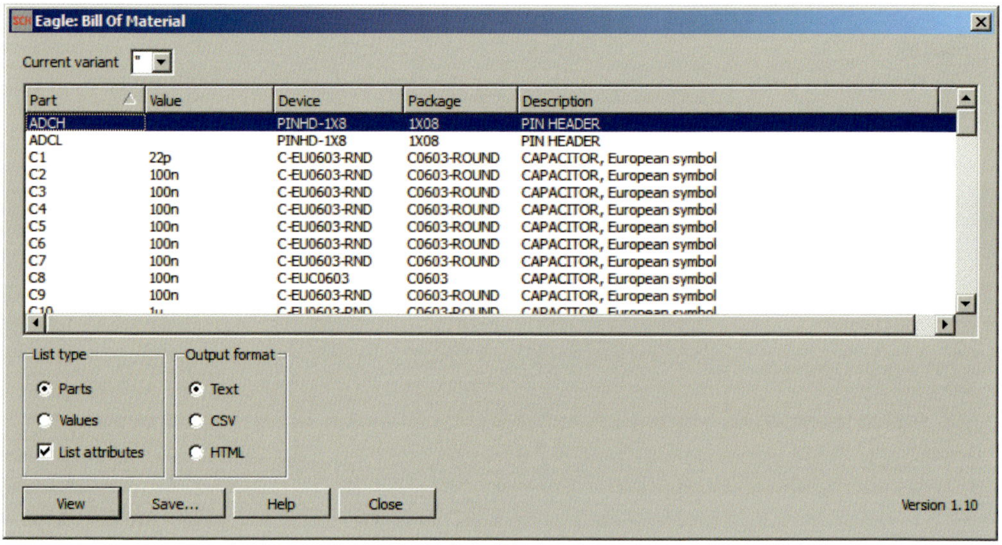

Figure 3-20 Bill of Materials Dialog

The exported file may list the components in order of either the Parts' Name or their Value. The format of the file may be selected as either: Text, CSV or HTML.

Naming of Objects in EAGLE

Nearly all objects in EAGLE are given a name. This may be assigned by EAGLE automatically, or assigned by the user. The user is able to edit an object's name at any time by using the NAME command

Name Length

Names of objects in EAGLE may have any desired length. There is no limit. The user should, however, consider readability of the object names within a drawing when naming devices.

Forbidden and Special Characters

There are a number of characters which are *not allowed* to be used within names. These are:

' ' spaces
';' semi-colons
' ¨ ' umlauts

Quotation marks and other characters (above 127 in the ASCII table) *should be avoided* as far as possible.

Device names should *not* contain:
'?' question marks
'*' asterisks

These characters are used as placeholders for Package variants (?) and technologies (*).

Bus or *Partbus* names must not contain colons, commas or square brackets.

Other names
Other special characters include the '=', '~' (tilde) and '!'. These have particular meaning under certain circumstances. The reader should refer to the help file in specific reference to the TEXT command to understand these specific uses.

Chapter 4 • EAGLE Window Commands

This section of the book describes the most commonly used commands of EAGLE; and is grouped in the context of how the command is used within the application. These commands will normally be entered on the command line of the user interface; however some commands may be activated via a menu item or icon.

Author's Note: Some material in this chapter is taken directly from a number of EAGLE documentation sources. This has been done in order present this information in a more convenient, accessible and integrated form; and to relate it contextually to illustrated user actions.
The author acknowledges that full ownership and rights of this material reside with Cad-SoftComputer GmbH.

Commands for Changing Modes or Files

This section discusses the most frequently used file manipulation commands. They apply to all EAGLE modules, except where indicated.

OPEN

Function
Opens a library for editing.

Syntax
OPEN library_name

See also CLOSE, USE, EDIT, SCRIPT

The OPEN command is used to open an existing library or create a new library. Once the library has been opened or created, an existing or new symbol, device, or package may be edited.

This command is mainly used in script files.

Examples
The command:

```
OPEN linear
```

would open the library 'linear.lbr' in a new window.

CLOSE

Function
Closes an editor window.

Syntax
`CLOSE`

See also OPEN, EDIT, WRITE, SCRIPT

The CLOSE command is used to close an editor window. Upon using this command, if the drawing the user is currently editing has been modified, EAGLE will prompt the user to choose whether they wish to save it or not.

This command is mainly used in script files.

QUIT

Function
Quits the program

Syntax
`QUIT`

This command ends the editing session. If any changes have been made but the drawing has not yet been saved, a popup menu will ask the user if the user want to save the drawing/library first.
The user can also exit from EAGLE at any time by pressing **Alt+X**.

EDIT

Function

Loads an existing drawing to be edited or creates a new drawing.

Syntax

```
EDIT name
EDIT name.ext
EDIT .ext
EDIT .sX [ .sY ]
```

See also OPEN, CLOSE, BOARD

The EDIT command is used to load a drawing, or if a library has been opened with the OPEN command, to load a package, symbol, or device for editing.

`EDIT name.brd`	loads a board
`EDIT name.sch`	loads a schematic
`EDIT name.pac`	loads a package
`EDIT name.sym`	loads a symbol
`EDIT name.dev`	loads a device
`EDIT .s3`	loads sheet 3 of a schematic
`EDIT .s5 .s2`	moves sheet 5 before sheet 2 and loads it (if sheet 5 doesn't exist, a new sheet is inserted before sheet 2)
`EDIT .s2 .s5`	moves sheet 2 before sheet 5 and loads it (if sheet 5 doesn't exist, sheet 2 becomes the last sheet)

The EDIT command without parameters will cause a file dialog (in board or schematic mode) or a popup menu (in library mode) to appear from which the user can select the file or object.

To change from schematic to a board with the same name the command

```
EDIT .brd
```

can be used. In the same way to change from board to schematic use the command

```
EDIT .sch
```

To edit another sheet of a schematic the command

```
EDIT .sX
```

(X is the sheet number) or the combo box in the action toolbar of the editor window where the command can be used. If the given sheet number doesn't exist, a new sheet is created.

The user can also switch between sheets by clicking on an icon of the sheet thumbnail preview. Using Drag&drop in the thumbnail preview allows the user to reorder sheets.

Symbols, devices or packages may only be edited if a library is first opened with the OPEN command.
EDIT loads files from the project directory.

The EDIT command is also used to create or edit modules within a schematic. The user should also refer to the `Module` command.

`EDIT name.mod`	loads (or creates) a module within a schematic
`EDIT name.m2`	loads (or creates) sheet 2 of module
`EDIT .m3`	loads (or creates) sheet 3 of the current module
`EDIT .s2 modY.m1`	moves sheet 2 before sheet 1 of module 'modY' and loads it
`EDIT modX.m3 modY.m1`	moves sheet 3 of module 'modX' before sheet 1 of module 'modY' and loads it

WRITE

Function
Saves the current drawing or library.

Syntax
```
WRITE;
WRITE name
WRITE @name
```

The WRITE command is used to save a drawing or library. If 'name' is entered, EAGLE will save the file under the new name.

The file name may also be entered with a pathname if it is to be saved in another directory. If no pathname is given, the file is saved in the project directory.

If the new name is preceded with a @, the name of the loaded drawing will also be changed accordingly. The corresponding board/schematic will then also be saved automatically under this name and the UNDO buffer will be cleared.

If WRITE is selected from the menu, a popup window will appear asking for the name to use (current drawing name is default). This name may be edited and accepted by clicking the OK button. Pressing the ESCAPE key or clicking the CANCEL button cancels the WRITE command.

To assure consistency for Forward&Back Annotation between board and schematic drawings, the WRITE command has the following additional functionality:

- when a board/schematic is saved under the same name, the corresponding schematic/board is also saved if it has been modified.

- when a board/schematic is saved under a different name, the user will be asked whether they also want to save the schematic/board under that (different) name. Saving a drawing under a different name does not clear the "modified" flag.

EXPORT

Function
Generates a data file for external use.

Syntax
```
EXPORT SCRIPT filename;
EXPORT NETLIST filename;
EXPORT NETSCRIPT filename;
EXPORT PARTLIST filename;
EXPORT PINLIST filename;
EXPORT DIRECTORY filename;
EXPORT IMAGE filename|CLIPBOARD [MONOCHROME|WINDOW] resolution;
```

See also SCRIPT, RUN

The EXPORT command is used to provide an ASCII text file which can be used to, for example, transfer data from EAGLE to other programs, or to generate an image file from the current drawing.

By default the output file is written into the Project directory.
The command generates the following output files:

SCRIPT
A library previously opened with the OPEN command will be output as a script file. When a library has been exported and is to be imported again with the SCRIPT command, a new library should be opened in order to avoid duplication — e.g. the same symbol is defined more than once. Reading script files can be accelerated if the command

```
Set Undo_Log Off;
```

is used before executing the EXPORT command.

NETLIST
Generates a netlist for the loaded schematic or board. Only nets which are connected to elements are listed.

NETSCRIPT
Generates a netlist for the loaded schematic in the form of a script file. This file can be used to read a new or changed netlist into a board where elements have already been placed or previously routed tracks have been deleted with DELETE SIGNALS. Note that while reading such a script into a board no schematic that is consistent with this board may be loaded.

PARTLIST
Generates a component list for schematics or boards. Only elements with pins/pads are included.

PINLIST
Generates a list with pads and pins, containing the pin directions and the names of the nets connected to the pins.

DIRECTORY
Lists the directory of the currently opened library.

IMAGE
Exporting an *IMAGE* generates an image file with a format corresponding to the given file-name extension. The following image formats are available:

`.bmp`	Windows Bitmap Files
`.png`	Portable Network Graphics Files
`.pbm`	Portable Bitmap Files
`.pgm`	Portable Grayscale Bitmap Files
`.ppm`	Portable Pixelmap Files
`.tif`	TIFF Files
`.xbm`	X Bitmap Files
`.xpm`	X Pixmap Files

The *resolution* parameter defines the image resolution (in 'dpi').
If *filename* is the special name, type in CLIPBOARD (upper or lowercase doesn't matter) and the image will be copied into the system's clipboard.
The optional keyword *MONOCHROME* creates a black & white image.
The optional keyword *WINDOW* creates an image of the currently visible area in the editor window. Without this keyword, the image will contain the entire drawing.

Further formats
A lot of further formats like DXF or Hyperlynx can be exported by ULPs. They can be started from command lines using the RUN command. Under 'File/Export' a number these format exports are also available.

USE

Function
Marks and loads a library for use. The user may then select objects from this library and place them into drawings.

Syntax

```
USE
USE -*;
USE library_name..;
```

See also ADD, REPLACE commands

The USE command marks a library for later use with the ADD or REPLACE command.

If the user activates the USE command without a parameter, a file dialog will appear that lets the user select a library file. If a path for libraries has been defined in the "Options/Directories" dialog, the libraries from the first entry in this path are shown in the file dialog.

The special parameter '-*' causes all previously marked libraries to be dropped.
library_name can be the full name of a library or it can contain wildcards. If library_name is the name of a directory, all libraries from that directory will be marked. The suffix .lbr can be omitted.

Note: when adding a device or package to a drawing, the complete library information for that object is copied into the drawing file, so that the user does not need to access the library if the drawing is to be changed later.

Changes in a library have no effect on existing drawings. See the UPDATE command if the user want to update parts from modified libraries.

Using Libraries via the Control Panel
Libraries can be easily marked for use in the Control Panel by clicking on their activation icon (which changes its color to indicate that this library is being used), or by selecting "Use" from the library's context menu. Through the context menu of the "Libraries" entry in the Control Panel it is also possible to use *all* of the libraries or *none* of them.

Used Libraries and Projects

The libraries that are currently in use will be stored in the project file (if a project is currently open).

Examples

`USE`	opens the file dialog to choose a library
`USE -*;`	drops all previously marked libraries
`USE demo trans*;`	marks the library demo.lbr and all libraries with names matching trans*.lbr
`USE -* /eagle/lbr;`	first drops all previously marked libraries and then marks all libraries from the directory /eagle/lbr

REMOVE

Function

Deletes files, devices, symbols, packages, and sheets.

Syntax

```
REMOVE name
REMOVE name.Sxx
```

See also OPEN, RENAME commands.

Files

The REMOVE command is used to delete the file name if EAGLE is being used in board or schematic editing mode.

Devices, Symbols, Packages

The REMOVE command is used to delete the device, symbol or package "name" from the presently opened library. The name may include an extension (for example REMOVE name. pac). If the name is given without extension, the user has to be in the respective mode to remove an object (i.e. editing a package if the user wants to remove packages).

Symbols and packages can be erased from a library only if not used by a device.

Note: REMOVE used within a library clears the UNDO buffer.

Sheets

The REMOVE command may also be used to delete a sheet from a schematic. The name of the presently loaded schematic can be omitted. The parameter xx represents the sheet number, for example:

```
REMOVE .S3
```

deletes sheet number 3 from the presently loaded schematic.

If the user deletes the currently loaded sheet, sheet number 1 will be loaded after the command has been executed. All sheets with a higher number than the one deleted will be assigned a number reduced by one.

Commands to Change the Screen Display and User Interface

ASSIGN

Function
Modify key assignments.

Syntax
```
ASSIGN
ASSIGN function_key command..;
ASSIGN function_key;
function_key = modifier+key
```

The options are as follows:

`modifier`	any combination of S (Shift), C (Control), A (Alt) and ⌘ (Cmd, Mac OS X only)
`key`	representations of keys in the ranges; F1..F12, A-Z, 0-9, BS (Backspace)

If `key` is one of A-Z or 0-9, the modifier must contain at least A, C or M.

The ⌘ modifier is only available on **Mac OS X**.

See also SCRIPT, KeyboardandMouse

The ASSIGN command can be used to define the meaning of the function keys F1 through F12, the letter keys A thru Z, the (upper) digit keys 0 thru 9 and the backspace key (each also in combination with modifier keys).

Keys can be assigned a single command, or significantly, multiple commands. The command sequence to be assigned should be enclosed in apostrophes.

If assignmed to a letter key together with the modifier A, (e.g. Alt+F), a corresponding hotkey from the pulldown menu will no longer be available.

To remove an assignment from a key, the user may enter the ASSIGN command with only the function_key code, omitting the command.

Note: any special operating system function assigned to a function key, will be overwritten by the ASSIGN command (depending on the operating system, ASSIGN may not be able to overwrite certain function keys).

The ASSIGN command without parameters displays the present key assignments in a dialog, as shown in Figure 41, which allows the user to modify these settings.

The values assigned to function keys may also be viewed from within a Schematic or PCB Layout Window by using the sub-menu: Options ▷ Assign, again, activating the dialog show in Figure 4-1.

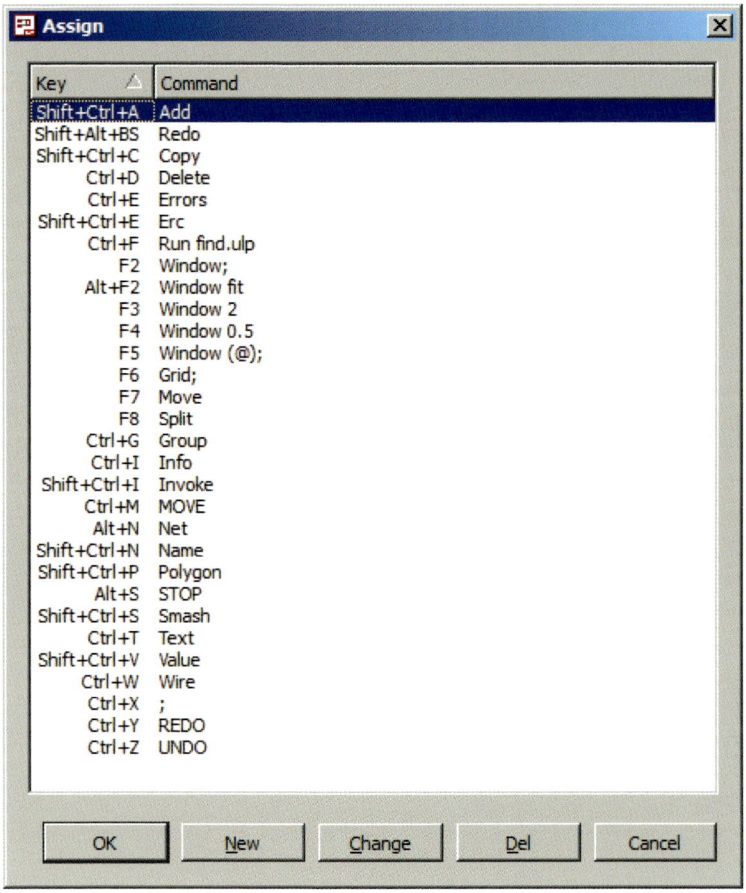

Figure 4-1: function key assignment dialog

Examples

```
ASSIGN F7 'change layer top; route';
ASS A+F7 'cha lay to; rou';
ASSIGN CA+R 'route';
```

The first two examples have the same effect, since EAGLE allows abbreviations not only with commands but also with parameters (only if they are unambiguous).

Note: in these examples, the change layer top command is terminated by a semicolon, but not the route command. The reason is that in the first case, the command already contains all the necessary parameters, while in the second case coordinates still have to be added (usually with the mouse). Therefore the ROUTE command must not be deactivated by a semicolon.

Define Command Menu

The user may assign the MENU command to a key. The separator character in the MENU command (semicolon) has to be enclosed in three pairs of apostrophes as follows:

```
ASSIGN C+F10 menu add mov rou ''';''' edit;
```

This semicolon will appear in the new menu.

CHANGE

Function

Changes parameters of an object.

Syntax

```
CHANGE option.
```

Mouse keys

Ctrl+Right-Click changes parameter of the group.

The CHANGE command is used to change or preset properties of objects within EAGLE.

The objects are clicked on with the mouse after the desired parameters have been selected from the CHANGE command menu (as shown in Figure 4-2) or have been typed in from the keyboard.

A complete list of all the parameters that may be changed are given in Table 4-1.

Parameters adjusted with the CHANGE command remain as preset properties for objects added later.

All values in the CHANGE command are used according to the actual grid unit.

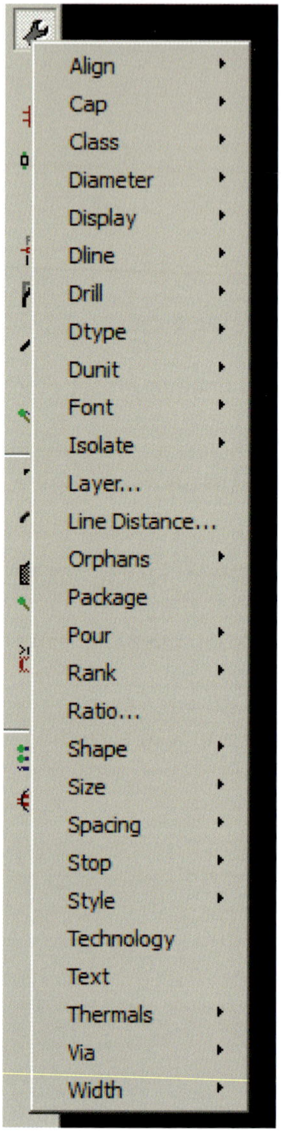

Figure 4-2: CHANGE command parameter menuChange Groups

When the CHANGE command with a group, the group should first be identified with the GROUP command, before entering the CHANGE command (with appropriate parameters). Right-Click is then used to execute the changes.

<table>
<tr><td>Layer</td><td>CHANGE LAYER name | number</td></tr>
<tr><td>Text</td><td>CHANGE TEXT [text]</td></tr>
<tr><td>Text height</td><td>CHANGE SIZE value</td></tr>
<tr><td>Text thickness</td><td>CHANGE RATIO ratio</td></tr>
<tr><td>Text line distance</td><td>CHANGE LINEDISTANCE value</td></tr>
<tr><td>Text font</td><td>CHANGE FONT VECTOR | PROPORTIONAL | FIXED</td></tr>
<tr><td>Text alignment</td><td>CHANGE ALIGN BOTTOM | LEFT | CENTER | TOP | RIGHT</td></tr>
<tr><td>Wire width</td><td>CHANGE WIDTH value</td></tr>
<tr><td>Wire style</td><td>CHANGE STYLE value</td></tr>
<tr><td>Arc cap</td><td>CHANGE CAP ROUND | FLAT</td></tr>
<tr><td>Pad shape</td><td>CHANGE SHAPE SQUARE | ROUND | OCTAGON | LONG | OFFSET</td></tr>
<tr><td>Pad/via/SMD flags</td><td>CHANGE STOP | CREAM | THERMALS | FIRST OFF | ON</td></tr>
<tr><td>Pad/via diameter</td><td>CHANGE DIAMETER diameter</td></tr>
<tr><td>Pad/via/hole drill</td><td>CHANGE DRILL value</td></tr>
<tr><td>Via layers</td><td>CHANGE VIA from-to</td></tr>
<tr><td>SMD dimensions</td><td>CHANGE SMD width height</td></tr>
<tr><td>SMD roundness</td><td>CHANGE ROUNDNESS value</td></tr>
<tr><td>Pin parameters</td><td>CHANGE DIRECTION NC | IN | OUT | IO | OC | HIZ | SUP | PAS | PWR
CHANGE FUNCTION NONE | DOT | CLK | DOTCLK
CHANGE LENGTH POINT | SHORT | MIDDLE | LONG
CHANGE VISIBLE BOTH | PAD | PIN | OFF
CHANGE SWAPLEVEL number</td></tr>
<tr><td>Polygon parameters</td><td>CHANGE THERMALS OFF | ON
CHANGE ORPHANS OFF | ON
CHANGE ISOLATE distance
CHANGE POUR SOLID | HATCH | CUTOUT
CHANGE RANK value
CHANGE SPACING distance</td></tr>
<tr><td>Gate parameters</td><td>CHANGE SWAPLEVEL number
CHANGE ADDLEVEL NEXT | MUST | ALWAYS | CAN | REQUEST</td></tr>
<tr><td>Net class</td><td>CHANGE CLASS number | name</td></tr>
<tr><td>Package</td><td>CHANGE PACKAGE part_name [device_name] | 'device_name' [part_name]</td></tr>
<tr><td>Technology</td><td>CHANGE TECHNOLOGY part_name [device_name] | 'device_name' [part_name]</td></tr>
<tr><td>Attribute display</td><td>CHANGE DISPLAY OFF | VALUE | NAME | BOTH</td></tr>
<tr><td>Frame parameters</td><td>CHANGE COLUMS value
CHANGE ROWS value
CHANGE BORDER NONE | BOTTOM | RIGHT | TOP | LEFT | ALL</td></tr>
<tr><td>Label</td><td>CHANGE XREF OFF | ON</td></tr>
<tr><td>Dimension type</td><td>CHANGE DTYPE value</td></tr>
<tr><td>Dimension unit</td><td>CHANGE DUNIT [MIC | MM | MIL | INCH] [OFF | ON] [precision]</td></tr>
<tr><td>Dimension line</td><td>CHANGE DLINE width [extension_width [extension_length [extension_offset]]] (extension values can be set to AUTO; unchanged preceding values can be skipped with '-')</td></tr>
</table>

Table 4-1: EAGLE parameters that can be changed

DISPLAY

Function
Selects the visible layers in a drawing.

Syntax

```
DISPLAY
DISPLAY [option] layer_number.
DISPLAY [option] layer_name.
```

Valid options are: `ALL`, `NONE`, `LAST`, `?` and `??`

See also LAYER, PRINT

The DISPLAY command is used to choose the visible layers. As parameters, the layer number and the layer name are allowed (even mixed). If the parameter ALL is chosen, all layers become visible. If the parameter NONE is used, all layers are switched off.

Note:

i. only those signal layers (1 - 16) that have been configured into the layer setup in the DesignRules dialog are available for display.

ii. avoid naming layers ALL and NONE; as well as names starting with a "-".

If the parameter LAST is given, the previously visible layers will be displayed.

Some commands (PAD, SMD, SIGNAL, ROUTE) automatically activate certain layers. If the DISPLAY command is invoked without parameters, a dialog is presented which allows the user to adjust all layer settings.

Examples

```
DISPLAY NONE BOTTOM;
```

This command selects only the Bottom layer for display.

```
DISPLAY TOP -BOTTOM -3;
```

In this example the Top layer is displayed, while the Bottom layer and the layer with the number 3 are not shown on the screen. The command syntax determines that if the layer name or layer number includes a negative sign, it will be filtered out.

Undefined Layers
The options '?' and '??' can be used to control what happens if an undefined layer is given in a DISPLAY command. The '?' and '??' options may appear any number of times and in any sequence.

Any undefined layers following a '?' will cause a warning and the user can either accept it or cancel the entire DISPLAY command.
Undefined layers following a '??' will be silently ignored. This is most useful for writing script files that can handle any drawing, even if a particular drawing doesn't contain some of the listed layers.

For example:

```
DISPLAY TOP BOTTOM ? MYLAYER1 MYLAYER2 ?? OTHER WHATEVER
```

the two layers TOP and BOTTOM are required and will cause an error if either of them is missing.

`MYLAYER1` and `MYLAYER2` will just be reported if missing, allowing the user to cancel the operation, and `OTHER` and `WHATEVER` will be displayed if they are there, otherwise they will be ignored.

Pads and Vias
If pads or vias have different shapes on different layers, the shapes of the currently visible (activated with DISPLAY) signal layers are displayed on top of each other.

If the color selected for layer 17 (Pads) or 18 (Vias) is 0 (which represents the current background color), the pads and vias are displayed in the color and fill style of the respective signal layers. If no signal layer is visible, pads and vias are not displayed.

If the color selected for layer 17 (Pads) or 18 (Vias) is not the background color and no signal layers are visible, pads and vias are displayed in the shape of the uppermost and undermost layer.

The above also applies to printouts made with the PRINT command.

Selecting Objects
If the user wants to select certain objects or elements (e.g. for use with, say, the MOVE or DELETE commands) the corresponding layer must be visible. Elements *can only* be selected if the *tOrigins* (or *bOrigins* with mirrored elements) layer is visible.

Parameter Aliases

Parameter aliases can be used to define certain parameter settings to the DISPLAY command, which can later be referenced by a given name. The aliases can also be accessed by **Left-Click** (and hold) on the DISPLAY icon until the list pops up, or simply **Right-Click**.

The syntax to handle these aliases is:

`DISPLAY = name parameters`

This command defines the alias with the given name to expand to the given parameters. The name may consist of any number of letters, digits and underscores, and is treated case insensitive.
It must begin with a letter or underscore and may not be one of the option keywords.

`DISPLAY = name @`

Defines the alias with the given name to expand to the current parameter settings of the command.

`DISPLAY = ?`

Asks the user to enter a name for defining an alias for the current parameter settings of the command.

`DISPLAY = name`

Opens the DISPLAY dialog and allows the user to select a set of layers that will be defined as an alias under the given *name*.

`DISPLAY = name;`

Deletes the alias with the given *name*.

`DISPLAY name`

Expands the alias with the given name and executes the DISPLAY command with the resulting set of parameters. The name may be abbreviated and there may be other parameters before and after the alias (even other aliases).

Note: where name is an abbreviation, aliases have precedence over other parameter names of the command.

Example:

`DISPLAY = MyLayers None Top Bottom Pads Vias Unrouted`

This command defines the alias "MyLayers" which will display just the layers : Top, Bottom, Pads, Vias and Unrouted (without the "None" parameter the given layers would be displayed *in addition to* the currently visible layers).

The alias may be abbreviated in use e.g. DISPLAY my; and is case insensitive.

GRID

Function
Defines grid parameters for a drawing.

Syntax
```
GRID option..;
GRID;
```

Keyboard
F6: GRID; turns the grid on or off.

See also SCRIPT
The GRID command is used to specify the grid and the current unit of measurement used in the drawing. When given without an option, this command switches between GRID ON and GRID OFF.

The following options for the GRID command are given in Table 4-2.

`GRID ON;`	Displays the grid on the screen
`GRID OFF;`	Turns off displayed grid
`GRID DOTS;`	Displays the grid as dots
`GRID LINES;`	Displays the grid as solid lines
`GRID MIC;`	Sets the grid units to micron
`GRID MM;`	Sets the grid units to mm
`GRID MIL;`	Sets the grid units to mil
`GRID INCH;`	Sets the grid units to inch
`GRID FINEST;`	Sets the grid to the finest possible value
`GRID grid_size;`	Defines the distance between the grid points in the actual unit
`GRID LAST;`	Sets grid to the most recently used values
`GRID DEFAULT;`	Sets grid to the standard values
`GRID grid_size grid_multiple;`	grid_size = grid distance grid_multiple = grid factor
`GRID ALT ...;`	Defines the alternate grid

Table 4-2 GRID command options

Examples

```
Grid mm;
```

Sets the grid units to millimeters.

```
Grid Last;
```

Sets the grid to the last grid definition (despite the user not knowing the prior definition itself).

```
GRID mm 1 10;
```

This example specifies that the distance between the grid points is 1 mm and that every 10th grid line will be displayed.

The GRID command may contain multiple parameters, as in :

```
GRID inch 0.05 mm;
```

Here the grid distance is first defined as 0.05 inch. Then the coordinates of the cursor are chosen to be displayed in mm.

```
GRID DEFAULT;
```

This example sets the grid to the standard value for the current drawing type.

```
GRID mil 50 2 lines on alt mm 1 mil;
```

The above defines a 50 mil grid displayed as lines (with only every 2nd line visible), and sets the alternate grid size to 1 mm, but displays it in mil.

Pressing the Alt key switches to the alternate Grid. This can typically be a finer grid than the normal one, which allows the user to finely position an object in a densely populated area (i.e. where the normal grid might be too coarse). The alternate grid remains active as long as the Alt key is held pressed down.

Parameter Aliases

Parameter aliases can be used to define certain parameter settings for the GRID command, which can later be referenced by a given name. The aliases can also be accessed by **Left-Click** (and hold) on the DISPLAY icon until the list pops up, or simply **Right-Click**.

The syntax to configure these aliases is:

```
GRID = name parameters
```

Defines the alias with the given name to expand to the given parameters. The name may consist of any number of letters, digits and underscores, and is case insensitive. It must begin with a letter or underscore and may not be one of the option keywords.

```
GRID = name @
```

Defines the alias with the given name to expand to the current parameter settings of the command.

```
GRID = ?
```

Asks the user to enter a name for defining an alias for the current parameter settings of the command.

```
GRID = name
```

Opens the GRID dialog and allows the user to adjust the grid parameters and define an alias for them under the given name.

```
GRID = name;
```

Deletes the alias with the given name.

```
GRID name
```

Expands the alias with the given name and executes the GRID command with the resulting set of parameters. The name may be abbreviated and there may be other parameters before and after the alias (even other aliases).

Note: where name is an abbreviation, aliases have precedence over other parameter names of the command.

Example:

```
GRID = MyGrid inch 0.1 lines on
```

Defines the alias "MyGrid" which, when used as in:

```
GRID myg
```

will change the current grid to the given settings.

The alias may be abbreviated in use e.g. myg instead of MyGrid,and is case insensitive.

MENU

Function
Allows the user to customize the textual command menu.

Syntax
```
MENU option ..; MENU;
```

See also ASSIGN, SCRIPT

This is a useful command and allows the user to customize the user interface to individual and specific requirements.

The MENU command can be used to create a user specific command menu.

The complete syntax specification for the `option` parameters is:

```
option    := command | submenu | delimiter
command   := [ icon ] text1 [ ':' text2 ]
submenu := [ icon ] text '{' option [ '|' option ] '}'
icon     := '[' filename ']'
delimiter := '---'
```

The special option '---' can be used to insert a delimiter, which may be useful for grouping buttons.

The ';' entry should always be added to the end of the MENU command. It is used to terminate this, and many other, EAGLE commands.

The command MENU; switches back to the default text menu.

A menu option can be a simple command, as:

```
MENU Display Grid;
```

which would set the menu to the commands Display and Grid, and configure a menu within the drawing as shown in Figure 4-3.

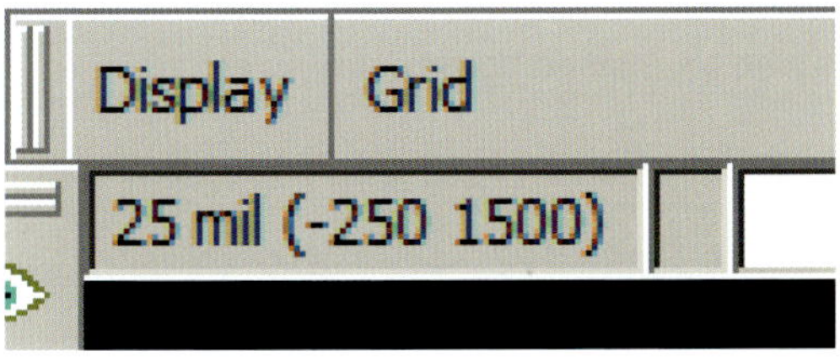

Figure 4-3: Simple MENU command

In this example Display and Grid are interpreted both as menu text and as commands.
It can also be used as a submenu button as in
MENU 'Grid { Fine : Grid inch 0.001; | Coarse : Grid inch 0.1; }';
which would define a button labeled Grid that, when clicked, opens a submenu with the two options Fine and Coarse. This is illustrated in Figure 4-4.

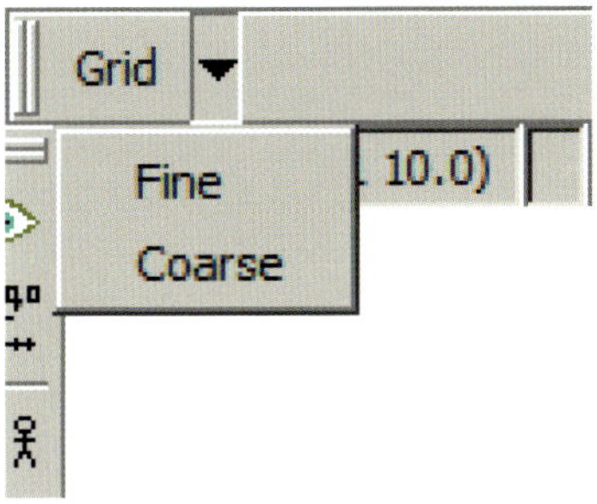

Figure 4-4: A sub-menu using the MENU command

Note: The '|' character is only necessary as a separator in submenu entries (see the submenu syntax above).

A command button can also incorporate, and display, an icon by preceding the button text with the path and file name of an icon (enclosed in square brackets) as in:

```
MENU '[/path/to/myicon.png] Set a fine grid : Grid inch 0.001;';
```

Here the button will display only the specified icon, and "Set a fine grid" will be used as a "tool tip" that is displayed when the mouse cursor is moved over the button. The filename does not need to be enclosed in quote characters (like for masking spaces). If the icon's file name doesn't include a directory path, it is searched for in the current working directory and in the EAGLE 'bin' directory.

The menu command may be an aliased command, as in:

```
MENU 'MyDisp : Display None Top Bottom Pads Vias;' 'MyGrid : Grid mil 100 lines on;';
```

This example would set the menu to show the command aliases MyDisp and MyGrid and actually execute the command sequence following the ':' for of each option (text2, see the command syntax above) when the respective button is clicked.

A complex example of the MENU command follows:

```
MENU '[draw.png] Draw {\
  Wire
    {\
      Continous : CHANGE STYLE Continuous; WIRE |\ DashDot :
      CHANGE STYLE DashDot; WIRE |\
      Help : HELP WIRE;\
    }|\
  Rectangle
    {\
      RECT |\
      Help : HELP RECT; \
    }\
  }\
[export.png] Export
  {\
    Script : EXPORT SCRIPT |\ Image :
    EXPORT IMAGE\
  }\
MyScript : SCRIPT MyScript.scr;';
```

This menu consists of the 3 entries: Draw, Export and MyScript, where Draw and Export have submenus and are supplied with icons.

Draw consists of the submenus Wire and Rectangle where: the Wire submenu comprises the entries Continuous, DashDot and Help; and the Rectangle submenu consists of the entries RECT (text and command RECT) and Help.

The Export submenu has the entries Script and Image.

Myscript simply consists of an entry which runs the user script file `MyScript.scr`.

Note:

i. any *option* that consists of more than a single word, or that might be interpreted as a command, must be enclosed in single quotes.

ii. if the MENU command is used in a script to define a complex menu, and the menu definitions spread over several lines to make them more readable, those lines are required to be terminated with a backslash character ('\'). For example:

```
MENU 'Grid  {\
             Fine : Grid inch 0.001; |\
             Coarse : Grid inch 0.1;\
           }';
```

SET

Function
Allows the user to modify and set system parameters

Syntax
```
SET
SET options;
```

Parameters which affect the behavior of the program, the screen display, or the user interface can be specified with the SET command. The precise syntax is described below.

A dialog in which all the parameters can be set appears if the SET command is entered without parameters.

User Interface

Snap function	`SET SNAP_LENGTH number;`
	
	This sets the limiting value for the snap function in the ROUTE command (using the current unit). The default is 20 mil.
	
	If tracks are being laid with the ROUTE command to pads that are not on the grid, the snap function will ensure that a route will be laid to the pad within the snap-length.
	
	`SET CATCH_FACTOR value;`
	
	Defines the distance from the cursor up to which objects are taken into account when clicking with the mouse. The value is entered relative to the height (or width, whichever is smaller) of the presently visible part of the drawing.
	
	This applies to a zoom level that displays at least a range of 4 inches and increases logarithmically when zooming further in. A value of 0 turns this limitation off.
	
	Values < 1 are interpreted as factor, values ≥ 1 as a percentage. The default is 0.05 (5%).
	
	`SET SELECT_FACTOR value;`
	
	This setting controls the distance from the cursor within which nearby objects will be suggested for selection. The value is entered relative to the height (or width, whichever is smaller) of the presently visible part of the drawing.
	
	Values < 1 are interpreted as factor, values ≥ 1 as a percentage. Default is 0.02 (2%).

Menu contents	`SET USED_LAYERS name | number;`
	
	Specifies the layers which will be shown in the associated EAGLE menus. See the example file mylayers.scr.
	
	The layers: Pads, Vias, Unrouted, Dimension, Drills and Holes will in any case remain in the menu, as will the schematic layers. Any used signal layers also remain in the menus. SET Used_Layers All activates all layers.
	
	`SET WIDTH_MENU value..;`
	`SET DIAMETER_MENU value..;`
	`SET DRILL_MENU value..;`
	`SET SMD_MENU value..;`
	`SET SIZE_MENU value..;`
	`SET ISOLATE_MENU value..;`
	`SET SPACING_MENU value..;`
	`SET MITER_MENU value..;`
	
	The content of the associated popup menus can be configured with the above command for the parameters *width* etc. A maximum of 16 values is possible for each menu (16 value-pairs in the SMD menu). Without any values (as in `SET WIDTH_MENU;`) the program default values will be restored.
	
	Example:
	`Grid Inch;`
	`Set Width_Menu 0.1 0.2 0.3;`

Context menus	`SET CONTEXT` objecttype text commands;
	
	For selectable object types, context menus (right mouse button) can be extended by arbitrary entries.
	
	Here objecttype is not case sensitive; text is the menu text; commands is the command sequence that is executed after click on the menu entry.
	
	Empty spaces are possible if the expression is set within apostrophes. If apostrophes are required in the string, then these must be doubled (see TEXT).
	
	Example:
	`SET CONTEXT Element Export 'run myexport.ulp';`
	
	This example adds, to the context menu for elements, an Export entry, which starts a named ULP (myexport.ulp).
	
	An existing user-defined entry may also be overwritten.
	
	The settings are stored in the eaglerc file. The number of entries is unlimited.
	
	Deletion of entries:
	
	`SET CONTEXT objecttype; deletes all entries for this object type.`
	
	`SET CONTEXT; all user defined menu entries are deleted.`
	
	All selectable object types are supported. These are: attribute, circle, dimension, element, frame, gate, hole, instance, junction, label, pad, pin, rectangle, SMD, text, via and wire.

Bend angle for wires	`SET WIRE_BEND bend_nr;`
	bend_nr can be one of:
	0 Starting point - horizontal - vertical - end
	1 Starting point - horizontal - 45° - end
	2 Starting point - end (straight connection)
	3 Starting point - 45° - horizontal - end
	4 Starting point - vertical - horizontal - end
	5 Starting point - arc - horizontal - end
	6 Starting point - horizontal - arc - end
	7 "Freehand" (arc that fits to wire at start, straight otherwise)
	8 Route short end of airwire in FollowMe Router
	9 Route both ends of airwire in FollowMe Router
	
	Note that 0, 1, 3 and 4 may contain additional miter wires (see MITER).
	
	`SET WIRE_BEND @ bend_nr ...;`
	
	Defines the bend angles that shall be actually used when switching with the right mouse button.
	
	`SET WIRE_BEND @;`
	
	Switches back to using all bend angles.

Screen Display

Color for grid lines	`SET COLOR_GRID color;`
Layer color	`SET COLOR_LAYER layer color; SET`
Fill pattern for layer	FILL_LAYER layer fill;
Grid parameters	`SET MIN_GRID_SIZE pixels;` The grid is only displayed if the grid size is greater than the set number of pixels.
Min. text size shown	SET MIN_TEXT_SIZE size; Text less than size pixels high is shown as a rectangle on the screen. The setting 0 means that all text will be displayed readably.
Net wire display	`SET NET_WIRE_WIDTH width;`

Pad display	`SET DISPLAY_MODE REAL | NODRILL;`
	REAL: Pads are displayed as they will be plotted. NODRILL: Pads are shown without drill hole.
	`SET PAD_NAMES OFF | ON;`
	Pad names are displayed/not displayed. SET

Bus line display	`BUS_WIRE_WIDTH width; SET`
DRC-Parameter	`DRC_FILL fill_name;`
Polygon calculation	`SET POLYGON_RATSNEST OFF | ON;` `See POLYGON command.`
Vector font	`SET VECTOR_FONT OFF | ON;` See TEXT command.
Cross-reference labels	`SET XREF_LABEL_FORMAT string;` See LABEL command.
Part cross- references	`SET XREF_PART_FORMAT string;` See TEXT command.

Mode parameters

Package check	`SET CHECK_CONNECTS OFF | ON;` The ADD command checks whether every pin has been connected to a pad (with CONNECT). This check can be switched off. Nevertheless, no board can be generated from a schematic if a device is found which does not have a package.
REPLACE mode	`SET REPLACE_SAME NAMES | COORDS;`
UNDO buffer on/off	`SET UNDO_LOG OFF | ON;`
Wire optimizing	`SET OPTIMIZING OFF | ON;` If set on, wires which lie in one line after a MOVE, ROUTE or SPLIT are subsumed into a single wire. See also OPTIMIZE.
Net wire termination	`SET AUTO_END_NET OFF | ON;` Automatic ending of nets or busses. See NET or BUS.
Automatic junctions	`SET AUTO_JUNCTION OFF | ON;` Automatic setting of junctions. See JUNCTION.
Automatic confirmation	`SET CONFIRM OFF | NO | YES;` Allows confirmation dialogs to be handled automatically (see below for details).

Colors

There are three *palettes* for black, white and colored backgrounds, respectively. Each palette has 64 color entries, which can be set to any ARGB value. The palette entry number 0 is used as the background color (in the "white" palette this entry cannot be modified, since this palette will also be used for printing, where the background is always white).

The color palettes can be modified either through the dialog under *Options* ▷ *Set* ▷ *Colors* or by using the command:

```
SET PALETTE index argb
```

where *index* is a number in the range 0.63, and *argb* is a hexadecimal value defining the Alpha, Red, Green and Blue components of the color, like 0xFFFFFF00 (which would result in a bright yellow).

The alpha component defines how "opaque" the color is. A value of 0x00 means it is completely transparent (i.e. invisible), while 0xFF means it is totally opaque. The alpha component of the background color is always 0xFF.

Note: the ARGB value must begin with "0x",otherwise it could be misinterpreted as a decimal number.

The user can use the command:

```
SET PALETTE BLACK|WHITE|COLORED
```

to switch to the black, white or colored background palettes, respectively.

Note: there will be no automatic window refresh after this command. The user should execute a WINDOW; command after using this.

By default only the palette entries 0.15 are used and they contain the colors listed below. The palette entries are grouped into "normal" and "highlight" colors. There are always 8 "normal" colors, followed by the corresponding 8 "highlight" colors.

Therefore colors 0.7 are "normal" colors, 8.15 are their "highlight" values, 16.23 are another 8 "normal" colors with 24.31 being their "highlight" values and so on. The "highlight" colors are used to visualize objects, for instance in the SHOW command.

The actual color names, together with their respective Color number, which can be used instead of the color names, are given in Table 4-3.
Fill specifies the style with which wires and rectangles in a particular layer are to be filled. Similarly, the fill type and corresponding number are given in Table 4-3.

Automatic Confirmation
EAGLE may prompt the user with informational or warning messages, or requires a decision on how to proceed. This may be unwanted in automated processes (like script files). The command:

```
SET CONFIRM YES
```

will automatically confirm every message dialog as if the user had clicked on the "positive" button ("OK" or "Yes"). The dialog itself is not even presented to the user.
Similarly, the command:

```
SET CONFIRM NO
```

acts as if the user had clicked on the "negative" button ("No"), if such a button is present. Otherwise it just confirms the dialog.
Finally, the command:

```
SET CONFIRM OFF
```

turns off automatic confirmation. If automatic confirmation is not turned off explicitly, it will automatically fall back to `OFF`, the next time the editor window accepts some interactive input from the user.

Note: Care should be exercised when using this command, particularly when in employed within script files. The result may be that important messages are overlooked and that the results may be entirely unexpected.

Color Number	Color parameter	Fill parameter
0	Black	Empty
1	Blue	Solid
2	Green	Line
3	Cyan	LtSlash
4	Red	Slash
5	Magenta	BkSlash
6	Brown	LtBkSlash
7	LGray	Hatch
8	DGray	XHatch
9	LBlue	Interleave
10	LGreen	WideDot
11	LCyan	CloseDot
12	LRed	Stipple1
13	LMagenta	Stipple2
14	Yellow	Stipple3
15	White	Stipple4

Table 4-3: Numbering of Color and Fill options

WINDOW

Function
Allows the user to Zoom in and out of a drawing.

Syntax
```
WINDOW;
WINDOW Left-Click;
WINDOW 2x Left-Click;
WINDOW 3x Left-Click
WINDOW scale_factor
WINDOW FIT
WINDOW LAST
```

Mouse keys
Left&Drag defines a rectangular window (shortcut for "**3x Left-Click;**").

Keyboard

	`Alt+F2: WINDOW FIT`	Fit drawing on the screen
	`F2: WINDOW;`	Redraw screen
	`F3: WINDOW 2`	Zoom in by a factor of 2
	`F4: WINDOW 0.5`	Zoom out by a factor of 2
	`F5: WINDOW (@);`	Cursor position is new center (if a command is active)

The WINDOW command is used to zoom in and out of the drawing and to change the position of the drawing on the screen. The command can be used with up to three left mouse clicks. If there are fewer, the command must be terminated with a semicolon.

Viewing the complete drawing
Using the command:

```
WINDOW FIT;
```

the user can adjust the parameters such that the drawing fills the entire screen.

Refreshing the Screen

After making adjustments or changing the screen, the user may refresh or re-draw it by using the command:

```
WINDOW;
```

Zooming in and out

The drawing may be magnified or reduced using the 'zoom' functionality of the WINDOW command.
Specifically,

```
WINDOW 2;
```

Makes the elements appear twice as large, while

```
WINDOW 0.5;
```

reduces the size of the elements by a factor of two.

Further, the user may specify an integer or real number as the argument to the WINDOW command to scale the view of the drawing by the amount entered. The center of the window remains the same.

Defining rectangles, a new center and zooming

When used with one point, the WINDOW command causes that point to become the center of a new screen display of the drawing. The scaling of the drawing remains the same. The user may also adjust the work area sliders (at the side and bottom of the window area) to move the visible area of the drawing. The function key F5 causes the current position of the cursor to be the new center.

The WINDOW command with two points defines a rectangle with the specified points at opposite corners. The rectangle expands to fill the screen, providing a close-up view of the specified portion of the drawing.

The WINDOW command may also be used with three points. The first point defines the new center of the drawing and the display becomes either larger or smaller, depending on the ratios of the spacing between the other points. In order to zoom in, the distance between point 1 and point 3 should be greater than the distance between point 1 and 2; to zoom out place point 3 between points 1 and 2.

Very large zoom factors

By default the maximum zoom factor is limited in such a way that an area of 1mm (about 40mil) in diameter will be shown using the full editor window. If further magnification is required, the user may uncheck *Options ▷ User interface ▷ Limit zoom factor*, allowing a functional 'zoom in' until the finest editor grid can be seen.

Note: When zooming very far into a drawing, the following things may happen:

i. Texts that are not using the vector font may not be shown if they are larger than the editor window.

ii. Circles and Arcs are approximated and therefore may not appear at their exact location (especially if they have a very small width).

iii. Whether or not the finest grid will be visible when zooming all the way in depends on the screen resolution, the editor window size and the value of *Options ▷ Set ▷ Misc ▷ Min. visible grid size.*

Back to the previous window
The user may revert back to the previous window selection by using:

```
WINDOW LAST;
```

This is achieved by EAGLE storing a window selection with every WINDOW command, except for zoom-only WINDOW commands and modifications of the window selection with the mouse.

Refreshing the screen
If the WINDOW command is used, followed by a semicolon, EAGLE redraws the screen without changing the center or the scale. This is useful if error messages cover part of the drawing or the display has become corrupted.

Parameter Aliases
Parameter aliases can be used to define certain parameter settings to the WINDOW command, which can later be referenced by a given name.

The aliases can also be accessed by **Left-Clicking** on the "WINDOW Select" button  and holding the mouse button pressed until the list pops up. A right click on the button also pops up the list.

The syntax to handle these aliases is:

`WINDOW = name parameters`

Defines the alias with the given name to expand to the given parameters. The name may consist of any number of letters, digits and underscores, and is case insensitive. It must begin with a letter or underscore and may not be one of the option keywords.

`WINDOW = name @`

Defines the alias with the given name to expand to the current window selection.

`WINDOW = ?`

Asks the user to enter a name for defining an alias for the current window settings.

`WINDOW = name`

Allows the user to select a window that will be defined as an alias under the given name.

`WINDOW = name;`

Deletes the alias with the given name.

`WINDOW name`

Expands the alias with the given name and executes the WINDOW command with the resulting set of parameters. The name may be abbreviated and there may be other parameters before and after the alias (even other aliases).

Note: where name is an abbreviation, aliases have precedence over other parameter names of the command.

Example:
The command:

```
WINDOW = MyWindow (0 0) (4 3);
```

defines the alias "MyWindow" which, when used in:

```
WINDOW myw
```

will zoom to the given window area. Note the abbreviated use of the alias and the case insensitivity.

Commands for Editing Drawings or Libraries

ADD

Function

Add elements into a drawing.
Add symbols into a device.

Syntax

```
ADD package_name[@library_name] [name] [orientation]..
ADD device_name[@library_name] [name [gate]] [orientation]..
ADD symbol_name [name] [options]..
```

Mouse keys

center-click mirrors the part.
Right-Click rotates the part.
shift+right reverses the direction of rotation.

Parameters

Name

The `package_name`, `device_name` or `symbol_name` parameter is the name under which the package, device or symbol is stored in the library.

Gate

The name of the gate from a device to be added.

Orientation

This parameter defines the orientation of the object in the drawing. Objects are normally rotated using the right mouse button. In script files, textual descriptions of this parameter are used:

```
[S][M]Rnnn
```

`S` sets the Spin flag, which disables keeping texts readable from the bottom or right side of the drawing (only available in a board context)

`M` sets the Mirror flag, which mirrors the object about the y -axis

`Rnnn` sets the Rotation to the given value, which may be in the range 0.0...359.9 (at a resolution of 0.1 degrees) in a board context, or one of 0, 90, 180 or 270 in a schematic context (angles may be given as negative values, which will be converted to the corresponding positive value)

The key letters `S`, `M` and `R` may be given in upper or lower case, and R must be at least followed by a number.

If the Mirror flag is set in an element as well as in a text within the element's package, they cancel each other out. The same applies to the Spin flag.

See also UPDATE, USE, INVOKE Commands

The ADD command fetches a circuit symbol (gate) or a package from the active library and places it into the drawing.
During device definition, the ADD command fetches a symbol into the device.

Usually the user clicks the ADD command and selects the package or symbol from the menu which opens. If necessary, parameters can now be entered via the keyboard.
If `device_name` contains wildcard characters ('*' or '?') and more than one device matches the pattern, the ADD dialog will be opened and the specific device can be selected from the list.

Note: The Description checkbox in the ADD dialog will be unchecked after any ADD command with a `device_name` has been given in the command line, no matter if it contains wildcards or not. This is because a `device_name` entered in the command line is only searched for in the device names, not in the descriptions.

The package or symbol is placed with the left button and rotated with the right button. After it has been placed, another copy is immediately available; attached to the cursor.

If there is already a device or package with the same name (from the same library) in the drawing, and the library has been modified after the original object was added, an automatic library update will be started and the user will be asked whether objects in the drawing should be replaced with their new versions.

Note: The user should always run a Design Rule Check (DRC) and an Electrical Rule Check (ERC) after a library update has been performed!

Fetching a Package or Symbol into a Drawing

Wildcards
The ADD command can be used with wildcards ('*' or '?') to find a specific device. The ADD dialog offers a tree view of the matching devices, as well as a preview of the device and package variant.

To add directly from a specific library, the command syntax
ADD `devicename@libraryname` can be used. `devicename` may contain wildcards and libraryname can be either a plain library name (like "ttl" or "ttl.lbr") or a full file name (like "/home/mydir/myproject/ttl.lbr" or "../lbr/ttl"). In case of blanks in the file name, the whole expression has to be enclosed by apostrophes (like ADD 'DEV1A@/home/my dir/ttl.lbr').

Names

The `package_name`, `device_name` or `symbol_name` parameter is the name under which the package, device or symbol is stored in the library. It is usually selected from a menu. The name parameter is the name which the element is to receive in the drawing. If the name could be interpreted as an orientation or option, it must be enclosed in single quotes. If a name is not explicitly given it will receive an automatically generated name.

Example:

`ADD DIL14 IC15` **Left-Click**

fetches the DIL14 package to the board and gives it the name IC15 (Figure 4-5).

If no name is given in the schematic, the gate will receive the prefix that was specified in the device definition with PREFIX, expanded with a sequential number (e.g. IC1).

Addlevel

The following alternatives are available for this parameter:

Next	If a device has more than one gate, the symbols are fetched into the schematic with an Addlevel of Next.
Must	If any symbol from a device is fetched into the schematic, then a symbol defined with an Addlevel of 'Must' must also appear. This happens automatically. It cannot be deleted until all the other symbols in the device have been deleted. If the only symbols remaining from a device are MUST symbols, the DELETE command will delete the entire device.
Always	Like Must, although a symbol with an Addlevel of 'Always' can be deleted and brought back into the schematic with INVOKE.
Can	If a device contains 'Next' gates, then 'Can' gates are only fetched if explicitly called with INVOKE. A symbol with an Addlevel of Can is only then fetched into the schematic with ADD if the device only contains 'Can' gates and 'Request' gates.
Request	This property is usefully applied to devices' power symbols. 'Request' gates can only be explicitly fetched into the schematic (using the INVOKE command) and are not internally counted. The effect of this is that in devices with only one gate and one voltage supply symbol, the gate name is not added to the component name.

Example:

`ADD PWR 0 REQUEST .`

fetches the PWR symbol (e.g. a power pin symbol), and defines a Swaplevel of 0 (not swappable) and the Addlevel Request for it.

Swaplevel

The swaplevel is an integer number, to which the following rules apply:

0 The symbol (gate) cannot be swapped with any other in the schematic.
>0 The symbol (gate) can be swapped with any other symbol of the same type in the schematic that has the same swaplevel (including swapping between different devices).

Default: 0

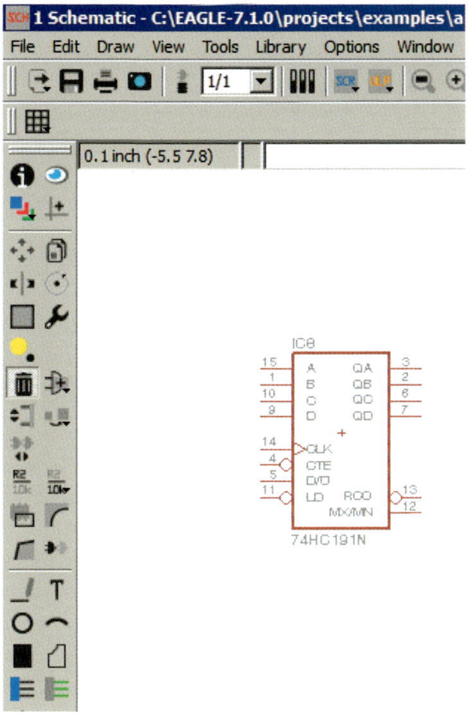

Figure 4-5: Placing a package into a drawing

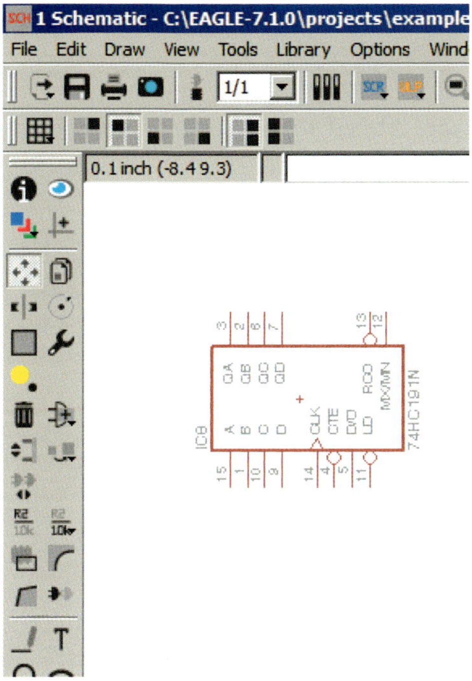

Figure 4-6: Placing a package into a drawing using rotation and co-ordinates

Particular Gates

To fetch a particular gate of a newly added device, the name of that gate can be given following the part name.

For instance:

```
ADD 7400 IC1 A
```

This is mainly useful if a schematic is to be generated through a script.

Note: that if a particular gate is added, no other gates with add level MUST or ALWAYS will be fetched automatically, and the user will have to use the INVOKE command to invoke at least the MUST gates (otherwise the ElectricalRuleCheck will report them as missing).

Examples:

`R0`	no rotation
`R90`	rotated 90° counterclockwise
`R-90`	rotated 90° clockwise (will be converted to 270°)
`MR0`	mirrored about the y-axis
`SR0`	spin texts
`SMR33.3`	rotated 33.3° counterclockwise, mirrored and spin texts

Default: `R0`

Example:

```
ADD DIL16 R90 (0 0);
```

places a 16-pin DIL package, rotated 90 degrees counterclockwise, at coordinates (0 0) i.e. the DATUM point (see Figure 4-6)

Fetch Symbol into Device

During device definition, the ADD command fetches a previously defined symbol into the device. Two parameters (swaplevel and addlevel) are available for definition, and may be entered into any sequence. Both can be preset and changed with the CHANGE command. The value entered with the ADD command is also retained as a default value.

ARC

Function
Draw an arc of variable diameter, width, and length.

Syntax
`ARC ['signal_name'] [CW | CCW] [ROUND | FLAT] [width]`

Mouse keys
center-click selects the layer.
Right-Click changes the orientation.

Parameters
`Signal Name`

The `signal_name` parameter is intended mainly to be used in script files that read in generated data.

If a `signal_name` is given, the arc will be added to that signal and no automatic checks will be performed.

The parameters `CW` and `CCW` enable the user to define the direction of the arc (clockwise or counterclockwise).

`ROUND` and `FLAT` define whether the arc endings are round or flat, respectively.
`Width`. The parameter "width" defines the thickness of the drawn line (ARC)
These parameters are also accessible using the parameter toolbar illustrated in Figure 4-7.

Figure 4-7: ARC command parameter toolbar

See also CHANGE, WIRE, CIRCLE commands

The ARC command, followed by three mouse clicks on a drawing, draws an arc of defined width. The first point defines a point on a circle, the second its diameter. Entering the second coordinate reduces the circle to a semi-circle, while the right button alters the direction from first to second point. Entry of a third coordinate truncates the semi-circle to an arc extending to a point defined by the intersection of the circumference and a line between the third point and the arc center.

CAUTION: The use of signal_name should be used with great care because it could result in short circuits if an arc is placed in such a way that it would connect different signals. The user should run a Design RuleCheck_after using the ARC command with the `signal_name` parameter!

The parameter "width" defines the thickness of the drawn line. It can be changed or pre-defined with the command:

```
CHANGE WIDTH width;
```

The adjusted width is identical to the line width for wires.

Arcs with angles of 0 or 360 degrees or a radius of 0 are not accepted. Example for text input:

```
GRID inch 1;
ARC CW (0 1) (0 -1) (1 0);
```

generates a 90 degree arc with the center at the origin.

Figure 4-8 illustrates the use of the ARC command icon. The parameter bar also shows the command parameters available to the user and include, from left to right; Layer, Width, CW/CCW and Round/Flat end.

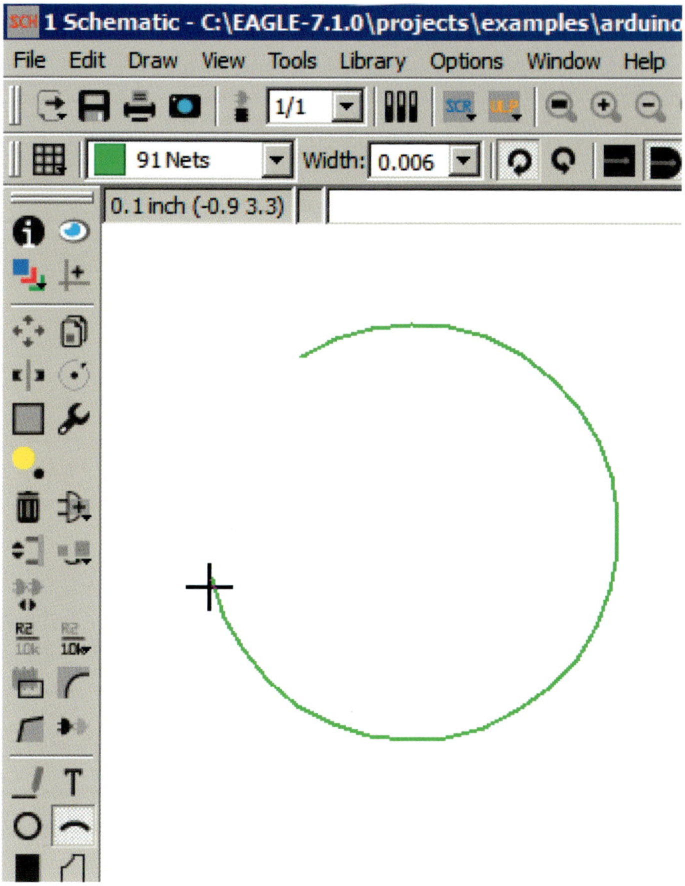

Figure 4-8: Using the ARC command icon

ATTRIBUTE

Function
Allows the user to create and modify a definition of attributes for parts.

See also TECHNOLOGY, NAME, VALUE, SMASH, TEXT

Syntax

```
ATTRIBUTE name [ 'value' ] [ options ]
ATTRIBUTE part_name attribute_name
ATTRIBUTE part_name attribute_name 'attribute_value'
[ [ orientation ] • ]
ATTRIBUTE part_name attribute_name DELETE ATTRIBUTE * [ name [ 'value' ] ]
ATTRIBUTE * name DELETE
ATTRIBUTE ..
```

Parameters

`Name`
The name may consist of any letters, digits, '_', '#' and '-' and may have any length; the first character must not be '-', though. Names are not case sensitive.

`Value`
The value may contain any characters and must be enclosed in single quotes.

`Options`
The valid types of options are:

`delete`	Delete the attribute with the given name from all technology variants (in this case there must be no 'value').
`variable`	Mark this attribute as variable, so that it can be overwritten in the schematic (this is the default).
`constant`	Attributes marked as constant cannot be overwritten in the schematic (unless the user insists).

Options may be abbreviated and are case insensitive.

`Orientation`
This parameter is defined similarly as for the ADD command.

An attribute is an arbitrary combination of a name and a value, which can be used to specify any kind of information for a given part.

Attributes can be defined in the library (for individual devices), in the schematic (for an actual part) or in the board (for an actual element). Attributes defined on the device level will be used for every part of that device type in the schematic. In a schematic, additional attributes can be defined for each part, and existing attributes from the devices can be overwritten with new values (if the attributes have been defined as variable). An element in the board has all the attributes of its corresponding part, and can have further attributes of its own.

Using Attributes in a Schematic Drawing

In a schematic, the ATTRIBUTE command can be used to assign attributes to a part, in which case the value of such an attribute overwrites the value of the attribute with the same name in the library (if the device has such an attribute and allows overwriting). A part may also be given attributes that are not defined in the library at all.

For a fully textual definition of an attribute, the following syntax can be used:

```
ATTRIBUTE part_name attribute_name 'attribute_value'     orientation
```

If no coordinates are given (and the command is terminated with a ';'), the behavior depends on whether the given attribute already exists for that part (either in the device or in the schematic). If the attribute already exists, only its value will be changed. If it doesn't exist yet, a new attribute with the given name and value will be placed at the origin of the selected gate of the part.

To delete an attribute from a part, the command:

```
ATTRIBUTE part_name attribute_name DELETE
```

can be used.

When defining attributes via the command line or a script, use the CHANGE DISPLAY command to define which parts of the attribute (name, value, both or none of these) shall be visible.

Selecting the ATTRIBUTE command and clicking on a part shows a dialog in which all attributes of that part are listed and can be edited. This can be seen in Figure 4-9 where the Attributes of switch S1 are displayed.

Note that in case of a multi-gate part, one of the gates (i.e. "instances") is selected. When selecting a gate via a mouse click, the intended gate is clear. However, when selecting a gate via `part_name`, the full name consisting of the part and gate name should be given. While a specific part can only have one attribute with a given name, the attribute can be attached to any or all of its gates. If only the part name is given, the first visible gate will implicitly be selected.

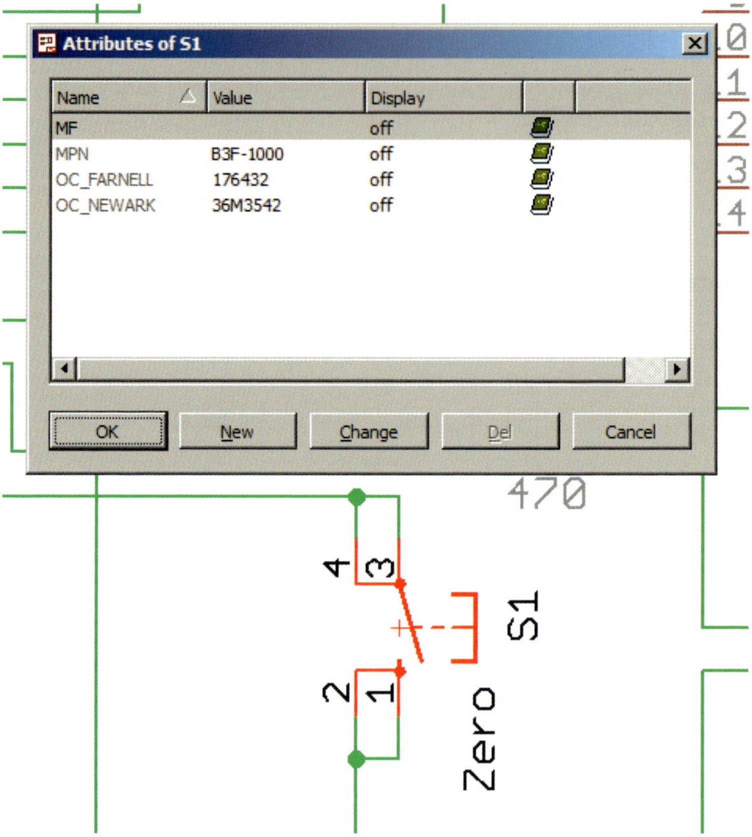

Figure 4-9: The ATTRIBUTE dialog

Attributes used in a Library

In a library the ATTRIBUTE command can be used to define the attributes of a given technology variant, using the syntax

```
ATTRIBUTE name [ 'value' ] [ options ]
```

An already existing attribute can be switched between *variable* and *constant* without the need to repeat its value, as in

```
ATTRIBUTE ABC '123'    (variable by default)
ATTRIBUTE ABC constant (ABC retains its value '123')
```

If the value of an attribute is changed, its *constant/variable* setting remains unchanged (unless explicitly given).

Some special attribute names are not allowed, since they would interfere with the already existing text variables. If an attribute named VALUE is defined, its value will be used to initialize the actual value when placing a part in a schematic (in case the device set has 'Value On').

Figure 4-10 illustrates the use of ATTRIBUTE within a library; where the attributes of the Device '74*05' are displayed for all variants of technologies.

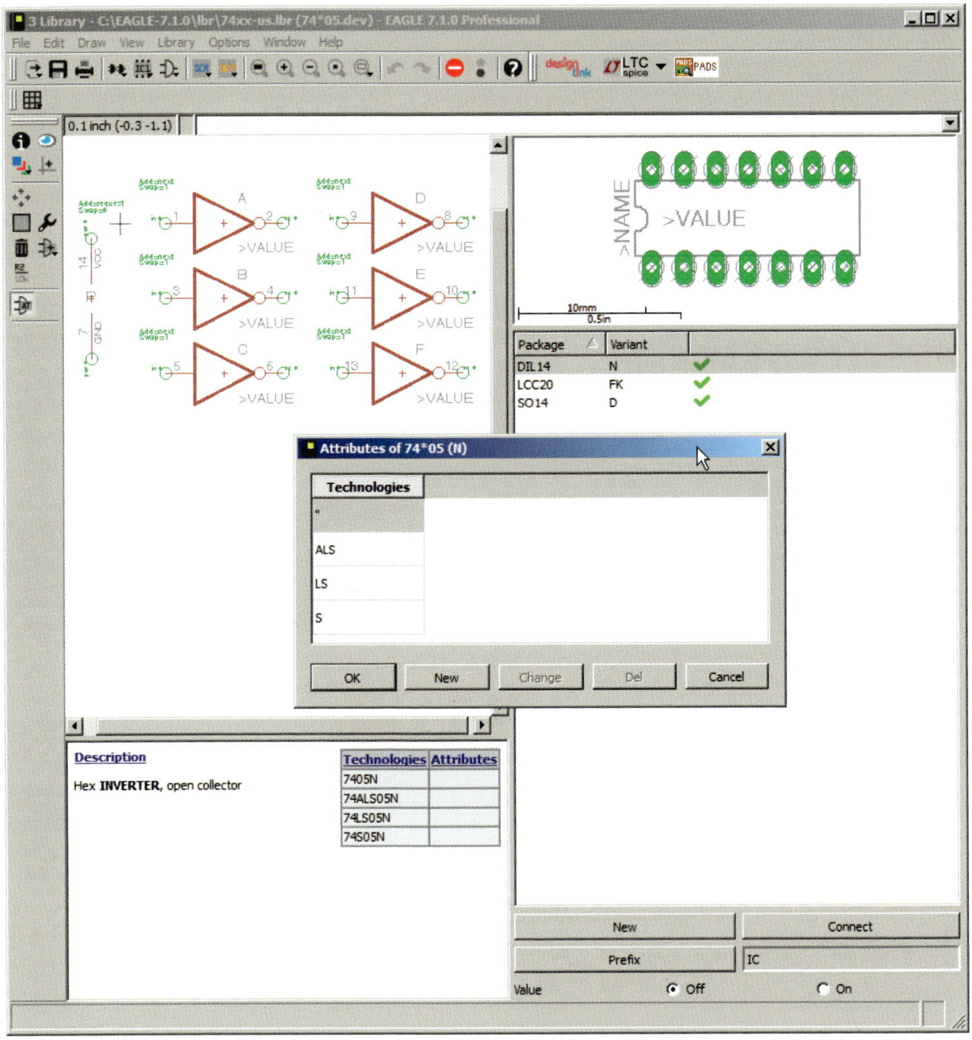

Figure 4-10: The ATTRIBUTE dialog within the Library

Attributes in a Board

In a board, attributes can be assigned to elements with the ATTRIBUTE command, much the same as in schematics. By default, elements have all the attributes that are defined for their part in the schematic (and their device in the library). Attributes with the same name for a given element/part pair will always have the same value (through Forward&Back Annotation). Elements may also have additional attributes that are not present in the schematic or library.

Global Attributes

Global attributes can be defined in boards and schematics by using '*' as the part name (which implies that this attribute applies to *all* parts). Alternatively global attributes can be defined through the menu option *Edit* ▷ *Global attributes.* The global attributes of board and schematic are handled separately and are not connected via Forward&Back Annotation.

An example of a global Attribute could be the author of a drawing, and can be used in the title block of a drawing's frame. It will be shown on every schematic sheet that has a drawing frame that contains a `textvariable` with the same name.

Example of defining Attributes

Before defining an attribute, the package and technology must be selected first (in case there is more than one). Then the attributes for that technology can be defined.
As an example:

```
PACKAGE N;
TECHNOLOGY LS;
ATTRIBUTE PartNo '12345-ABC';
ATTRIBUTE Temp '100K' constant;
ATTRIBUTE Remark 'mount manually';
```

CIRCLE

Function
Adds circles to a drawing.

Syntax

```
CIRCLE [center, circumference]
CIRCLE width
```

Mouse keys

center-click selects the layer.

See also CHANGE, WIRE

The CIRCLE command is used to create circles. Circles in the layers tRestrict, bRestrict, and vRestrict define restricted areas. They should be defined with a width of 0 (zero).

The width parameter defines the width of the circle's circumference and is the same parameter as that used in the WIRE command. The width can be changed with the command:

```
CHANGE WIDTH width;
```

where *width* is the desired value in the current unit. A circle defined with a width of 0 will be filled.

Example
The commands

```
GRID inch 1;
CIRCLE (0 0) (1 0);
```

generate a circle with a radius of 1 inch and the center at the origin.

Figure 4-11 illustrates the use of the CIRCLE command with the circle being drawn in the 'Nets' layer with a width of 0.006 inches.

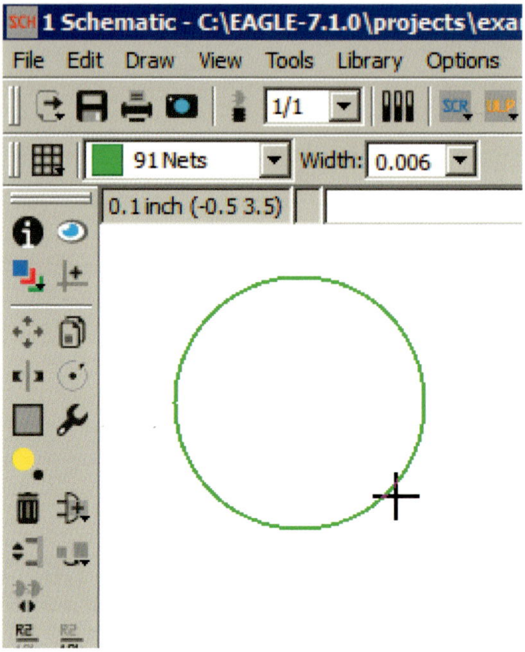

Figure 4-11: Drawing a circle in a schematic diagram

CLASS

Function

Define and use net classes.

Syntax

```
CLASS
CLASS number|name
CLASS number [name [width [clearance [drill] ] ] ] [number:clearance..]
```

See also DesignRules, NET, SIGNAL, CHANGE

The CLASS command is used to define or use net classes. Without parameters, EAGLE displays a dialog in which the net classes can be defined (as shown in Figure 4-12) The user is able to program and set any number of such Net classes.

If only a number or name is given, the net class with the given number or name is selected and will be used for subsequent NET and SIGNAL commands.

If both a number and a name are given, the net class with the given number will be assigned all the following values and will also be used for subsequent NET and SIGNAL commands. If any of the parameters following name are omitted, the net class will keep its respective value.

If number is negative, the net class with the absolute value of number will be cleared. The default net class 0 cannot be cleared.

Net class names are case insensitive (i.e. 'SUPPLY' would be the same as 'Supply' or 'SuPpLy').

Using several net classes in a drawing increases the time the Autorouter needs to do its job. Therefore the user should use as few net classes as possible. Only the number of net classes actually used by nets or signals are relevant here, not the number of defined net classes.

In order to avoid conflicts when performing Cut& Paste operations between drawings, the user should take care to define the same net classes under the same numbers in all drawings.

The Autorouter processes signals sorted by their total width requirements (Width plus Clearance), starting with those that require the most space. The bus router only routes signals with net class 0.

The net class of an existing net/signal can be changed with the CHANGE command.

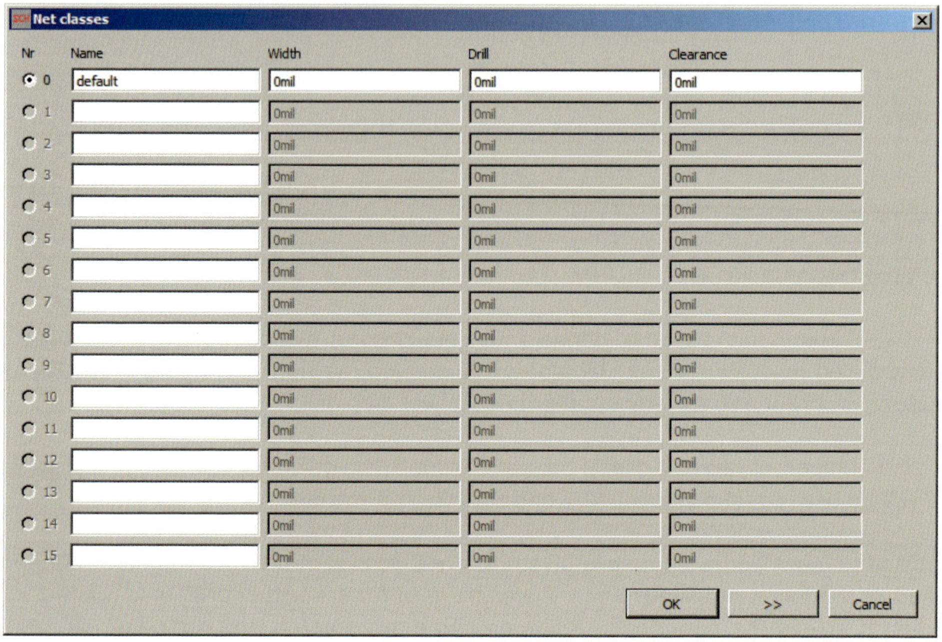

Figure 4-12: Dialog for setting up Net classes

Parameters

Width
The Width parameter defines a minimum width that all objects in this net class must have.

Clearance
The *Clearance* parameter defines the minimum clearance between objects of different signals in this net class and objects in other net classes.

Drill
The *Drill* parameter defines a minimum drill size that all objects in this net class must have (only applies to objects that actually have a drill parameter, like pads and vias).

Clearance between net classes

If a clearance is given in the form `number:clearance`, it defines the minimum clearance between signals in this net class and signals in the net class with the given `number`.
The command

```
CLASS 3 1:0.6mm 2:0.8mm
```

defines a minimum clearance of 0.6mm between signals in net classes 1 and 3, and one of 0.8mm between signals in net classes 2 and 3. Note that the numbers in `number:clearance` must be less than or equal to the number of the net class itself ('3' in the above example), so

```
CLASS 3 1:0.6mm 2:0.8mm 3:0.2mm
```

would also be valid, whereas

```
CLASS 3 1:0.6mm 2:0.8mm 3:0.2mm 4:0.5mm
```

would *not* be allowed.

COPY

Function

Copy objects or elements.

Syntax

```
COPY...
COPY deviceset@library [name]
COPY package@library [name]
```

Mouse keys

Ctrl+Left-Click selects an object at its origin and places the copied object.
Ctrl+Right-Click selects the group.
center-click mirrors the selected object or the group.
Right-Click rotates the selected object or the group.
Shift+Right-Click reverses the direction of rotation.

See also GROUP, CUT, PASTE, ADD, INVOKE, POLYGON

The COPY command is used to copy objects within the same drawing, or between libraries.

EAGLE will generate a new name for the copy but will retain the old value. When copying signals (wires), buses, and nets the names are retained, but in all other cases a new name is assigned.

Copying to the system's clipboard

The COPY command in EAGLE V6 allows the user to copy: objects within drawings, objects between libraries and the current group into the system's clipboard. (Previous versions of EAGLE did not provide the latter functionality).

Copying Wires

Copied wires or polygons, belonging to a signal, will retain the same signal characteristics. This can lead to the following erroneous situations:

- If two wires overlap after the use of the COPY command, the DRC will not register an error.

- If a net or bus wire is copied in a schematic, it belongs to the same segment as the original wire, *even if there is no visible connection*. This can lead to unexpected effects, for instance when renaming them later. Therefore COPY should not be used with net or bus wires, respectively.

Copying Parts

When copying a part in a schematic, a new instance of the complete part will always be added, even if only a single gate of a multi-gate part is selected. In addition to the selected gate, any other gates of that device which have Add-Level MUST or ALWAYS, will automatically be invoked.

If the user requires another gate of a multi-gate part, they should use the INVOKE_command instead of the COPY command.

Copying library objects

By using the forms: `COPY deviceset@library` or `COPY package@library` the user can copy a device set or a package from a given library into the currently loaded library. '`library`' can be either a plain library name or a file path (see the ADD_command).
In case of ambiguity the user may add the suffix `[.dev]` for device sets or `[.pac]` for packages. If an additional `name` is given, the copied object will be given that name. This can also be done through the library objects' context menu_or, alternatively, via Drag&Drop from the Control Panel's tree view.

Note: any existing library objects (device sets, symbols or packages) used by the copied library object will be automatically updated.

Copying a group

Copying a group is done by selecting the group and then COPYing it with the command icon, and then using Right-Click. (This is the same operation as an implicit CUT operation, immediately followed by a PASTE.)

Copying objects to another sheet

To copy objects to another sheet of the same schematic, the user first needs to GROUP the objects, then execute a COPY (or CUT), switch to the target sheet and then execute a PASTE command.

CUT

Function
Copies a defined group into the system clipboard.

Syntax
CUT
CUT;

See also PASTE, COPY, GROUP
Parts of a drawing (or even a whole board) can be copied onto other drawings by means of the commands CUT and PASTE.

To use this command, the user must define a group (using the GROUP command); then invoke the CUT command, followed by a reference point to put the selected objects into the buffer

The 'CUT;' syntactical form automatically sets the reference point at the center of the selected objects (snapped to the grid).

The user then changes to another drawing (using EDIT) and copies the contents of the buffer into the new drawing by executing the PASTE command.

Reference Point
A reference point is set using either a mouse click or with co-ordinates (x y). If the user clicks the mouse after invoking the CUT command, the position of the mouse cursor defines the reference point for the group, i.e. when using the PASTE command; the mouse cursor will be at the exact center position of the group.

DELETE

Function
Deletes objects from within Schematic & Layout drawings and Libraries.

Syntax
```
DELETE..
DELETE name ..
DELETE SIGNALS
```

Mouse keys
Ctrl+Left-Click
Shift+ Left-Click deletes higher level object.
Ctrl+Left-Click deletes a wire joint.
Ctrl+Right-Click deletes a group.

See also RIPUP, DRC, GROUP

The DELETE command is used to delete a selected object.

Parts, pads, SMDs, pins and gates can also be selected by their name, which is especially useful if the object is outside the currently shown window area.

Note: when selecting a multi-gate part in a schematic by name, the user will need to enter the full instance name, consisting of part and gate name.

Attributes of parts can be selected by entering the concatenation of part name and attribute name (e.g. as in `R5>VALUE`).

With active Forward&BackAnnotation, no wires or vias can be deleted from a signal that is connected to components in a board. Also, no components can be deleted that have signals connected to them. Such modifications must be done in the schematic.

Deleting GROUPS
Clicking the right mouse button deletes a previously defined GROUP.

After deleting a group it is possible that airwires which have been newly created by the removal of a component, may be "left over", because they were not part of the original group. In such instances the user should re-calculate the airwires with the RATSNEST command.

Use the RIPUP command to convert an already routed connection back into an airwire. The DELETE command has no effect on layers that are not visible (refer to DISPLAY). The DRC might generate error polygons which can only be deleted with DRC CLEAR.

Deleting Wire Joints

If the DELETE command is invoked with the `Ctrl` key pressed, while being applied to the joining point of two wires, these wires will be combined to form one straight wire. This action will only work if: the two wires are in the same layer; have the same width and line style and both have round endings (in case of arcs).

Deleting Polygon Corners

The DELETE command deletes one corner at a time from a polygon. The whole polygon is deleted if there are only three corners left.

Deleting Components

Components can be deleted only if the tOrigins layer (or bOrigins with mirrored components) is visible *and* if no signals are connected to the component (while Forward&BackAnnotation is activated).

Please note that an element may appear to be **not** connected (no airwires or wires connect to any of its pads) while in fact it **is** connected to a supply voltage (say, through an implicit power pin). In such a case the user can **only** delete the corresponding part in the schematic.

Deleting Junctions, Nets, and Buses

The following rules apply for deleting these objects:

- If a bus is split into two parts, both retain the initial name.
- If a net is split into two parts, the larger part retains the initial name while the smaller part is assigned a new (generated) name.
- After the DELETE command, labels belong to the segment next to them.
- If a junction point is deleted, the net is separated at this location. The user should check the names of the segments by using the SHOW command.

Deleting Supply Symbols

If the last supply symbol of a given type is deleted from a net segment that has the same name as the deleted supply pin, that segment is assigned a newly generated name (if there are no other supply symbols still attached to that segment) or the name of one of the remaining supply symbols.

Deleting Signals

If the user DELETES wires (tracks) or vias belonging to a signal, the command behaves in 3 possible ways. These are:

- The signal is split into two parts. EAGLE will generate a new name for the smaller part of the signal and keep the previous name for the larger one.
- The signal is deleted from one end. The remaining part of the signal will retain the previous name.
- The signal had only one airwire. It will be deleted completely and its name will no longer exist.

After wires or vias have been deleted from a signal which contains polygons, all polygons 'belong' to the signal while retaining the original name (which is usually the bigger part).

Deleting all Signals

DELETE SIGNALS can be used to delete all signals on a board. This is useful if the user wants to read in a new or changed netlist (see EXPORT). Only those signals which are connected to pads are deleted.

If the user wishes to delete a part that has the name SIGNALS, the name needs to be written within single quote marks.

Deleting higher level objects

If the Shift key is pressed when clicking on an object, the object that is hierarchically above the selected one will be deleted. This applies to the following objects:

`Gate`	Deletes the entire part containing this gate (even if the gates are spread over several sheets). If Forward&BackAnnotation annotation is active, the wires connected to the element in the board will not be ripped up (as opposed to deleting a single gate), except for those cases where a pin of the deleted part is only connected directly to one single other pin and no net wire.
`Polygon Wire`	Deletes the entire polygon
`Net/Bus Wire`	Deletes the entire net or bus segment

Note : The DELETE operation can be reversed by using the UNDO_command !

DESCRIPTION

Function
Defines the description of a drawing or a library object.

Syntax
DESCRIPTION [*]
DESCRIPTION [*] description_string;

See also CONNECT, PACKAGE, VALUE

This command is used to define or edit the description of a drawing or a library object.

The `description_string` may contain *html*_tags.

The first non-blank line of `description_string` will be used as a short descriptive text (headline) in the Control Panel pane.

The DESCRIPTION command without a parameter opens a dialog in which the text can be edited. The upper pane of this dialog shows the formatted text, in case it contains HTML tags, while the lower pane is used to edit the raw text. At the very top of the dialog the *headline* is displayed as it would result from the first non-blank line of the description. The headline is stripped of any HTML tags.

By default the DESCRIPTION command works on the description of the object that is currently edited; like a device set, package, symbol, board or sheet. If, in a library, there is no currently edited object (as can be the case after it has been newly loaded) the description of the library will be changed.

To explicitly access the description of a library, even if a device, package or symbol is already being edited, enter the asterisk character ('*'), as the first parameter to the DESCRIPTION command. This is also the way to access the description of a schematic, as opposed to the description of an individual sheet.

Example
```
DESCRIPTION '<b>Quad NAND</b><p>\nFour NAND gates with 2 inputs each.';
```

This would result in:

Quad NAND
Four NAND gates with 2 inputs each.

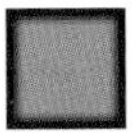

GROUP

Function
Defines a group of objects.

Syntax
```
GROUP
GROUP ALL
GROUP;
```

Mouse keys
Left&Drag defines a rectangular group.
Shift+Left-Click adds the new group to an existing one.
Ctrl+Left-Click toggles the group membership of the selected object.
Ctrl+Shift+Left-Click toggles the group membership of the higher level object.
Right-Click closes the group polygon.

See also CHANGE, CUT, PASTE, MIRROR, DELETE

The GROUP command is used to define a group of objects for a subsequent command. Further, a whole drawing or an element can be defined as a group.

Objects are selected (after activating the GROUP command) by:

i. Using Click&Drag to create a rectangle or;
ii. By drawing a polygon with the mouse.

Only objects from displayed layers can become part of the group.

The keyword **ALL** can be used to define a group that includes the entire drawing area.

The group includes:

- all objects whose origin is inside the polygon
- all wires with at least one end point inside the polygon
- all circles whose center is inside the polygon
- all rectangles with any corner inside the polygon

Moving a Group
In order to move a group it is necessary to select the MOVE command as the subsequent command to the GROUP command. The MOVE command is then invoked with the right mouse button. Figure 4-13 shows what appears when this technique is used.

When moving wires (tracks) with the GROUP command that have only one end point in the polygon, this point is moved while the other one remains at its previous position.

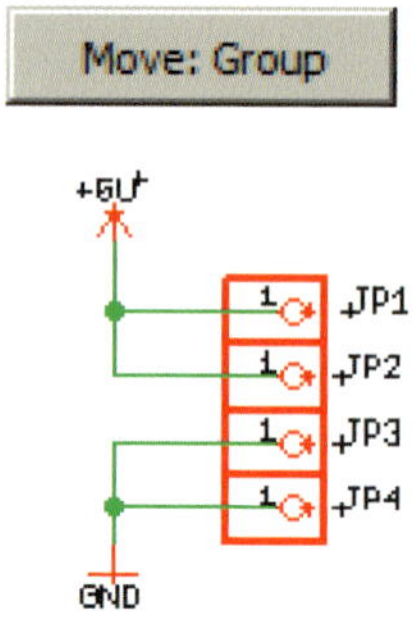

Figure 4-13: Using the Right-Click to MOVE a GROUP

The group definition remains in force until a new drawing is loaded or the command

```
GROUP;
```

is executed (which terminates the GROUP command).

Extending the group

If the user presses the **Shift** key together with any mouse click when defining the group, the newly defined group will be added to the existing group (if any).

Individual objects

The user can toggle the group membership of an individual object, by **Left-Clicking** on it with the **Ctrl** key pressed. If the user also presses the **Shift** key when doing so, the group membership of the next higher level object is toggled. For instance, when clicking on a net wire in a schematic with the GROUP command and **Ctrl+ Shift** pressed, the group membership of the entire segment will be toggled.

ERC

Function

Performs an Electrical Rule Check and Consistency on a layout board and its corresponding schematic

Syntax

ERC

See also DRC, ERRORS, Consistency Check

This command is used to test schematics for electrical errors. The result of the check is presented in the ERRORS dialog.

Consistency Check

The ERC command performs a Consistency Check between a schematic and its corresponding board, provided the board file has been loaded before starting the ERC. As a result of this check ,the automatic Forward&BackAnnotation will be turned on or off, depending on whether the files have been found to be consistent or not.

NOTE: the ERC detects inconsistencies between the implicit power and supply pins in the schematic and the actual signal connections in the board. Such inconsistencies can occur if the supply pin configuration is modified after the board has been created with the BOARD command. Since the power pins are only connected "implicitly", these changes cannot always be forward annotated. If such errors are detected, Forward&BackAnnotation will still be performed, but the supply pin configuration should be checked.

ERRORS

Function
Shows the errors found by the ERC or DRC command.

Syntax
```
ERRORS
ERRORS CLEAR
```

Mouse keys

2xLeft-Click on an error entrycenters the drawing to the area where the error is located Checking the "Centered" checkbox causes this to happen automatically.

See also ERC, DRC

The command ERRORS is used to show the errors found by the Electrical Rule Check (ERC) or the Design Rule Check (DRC).

The errors found by DRC are displayed as error polygons in the respective layers, and can be browsed through with the ERRORS_command.

The ERRORS dialog window is shown in Figure 4-14 in which all the errors are listed. Selecting an entry with the **Left-Click** causes the error to be marked in the editor window, and with a rectangle and a line from the upper left corner of the screen. An example of an error polygon is illustrated in the white square, with a connecting line, in the same figure with the highlighted entry as the cause of the error.

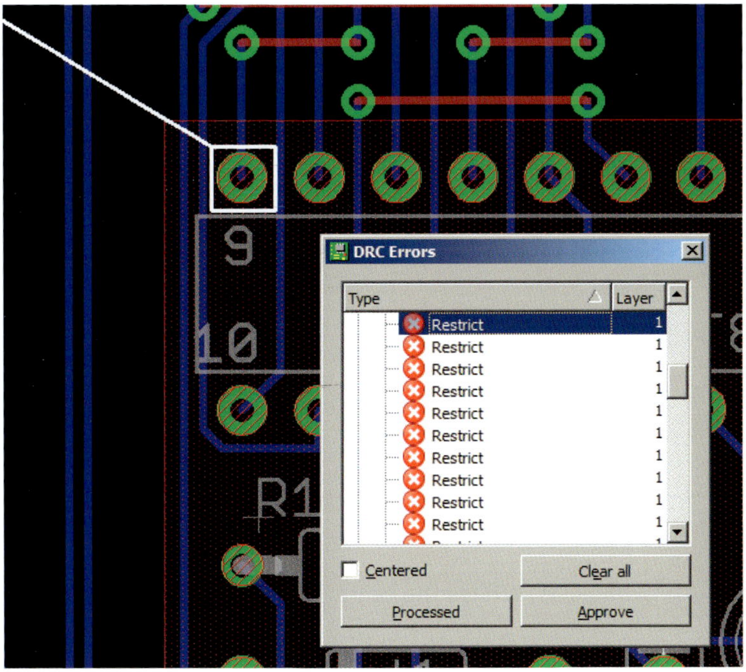

Figure 4-14: DRC error polygon and dialog

The list view of the ERRORS dialog contains up to four sections that contain *Consistency errors*, *Errors*, *Warnings* and *Approved* messages, respectively.

Marking a message as processed

The Processed button marks a message as processed. The message remains in the list, but the error indicator is removed from the editor window (except if the list entry is selected). This can be used to mark messages as "done" after fixing the related problem, without having to run the check again. After the next ERC/DRC command execution, the message will be either removed, or marked as unprocessed if the problem still persists.

Approving a message

If an error or warning can't be fixed, but apparently doesn't matter (which the user has to decide), it can be moved to the *Approved* section by pressing the *Approve* button. Messages in that section will not draw error indicators in the editor window (except if the list entry is selected) and are implicitly marked as "processed". If any of these messages no longer apply after the next ERC/DRC, they will be deleted. All approved messages are stored in the drawing file, so that it is documented which ones have been explicitly approved by the user.

Note: consistency errors cannot be approved - they always have to be fixed in order to activate *Forward&BackAnnotation.*

The user may delete all error polygons by using the command:

```
ERRORS CLEAR
```

HOLE

Function
Add a drill hole (non-conducting) to a board or package.

Syntax

```
HOLE [drill]
HOLE [drill] [(co-ordinates)]
```

See also VIA, PAD, CHANGE

This command is used to define a hole e.g. a mounting hole that has no electrical connection between the different layers in a board or in a package.

The parameter `drill` defines the diameter of the hole in the actual unit. It may be up to 0.51602 inch (13.1 mm).

The parameter `(co-ordinates)` defines the center position of the hole in actual units.

Examples

```
HOLE 0.20
```

If the actual unit is "inch", the hole will have a diameter of 0.20 inch.

```
HOLE 0.15 (5 8.5) ;
```

Place a hole with drill diameter 0.15 at position (5, 8.5).

The entered value for the diameter (also used for via-holes and pads) remains as a presetting for successive operations. It may be changed with the command:

```
CHANGE DRILL value
```

A hole can only be selected if the Holes layer is displayed.

A hole generates a symbol in the Holes layer as well as a circle with the diameter of the hole in the Dimension layer. The relation between certain diameters and symbols is defined in the *Options ▷ Set ▷ Drill* dialog. The circle in the Dimension layer is used by the Autorouter. It will ensure a (user-defined) minimum distance is kept between via-holes/wires and dimension lines, it will also automatically maintain this distance to the hole.

In the layers *tStop* and *bStop*, holes generate the solder stop mask, whose diameter is determined by the *DesignRules*.

An example of the HOLE command used on a board is shown in Figure 4-15.

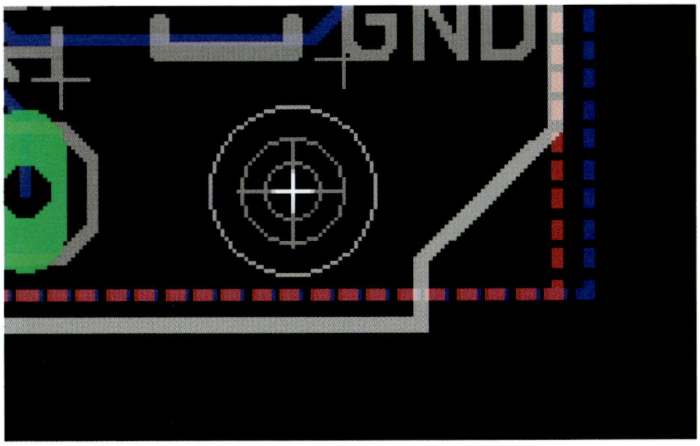

Figure 4-15: Placing a HOLE on a PCB

LAYER

Function
Changes and creates/defines layers within a drawing.

Syntax
```
LAYER layer_number
LAYER layer_name
LAYER layer_number layer_name
LAYER [??] -layer_number
```

See also DISPLAY

Choose Drawing Layer
The LAYER command with one parameter is used to change the current layer, i.e. the layer onto which wires, circles etc. will be drawn.

If the LAYER command is selected from the menu or a toolbar, a popup dialog will appear (as shown in Figure 4-16) in which the user may change to the desired layer for working; or add, delete or edit an existing layer within the current drawing.

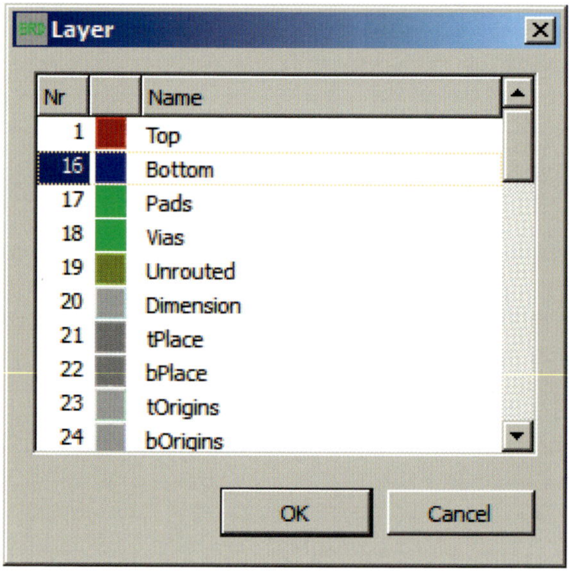

Figure 4-16: the LAYER dialog

If entered from the command line, 'layer_number' may be the number of any valid layer, and 'layer_name' may be the name of a layer (as displayed in the popup dialog).

Note:
- Only those signal layers (1 through 16) are available that have been setup in the Design Rules.
- Certain layers are not available in all modes.

Defining Layers
The LAYER command with two parameters:

```
LAYER layer_number layer_name
```

is used to define a new layer or to rename an existing one.

Example
```
LAYER 101 SAMPLE;
```

would define a new layer with layer number 101 and layer name SAMPLE.
If the user defines his or her own layers, they should use only layer_number greater than 100. Numbers below this may be assigned for special purposes in later EAGLE versions.

If a package contains layers not yet specified in the board, these layers are added to the board as soon as the package is placed into the board (using the ADD or REPLACE commands).

Delete Layers
The LAYER command syntax with the minus sign and a layer_number:

```
LAYER [??] -layer_number
```

deletes the layer with the specified number.
Layers to be deleted must be empty. If the target layer is not empty then the program generates the error message:

```
"layer is not empty: #"
```

where "#" represents the layer number.

To avoid any error messages in a layer delete operation, the user may use the '??' option. This may be useful in scripts that try to delete certain layers. However, care should be taken in using this option, since it essentially ignores and overrides any error messages. It will unconditionally delete the specified layer.

Example

```
LAYER -103;
```

deletes the layer number 103.

```
LAYER ?? -103;
```

deletes the layer number 103 without showing any warnings or error messages..

Pre-defined EAGLE Layers

EAGLE preserves a number of pre-defined Layers, which have pre-set numbers and purposes within the application. It is possible to change the names of these pre-defined layers, but their functions (related to their number) remain the same. These Layers are listed in Table 4-4 and Table 4-5.

Layer No.	Layer Name	Layer Function
1	Top	Tracks, top side
2	Route2	Inner layer
3	Route3	Inner layer
4	Route4	Inner layer
5	Route5	Inner layer
6	Route6	Inner layer
7	Route7	Inner layer
8	Route8	Inner layer
9	Route9	Inner layer
10	Route10	Inner layer
11	Route11	Inner layer
12	Route12	Inner layer
13	Route13	Inner layer
14	Route14	Inner layer
15	Route15	Inner layer
16	Bottom	Tracks, bottom side
17	Pads	Pads (through-hole)
18	Vias	Vias (through-hole)
19	Unrouted	Airwires (rubberbands)
20	Dimension	Board outlines (circles for holes)
21	tPlace	Silk screen, top side
22	bPlace	Silk screen, bottom side
23	tOrigins	Origins, top side
24	bOrigins	Origins, bottom side
25	tNames	Service print, top side
26	bNames	Service print, bottom side
27	tValues	Component VALUE, top side
28	bValues	Component VALUE, bottom side
29	tStop	Solder stop mask, top side
30	bStop	Solder stop mask, bottom side
31	tCream	Solder cream, top side
32	bCream	Solder cream, bottom side
33	tFinish	Finish, top side
34	bFinish	Finish, bottom side
35	tGlue	Glue mask, top side
36	bGlue	Glue mask, bottom side
37	tTest	Test and adjustment inf., top side
38	bTest	Test and adjustment inf. bottom side
39	tKeepout	NO-GO areas for components, top side
40	bKeepout	NO-GO areas for components, bottom side
41	tRestrict	NO-GO areas for tracks, top side
42	bRestrict	NO-GO areas for tracks, bottom side
43	vRestrict	NO-GO areas for via-holes
44	Drills	Conducting through-holes
45	Holes	Non-conducting holes
46	Milling	Milling
47	Measures	Measures
48	Document	General documentation
49	Reference	Reference marks
51	tDocu	Part documentation, top side
52	bDocu	Part documentation, bottom side

Table 4-4 Pre-defined Layout Layers

91	Nets	Nets
92	Busses	Buses
93	Pins	Connection points for component symbols with additional information
94	Symbols	Shapes of component symbols
95	Names	Names of component symbols
96	Values	Values/component types
97	Info	General information
98	Guide	Guide lines

Table 4-5 Pre-defined Schematic Layers

MIRROR

Function

Mirrors (transforms) objects and groups.

Syntax

```
MIRROR •..
MIRROR name..
```

Mouse keys

Ctrl+Right-Click mirrors a group.

See also ROTATE, LOCK, TEXT

Using the MIRROR command, objects may be mirrored (transformed into their reflection) about the vertical axis. This may be used, for example, to transform components so that they may be placed on the reverse side of a board.

Parts, pads,SMDs and pins may also be selected by their name, which is especially useful if the object is outside the currently shown window area.

Attributes of parts can be selected by entering the concatenation of part name and attribute name, as in e.g. `R5>VALUE`.

Components can be mirrored only if the appropriate tOrigins/bOrigins layer is visible. When packages are selected for use with the MIRROR command, connected wires on the outer layers are mirrored too. The user should take care when using this latter application, since short circuits may be created inadvertently. See Figure 4-17 and Figure 4-18 for an example of this transform.

Note: any objects on inner layers (2...15) do not change their layer after they are mirrored. This also applies to vias.

Parts cannot be mirrored if they are locked; or, in the case of a limited edition of EAGLE, if any of their connected pads would extend outside the allowed area.

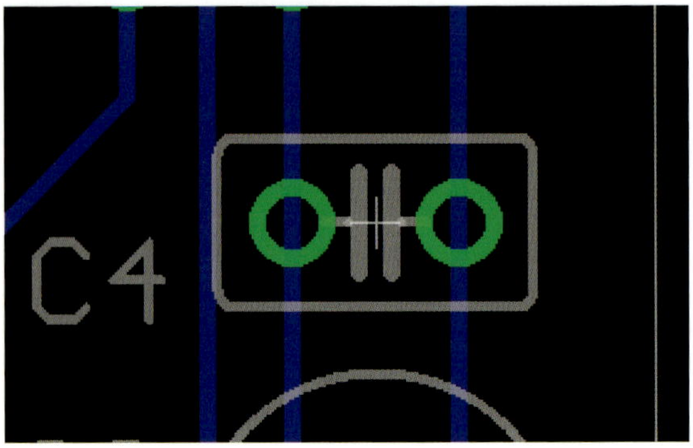

Figure 4-17: Component prior to MIRROR command

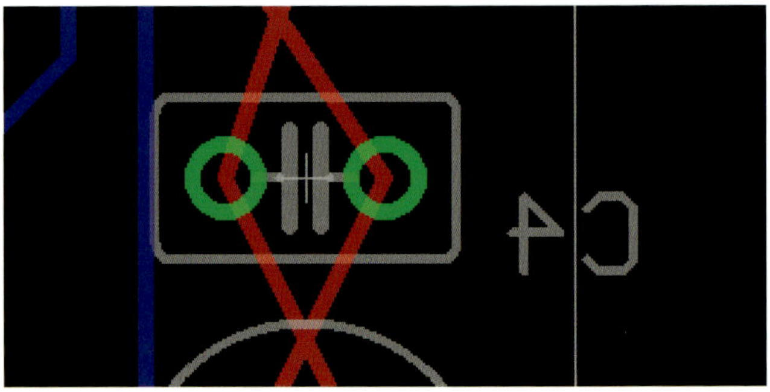

Figure 4-18: Component after the MIRROR command

Mirror a Group

In order to mirror a group of elements, the group should be first defined using the GROUP command and polygon in the usual manner. The MIRROR command is then selected and

the **Right-Click** mouse button is used to execute the change. The group will be mirrored about the vertical axis through the next grid point. This can be seen in Figure 4-19 and Figure 4-20.

Wires, circles, pads and polygons may not be individually mirrored unless included in a group.

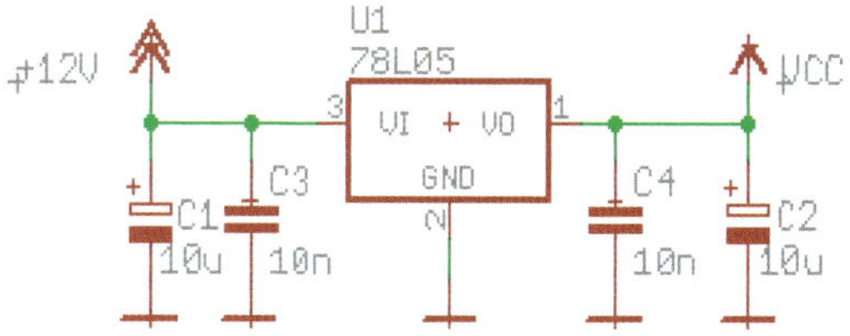

Figure 4-19: GROUP prior to MIRROR command

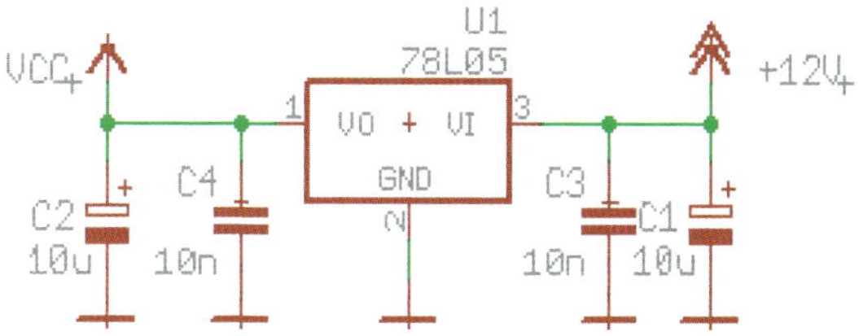

Figure 4-20: GROUP after the MIRROR command

Mirror Text

Text on the solder side of a pc board (*Bottom* and *bPlace* layers) is mirrored automatically so that it is readable when the user looks at the solder side of the board. An example of this in a board can be seen in Figure 4-21.

Mirrored text in a schematic will be printed on the other side of its origin point, but it will still remain normally readable.

Figure 4-21: text MIRRORed on the solder side of a PCB layout

MITER

Function
Miters wire joints.

Syntax
```
MITER [radius]
```

Mouse keys

Left&Drag dynamically modifies the miter.
Right-Click toggles between round and straight mitering.

See also SPLIT, WIRE, ROUTE, POLYGON

The MITER command can be used to take the edge off a point where two wires join. The two existing wires need to be on the same layer and must have the same width and wire style.

When the command is actioned, a parameter is displayed in the window main parameter toolbar, as shown in Figure 4-22. This toolbar displays the miter style and allows the user to set the miter radius.

Figure 4-22: the MITER parameter toolbar

Mitering a point
If the user selects a point where exactly two straight wires join, an additional wire will be inserted between these two wires, according to the given `radius`. If the user then Click&Drags on such a point with the left mouse button, they can define the mitering wire dynamically.

Mitering a wire
If the user selects a wire (which may also be an arc) somewhere in the middle between its end points, and that wire is connected to exactly two other straight wires (one at each end), then the selected wire will be "re-mitered" according to the set `radius`. If the user Click&Drags on such a wire with the left mouse button, the wire mitering will be defined dynamically.

Straight versus round mitering

If `radius` is positive, the inserted wire will be an arc with the given radius; if it is negative, a straight wire will be inserted. The user can toggle between round and straight mitering by using the **Right-Click** action.

Miter radius and wire bend style

The `radius` specified in the MITER command will be used in all other commands that draw wires; and where that command employs wire bend styles of 90 or 45 degrees (e.g. SPLIT or ROUTE commands).

If the user sets the round mitering parameter, it will apply to both the 90 and 45 degree bend styles; or in the case of straight mitering, only the 90 degree bend styles will be affected.

MOVE

Function
Moves objects and elements.

Syntax
```
MOVE ..
MOVE name
```

Mouse keys

Ctrl+Left-click selects an object at its origin or modifies it.
Ctrl+Right-Click selects the group.
Left-Click&Drag immediately moves the object.
Ctrl+Right&Drag immediately moves the group.
Center mirrors the selected object or the group.
Right-Click rotates the selected object or the group.
Shift+Right-Click reverses the direction of rotation.

Keyboard
F7: activates the MOVE command.

See also GROUP, LOCK, RATSNEST

The MOVE command is used to move objects within a drawing or between sheets in a drawing.

If an object is selected with the left mouse button and the button is not released, the object can be moved immediately ("Click&Drag"). The same applies to groups when using the right mouse button.

Note: it is not possible to rotate or mirror the object while attempting to MOVE it.

Parts, pads, SMDs, pins and gates can be selected by their name. This form of the command is useful if the object is outside the currently displayed window area, or the area is congested with elements, making manual mouse selection difficult.

Parts cannot be moved if they are locked, or if any of their connected pads would extend outside the allowed area (where a limited edition of EAGLE is being used).

Elements can be moved only if the appropriate *tOrigins/bOrigins* layer is visible. The MOVE command has no effect on layers that are not visible.
Attributes of parts can be selected by entering the concatenation of part name and attribute name e.g. `R5>VALUE`.

Moving Wires

The ends of wires (tracks) that are connected to an element cannot be moved. When moving elements, connected wires (tracks) that belong to a signal are also moved. Care should be taken as this could create short circuits.

If, following a MOVE command, two wires from different signals are shortened together, they are retained as separate signals and the error will be flagged by the DRC command.

Moving Groups

In order to move a group, and before selecting the MOVE command, the objects are selected in the normal way (using the GROUP command and polygon). The user may then:

- **Right-Click** to activate the context menu and then `Left-Click the MOVE:GROUP` entry;
- **Ctrl+Right-Click** to active the MOVE command.

In any case the entire group can now be moved, and rotated with **Right-Click**.

Considerations when working within Schematics

Note that when selecting a multi-gate part in a schematic by name, the user will need to enter the full instance name consisting of part and gate name.

If a supply pin (*Direction Sup*) is placed on a net, the pin name is allocated to this net. Pins placed on each other are connected together.

If unconnected pins of an element are placed on nets or pins then they are connected to them.

If nets are moved over pins they are not connected to them.

Selecting objects at their origin

Normally a selected object remains within the grid on which it has been originally placed. If the user presses `Ctrl` while selecting an object, the point where the object is selected is pulled towards the cursor and snapped into the current grid.
The following actions are performed when using `Ctrl` and selecting other objects:

i. Wire
   If a *wire* is selected with `Ctrl` pressed, somewhere in the middle (not at an end point), the end points stay fixed and the wire can be bent; forming an arc. In the same way the curvature of an arc (which is basically a wire) can be modified.
ii. Rectangles
   If a *rectangle* is selected at one of its corners with `Ctrl` pressed, the user may resize both the rectangle's width and height. Selecting an edge of the rectangle with `Ctrl` pressed, allows the user to resize the rectangle's width or height, respectively. Selecting the rectangle at its center with `Ctrl` pressed, pulls it towards the cursor and snaps it into the current grid.

iii. Circles
If a *circle* is selected at its circumference with `Ctrl` pressed, the center stays fixed and the user can resize the circle's diameter. Selecting the center point this way pulls the circle towards the cursor and snaps it into the current grid.

Move part of a sheet to another sheet
The user may move part of a sheet to another sheet of the same schematic without affecting the board (despite Forward&BackAnnotation_being active). This is performed as follows:

i. defining the GROUP that contains the objects to be moved;
ii. selecting the group with the MOVE command;
iii. switch to the desired sheet with the MOVE command still active, and with the group attached to the cursor; and place the GROUP with **Left-Click.**

All the affected objects in this operation will be transferred from the original sheet to the current, new sheet.

Note: that only wires that have both ends in the group will be transferred. Any part that is transferred takes all its electrical connections with it, even if a net wire attached to one of its pins is not transferred (due to the other end of the wire not being included in the group). In case a pin in the new sheet has an electrical connection, but no other pin, wire or junction attached to it to make this visible, a junction will be automatically generated at this point.

 NAME

Function
Displays and changes names of elements.

Syntax
```
NAME..
NAME new_name
NAME old_name new_name
```

See also SHOW, SMASH, VALUE

The NAME command is used to display or edit the name of the selected object.

Parts, elements, pads, SMDs, pins and gates can also be selected by their name, which is especially useful if the object is outside the currently shown window area. Other object types (e.g. nets, busses, signals) have to be clicked first.

Automatic Naming
EAGLE generates names automatically: E$.. for elements, S$.. for signals, P$.. for pads, pins and SMDs. In general, it is convenient to substitute commonly used names (e.g. 1...14 for a 14-pin dual inline package) in place of these automatically generated names.

Automatic naming of parts can be controlled with the PREFIX Command.

Note: In versions of EAGLE prior to V6.x, names that started with a '$' were treated specially (i.e. Supply Layers commenced with '$'). This is no longer the case.

Schematic
If nets or buses are to be renamed, the program has to distinguish between three cases because they can consist of several segments placed on different sheets. Thus, a menu will ask the user to enter the new name and select the action to be taken. These questions appear in a popup dialog (as shown in Figure 4-23) and can be answered either by selecting the appropriate item with the mouse or by pressing the appropriate hot key (T, E, A).

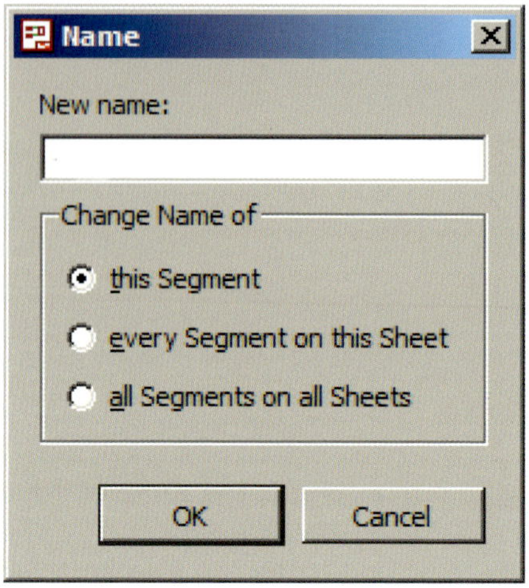

Figure 4-23: the NAME dialog for a net

Polygon

When renaming a signal polygon in a board, the user may choose whether to rename only this polygon (and thus move it from one signal into another), or to give the entire signal a different name.

Library

When in library edit mode, the NAME command is used to display or edit the name of the selected pad, SMD, pin or gate.

PASTE

Function
Copies the contents of the clipboard or a drawing file to an open drawing.

Syntax
```
PASTE [ orientation ]
PASTE [ orientation ] [ offset ] filename
```

Mouse keys
Center-Click mirrors the contents of the clipboard.
Right-Click rotates the contents of the clipboard.
Shift+Right-Click reverses the direction of rotation.

See also CUT, COPY, GROUP

See the ADD command for an explanation of `orientation`.

Using the commands GROUP, CUT, and PASTE, parts of a drawing/library can be copied to the same or different drawings/libraries. When using the PASTE command, the following points should be observed:

- CUT/PASTE cannot be used in device editing mode.
- Elements and signals on a board can only be copied to a board.
- Parts, buses and nets on a schematic can only be copied to a schematic.
- Pads and SMDs can only be copied from package to package.
- Pins can only be copied from symbol to symbol.
- When copying elements, signals, pads, SMDs and pins, a new name is allocated if the previous name is already used in the new drawing.
- Buses retain the same names.
- Nets retain the same name as long as one of the net segments has a label, or is connected to a supply pin. Otherwise a new name is generated if the previous name is already in use.
- To prevent the file name being mistaken for an orientation or an offset value, it can be enclosed in single quotes.

If there exists modified versions of devices or packages in the clipboard, an automatic library update will be started to replace the objects in the schematic or board with the ones from the clipboard.

Note: The user should always run a DesignRuleCheck (DRC) and an ElectricalRuleCheck (ERC) after a library update has been performed!

Pasting from a file
If a file name is given in the command line, the contents of that file are pasted into the currently open drawing. (Both files should be in the same directory).

If the given file is one of a consistent board/schematic pair, both files will be pasted into the corresponding drawings of the currently open project.

Example
The following example shows the use of an `offset`, which adds the given value to all part and net names in the pasted files (unless they retain their name, see below).

Assume the user has a consistent board/schematic pair that contains the design of an amplifier, where the schematic may consist of several sheets. The user wishes to place this amplifier twice into the project.

This is achieved by using the following commands:

```
PASTE 100 amplifier.sch
PASTE 200 amplifier.sch
```

As a result, the first amplifier channel will have all parts and nets named starting at 100, while the second one will have them start at 200. If no offset is given, new names are generated as necessary.

Just like in a normal PASTE operation, when pasting from a file, nets that have a label or are connected to a supply pin, retain their name while all others will acquire newly generated names. A net will retain its name if it is labeled or connected to a supply pin on one sheet, despite appearing on several sheets.

Unless the PASTE operation is done in a script file, a dialog, as shown in Figure 4-24, will be offered that displays all the net names. By clicking on the names in the "New name" column the user may edit individual net names. Icons indicate whether a net in the pasted drawing has a label or a supply pin, and whether the net will be connected to an existing net with the same name in the edited drawing.

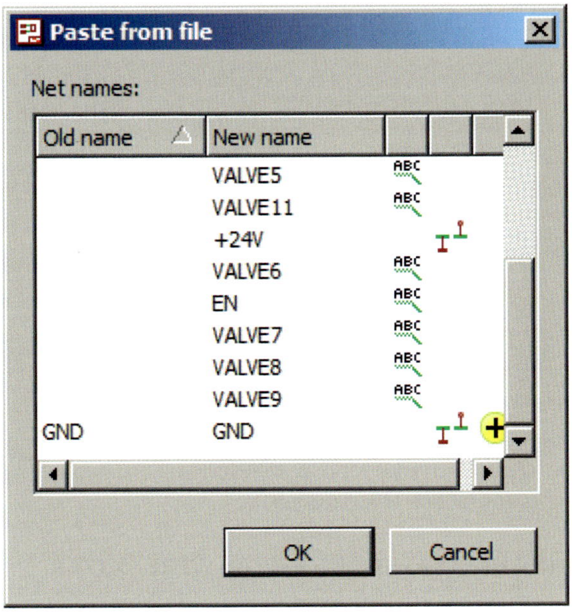

Figure 4-24: the NAME dialog for a net

If the user pastes a schematic into a schematic drawing, all sheets of the pasted schematic will be added as separate, new sheets to the edited drawing. (Note: this is not possible in the Light Edition, which can handle only a single schematic sheet).

When pasting into a board drawing, the corresponding board (if any) will be placed below the existing content of the edited board drawing. If explicit control is required over where the board is placed, one can perform the PASTE operation in the board; in which case the schematic sheets will be added just the same, but the board will be attached to the mouse cursor and may then be placed exactly where it is required.
The user can also paste from a file using Drag&Drop, by pressing the Ctrl key when dropping the file.

POLYGON

Function

Draws polygon areas within drawings.

Syntax

```
POLYGON [signal_name] [width] [curve | @radius]
```

Mouse keys

Center-Click selects the layer.
Right-Click changes the wire bend style (see SET *Wire_Bend*).
Shift+Right-Click reverses the direction of switching bend styles.
Ctrl+Right-Click toggles between corresponding bend styles.
Ctrl+Left-Click when placing a wire end point defines arc radius. **Left-Click** twice at the same point closes the polygon.

See also CHANGE, DELETE, RATSNEST, RIPUP, WIRE, MITER

Naming

A polygon with a name beginning with a digit (as in `0V`), must be enclosed single quotes to distinguish it from a *Width* value.

Curve , @radius

If the `curve` or `@radius` parameter is used, an arc can be drawn as part of the polygon definition (see the detailed description in the WIRE command).

The POLYGON command is used to draw polygon areas within drawings. When the command is invoked, the parameter toolbar, given in Figure 4-25 (split into 2 sections), is displayed. This toolbar includes the following parameters: Layer, Miter, Width, Pour, Thermals, Orphans, Isolate, Spacing and Rank.

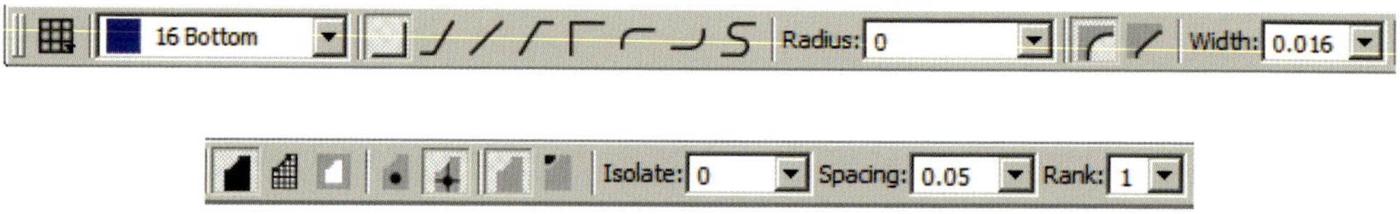

Figure 4-25: the POLYGON parameter toolbar (split)

Layers

Layers are treated elsewhere in this book. Polygons in the layers Top, Bottom, and (Route2 to Route15) are treated as signals. Polygons in the layers *t/b/vRestrict* are protected areas for the Autorouter.

Miter
See the MITRE command for this functionality.

Width
This is the line thickness, in the current units, with which the polygon is drawn. The user should select the largest possible width to avoid unnecessary quantities of data at time of manufacture. A finer line width permits the polygon to have a more complex shape.

If the wire width is lower than the resolution of the output driver in the CAM Processor, a warning is issued.

The polygon *Width* should always be larger than the hardware resolution of the output device. For example when using a Gerber photoplotter with a typical resolution of 1 mil, the polygon *width* should not be smaller than, say, 6 mil. Typically the polygon *Width* should be set in the same range as other wires in the drawing.

Pour
Pour specifies the filling type: the whole area (*Solid*) or a grid (*Hatch*).

There is a special type; *Cutout*, that may be used to define polygons that get subtracted from all other signal polygons within the same layer. This type is suitable for cutouts (i.e. restricted areas) in polygons in inner signal layers.

Thermals:
Thermals determines whether pads in the polygon are connected via Thermal symbols, or are completely connected to the copper plane. This also applies to vias, assuming that the option has been activated in the Design Rules.

The width of the thermal connectors is calculated as the half of the pad's drill diameter. The width has to be between the limits of a minimum of the wire width and a maximum of twice the wire width of the polygon. The length of the thermal connectors is defined by the Thermal isolation value in the Design Rules' Supply tab.

Orphans
The Orphans parameter determines if a polygon may contain areas (islands) which are not electrically connected to the polygon's signal. If Orphans is set *Off*, such unconnected areas will not be drawn.

Isolate
The Isolate parameter defines the value that the polygon must maintain with respect to all other objects not part of its signal. If higher values are defined for special objects in the Design Rules or net classes, the higher values apply.
In the case of polygons with different Ranks, *Isolate* always refers to the drawn contour which is shown in the outline mode of the polygon, even if the calculated polygon has got another contour, for example, due to a wire that supersedes the polygon. The actual clearance can become greater than the given *Isolate* value.

Spacing
If the option *Hatch* is chosen for *Pour*, this value determines the spacing of the grid lines.

Rank
Overlapping polygons must not create any short circuits. *Rank* can therefore be used to determine which polygons are to be subtracted from others. A polygon with rank = 1 has the highest priority in the Layout Editor, no other polygon drawn in the layout is ever subtracted from it, while one with rank = 6 has the lowest priority. As soon as there is an overlap with a higher rank, the appropriate area is cut out from the polygon with rank = 6. This scenario in a board is illustrated in Figure 4-26 and Figure 4-27.

Polygons with the same rank are compared by the DRC. The rank property works only for polygons with different signals. For overlapping polygons with the same signal name it is without effect. They will be drawn one over the other.

Polygons that are created in the Package Editor, and not assigned to a signal, will be subtracted from all other polygons. There is no rank parameter available.

The parameters *Isolate* and *Rank* only have a meaning for polygons in layers Top...Bottom.

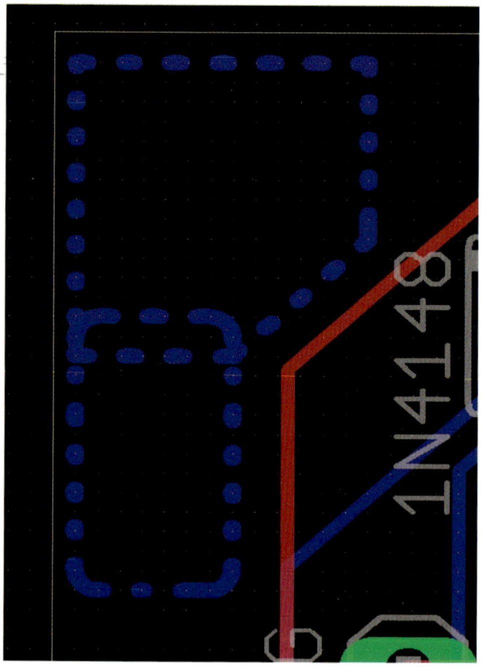

Figure 4-26: POLYGONs with different Ranks

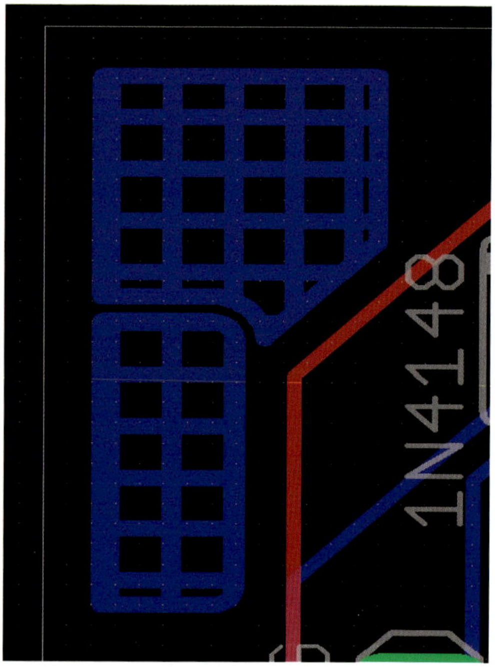

Figure 4-27: POLYGONs after Rank calculation

Polygon Modes of display

Polygons belonging to a signal can be displayed in two different modes:

- Outlines — only the outlines, as defined by the user, are displayed.
  In "outlines" mode a polygon is drawn with dotted wires, so that it can be distinguished from other wires. The board file contains only the "outlines".

- Real mode — all of the areas are visible, as calculated by the program.
  The default display mode is "outlines" as the calculation is a time consuming operation. When a drawing is generated with the CAM Processor all polygons are calculated.

The calculation of the polygons is initiated by the RATSNEST command (this can be turned off with `SET POLYGON_RATSNEST OFF;`). **Left-Clicking** the STOP button terminates the calculation of the polygons. Already calculated polygons are shown in "real mode", all others are shown in "outline mode".

The RIPUP command changes the display mode of a polygon to "outline". CHANGE operations re-calculate a polygon if it was shown in "real mode" before.

Other commands when used with Polygons

Polygons are selected at their edges (like wires). SPLIT: Inserts a new polygon edge.

DELETE	Deletes a polygon corner (if only three corners are left the whole polygon is deleted).
CHANGE LAYER	Changes the layer of the whole polygon.
CHANGE WIDTH	Changes the parameter width of the whole polygon.
MOVE	Moves a polygon edge or corner (like wire segments).
COPY	Copies the whole polygon.
NAME	If the polygon is located in a signal layer the name of the signal is changed.

RECT

Function
Adds rectangles to a drawing.

Syntax
```
RECT [orientation]
```

Mouse keys
Center-Click selects the layer.

See also CIRCLE

The RECT command is used to add rectangles to a drawing. The two points define two opposite corners of the rectangle. **Center-Clicking** changes the layer to which the rectangle is to be added.

The `orientation` parameter may be any angle in the range `R0...R359.9` (see description in the ADD command). The `S` and `M` flags can not be used here.
Note: the coordinates are always defined at an orientation of `R0`.
The alternative of entering an orientation in the RECT command is mainly for use in scripts, where the rectangle data may have been derived through a User Language Program from the UL_RECTANGLE object. When entering a non-zero orientation interactively, the corners of the rectangle may not appear at the actual cursor position; in which case the user should employ the ROTATE command to interactively rotate a rectangle.

Rectangles and Signals
Rectangles in the signal layers *Top*, *Bottom*, or *Route2* to *Route15* do not belong to signals. Therefore the DRC reports errors if they overlap with wires, pads etc.

Restricted Areas
If used in the layers *tRestrict*, *bRestrict*, or *vRestrict*, the RECT command defines restricted areas for the Autorouter.

ROTATE

Function
Rotates objects.

Syntax

```
ROTATE orientation
ROTATE orientation 'name' ..
```

Mouse key

Ctrl+Right-Click	rotates the group.
Left-Click &Drag	rotates the object by any angle.
Ctrl+Right-Click &Drag	rotates the group by any angle.

See also ADD, MIRROR, MOVE, LOCK, GROUP

The ROTATE command is used to change the orientation of objects.

If `orientation` (see the description given for the ADD command) is given, that value will be added to the orientation of the selected object instead.

Prefixing `orientation` with the character '=' causes the value not to be added, but instead set absolutely.

Parts, pads, SMDs and pins can also be selected by their name, which is especially useful if the object is outside the currently shown window area. For example:

```
ROTATE =MR90 IC1
```

would set the orientation of element IC1 to MR90, regardless of its previous setting.
The quotes around `name` are necessary to distinguish it from an orientation parameter as in:

```
ROTATE R45 'R1'
```

They can be omitted if the context is clear.

Alternatively the user may use **Left-Click &Drag** to rotate an object through any angle. This is achieved as follows:

Left-Click on the object and move the mouse (i.e. `Drag` with the mouse button held down) away from the object. After having moved the mouse a short distance, the object will start rotating. Move the mouse until the desired angle has been reached and then release the mouse button.

The ROTATE command may be cancelled by pressing the ESCape key (while still holding the mouse button pressed).

The same operation can be applied to a group by using the right mouse button. The group will be rotated around the point where the right mouse button has been pressed down.

Parts cannot be rotated if they are locked, or if any of their connected pads would extend outside the allowed area (in the case where the limited edition of EAGLE is being used).

Elements

When rotating an element, the wires (tracks) connected to the element are moved at the connection points. Care should be taken to avoid short circuits.

Elements can only be rotated if the appropriate *tOrigins/bOrigins* layer is visible.

Text

Text is always displayed so that it can be read from the bottom or from the right - even when rotated. Therefore after every two rotations it appears the same way, but the origin has moved from the lower left to the upper right corner. This may be the case if a text appears to be unable to be selected!

If the required result is text that is printed "upside down" in a layout, the "Spin" flag needs to be set for that text.

SMASH

Function
Separates text variables and attributes from parts or elements.

Syntax
SMASH..
SMASH name ..

Mouse keys

Ctrl+Right-Click	smashes the group.
Shift+Left-Click	reverses the text separation ("un-smashes" the part).
Ctrl+Shift+Right-Click	reverses the text separation for the group.

See also NAME, VALUE, TEXT, ATTRIBUTE

The SMASH command is used to operate on parts or elements, so that the text parameters (which indicate name, value or attributes) may be manipulated independently. The text may then subsequently be placed in a new and more convenient location with the MOVE command.

Parts and elements may also be selected by their name, which is especially useful if the object is outside the currently displayed window area.

Note: when selecting a multi-gate part in a schematic by name, the user will need to enter the full instance name, consisting of part and gate name.

Use of the SMASH command allows the text to be treated like any other text, e.g. CHANGE SIZE, ROTATE, etc., but the actual text may not be changed.

A SMASH command can be reversed (i.e. "un-smashed") by using the **Shift+Left-Click** key combination (after activating the SMASH command).

SPLIT

Function

Splits wires and polygon edges into segments.

Syntax

SPLIT [curve | @radius]..

Mouse keys

Left-Click	defines the point where a spilt is commenced
Right-Click	changes the wire bend style (see SETWire_Bend).
Shift+Right-Click	reverses the direction of switching bend styles.
Ctrl+Right-Click	toggles between corresponding bend styles.
Ctrl+Left-Click	when placing a wire end point defines arc radius.

Keyboard

F8: SPLIT	activates the SPLIT command.

See also MITER, MOVE, OPTIMIZE, SET

The SPLIT command is used to divide a wire (or segment) or a polygon edge into two segments in order, for example, to introduce a bend or to re-align a track. This means the user may split wires into parts that can be moved with the mouse during the activation of the SPLIT command.

The user defines the point at which the wire is split using the **Left-Click**. The shorter of the two new segments follows the current wire bend rules and may therefore, itself, become two segments (see SET Wire_Bend); the longer segment is a straight segment which runs to the next end point. Figure 4-28 and Figure 4-29 illustrate the use of the SPLIT command on a top track of a PCB.

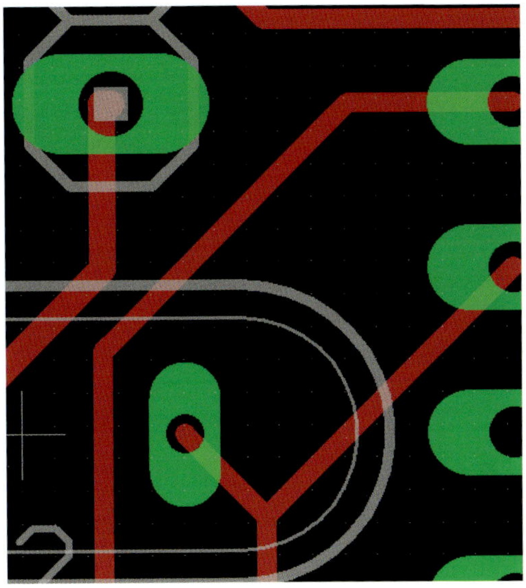

Figure 4-28: track prior to SPLIT operation

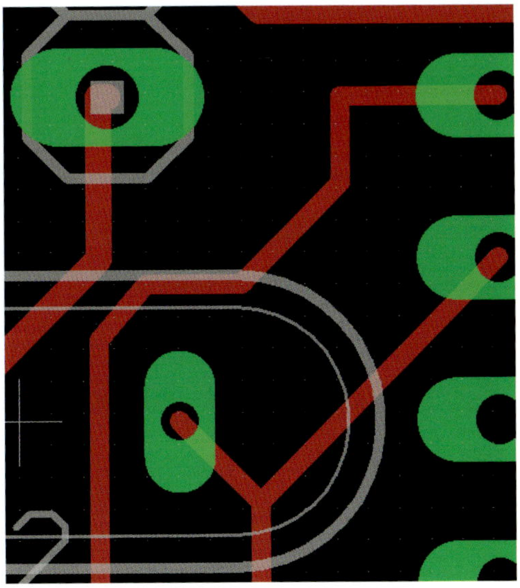

Figure 4-29: track after a SPLIT operation

If the `curve` or `@radius` parameter is given, an arc can be drawn as part of the wire segment (see the detailed description in the WIRE command).

On completion of the SPLIT command, the segments are automatically rejoined if they are in line. This may be overridden with the SET command i.e. using `SET OPTIMIZING OFF;`
The user may also employ the SPLIT command to reduce the width of a segment. This is done by selecting the SPLIT command, marking the part of the wire which is to be reduced with **2x Left-Click**, and using the command:

```
CHANGE WIDTH width
```

to change the segment's width. To complete the change the user actions a **Left-Click** on the segment (see Figure 4-30 and Figure 4-31).

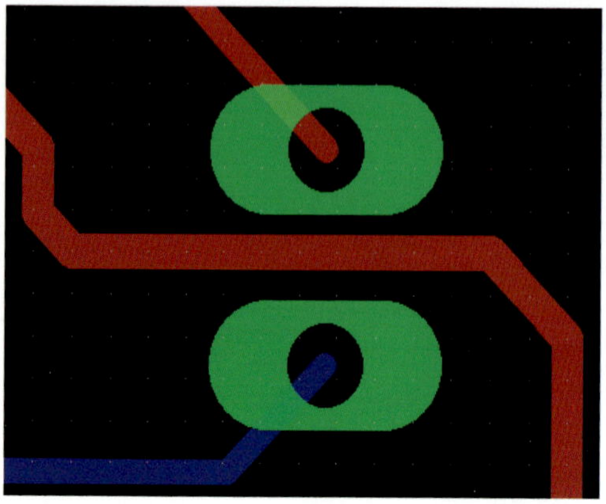

Figure 4-30: track prior to a CHANGE WIDTH operation

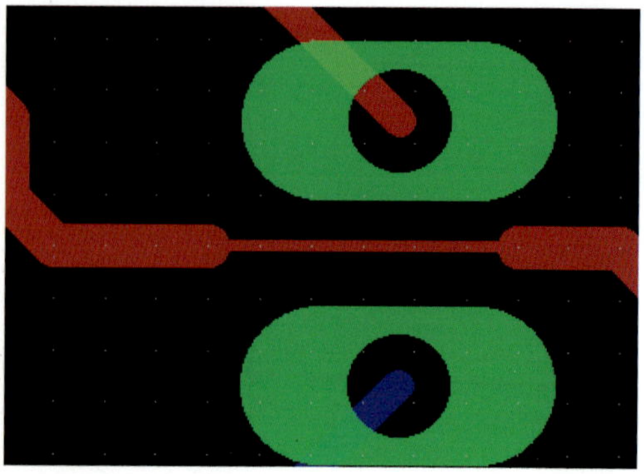

Figure 4-31: track after a CHANGE WIDTH operation

TEXT

Function
Used to add text to a drawing.

Syntax
```
TEXT any_text [orientation]..
TEXT 'any_text' [orientation]
```

Mouse keys
Center-Click selects the layer.
Right-Click rotates the text.
Shift+Right-Click reverses the direction of rotation.

See also CHANGE, MOVE, MIRROR, PIN, ROTATE, ATTRIBUTE

The TEXT command is used to add text to a library element or drawing. When the command is invoked, the required text is entered in a dialog box.

When entering several text strings, it is not necessary to invoke the command each time, as the text command remains active after placing text with the mouse.

While the TEXT command is active, the TEXT parameter toolbar is displayed (as in Figure 4-32).

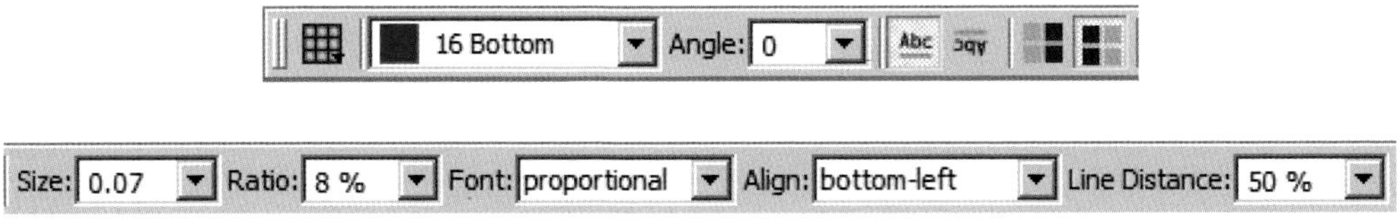

Figure 4-32: the TEXT parameter toolbar (split)

The parameters under the user control are: Layer, Angle, Spin Flag, Font Size, Font Ratio, Font Type, Text Alignment.

Special Characters
The parameter `any_text` does not quite literally mean any text. Some restrictions apply.

If the text parameter contains several successive blanks or a semicolon, the whole text string must be enclosed in single quotes. Further, if the text contains single quotes, then each quote mark itself has to be enclosed in single quotes. If apostrophes are required in the text then, they too, must each be enclosed in single quotes.

Orientation

The orientation of the text may be defined by the TEXT command (`orientation`) using the usual definitions as listed in the ADD_command (`R0, R90` etc.). **Right-Clicking** will rotate the text and the **Center-Click** will change the current layer.

The text `Orientation` may also be set using the 'Angle' section in the parameter toolbar. This section allows the user to either enter the numeric value (in degrees) of rotation or, by using the drop-down menu, pick from the pre-set values of 90, 180, 270.

Text is always displayed so that it can be read from in front or from the right - even if rotated. Therefore after every two rotations it appears the same way, but the origin has moved from the lower left to the upper right corner.

Next to, and to the right of, the Angle box are the buttons for the Spin and Mirror flags respectively. If the user selects the lefthand Spin icon, the *Spin flag is off* (by default). This means that text is always displayed readable from the right or from the bottom side of the drawing. If the spin flag is active (i.e. the righthand *Spin flag on* icon is marked) the text can be displayed in any orientation/rotation, including upside down.

The reading direction for vertical text can be changed from "up" to "down" in the user interface dialog. If the text is to be printed "upside down", the user may set the "Spin" flag for that text.

The *Mirror* icons are used with components to determine where a component is placed: on the top (default) or on the bottom side of the board. If a component is placed on top, the lefthand icon is active. If the user wants to place it on the bottom side, the user **Left-Clicks** onto the righthand *Mirrored* icon.

Text Height & Thickness

The height and thickness of characters can be changed using the CHANGE command or the relevant section of the parameter toolbar.

Size

The size of the text can be changed using;

```
CHANGE SIZE text_size
```

or by using the *Size* drop-down menu. The user enters the required size or selects the option from the drop-down.

Ratio

The thickness is expressed as a ratio. This ratio is the line thickness as a % of the text height. The user may employ the CHANGE command;

```
CHANGE RATIO ratio
```

or use the *Ratio* section of the parameter toolbar.

Text Font

Text may have three different fonts:

`Vector`	the program's internal vector font
`Proportional`	a proportional pixel font (usually 'Helvetica')
`Fixed`	a monospaced pixel font (usually 'Courier')

The text font can be changed with the CHANGE command, as follows:

```
CHANGE FONT VECTOR|PROPORTIONAL|FIXED
```

The program attempts to reproduce text, with `FONT` set to other than `Vector`, as faithfully as possible. However, since the actual font is drawn by the system's graphics interface, `Proportional` and `Fixed` fonts may be output with different sizes and/or lengths.

If the option "Always vector font" is set in the user interface dialog, all text will always be displayed and printed using the built-in vector font, independent of the settings of the individual text, and for each drawing. This option is useful if the system does not display correctly when the other fonts are used.

When creating a new board or schematic, the current setting of this option is stored in the drawing file. This ensures that the drawing will be printed with the correct setting if it is transferred to another system with a different setting of this option.

The user may use the SET VECTOR_FONT OFF|ON command to change the setting in an existing board or schematic drawing.

When creating output files with the CAM Processor, text will always be drawn with `Vector` font. Other fonts are not supported.
The `RATIO` parameter has no meaning for text fonts other than `Vector`.

Text Alignment

The *Align* (text alignment) parameter defines where the origin of the text block shall be put within the text.

The user may use the drop-down menu to change the alignment parameter, or alternatively use the CHANGE command as follows;

```
CHANGE ALIGN TOP CENTER; TEXT 'ABC'
```

which draws the text ABC with the origin at its top/center.

There are nine different possible alignments, which consist of combinations of the keywords `left`, `bottom`, `center`, `right` and `top`. These keywords can be given in any sequence, but only the last one of left/right and top/bottom will be taken into account for the respective direction. The center keyword only applies to those directions where no other keyword has been given. The default is left and bottom.

Line Distance

The line distance parameter determines the spacing between the lines of a segment of multi-line text.

If the user enters text within the TEXT command dialog window, they may extend this to several lines by using the `Shift + Enter` key at the end of each line. The distance between these lines of text can be set with the line distance parameter. This distance is set as a percentage of the text size.

The constraints of these parameters are:

- Maximum text height: 2 inches
- Maximum text thickness: 0.51602 inch (13.1 mm)
- Ratio: 0...31 (% of text height)
- Line distance: 0...250 (% of text height).

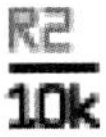

VALUE

Function
Allows the user to display and edit values of an element.

Syntax
```
VALUE ..
VALUE value ..
VALUE name value ..
VALUE ON;
VALUE OFF;
```

See also NAME, SMASH, VARIANT

In Boards and Schematics
Elements can be assigned a value, e.g. '1k' for a resistor or '10uF' for a capacitor. This is done with the VALUE command. The command selects an element and opens a popup menu that allows the user to enter or change a value.

Using the syntax :
```
VALUE value
```

the user may enter a value before selecting an element. All of the subsequently selected elements will be assigned this value. This is useful if the user wishes to place a series of components with the identical values e.g. a number of resistors which have the same value.

For the syntax:
```
VALUE name value ..
```

where the parameters name and value are specified, the element name receives the specified value. The VALUE command can only be used in the default assembly variant. If a change of value is required of another assembly variant, the user should use the VARIANT command.

Example
```
VALUE R1 10k R2 100k
```

In this case more than one element has been assigned a value. This alternative can be used in script files as follows:

```
VALUE R1 10k \
R2 100k \
R3 5.6k \
C1 10uF \
C2 22nF \
...
```

(Note: the '\' prevents the following line from being mistaken for an EAGLE key word.)

In Device Mode

If the VALUE command is used in the device edit mode, the parameters ON and OFF may be used:

`On` Permits the actual value to be changed in the schematic.

`Off` Automatically enters the actual device name into the schematic (e.g.74LS00N). The user can only modify this value after a confirmation.

WIRE

Function
Adds wires (tracks) to a PCB drawing.

Syntax
```
WIRE ['signal_name'] [width] .
WIRE ['signal_name'] [width] [ROUND | FLAT] [curve | @radius].
```

Mouse keys

Left-Click	commences drawing a wire; double Left-Click terminates it.
Center-Click	selects the layer for the wire.
Right-Click	changes the wire bend style (see SET Wire_Bend).
Shift+Right-Click	reverses the direction of switching bend styles.
Ctrl+Left-Click	when starting a wire snaps it to the next existing wire end point.; when placing a wire end point defines arc radius.
Ctrl+Right-Click	toggles between corresponding bend styles.

See also MITER, SIGNAL, ROUTE, CHANGE, NET, BUS, DELETE, RIPUP, ARC

The WIRE command is used to add wires (tracks) to a PCB layout drawing. The wire begins at the first point specified and runs to the second. (Additional points added to the wire draw extra wire segments.) To complete the wire, the user executes two **Left-Clicks** at the same position.

Starting a WIRE with **Ctrl+Left-Click** snaps the starting point of the new wire to the coordinates of the closest existing wire. This is especially useful if the existing wire is off grid. It also adjusts the current width, layer and style to those of the existing wire.
Depending on the currently active wire bend, one or two wire segments will be drawn between every two points.

Signal name
The `signal_name` parameter is intended mainly to be used in script files that read in generated data. If a `signal_name` is given, all subsequent wires will be added to that signal and no automatic checks will be performed.

This feature should be used with great care due to the risk of creating short circuits i.e. a wire could be placed in a way that it would connect different signals. The user is advised to run a DesignRule Check after using the WIRE command while including the `signal_name` parameter.

When the WIRE command is executed, the parameter toolbar is displayed as shown in Figure 4-33.

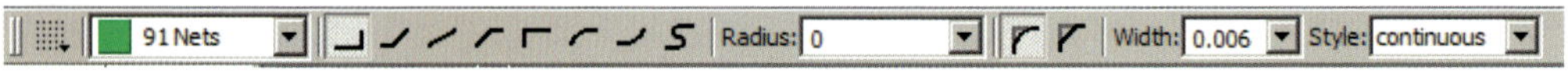

Figure 4-33: the WIRE parameter toolbar

Signal Layers for Wires

The leftmost parameter in the toolbar allows the user to specify the layer in which the wire will be placed.

Wires (tracks) in the layers Top, Bottom, and ROUTE2...15 are treated as signals. If a wire is drawn in either of these layers starting from an existing signal, then all of the segments of this wire belong to that signal (only if the center of the wire is placed exactly onto the center of the existing wire or pad).

If the user terminates a drawing operation with a wire segment connected to a different signal, then EAGLE will ask the user to confirm that the two signals are to be connected.

Note: EAGLE treats each wire segment as a single object (e.g. when deleting a wire). When the WIRE command is active; the use of **Center-Click** may be used to change the layer on which the wire is drawn.

WARNING: The WIRE command should not be used for nets, buses, and airwires. See the NET, BUS and SIGNAL commands for further details.

Wire bend style

The wire bend style essentially defines the angle between the segments; and can be changed with the **Right-Click** action. The toolbar option for this parameter is shown in Figure 4-34. **Shift+Right-Click** reverses the direction in which the bend styles are selected, and the **Ctrl+Right-Click** makes it toggle between corresponding bend styles.

Figure 4-34: WIRE bend style parameter

Miter radius

The *radius* parameter specified is used where the command employs wire bend styles of 90 or 45 degrees. If the user sets the round mitering parameter, it will apply to both the 90 and 45 degree bend styles; or in the case of straight wires; only the 90 degree bend styles will be affected.

If *radius* is positive, the inserted wire will be an arc with the given radius; if it is negative, a straight wire will be inserted.

Miter style

The miter style parameter toolbar option is shown in Figure 4-35. This parameter can be selected to commence the action of a round- or straight- miter wire,

Figure 4-35: miter style parameter option

The user can toggle between round and straight mitering by using the **Right-Click** action.

Wire Width

Entering a number after activating the WIRE command changes the width of the wire (in the present unit) which can be up to 0.51602 inch (13.1 mm).

The wire width can be changed with the command:

```
CHANGE WIDTH width
```

at any time.

Alternatively, this can also be done using the drop-down menu for the *Width* parameter.

Wire Style

Wires can have one of the following *styles*:

- Continuous
- LongDash
- ShortDash
- DashDot

The wire style can be changed with the CHANGE command, or by using the drop-down menu for the Style parameter.

Commands for Editing Boards

AUTO

Function
Starts the Autorouter module.

Syntax
```
AUTO;
AUTO signal_name..; AUTO ! signal_name..;
AUTO ..;
AUTO FOLLOWME
AUTO LOAD|SAVE filename;
```

See also SIGNAL, ROUTE, WIRE, RATSNEST, SET

Example
```
AUTO ! GND VCC;
```

In every case the semicolon is necessary as a terminator.

The AUTO command activates the integrated Autorouter module of EAGLE.

If signal names are specified or signals are selected with the mouse, only these signals are routed.

Without parameters the command will try to route all signals. If a "!" character is specified all signals are routed except the signals following the "!" character. The "!" character must be the first parameter and must show up only once.

The LOAD and SAVE options can be used to load the Autorouter parameters from or save them to the given file. If *filename* doesn't have the extension ".ctl" it will be appended automatically.

Without any parameters (or if no terminating ';' is given), the AUTO command opens a dialog in which the parameters that control the routing algorithm can be configured (as shown in Figure 4-36).

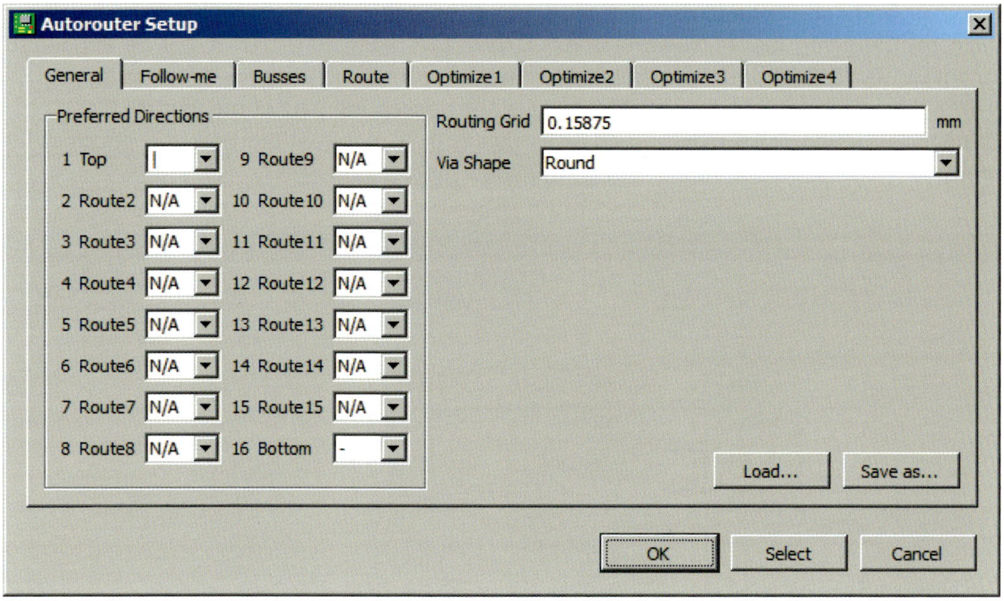

Figure 4-36: AUTO command parameters dialog

Autorouter Parameters

The Autorouter is controlled by a number of parameters, these are:

- The values in the current Design Rules
- the net classes
- special Autorouter control parameters

The Design Rules specify the minimum clearances (DRC commands for setting Clearance and Distance), the via diameter (Restring setting) and the hole diameter of the vias (Sizes setting). The minimum track width is also specified.

The net classes if any are defined specify special minimum clearances, track widths and the hole diameters for vias carrying particular signals.

The range of special cost factors and control parameters that can be changed via the Autorouter menu. These can be seen in the various tab sections in Figure 4-36. They affect, among other things, the route given to tracks during automatic routing. Default values are provided by the program. These control parameters are saved in the BRD file when the layout is saved.

The LOAD and SAVE options can be used to load the Autorouter parameters from, or save them to, the given file. If *filename* doesn't have the extension ".ctl" it will be appended automatically. This allows a particular set of parameters to be used for different layouts. Neither Design Rules nor the data for various net classes are part of the control file.
The special option FOLLOWME, opens this dialog in a mode where only the parameters controlling the Follow-me router can be modified (as in Figure 4-37).

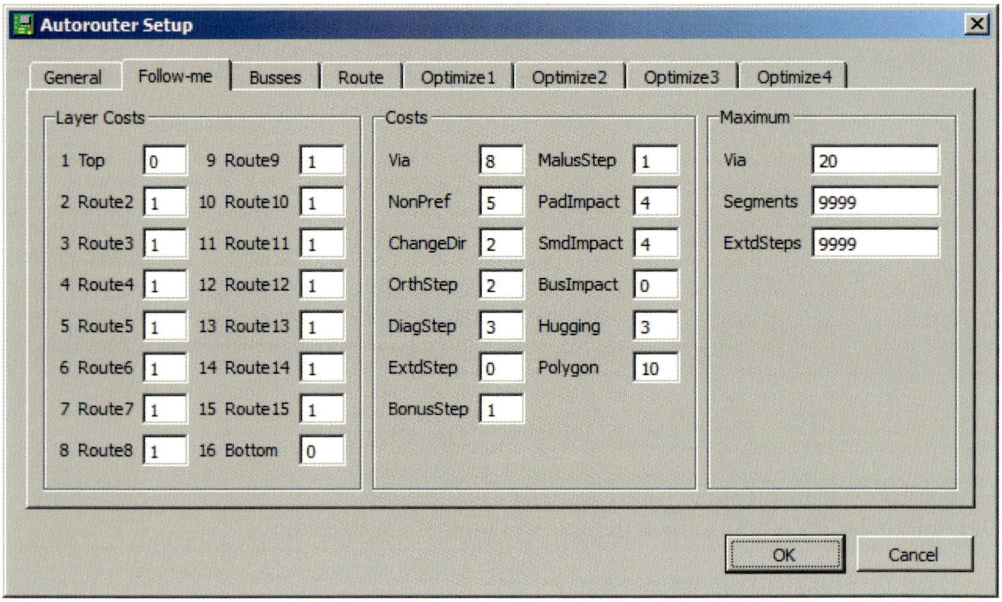

Figure 4-37: AUTO 'Follow-me' parameters dialog

Use of Wildcards

If a `signal_name` parameter is given, the characters '*', '?' and '[]' are wildcards and have the following meaning:

`*` matches any number of any characters
`?` matches exactly one character
`[...]` matches any of the characters between the brackets

If any of the above characters are to be matched exactly, they must be enclosed in brackets. For example, `abc[*]ghi` would match `abc*ghi` and not `abcdefghi`.

A range of characters may also be referenced by `[a-z]`, which results in any character in the range `'a'...'z'`.

Polygons

When the Autorouter is started all Polygons are calculated.

Protocol File
A protocol file (*name.pro*) is generated automatically.

Board Size
The Autorouter puts a rectangle around all objects in the board and takes the size of this rectangle as the routing area. Wires in the Dimension layer are border lines for the Autorouter.

This allows the user to delimit the route area with closed lines, and draw in this layer with the WIRE command. In practice, the outline for the board is drawn in the Dimension layer with the WIRE command, and the components are then placed within this area.

Signals
Signals defined with EAGLE's SIGNAL command, polygons, and wires drawn within the Top, Bottom, and ROUTE2...15 layers, are recognized by the Autorouter.

Restricted Areas
Objects in the layers *tRestrict*, *bRestrict*, and *vRestrict* are treated as restricted areas for the Top and Bottom side and for vias respectively.
The Autorouter can be excluded from using a layer by selecting "N/A" in the Preferred Direction field (see Figure 4-36).

Cancelling the Autorouter

If Autorouter is cancelled (by **Left-Click** ), any airwires that have not yet been routed, are not automatically recalculated. The RATSNEST command should be used to do this.

The Autorouter Process
The routing process involves a number of separate basic steps:

Bus Router
Normally the bus router starts first.
This sub-process deals with signals which can be routed in the preferred direction with only slight deviation in x and y direction allowed. The bus router takes only those signals into consideration that belong to net class 0.
This step may be omitted.

Routing Pass
The second sub-process commences the actual routing pass and uses parameters which make a 100% routing as likely as possible. A large number of vias are deliberately allowed to avoid paths becoming blocked.

Optimization
The last sub-process allows for any number of optimization passes to be made. The parameters are setup to remove superfluous vias and to smooth the track paths.

During the optimization passes, tracks are removed and rerouted one at a time. This can, however, lead to a higher degree of routing, since it is possible for new paths to be freed by the changed path of a previous track re-alignment.

The number of optimization passes must be specified before starting the Autorouter. It is not possible to optimize at a later stage. Once the routing job has been completed all the tracks are considered to have been 'prerouted', and may no longer be changed.

Any of these sub-processes may be separately activated or deactivated.

DRC

Function
The DRC command checks the board design rules.

Syntax
```
DRC
DRC ;
DRC LOAD|SAVE filename;
DRC *
```

See also DesignRules, CLASS, SET, ERC, ERRORS

The command DRC checks a board against the current set of DesignRules.

Note: electrically irrelevant objects (wires in packages, rectangles, circles and texts) are not checked against each other for clearance errors; mechanical or otherwise.
Without parameters, the DRC command opens a Design Rules dialog in which the board's Design Rules can be defined, and from which the actual check can be started. This is shown in Figure 4-38.

Setting the Design Rules is captured by the UNDO/REDO function.

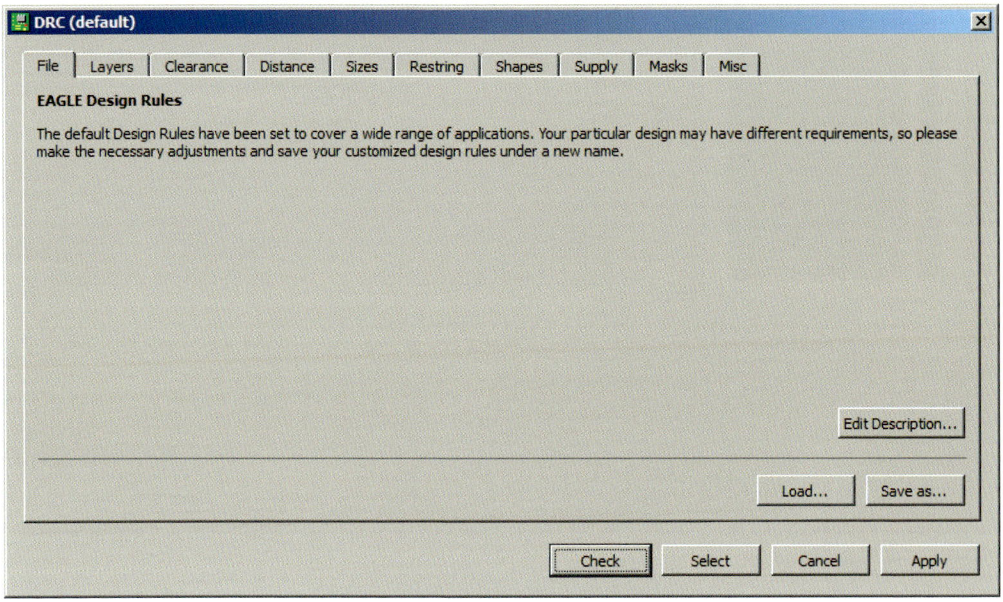

Figure 4-38: DRC command dialog

If two coordinates are given in the DRC command (or if the Select button is clicked in the Design Rules dialog) all checks will be performed solely in the defined rectangle. The rectangle is defined by using the left mouse key and dragging from one corner of the desired area to the other. Only errors that occur (at least partly) in this area will be reported.

The `LOAD` and `SAVE` options can be used to load the Design Rules from, or save them to, the given file. If `filename` doesn't have the extension ".dru" it will be appended automatically. This can be used to load design rules supplied by the target PCB production facility.

If the DRC command is given an asterisk character ('*') as the first parameter, the Design Rules dialog will be opened and allow editing the Design Rules, without triggering an actual check when the dialog is confirmed.

Layers parameter

This parameter is used to define the number of signal layers and the kind of vias (Blind or Buried vias) to be incorporated in the board design. An example of the Layers section of the DRC dialog is shown in Figure 4-39.

The Setup line contains the mathematical expression which defines the proper structure of the board, the appropriate combination of cores and 'pre-pregs' and the resulting facilities for vias.

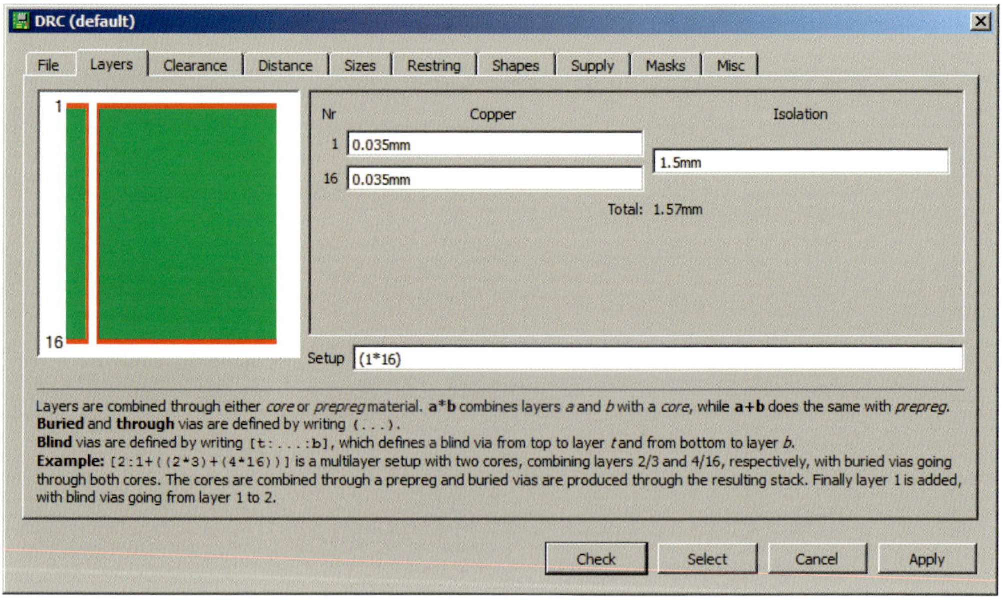

Figure 4-39: Layers section of DRC dialog

In most cases (for simple two or more layer boards) the vias are drilled through all layers. Figure 4-39 shows the default setup for a two layer board.

The expression in the *Setup* field defines the structure of the board. In this example '`(1*16)`' defines one core with layers 1 and 16, which can be connected with vias. Parentheses around the expression define throughhole (continuous) vias.

Examples:

1 layer board:

`16` a board with only one layer; 16 - no vias.

4 layer board , vias through all layers:

`(1*2+3*16)` a board with two cores which are affiliated with each other.

6 layer board, vias through all layers:

`(1*2+3*4+5*16)` a board with three cores which are affiliated with each other.

The fields for *Copper* and *Isolation* are used to define the thickness of copper and isolation layers. These settings are only relevant for complex multilayer boards that use Blind or Micro vias.

Clearance parameter

Clearance refers to the minimum distances between tracks, pads, SMDs and vias of different signals, and between SMDs, pads and vias of the same signal. This dialog is illustrated in Figure 4-40.

Setting the values for *Same signal* checks to 0, disables the respective check.
If a net belongs to a special net class, the values for *Clearance* and for the drill diameter of vias (Drill), defined by means of the CLASS command, are taken into consideration, provided these values are higher than those given in the Design Rules (*Clearance* and *Minimum Drill* in the *Sizes* tab).

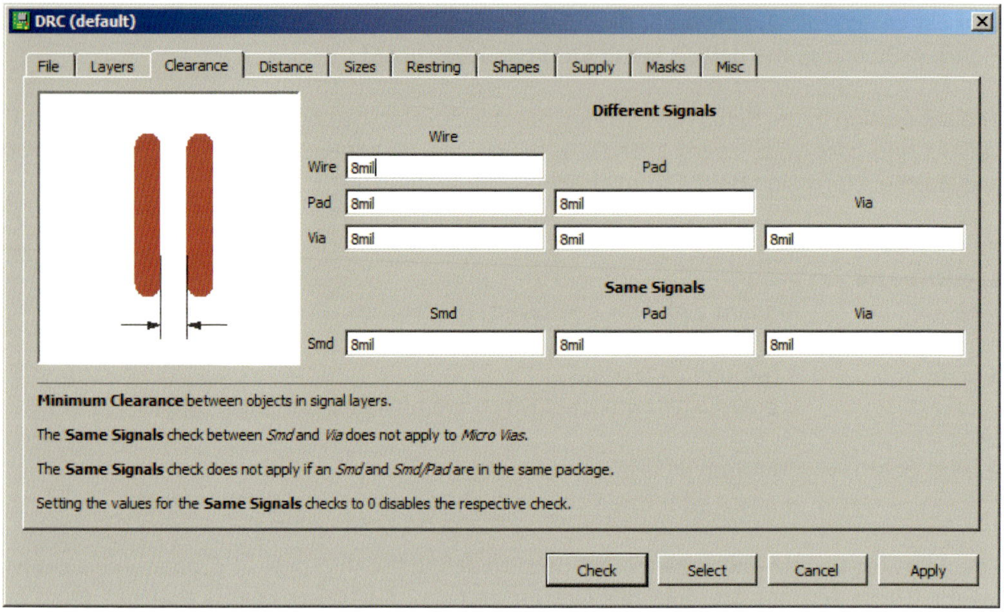

Figure 4-40: Clearance section of DRC dialog

Distance parameter

Distance allows settings to be made for the minimum distances between objects in layer 20, *Dimension*, in which the board outline is usually drawn, and between holes. This parameter is set in the *Distance* dialog tab shown in Figure 4-41.

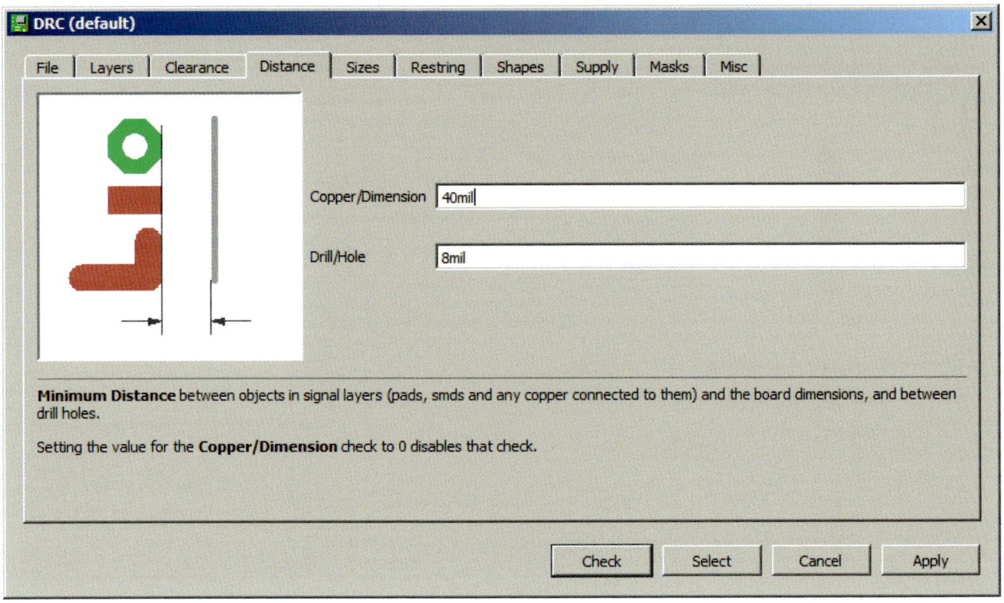

Figure 4-41: Distance section of DRC dialog

Sizes parameter

The minimum values for track width and for hole diameter allowed in the layout are set in this section; shown in Figure 4-42.

For micro vias the minimum drill diameter is setup in the line *Min. MicroVia*. Setting this value higher than the value in *Minimum Drill* means that there are no micro vias used (default). This means: If the drill diameter is between the value for *Min. MicroVia* and *Minimum Drill,* the via is considered a micro via.

Also, the aspect ratio of drill depth to drill diameter for boards that contain Blind Vias is set here. For example if the board manufacturer specifies an aspect ratio of `1:0.5` the correct entry would be the value `0.5` in the line *Min. Blind Via Ratio*.

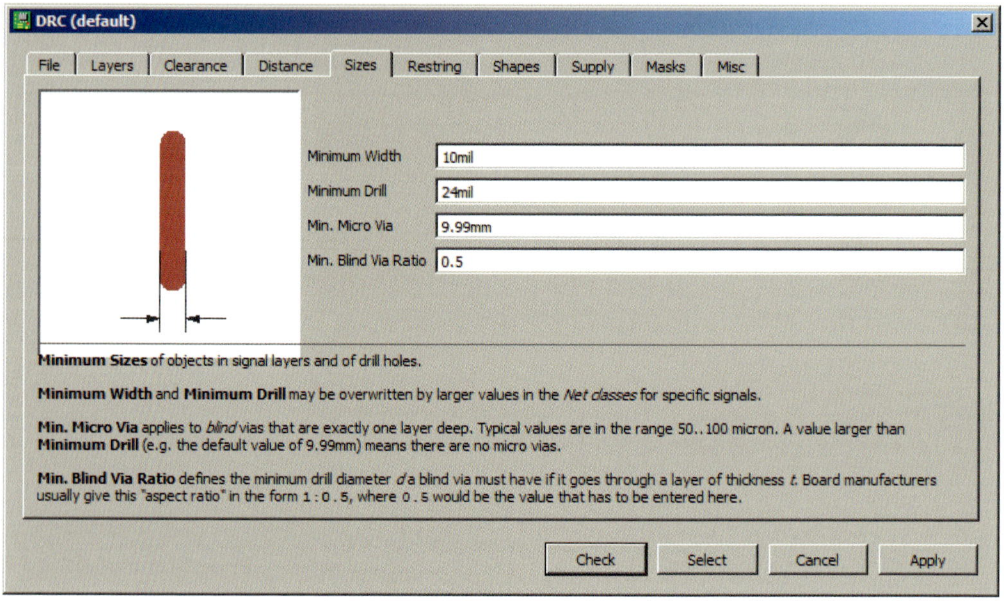

Figure 4-42: Sizes section of DRC dialog

Restring parameter (Pad and Via Diameter)

The settings made under *Restring* determine the width of the ring remaining at pads, vias, and micro vias. These parameters can be set in the Restring section of the DRC dialog as shown in Figure 4-43.

The remaining ring refers to the ring of copper that remains around a hole after a pad or via has been drilled. Different selections can be made for the width of the remaining ring in the inner and outer layers. Pads may also differ between the *Top* and *Bottom* layers.

Usually the parameter value is expressed as a percentage of the hole diameter. Minimum and maximum values can additionally be specified.

Effects of changes to parameters can be immediately and directly seen in the layout by clicking the Apply button.

If different parameter values for the upper and lower layer are required(or different shapes, see *Shapes* tab), it is recommended to set the layer color for layers 17, *Pads*, and 18, *Vias*, the same as the background color (black or white). This will allow the real size and shape of the pad/via to be displayed in its respective layer.

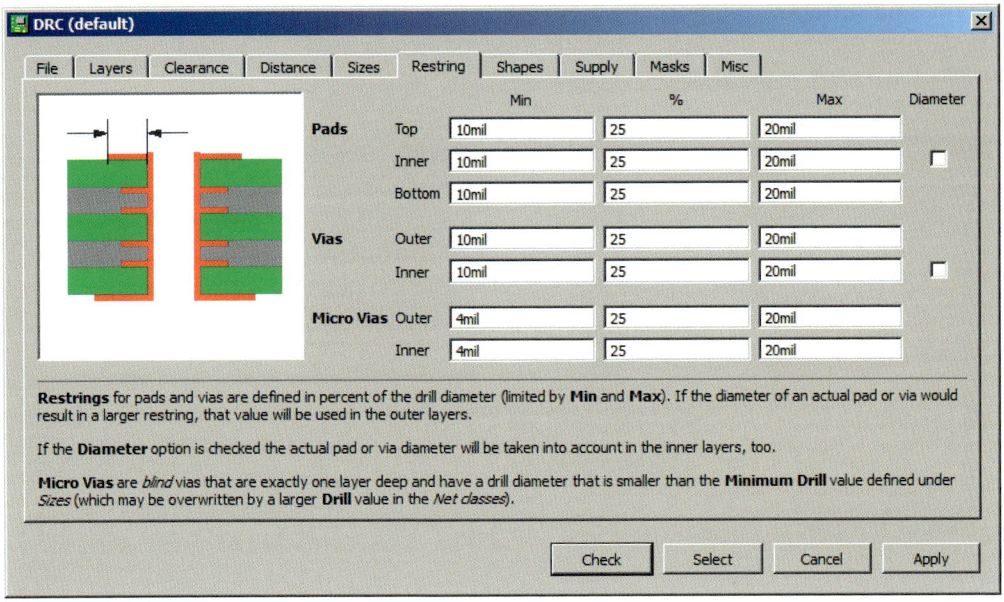

Figure 4-43: Restring section of DRC dialog

The *Diameter* check box allows for the case where the defined diameter for a pad in the library, or for a via in the Layout Editor, is to be taken into consideration for inner layers of the board. Checking this box will activate this option.

This option can be used if a predefined pad or via diameter exceeds the value calculated by the Design Rules. Otherwise the pad or via in the inner layers would be smaller than in the outer layers. If the required result is that pads/vias should have the same diameter in all layers, then the *Diameter* option should be set.

The *Diameter* option is set off, by default, for newly created boards, but will be set on for boards that are updated from version 3.5 or prior (because in these versions pads and vias had the same diameter in all layers). Thus, the update process does not change the original layout.

Shapes parameter

The *Shapes* section of the Design Rules is shown in Figure 4-44 . This parameter is used to modify the outline shape of SMDs and pads.

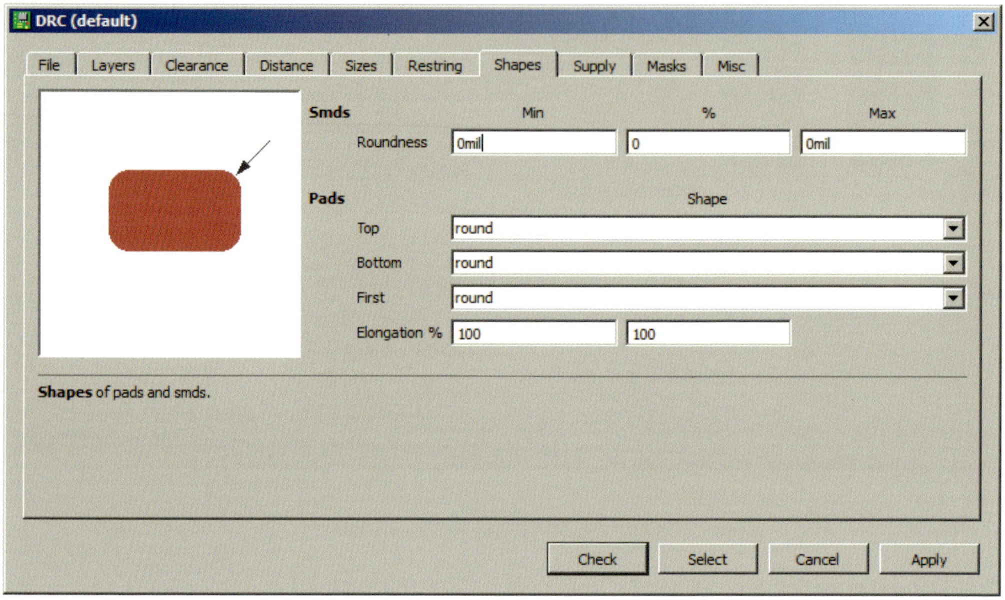

Figure 4-44: Shapes section of DRC dialog

SMDs:

A rounding factor can be specified here for SMD pads.

Figure 4-45 illustrates the effect that setting this value has on SMD pads. The value shown range (left to right) between 0 % (no rounding) and 100 % (maximum rounding).

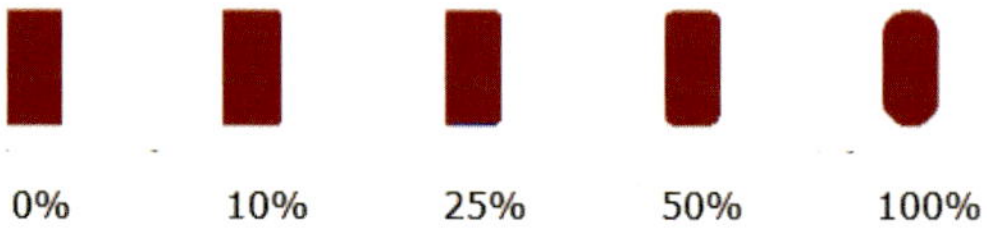

Figure 4-45: SMD pad rounding factor

Pads:

This configuration area is where the form of the pads is specified. It is possible to give different settings for the top and bottom layers.

Pads can have one of the following forms:

- As in library (adopts the form defined in the Package Editor)
- round
- square
- octagon
- Not special (applies to the First pad only)

Pads and Vias within inner layers are always round, regardless of their shape in the Top or Bottom layers. Their diameter is determined by the restring settings.
Elongation defines the aspect ratio of length to width of Long and Offset pads (as illustrated in Figure 4-46); this ratio being given in percent. Click with the mouse into the field Long or Offset and the image on the left shows the corresponding calculation rule.
An Elongation ratio of 100 % is equivalent to an aspect ratio of 2:1; 0 % results in a normal octagon pad with an aspect ratio of 1:1. The maximum ratio is 200 % (ratio 4:1).

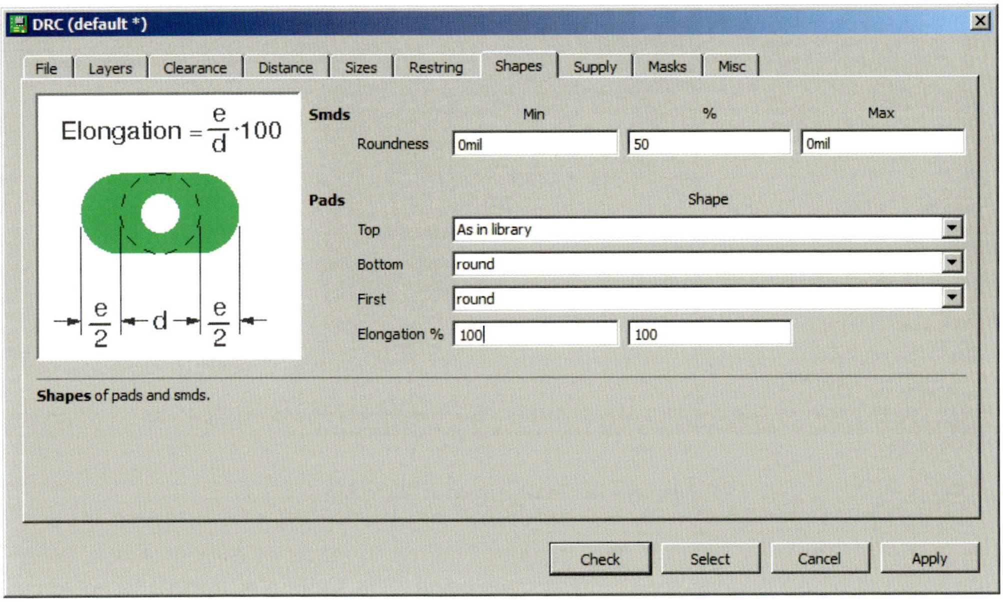

Figure 4-46: pad elongation ratio

If pads or vias have different shapes on different layers, the shapes of the currently visible (activated with DISPLAY) signal layers are displayed on top of each other.

If the color selected for layer 17, *Pads*, or 18, *Vias*, is 0 (which represents the current background color), the pads and vias are displayed in the color and fill style of their respective layers. If no signal layer is visible, pads and vias are not displayed.

If the color selected for layer 17, *Pads*, or 18, *Vias*, is not the background color and no signal layers are visible, pads and vias are displayed in the shape of the top and bottom layer. These conditions also apply to printouts made with the PRINT command.

Supply parameter

The Supply parameter specifies the settings for Thermal symbols. This section is shown in Figure 4-47.

The value for Thermal isolation determines the distance between a polygon and the restring of the pad or via that is joined to the polygon through a Thermal symbol.

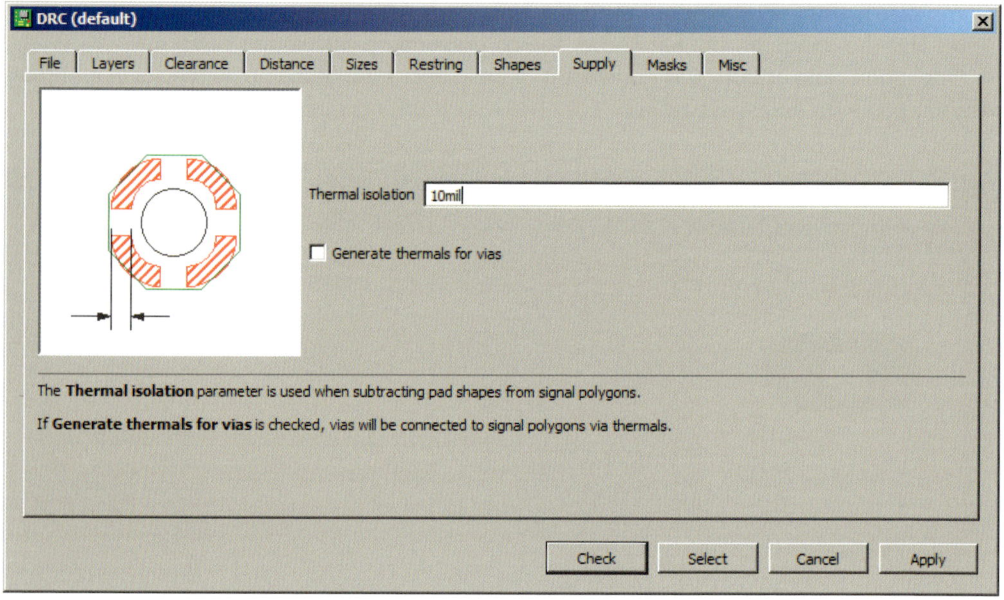

Figure 4-47: Supply section of DRC dialog

The 'Generate thermals for vias' flag, enables Thermal symbols at through holes. Otherwise vias will be fully connected to the copper plane. The same also applies to polygons. (This option can be disabled for individual polygons by using the command 'CHANGE THERMALS OFF' then **Left-Click** on the polygon's contour).
Pads or SMDs marked with the flag NOTHERMALS (CHANGE THERMALS OFF) in the Package Editor, will be effectively connected without Thermal symbols.

Masks parameter

Settings for the oversized measurement of the solder stop mask (Stop) and the solder cream mask (Cream) are made here. This parameter is set in the section shown in Figure 4-48.

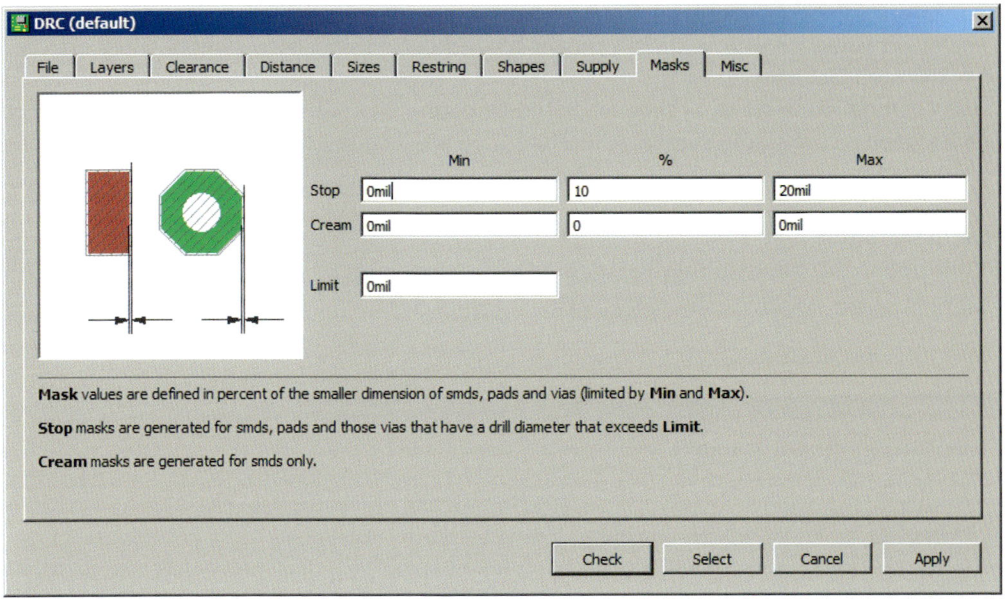

Figure 4-48: Masks section of DRC dialog

Stop

Where values are specified in percent, and where the SMDs and pads are set as the *Long* or *Offset* form of *Shape*, the smaller dimension is the significant one. The values are constrained by minimum and maximum values.
The solder stop mask is drawn in layers 29, *tStop*, or 30, *bStop*.

Cream

The value for *Cream* is given positively, as is *Frame*, although its effect is to reduce the size of the solder cream mask (cream frame).

The solder cream mask is only generated for SMDs, and is displayed on layer 31, *tCream*, or layer 32, *bCream*.

Setting the flag *STOP* or *CREAM* (only for SMD) to *OFF* for a pad or SMD at the Package definition forbids EAGLE to generate a solder stop mask or a cream frame for it.

Limit

The Limit option determines, together with the hole diameter, whether or not a via is to be covered with solder stop lacquer.
For vias with hole diameters below the *Limit,* the *STOP* flag can be set (CHANGE STOP ON). EAGLE will then generate a solder stop mask.

Example

The default value for *Limit* is 0. This means all vias get a solder stop symbol. They are free of solder stop lacquer.

If the *Limit* option is set to 24 then all plated-through holes with diameters ≤ 24 mil do not get assigned a solder stop symbol (therefore they are lacquered). However vias with larger hole diameters (i.e. > 24 mil) get a solder stop symbol.

Misc parameter

In this option tab the user may select/deselect various checks which are made by the Design Rule Check function. This is displayed in Figure 4-49.

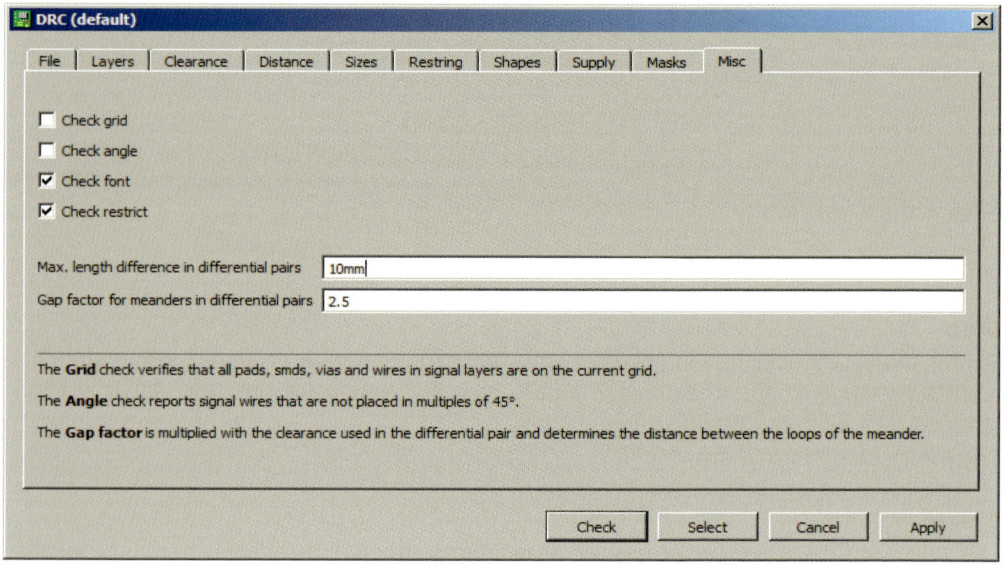

Figure 4-49: Miscellaneous section of DRC dialog

Check grid

This option examines whether objects lie precisely on the grid currently set by the GRID command. However, interpretation is required when using this test since, often; Devices built to both metric and imperial grids are in use at the same time. No common grid can be found in such a case.

Check angle

This option ensures that all tracks are laid at whole multiples of 45 degrees.
Default setting: OFF

Check font

This can be used to select or de-select the font check.
The DRC checks if texts are written in vector font. Any text which is nonvector font is marked as an error. This check is necessary because the CAM Processor *only works with vector fonts* for the generation of manufacturing data.

Default setting: ON.

Check restrict

This option is used can be used to ensure that copper objects are not to be checked against restricted areas drawn in layers 39, *tRestrict*, and 40, *bRestrict*. If restricted areas and copper objects are defined in a common Package, EAGLE does not check them against each other. Restricted areas that are defined by cutout polygons are ***not*** checked by DRC!
Default setting: ON

LOCK

Function
Locks the position and orientation of a part, or group of parts, in a board.

Syntax
```
LOCK .
LOCK name ..
```

Mouse keys
Ctrl+Right-Click	applies the command to the group.
Shift+Left-Click	reverses the lock operation ("unlocks" the part).
Ctrl+ Shift+Right-Click	"unlocks" all parts in the group.

See also MIRROR, MOVE, ROTATE SMASH

The LOCK command can be applied to parts (or group of parts) in a board, and prevents them from being moved, rotated, or mirrored. This can be applied to objects like connectors, which need to be mounted at a particular location and must not be inadvertently moved.

After activating the LOCK command, the origin of a locked part is displayed as an 'x' in order to provide a visual indication that the part is locked.
Parts can also be selected by their name so that an object, which is outside the currently shown window area, may be locked.

If a group is moved and it contains locked parts, these parts (together with any wires ending at their pads) will not move with the group.

Detached text connected to a locked part may still be moved individually, but it will not move with a group.

MEANDER

Function
Balance lengths of differential pairs and increase the length of a signal segment.

Syntax
```
MEANDER [length]..
```

Mouse keys
Ctrl+Left-Click measures the length of the selected signal segment.
Ctrl+Shift+Left-Click measures the maximum length of the selected signal segments.
Right-Click toggles between symmetrical and asymmetrical meanders.

See also ROUTE

The MEANDER command can be used to balance the lengths of signals forming a differential pair.

To use this command the user **Left-Clicks** on a wire of a differential pair and moves the mouse cursor away from the selection point. If there is a difference in the length of the two signals, and the current mouse position is far enough away from the selection point, a "meander" shaped sequence of wires will be drawn that increases the length of the shorter signal segment. An example of the use of the MEANDER command is shown in Figure 4-50 and Figure 4-51. An indicator attached to the mouse cursor shows the target length (which is the length of the longer signal segment), as well as the deviation (in percent) of the two signals from the target length.

The meander starts at the first click point and extends to the second point the mouse is moved to. The maximum (perpendicular) size of the meander is defined by the distance of the mouse to the meandered wire.
If a single meander isn't enough to balance the lengths, further meanders may be added at different locations.

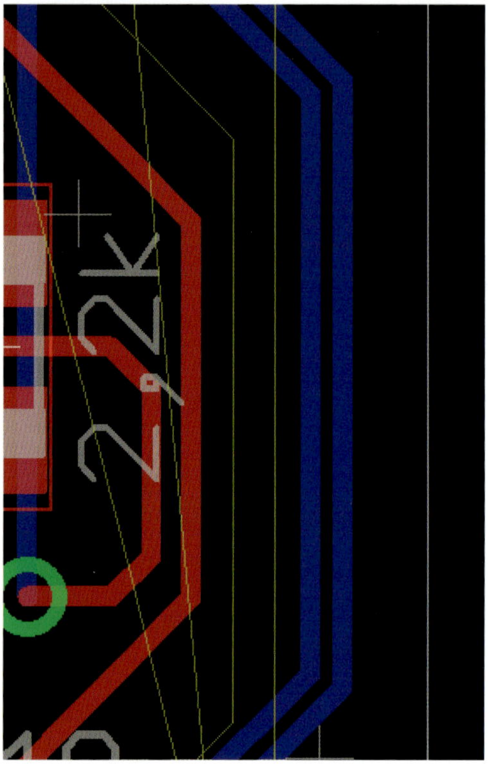

Figure 4-50: a differential pair

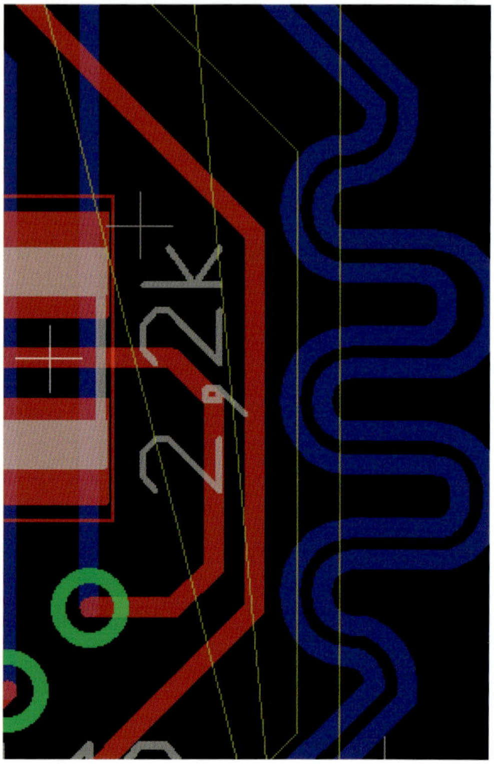

Figure 4-51: a MEANDERed differential pair

Measuring signal lengths

By using the **Ctrl+Left-Click** combination on a signal wire, the length of that signal segment will be measured and displayed on the screen in a little indicator near the mouse position.

This may be used as a target length for MEANDERing another segment.

Using the **Ctrl+Shift+Left-Click** combination, the maximum length of this or any previously selected segments will be taken. This can be used to easily determine the maximum length of several bus signals, and then MEANDERing each of them to that length.

At any time the user can enter a value in the command line to set the target length.

When MEANDERing a differential pair with a given target length, the meander first tries to balance the length of the two signal segments that form the differential pair, and then increase the total length of both segments.

The target length may be reset by restarting the MEANDER command or entering a value of `0` in the command line.

Length tolerance

The value defined in the Design Rules under *"Misc/Max. length difference in differential pairs"* is used to select the color, when displaying the length deviations, while drawing a meander. If the percentage is shown in green, the respective segment lies within the given tolerance. Otherwise the percentage is displayed in red. The default for this parameter is 10mm.

OPTIMIZE

Function
Joins wire segments on a board.

Syntax
```
OPTIMIZE;
OPTIMIZE signal_name ..
OPTIMIZE..
```

Mouse keys
Ctrl+Right-Click optimizes the group.

See also SET, SPLIT, MOVE, ROUTE

The OPTIMIZE command (which is only applicable for use in a board drawing) joins wire segments which lie in one straight line. The individual segments must be on the same layer and have the same width. This command is useful for reducing the number of objects in a drawing and to facilitate moving a complete track instead of individual segments.

If signal names are given, or a signal is selected, the command affects only the respective signals e.g. `OPTIMIZE VCC`

Note: that when selecting an object with the mouse (or selecting a group) only actual signal wires are optimized. To optimize all wires in a board drawing, the command

```
OPTIMZE;
```

is used.

Automatic Optimization
Wire optimization takes place automatically after MOVE, SPLIT, or ROUTE commands, unless it is disabled with the command:

```
SET OPTIMIZING OFF;
```

or the user has **2xLeft-Click** with the SPLIT command.

The OPTIMIZE command works in any case, whether Optimizing is enabled or disabled.

RATSNEST

Function
Calculates the shortest possible airwires and polygons in a board drawing.

Syntax
```
RATSNEST
RATSNEST signal_name ..
RATSNEST ! signal_name ..
```

See also SIGNAL, MOVE, POLYGON, RIPUP

The RATSNEST command evaluates the airwire connections in a layout board in order to achieve the shortest possible paths. For example; this command could be used after components have been moved, or after reading a netlist via the SCRIPT command, to optimize the length of airwires.

The RATSNEST command also calculates all polygons belonging to a signal. This is necessary in order to avoid the calculation of airwires for pads already connected through polygons. All of the calculated polygon areas are then being displayed in the "real mode". The user may switch back to the faster "outline mode" with the RIPUP command.

The automatic calculation of the polygons can be turned off with

```
SET POLYGON_RATSNEST OFF;
```

Note: The RATSNEST command does not mark the board drawing as modified, since the calculated polygon data (if any) is not stored in the board, and the recalculated airwires do not constitute a modification of the drawing.
Zero length airwires

If two or more wires of the same signal, on different routing layers, end at the same point without being connected through a pad or a via, a zero length airwire is generated. This will be displayed as an X-shaped cross in the Unrouted layer. The same applies to SMDs that belong to the same signal and are placed on opposite sides of the board.

Such zero length airwires can be picked up with the ROUTE command just like ordinary airwires. They may also be handled by placing a VIA at that point.

Hiding selected airwires
During the board layout process it may be convenient to hide the airwires of selected signals, for instance if these will later be connected through a polygon. Typically this could be supply signals, which typically have a lot of airwires that will never be routed explicitly and would obscure the other signals' airwires.

To hide airwires, the RATSNEST command can be given the exclamation mark ('!'), followed by a list of signals, as in:

```
RATSNEST ! GND VCC
```

which would hide the airwires of the signals GND and VCC.

The airwires may be displayed again by using the RATSNEST command without the '!' character, and the list of signals:

```
RATSNEST GND VCC
```

This will activate the display of the airwires of the signals GND and VCC and also recalculates them. This form of the command may be used to recalculate the airwires (and polygons) of particular signals this way.

The signal names may also contain wildcards, and the two variants may be combined, as in:

```
RATSNEST D* ! ?GND VCC
```

which would recalculate and display the airwires of all signals with names beginning with 'D', and hide the airwires of all the various GND signals (like AGND, DGND etc.) and the VCC signal.

Note: The RATSNEST command is processed from left to right, so in case there is a DGND signal the example would first process it for display, but then hide its airwires.

To display all airwires the following command is used:

```
RATSNEST *
```

REPLACE

Function
Replace a part in a drawing.

Syntax
```
REPLACE ..
REPLACE device_name[@library_name] ..
REPLACE part_name device_name[@library_name] ..
REPLACE package_name ..
REPLACE element_name package_name ..
```

See also SET, UPDATE
The REPLACE command can be used to replace a part with a different device (even from a different library). However, the old and new devices must be compatible i.e. their used gates and connected pins/pads must match, either by their names or their coordinates.

Without parameters, the REPLACE command opens a dialog (as shown in Figure 4-52) from which a device can be selected from all libraries that are currently in use. After such a device has been selected, subsequent mouse clicks on parts will replace those parts' devices with the selected one if possible.

If a `device_name` is given, that device will be used for the replace operation. With both a `part_name` and a `device_name`, the device of the given part will be replaced (this is useful when using scripts).

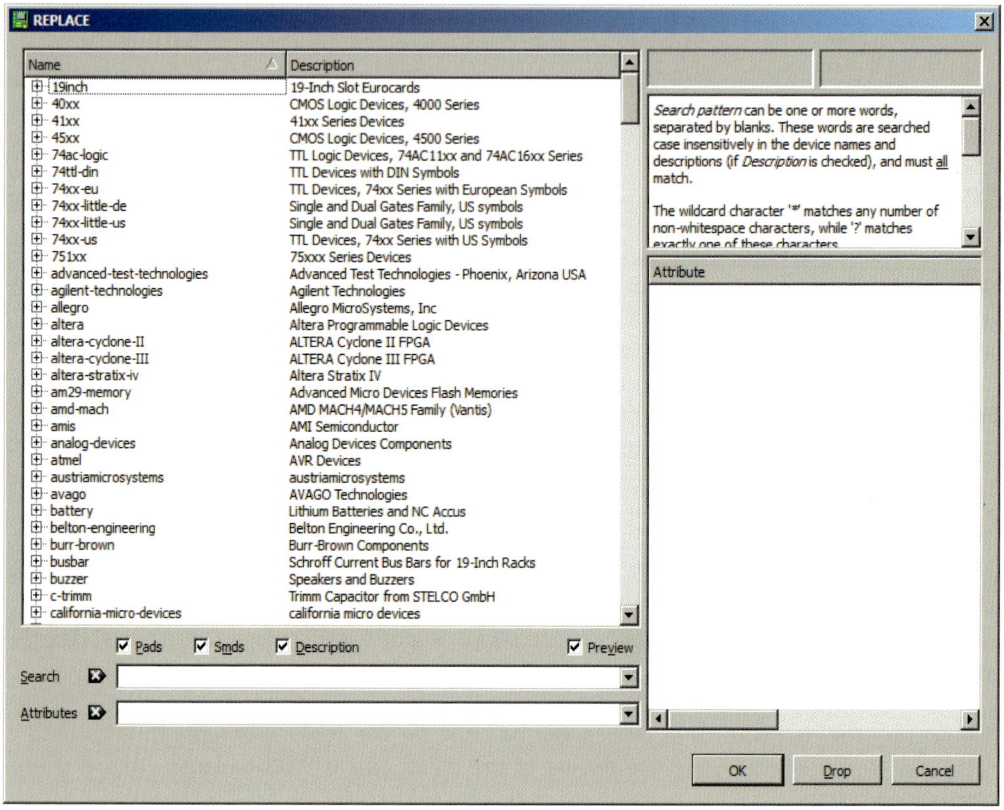

Figure 4-52: REPLACE command dialog

If a `library_name` is given and it contains blanks, the whole `device_name@library_name` needs to be enclosed in single quotes.

If only a board is being edited (without a schematic), or if elements in the board are being replaced that have no matching part in the schematic, the REPLACE command has two different modes that are chosen by the SET command.

i. The 'names' (default) mode is activated by the command:

```
SET REPLACE_SAME NAMES;
```

This mode requires that the new package must have the same pad and SMD names as the old one. It may be taken from a different library and it may contain additional pads and SMDs. The position of pads and SMDs is irrelevant.

ii. The second 'co-ordinates' mode is activated by the command:

```
SET REPLACE_SAME COORDS;
```

In this mode, pads and SMDs of the new package must be placed at the same coordinates as in the old one (relative to the origin). Pad and SMD names may be different. The new package may be taken from a different library and may contain additional pads and SMDs.
Pads of the old package connected with signals must be present in the new package. If this condition is true the new package may have less pads than the old one.

If there is already a package with the same name (from the same library) in the drawing, and the library has been modified after the original object was added, an automatic library update will be started and the user will be asked whether objects in the drawing should be replaced with their new versions.
REPLACE only functions when the appropriate *tOrigins/bOrigins* layer is displayed.

Note: A REPLACE operation automatically updates all involved library objects where required. This means that other parts (on other schematic sheets or in other locations on the board) may also be changed. The user should always run a DesignRuleCheck (DRC) and an ElectricalRuleCheck (ERC) after a REPLACE operation!

RIPUP

Function

Changes routed wires and vias into airwires.
Changes the display of polygons to "outlines".

Syntax

```
RIPUP;
RIPUP [ @ ] [ ! ] ..
RIPUP [ @ ] [ ! ] signal_name..
```

Mouse keys

Ctrl+Right-Click rips up a group.

See also DELETE, GROUP, POLYGON, RATSNEST

The RIPUP command changes routed wires (tracks) into airwires. That can be executed in the following cases:

- all signals `RIPUP;`
- all signals except particular instances `RIPUP ! GND VCC;`
- one or more signals `RIPUP D0 D1 D2;`
- certain segments (chosen with one or multiple **Left-Clicks**)
- all polygons `RIPUP @;`
- all polygons of specific signals `RIPUP @ GND VCC;`
- all polygons except those of certain signals `RIPUP @ ! GND VCC;`

Selecting an airwire with RIPUP converts all adjacent routed wires and vias into airwires, up to the next pad, SMD or airwire.

Examples:

```
RIPUP signal_name..
```

rips up the complete signal "signal_name" (several signals may be listed, e.g. `RIPUP D0 D1 D2;`).

```
RIPUP ..
```

rips up segments selected by the mouse click up to the next pad/SMD.

```
RIPUP;
```

removes only signals which are connected to elements (e.g. board crop marks are not affected). The same applies if RIPUP is used on a group.

Note: in all cases the RIPUP command ***only*** acts on objects that are in layers ***that are currently visible***.

Use of Wildcards

If a `signal_name` parameter is given, the characters '*', '?' and '[]' are wildcards and have the following meaning:

`*` matches any number of any characters
`?` matches exactly one character
`[...]` matches any of the characters between the brackets

If any of the above characters are to be matched exactly, they must be enclosed in brackets. For example, `abc[*]ghi` would match `abc*ghi` and not `abcdefghi`.
A range of characters may also be referenced by `[a-z]`, which results in any character in the range `'a'...'z'`.

Polygons

If the RIPUP command with a name is applied to a signal which contains a polygon, the polygon will be displayed with its outline. The user may action the RATSNEST_command to have polygons displayed in the "real mode" again.

ROUTE

The Route command allows the user to route signals manually on a PCB board layout.

Syntax

```
ROUTE [width] [curve | @radius]..
ROUTE name ..
```

Mouse keys

The ROUTE command offers several options with the different mouse buttons, also in combination with the **Ctrl** and **Shift** keys.

Ctrl +Left-Click	allows the user to commence the routing at any given point along a wire or, at a via
Shift+Left-Click	before selecting an airwire, and if the airwire begins at an already existing wire with a different width to that specified, the new wire adopts the width of the existing wire
Center-click	selects the layer
Right-Click	changes the wire bend style
Shift + Right-Click	reverses the direction of switching bend styles
Ctrl + Right-Click	toggles between corresponding bend styles
Shift + Left-Click	places a via at the current cursor position while routing a trace
Ctrl + Left-Click	defines arc radius when placing a wire's end point

See also AUTO, UNDO, WIRE, MITER, SIGNAL, SET, RATSNEST

The ROUTE command activates the manual router which allows the user to convert airwires (unrouted connections) into real wires (tracks).

Parameters

The `width` parameter determines the width of the track to be placed. This may be specified explicitly both in magnitude and units e.g. `ROUTE 0.5mm`.

If the `curve` or `@radius` parameter is used, an arc can be drawn as part of the track (a comprehensive description of these parameters is given in the EAGLE help file as part of the WIRE command).

If a `name` parameter is used, the airwire of that signal that is closest to the mouse cursor is selected. To prevent the `name` parameter being interpreted as a `width`, `curve` or `@radius` it has to be written in single quotes e.g. `ROUTE 'GND'`.

Note: A more comprehensive overview of the functionality of the ROUTE command is given in chapter 6: Using EAGLE's ROUTE command and Follow-Me router.

SIGNAL

Function
Defines signals to establish basis for airwires.

Syntax
SIGNAL .
SIGNAL signal_name..
SIGNAL signal_name element_name pad_name..;

See also AUTO, ROUTE, NAME, CLASS, WIRE, RATSNEST, EXPORT

The SIGNAL command is used to define signals between end points. A signal therefore represents an electrical connection, on a board, between two pads associated with an element or object. The user must define a minimum of two element_name/pad_name pairs, otherwise no airwire can be generated for that signal.

The SIGNAL command can only be used in a PCB layout drawing where there is no corresponding schematic. This is because EAGLE is unable to draw a referring net in the schematic, and so consistency between them would be compromised.

Mouse Input
To define the 'pad pairs' the user selects (with **Left-Click**) the pads of the elements to be connected. EAGLE displays the part signals as airwires in the Unrouted layer.

Text Input
Signals may also be defined completely by using text input via the keyboard on the command line or script file.

If the command is input with `signal_name` the signal will be allocated the specified name. For example the command:

```
SIGNAL GND IC1 7 IC2 7 IC3 7;
```

connects pad 7 on all IC1, IC2 & IC3.

A script file may be used (which has extension *.scr) to generate a whole netlist. This file should include all of the necessary SIGNAL commands in the format shown above.

On-line Check
If the SIGNAL command is used to connect pads (or SMDs) that already belong to different signals, a popup menu will appear and ask if the user wants to connect the signals together, and which name the signal should be assigned.

VIA

Function
Allows the user to add vias to a board.

Syntax
```
VIA ['signal_name'] [diameter] [shape] [layers] [flags] •..
```

See also SMD, CHANGE, DISPLAY, SET, PAD and Design Rules

When the VIA command is active, a via symbol is attached to the cursor. **Left-Click** places a via at the current cursor position. The via is added to a signal if it is placed on an existing signal wire. If the user attempts to connect different signals, EAGLE will ask the user for confirmation to connect them.

Signal name
The `signal_name` parameter is intended mainly to be used in script files that read in generated data. If a `signal_name` is given, all subsequent vias will be added to that signal, and no automatic checks will be performed.

Note: This feature should be used with great care, since it has the potential to create short circuits, if a via is placed in a way that it would connect wires belonging to different signals.

The user should run a Design Rule Check after using the VIA command with the `signal_name` parameter.

When activated, the Via command opens the parameter toolbar shown in Figure 4-53.

Figure 4-53: Via parameter toolbar

Shape
A via can have one of the following shapes:
• Square
• Round
• Octagon

These shapes only apply to the outer layers (Top and Bottom). In inner layers the shape is always "round".

Layers

The `layers` parameter defines the layers this via shall cover. The syntax is `from-to`, where 'from' and 'to' are the layer numbers that would be covered, e.g. `2-7` would create a via that goes from layer 2 to layer 7 (`7-2` would have the same meaning). If that exact via is not available in the layer setup of the *Design Rules*, the next longest via will be used (or an error message will be issued in the case where no such via can be set).

Via diameter

Entering a number changes the diameter of the via (in the units in-use at the time) and that value remains in use for subsequent via placements. Via diameters can be up to 0.51602 inch (13.1 mm).

Drill diameter

The drill diameter of the via is the same as the diameter set for pads. It can be changed with:

```
CHANGE DRILL diameter
```

Vias generate drill symbols in the Drills layer and the solder stop mask in the *tStop/bStop* layers.

Both the `diameter` and `shape` parameters can be entered while the VIA command is active; or it can be changed with the CHANGE command. The shape then remains valid for subsequent placements of vias.

Note: the actual shape and diameter of a via will be determined by the *Design Rules* of the board within which the via is used.

Flags

The STOP *flag* can be used to control the appearance of a via.
By default a via with a drill diameter that is ≤ the value of the *Design Rules* parameter "Masks/Limit" will not have a solder stop mask. The STOP flag can be used to force a solder stop mask for a via, so as to always generate the solder stop mask.

Commands for Editing Schematics

BOARD

Function
Generates a board layout drawing from a schematic.

Syntax
`BOARD [ grid ]`

See also EDIT

The command BOARD is used to generate a board layout from a schematic drawing. If the board already exists, it will be loaded into a board window.

If the board does not exist, the user will be asked whether to create that new board. If a `grid` parameter is given, the parts on the board will be placed within the given raster, as in:

```
BOARD 5mm
```

which would place the parts in a 5 millimeter grid plane (the default is 50mil). The number must be specified with a unit, and the maximum allowed value is 10mm.

The BOARD command will never overwrite an existing board file. In order to create a new board file to replace an existing file of the same name, the existing file must be removed first.

Creating a board from a schematic
The first time a board file is edited, EAGLE checks if there is a schematic with the same name, in the same directory, and gives the user the choice of creating the board from that schematic.

If a schematic drawing window is open and the user wants to create a board, the user would type:

```
edit .brd
```

in the editor window's command line.

All relevant data from the schematic file (of style `<name>.sch`) will be used to generate a board file (of style `<name>.brd`). The new board is loaded automatically as an empty card with a size of 160x100mm (the Light edition has a size limit of 100x80mm). All packages and connections are shown on the left side of the board. Supply pins are already connected.

A board file cannot be generated:

i. if there are gates in the schematic from a device for which no package has been defined, EAGLE will generate an error message: "device name has no package".

ii. if there are gates in the schematic from a device for which not all pins have been assigned to related pads of a package, EAGLE will generate an error message:"device name has unconnected pins".

BUS

Function
Draws buses in a schematic.

Syntax

```
BUS [bus_name] [curve | @radius]..
```

Mouse keys

Right-Click	changes the wire bend style.
Shift+Right-Click	reverses the direction of switching bend styles.
Ctrl+Right-Click	toggles between corresponding bend styles.

See also NET, NAME, SET

The command BUS is used to draw bus connections onto the Bus layer of a schematic diagram. `bus_name` has the following form:

SYNONYM:partbus,partbus,..

where SYNONYM can be any name, `partbus` is either a simple net name or a bus name range of the following form:

Name[LowestIndex..HighestIndex]

where the following condition must be met: `0 <= LowestIndex <= HighestIndex <= 511`

If a name is used with a range, that name must not end with digits. This usage may result in ambiguous assignment of the digits to either the Name or to the range indexes.

If a bus wire is placed at a point where a bus wire already exists, the current bus wire will be ended at that point. This function can be disabled with "`SET AUTO_END_NET OFF;`", or by unchecking *Options ▷ Set ▷ Misc ▷ Auto end net and bus*.

If the `curve` or `@radius` parameter is given, an arc can be drawn as part of the bus (see the detailed description in the WIRE command).

Examples

```
A[0..15]
RESET
DB[0..7],A[3..4]
ATBUS:A[0..31],B[0..31],RESET,CLOCK,IOSEL[0..1]
```

If no `bus_name` parameter is used, a name of the form B$1 is automatically allocated. This name can be changed with the NAME command at any time.

The line width used by the bus can be defined with, for example:

```
SET Bus_Wire_Width 40;
```

will set the line width 40 mil. (the default is 30 mil).

Inverted signals

The name of an inverted ("active low") signal can be displayed overlined if it is preceded with an exclamation mark ('!'), as in:

ATBUS:A[0..31],B[0..31],!RESET,CLOCK,IOSEL[0..1]

would result in:

ATBUS:A[0..31],B[0..31],$\overline{\text{RESET}}$,CLOCK,IOSEL[0..1]

GATESWAP

Function
Swaps equivalent gates, within a device, within a schematic.

Syntax
GATESWAP..;
GATESWAP gate_name gate_name..;

See also ADD

Using this command, two gates may be swapped within a schematic. Both gates must be identical, with the same number of pins and must be allocated the same Swaplevel in the device definition. They do not, however, need to be in the same device.

The name used in the GATESWAP command is the displayed name on the schematic (e.g. U1A for gate A in device U1).

Example
The command:

```
GATESWAP IC3A IC3B ;
```

would swap the gates A and B within device IC 3. The effect of this command is shown in Figure 4-54 and Figure 4-55: Device gates to be swapped Figure 4-55: Gates after the GATESWAP command

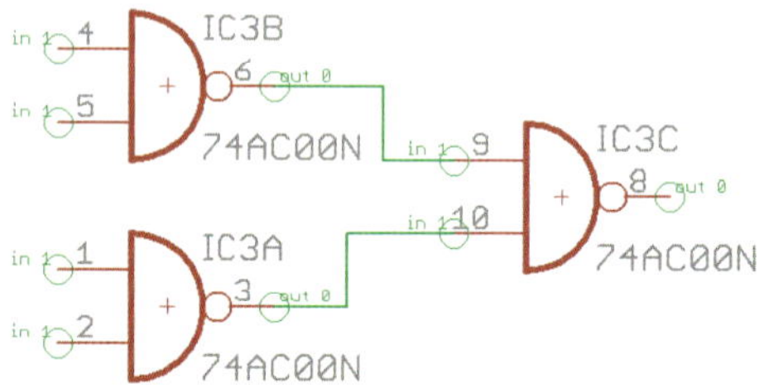

Figure 4-54: Device gates to be swapped

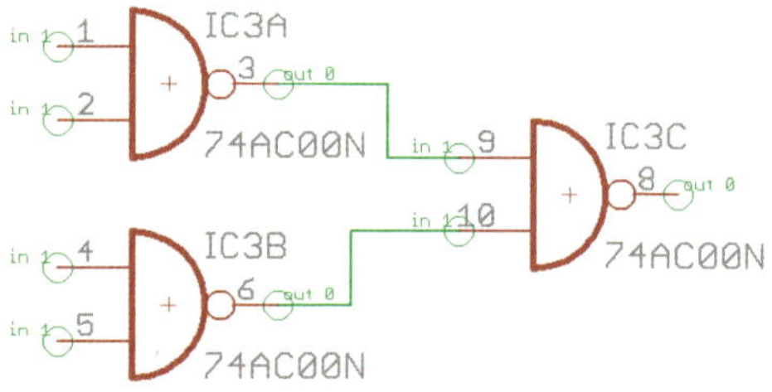

Figure 4-55: Gates after the GATESWAP command

If a device is not used after the GATESWAP command, it is deleted automatically from the drawing.
Gates may not be swapped if their Swaplevel is 0.

INVOKE

Function
Call a specific symbol from a device.

Syntax
```
INVOKE orientation
INVOKE part_name gate_name orientation
```

Mouse keys

Center-click	mirrors the gate. Right rotates the gate.
Shift + Right-Click	reverses the direction of rotation.

See also COPY, ADD

The INVOKE command is used to select a particular gate from a device which is already in use, and place it into the schematic.

Gates may be activated in any of the following ways:
- Enter the part name (e.g. IC5) and select the gate from the popup dialog that appears.
- Define device and gate name from the keyboard (e.g. INVOKE IC5 POWER).
- Select an existing gate from the device with the mouse and then select the desired gate from the popup menu which appears, as shown in Figure 4-56

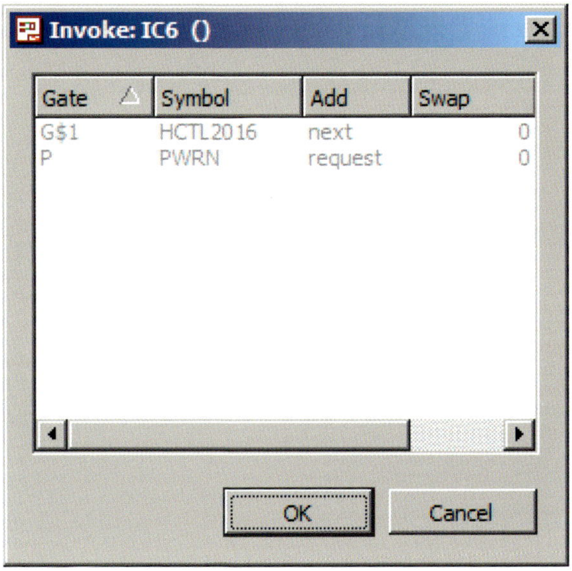

Figure 4-56: Invoke command dialog

The final **Left-Click** positions the new gate.

If an already invoked gate is selected in the dialog, the default button changes to "Show", and a **Left-Click** on it zooms the editor window in on the selected gate, switching to a different sheet if necessary.

See the ADD command for an explanation of Addlevel and Orientation.

Gates on Different Sheets

If a gate from a device on a different sheet is to be added to the current sheet, the name of the part must be specified in the INVOKE command. In this case the rightmost column of the popup menu shows the sheet numbers where the already used gates are placed.

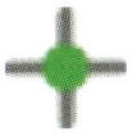

JUNCTION

Function
Places a dot at intersecting nets in a schematic.

Syntax
JUNCTION..

See also NET

This command is used to draw a connection dot at the intersection of nets which are to be connected together. Junction points may be placed only on a net. If placed on the intersection of different nets, the user is given the option to connect the nets. The JUNCTION command can be seen in use in Figure 4-57.

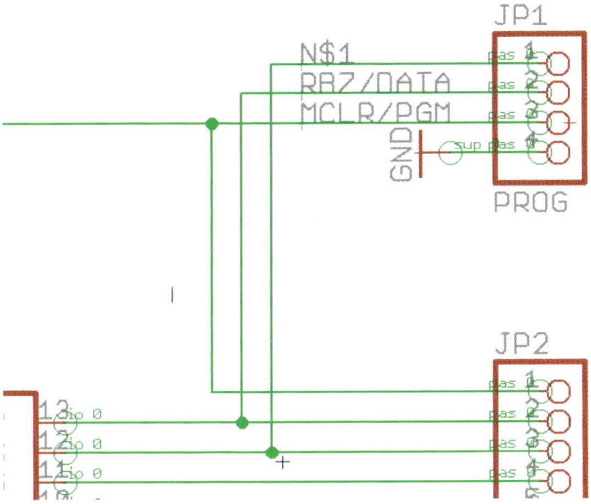

Figure 4-57: The JUNCTION command in use

If a net wire is placed at a point where there are at least two other net wires and/or pins, a junction will automatically be placed. This function can be disabled with "`SET AUTO_JUNCTION OFF;`", or by unchecking "*Options ▷ Set ▷ Misc ▷ Auto set junction*".

LABEL

Function
Allows user to attach a text label to a bus or a net.

Syntax
```
LABEL [XREF] [orientation]
```

Mouse keys
Center-click selects the layer of the label.
Right-Click rotates the label.
Shift+Right-Click reverses the direction of rotation.

See also NAME, BUS, FRAME

Bus or net names may be placed in a schematic drawing in any location by using the LABEL command.
Left-Clicking on the icon, and then the net, commences the LABEL command. The relevant label attaches itself to the mouse cursor and may be rotated, changed to another layer, or moved to a different location.
Left-Click defines the location of the label.

Buses and nets may have any number of labels. Labels cannot be changed with "CHANGE TEXT" command.

Labels are handled by the program as text, but their value corresponds to the name of the appropriate bus or net. If a bus or net is renamed with the NAME command, all associated labels are renamed automatically.

If a bus, net, or label is selected with the SHOW command, all connected buses, nets and labels are highlighted.

When the command is invoked, the parameter toolbar, given in Figure 4-58, is displayed. This toolbar includes the following parameters: *Layer*, *Xref*, *Rotation* (4 positions), *Mirror*, *Size*, *Text Ratio*, *Font Type.*

Figure 4-58: The LABEL parameter toolbar

Layers
This is the layer in which the Label is to be placed. The default is *95 Names*.

Xref

This parameter changes the style of the label. The left-most parameter, *Xref off* , determines that the label is to be on one drawing sheet. The right-most parameter, *Xref on* , determines that the label is to connect to another drawing sheet.

Figure 4-59 illustrates the LABEL command in use, with the *Xref* parameter set *off*.

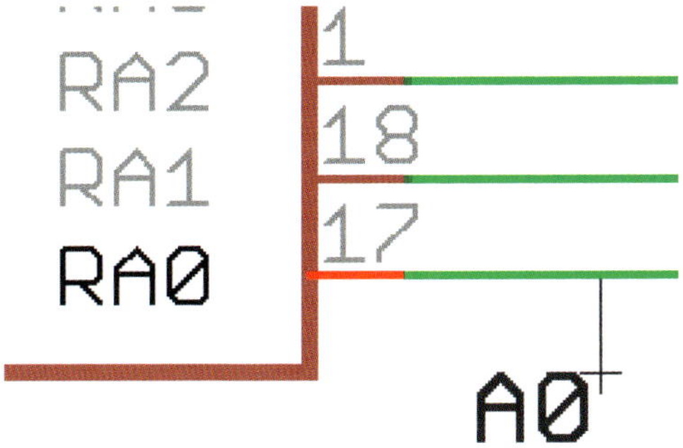

Figure 4-59: The LABEL command in use

Rotation
There are 4 pre-set rotations; No Rotation and Rotation by 90, 180 and 270 degrees respectively.
The orientation of the label may also be defined textually using the usual definitions as listed in the ADD command (R0, R90 etc.).

Size
The size parameter sets the size of the label text in the prevailing units.

Ratio
The thickness of the text is expressed as a ratio. This ratio is the line thickness as a % of the text height.

Font
Label Text may have three different fonts: *Vector, Proportional and Fixed*. These are outlined in the description of the TEXT command.

Using Cross-reference labels

If the optional keyword XREF is given, to set that parameter on, the label will be a "cross-reference" label. Cross- reference labels can be used in multi-sheet schematics to indicate the next sheet a particular net appears on.

Note: this is only applicable to nets.

Figure 4-60 illustrates the LABEL command in use, with the *Xref* parameter set *on.*

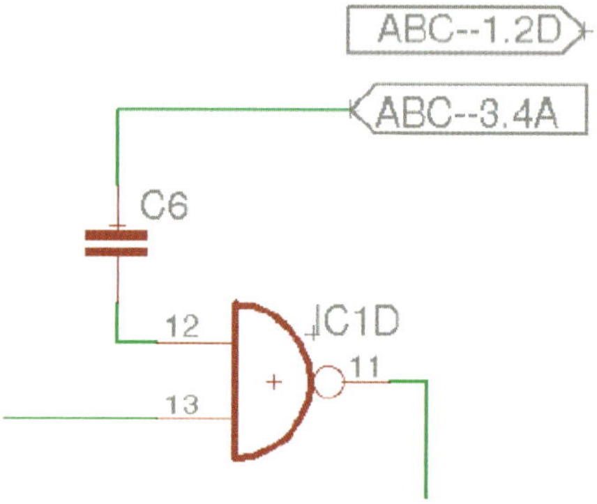

Figure 4-60: The LABEL command with Xref parameter set on

The XREF keyword is mainly for use in scripts. Normally the setting is taken from what has previously been set, or by clicking on the *Xref* button in the parameter toolbar.

The format in which a cross-reference label is displayed can be controlled through the "Xref label format" string, which is defined in the "*Options* ▷ *Set* ▷ *Misc* " dialog, or with the SET command. The following placeholders are defined, and can be used in any order:

%F enables drawing a flag border around the label
%N the name of the net
%S the next sheet number
%C the column on the next sheet
%R the row on the next sheet

The default format string is "%F%N/%S.%C%R". Apart from the defined placeholders the user may use any other ASCII characters.

MODULE

Function
Creates a module. Adds module instances into a schematic diagram.

Syntax

```
MODULE [[width height] 'module_name'] ['module_instance_name'] [+offset]
[orientation] ..
MODULE 'variant_name@module_name' ['module_instance_name'] [+offset]
[orientation] ..
```

Mouse keys

Center-click	mirrors the module instance.
Right-Click	rotates the module instance.
Shift+Right-Click	reverses the direction of rotation.
Ctrl+Left-Click	used with MOVE to move and re-size a Module

See also NAME, PORT, PREFIX

The MODULE command is used to create modules used in hierarchical schematics and to add module instances into a sheet. If `+offset` is given, the current module instance will use this offset for naming the elements. The value has to be a multiple of 100 (e.g. +100).

Note: this is only supported for module instances in the main schematic.

The `orientation` of the module instance may be defined textually using the usual definitions as listed in the ADD command (R0, R90 etc.).

A module instance adds the parts and nets of that module to the master board (i.e. the level one 'above' it in the hierarchy). Net names are composed using the module name and the net name (e.g. 'MODULE1:N$1').

If a net is exported through a PORT, it could be overwritten with a net connected to this port. Part names of a module instance with an offset, are generated by adding this offset (e.g. 'R17' with offset '100' becomes 'R117'). If no offset is set, part names are composed the same way as net names (e.g. 'MODULE1:R17').

In order to choose a specific assembly variant of the module, its name has to be prefixed to the module name, as in: `variant_name@module_name` (e.g. 'V1@ABC').

Names
Module instance names are generated automatically and may be modified with the NAME command.

Size

The size of a module is set if `width` and `height` are given before the module name.

Edit

The MOVE command can be used to edit the module symbol. The border of the module symbol can be selected with **Ctrl+Left-Click** for resizing it.

NET

Function
Draws nets on a schematic.

Syntax
```
NET [net_name] [curve | @radius]•..
```

Mouse keys
Right-Click changes/selects the wire bend style.
Shift+Right-Click reverses the direction of switching bend styles.
Ctrl+Right-Click toggles between corresponding bend styles.

See also BUS, NAME, CLASS, SET

The net command is used to draw individual connections (nets) onto the Net layer of a schematic drawing. **Left-Click** marks the starting point for the net; the second **Left-Click** marks the end point of a segment. **2 x Left-Click** on the same point terminates the net command.

If a net wire is placed at a point where there is already another net or bus wire or a pin, the current net wire will be ended at that point. This function can be disabled with "`SET AUTO_END_NET OFF;`", or by unchecking *"Options ▷ Set ▷ Misc ▷ Auto end net and bus"*.

If a net wire is placed at a point where there are at least two other net wires and/or pins, a junction will automatically be placed. This function can be disabled with "`SET AUTO_JUNCTION OFF;`", or by unchecking *"Options ▷ Set ▷ Misc ▷ Auto set junction"*.

If the `curve` or `@radius` parameter is given, an arc can be drawn as part of the net (see the detailed description in the WIRE command).

Parameters
Upon activation, the NET command displays the parameters toolbar as shown in Figure 4-61.

Figure 4-61: The NET command parameter toolbar

The parameters than can be set from the toolbar, from left to right, are: *Wire Bend Style, Radius, Miter Style and Net Class.*

Wire Bend Style

The wire bend style essentially defines the angle between the segments; and can be changed with the **Right-Click** action. **Shift+Right-Click** reverses the direction in which the bend styles are selected, and the **Ctrl+Right-Click** makes it toggle between corresponding bend styles.

The Wire Bend Style 0 may be used draw an ARC with NET.

Radius

The *radius* parameter specified is used where the command employs wire bend styles of 90 or 45 degrees. If the user sets the round mitering parameter, it will apply to both the 90 and 45 degree bend styles; or in the case of straight wires, only the 90 degree bend styles will be affected.

If *radius* is positive, the inserted Net will be an arc with the given radius; if it is negative, a straight Net will be inserted.

Miter style

The miter style parameter toolbar option is used to effect the action of a round- or straight-miter Net.

Net Style

Wires can have one of the following *styles*:

- Continuous
- LongDash
- ShortDash
- DashDot

The Net style can be changed with the CHANGE command, or by using the drop-down menu for the Style parameter.

Net class

The Net class parameter sets the value of the Net class for the Net to be drawn. The default for all Nets is 0.

The values for Net classes are configured in the *"Edit ▷ Net classes.."* dialog.

Net Names

If the NET command is used with a net name then the net is named accordingly.

If no net name is included in the command line and the net is not started on a bus, then a name in the form of N$1 is automatically allocated to the net.

Nets or net segments that run over different sheets of a schematic, and use the same net name, are connected.

Net names should not contain a comma (','), since this is the delimiting character used in busses.

Line Width

The width of the line drawn by the net command may be changed using the SET command e.g.

```
SET NET_WIRE_WIDTH width;
```

(The default width is 6 mil).

Inverted signals

The name of an inverted ("active low") signal can be displayed overlined if it is preceded with an exclamation mark ('!'), as in:

`!RESET` which would result in: $\overline{\text{RESET}}$

Select Bus Signal

If a net is started on a bus, a popup menu opens from which one of the bus signals can be selected. The net then is named accordingly and becomes part of the same signal. If the bus includes several part buses, a further popup menu opens from which the relevant part bus can be selected. This is shown in Figure 4-62.

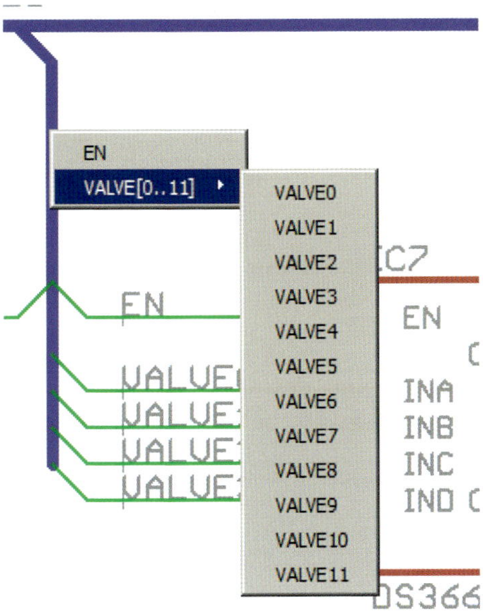

Figure 4-62: using a NET command on a bus

PINSWAP

Function
The PINSWAP command allows the user to swap two pins or pads of a device.

Syntax
```
PINSWAP•. .
```

See also PIN

The PINSWAP command is used to swap pins, within the same symbol, which have the same *Swaplevel* (and must be > 0). If a board is tied to a schematic via *BackAnnotation* two pads can only be swapped if the related pins are swappable.

On a board without a schematic, this command permits two pads in the same package to be swapped. The *Swaplevel* is not checked in this case.

The PINSWAP command is only executed with mouse operations (not as a script command).

The result of using the PINSWAP command can be seen in Figure 4-63 and Figure 4-64.

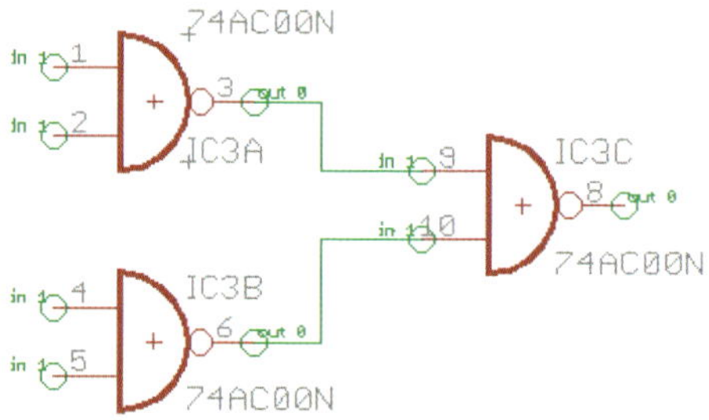

Figure 4-63: Circuit to be Pinswapped

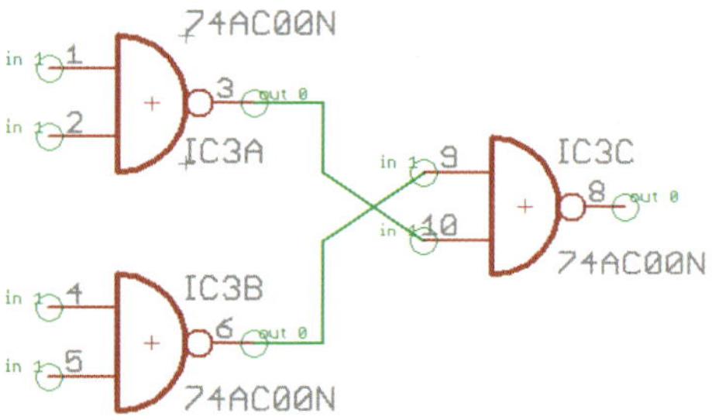

Figure 4-64: Circuit after Pinswap

Note: Wires attached to the swapped pins are moved with the pins, and may create short circuits. It is advised that a DRC is run to detect any possible errors.

PORT

The PORT command is used to add ports to a module.

Function
Adds ports to modules.

Syntax
```
PORT 'module_instance_name' 'net_name' options ..
PORT 'module' 'net_name' options ..
PORT 'module' 'net_name' options|DELETE
```

See also MODULE

The PORT command is used to add ports to modules used in hierarchical schematics. The position and orientation of the PORT are calculated automatically, and based on the positioning with reference to the closest side of module symbol.

A port carries a net of a module to the outside and defines a connection point for another net. The net connected to the port provides the common name and class.

A port with a bus name carries all nets of that bus simultaneously to the outside and defines a connection point for a proper bus.

If a net of a MODULE has an external connection through a PORT, the net class of the net on this port overrides the net class of the net in the module.

Names
The port name has to be chosen according to the net name within that module, which should be exported. The port name may also be a simple bus name like 'PA[0..7]'.

Options

Direction
The Direction indicates the logical direction of signal flow or function of the PORT. This parameter is essential for the Electrical Rule Check (ERC) and for the automatic wiring of the power supply pins. The following alternatives are valid for the Direction option:

Direction Symbol	Functionality
NC	not connected
In	input
Out	output (totempole)
IO	in/out, bidirectional (default)
OC	open collector or open drain
Hiz	high impedance(3State) output
Pas	passive
Pwr	power pin (Vcc, Gnd, Vss ...), supply voltage input

The direction of already existing ports can be changed within a module.

Commands for Editing Libraries

CONNECT

Function
Used to assign package pads to element/gate pins.

Syntax

```
CONNECT
CONNECT [ ALL | ANY ] gate_name.pin_name pad_name..
CONNECT [ ALL | ANY ] pin_name pad_name..
```

See also PREFIX, OPEN, CLOSE, SCRIPT

This command is used in the device editing mode in order to define the relationship between the pins of a gate and the pads of the corresponding package in the library.

NOTE: the package to be used should first be defined by actioning the PACKAGE command. If the CONNECT command is invoked without parameters, a dialog is presented which allows the user to interactively assign the connections. An example of this dialog is shown in Figure 4-65.

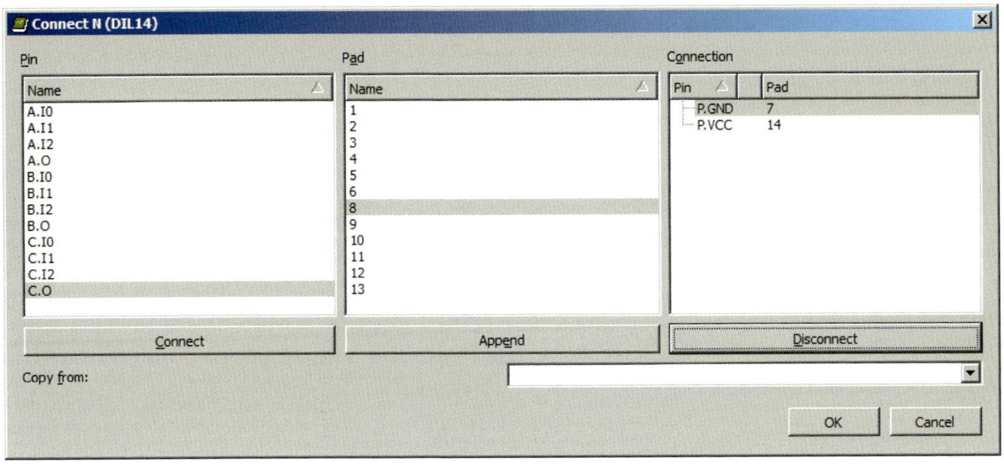

Figure 4-65: CONNECT command dialog

In the CONNECT dialog the buttons function as follows:

`Connect` creates a new connection between the selected pin and the selected pads. The user may select more than one pad, in which case all of these pads will be connected to the selected pin. (the user may use the Ctrl and Shift keys in the usual way to mark/select more than one pad).

`Append` adds the selected pads to the current connection

`Disconnect` removes the selected connection and puts the pin and pads back in their separate lists, keeping them selected so that it is easy to make modifications.

If a connection contains more than one pad, an icon in the right-hand Connection pane

indicates whether ANY  or ALL  of these pads need to be externally connected to a signal.

Examples

Device with one Gate

If only one gate is included in a device, the parameter gate_name can be dropped, e.g.:

```
CONNECT gnd 1 rdy 2 phi1 3 !irq 4 nc1 5...
```

(Note: "!" is used to indicate inverted data signals.)
would connect the following pins to pads:

gnd → 1
rdy → 2
phi1 → 3
$\overline{\texttt{irq}}$ → 4
nc1 → 5

Devices with several Gates

If several gates are present in a device, the parameters must be entered with gate_name, pin_name and pad_name each time.

For example:

The following are connections for which four NAND gates of a 7400 device are allocated. The device includes five gates: A, B, C, D, and PWR. The gate inputs are named I1 and I2 while the output is named O.

```
CONNECT A.I1  1 A.I2 2 A.O 3;
CONNECT B.I1  4 B.I2 5 B.O 6;

CONNECT C.I1  13 C.I2 12 C.O 11;
CONNECT D.I1  10 D.I2 9 D.O 8;
```

```
CONNECT PWR.gnd 7;
CONNECT PWR.VCC 14;
```

The CONNECT command may be repeated as often as required. It may be used with all pin/pad connections or with only certain pins. Each new CONNECT command overwrites the previous conditions for the relevant pins.

Several Pads connected to the same Pin

Some parts, like power amplifiers or BGA chips, may have several pads that are connected internally. This may be done for better heat dissipation or to allow for higher currents. The CONNECT command can handle these cases by simply listing all related pad names, separated by blanks (and therefore enclosed in single quotes).

Examples:

```
CONNECT ALL I1 '1 3 5';
```

In this example the pin `I1` is connected to the three pads; `1`, `3` and `5`. If the pin `I1` is connected to a net in the schematic, all three pads must be explicitly connected to the corresponding signal in the board.

The  symbol would be displayed in the Connection pane of the dialog.

```
CONNECT ANY O1 '2 4 6';
```

In this example, the keyword `ANY` indicates that any one (or even all) of the pads `2`, `4` or `6` can be connected to the signal. It is even allowed to use this internal connection as a "bridge" by connecting one segment of the signal to, say, pad `2`, while connecting the rest of the signal to pad `6`, without any explicit external connection between these two pads.

The  symbol would be displayed in the Connection pane of the dialog.

Note: when designing a library part and using `ANY` in a CONNECT command, the user should ensure that the part will be able to handle cross currents running through its pads. If there is any doubt, the user should employ the `ALL` option (which is the default and may be omitted).
If a pin name would conflict with one of the keywords `ALL` or `ANY`, the pin name needs to be enclosed with single quotes. As soon as one of these keywords appears in a CONNECT command, it applies to all pin/pad connections that follow it, until a different keyword is seen. This can be seen in the example:
CONNECT 'A' '1' 'B' '2' ANY 'C' '3 4 5 6' 'D' '7 8' ALL 'E' '9 10 11';
The RATSNEST and AUTO command will handle the `ALL` and `ANY` cases appropriately.

PACKAGE

Function
Defines a package variant for a device.

Syntax
```
PACKAGE
PACKAGE pname vname
PACKAGE pname@lname vname
PACKAGE name
PACKAGE -old_name new_name

PACKAGE -name
```

See also CONNECT, TECHNOLOGY, PREFIX

This command is used in the device edit mode to define, delete or rename a package varant. In the schematic or board editor the PACKAGE command behaves exactly like the command "CHANGE PACKAGE".

Without parameters a dialog is opened that allows the user to select a package and define this variant's name. This is shown in Figure 4-66.

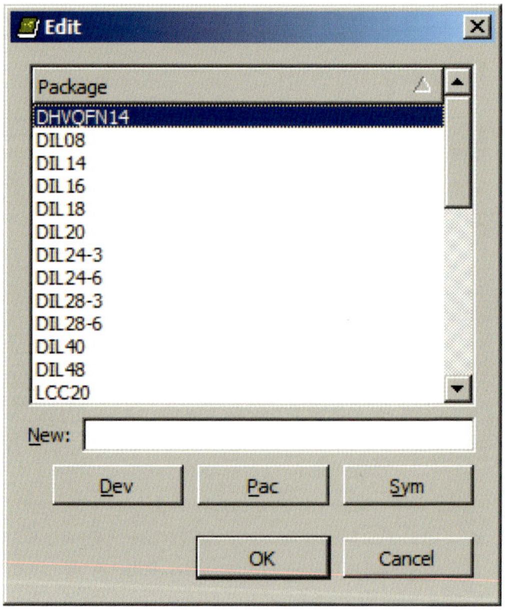

Figure 4-66: PACKAGE command dialog

The parameters `pname vname` assign the package `pname` to the new variant `vname`.

The notation `pname@lname vname` fetches the package `pname` from library `lname` and creates a new package variant. This can also be done through the library objects' context menu or via *Drag&Drop* from the Control Panel's tree view.

The single parameter `name` switches to the given existing package variant. If no package variants have been defined yet, and a package of the given name exists, a new package variant named '' (an 'empty' name) with the given package will be created (this is for compatibility with version 3.5 of EAGLE).

If `-old_name new_name` is given, the package variant `old_name` is renamed to `new_name`.
The single parameter `-name` deletes the given package variant.

The name of a package variant will be appended to the device set name to form the full device name. If the device set name contains the character '?', that character will be replaced by the package variant name.
Note: the package variant is processed after the technology, so if the device set name contains neither a '*' nor a '?' character, the resulting device name will consist of:

device_set_name + technology + package_variant.

Devices without packages
Devices can also be created without assigning a package, for example for frames, supply devices, external or other devices that only make sense in a schematic. This can be done by creating a device set with adequate gates, technologies and attributes (if necessary) without using the PACKAGE command. If saved, a packageless variant is created (with empty string as variant name). As soon as a package is assigned, the packageless variant gets overwritten by this and no further packageless variants can be created.

As soon as gates contain pins, packageless devices only make limited sense (e.g. supply devices).

Supply devices
In order to use supply symbols in schematics, packageless supply devices are common. The device usually consists of exactly one symbol with a *Sup* pin (see the PIN command).

PAD

Function
Adds pads to a package.

Syntax

```
PAD [diameter] [shape] [orientation] [flags] ['name']•..
```

Mouse keys

Right-Click rotates the pad.
Shift+Right-Click reverses the direction of rotation.

See also SMD, CHANGE, DISPLAY, SET, NAME, VIA, DesignRules

The PAD command is used to add pads to a package. When the PAD command is active, a pad symbol is attached to the cursor and can be moved around the screen. **Left-Click** places a pad at the current position. Entering a number changes the diameter of the pad (in the actual unit). Pad diameters can be up to 0.51602 inch (13.1 mm).

Parameters
Pads may have the following individual properties: *Shape*, *Diameter*, and *Drill* (hole diameter) and *Orientation*. These are illustrated in the parameter toolbar shown in Figure 4-67.

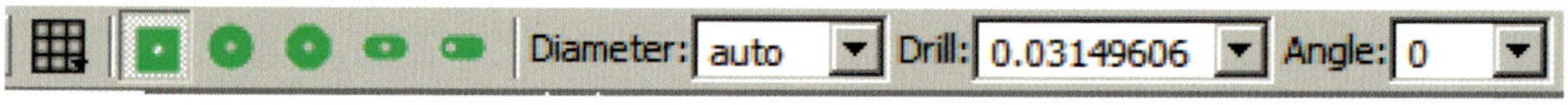

Figure 4-67: PAD command parameter toolbar

Shape
Available alternative shapes are: Square, Round, Octagon, Long, and Offset (Long with offset drill).

These shapes only apply to the outer layers (Top and Bottom). In inner layers the shape is always "round".

With elongated pads, the given diameter defines the smaller side of the pad. The ratio between the two sides of elongated pads is given by the parameter Shapes/Elongation in the DesignRules of the board (default is 100%, which results in a ratio of 2:1).

The pad shape or diameter can be selected while the PAD command is active, or it can be changed with the CHANGE command, e.g.:

```
CHANGE SHAPE OCTAGON
```

Note: the actual shape and diameter of a pad will be determined by the DesignRules of the board the part is used in.

Diameter
The pad diameter usually is defined with the standard value auto (respectively 0), since the size is finally determined in the layout by means of the Design Rules, Restring tab. The pad appears in the library with the default value of 55 mil.
The user may also specify and assign an individual value. For example:

```
PAD 70 mil
```

would restrict the diameter of the pad on the board to be ≥ 70 mil (independent of the calculated value of the Design Rules). The user would select this value when the PAD command is active (i.e. the pad is attached to the mouse cursor) by using the parameter toolbar.

Drill
It is also possible to specify the drill hole diameter. This is selected from the drop-down menu, or as a numeric value entered in the *Drill* field.

The drill size may also be changed using the CHANGE command. The existing values then remain in use for successive pads.

Because displaying different pad shapes and drill holes in their real size slows down the screen refresh, EAGLE allows the user to change between real and fast display mode by the use of the SET commands:

```
SET DISPLAY_MODE REAL | NODRILL;
```

Orientation
The `orientation` may be set to any angle in the range R0...R359.9. The angle may be selected from the drop-down menu, or as a numeric value entered in the *Angle* field.

Flags
The following flags can be used to control the appearance of a pad:

`NOSTOP` don't generate solder stop mask
`NOTHERMALS` don't generate thermals
`FIRST` this is the "first" pad (which may be drawn with a special shape)

By default a pad automatically generates solder stop mask and thermals as necessary. However, in special cases it may be desirable to have particular pads not do this. The above NO...options in `flags` can be used to suppress these features.

If the DesignRules of a given board specify that the "first pad" of a package shall be drawn with a particular shape, the pad marked with the `FIRST` flag will be displayed that way.

A newly started PAD command resets all flags to their defaults. Once a flag is given in the command line, it applies to all following pads placed within this PAD command (except for `FIRST`, which applies only to the pad immediately following this option).

Pad Names

Pad names are generated by the program automatically and can be changed with the NAME command. The name can also be defined in the PAD command.
Pad name display can be turned on or off by means of the command:

```
SET PAD_NAMES OFF | ON;
```

This change will become visible after the next screen refresh.

PIN

Function
Defines connection points for symbols.

Syntax
`PIN 'name' options`

Mouse keys
Right-Click rotates the pin.
Shift+Right-Click reverses the direction of rotation.

See also NAME, SHOW, CHANGE

The PIN command is used while editing a symbol to define a connection point to that symbol.

Using the PIN Command
The PIN command is used to define connection points on a symbol for nets. Pins are drawn onto the Symbols layer while additional information appears on the Pins layer. Individual pins may be assigned various options in the command line. The options can be listed in any order or omitted. In this case the default options are valid.

If a name is used in the PIN command, it must be enclosed in apostrophes. Pin names can be changed in the symbol edit mode using the NAME command.

Automatic Naming
Pins may be automatically numbered in the following way. In order to place the pins `D0...D7` on a symbol, the first pin is placed with the following command:

```
PIN 'D0' *
```

and the location for the other pins is defined with `Left-Click` for each.

Pins with the same Name
If it is required to define several pins in a component with the same name, the following procedure can be used:

For example, suppose that three pins are required for the ground signal , and named 'GND'. The pins are allocated the names GND@1, GND@2 and GND@3 during the symbol definition. Then, only the characters before the "@" sign appear in the schematic.

It is not possible to add or delete pins in symbols which are already used by a device, because this would change the pin/pad allocation defined with the CONNECT command.

Pin Lettering
The position of pin and pad names, or the text size, on a symbol, relative to the pin connection point, can not be changed.

Note: When defining new symbols, the user is encouraged to ensure that their size is consistent with existing symbols.

Inverted pins
The name of an inverted pin ("active low") can be displayed overlined if it is preceded with an exclamation mark ('!'), as in

```
!RESET
```

would result in:

$\overline{\text{RESET}}$

Upon activation the PIN command displays a parameter toolbar which is shown in Figure 4-68.

Figure 4-68: PIN command parameter toolbar

Options
There are a number of options that may be modified using this toolbar. These parameters are given in Table 4-6 , and are represented (left to right) by the consecutive partitions of the parameter toolbar.

Orientation	defines the PIN rotation in increments of 90 degrees
Function	gives a graphic representation of the PIN and its logical function
Length	configures the length of the pin used in the symbol
Visible	defines the visibility of the pin / pad name
Direction	defines the direction of signal flow or function
Swaplevel	indicates the integer of the swap level number

Table 4-6: PIN Command Options

These options are defined as follows:

Orientation
This is the orientation of the pin. When placing pins manually, **Right-Click** rotates the pin anti-clockwise. The parameter "orientation" is mainly used in script files. The alternatives are:

i. R0 connection point on the right
ii . R90connection point above
iii. R180 connection point on the left
iv. R270 connection point below

The default value is: R0

Function
The graphic representation of the pin's functionality:

i. None no special function
ii. Dot inverter symbol
iii. Clk clock symbol
iv. DotClk inverted clock symbol

The default value is: None

Length
Length (in inches) of the pin symbol:

i. Point pin with no connection or name
ii. Short 0.1 inch long connection
iii. Middle 0.2 inch long connection
iv. Long 0.3 inch long connection

The default value is: Long

Name Visibilty
This parameter defines if the pin and/or pad name are visible in the schematic:

i. Off pin and pad name not drawn
ii. Pad pad name drawn, pin name not drawn
iii. Pin pin name drawn, pad name not drawn
iv. Both pin and pad name drawn

The default value is: Both

Direction

This option defines the logical direction of signal flow or function of the PIN. It is essential for the Electrical Rule Check (ERC) and for the automatic wiring of the power supply pins. The following alternatives may be used, and selected from the drop-down menu in the parameter toolbar:

i. NC not connected
ii. In input
iii. Out output (totem-pole)
iv. IO in/output (bidirectional)
v. OC open collector or open drain
vi. Hiz high impedance output (e.g. 3-state) Pas passive (for resistors, capacitors etc.)
vii. Pwr power input pin (e.g. V_{CC}, GND, V_{SS}, V_{DD}, etc.)
viii. Sup general supply pin (e.g. for ground symbol)

The default value is: IO

Swaplevel

An integer number whose pins may be swapped with another. The allocation of a number greater than 0, indicates that a pin may be swapped with any other in the same symbol with the same swaplevel number. Swaplevel = 0 indicates that a pin can not be swapped with another. See the PINSWAP command.

Example: The inputs of a NAND gate could be allocated the same swaplevel number as they are all identical.

The default value is: 0

Predefined options with CHANGE

All options may be predefined with CHANGE commands. The options remain in force until edited by a new PIN or CHANGE command.

The SHOW command may be used to show pin options such as Direction and Swaplevel.

PREFIX

Function
Defines the prefix for a symbol name in generated symbol names.

Syntax
```
PREFIX prefix_string;
```

See also CONNECT, PACKAGE, VALUE

This command is used in the device editor mode to determine the initial characters of automatically generated symbol names, when a symbol is placed in a schematic using the ADD command.

Upon activation the PIN command displays a parameter dialog which is shown in Figure 4-69. This allows the user to enter the required prefix characters.

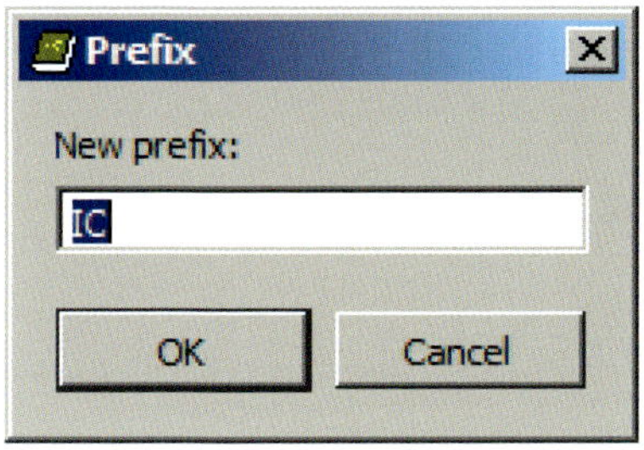

Figure 4-69: PREFIX command dialog

Example

```
PREFIX U;
```

If this command is used when editing, for example, a 7400 device, then gates which are later placed in a schematic using the ADD command will be allocated the names U1, U2, U3 in sequence. These names may be changed at any time with the NAME command.

REMOVE

Function
Deletes files, devices, symbols, packages, and sheets in a library.

Syntax
```
REMOVE name
REMOVE name.Sxx
```

See also OPEN, RENAME

Removing Files
The REMOVE command is used to delete the file `name` in the board or schematic editing modes.

Removing Devices, Symbols, Packages
The REMOVE command is used to delete the device, symbol or package '`name`' from the currently open library. The name may include an extension (for example REMOVE `name.pac`). If the name is given without extension, the user must be in the respective mode to remove an object (i.e. in package edit mode if the intent is to remove packages).

Symbols and packages can be erased from a library only if they are not being used by a device.

WARNING: Using REMOVE in a library clears the UNDO buffer, and so can not be undone.
Removing Sheets

The REMOVE command may also be used to delete a sheet from a schematic. The name of the presently loaded schematic can be omitted. The parameter `xx` represents the sheet number, for example:

```
REMOVE .S3
```

deletes sheet number 3 from the currently loaded schematic.

If the currently loaded sheet is deleted, sheet number 1 will be loaded after the command has been executed. All sheets with a higher number than the one deleted, will be assigned a new number (i.e. reduced by one).

RENAME

Function
Renames symbols, devices or packages in a library.

Syntax
```
RENAME old_name new_name;
```

See also OPEN

The RENAME command is used to change the name of a symbol, device or package. The appropriate library must already be open (by using the OPEN command) before use.

The names may include extensions (for example **RENAME name1.pac name2[.pac]**.
Note: the extension is optional in the second parameter.

If the first parameter is given without extension, the user must be in the respective mode to rename an object (i.e. in package edit mode if the intent is to rename packages).

WARNING: RENAME clears the UNDO buffer, and so cannot be undone.

SMD

Function
Adds SMD (surface mount device) pads to a package.

Syntax
```
SMD [x_width y_width] [-roundness] [orientation] [flags] ['name']..
```

Mouse keys
Center-click selects the layer.
Right-Click rotates the SMD.
Shift+Right-Click reverses the direction of rotation.

See also PAD, CHANGE, NAME, ROUTE, DesignRules

The SMD command is used to add pads for surface mount devices to a package. When the SMD command is active, an SMD symbol is attached to the cursor. **Left-Click** places an SMD pad at the current position.

Upon activation, the SMD command displays the parameter toolbar illustrated in Figure 4-70.

Figure 4-70: SMD command parameter toolbar

Layer
The user may select the Layer for the SMD. The options are *Top* and *Bottom.* **Center-click changes the layer onto which the SMD pad will be drawn.**

Size
Entering numbers, or selecting a combination from the drop-down menu, changes the x- and y- width of the SMD pad (which can be up to 0.51602 inch or 13.1 mm). These parameters remain in force for successive SMD commands and can be changed with the CHANGE command.

Roundness
The `roundness` has to be entered as an integer number between `0` and `100`, with a negative sign to distinguish it from the width parameters. A value of `0` results in fully rectangular SMDs, while a value of `100` makes the corners of the SMD fully round. For example, the command:

```
SMD 50 50 -100 '1'
```

would create a completely round SMD named '1' at the given **Left-Click** position. This can be used to create BGA (Ball Grid Array) pads.

Orientation

The `orientation` (see description in ADD command) may be any angle in the range `R0`... `R359.9`. The angle may also be entered in the dialog field or selected from the drop-down menu.

Names

SMD names are generated automatically and may be modified with the NAME command. Names may be included in the SMD command if enclosed in single quotes.

Flags

The following flags can be used to control the appearance of an SMD:

`NOSTOP`	don't generate solder stop mask
`NOTHERMALS`	don't generate thermals
`NOCREAM`	don't generate cream mask

By default an SMD automatically generates solder stop mask, cream mask and thermals as necessary. However, in special cases it may be desirable to have particular SMDs not do this.

The above `NO...` flags can be used to suppress these features.

A newly started SMD command resets all flags to their defaults. Once a flag is given in the command line, it applies to all subsequent SMDs placed within this SMD command.

Single SMDs

Single SMD pads in boards can only be used by defining a package with one SMD.

Modifying SMD Packages

It is not possible to add or delete SMDs in packages which are already used by a device, because this would change the pin/SMD allocation defined by the CONNECT command.

TECHNOLOGY

Function
Defines the possible *technology* parts of a device name.

Syntax

```
TECHNOLOGY name ..;
TECHNOLOGY -name ..;
TECHNOLOGY -* ..;
```

See also PACKAGE, ATTRIBUTE

This command is used in the device editor mode to define the alternate *technology* parts of a device name. In the schematic or board editor, the TECHNOLOGY command behaves exactly like "CHANGE TECHNOLOGY".

When activated, the TECHNOLOGY command opens a dialog, listing the alternative technologies for the selected device. Figure 4-71 shows the dialog for the 7400 (Quad 2-input NAND gate), from the loaded library; 74xx-us.lbr.

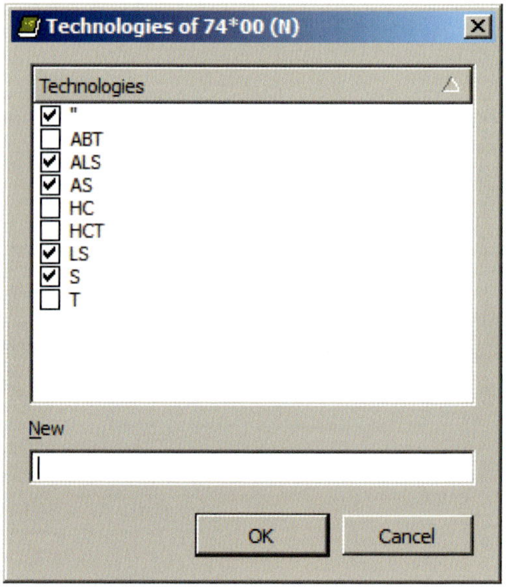

Figure 4-71: TECHNOLOGY command dialog

Note: the Technologies dialog contains *all* technologies from *all* devices in the loaded library. The currently referenced technologies are those for which the current device has checked in the check box.

One name given in the TECHNOLOGY command will be used to replace the '*' in the device set name when an actual device is added to a schematic. The term *technology* stems from the main usage of this feature in creating different variations of the same basic device; all of which have the same schematic symbol(s), package, and pin/pad connections. They only differ in a part of their name, which for the classic TTL devices, is related to their different technologies, like 'L', 'LS' or 'HCT'.

The TECHNOLOGY command can only be used if a package variant has been selected with the PACKAGE command.
If no '*' character is present in the device set name, the technology will be appended to the device set name to form the full device name.

Note: the technology is processed before the package variant, so if the device set name contains neither a '*' nor a '?' character, the resulting device name will consist of:

```
device_set_name+technology+package_variant.
```

The names listed in the TECHNOLOGY command will be added to an already existing list of technologies for the current device. Starting a name with '-' will remove that name from the list of technologies. If a name is required that begins with '-', it has to be enclosed in single quotes. Using -* removes all technologies.

Only ASCII characters in the range 33..126 may be used in technologies (lowercase characters will be converted to uppercase).

The special "empty" technology can be entered as two single quotes ('', an empty string).

Example
In a device named '74*00' the command:

```
TECHNOLOGY -* '' L LS S HCT;
```

would first remove any existing technologies and then create the individual technology variants

```
7400
74L00
74LS00
74S00
74HCT00
```

Miscellaneous Commands

HELP

Function

Provides the user with Help for general access or for the current command.

Syntax

```
HELP
HELP command
```

Keyboard

`F1`: HELP activates the context sensitive help.

This command opens a context sensitive help window as shown in Figure 4-72.

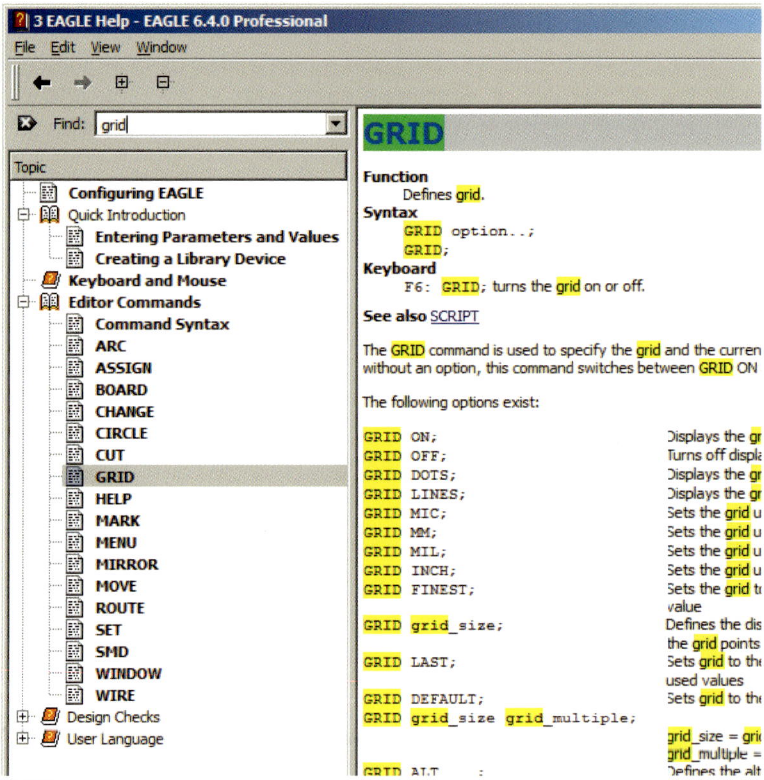

Figure 4-72: HELP command window

A `command` name within the HELP command shows the help page of that command.

Example

```
HELP GRID;
```

displays the help page for the GRID command, again as shown in Figure 4-72.

INFO

Function
Display and modify object properties.

Syntax
`INFO..`
`INFO name ..`

See also CHANGE, SHOW

The INFO command displays further details about an object's properties on screen: e.g. wire width, layer number, text size etc. It is also possible to modify properties in this dialog. An example is shown in Figure 4-73, displaying the properties of IC1.

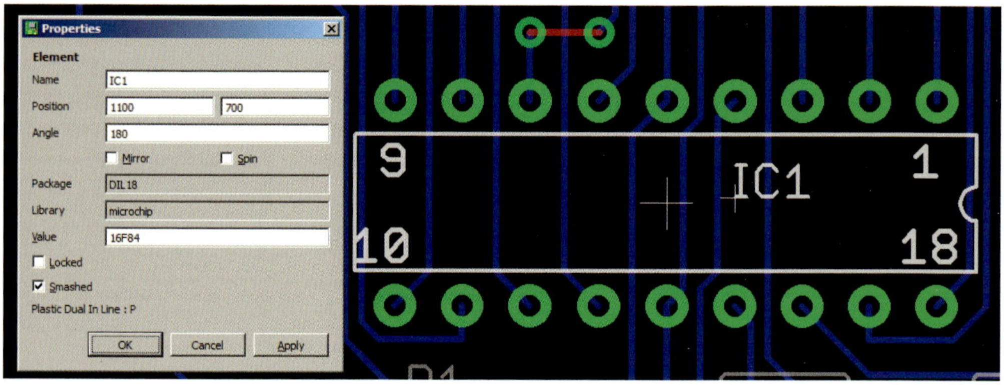

Figure 4-73: the INFO command dialog

Parts, pads, SMDs, pins and gates can also be selected by their name, which is especially useful if the object is outside the currently shown window area.

Note: when selecting a multi-gate part in a schematic by name, the user will need to enter the full instance name, consisting of part and gate name e.g. `INFO IC10C` would display the information for part IC10, gate C.

Attributes of parts can be selected by entering the concatenation of part name and attribute name, as in; `R5>VALUE`.

MARK

Function
Defines a mark on the drawing area.

Syntax

```
MARK
MARK;
```

See also GRID

The MARK command allows the user to define a point on the drawing area and display the coordinates of the mouse cursor, relative to that point, at the upper left corner of the screen (with a leading 'R' character).

This command may be used to set a datum for the complete drawing; and is especially useful when board dimensions or cutouts need to be defined.
Entering `MARK;` turns the mark on or off.

Note: To ensure accurate placement of the MARK, a sufficiently fine enough grid should be chosen and set, prior to activation of the command.

PRINT

Function

Prints a drawing to the system printer.

Syntax

```
PRINT [factor] [-limit] [options] [;]
```

The PRINT command prints the currently edited drawing to the system printer.

The `factor` parameter is used to scale the output.

The `limit` parameter is the maximum number of pages required for the output. The number has to be preceded with a '-' to distinguish it from the `factor` parameter. Where the drawing does not fit on the given number of pages, the factor will be reduced until it fits. Set this parameter to `-0` to allow any number of pages (and thus making sure the printout uses exactly the given scale factor).

The following `options` exist:

`MIRROR`	mirrors the output
`ROTATE`	rotates the output by 90°
`UPSIDEDOWN`	rotates the drawing by 180°
`ROTATE`	rotates the drawing is rotated by a total of 270°
`BLACK`	ignores the color settings of the layers and prints everything in black
`SOLID`	ignores the fill style settings of the layers and prints everything in solid
`CAPTION`	prints a caption at the bottom of the page
`FILE`	prints the output into a file; the file name must immediately follow this option
`PRINTER`	prints to a specific printer; the printer name must immediately follow this option
`PAPER`	prints on the given paper size; the paper size must immediately follow this option
`SHEETS`	prints the given range of sheets; the range (from-to) must immediately follow this option
`WINDOW`	prints the currently visible window selection of the drawing
`PORTRAIT`	prints in portrait orientation
`LANDSCAPE`	prints in landscape orientation

Colors and fill styles are used as they have been set in the editor window. This can be changed with the `SOLID` and `BLACK` options. The color palette used for the printout is always that for a white background.

If pads and vias are to be printed as "filled" (i.e. without the drill holes being visible), the command:

```
SET DISPLAY_MODE NODRILL;
```

should be used.

Note: polygons in boards will *not* be automatically calculated when printing via the PRINT command. Only the outlines will be drawn.
To print polygons in their calculated shape, the `RATSNEST` command should be used before printing.

If any of the options `MIRROR` through to `CAPTION` is preceded with a '-' (hyphen) that option is turned off (where it has been currently on from a previous PRINT). A '-' by itself turns off all options.

The `FILE` option can be used to print the output into a file. If this option is present, it must be immediately followed by the name of the output file.

If the output file name has an extension of "`.pdf`" (case insensitive), a PDF file will be created. A PDF file can also be created by selecting "Print to File (PDF)" from the "Printer" combo box in the print dialog. Text in a PDF file can be searched in a PDF viewer, provided the vector font is not used.

If the output file name has an extension of "`.ps`" (case insensitive), a Postscript file will be created.
If the file name is only an "`*`" or "`*.ext`" (an asterisk followed by an extension, as in "`*.pdf`", for instance), a file dialog will be opened that allows the user to select or enter the actual file name.

If the file name is only an extension, as in "`.pdf`", the output file name will be the same as the drawing file name, with the extension changed to the given string.

The file name may contain one or more of the following placeholders (or metadata), which will be replaced with the respective string:

`%E` the loaded file's extension (without the '.')
`%N` the loaded file's name (without path and extension)
`%P` the loaded file's directory path (without file name)
`%%` the character '%'

For example, the file name
`%N.cmp.pdf`
would create `boardname.cmp.pdf`.

If both the FILE and the PRINTER options are present, only the last one given will be taken into account.

If the PRINT command is used without any options, the print dialog is opened (as shown in Figure 4-74)

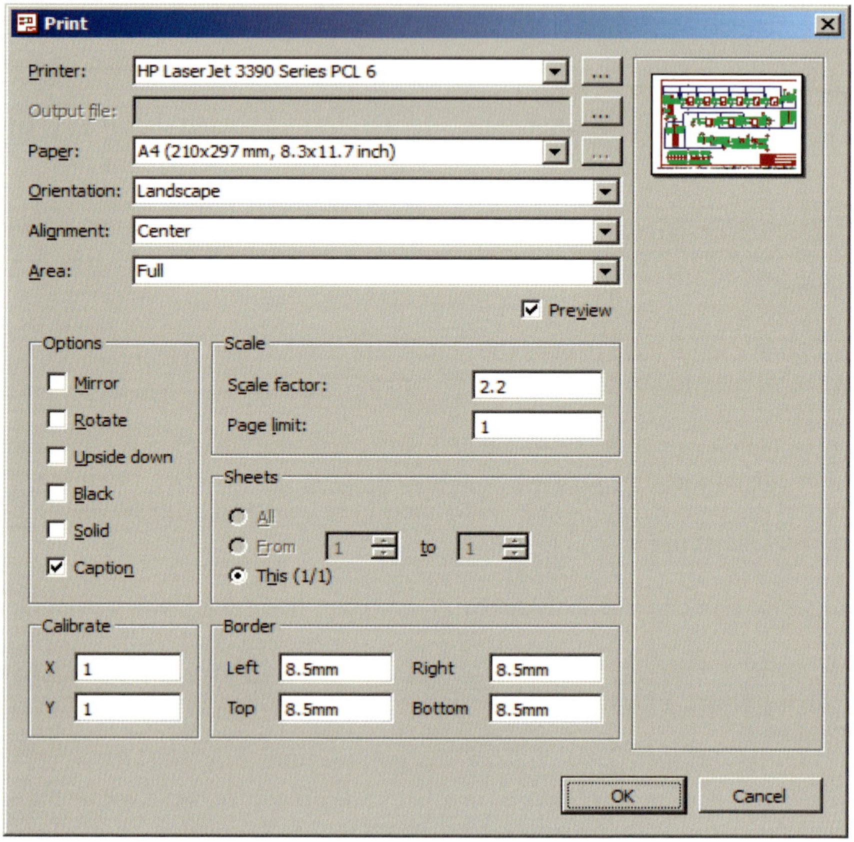

Figure 4-74: the PRINT command dialog

Printing to a given paper size

The `PAPER` option defines the size of the paper to print on. It must be immediately followed by one of the paper size names listed in the *Paper* combo box of the PRINT dialog, like `A4`, `Letter` etc. If a custom paper size shall be set, it has to be given in the format:

```
Width x Height Unit
```

(without blanks), as in

```
PRINT PAPER 200x300mm
PRINT PAPER 8.0x11.5inch
```

`Width` and `Height` can be floating point numbers, and the *Unit* may be either `mm` or `inch` (the latter may be abbreviated as `in`). Paper names must be given in full, and are case insensitive.

If both the `PRINTER` and `PAPER` options are used, the `PRINTER` option must be given first. Custom paper sizes may not work with all printers. They are mainly for use with Postscript or PDF output.

Printing a range of sheets

The `SHEETS` option can be used to print a range of sheets from a schematic. The range is given as two numbers, delimited by a '-', as in `2-15`. Without this option, only the currently edited sheet is printed.

To print all sheets, the range `ALL` can be used (which is case insensitive, but must be written in full). A range can also consist of just a single number, as in `42`, which will print exactly that sheet.

Examples

`PRINT`	opens the print dialog_allowing the user to set print options
`PRINT;`	immediately prints the drawing with the default options
`PRINT - MIRROR BLACK SOLID;`	prints the drawing mirrored, with everything in black and solid
`PRINT 2.5 -1;`	prints the drawing enlarged by a factor of 2.5, but ensuring that it does not exceed one page
`PRINT FILE .pdf;`	prints the drawing into a PDF file with the same name as the drawing file
`PRINT SHEETS 2-15 FILE .pdf;`	prints the sheets 2 through 15 into a PDF file with the same name as the drawing file

REDO

Function
Executes a command that was reversed by UNDO.

Syntax
`REDO;`

Keyboard
`F10 or Shift+Alt+BS` execute the REDO command.

Note: These key assignments may be modified by using the ASSIGN command.

See also UNDO, Forward&BackAnnotation

This command allows the user to reverse previous actions performed with the UNDO command. These actions can be executed again by the REDO command.

UNDO and REDO operate with a command memory which exists back to the last EDIT, OPEN or REMOVE command.

UNDO/REDO is completely integrated within Forward&Back Annotation.

ULP RUN

Function

Executes a User Language Program (ULP) file.

Syntax

```
RUN file_name [argument ...]
```

See also SCRIPT

The RUN command starts the User Language Program from the file `file_name`.
The optional `argument` list is available to the ULP through the Built-in Variables `argc` and `argv`; where `argc` is an integer containing the number of arguments passed to the RUN command and `argv` is a string containing the arguments passed to the ULP.

Running a ULP from a script file

If a ULP is executed from a script file and the program returns an integer value other than `0` (either because it has been terminated through a call to the exit() function, or because the STOP button was clicked), execution of the script file will be terminated.

Editor commands resulting from running a ULP

A ULP can also use the exit() function with a `string` parameter to return a command string back to the editor window.

Note: For detailed information on The EAGLE User Language, the user should refer to the Appendix at the end of this book titled; 'EAGLE User Language Reference Manual'.

SCRIPT

Function
Executes a script command file.

Syntax
```
SCRIPT file_name;
```

See also SET, MENU, ASSIGN, EXPORT, RUN

The SCRIPT command is used to execute sequences of commands that are stored in a script file. If SCRIPT is typed in at the keyboard and 'file_name' has no extension, the program automatically uses '.scr'. If the SCRIPT command is selected with the mouse, a popup menu will show all of the files which have the extension '.scr' so that they can be selected and executed (as shown in Figure 4-75).

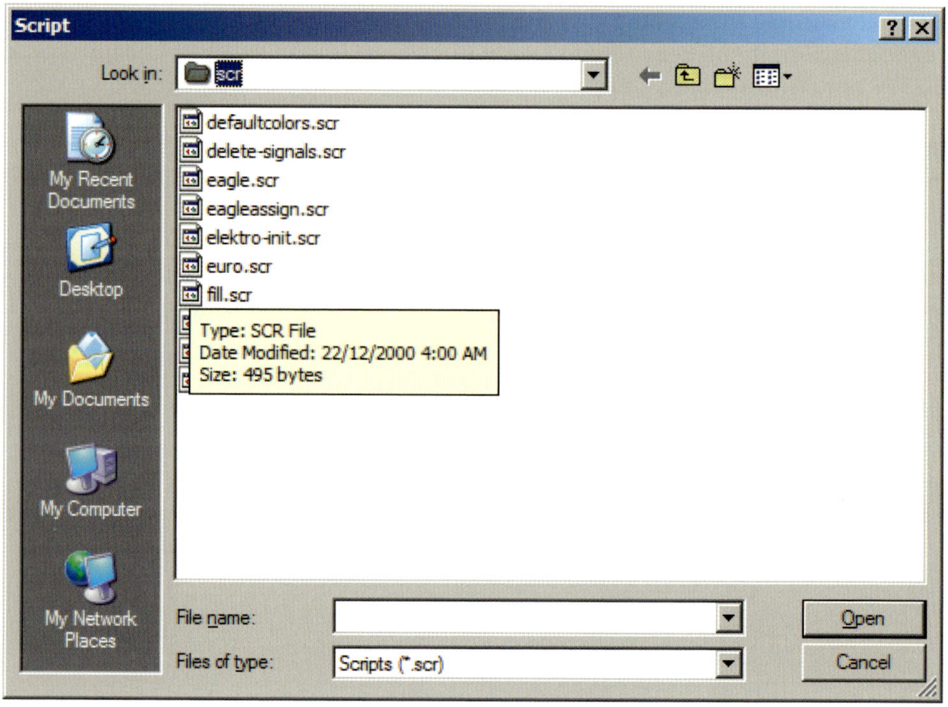

Figure 4-75: the SCRIPT command selection

Examples

`SCRIPT nofill`	executes nofill.scr
`SCRIPT myscr.`	executes myscr (no Suffix)
`SCRIPT myscr.old`	executes myscr.old

Script files contain sequences of commands (according to strict syntax rules) that enable the user to configure and tailor the functionality of EAGLE to suit individual user preferences. The following are examples of the application of script files:

i. the specification of specific colors and fillpatterns for all layers e.g. in the script file *defaultcolors.scr.* An extract from this file is shown in Figure 4-76.
ii. contain netlists converted from the data of other programs
iii. change the command menu or sub-menus
iv. assign keys to command or to even run scripts or ULPs
v. load pc board shapes

Script files can be created with a simple text editor. The development of customized script files requires knowledge of the EAGLE command language and the precise functioning and the syntax of the individual EAGLE commands.

```
# Set the default colors:

set palette black;

set palette 0 0xFF000000;
set palette 1 0xB43232C8;
set palette 2 0xB432C832;
set palette 3 0xB432C8C8;
set palette 4 0xB4C83232;
set palette 5 0xB4C832C8;
set palette 6 0xB4C8C832;
set palette 7 0xB4C8C8C8;
set palette 8 0xB4646464;
set palette 9 0xB40000FF;
set palette 10 0xB400FF00;
set palette 11 0xB400FFFF;
set palette 12 0xB4FF0000;
set palette 13 0xB4FF00FF;
set palette 14 0xB4FFFF00;
set palette 15 0xB4FFFFFF;

set palette colored;

set palette 0 0xFFEEEECE;
set palette 1 0xB4000080;
set palette 2 0xB4008000;
set palette 3 0xB4008080;
set palette 4 0xB4800000;
set palette 5 0xB4800080;
set palette 6 0xB4808000;
set palette 7 0xB4808080;
set palette 8 0xB4C0C0C0;
set palette 9 0xB40000FF;
set palette 10 0xB400FF00;
set palette 11 0xB400FFFF;
set palette 12 0xB4FF0000;
set palette 13 0xB4FF00FF;
set palette 14 0xB4FFFF00;
set palette 15 0xB4000000;
```

Figure 4-76: extract from ***defaultcolors.scr*** script file

Script Files created by ULPs
Many User Language programs (ULP) create script files that can be read in order to modify a layout or a schematic.

EAGLE may output an entire library, for instance, as a script file with the aid of the EXPORT command (*Script* option). This file can be modified with a text editor, after which it can be read in again. This allows changes to be made to a library quite easily.

A comment line in a script file commences with the '#'character.

The execution of a script file can be stopped by **Left-Clicking** the Stop icon in the action toolbar.

Script Files and Data Import
The SCRIPT command makes a universal tool available to the EAGLE user for data import.

Since every EAGLE operation can be carried out with the aid of text commands, all types of data can be imported with the aid of a script file. A script file can, in turn, call other script files.

Continued Lines
SCRIPT files contain one or more commands in every line according to the syntax rules. The use of the '\' character at the end of a command line, ensures that the first word of the next line is not interpreted as a command.

Set Default Parameters
The SCRIPT file eagle.scr (if it exists in the project directory or in the script path) is executed each time a new drawing is loaded into an editor window (or when the drawing type is changed in a library).

Script Labels
The default SCRIPT file eagle.scr makes use of labels of the form
`BRD:`

This is illustrated in the script file shown in Figure 4-77, where BRD is one of SCH, BRD, LBR, DEV, PAC and SYM. This ensures that only the appropriate section is executed in the editor. The label must be at the beginning of the line.

For example, when a new board is opened, only the section starting with '`BRD:`' is executed (until the next label, if any).

```
# This file can be used to configure the editor windows.
Assign A+F3 'Window 4;';
Assign A+F4 'Window 0.25;';
Assign A+F7 'Grid mm;';
Assign A+F8 'Grid inch;';
Menu '[designlink22.png] Search and order {\
General : Run designlink—order.ulp —general; |\
Schematic : Run designlink—order.ulp; \
}';
BRD:
#Menu Add Change Copy Delete Display Grid Group Move \
#Name Quit Rect Route Script Show Signal Split \
#Text Value Via Window ';' Wire Write Edit;
Grid inch 0.05 on;
Grid alt inch 0.01;
Set Pad_names on;
Set Width_menu 0.008 0.01 0.016;
Set Drill_menu 0.024 0.032 0.040;
Set Size_menu 0.05 0.07 0.12;
Set Used_layers 1 16 17 18 19 20 21 22 23 24 25 26 \
27 28 39 40 41 42 43 44 45;
SCH:
Grid Default;
Change Width 0.006;
#Menu Add Bus Change Copy Delete Display Gateswap \
#Grid Group Invoke Junction Label Move Name Net \
#Pinswap Quit Script Show Split Value Window ';' \
#Wire Write Edit;
LBR:
#Menu Close Export Open Script Write ';' Edit;
DEV:
Grid Default;
#Menu Add Change Copy Connect Delete Display Export \
#Grid Move Name Package Prefix Quit Script Show \
#Value Window ';' Write Edit;
SYM:
Display all;
Grid Default On;
Change Width 0.010;
#Menu Arc Change Copy Delete Display Export \
#Grid Group Move Name Paste Pin Quit Script \
#Show Split Text Value Window ';' Wire Write Edit;
PAC:
Grid Default On;
Grid Alt inch 0.005;
Change Width 0.005;
Change Size 0.050;
Change Smd 0.039 0.039;
#Menu Add Change Copy Delete Display Grid Group \
#Move Name Pad Quit Script Show Smd Split Text \
#Window ';' Wire Write Edit;
```

Figure 4-77: an eagle.scr script file

This script file functionality also offers the user the ability to construct editor-specific menus by using the MENU command.

Note: For detailed information on The EAGLE User Language, the user should refer to the Appendix at the end of this book titled; 'EAGLE User Language Reference Manual'.

SHOW

Function
Highlights an object in a drawing.

Syntax
```
SHOW ..
SHOW name..
SHOW @ name..
```

Mouse keys
Ctrl+Left-Click toggles the show state of the selected object.

See also INFO

The SHOW command is used to highlight objects. Details are listed in the status bar. Complete signals and nets can be highlighted with the SHOW command. If a bus is selected, all nets belonging to that bus will also be highlighted.

Multiple Objects
If the user selects different objects with the SHOW command, every single object is highlighted separately. More than one object may be highlighted by **Ctrl+Left-Click** when selecting the objects. Ctrl+Left-Clicking on an object that is already highlighted will be de-selected (and not highlighted).

If the command line form is used, and several names are entered in one line, all matching objects are highlighted at the same time.

Small Objects
If the `@` character is given in the command line, a pointer rectangle is drawn around the shown object (as shown in Figure 4-78). This is helpful in locating small objects that do not display well just through highlighting. If more than one object is shown, the rectangle is drawn around all the objects. It may be necessary to zoom out (or do a WINDOW FIT command) in order to see the pointer. If an object with the literal name `@` shall be shown, the name must be enclosed in single quotes.

Cross Probing
With active Forward&BackAnnotation set, an object that is highlighted with the SHOW command in a board, will also be highlighted in the schematic; and vice versa.

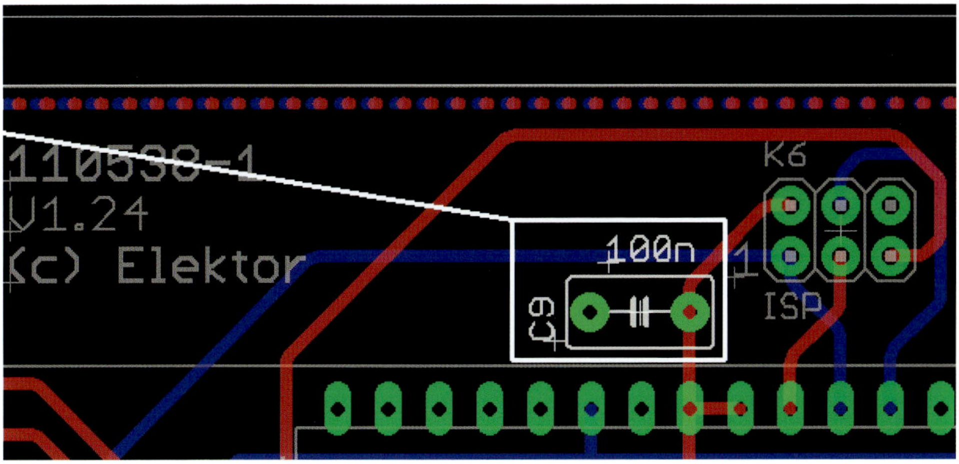

Figure 4-78: the SHOW command highlights a specific device

UNDO

Function
Cancels or reverses previous commands.

Syntax
```
UNDO
UNDO LIST
```

Keyboard
`F9: UNDO` execute the UNDO command.
`Alt+BS: UNDO`

See also REDO, SET, Forward&BackAnnotation

The UNDO command allows the user to cancel or reverse the effect of previously executed commands. This is especially useful if the user has accidently deleted objects. Multiple UNDO commands cancel the corresponding number of commands until the last EDIT, OPEN or REMOVE command is reached.

The UNDO command uses up memory space. If the user's system is short of memory, this function may be switched off with the SET command, as in:

```
SET UNDO_LOG OFF;
```

UNDO/REDO is completely integrated within Forward&Back Annotation.

UNDO buffer dialog
The user may use the option `LIST` in the UNDO command opens a dialog that contains the entire contents of the undo buffer. This is shown in Figure 4-79.

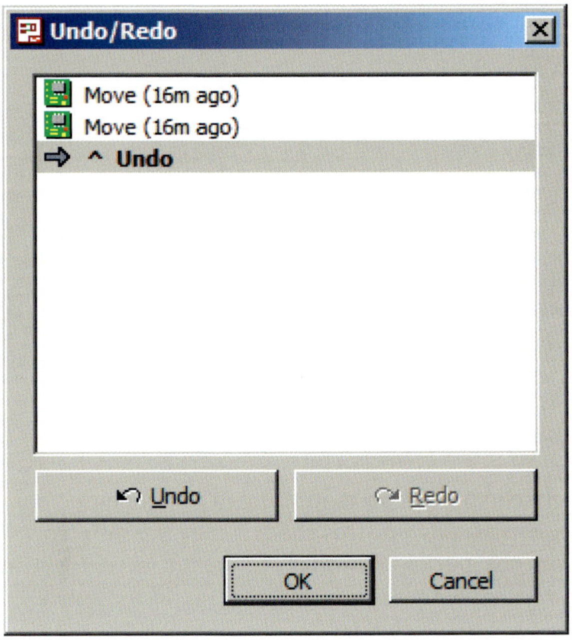

Figure 4-79: the UNDO/REDO dialog

Alternatively, it is possible to access the Undo/Redo list from the menu using *Edit ▷ Undo/Redo list...*, again opening the dialog.

This dialog allows the user the option of restoring changes to anywhere in the list by navigating through the list of undo/redo steps (by Click&Dragging the list delimiter), or by directly clicking on any given step in the revision history. If there are several steps between the current delimiter position and the clicked list item, all steps in between will be executed in the proper sequence. Moving upward in the list means performing UNDO, moving downward results in REDO.

The icon at each list item indicates in which drawing this particular command has been executed.

If the user confirms this dialog with "OK", the drawing will be left in the condition as selected in the list. If the user cancels the dialog, it will be restored to the state it had before the dialog was opened.

NOTE: By executing UNDO towards the beginning of the list, and subsequently executing any new command, the user would truncate the UNDO buffer, losing all prior changes. ***This cannot be reversed.***

UPDATE

Function
Updates library objects.

Syntax
```
UPDATE UPDATE;
UPDATE library_name..;
UPDATE package_name@library_name..;
UPDATE +@ | -@ [library_name..];
UPDATE old_library_name = new_library_name;
```

See also ADD, REPLACE

The UPDATE command checks the parts in a board or schematic against their respective library objects, and automatically updates them if they are different. If UPDATE is invoked from the library editor, the packages within the loaded library will be updated from the given libraries.

If the UPDATE command is activated without a parameter, a file dialog will be presented to select the library from which to update.

If one or more libraries are given, only parts from those libraries will be checked. The library names can be either a plain library name (like 'ttl' or 'ttl.lbr') or a full file name (like '/home/mydir/myproject/ttl.lbr' or '../lbr/ttl').

If a library_name contains blanks, it needs to be enclosed in single quotes.

Updating a board or schematic
If the command is terminated with a ';', but has no parameters, all parts will be checked.

If the first parameter is '+@', the names of the given libraries (or all libraries if none are given) will have a '@' character appended, followed by a number. This can be used to make sure the libraries contained in a drawing will not be modified when a part from a newer library with the same name is added to the drawing. Library names that already end with a '@' character, followed by a number, will not be changed.

If the first parameter is '-@', the '@' character (followed by a number) of the given libraries (or all libraries if none are given) will be stripped from the library name. This only works if there is no library with that new name already in the drawing.

Note: 'UPDATE +@;' followed by 'UPDATE -@;' (and vice versa) does not necessarily result in the original set of library names, because the sequence in which the names are processed, depends upon the sequence in which the libraries are stored in the drawing file.

The libraries stored in a board or schematic drawing are identified only by their base name (e.g. 'ttl'). When considering whether an update shall be performed, only the base name of the library file name will be taken into account. Libraries will be searched in the directories specified under "Libraries" in the directories dialog, from left to right. The first library of a given name that is found will be taken.

Note: the library names stored in a drawing are case insensitive. It is irrelevant whether a specific library is currently "in use". If a library is not found, no update will be performed for that library and EAGLE will not issue an error message.

Using the UPDATE command in a schematic or board that is connected via active *Forward&BackAnnotation* will act on both the schematic and the board.

When used with the format; `old_library_name = new_library_name` (at least one blank must precede and follow the '=' character), the UPDATE command locates the library named `old_library_name` in the current board or schematic, and updates it with the contents of `new_library_name`.

Note: `old_library_name` must be the pure library name, without any path, while `new_library_name` may be a full path name. If the update was performed successfully, the library in the current board/schematic file will also be renamed accordingly. This whole operation is only possible if `new_library_name` has not yet been used in the current board or schematic.

Note: A DesignRuleCheck (DRC) and an ElectricalRule Check (ERC) should always be run after a library update has been performed in a board or a schematic.

Updating a library

Using the UPDATE command in a library replaces all packages within that library with the versions from the given libraries.

By specifying the package name format (i.e. `package_name@library_name`) the user may specify that only a particular package be replaced.

Chapter 5 • Using EAGLE's Library Manager & Editor

The EAGLE application is supplied with a large number of library files containing components ranging from small surface mount devices through to large board mounted hardware (like connectors and sockets). This can be seen simply by expanding the tree view of the 'Libraries' entry of the EAGLE Control Panel.

As the user develops a circuit and realizes this design in the schematic and PCB layout respectively, components are accessed from the appropriate libraries and inserted into the (schematic or layout) drawing. The target drawing file will then contain all necessary information about those included components. This precludes the need to distribute libraries when sending the drawings to reviewers or to a PCB fabricator.

EAGLE provides a powerful editor for creating and manipulating components and their constructs (i.e. Package, Symbol and Device).

Library and Component Management

EAGLE's Library Editor enables the user to manage libraries, parts and components in order to tailor the application to most needs, or conversely, to create a specific library for a particular project environment.

A library contains the basic elements of an electronic/electrical component, which comprise the following:

- **Package:** the footprint of the component when used in the layout drawing
- **Symbol**: the representation of the functional description of the component which is used in the schematic drawing
- **Device** the real component, consisting of a combination of symbols and packages

The Library Editor allows the user to create, copy, edit and delete any library elements within any library.
For example, elements may be created from nothing, or they may be copied from an existing combination of elements to create a wholly new component. Therefore all elements may be freely manipulated with the Library Editor.

This can be done from the Library Editor window by **Left-Clicking**  (on the left-hand side of the window), which will open the component Edit window (as shown in Figure 5-1). It is from here that Packages, Symbols and Devices may be edited and created.

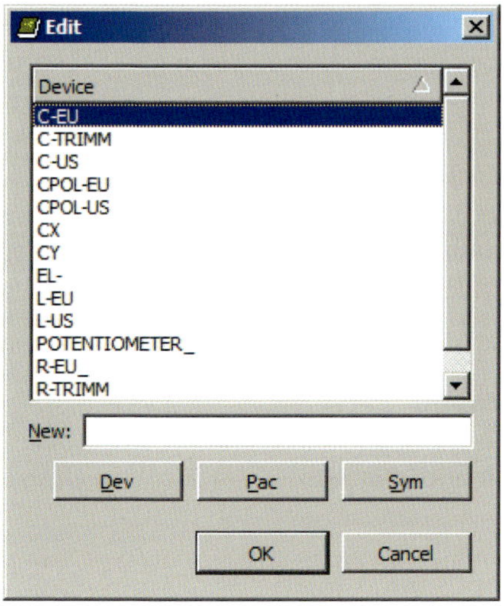

Figure 5-1: the component Edit window

Overview of Defining a Complex Device or Component

Using a combination of EAGLE's functionality; the Library Manager and the Package and Symbol Editors, it is possible to construct complex components for use in PCB design.

Initially we will outline here, a summary of the steps required to create a new component for inclusion into a library:

Creating a new or use an existing library

The user may choose to

i. create a new library using File ▷ New ▷ Library from the menu toolbar in the EAGLE Control Panel.

or

ii. expand an existing library using File ▷ Open ▷ Library from the menu toolbar in the EAGLE Control Panel (or alternatively use the context menu within the Control Panel's tree view).

Creating the housing or packaging

The next step is to create the package or housing for the new component. This may be copied into the open library, from another library, using EAGLE's COPY command or by Drag&Drop from the Control Panel.

However, if the package does not exist, the user might need to create their own package library element. In general there exists two major types of packages: pinleaded and SMD (surface mount devices). Of course as advances are made in the component packaging industry, other types of packaging technologies will emerge.

The overall process of creating a package is similar to both types of connection. In general, the basic stages for package construction are:

Edit package
Open the package Editor and create a new package within the dialog, naming it accordingly.

Set the grid parameters
Set the appropriate grid parameters for the package. These are determined by the type of package (e.g. 0.1 inch for DIL packages). It is advised to set an alternative grid in another linear measure (e.g. inches with alternative millimeters).

Place the Pins/SMD Pads
Using the Pad or Pin command place the pins/pads according to the specifications in the package datasheet. Select the appropriate parameters/options for each contact type (i.e. diameter, shape, orientation etc. for Pads; x_width, y_width, roundness etc. for SMD pads).

Name the Pins/Pads
EAGLE normally automatically names Pins/Pads as they are placed. This can be turned on or off and can be set by Options ▷ Set ▷ Misc menu and choosing the *Display pad names* option.

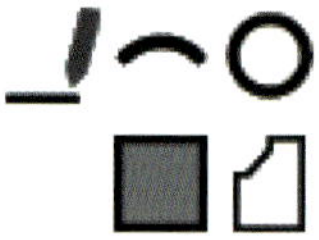

Draw the Silk Screen

The silk screen is important insofar as it is the visible indicator to the PCB fabricator and user of the board, as to package placements on the board. Care should be taken to avoid screening over potential solder areas.
The silk screen is normally created in the print layer21, *tPlace* ; although other silk screening may be placed in layer 51, *tdcou* for additional documentation purposes.

T

Specify the Package Name and Value

The user may label the package using the TEXT command to write '>NAME' on the package drawing, in layer 25, *tNames*. This is a reserved text variable for EAGLE.

Similarly, the user should enter '>VALUE' in layer 27, *tValues* as the variable placeholder for the Device value.

Text for Names and Values should use vector fonts so that the finished board reflects the Layout Editor drawing.

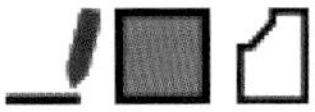

Specify forbidden areas

The user should, if required, Draw restricted areas in layers 41, *tRestrict*, 42, *bRestrict*, or 43, *vRestrict*; or in layers 39, *tKeepout*, or 40, *bKeepout*. This is done by using the RECT or POLYGON commands to cover the complete component, or by drawing a frame around the Package with the WIRE command. This process sets up the drawing for DRC to check that components are correctly spaced, and for the Autorouter to function appropriately.

Locate the package origin

The coordinate origin of the Package should be close to the geometric middle of the drawing. If required, the package may be re-aligned by using the combination of GROUP and MOVE commands, first ensuring that all layers of the drawing are visible (using DISPLAY ALL).

Edit the description

The user may edit the Package description (**Left-Click** on *Description* in the description box). A dialog window opens allowing the description text to be entered in plain or HTML format. EAGLE works with a subset of HTML tags that allow the text to be formatted. This text is accessed by the Layout Editor's ADD dialog search facility.

Creating the logic symbol

The user may copy a Symbol element from one library to another using *Drag&Drop* or by using the COPY command (but not from the Control Panel directory tree).
Similar to the process of creating a Package, the user is also able to create a Symbol from first principles. The steps are as follows:

Edit the Symbol

Open the Symbol Editor and create a new package from within the dialog naming it accordingly.

Set the grid parameters

Set the grid parameters for the Symbol to 0.1 inch. This will ensure that Pins and Nets are coincident on the same grid and that EAGLE can establish electrical connection between them in the schematic drawing.

Place the Pins

Select the PIN command; specify the pin properties (using the parameter toolbar) and then place the pins. Center the overall Symbol diagram around the coordinate origin (avoid placing the origin directly under a pin connection point).

Name the Pins/Pads

Using the NAME Command name the Pins as desired.

Draw the Symbol

Use the WIRE, ARC and CIRCLE commands to draw the Symbol in layer 94, *Symbols*. The standard line thickness for the Symbol Editor is 10 mil, although any other line thickness may be selected.

Specify the Symbol Name and Value

Using the TEXT command, the user should add the text variables;
>NAME
in layer 95, *Names,* and
>VALUE
in layer 96, *Values* in appropriate positions in the Symbol diagram. These can be re-located later using the SMASH command.

Edit the Symbol description

The user may edit the Symbol description (Left-Click on *Description* in the description box). A dialog window opens allowing the description text to be entered in plain or HTML format.

Create the power supply symbol

All multi-gate devices require a power supply symbol. This is essentially the same process as that given above to create a symbol.

The particular parameters for a power supply symbol are:

i. placing pins – both pins should have a *Direction* of PWR (and of course are placed in layer 93, *Pins*);
ii. the pins should be named according to the signal they will carry e.g. GND or VCC.
iii. The pin property *Visible* should be set to *Pad* to ensure the Name is visible when placed in the layout drawing.
i. the power supply Symbol does not require a *Value* text variable

Associating the Packages and Symbols to form a Device set

This stage involves combining Packages and Symbols into an associated set, so that it reflects the finished component to be utilized in schematic and layout drawings.
So, defining a Device set comprises the following steps:

Open a new Device
Commence by selecting the edit Device icon. Enter the name of the new Device and accept it. This opens the Device Editor window.

Add Symbols to the Device
In this step the user fetches the required logic and power supply symbols from the currently in-use libraries.

Name the Gates
Gates are those Symbols that are used within a device. EAGLE, by default, generates names for these gates, but may be reassigned by the user.

Specify the Addlevel and Swaplevel
The Addlevel and Swaplevel parameters are used when placing the symbol into a schematic drawing. The former parameter determines how EAGLE labels a Device's gates as they are fetched and the latter parameter controls how a Device's gates may be swapped within the schematic.

Choose the Package Variants

In the Device Editor window (**Left-Click** on New in the lower right-hand corner). Select the Package required for this Device and confirm.

A list of Package variants will be displayed. Confirming from the list will allow for Technologies to be defined and the CONNECT command to be called (as well as other options).

Assign the Pins/Pads

Calling the CONNECT command (**Left-Click** on Connect) opens the CONNECT dialog, which defines the interconnection between Pins and Pads; and the way in which nets in the schematic drawing are converted to signal lines in the PCB layout.

Define Technologies

Technologies are also defined at this stage by selecting from the context menu activated from the Package listing. In order to add different technologies, the Device name should include a '*' character as a placeholder for the Device name. A technology variant is chosen from the 'Technologies' listing in the Description box (lower pane of the Device Editor window).

State the Device prefix and value

The prefix of the Device is named by **Left-Clicking** on Prefix. The text is entered in the variable field.

The setting of 'Value' (radio buttons at the bottom of the Device Editor window) determines whether the VALUE command can be used to alter the value of the Device in the schematic diagram and in the layout.

Describe the Device

Enter a description of the new Device to assist the user when utilizing this component in a new design.

In the latter part of this chapter we will use a set of examples to illustrate how Devices or Components may be created.

Creating a New Library

A new library may be created by using the File ▷ New ▷ Library menu selection from the Control Panel main menu. Upon execution this process opens a new library window, as shown in Figure 5-2.

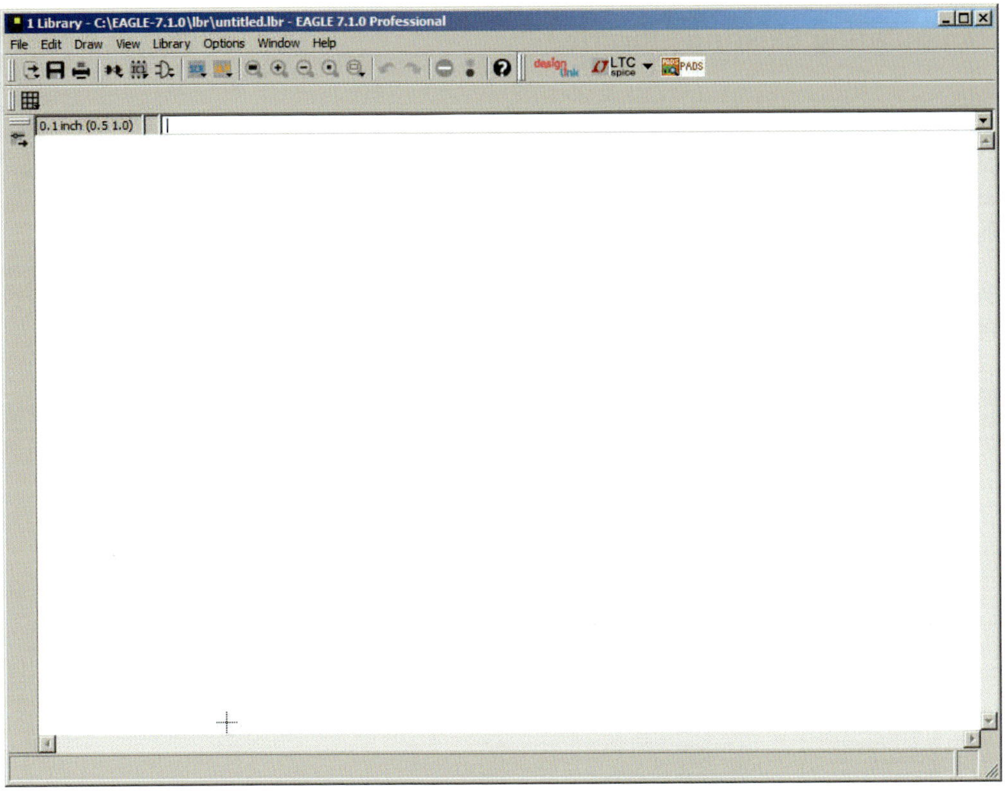

Figure 5-2: new Library window

It is from this window that the library will be managed.
An alternative method of opening a new (or existing) library is to use the OPEN command from within a drawing. For example, to create a new library, the command:

```
OPEN my_new_library
```

would open a new library window named '`my_new_library.lbr`'.

To save this new library the user simply uses any of; the WRITE command, File ▷ Save, Ctrl-S or **Left-Click** .

Manipulating Existing Libraries

Libraries that already exist in the EAGLE portfolio may be manipulated directly from the Control Panel by using a context menu. The user simply selects the library to be manipulated (by **Left-click**) and then executes a **Right-Click** to bring up the context menu. This is illustrated in Figure 5-3.

From here the user may Open, Rename, Copy, Delete or Use the selected library, by selecting the option within this context menu.

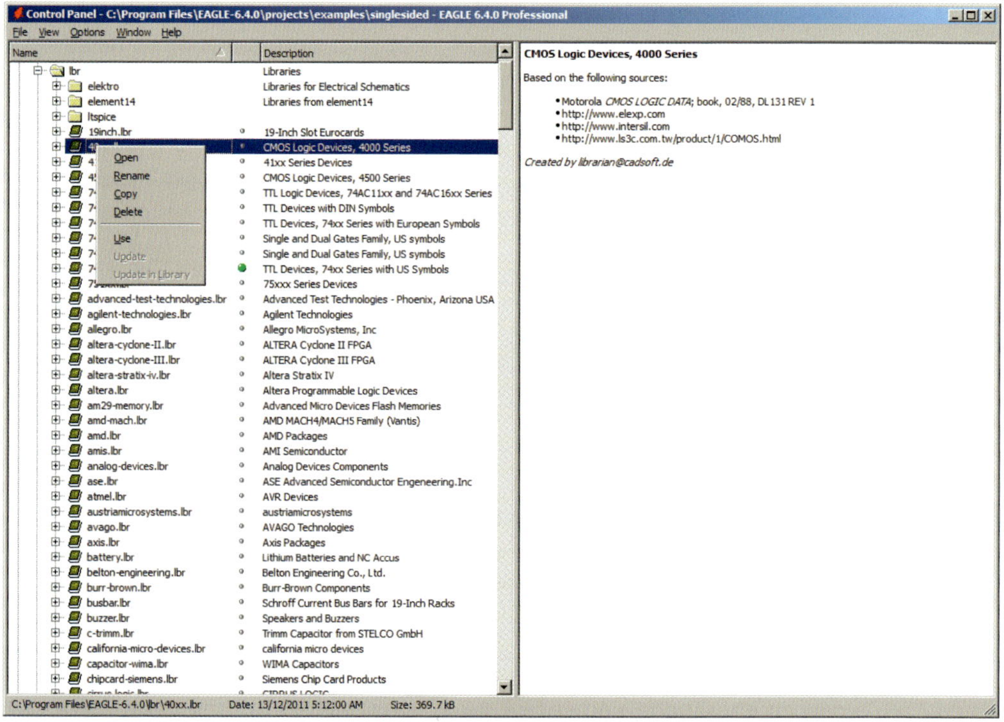

Figure 5-3: Library context menu

Manipulating Library Elements

The Library Editor allows the user to manipulate elements within a single library or between different libraries. Elements may be copied between, and removed from, libraries as the user chooses.

Copying Library Elements within a Library

It is possible to copy a Symbol or Package (but not Devices), in a library to another new definition within the same library. This can be done using the GROUP, COPY, and PASTE commands. After the copy has been completed the element may be edited as required.

Example

The following outlines the procedure to copy an element within the library 'rcl.lbr':

Open the Library

To open the library within which the Element is to be copied, use the menu File ▷ Open ▷ Library in the Control Panel to open the library rcl.lbr, or select the entry Open from its context menu of the tree view, as shown in Figure 5-3.

The reader should note that upon selecting a library in the left-hand pane of the Control Panel, a comprehensive description of the library is given in the right hand pane.

Copy the existing Element

In this example we will copy the 'R-US' symbol within the library. The steps are:

i. Open the symbol using Library ▷ Symbol or use the edit-symbol icon ; and then select 'R-US' from the list (as in Figure 5-4).

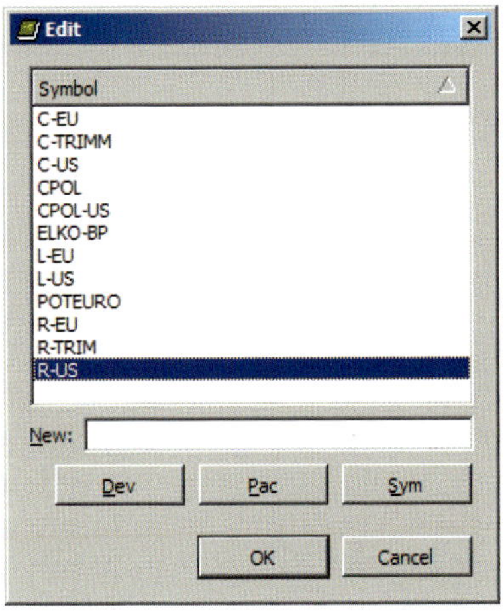

Figure 5-4: the Symbol edit window

After selection, the result will be shown in the library editor window, as in Figure 5-5.

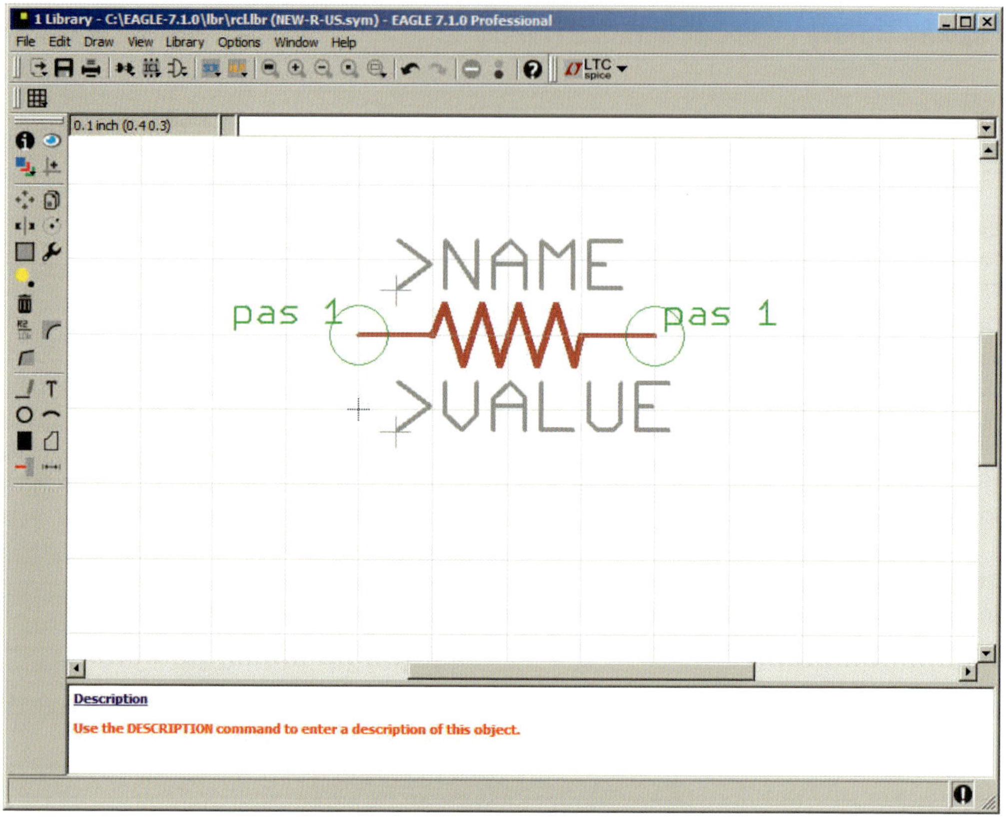

Figure 5-5: the Symbol in the Library Editor window

ii. Ensure all layers are displayed by using the '`DISPLAY ALL;`' command or by using the Layers icon and selecting '`All`'.

iii select all objects by using the `GROUP ALL;` command

iv. copy the Symbol using either the COPY command or by **Left-Clicking** on .

Create New Element

The copied symbol may now be transferred into a newly created one within the library, as follows:

i. Create the new symbol by using Library ▷ Symbol or use the edit-symbol icon ;

ii. enter the name '`NEW-R-US`' in the '`New:`' field of the Symbol edit window (as in Figure 5-4). Then **Left-Click** on `OK`.

iii. paste the copied Symbol data into this new window by: **Left-Click** on  and then by **Left-Clicking** at the new Symbol's reference point; or by using the PASTE command.

The newly created Symbol may now be edited normally.

Note:

- Devices can not be copied within a library.
- Defining a new library element can not be cancelled by UNDO.

Copying Library Elements between Libraries

Copying Devices and Packages

Using the Library Editor it is possible to copy elements from one library to another. Devices and Packages may be copied directly from the Control Panel directory tree, but Symbols can not.

Two methods exist by which the user may copy an element from one library to another; these are: via the Control Panel (using *Drag&Drop*) or by using the COPY command.

Copying via the Control Panel

To effectively use the *Drag&Drop* method for copying, the user must have the Control Panel (with the Libraries file tree expanded) and the Library Editor windows open together.

Example

Figure 5-6 shows this configuration where the Control Panel has the `40xx.lbr` library expanded and the editor window for a new library (`untitled.lbr`) open.

To copy, say, the 4001 Quad 2-input NOR device to the new library, the user should do the following:

i. select and **Left-Click** on the `4001` device.

ii. *Drag&Drop* by holding the left mouse button while moving the mouse so that the icon is positioned in the new Library Editor window

iii. place the copied device by releasing the left mouse button.

Alternatively, the user may simply use the context menu (**Right-Click** on the Device in the library tree) and choose the '`Copy to Library`' option.

In either case, the device will appear in the new library's edit window, as shown in Figure 5-7. The device, complete, with all associated Symbols and Packages, will be copied to the library.

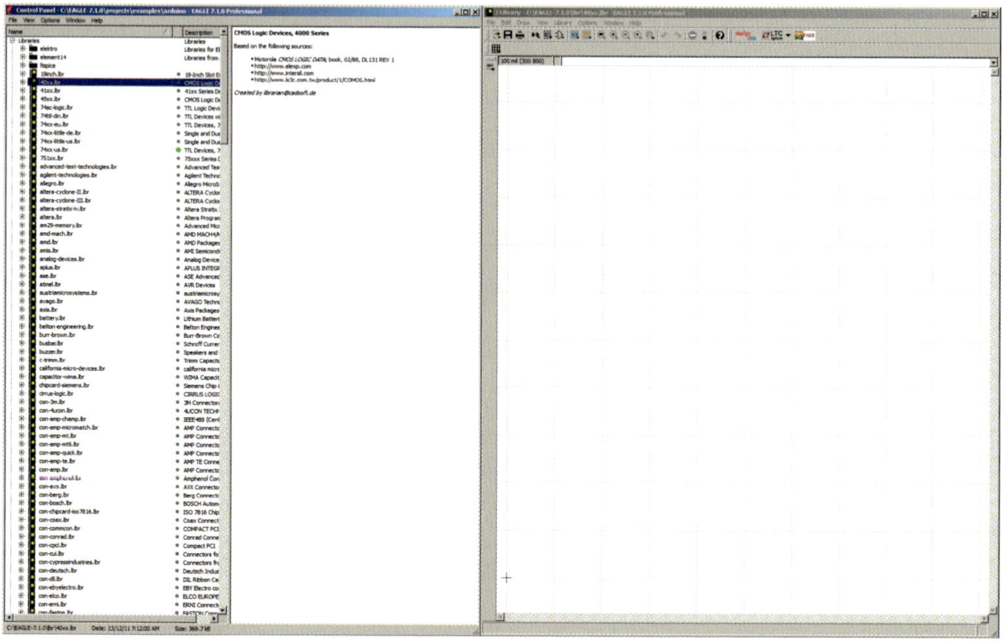

Figure 5-6: Simultaneous Control Panel and Library Editor windows open

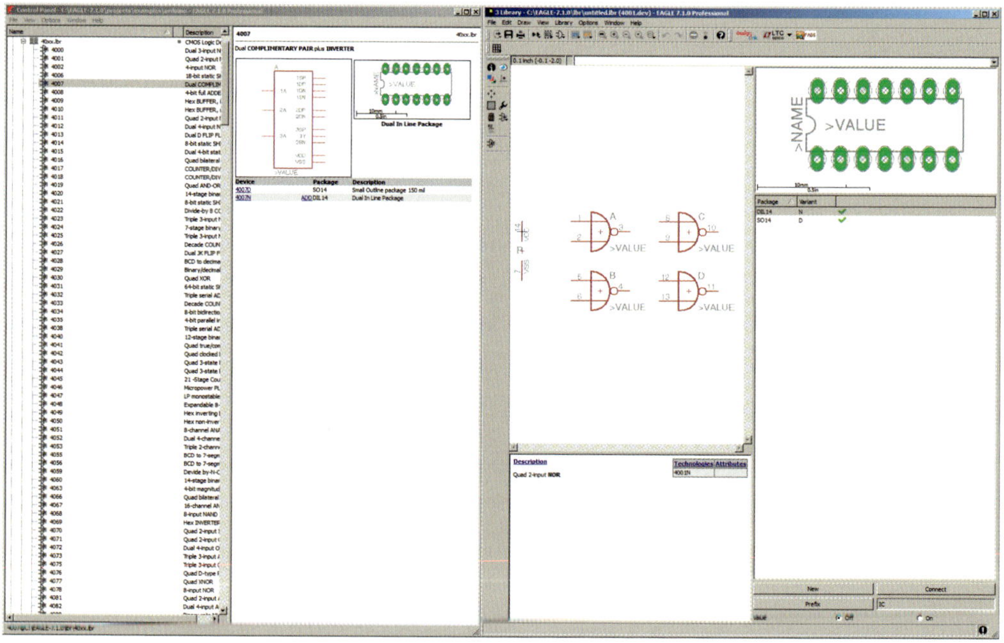

Figure 5-7: 4001 device copied to new Library Editor window

Copying using the COPY command
From within the current (new) library, and using the COPY command syntax:

```
COPY deviceset@library [name]
COPY package@library [name]
```

it is possible to copy a device or a package from another EAGLE library.

Example
The following command:

```
COPY 4001@40xx.lbr new-4001
```

would copy the device (4001 Quad 2-input NOR) from the `40xx.lbr` library into the currently open library, renaming it '`new-4001`'.
The whole path may be specified for the source library, as in:

```
COPY 4001@d:\eagle\lbr\40xx.lbr new-4001
```

Copying Packages is almost identical to the process for copying Devices. However, there exist some differences in the method. These are:

i. If the Package is already in use in a Device, and the position or the name of one or more pads/SMDs changes, EAGLE prompts the user with a message requesting the mode in which pads/SMDs are to be replaced.

ii. If the numbering and position of the pads are unchanged but the order is changed in the new package, EAGLE will request the user to select the appropriate update mode. Depending on the selection the pin/pad connections of the Device may change (see the CONNECT command).

Copying Symbols
Symbols are not displayed in the tree view of the Control Panel, so it is not possible to copy them from this source into the Library Editor.

Therefore, Symbols can only be copied from one library into another using the same method as for copying within the same library. Hence, the user should utilize the GROUP, COPY, and PASTE commands employing the technique described in the previous section.

The only difference in the procedure for copying a Symbol within a library is that the user must open the target library (File/Open) after executing the COPY command. The user may then define a new Symbol that may have the same (or another name) as before.

In summary:

i. OPEN the source library and EDIT the Symbol using Library ▷ Symbol (or use edit-symbol  icon).

ii. DISPLAY all layers

iii. Select all objects with GROUP ALL;

iv **Left-Click** onto  (COPY)

v . OPEN the target library with File ▷ Open from the Control Panel menu

vi. EDIT  a new Symbol in the target library

vii. Use the PASTE  command to place the copied Symbol into the new Symbol

viii Save the library with File ▷ Save 

Deleting and Renaming Library Elements

Deleting Elements

All elements (Devices, Symbols and Packages) can be deleted from a library using the REMOVE command e.g. REMOVE IR-2

Packages and Symbols can be removed only if they are not already in use in one of the library's Devices. If this is the case the message *Package is in use!* or *Symbol is in use!* Is displayed as in Figure 5-8.

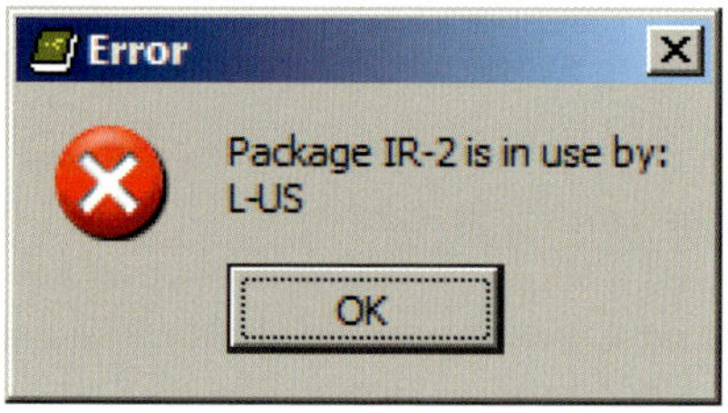

Figure 5-8: Error display for an attempted removal of in-use Package

To overcome this state, the user must first REMOVE the corresponding Device or, alternatively, delete the particular Package or Symbol in the Device (set).

Example:
The user wishes to remove the Package named DIL16. The procedure is as follows:
Open the menu using Library ▷ Remove or use the command:

```
REMOVE DIL16;
```

In either case a dialog window opens (see Figure 5-9) where the user enters the name of the element to be deleted.

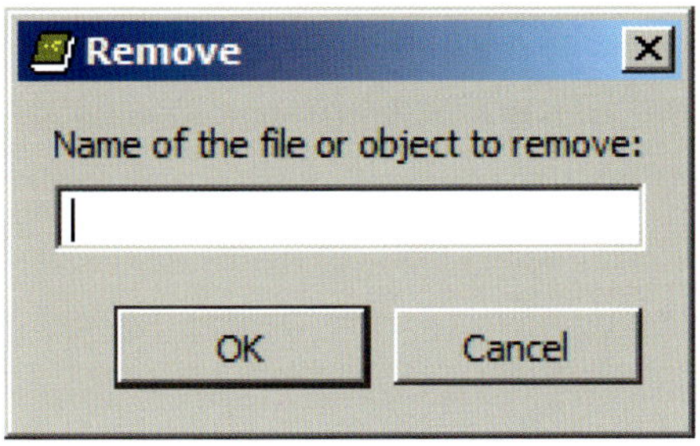

Figure 5-9: element removal dialog

Renaming Elements

All elements (Devices, Symbols and Packages) can be renamed within a library using the RENAME command.

Example:
To rename the Package `DIL08` to '`DIL-08`'the steps are as follows:

i. `OPEN` the source library and EDIT the Package using Library ▷ Package

   (or use edit-package 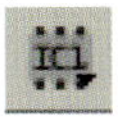 icon)

ii. In the open dialog window, select the DIL08 entry and **Left-Click** OK

ii. Use the Library ▷ Rename ...menu option or the command:

```
RENAME DIL08
```

   In either case, a dialog window will open (see Figure 5-10) to allow the user to enter the new Package name.

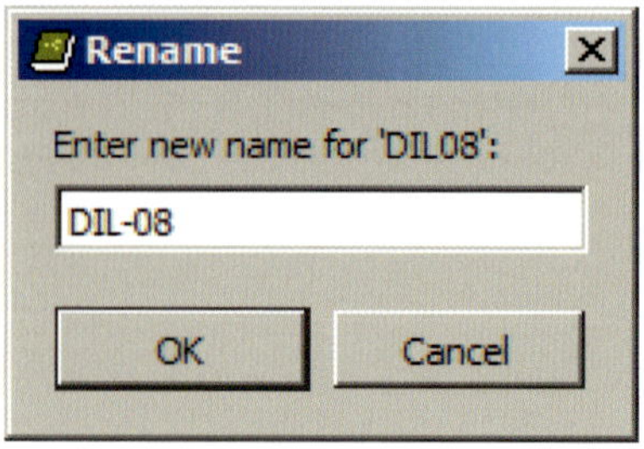

Figure 5-10: rename element dialog

A shorthand method of performing the same function may be achieved with the command:

```
RENAME DIL08 DIL-08;
```

An efficient method of renaming any element (Device, Symbol, or Package) is to use the command format

```
RENAME old_name new_name;
```

where

```
old_name = text [.dev]|[.pac]|[.sym].
```

The above could therefore be executed with the command:

```
RENAME DIL08.PAC DIL-08;
```

without having to perform steps i and ii above (i.e. switching to the element's edit mode prior to using the command).

Updating Packages in Libraries

Individual Libraries contain Packages that are integral to a Device definition. These Packages may be identical, and may also exist in many libraries. In order to keep these Package specifications uniform over all libraries, the user is able to replace all Packages within a library with those from another library, by using the UPDATE command.

Example:
A set of uniquely defined Packages (say, for special applications or requirements) may be incorporated in a custom-built package or library. These could be transferred to other libraries using the UPDATE command.

The procedure is:

i. `OPEN` the target library to be updated with File ▷ Open ▷ Library or from the context menu of the tree view of the Control Panel

ii. Use the menu action Library ▷ Update to select the source library from which to transfer Packages.

iii. When complete, EAGLE reports the update in the status bar with the messages:

Update: finished library modified!

or

`Update: finished  nothing to do` (i.e. if there was nothing to replace).

The UPDATE command may be used for this procedure, as in:

```
UPDATE ref-packages.lbr
```

updates the open library with Packages from the library '`refpackages.lbr`'.

```
UPDATE ref-packages.lbr rcl.lbr SMD-special.lbr
```

transfers Packages from the different libraries '`ref-packages.lbr`',' `rcl.lbr`', and '`SMD-special.lbr`'.

```
UPDATE SO14@ref-packages
```

Updates a single Package, '`SO14`'from the source library '`ref-packages.lbr`'

Note: The extension `.lbr` is not requied.

Creating New Components – A Tutorial

There is an ever-increasing need for EAGLE library components as manufacturers produce their own new products. This demand is frequently not met, since providing such libraries is often an afterthought for the manufacturer's technical support department. Accordingly, the EAGLE user is left with no choice but to create his/her own components and library elements.

As mentioned in the introduction to this chapter, a component is made up of a series of Symbols and Packages. When configured in a Device these become actual components.

This chapter will guide the user through the steps required to create new components using a series of examples. (It is assumed that the reader has a working knowledge of EAGLE and the use of EAGLE commands or icons-as-commands. Guidelines in this chapter are not 'click-by-click' instructions.) Following will be 3 ***fictitious*** components requiring creation of a new symbol or package and are:

the Quirkistor	a new device in a simple 2 pins and rectangular housing. It is a bi-directional unit with passive functionality, requiring no power supply.
the Kunda-buffer	another new device. It is an analogue series buffer with one input and 4 in-line outputs and comes in 2 standard packages: SOIC8 and DIL8
the Gizzy-gate	this well-known digital logic element is configured with 2-input, 1-output per gate. The configuration is octal and is unusually packaged in an SMD package with 32 pins.

Creating the New Library

For these examples a new library should be created. The simplest way to perform this is to: from the Control Panel main menu, the user would action File ▷ New ▷ Library and then save the library with the name, for example, '`new_test_library`'

This will create a new library named '`new_test_library.lbr`'. It is in this library that the following example components will be created.

Creating the 'Quirkistor' Component

The 'Quirkistor' is an analogue component with bidirectional functionality and is housed in the same package as a conventional resistor. The basis for this component can be derived from the VARISTOR symbol and a standard resistor packaging.

The first step is to define the package for this device. It is a power device and will be housed in an axial-leaded package. This example will use the pre-existing specification, `'CA0001', from the library 'resistor-power.lbr'`.

Step 1 - Copy the package to the new library
As described previously, the user may copy the package to the new library, or use the following method:

i. If not still open, open the library '`new_test_library.lbr`' (this is the target library)

ii. From the command line in the new library, copy the required Package using the command:

```
COPY CA0001@resistor-power.lbr
```

This will copy/insert the Package specifications into the new library, the new window appearing as in Figure 5-11.

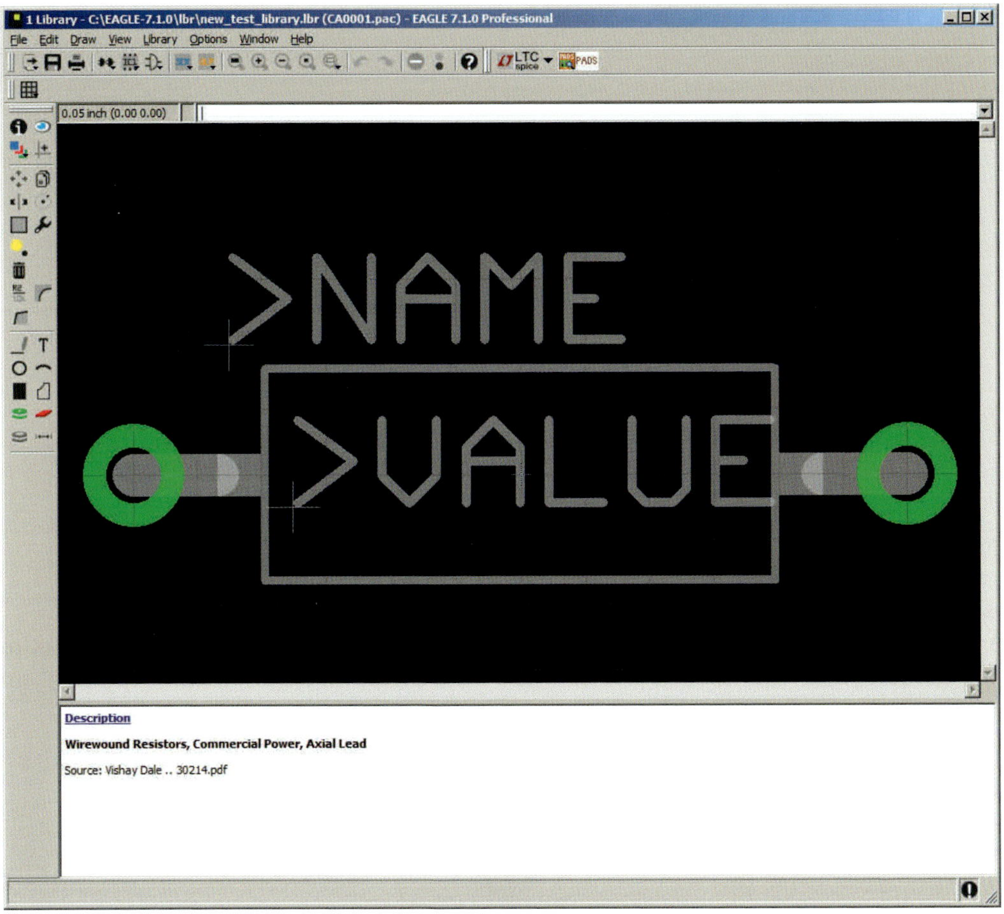

Figure 5-11: copied resistor package

iii. The description in the lower pane of this window is that of the copied resistor package. This description can be modified by **Left-**Clicking on Description and editing the description data as shown in Figure 5-12.

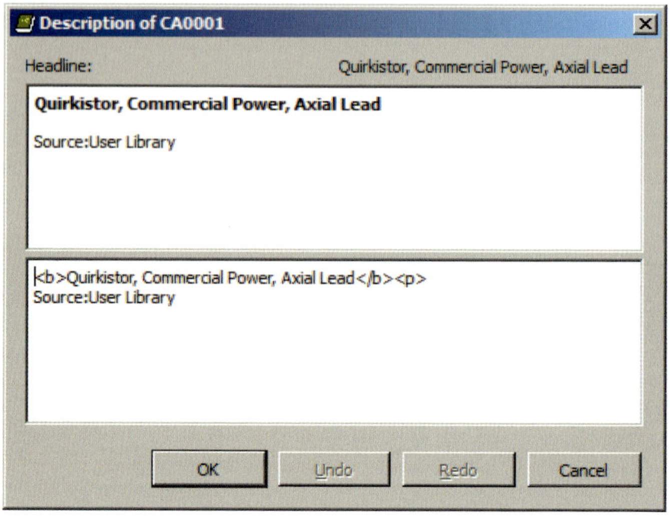

Figure 512: editing the package description

iv. save the new library by using File ▷ Save, Ctrl-S or **Left-Click** .

Step 2 – Create a new Symbol from a copied Symbol

In this step the user will copy a Symbol from an existing library and edit that symbol to transform it into a 'Quirkistor' Symbol. This is done by copying the Symbol 'VARISTOR' from the library 'varistor.lbr' to our new library.

The steps are:

i. OPEN the source library ('varistor.lbr') and EDIT the Symbol ('VARISTOR') using Library ▷ Symbol (or use edit-symbol  icon)

ii. execute the command DISPLAY ALL; to display all layers

iii. select all of the objects with the command GROUP ALL

At this point the symbol edit window in the varistor.lbr library should look like Figure 5-13.

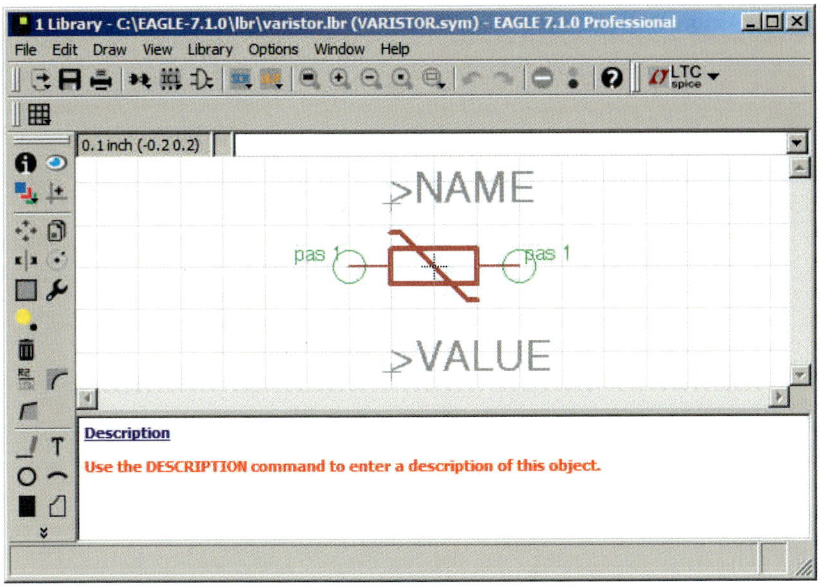

Figure 5-13: copying the VARISTOR symbol

iv. **Left-Click** onto  (COPY)

v. OPEN the target library (new_test_library.lbr) with File ▷ Open from the Control Panel menu

vi. EDIT  a new Symbol in the target library and name it 'QUIRKISTOR'. Confirm the new name when EAGLE pops up the warning 'Create new symbol 'QUIRKISTOR'? '

vii. Use the PASTE  command to place the copied Symbol into the new Symbol window.

viii. Save the library with File ▷ Save or Left-Click 

ix. Add the required text to the symbol
Our example 'QUIRKISTOR' symbol differs from the standard varistor only in that it has a 'Q' within the rectangular 'body' of the symbol. The user should use the TEXT command to add a 'Q' to the symbol diagram. Using the 'Alt' key (to access the alternate, finer grid) while positioning the character would be useful. The finished symbol is shown in Figure 5-14.

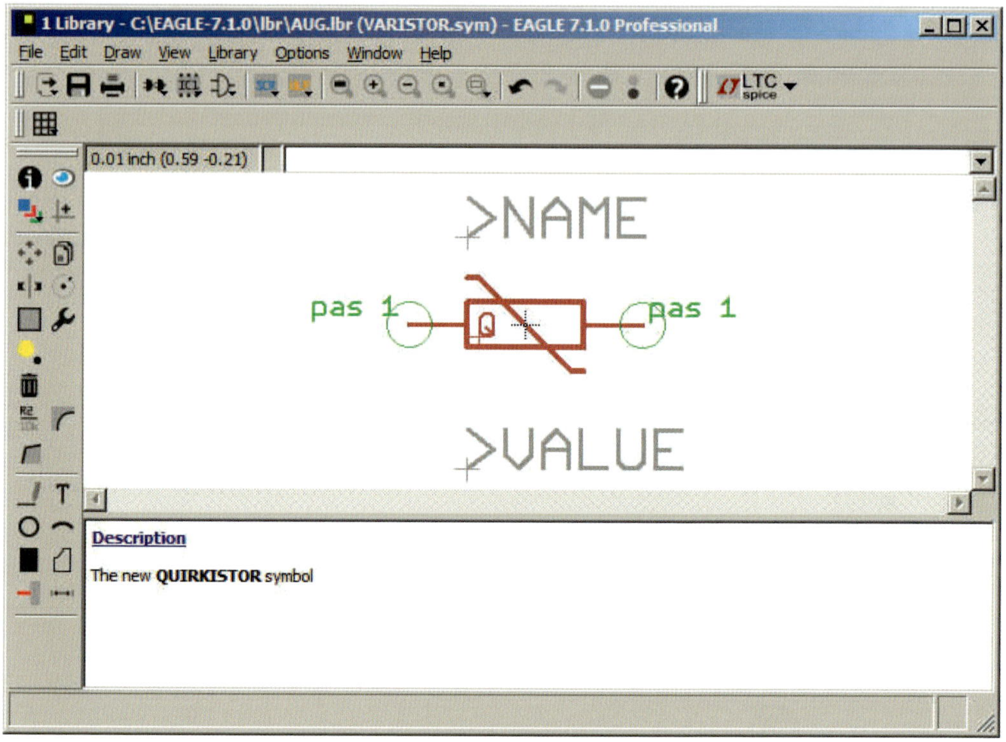

Figure 5-14: the new QUIRKISTOR symbol

Step 3 – Create the new QUIRKISTOR Device

The new Device can now be created by using these new elements (the package and the symbol). This Device will be named Q-06, and can be added to a drawing using this name. The steps to create this Device are:

Create the new Device using the edit-device icon  . A dialog will open and the user should enter the name 'Q-06' (see Figure 5-15).

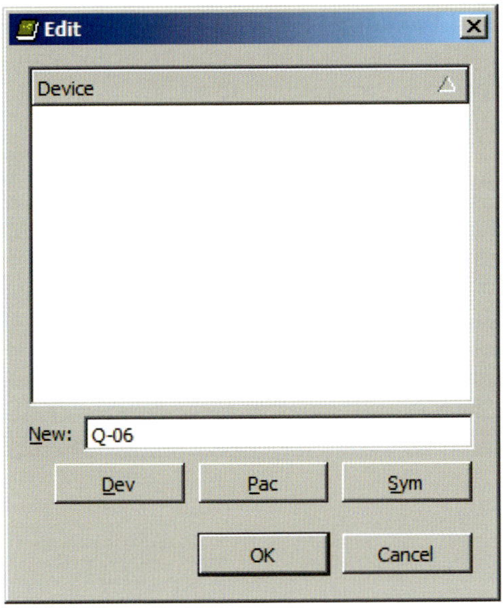

Figure 5-15: the edit Device dialog

After accepting the Device name, the user will see the screen shown in Figure 5-16.

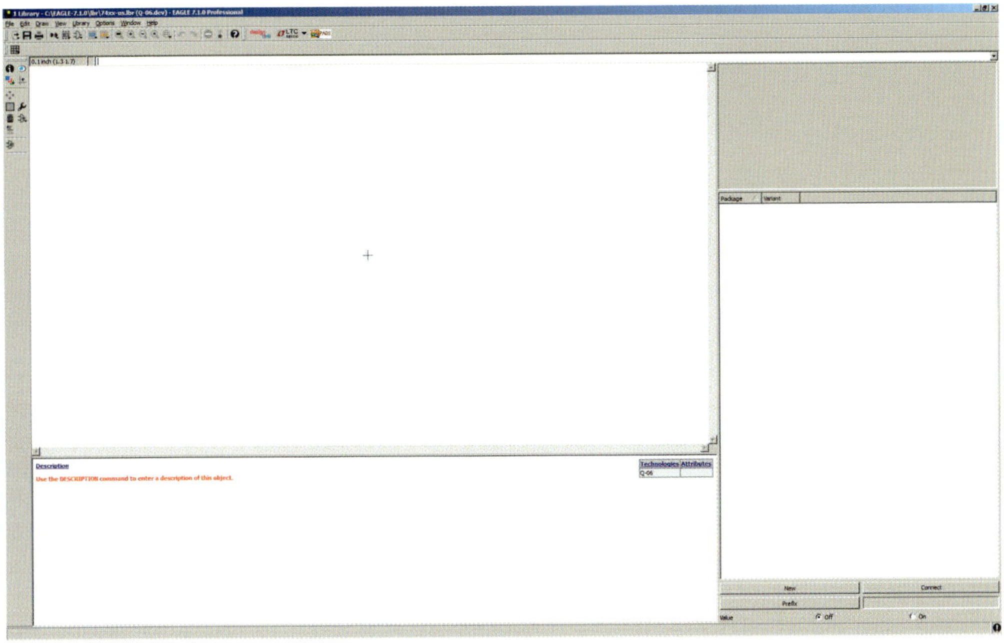

Figure 5-16: the new Device window

Step 4 – Add Symbol and Package to the QUIRKISTOR Device

The final step involves adding the required elements of Symbol and Package to the new QUIRKISTOR Device to realize a complete component.

i. Select the QUIRKISTOR Symbol using the ADD command  (***on the left-hand side of the window***) and then . This will open the Add dialog as shown in Figure 5-17. The user should select the QUIRKISTOR entry and **Left-Click** on 'OK'.

Figure 5-17: the Add Device dialog

ii. Set the *Addlevel* and *Swaplevel* of the Symbol using the parameter toolbar, as in Figure 5-18.

Figure 5-18: the Add parameter toolbar

iii. Place the Symbol by **Left-Clicking** onto the origin mark in the upper left hand pane, then **Left-Click** onto the STOP command. Adjust the display to fill the complete pane (see Figure 231 for the window display action command icons).

The user should next execute the command 'DISPLAY ALL;' to display all layers. The window should now appear as shown in Figure 5-19.

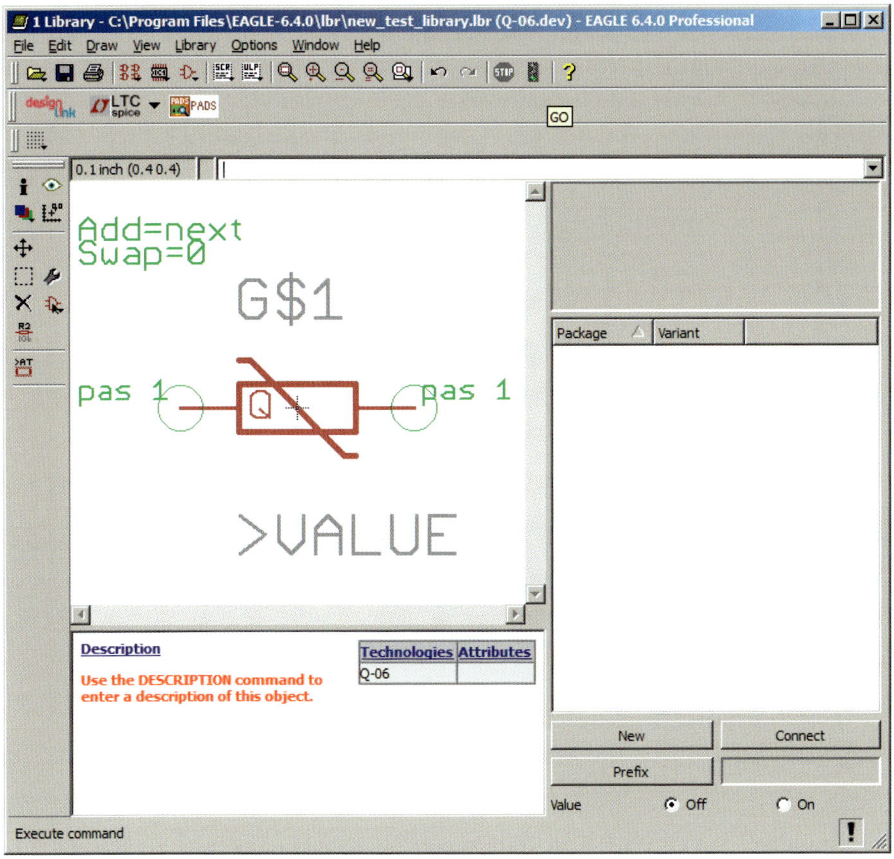

Figure 5-19: QUIRKISTOR Device with Symbol added

iv. Select the Package by **Left-Clicking** on 'New' (near bottom right-hand corner of the window) to open the package variant dialog (see Figure 5-20). The user may choose to enter a new name for the variant (in the entry field in the lower left corner of the dialog). In this example we have chosen 'Q6-CA01' as the variant name.

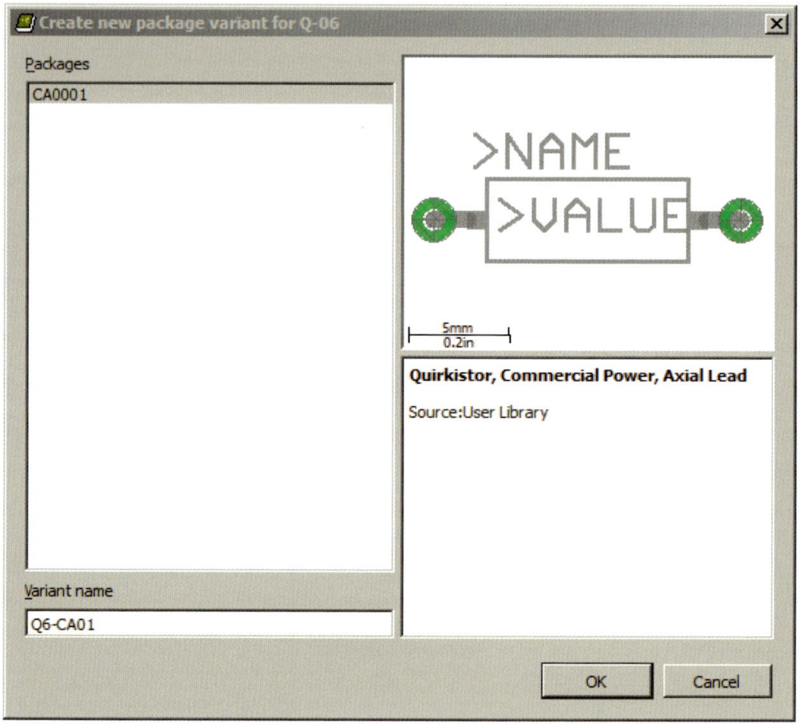

Figure 5-20: package variant dialog

After confirmation, the QUIRKISTOR Device window should appear as in Figure 5-21.

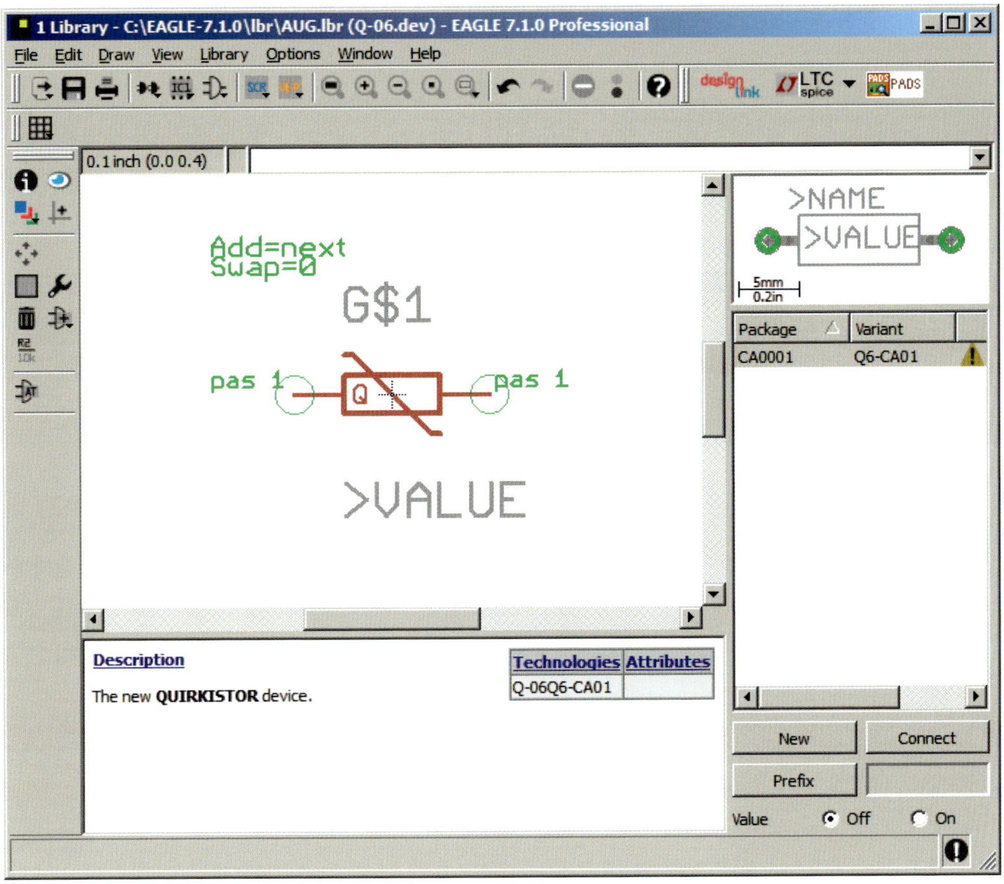

Figure 5-21: QUIRKISTOR Device with Symbol and Package variant added

Step 4 – Connect Pins and Pads in the Device

In order for the Device to properly 'function' the pins of the Symbol have to be 'connected' to the pads of the Package. (The 'warning'  symbol indicates that this is not done.) This is achieved by using either the CONNECT command or by simply **Left-Clicking** on the 'Connect' button (in the lower right hand of the Device window. In any case the CONNECT window pops up and will contain that shown in Figure 5-22.

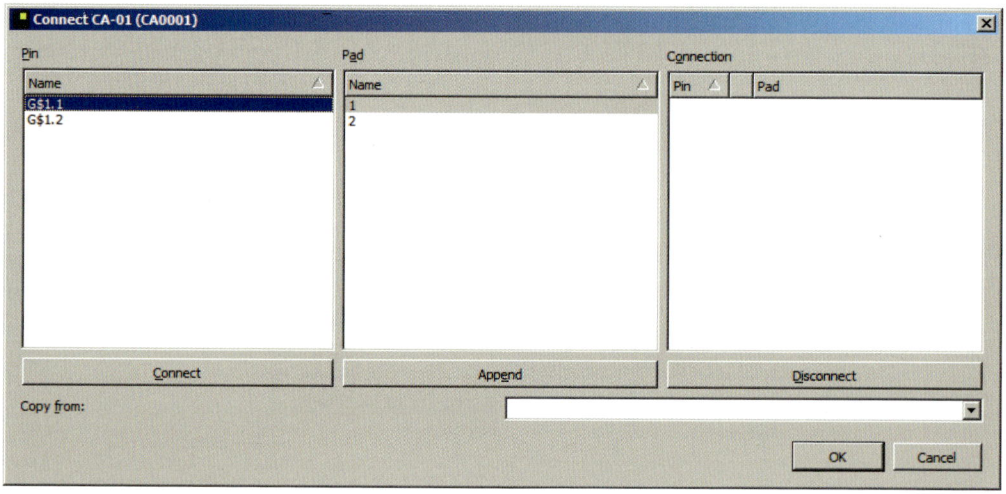

Figure 5-22: the CONNECT command window

Here the user will see that the QUIRKISTOR gate has been automatically identified as `G$1` and the pins `G$1.1` and `G$1.2` are listed in the Pin pane/column of the window.
The pad connections to the Package are listed in the Pad pane/column of the window.
To connect a Pin to a Pad the user simply selects (**Left-Click on**) an entry in the Pin column, then in the Pad column and finally **Left-Click** on 'Connect'. The result will be as in Figure 5-23.
To finish select 'OK'.

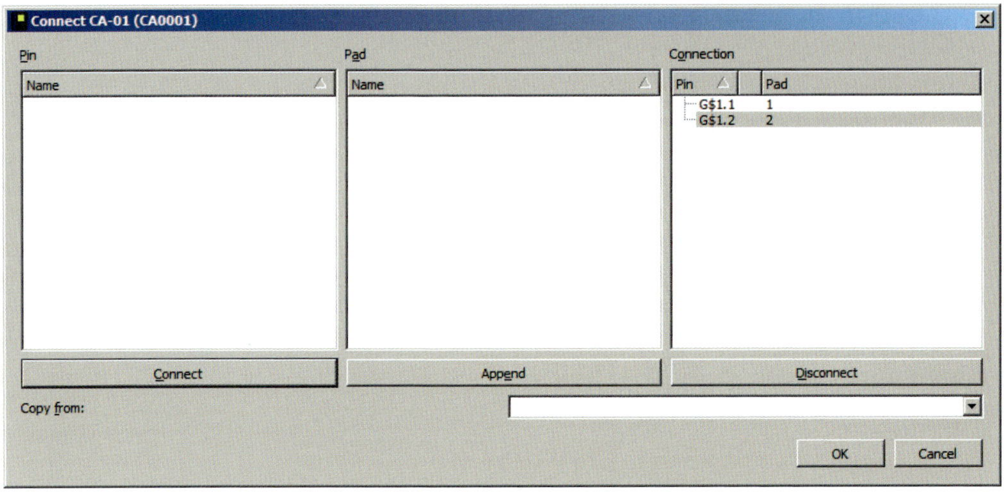

Figure 5-23: connected Pins and Pads for the device

Step 5 – Assign Prefix and Description to the Device

i. To properly designate the component, a prefix for it (and its like) needs to be assigned. EAGLE assigns an automatic suffix (i.e. x1, x2....xN). We will assign the prefix 'QK' to this device by using either the PREFIX command or **Left-Click** on 'Prefix'. In either case EAGLE will pop up the Prefix dialog to allow the user to enter the chosen prefix.

ii. The last operation is to edit the Description of the Device. This is not only useful to the human operator, but enhances productivity, since the EAGLE search facility (in the ADD command) accesses this text. Figure 5-24 shows the edit window for the Device Description. The user should note that certain HTML text may be used in this field. Complete by **Left-Clicking** on 'OK'.

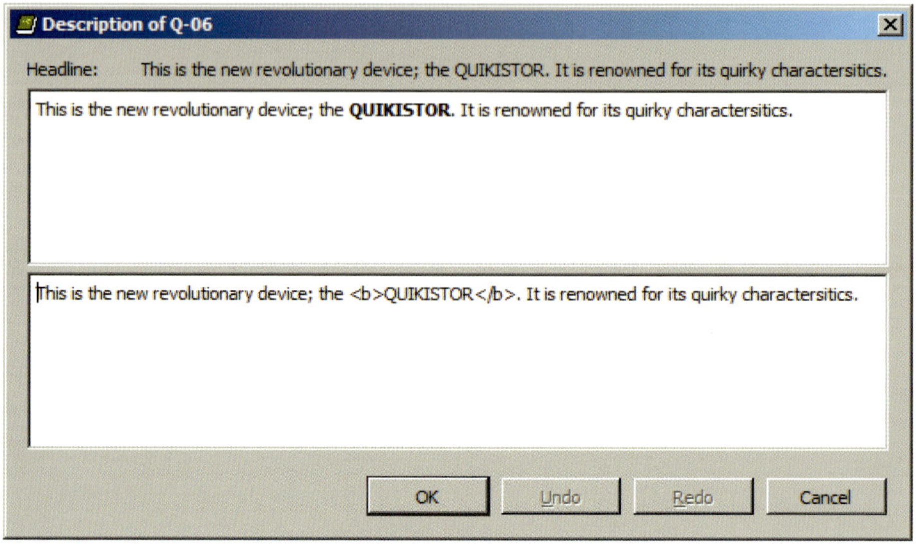

Figure 5-24: editing the Description of the Device

Step 6 – Save the Library

The final step is to save the library by using the WRITE command or **Left-Click** on . The completed Device is shown in Figure 5-25.

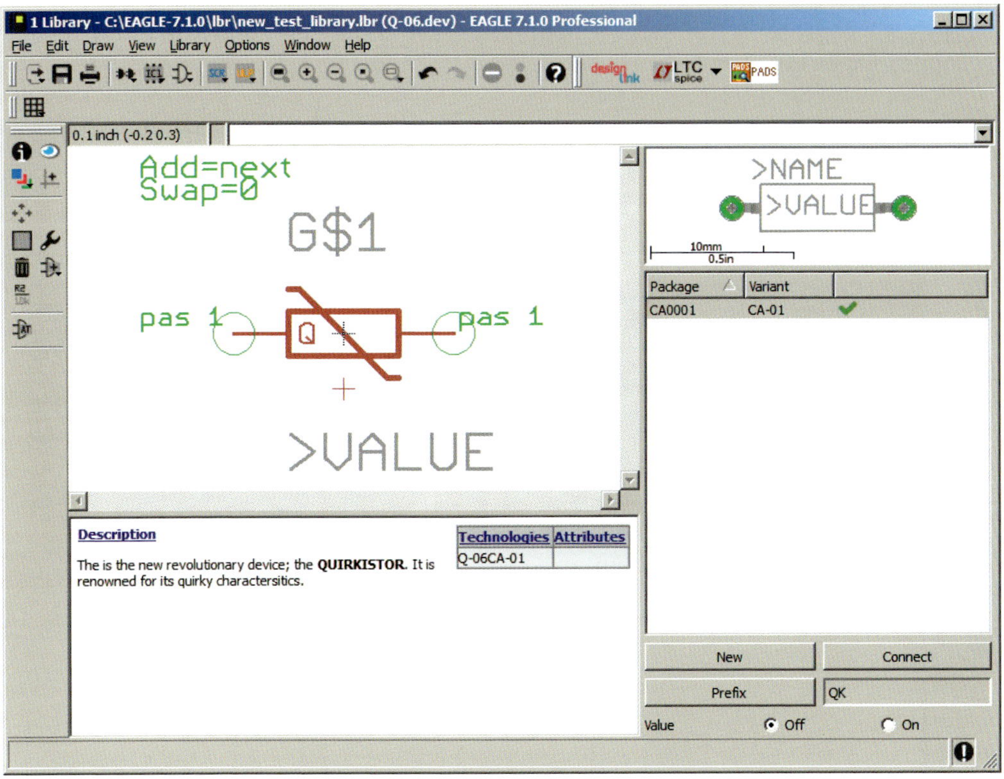

Figure 5-25: the completed QUIRKISTOR Device

Creating the 'Kunda Buffer' Component

The 'Kunda Buffer' is an analogue component with buffering (time delay) characteristics. It has a single input and 4 in-line outputs and comes in 2 standard packages: SOIC8 and DIL8.

The first step is to define the packages for this device. It is a small-signal, linear, analogue, low-power device and can be housed in a range of packages. This example will use the pre-existing specifications, '`SOIC8`' and '`DIL8`', from the library '`ref-packages.lbr`'.

Step 1 - Copy the packages to the new library

As described previously, the user may copy the package to the new library, or use the following method:

i. Open the library '`new_test_library.lbr`' (our nominated target library)

ii. From the command line in the new library, copy the first Package using the command:

```
COPY SOIC8@ref-packages.lbr
```

This will copy/insert the Package specifications into the new library, the new window appearing as in Figure 5-26.

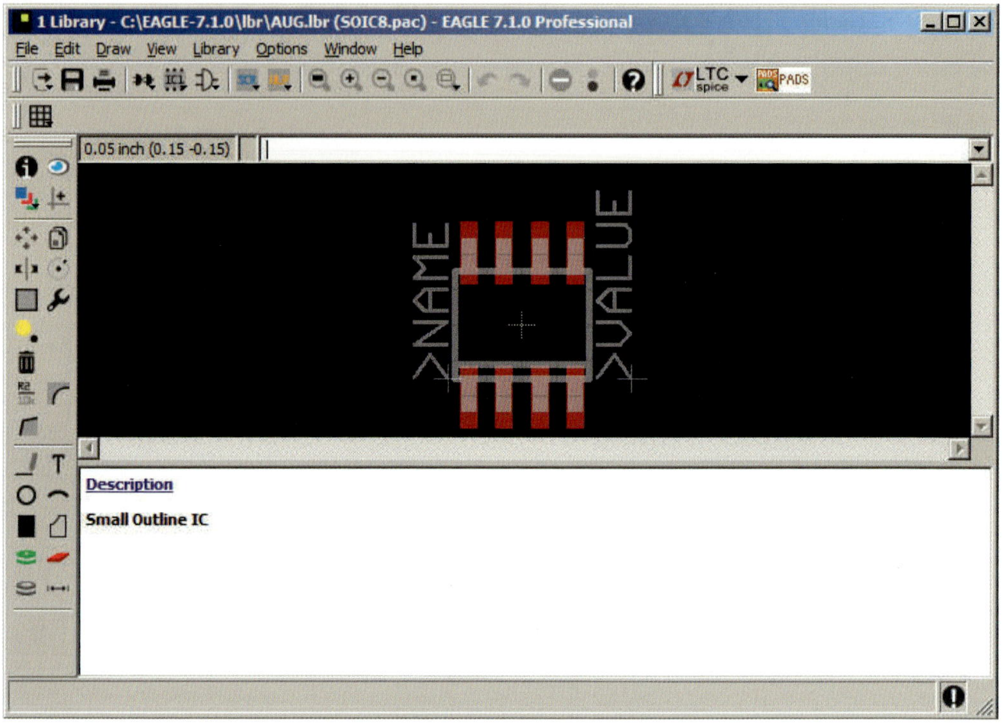

Figure 5-26: copied SOIC8 package

iii. Save the library by using File ▷ Save, `Ctrl-S` or `Left-Click` .

iv. Again, from the command line in the new library, copy the second Package using the command:

```
COPY DIL08@ref-packages.lbr
```

These Package specifications will also be copied into the new library, the new window appearing as in Figure 5-27.

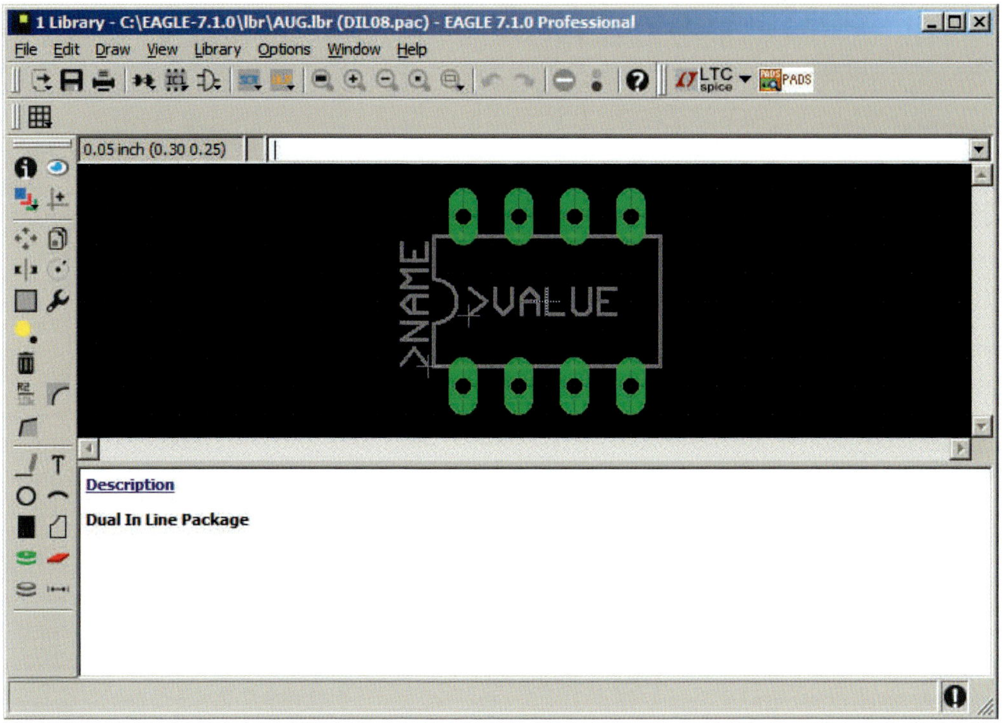

Figure 5-27: copied DIL08 package

v. Again, save the library by using File ▷ Save, `Ctrl-S` or **Left-Click** .

The user can check that the packages have been added to the library by using the Edit Package icon (**Left-Click** ).

Step 2 – Create a new Symbol

In this step the user will create a new Symbol (the 'Kunda Buffer') and add it to the library. The Symbol is illustrated in Figure 5-28.

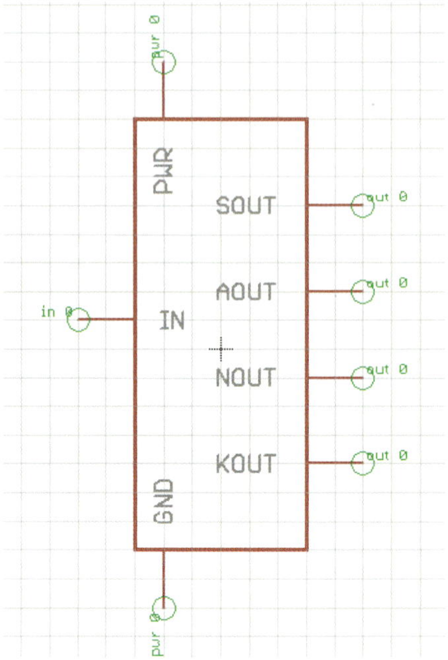

Figure 5-28: the Kunda Buffer Symbol

i. Create the new KUNDABUFFER Symbol using the EDIT command (or **Left-Click**). This will open the EDIT dialog as shown in Figure 5-15. The user should enter '`KUNDABUFFER`' in the '`New:`' entry field and **Left-Click** '`OK`'.

ii. Ensure that the correct Grid and Layers are selected by using the GRID command (or **Left-Click**), which should be set to `0.1` inch, and then the Layer command (or **Left-Click**), which should be set to '`94 Symbols`'. If not, simply **Left-Click** on the number 94.

iii. Draw the 'body' of the symbol using the WIRE Command or (**Left-Click**). The rectangle should be centered around the datum point marked on the screen.

Before commencing, the user should confirm that the settings match those displayed in Figure 5-29.

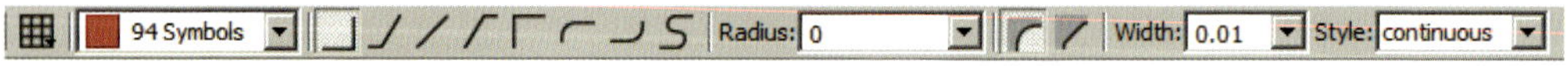

Figure 5-29: the WIRE command parameter toolbar

The completed rectangle should appear as in Figure 5-30.

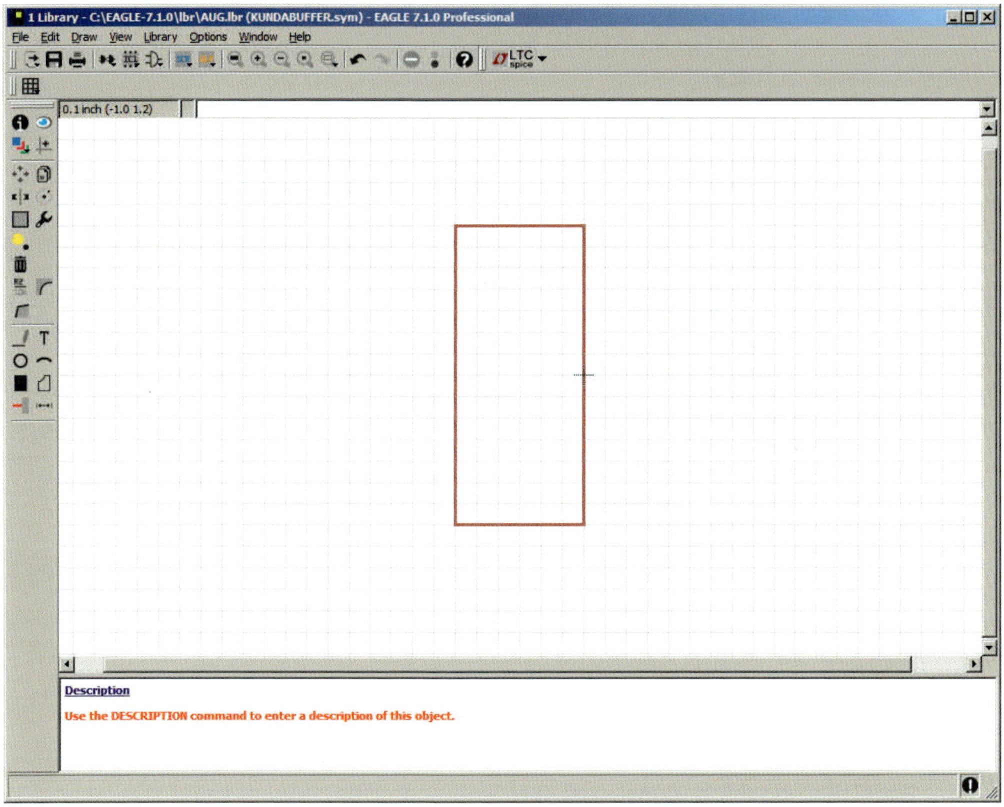

Figure 5-30: body of the new Symbol

iv. Add Pins to the Symbol using the PIN command (or **Left-Click** ).

a. Place the first Pin (the signal IN pin)on the left-hand side shown in Figure 5-28. Before doing so ensure that the PIN parameters are set as shown in the toolbar illustrated in Figure 5-31.

Figure 5-31: PIN parameter toolbar

The 'Direction' parameter is set to 'in' and the SwapLevel is '0'.

After placement, the properties of the pin may be edited by invoking the context menu for the pin (i.e. **Right-Click** on the pin and select '`Properties`'). The Properties dialog will be displayed (see Figure 5-32).

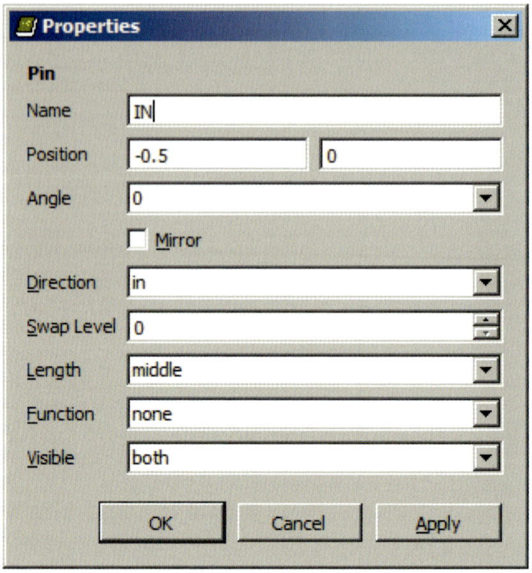

Figure 5-32: the PIN Properties dialog

For the first pin, the user should enter 'IN' into the 'Name' field of the dialog, then **Left-Cli**ck on 'OK'.

b. Place the remaining signal pins (i.e. xOUT) onto the Symbol using the technique outlined above. The pin may be rotated prior to placement using **Right-Click** of the mouse. All Properties remain the same except for 'Direction' (which should be changed to 'out'). Name the pins when they are placed, from within the Properties dialog as: KOUT, NOUT, AOUT and SOUT.

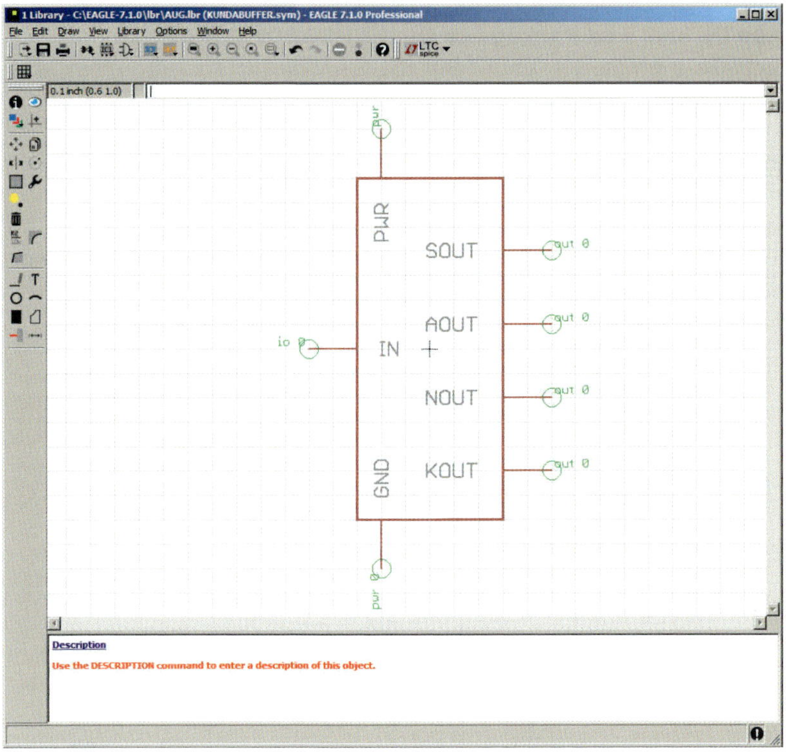

Figure 5-33: the KUNDABUFFER Symbol with pins

c. Place the power supply pins ('PWR' and 'GND') by, again, using a similar technique to the above. Their 'Direction' property should be set to 'pwr'; and is a special property which indicates a supply pin.

   When complete, the symbol should appear as in Figure 5-33.

Step 3 Create the new KUNDABUFFER Device

The step will add the Symbol and Packages to the new KUNDABUFFER Device to realize a complete component.

Create the new Device using the edit-device icon . A dialog will open and the user should enter the name 'KBUF-08' (the display will be similar to that shown in Figure 5-15). After accepting the Device name (**Left-Click** on 'OK'), the user will see the screen similar to that shown in Figure 5-16.

Step 4 - Add Symbol and Package to the KUNDABUFFER Device

Like our previous example we'll now add the Symbol and Package elements to the new KUNDABUFFER Device.

i. With the Device window still open, select the KUNDABUFFER Symbol using the ADD command  (on the left-hand side of the window). This will open the Add dialog as shown in Figure 5-34. The user should select the KUNDABUFFER entry and **Left-Click** on 'OK'. EAGLE will then display the Addlevel and Swaplevel parameter selectors in the left hand side of the parameter toolbar.

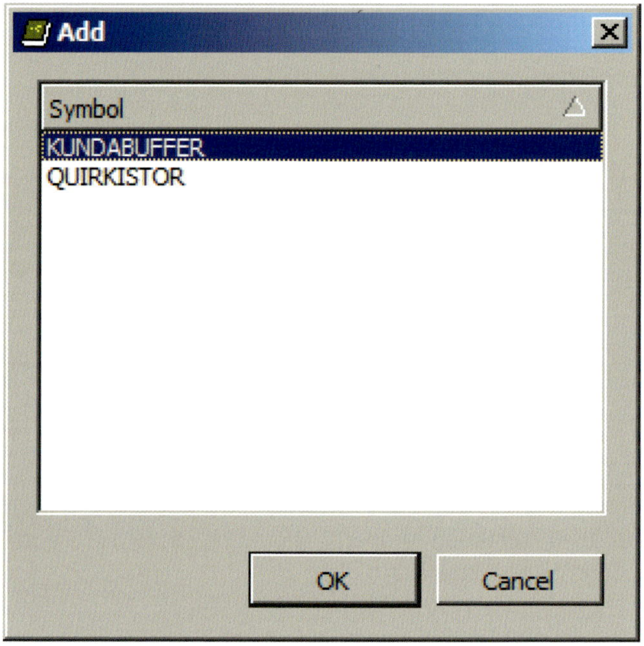

Figure 5-34: the Add Device dialog

ii. The user should set the *Addlevel* and *Swaplevel* of the Symbol using the parameter toolbar, as described in the previous example.

iii. Place the Symbol onto the origin mark in the upper left hand pane, using the STOP command and then adjust the display to fill the complete pane (see Figure 231 for the window display action command icons).

The window should now appear as shown in Figure 5-35.

iv. To add the packages, perform the actions as described in the previous example. Select the first Package by **Left-Clicking** on '`New`' (near bottom right-hand corner of the window) to open the package variant dialog (see Figure 5-36).

   a. The user should select the '`DIL08`' Package and enter '`DIL08`' in the 'Variant name' field, then **Left-Click** on '`OK`'.

   b. Similarly, the user should do the same to add the '`SOIC8`' package.

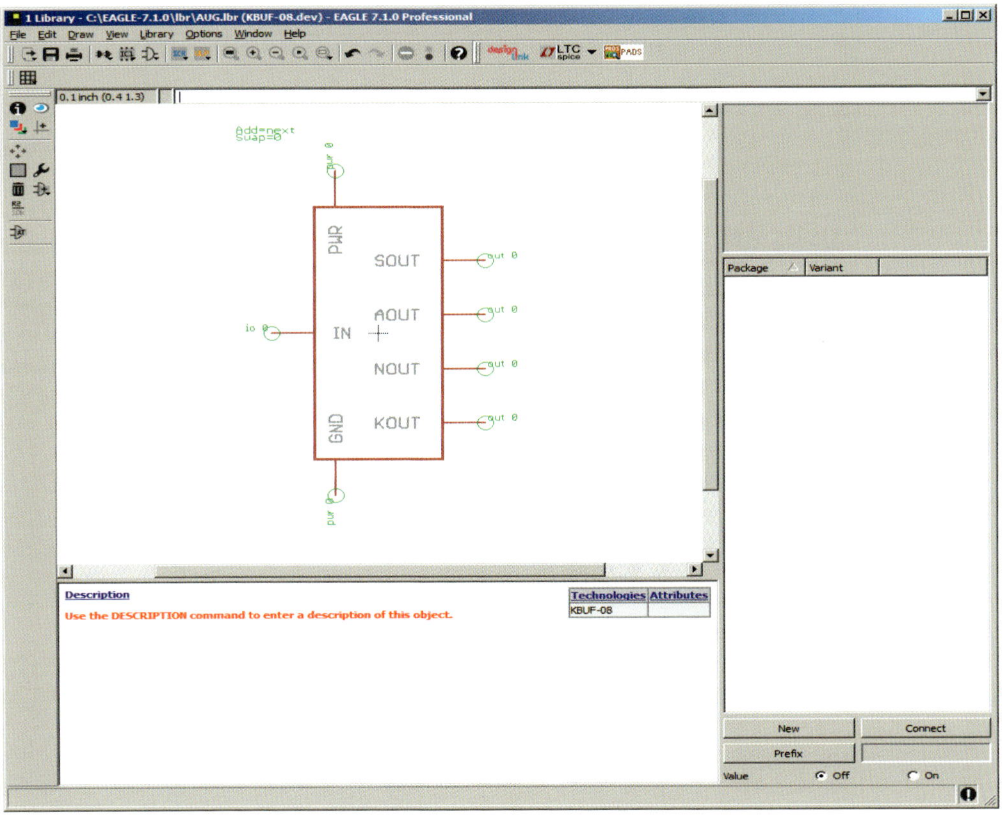

Figure 5-35: KUNDABUFFER Device with Symbol added

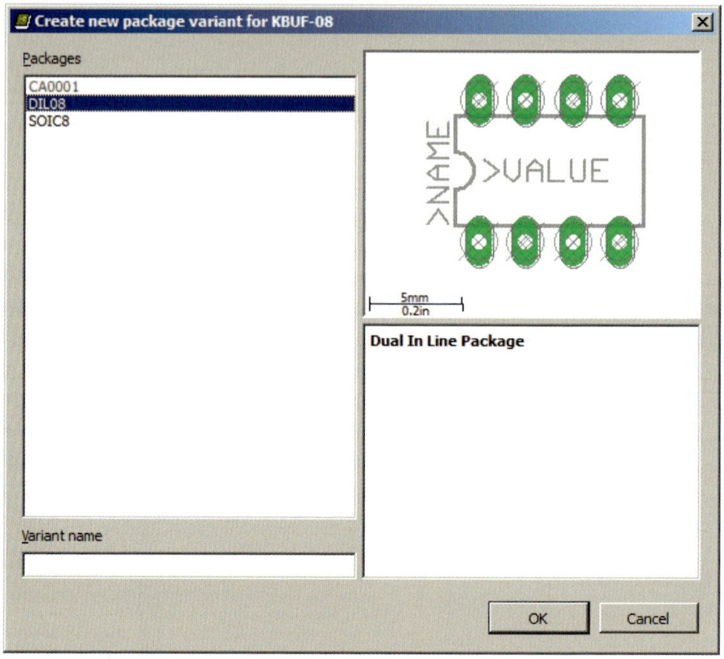

Figure 5-36: KUNDABUFFER package variant dialog

The KUNDABUFFER device window should now appear as in Figure 5-37.

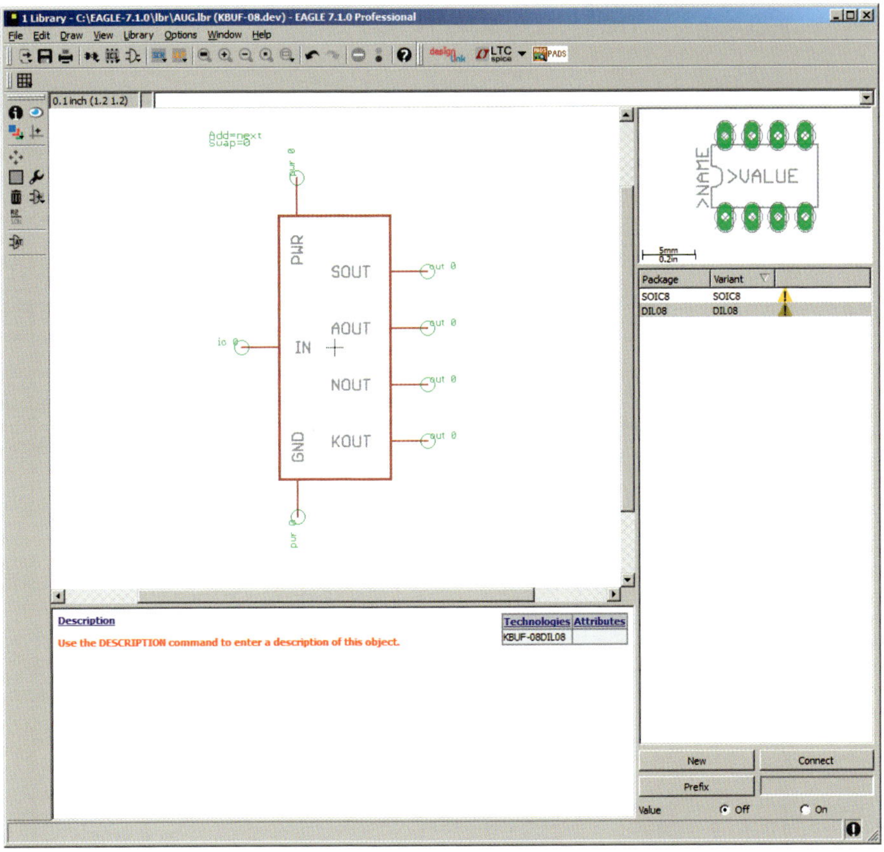

Figure 5-37: KUNDABUFFER device with package variants

Step 4 – Connect Pins and Pads in the Device

The user should now connect the pins to the package pads for each of the package variants (as described in Step 4, above, for the QUIRKISTOR).

Using the CONNECT command or button, make the appropriate connections. The user should select the '`G$1.AOUT`' pin, followed by Pad '`5`'. Make the connection by **Left-Clicking** on '`Connect`'. The user should similarly complete the remaining Pin-to-Pad connections given in Figure 5-38.

Since the pinout is the same (they are both 8 pin packages) the new layout appears in Figure 5-39 with the respective pins numbered accordingly.

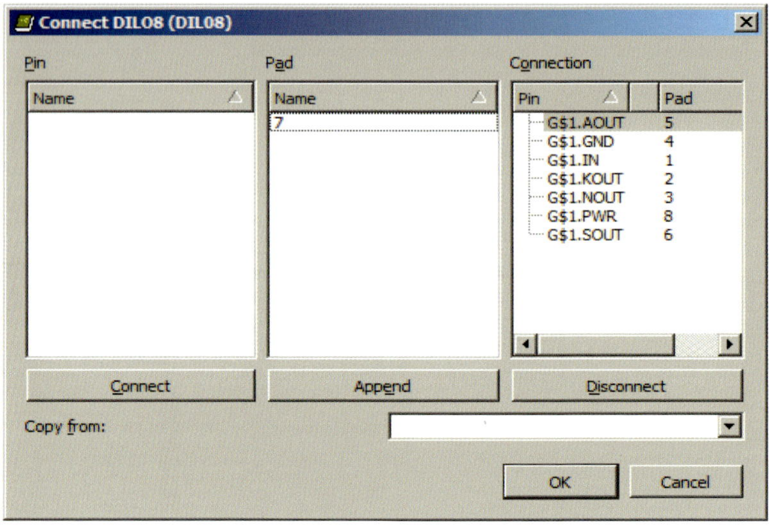

Figure 5-38: KUNDABUFFER Pin-Pad connections for package DIL08

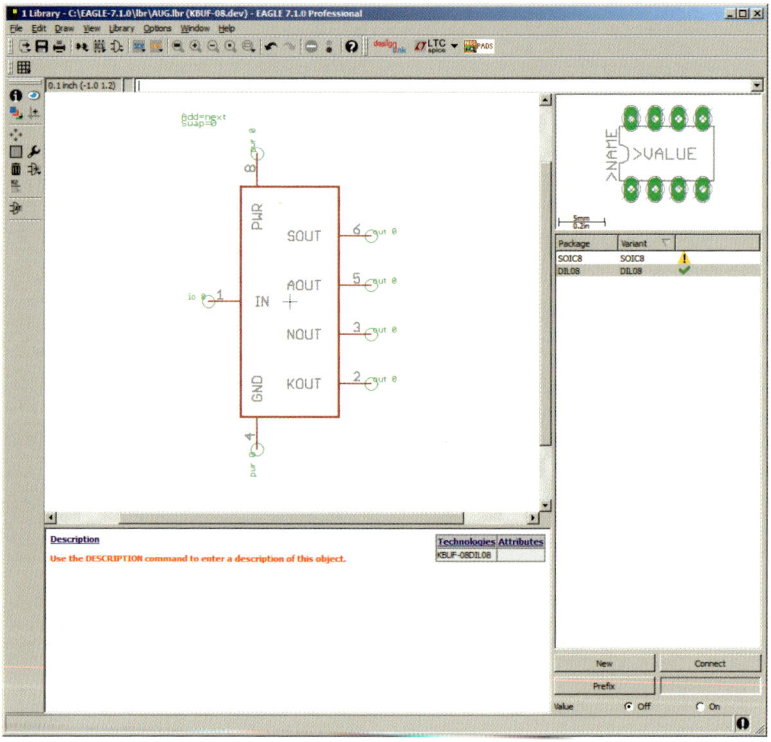

Figure 5-39: KUNDABUFFER Device window

Step 5 – Assign Prefix and Description to the Device

i. We will assign the prefix 'KB' to this device by using either the PREFIX command or **Left-Clicking** on '`Prefix`'. In either case EAGLE will pop up the Prefix dialog to allow the user to enter the chosen prefix.

ii. The last operation is to edit the Description of the Device. The user should complete this as described, similarly, in the first example.

The completed KUNDABUFFER device window should now appear as in Figure 5-40.

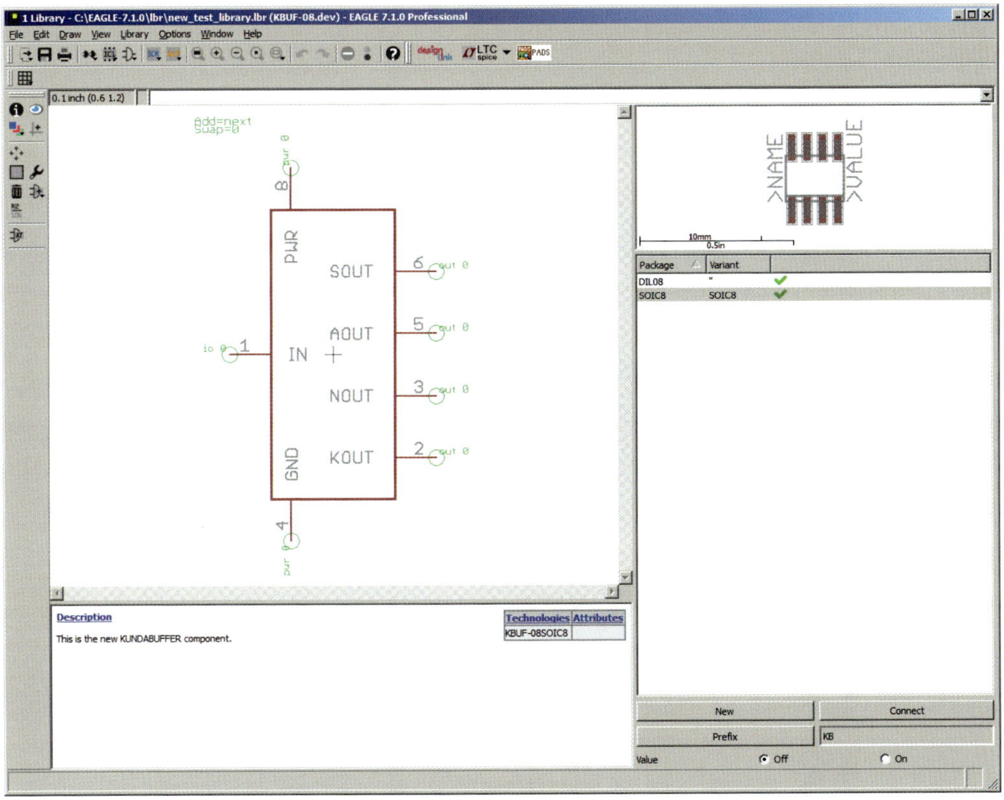

Figure 5-40: completed KUNDABUFFER Device window

Creating the 'GizzyGate' Device

This digital logic element is configured with 2-input, 1-output per gate and performs a unique logical transform. The gate configuration is octal and is only available in a 32-pin, TSOP Type II SMD package.

As with our first example this component will borrow from other component's package and symbol specifications.

Step 1 - Create a new Symbol from a copied Symbol

As described at the beginning of this chapter, the user may employ the same technique to copy a Symbol from an existing library and edit that symbol to transform it into the new 'GizzyGate' Symbol.

To do this:

i. `OPEN` the source library, '`74xx-us.lbr`', and EDIT the Symbol using Library ▷ Symbol (or use edit-symbol  icon) sequence to select and open symbol '`7486`. The window will appear as in Figure 5-41.

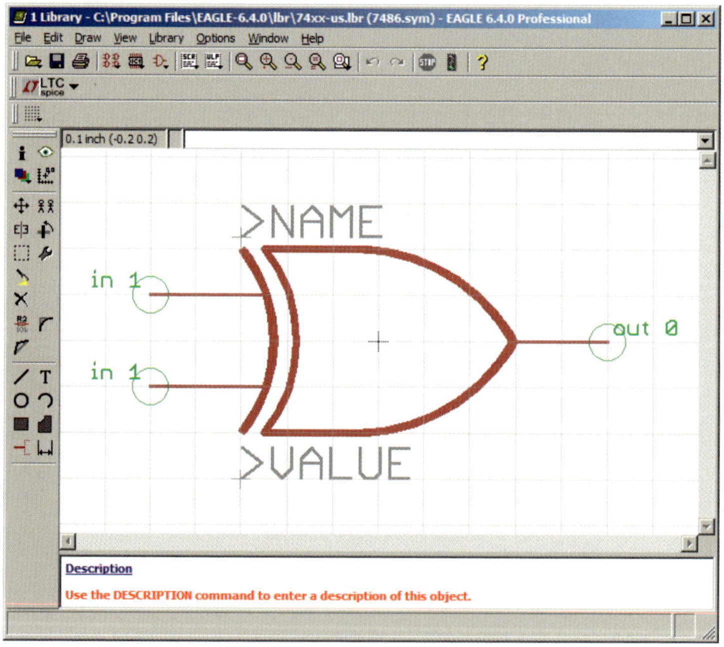

Figure 5-41: the 7486 symbol edit window

ii. use the 'DISPLAY ALL' command to display all the layers of the symbol.

iii. Select all objects in the symbol with the command 'GROUP ALL'.

iv. **Left-Click** onto  (COPY) to copy the symbol elements

v.. Now, open our own target library ('new_test_library.lbr') with File ▷ Open from the Control Panel menu

vi. Use the EDIT command (or **Left-Click** on ) to create the new Symbol in the target library. Name the new gate 'GIZZYGATE' by entering this in the 'New' name field and **Left-Click** on 'OK'

vii. Use the PASTE  command to place the copied Symbol into the new Symbol window.

viii. Save the library with File ▷ Save 

xi. Add the required text to the symbol

This GIZZYGATE symbol differs from the standard X-OR gate in that it has a 'G' within the 'body' of the symbol. The user should use the TEXT command to add a 'G' to the symbol diagram. Using the 'Alt' key (to access the alternate, finer grid) while positioning the character would be useful. The finished symbol is shown in Figure 5-42.

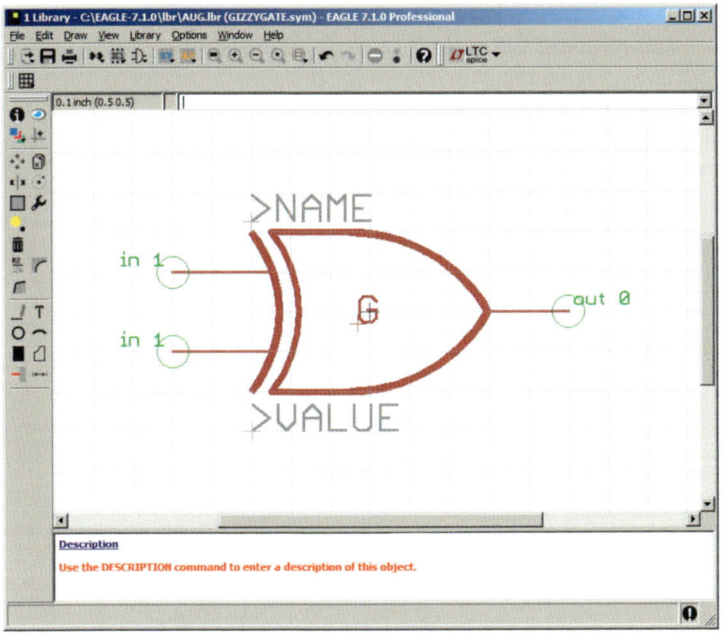

Figure 5-42: the GIZZYGATE symbol edit window

Step 2 - Create a new Power gate symbol

In this Device it will be necessary to define a special type of 'gate'; a Power Gate. This symbol allows the user to incorporate specific supply pins into the completed Symbol for the combined GIZZYGATE Device. This gate will be named 'PWRN' as is constructed as follows:

i. Use the EDIT command (or **Left-Click** on ) to create the new Symbol in the target library.
Name the new gate 'PWRN' by entering this in the 'New' name field and **Left-Click** on 'OK'

ii. Use the PIN command (or **Left-Click** ) to place 2 pins into the new symbol.

iii. Using the Properties dialog (**Right-Click** for the context menu), make changes to the pins according to the values shown in Table 5-1.

	Pin1	Pin2
Name	V+	GND
Direction	Pwr	Pwr
Swaplevel	0	0
Function	none	none
Visible	off	off

Table 5-1: Properties for PWRN gate pins

iv. The user should now add the relevant text to the symbol using the TEXT command

(or **Left-Click** on ). The 'V+' and 'GND' should be placed in the 95 Names layer and using the **Right-Click** mouse button for rotation and the 'Alt' key for fine grid placement. Similarly, the user may also 'label' the symbol (using the TEXT command) to insert the text variable '>NAME'.

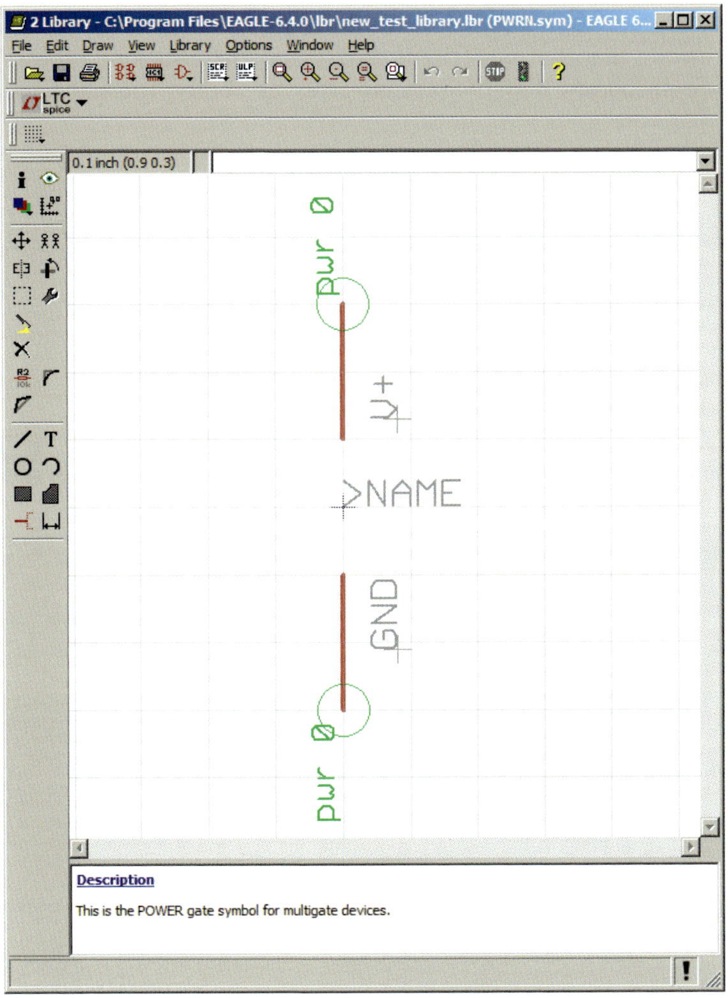

Figure 5-43: the PWRN gate symbol

The completed power gate symbol should appear similar to that shown in Figure 5-43.

v. The user may also edit the description (**Left-Click** on Description) to indicate the use of the device.

vi. Save the new gate/symbol with File ▷ Save (or **Left-Click** ).

Step 3 - Copy the package from another library

As described before, the user may (Drag& Drop) copy the package to the new library. In this instance we will borrow from the memory-sram.lbr library. The steps are as follows:

i. If not still open, open the library 'new_test_library.lbr'.

ii. From the command line in the new library, copy the required Package using the command:

```
COPY SOJ32-400@memory-sram.lbr
```

This will copy/insert the Package specifications into the new library, the new window appearing as in Figure 5-44.

iii. save changes to the library by using File ▷ Save, `Ctrl-S` or **Left-Click** .

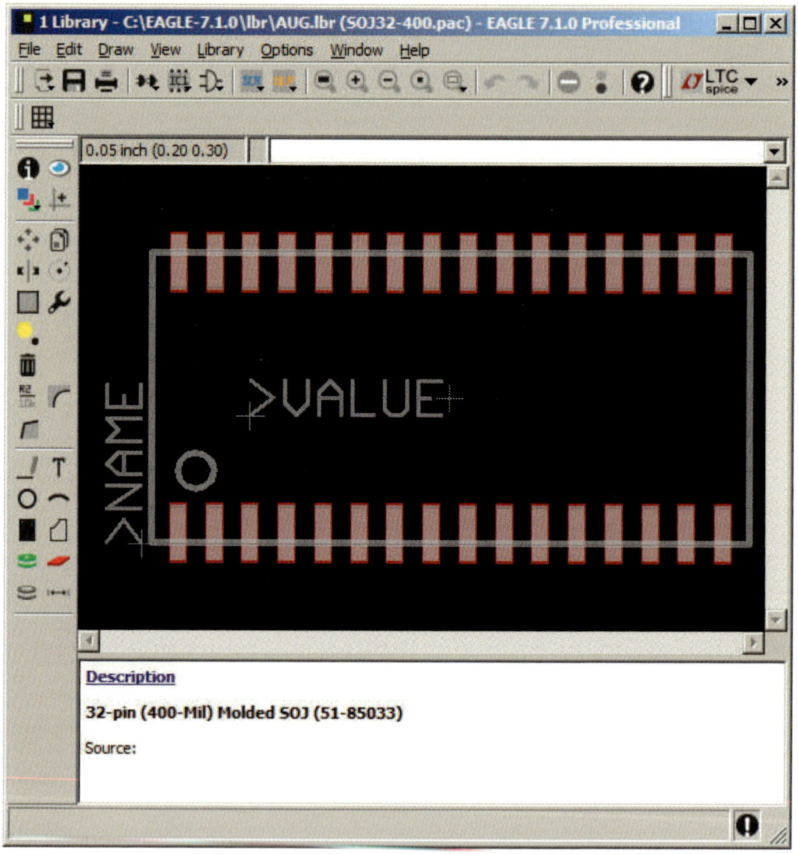

Figure 5-44: the 32 pin TSOP Type II SMD package

Step 4 – Include Symbol and Package to create the new GIZZYGATE Device
The new Device can now be created by using the above elements. This Device will be named 'GG-08', and can be added to a drawing using this name.

Creation of this component will require some extra work, since this is an octal device in a single package.

The steps to create the Device are:

a. Create the new Device using the edit-device icon  . A dialog will open and the user should enter the new device name 'GG-08' (the display will be similar to that shown in Figure 5-45).

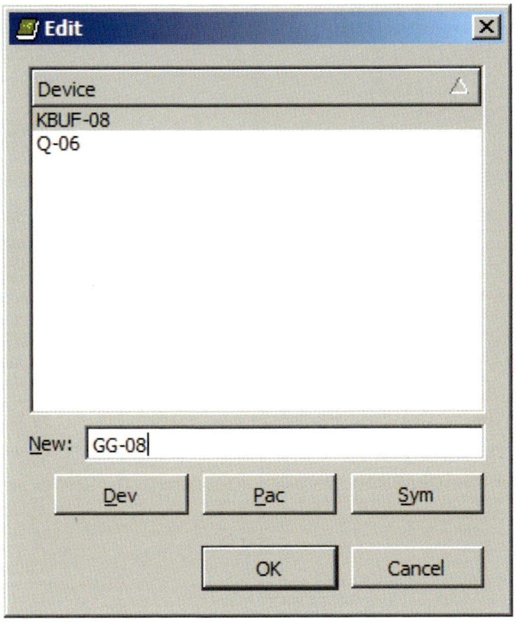

Figure 5-45: the Add Device dialog

After accepting the Device name (**Left-Click** on 'OK'), the user will see the screen similar to that shown in Figure 5-16.

Step 5 - Add Symbol and Package to the GIZZYGATE Device
In this step we'll add the Package first, since this is the simplest process. This is done by:

i. **Left-Click** on 'New' (near bottom right-hand corner of the window) to open the package variant dialog as shown in Figure 5-46.

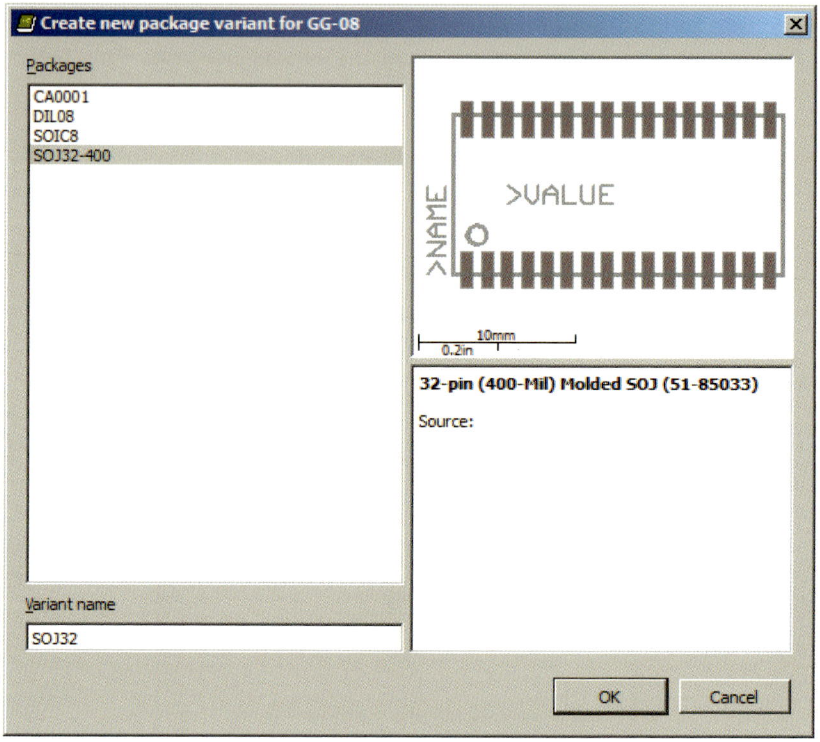

Figure 5-46: GIZZYGATE package variant dialog

The user should select the '`SOJ32-400`' Package and enter '`SOJ32`' in the 'Variant name' field, then **Left-Click** on '`OK`'. The user can verify that the Package has been included by the window, since it will display the package element as shown in Figure 5-47.

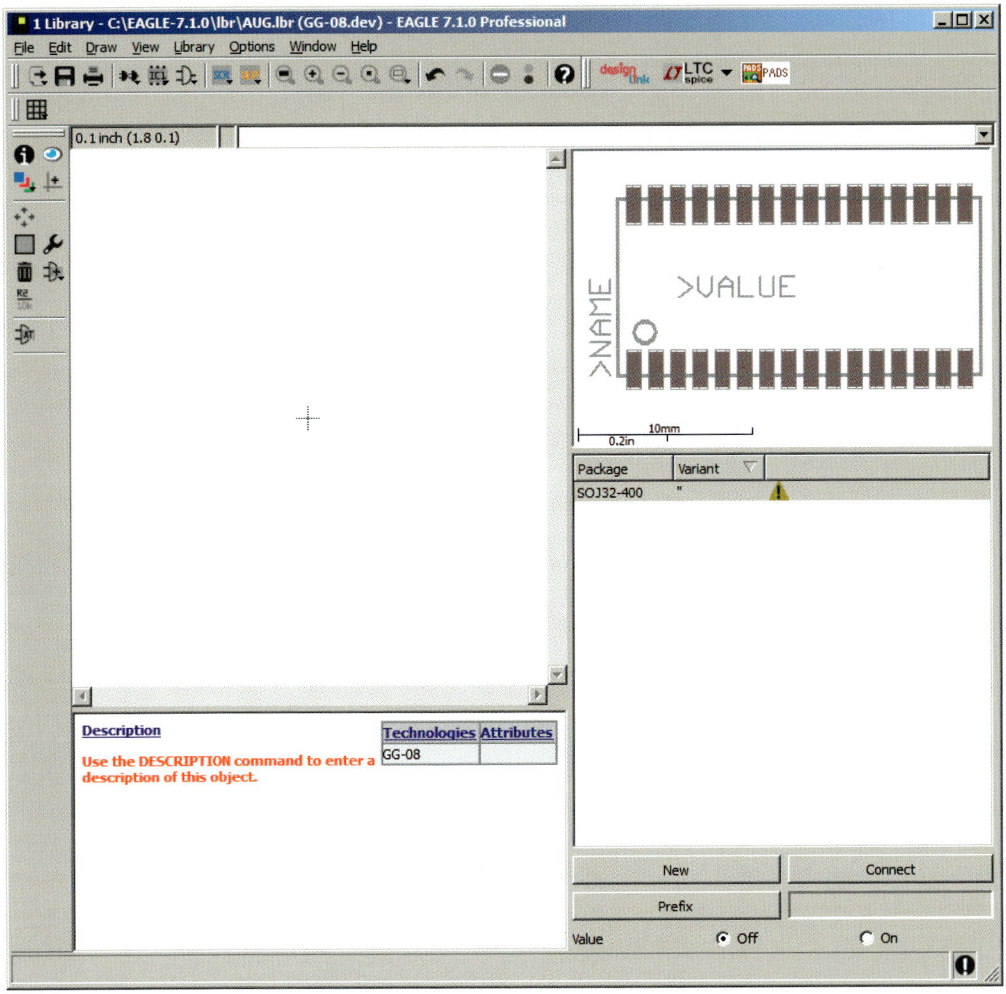

Figure 5-47: GIZZYGATE device with package variant

ii. The function of adding the Symbol is more complex and requires more steps than our previous examples. It involves using the basic GIZZYGATE symbol to construct the octal form of the device. This is done as follows:

a. With the Device window still open, select the GIZZYGATE Symbol using the ADD command  (on the left-hand side of the window). This will open the Add dialog as shown in Figure 5-34. The user should select the GIZZYGATE entry and **Left-Click** on 'OK'.

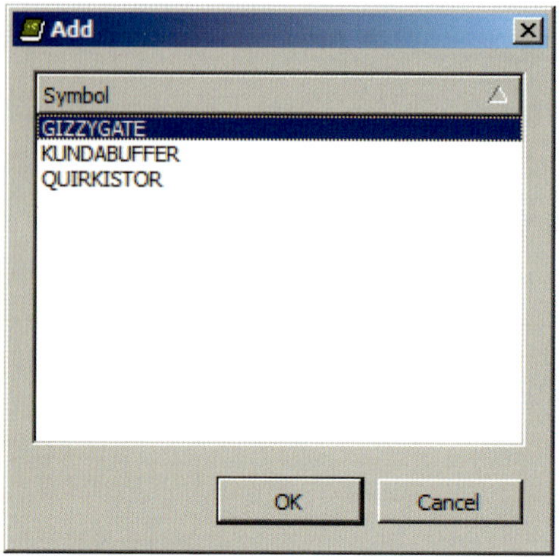

Figure 5-48: the Add Device dialog

b. The display will revert to the Device window with the GIZZYGATE Symbol 'attached' to the cursor; as in Figure 5-49.

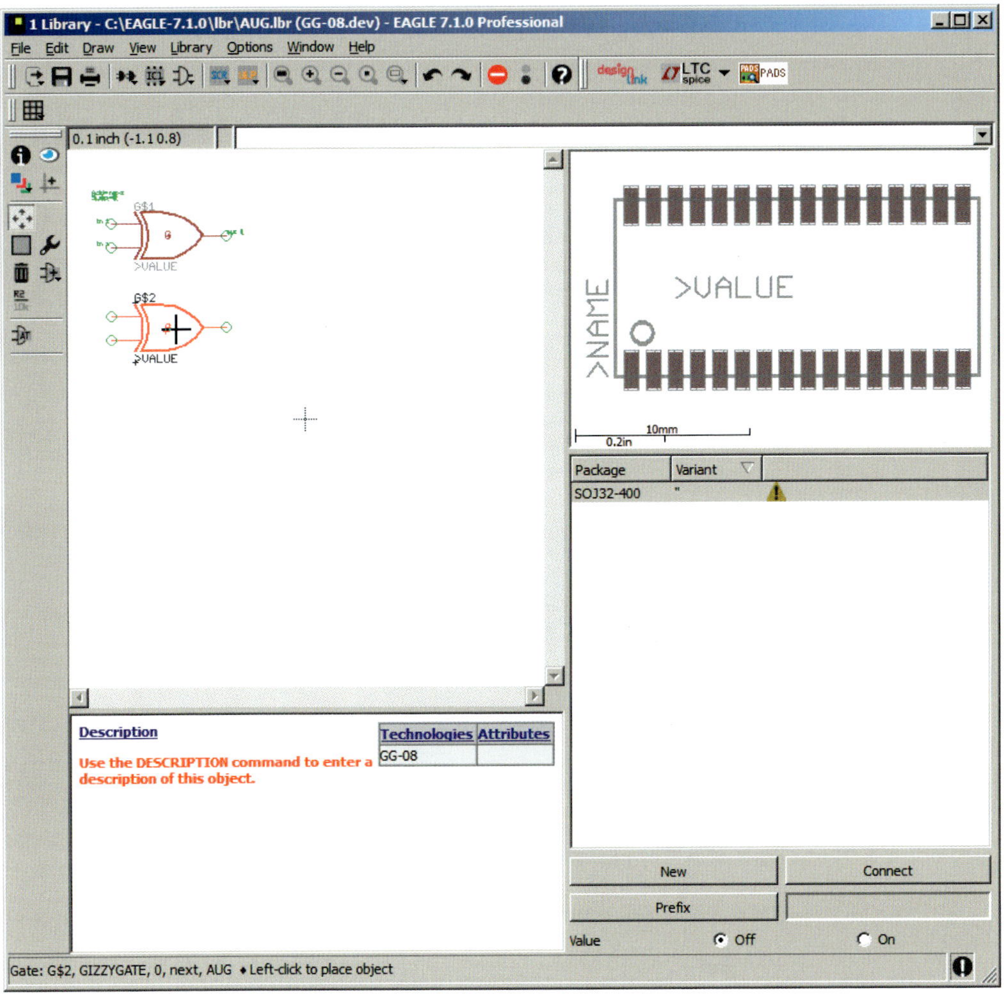

Figure 5-49: placing the GIZZYGATE symbol in the Device window

c. The user should place eight (8) of these symbols in the upper left-hand pane of the Device window. Terminate the sequence using the STOP icon (**Left-Click** on ). The window should now appear as in Figure 5-50.

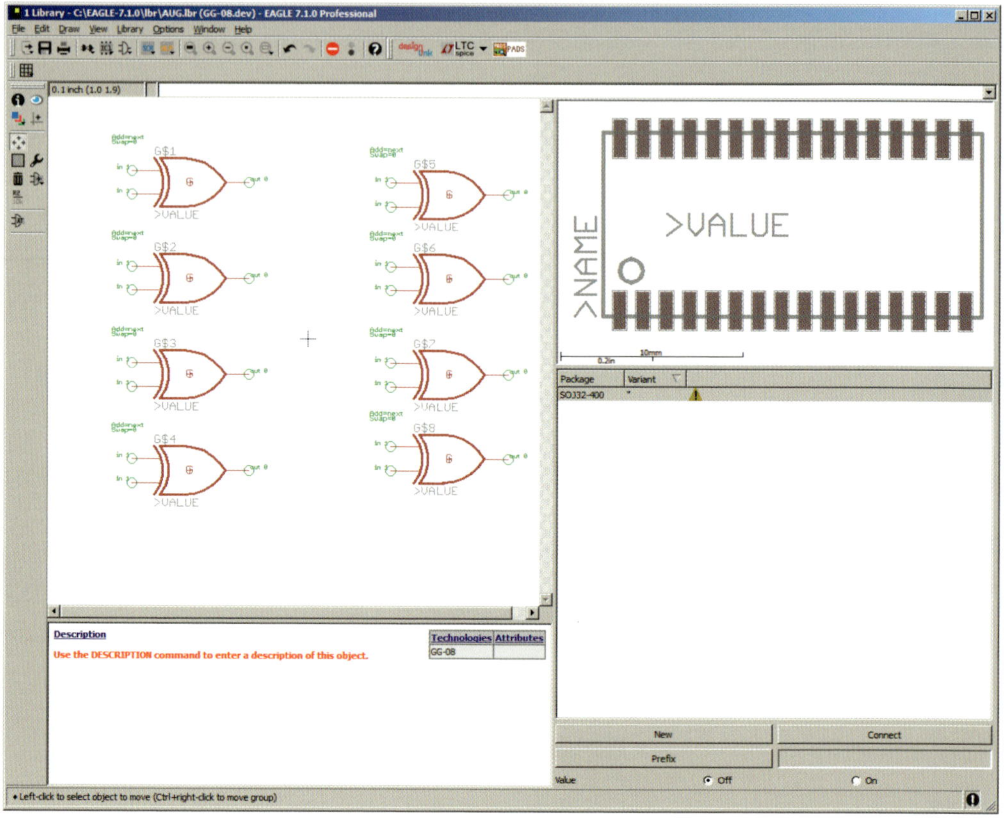

Figure 5-50: the Device window with GIZZYGATE symbols included

d. The last step is to place the PWRN symbol once. First, using the CHANGE command (or **Left-Click** on ) set the parameters: Addlevel – `Request` and Swaplevel – `0`.

Place the symbol and then, using the NAME command (or **Left-Click** on  and then Left-Click on the center + of the G$9 symbol), name it '`PWR`'.

The GIZZYGATE device window Symbol pane should now appear as in Figure 5-51.

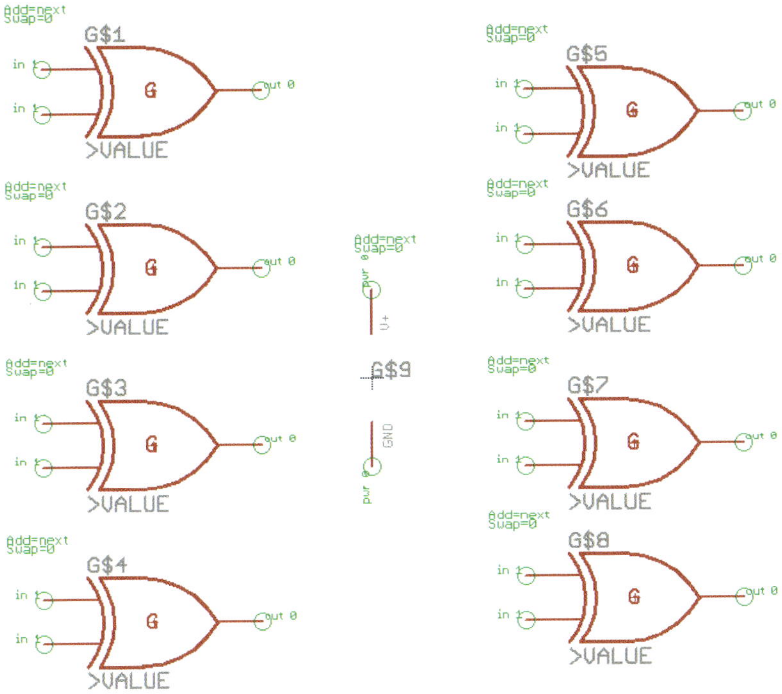

Figure 5-51: the completed GIZZYGATE Device symbol Pane

Step 6 – Connect Pins and Pads in the Device

The user should now connect the pins to the package pads (as described in Step 4, above, for the QUIRKISTOR).

Using the CONNECT command or button make the appropriate connections using those listed in Table 5-2.

Pad	Pin	Pad	Pin
1	G$1.I0	17	G$5.I0
2	G$1.I1	18	G$5.I1
3	G$1.O	19	G$5.O
4	G$2.I0	20	G$6.I0
5	G$2.I1	21	G$6.I1
6	G$2.O	22	G$6.O
7	N/C	23	N/C
8	G9.GND	24	V+
9	G$3.I0	25	G$7.I0
10	G$3.I1	26	G$7.I1
11	G$3.O	27	G$7.O
12	G$4.I0	28	G$8.I0
13	G$4.I1	29	G$8.I1
14	G$4.O	30	G$8.O
15	N/C	31	N/C
16	N/C	32	N/C

Table 5-2: Pin-pad connections for the GIZZYGATE device

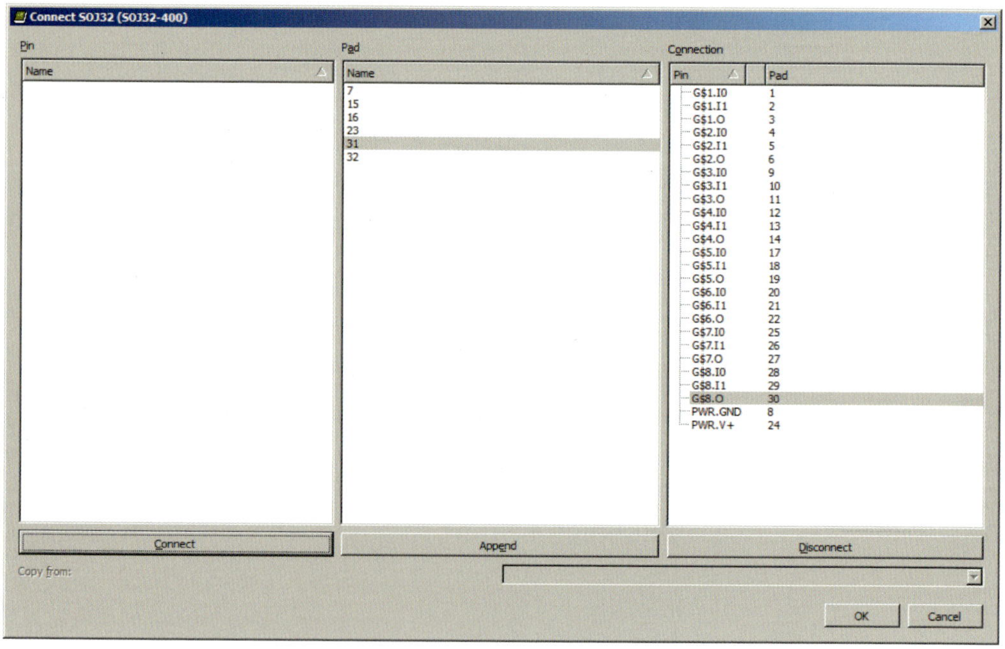

Figure 5-52: the connected pins for GIZZYGATE Device

Step 7 – Assign Prefix and Description to the Device

i We will assign the prefix 'GG' to this device by using either the PREFIX command or **Left-Click** on '`Prefix`'. In either case EAGLE will pop up the Prefix dialog to allow the user to enter the chosen prefix.

ii The last operation is to edit the Description of the Device. The user may complete this, as similarly described, in the previous examples.

iii. save changes to the library by using File ▷ Save, Ctrl-S or **Left-Click** .

The GIZZYGATE device window should appear as shown in Figure 5-53.

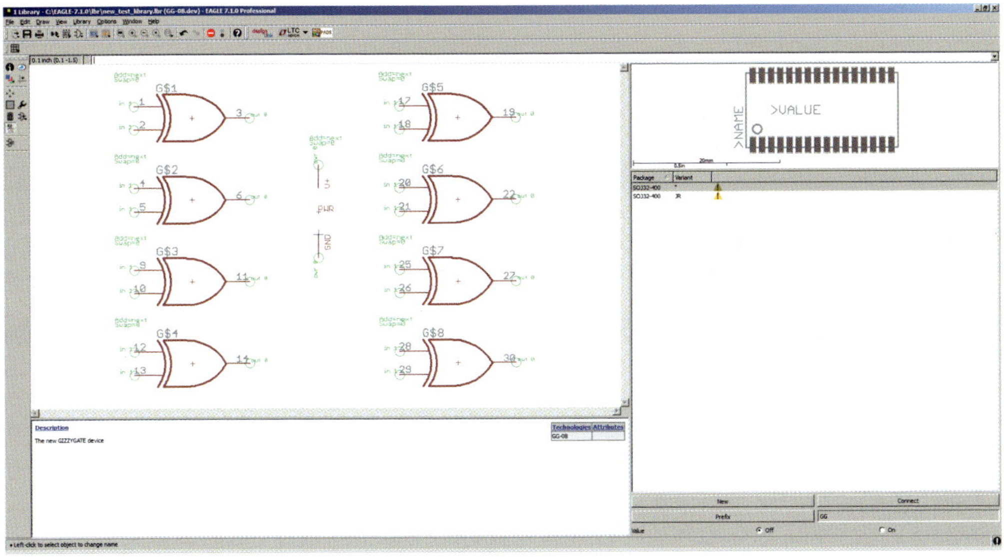

Figure 5-53: the completed GIZZYGATE device window

Labeling and Text Variables

EAGLE recognizes text variables in a symbol or package drawing by the presence of the '>' character. The variable is replaced, when used in a board or schematic, by the actual value of the element.

The valid text variables are:

Valid only for symbol	
>PART	Component name
>GATE	Gate name
>XREF	Part cross-reference
>CONTACT_XREF	Contact cross-reference

Valid only for symbol or package	
>NAME	Component name
>VALUE	Component Value / type 1

Valid only for symbol or schematic	
>SHEET	equivalent to ">SHEETNR/>SHEETS"
>SHEETNR	Sheet number of a schematic
>SHEETS	Total number of sheets in a schematic

Valid overall	
>ASSEMBLY_VARIANT	Name of the current assembly variant
>DRAWING_NAME	Drawing name
>LAST_DATE_TIME	Time of the last modification
>PLOT_DATE_TIME	Time of the plot creation

Of special note are the two text variables >NAME and >VALUE. As noted above, these can be used for labeling packages and symbols. They can be used as 'placeholders' for the actual name and value parameters when the element is edited into a drawing.
At that time, as stated in the NAME command section, names are allocated automatically according to certain rules for elements. They can be edited at any time using the NAME command.

Characteristics of Names

Length

There is no limit on the length of Names in EAGLE.

Special Characters

Names should not contain spaces, semicolons or umlauts. Quotation marks and other characters (above ASCII 127) should be avoided.

The exclamation mark ('!') is a special character for starting and ending the overscore of text e.g. The user should consult the TEXT command for details. If an exclamation mark is visibly required in the text, it needs to be preceded by a backslash e.g. NAME \!TEST names the selected object '!TEST'.

To have a backslash ('\') displayed in a name or text, it should be type twice within the NAME or TEXT command e.g. NAME \\TEST names the selected object '\TEST'.

More specifically for:
Device names

These must not contain either question marks or asterisks, since these characters are used as placeholders for Package variants (?) and technologies (*).

Pad Names
Commas must be avoided in pad names.

Partbus names
These must not contain colons (:), commas (,) or square brackets ([ ]).

Creating Package Variants

If the user does not find the appropriate Package variant in the current library, they may use Packages from another library. This requires using the PACKAGE command to copy the Package into the current variant and to subsequently define a new variant.

An example follows:

i. From within the Device Editor window, **Left-Click** on the 'New' button (lower right-hand part of dialog). A window opens that displays the Packages defined in this library (as shown in Figure 5-54.

ii. In the illustrated case, the selected package (`SOJ32-400`) is the only package capable of accommodating the GIZZYGATE device. If the user selects this variant, and names the new variant 'JR' (by entering '`JR`' in the 'Variant name' field and **Left-Click** on 'OK'), the new variant appears in the lower right-hand pane of the Device Editor window (as shown in Figure 5-55).

    At this point the user may invoke a context menu to allow: variants to be deleted, renamed or newly created; Technologies to be defined; the CONNECT command to be called; or the Package editor to be opened.

    The entry with the yellow exclamation mark ( ) means that the pin-pad assignment has yet to be made.

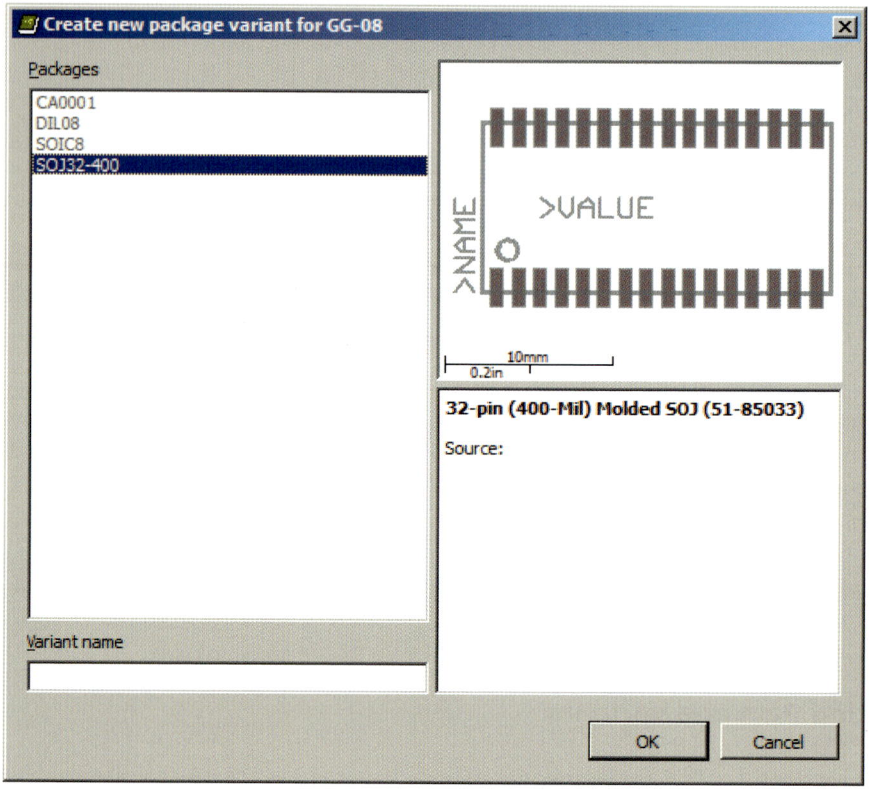

Figure 5-54: package variants for GIZZYGATE device

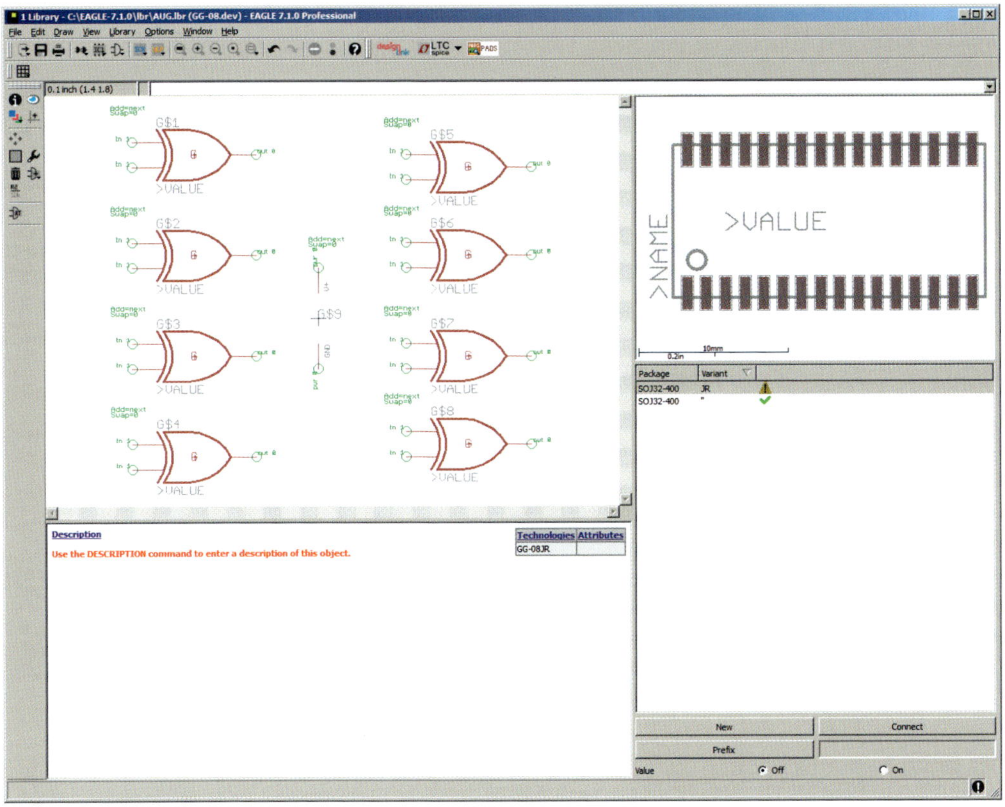

Figure 5-55: new package variant added to GIZZYGATE device

Use of the Addlevel & Swaplevel Parameters

There are two parameters applicable to gates and pins that determine their placement and interchangeability within a schematic diagram. They are the *Addlevel* and *Swaplevel* parameters respectively and are displayed above and left of the Gate in layer 93, Pins (see Figure 5-19).

These parameters may be specified at the time when a gate is added to a schematic (using the ADD command, in the parameter toolbar) or at a later time (by using the CHANGE command).

The Addlevel parameter

The *Addlevel* parameter is used to specify how gates are placed into a schematic diagram by the ADD command. The *Addlevel* defines, for instance, if a Gate is to be added to the schematic only on the user's request or by a pre-defined mechanism.

The following values apply to this parameter:

Next specifies that the symbols are fetched into the schematic in sequence. This means that the ADD command fetches the first unused 'Next' Gates first, before accessing a new device/component.

Must this forces the selected gate to be present in the diagram if another Gate from that component is present. 'Must' Gates cannot be deleted before all other Gates.

Always this value specifies Gates that are used as soon as a component is added.

Can 'Can' gates are only fetched when required.

Request This variable is used for power symbols.

The Swaplevel parameter

The Swaplevel determines whether a Device's Pins or Gates can be swapped within the schematic diagram. Pins or Gates that have the same *Swaplevel* can be exchanged with one another. These properties are specified either when the Symbol is defined or when the Device is created.

For Gates:

Swaplevel	Function
0	the Gate cannot be exchanged for another Gate in the Device
>0	the Gate can be swapped for another Gate within the schematic, in same Device, which has the same Swaplevel

The Swaplevel of a Gate may be found by means of the INFO command, or, alternatively via the context menu *Properties* entry.
The command used to swap gates within a Device is GATESWAP.

For Pins:
The Swaplevel of a Pin is similar to the function for a Gate.

Swaplevel	Function
0	the Pin cannot be exchanged for another Pin in the same Gate
>0	the Pin can be exchanged for another Pin with the same Swaplevel, defined within the same Symbol.

Example: Pins of a diode cannot be exchanged, and are therefore given Swaplevel=0; whereas Pins of a resistor should be assigned the same Swaplevel and >0, since they are interchangeable.

Multiple Pad to One Pin Connections

It is possible to connect one pin to several pads which share a common signal. This is done using the *Append* button in the connect dialog window.

The user technique is as follows:

i. The user marks one pin (in the 'Pin' column) and one pad (in the 'Pad' column) in the connect dialog as usual, and **Left-Clicks** on the 'Connect' button. The pin/pad connection now appears in the 'Connection' column.

ii. To add a further pad to this connection the user first marks the connection, then selects the pad to be added in the 'Pad' column, and **Left-Clicks** on the 'Append' button. (This can be repeated for more pads, if required). The names of the appended pads are displayed in the 'Connection' column.

As soon as the user establishes a multiple pad connection, a special icon is displayed in the 'Connections' column, located between *Pin* and *Pad* list. It informs the user about the mode, being either *All* or *Any* and is illustrated in Figure 5-56.

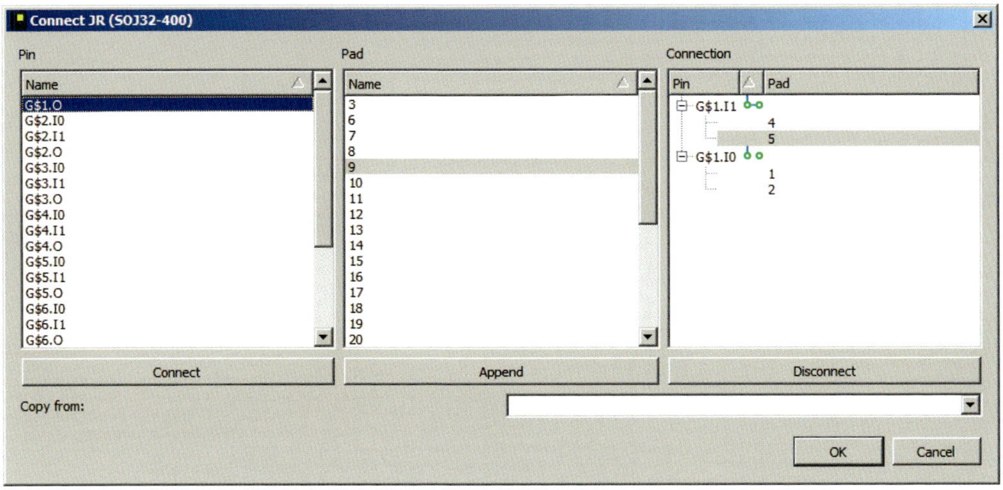

Figure 5-56: example multiple pin-pad connections in the GIZZYGATE device

These modes may be described as follows:

 All — All pads must be connected with traces. In the Layout editor the user will see all pads connected with airwires that have to be routed.

 Any — Only one of the pads will be connected by an airwire and has to be routed. In the routing process it is up to the user which pad is required to be connected with a trace. In this mode, internal connections of a device can be realized.

The user may **Left-Click** on this icon, in the Connection pane of the dialog, to toggle the mode. When such a connection item is expanded, all the pads are listed separately. The user may disconnect one of those pads by **Left-Clicking** on `Disconnect` with one of the pads selected – this will only disconnect that one pad.
The user should also refer to the CONNECT command.

Chapter 6 • Using EAGLE's ROUTE command and Follow-Me router

The EAGLE application provides the user with the ability to perform the routing of tracks automatically (using the Autorouter); manually by using the ROUTE command alone, or with the additional functionality of the 'follow-me' router.

The ROUTE command

This section discusses the application of the ROUTE command, which is activated by

Left-Clicking on .

Upon activation, the command's parameter toolbar is displayed (as shown in Figure 6-1). These parameters can be set prior to the commencement of routing a track (or trace); or dynamically, while the routing is in progress.

ROUTE Parameters

The ROUTE parameter toolbar is shown in Figure 6-1. The toolbar encompasses a number of parameters which determine how the command behaves. They are *Grid*, *Layer*, *Wire Bend Style*, *Miter Radius*, *Miter Style*, *Wire Width*, *Via Shape*, *Via Diameter* and *Drill Diameter*.

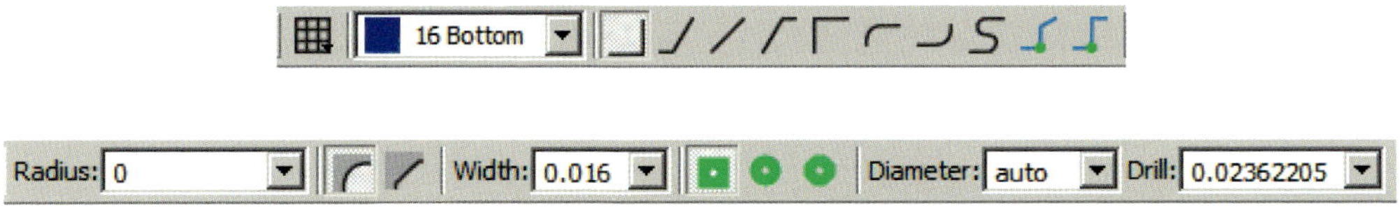

Figure 6-1: ROUTE parameter toolbar (split)

The parameters : *Grid*, *Layer*, *Wire Bend Style*, *Miter Radius*, *Miter Style* & *Wire Width* have the same functionality as described for the WIRE command.

The parameters : *Via Shape*, *Diameter* and *Drill* have the same functionality as described for the VIA command.

The route layer

The initial layer of a track is generally determined by the object from which the selected airwire starts i.e. the track adopts the currently selected layer if the object is in it, otherwise another layer of the commencement object will be adopted.

The **Center-click** mouse action may be used to change the track layer.

The wire width and via parameters

When selecting an airwire for routing , the wire width is determined by the setting in the Design Rules and the net class of the selected signal and the status of the flag Options ▷ Set ▷ Misc ▷ Auto set route width and drill. This is shown in Figure 6-2 . If this is set off (i.e. unchecked) the user is able to manually set the wire width from the drop-down menu in the parameter toolbar. Otherwise, if set on (i.e. checked), the width is automatically calculated and set. This option also controls the via Diameter and Drill parameters.

The width of an airwire that starts at an already existing track, may be automatically set to that track's width by using the key/mouse combination **Shift+Left-Click** before selecting the airwire.

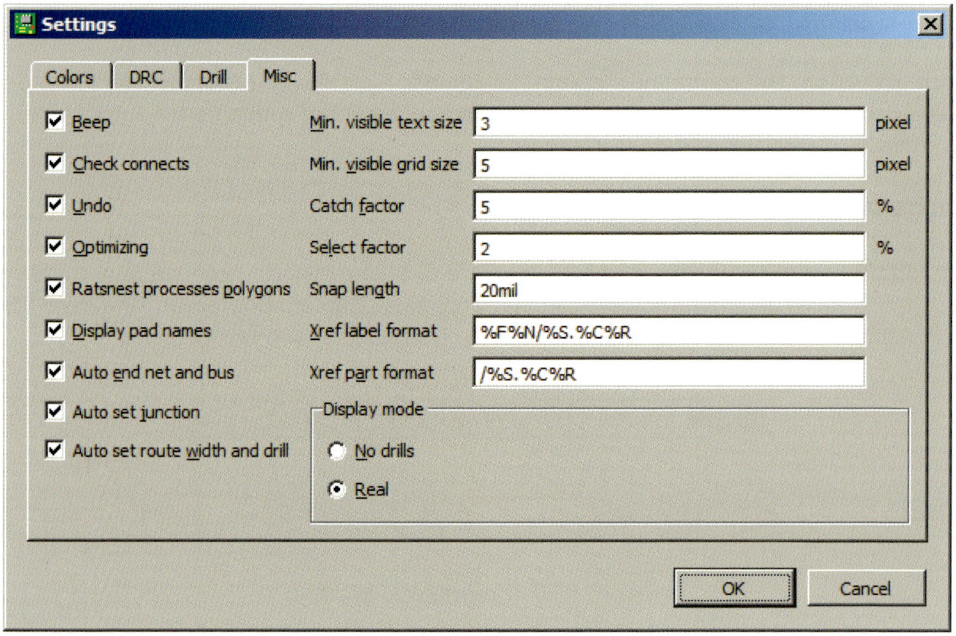

Figure 6-2: Options settings

The user can select a different wire trace width, while the airwire is attached to the cursor, by using the relevant SET command from the keyboard. The most recent track segment will be rerouted with the new width. e.g. `SET width 25`

The same comments apply to the via parameters (i.e. those displayed in the toolbar).

The Snap Function

The `Snap Length` option determines the distance within which a routed trace or wire automatically 'snaps' to the airwire's endpoint. While routing is in progress, the end point of the dynamically calculated airwire is always used as an additional snap point. So, if the remaining airwire has a length that is shorter than SNAP_LENGTH parameter, the routed wire automatically snaps to the airwire's end point, and remains there until the mouse pointer is moved at least SNAP_LENGTH away from that point. This minimum distance for this snap function can be defined by the `Snap Length` option in Figure 6-2.

Using the ROUTE command to place wires (tracks) manually

The user commences ROUTEing of the track by selecting an un-routed airwire connection with **Left-Click.** The end which is closest to the mouse cursor will be used as the starting

point. EAGLE then proceeds to replace one end of it by a wire (track). The airwire/signal name and net class is displayed in the status bar.

If the **Ctrl+Left-Click** key is pressed while selecting the starting point of the trace, and there is no airwire at that point, a new airwire will be created automatically. (The same key/mouse combination may also be used to start the wire at a via.) The starting point of that airwire will be a point on the selected wire or via, that is closest to the mouse cursor (possibly snapped to the nearest grid point).

During the routing process the track/trace wire can be moved around (also see the WIRE command) and further manipulated with a number of key/mouse combinations (see Table 6-1). The description in the previous sections above also outlines possible variations that may be made to the trace by using the ROUTE command parameters.

Mouse / key combination	ROUTE Function
Ctrl + Left-Click	allows the user to commence the routing at any given point along a wire or at a via
Shift + Left-Click	before selecting an airwire, and if the airwire begins at an already existing wire with a different width to that specified, the new wire adopts the width of the existing wire
Center-click	selects the layer
Right-Click	changes the wire bend style
Shift + Right-Click	reverses the direction of switching bend styles
Ctrl + Right-Click	toggles between corresponding bend styles
Shift + Left-Click	places a via at the current cursor position while routing a trace
Ctrl + Left-Click	defines arc radius when placing a wire's end point

Table 6-1: mouse/key combinations

If, during this process, the layer is changed and a via-hole is necessary, it will be added automatically as the wire is placed. When the complete connection has been routed a 'beep' will be given and the next unrouted connection may be selected for routing.

The far end of the airwire will dynamically point to a target segment that is different from the selected one. If the selected signal is already completely routed, the far end will point to the starting point instead. If the selected wire is an arc, the airwire will start at the closest end point of the wire.

Pads and SMDs which are part of the currently routed signal have the so called 'magnetic-pads' function. When routing near these elements the track obeys the 'snap-function' rules described above i.e. within a certain radius around the pad, the wire will be snapped to the pad's center automatically. If the cursor is moved from the pad, the track reverts to an airwire, and continues to follow the cursor.

If a via is to be generated **Shift + Left-Click** is used at this point, (if possible and the airwire has not already been completely routed). The generated via will have either the appropriate length or, if unable to be determined, will go from layer 1 through 16.

The user moves the mouse to the final position of the wire. The trace is then terminated by **Left-Click** to place the wire; at which point a new wire segment will be attached to the cursor. When a signal line has been completely laid, EAGLE confirms that there is a correct connection with a short beep as it is placed.

The Follow-me router

Setting Options and configuring the router

The follow-me router is constrained by a number of settings that are part of the overall configuration of the project. These are:

Design Rules
: the router obeys the Design Rule settings for Clearance, Distance and Size. The reader should refer to Figure 4-40, Figure 4-41 and Figure 4-42 respectively. The router also accommodates any particular values of net classes that may have been defined, together with the layer setup (in the DRC Layers tab shown in Figure 4-39).

Grid setting
: the grid setting in the layout editor is used by the router as its own grid and may be changed by using the GRID command and/or the Grid dialog.

Layer setting
: the current Layer is displayed in the parameter toolbar (as shown in Figure 6-1), and may be changed by the use of the drop-down menu in this toolbar.

Wire width & drill diameter

the follow-me router responds immediately to changes in the wire width and drill diameter of vias parameters. If the Auto Option is set (see Figure 6-2), as described above, the router adopts the given values from the Design Rules and net classes immediately when the airwire is selected.

Setting routing parameters

The user may set up the parameters that modify the routing strategy by using the command:

```
AUTO FOLLOWME
```

This action will invoke the Follow-me parameter Setup dialog as shown in Figure 6-3.

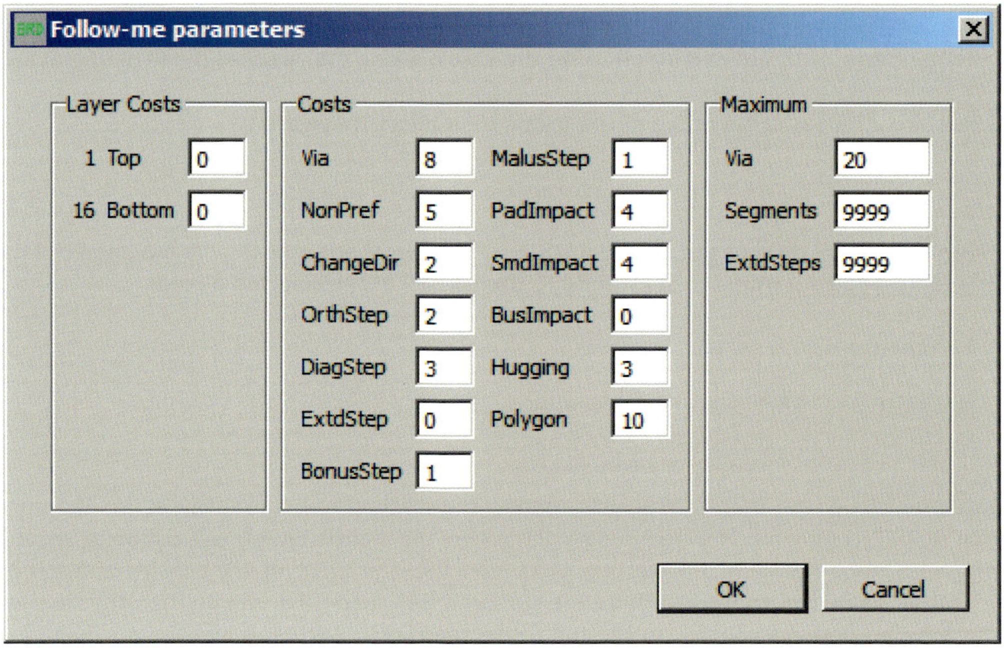

Figure 6-3: AUTO 'Follow-me' parameters dialog

The sections within this dialog are as follows:

Layer Costs & Costs

these parameters control the usage of each layer. The higher the value (from 0 up to 99), the more the layer is avoided. By default, EAGLE has set 'reasonable' values as initial values.

Maximum

these parameters simply control the following:

- Vias the maximum number that may be used to create a connecting track. If this value is set to 0, the Followme router is not allowed to set vias automatically. This may be manually overridden by changing the layer.
- Segments the maximum number of wire pieces that a track may comprise.
- ExtdSteps the number of steps that are allowed, at 45 degrees to the preferred direction, without a conflict with the limiting value of cfExtdStep.

Starting and using the Follow-me router

The EAGLE application provides the user with the ability to perform automatic routing of single tracks. This functionality is provided by the 'Follow-me' router, which draws on the full capability of EAGLE's Autorouter to complete the task.

The follow-me router is started after activating either by the ROUTE command from the command line, or by **Left-Clicking** on  ; then by invoking the required mode of operation.

There are 2 modes of operation of the follow-me router. These are :

partial mode (from one side)

is activated by  or the command '`set wire_bend 8`' and routes only the shorter side (i.e. the segment from the start point to the cursor) of the selected airwire.

full mode (from both sides)

is activated by  or the command '`set wire_bend 9`' and routes both sides of the selected airwire simultaneously.

In either mode ,the user commences routing the track in the same way as for the normal ROUTE command. However, using the follow-me router EAGLE will calculate an appropriate trace between the starting point and the end point of the airwire and trace. In partial mode the endpoint will be the cursor, in full mode this will be the other end of the airwire. More specifically, in the full mode the router calculates the trace simultaneously in both directions, establishing an end-to-end wire which replaces the selected airwire. An illustration of the partial mode of operation of the follow-me router is shown in Figure 6-4 , while using the follow-me router in the full mode is shown in Figure 6-5.

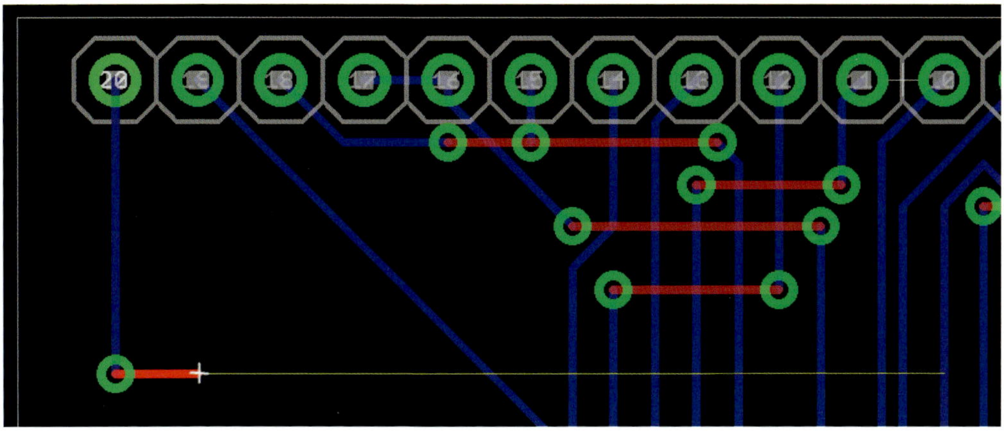

Figure 6-4: Operation of the follow-me router in partial mode

The former shows the red section of the track attached to the cursor, having been calculated from the starting point; pin 20. The latter shows the complete track calculated from pin 20 to another point (off the diagram bottom edge). The connection has already been made from the blue track to the terminating connection by using the red track and two vias.

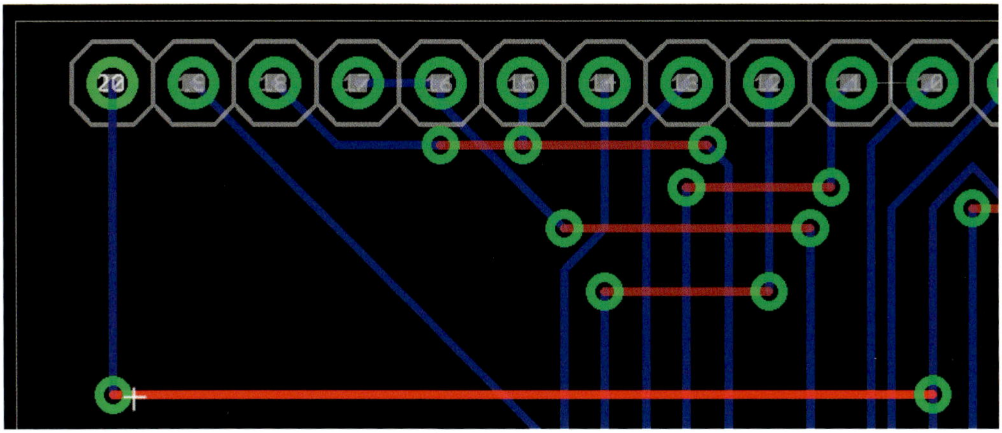

Figure 6-5: Operation of the follow-me router in full mode

Once the automatic routing process is complete, the airwire will be replaced by the actual routed wires and vias. If the routing can not be completed (for instance due to Design Rules restrictions), the cursor changes into a 'forbidden or X' sign. If the full mode (*bend style* 9) is used, it is possible that only one side of the airwire can be routed, while the other side can not.

The Follow-me router works by marking the grid point at the current mouse position as a starting point, and using the Autorouter to find a path from that point to any point along the signal segment at which the selected airwire ends (which is not necessarily the exact end point of the airwire). The starting point also considers the currently selected layer. The routing calculations may be influenced by changing the current layer and EAGLE may add vias at points it finds appropriate while the process continues.

When the mouse is moved, any previous result is discarded and a new calculation is started. The remaining part of the airwire is then calculated dynamically. This may result in the airwire pointing to another object which is part of the same signal which, in turn, depends upon the current cursor position.

At any point where the routing is deemed successful, the user should terminate the routing and fix the result with **Left-Click.**

Chapter 7 • Using New EAGLE V7 Features

Autorouter Features

In V7 of EAGLE, enhancements to the Autorouter module allow it to support the calculation of multiple autorouter jobs at a time, and for it to use multicore processors.

The enhanced features incorporate some new setup options including; the automatic choice of the routing grid, or automatically determining the preferred directions in the signal layers. The setting for *effort* determines the number of calculated routing jobs. Each of the proposed jobs can be customized.

Additionally, a new capability allows the user to select the socalled "TopRouter" as a kind of prerouter. It functions with a new gridless algorithm which first tries to establish the trace connections, and then uses the classic EAGLE Autorouter for optimization. By way of example, Figure 7-1 shows a sample PCB which has been routed without selecting the TopRouter capability, while Figure 7-2 shows exactly the same layout using the AutoRouter with the TopRouter capability selected.

This section does not discuss the Autorouter functionality, since it is already comprehensively explained in the EAGLE V7 Manual (see Chapter 7 – The Autorouter).

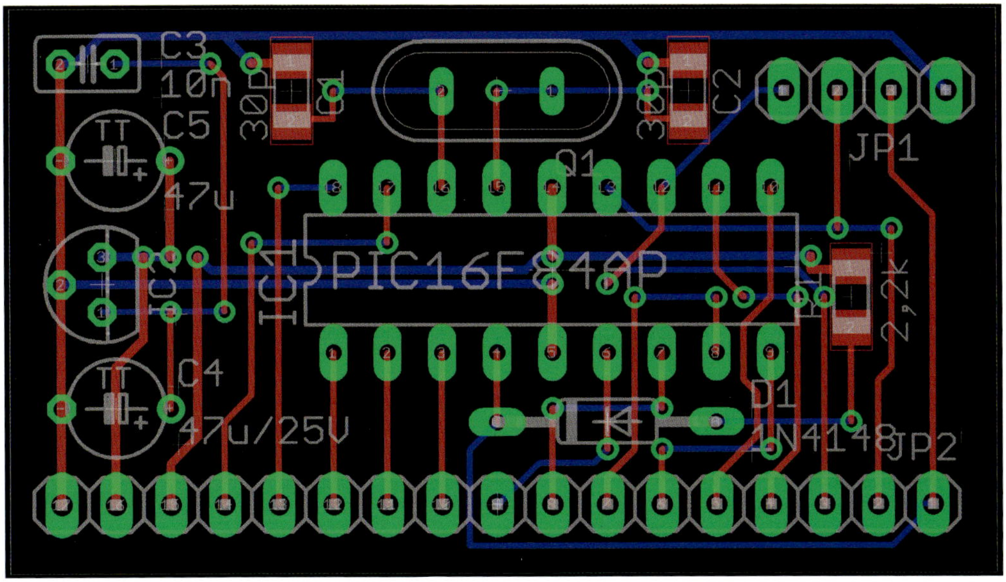

Figure 7-1: Sample PCB Layout executing the Autorouter without using the TopRouter

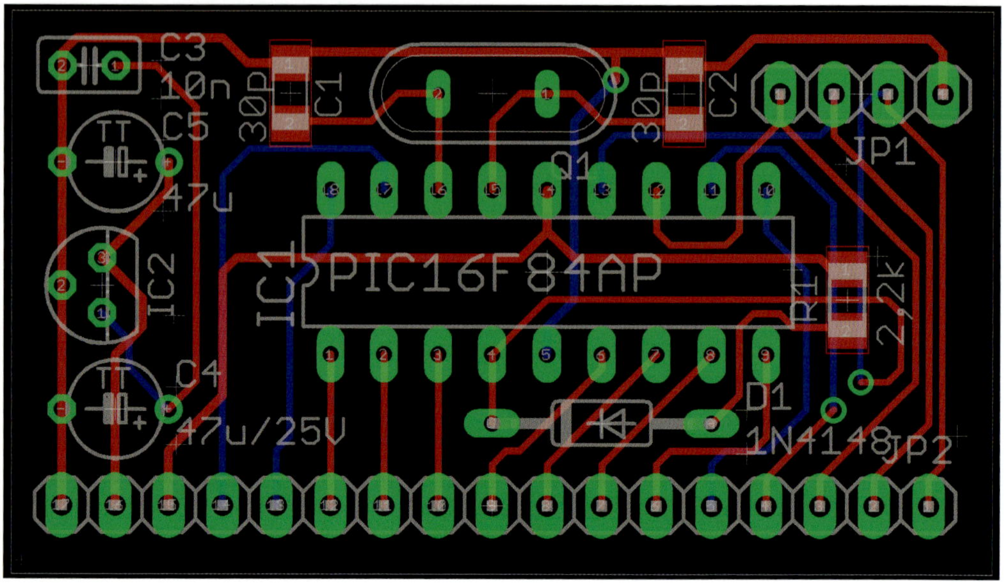

Figure 7-2: Sample PCB Layout executing the Autorouter and using the TopRoute

Hierarchical Schematics in EAGLE

One of the new features of EAGLE V7 is the ability to create a structured schematic, organized in a hierarchical form. It achieves this by using sub-units called 'Modules' and their functional interfaces called 'Ports'. The hierarchy can have any depth. The resultant PCB layout is comparable to the layout generated from a non- hierarchical schematic of the same design.

Figure 7-3 illustrates a project schematic which has been constructed using this hierarchical method. A brief examination of this project shows that it differs from a normal schematic diagram. It consists mainly of 'blocks', which are interconnected via nets at the interface points. In fact, the 'blocks' are examples (instances) of EAGLE *Modules* which have *Ports* for the interconnection of *Nets* (their behavior is somewhat similar to that of Pins).

Modules are schematics, represented by a 'block' in the higher level schematic diagram of the circuit. These blocks represent instances of the constituent circuit within the complete design and may be used repeatedly within that design. These can be seen in the Sheet toolbar of the main Schematic Editor window (see the left hand side of Figure 7-3).

Ports allow for the interconnection of Modules at the main circuit diagram, or at some other level i.e. schematics which make up a Module may themselves contain Modules. The depth of the diagram hierarchy may be arbitrarily deep.

So, in the top level circuit diagram of the Project, the Modules (instances) use a network (of Nets or simple Buses) to interconnect via Ports. A Port therefore serves as an interface for the nets within a module to the outside world (or the next level 'up' in the hierarchy)

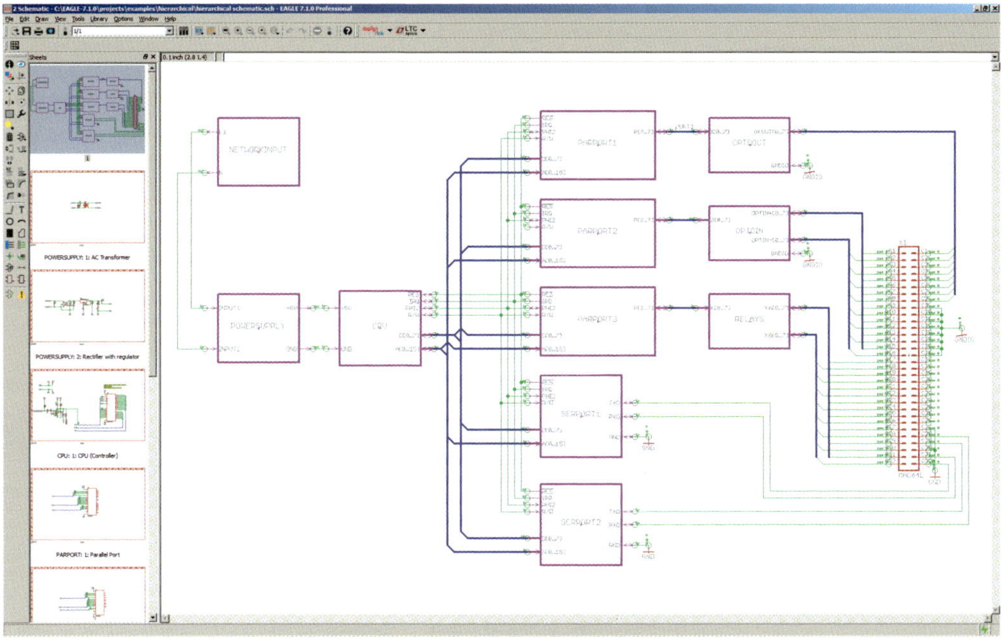

Figure 7-3: Editor window displaying a hierarchical schematic project

Working with the Hierarchical Schematics Elements

This section will illustrate the features and methods of working with the basic elements of the new hierarchical structure of EAGLE V7. The schematic in Figure 7-3 will serve as a reference for some following examples.

It is assumed that the reader has a working knowledge of EAGLE, in particular; how to create schematic diagrams with the Schematic Editor module of the EAGLE software.
For the purposes of this example, we assume that a new, blank schematic has been created. This will be used to illustrate how to work with the various elements of the hierarchical structure functionality.

Working with Modules

As stated previously, Modules are a building block of the hierarchical schematic drawing. In this section the process of creating, editing and deleting a Module will be illustrated.

Creating a Module

The first step in creating a hierarchical schematic is to create a Module. A module may be created within a schematic by using the command:

```
Module
```

or by using the icon  **+ Left-Click**, to place the module. EAGLE then opens the dialog shown in Figure 7-4.

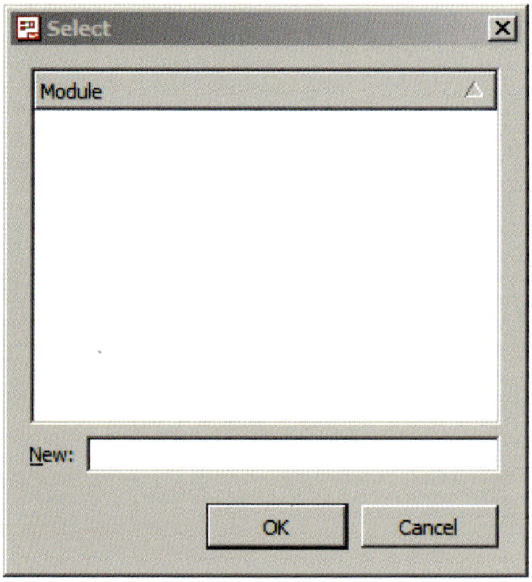

Figure 7-4: Module dialog

At this point the user may enter the name of the Module to be created. For this tutorial, we will name our module; 'NETWORKINPUT'. This should be placed in the diagram in the normal way (**Left-Click**).

Once a module has been created, the user may place further instances of that module by using the Module command. In this context EAGLE will display the Module selection dialog (as illustrated in Figure 7-5), and then allow the user to select an existing Module by name, or to create a new one.

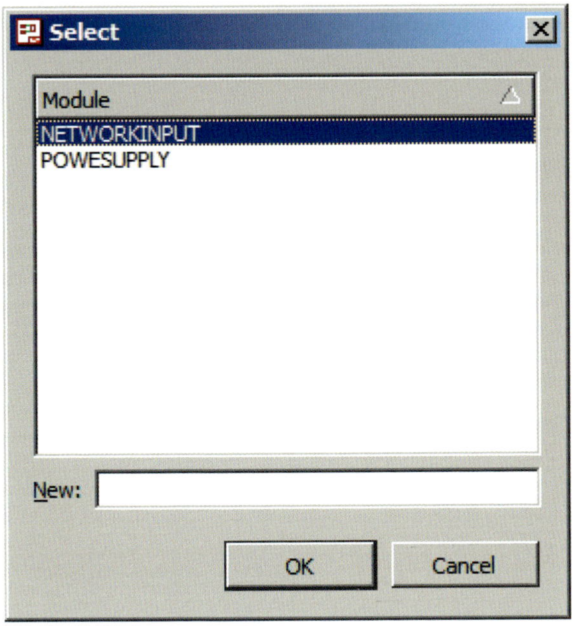

Figure 7-5: Module selection dialog while creating a Module

To continue our example, the user should place another, new Module into the schematic, naming this example 'POWERSUPPLY'. The resultant schematic editor window should appear as in Figure 7-6. The user should note the blank 'sheets' present, as entries in the Sheet toolbar to the left of the window,are both appropriately named.

Using the same Module command icon it is also possible to place multiple instances of the same Module into a schematic. This is illustrated in Figure 7-7 where 2 instances of the Module 'CPU' have been placed in the schematic, named 'CPU' and 'CPU1' respectively. The schematic for the actual 'CPU' Module can be seen on the left of the diagram, in the sheet toolbar.

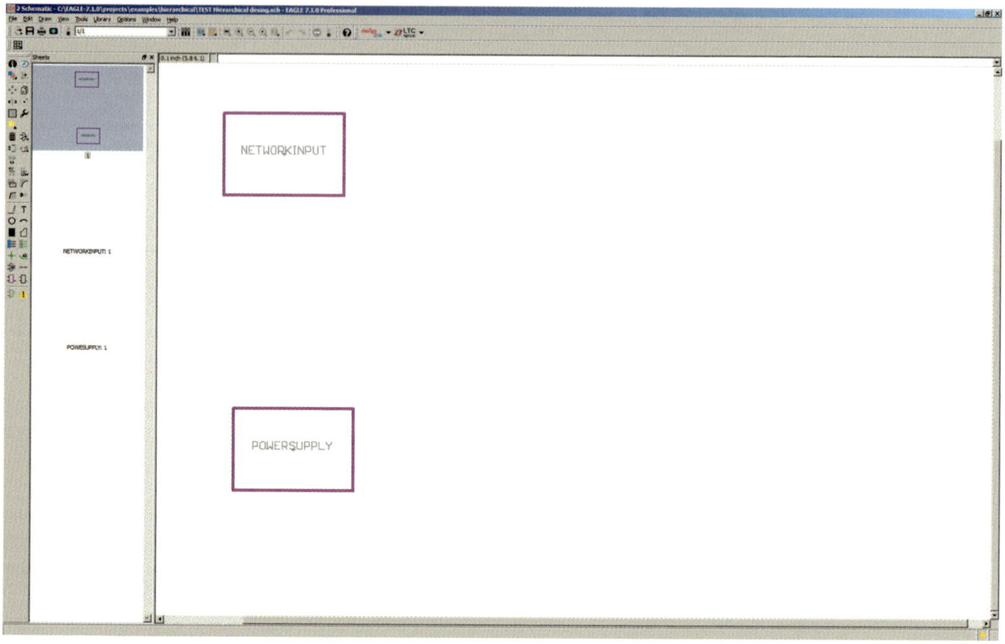

Figure 7-6: Modules in top level schematic

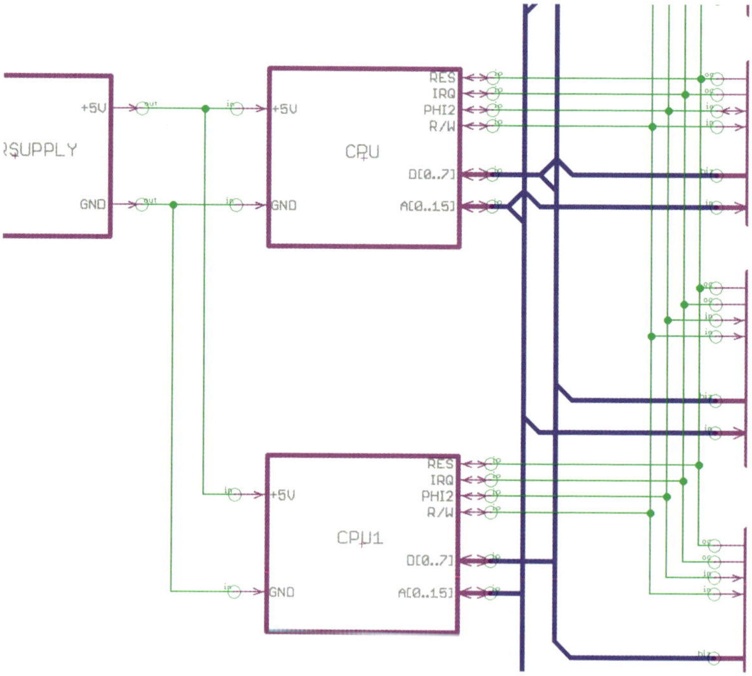

Figure 7-7: Multiple instances of a Module in a schematic

Editing a Module

When a module is edited using the icon in the context menu (see Figure 7-9)

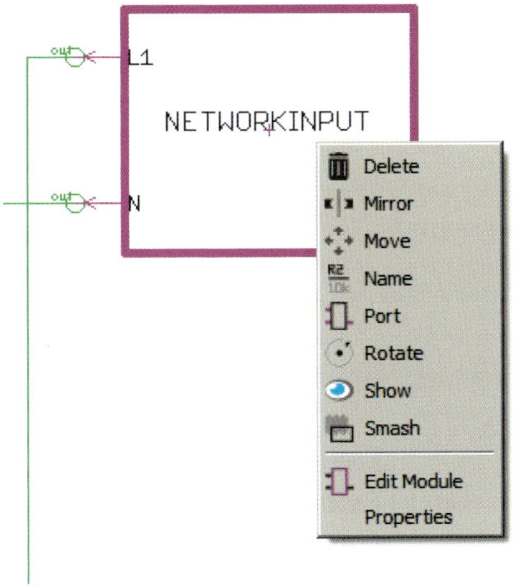

Figure 7-8: Context menu for editing a Module

or the EDIT command e.g.

```
EDIT NETWORKINPUT.mod
```

would open the `NETWORKINPUT` module for editing.

If the Module is empty, the schematic for the Module is opened ready for the user to create a new drawing. If the Module is not empty the exiting Module schematic is opened (at the first sheet if it is a multi-sheet schematic).

The Module schematic may then be created or edited in the normal process for such a drawing. Modules may be created which cover more than one sheet.

Using the Context Menu to edit modules from the Sheet toolbar.
In addition to the functionality within the menu illustrated in Figure 7-8, EAGLE offers a more comprehensive method of editing Modules by using the Context Menu within the Module itself. This can be seen in Figure 7-9.

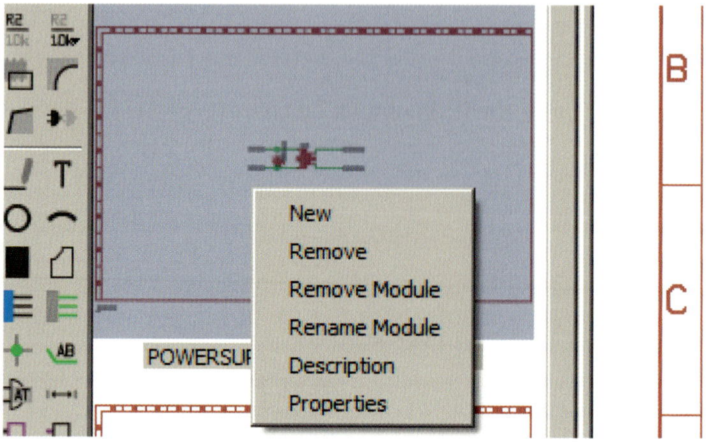

Figure 7-9: Context menu for editing Modules

Using this feature the user may:

- create a new additional module sheet
- remove a module sheet
- remove a complete module, with all its module instances, from the schematic
- edit the description of the module

  The description of a module can be formatted with HTML tags. The first line of the description will be displayed, in addition to the module name, in the module sheet preview and in the Sheet combo box.

- edit some properties of the module instance

Deleting a Module

A Module may be removed from a schematic by using the DELETE command, or using the command icon (), and subsequently selecting the Module with **Left-Click**.

Other Operations with Modules

If the user **Right-Clicks** on a Module in the schematic, a context menu will be displayed, as shown in Figure 7-10. This lists the relevant operations available to the user for manipulating a Module. Many of these have a similar function to that used on other schematic elements (components), namely; Delete, Mirror, Move, Name, Rotate Show and Smash. The 'Edit Module' entry is discussed below.

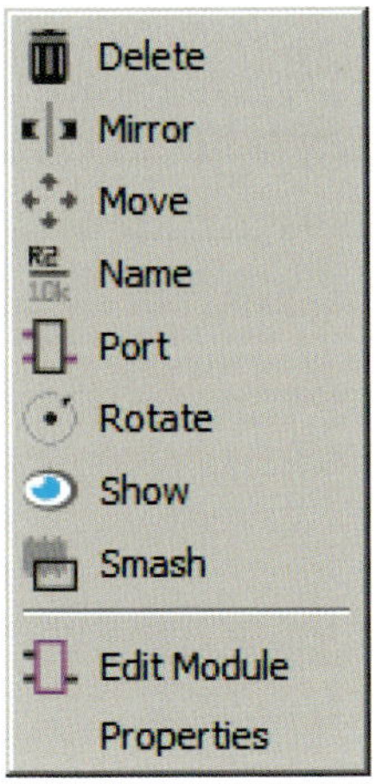

Figure 7-10: Module context menu

Properties of Modules

The Properties entry in the context menu requires special attention. Invoking this menu item on the CPU Module, displays the dialog shown in Figure 7-11. This comprises two sections; the Module instance (ModInst) and the Module definition itself (Module).

The upper part of the dialog (ModInst) displays the properties of this instance of the Module. Here the instance has the same name as the actual module. However, this may be re-named at any time using the NAME command.

The lower part of the dialog (Module) displays the properties of the Module itself. Importantly, it displays the Ports configured for this Module, together with their associated Direction.

In the *Properties* section, the user has the opportunity to define a prefix; and the size of the symbol, of the module instance, that represents the module in the schematic.

The Prefix defines the name of the module instances, similar to the prefix definition for a device in a library. For example; if the user chooses *'PS'* as a prefix for a module named *'Power_Supply'*, the name of the first module instance will be *PS1*, the second *PS2*, and so on. If there is no prefix defined, the module name + number will be used.

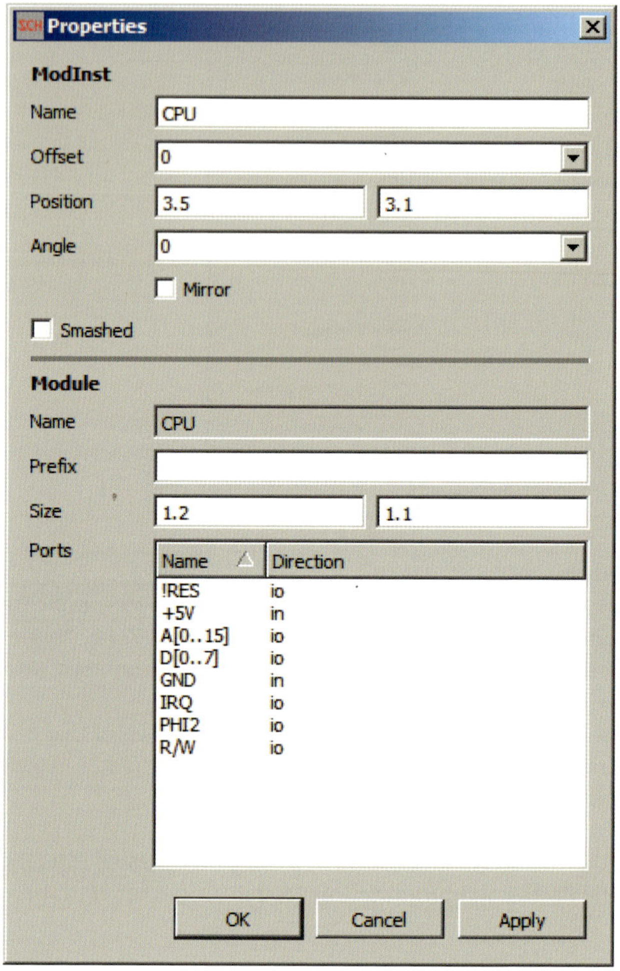

Figure 7-11: Properties of the CPU Module

Editing Module Sheets

The user may change the order of the module sheets by using *Drag&Drop* in the sheet preview toolbar.

It is also possible to move a schematic sheet from the main level 'down' into a module. The result is a corresponding new module sheet.

Further, sheets may be moved out of a module 'up' into the main schematic level.

Warning ! This can have a significant impact on the circuit design under certain circumstances, especially with its effect on the corresponding PCB layout.

Working with Ports

Ports may be manipulated using similar types of commands as employed with other elements; they may be created, edited, moved, and deleted.

Creating a Port

To create a port on a module, the user may use the

```
Port
```

command or use the icon  **+ Left-Click**, to place the port.

Before placing the port, EAGLE will display a dialog similar to that in Figure 7-12. This allows the user to select the Net that will be included in the Port 'interface' at the next higher level of the drawing hierarchy.

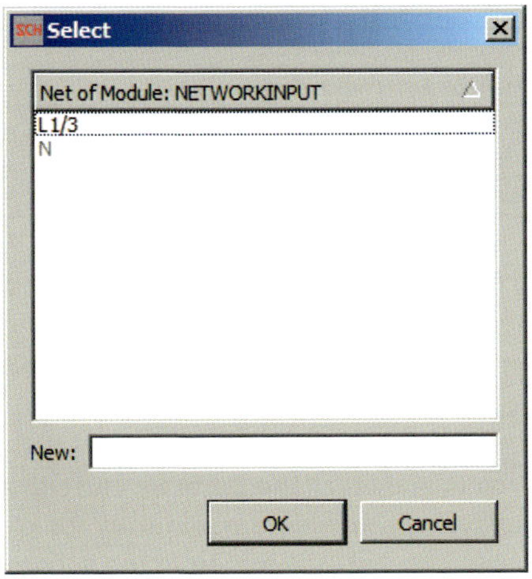

Figure 7-12: The Net dialog for a Port

Next, the user should choose the *Direction* from the parameter toolbar as illustrated in Figure 7-13.

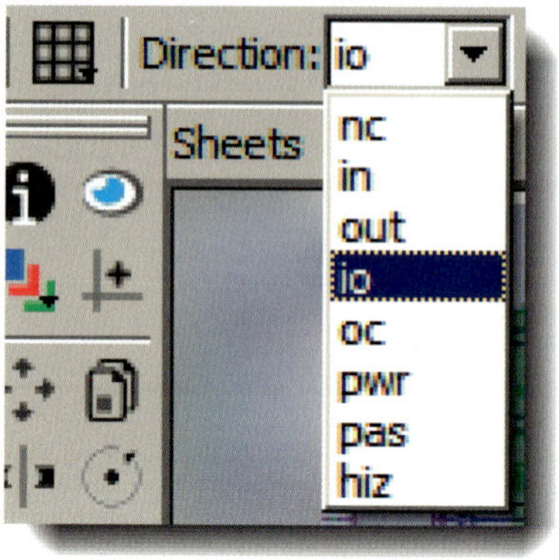

Figure 7-13: The Direction toolbar for Ports

The *Direction* parameter describes the logical direction of signal flow or function for the port. The valid options for the parameter are shown in Table 7-1:

Direction Symbol	Functionality
NC	not connected
In	input
Out	output (totempole)
IO	in/out, bidirectional (default)
OC	open collector or open drain
Hiz	high impedance(3State) output
Pas	passive
Pwr	power pin (Vcc, Gnd, Vss ...), supply voltage input

Table 7-1: Port Direction parameter and functionality

Prior to placement, the user may use the **Right-Click** function to rotate the port into the correct alignment.

After placement, the direction is shown at the ports by corresponding arrows. The connection point of the port is displayed in the same manner as for pins of components; in layer 93, *Pins*. This can be seen with any port contained in the schematic in Figure 7-7.

Editing a Port
Once placed, a Port may be moved and its Properties changed.

To move a Port, the user may use the `Move` command or the icon, then **Ctrl + Left-Click**, to place the port.

The Properties of a port may be changed by using the `Info` command or the icon, then **Ctrl + Left-Click**. This forces EAGLE to open the dialog shown in Figure 7-14, which illustrates the Properties dialog for Port AC1 on the 'POWERSUPPLY' Module. The drop-down menu may be used to change the Direction of the port.

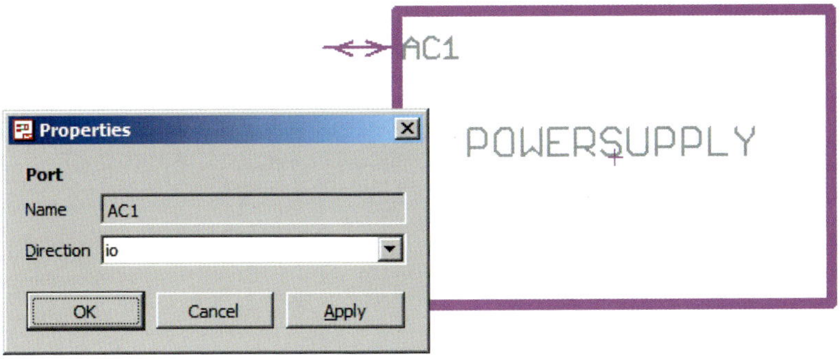

Figure 7-14: Properties of the AC1 Port

Deleting a Port

A Port may be removed from a schematic by using the `DELETE` command, or using the command icon ( ), and subsequently selecting the Port with **Ctrl + Left-Click**.

Appendix 1 • Useful Industry References

This Appendix brings together a collection of data from diverse sources to serve as a convenient reference point for the reader.

Some of this data is extracted from industry standards and presented in a form which is more useable and/or does not breach any intellectual property rights.

Standards in PCB design manufacture

The Association Connecting Electronics Industries (known as IPC – see www.ipc.org) is the pre-eminent industry body for reference in design, production and manufacturing of printed circuit boards in all their forms. This body, among other things, produces standards to which manufacturers refer, when consistency and quality assurance are essential.

The following page presents a 'road map' summary of the standards documents produced by the IPC. Some of these standards are referenced in sections of this book.

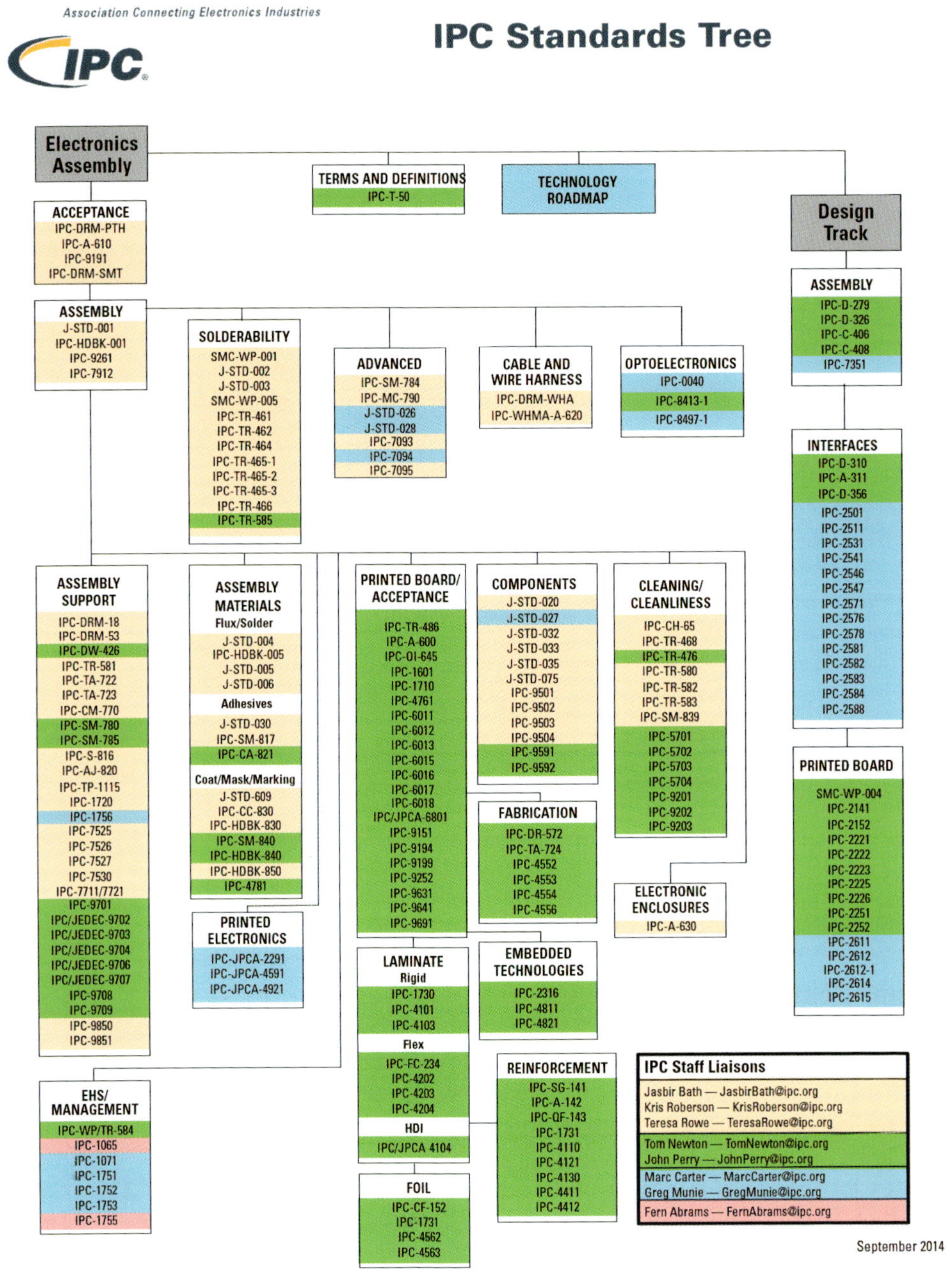

For more details on these standards, visit the IPC Document Revision Table located at www.ipc.org/revisions
IPC Headquarters • 3000 Lakeside Drive, Suite 309 S., Bannockburn, IL USA • www.ipc.org

Source IPC; www.ipc.org

Copper Foil in PCB Manufacture

When a PCB is manufactured, the fabricator uses copper 'foil' or sheeting which is laminated to the substrate material.
The industry uses *de facto* nomenclature which designates the characteristics of a particular weight, and subsequent thickness, of the copper when on the board. This nomenclature is given in Table A1-1.

Common Industry Nomenclature		Weight / Area	Weight / Area	Nominal Thickness	Nominal Thickness
Foil Designator	Weight Designator	(oz/ft^2)	(g/m^2)	(microns)	(mils)
E	5 µm	0.148	45.1	5.1	0.20
Q	9 µm	0.249	75.9	8.5	0.34
T	12 µm	0.350	106.8	12.0	0.47
H	½ oz	0.500	152.5	17.1	0.68
M	¾ oz	0.750	228.8	25.7	1.01
1	1 oz	1	305.0	34.3	1.35
2	2 oz	2	610.0	68.6	2.70
3	3 oz	3	915.0	102.9	4.05
4	4 oz	4	1220.0	137.2	5.40
5	5 oz	5	1525.0	171.5	6.75
6	6 oz	6	1830.0	205.7	8.10
7	7 oz	7	2135.0	240.0	9.45
10	10 oz	10	3050.0	342.9	13.50
14	14 oz	14	4270.0	480.1	18.90

Table A1-1 - Industry grades of Copper Foil Thickness

Derived from IPC-4101

Thermal design of PCB Traces

Of significant importance is the current carrying capacity of a trace, together with the attendant rise in temperature when carrying this same current. PCB designers need to know the thermal effects and limiting temperature rises of their trace specifications.

Guidelines for the thermal design of traces on PCB is documented in 'IPC-2221 Generic Standard on Printed Board Design'.

IPC-2221 recommendations are based on a general thermodynamic formula for the carrying capacity of a trace conductor for a given trace cross-section and temperature rise. The formula is:

$$I = k \times \Delta T^{\beta_1} A^{\beta_2}$$

where:
I = current in amps,
ΔT = change in Temperature above ambient, in degrees C,
A = cross sectional area in square mils, and
k, β_1 and β_2 are constants.

Another industry participant (UltraCAD Design, Inc. *www.ultracad.com*) has re-evaluated the standards since they were compiled and has derived a modified formula for the current carrying capacity of a trace where the area is expressed in width and thickness terms. This makes any calculation easier, since the cross section may be derived from the copper foil weight and the density of copper.

$$I = k \times \Delta T^{\beta_1} W^{\beta_2} Th^{\beta_3}$$

where:
W = the trace width in mils
Th = the trace thickness in mils
k, β_1, β_2 and β_3 are constants.

The values for the constants k, β_1, β_2 and β_3 vary according to environmental test conditions and the source publishing those test results. However, a conservative derivation could be used as follows for the case of internal and external traces:

Trace Type	*k*	β_1	β_2	β_3
Internal	0.024	0.440	0.760	0.540
External	0.048	0.440	0.760	0.540

Using the resulting formulae we have calculated the current limits in a trace for a given range of temperature rises (ΔT) and trace widths. These results are given in Tables 8-2 through 8-15 for industry grades of copper foil weights (thicknesses).

For ¼ oz copper

Current Limits for External Traces (Amperes)

Trace Width in MILS

ΔT temp rise in Deg C	10	20	30	40	50	60	70	80	90	100	110	120	130	140	150	160	170	180	190	200	210	220
1	0.154	0.261	0.356	0.442	0.524	0.602	0.677	0.749	0.819	0.888	0.954	1.020	1.084	1.146	1.208	1.269	1.329	1.388	1.446	1.503	1.560	1.616
2	0.209	0.354	0.482	0.600	0.711	0.817	0.918	1.016	1.112	1.204	1.295	1.383	1.470	1.555	1.639	1.721	1.802	1.882	1.961	2.039	2.116	2.192
3	0.250	0.424	0.576	0.717	0.850	0.976	1.098	1.215	1.329	1.439	1.548	1.653	1.757	1.859	1.959	2.057	2.154	2.250	2.344	2.438	2.530	2.621
4	0.284	0.481	0.654	0.814	0.965	1.108	1.246	1.379	1.508	1.634	1.756	1.876	1.994	2.110	2.223	2.335	2.445	2.554	2.661	2.766	2.871	2.974
5	0.313	0.530	0.722	0.898	1.064	1.222	1.374	1.521	1.663	1.802	1.938	2.070	2.200	2.327	2.453	2.576	2.697	2.817	2.935	3.052	3.167	3.281
6	0.339	0.575	0.782	0.973	1.153	1.324	1.489	1.648	1.802	1.953	2.099	2.243	2.384	2.522	2.657	2.791	2.923	3.052	3.180	3.307	3.432	3.555
7	0.363	0.615	0.837	1.041	1.234	1.417	1.594	1.764	1.929	2.090	2.247	2.400	2.551	2.699	2.844	2.987	3.128	3.267	3.404	3.539	3.673	3.805
8	0.385	0.652	0.888	1.104	1.309	1.503	1.690	1.870	2.046	2.216	2.383	2.546	2.705	2.862	3.016	3.168	3.317	3.464	3.610	3.753	3.895	4.035
9	0.406	0.687	0.935	1.163	1.378	1.583	1.780	1.970	2.154	2.334	2.509	2.681	2.849	3.014	3.176	3.336	3.493	3.648	3.802	3.953	4.102	4.250
10	0.425	0.719	0.979	1.218	1.444	1.658	1.864	2.063	2.257	2.445	2.628	2.808	2.984	3.157	3.327	3.494	3.659	3.822	3.982	4.140	4.297	4.451
11	0.443	0.750	1.021	1.271	1.505	1.729	1.944	2.152	2.353	2.549	2.741	2.928	3.112	3.292	3.470	3.644	3.816	3.985	4.152	4.318	4.481	4.642
12	0.460	0.780	1.061	1.320	1.564	1.797	2.020	2.236	2.445	2.649	2.848	3.043	3.234	3.421	3.605	3.786	3.965	4.141	4.315	4.486	4.655	4.823
13	0.477	0.808	1.099	1.368	1.620	1.861	2.092	2.316	2.533	2.744	2.950	3.152	3.349	3.543	3.734	3.922	4.107	4.289	4.469	4.647	4.822	4.996
14	0.493	0.834	1.135	1.413	1.674	1.923	2.162	2.393	2.617	2.835	3.048	3.256	3.460	3.661	3.858	4.052	4.243	4.431	4.617	4.801	4.982	5.162
15	0.508	0.860	1.170	1.456	1.726	1.982	2.228	2.466	2.697	2.922	3.142	3.357	3.567	3.774	3.977	4.177	4.374	4.568	4.760	4.949	5.136	5.321
16	0.522	0.885	1.204	1.498	1.775	2.039	2.293	2.537	2.775	3.006	3.232	3.453	3.670	3.882	4.091	4.297	4.500	4.700	4.897	5.091	5.284	5.474
17	0.537	0.909	1.237	1.539	1.823	2.094	2.355	2.606	2.850	3.088	3.320	3.547	3.769	3.987	4.202	4.413	4.621	4.827	5.029	5.229	5.427	5.622
18	0.550	0.932	1.268	1.578	1.870	2.148	2.415	2.672	2.923	3.166	3.404	3.637	3.865	4.089	4.309	4.526	4.739	4.950	5.157	5.362	5.565	5.765
19	0.563	0.954	1.299	1.616	1.915	2.199	2.473	2.737	2.993	3.243	3.486	3.725	3.958	4.187	4.413	4.635	4.853	5.069	5.281	5.491	5.699	5.904
20	0.576	0.976	1.328	1.653	1.958	2.250	2.529	2.799	3.061	3.317	3.566	3.810	4.048	4.283	4.514	4.741	4.964	5.184	5.402	5.617	5.829	6.039
21	0.589	0.997	1.357	1.689	2.001	2.298	2.584	2.860	3.128	3.389	3.643	3.892	4.136	4.376	4.612	4.843	5.072	5.297	5.519	5.739	5.955	6.170
22	0.601	1.018	1.385	1.724	2.042	2.346	2.637	2.919	3.192	3.459	3.718	3.973	4.222	4.466	4.707	4.944	5.177	5.406	5.633	5.857	6.078	6.297
23	0.613	1.038	1.413	1.758	2.083	2.392	2.690	2.977	3.256	3.527	3.792	4.051	4.305	4.555	4.800	5.041	5.279	5.513	5.745	5.973	6.199	6.422
24	0.625	1.058	1.439	1.791	2.122	2.437	2.740	3.033	3.317	3.594	3.864	4.128	4.387	4.641	4.891	5.136	5.379	5.617	5.853	6.086	6.316	6.543
25	0.636	1.077	1.465	1.823	2.160	2.482	2.790	3.088	3.377	3.659	3.934	4.203	4.466	4.725	4.979	5.230	5.476	5.719	5.959	6.196	6.430	6.662
26	0.647	1.095	1.491	1.855	2.198	2.525	2.839	3.142	3.436	3.722	4.002	4.276	4.544	4.807	5.066	5.321	5.571	5.819	6.063	6.304	6.542	6.777
27	0.658	1.114	1.516	1.886	2.235	2.567	2.886	3.194	3.494	3.785	4.069	4.347	4.620	4.888	5.151	5.410	5.665	5.916	6.164	6.409	6.652	6.891
28	0.668	1.132	1.540	1.917	2.271	2.608	2.933	3.246	3.550	3.846	4.135	4.417	4.694	4.966	5.234	5.497	5.756	6.012	6.264	6.513	6.759	7.002
29	0.679	1.149	1.564	1.947	2.306	2.649	2.978	3.296	3.605	3.906	4.199	4.486	4.768	5.044	5.315	5.582	5.846	6.105	6.361	6.614	6.864	7.111
30	0.689	1.167	1.588	1.976	2.341	2.689	3.023	3.346	3.659	3.964	4.262	4.554	4.839	5.120	5.395	5.666	5.934	6.197	6.457	6.714	6.967	7.218

Table A1-2 – Current Limits for ¼ oz copper external traces

For $^1/_3$ oz copper

Current Limits for External Traces (Amperes)

Trace Width in MILS

ΔT temp rise in Deg C	10	20	30	40	50	60	70	80	90	100	110	120	130	140	150	160	170	180	190	200	210	220
1	0.222	0.377	0.513	0.638	0.756	0.868	0.976	1.081	1.182	1.280	1.377	1.471	1.563	1.653	1.742	1.830	1.916	2.001	2.085	2.168	2.250	2.331
2	0.302	0.511	0.696	0.866	1.026	1.178	1.324	1.466	1.603	1.737	1.867	1.995	2.120	2.243	2.364	2.483	2.600	2.715	2.829	2.941	3.053	3.162
3	0.361	0.611	0.832	1.035	1.226	1.408	1.583	1.752	1.916	2.076	2.232	2.385	2.534	2.681	2.825	2.967	3.107	3.245	3.381	3.516	3.649	3.780
4	0.409	0.693	0.944	1.174	1.391	1.598	1.797	1.989	2.175	2.356	2.533	2.706	2.876	3.043	3.207	3.368	3.527	3.683	3.838	3.990	4.141	4.290
5	0.452	0.765	1.041	1.295	1.535	1.763	1.982	2.194	2.399	2.599	2.795	2.986	3.173	3.357	3.538	3.715	3.891	4.063	4.234	4.402	4.568	4.733
6	0.489	0.829	1.128	1.404	1.663	1.910	2.148	2.377	2.600	2.816	3.028	3.235	3.438	3.637	3.833	4.026	4.216	4.403	4.587	4.770	4.950	5.128
7	0.524	0.887	1.207	1.502	1.780	2.044	2.298	2.544	2.782	3.014	3.241	3.462	3.679	3.892	4.102	4.308	4.511	4.712	4.909	5.104	5.297	5.488
8	0.555	0.941	1.280	1.593	1.888	2.168	2.438	2.698	2.951	3.197	3.437	3.672	3.902	4.128	4.350	4.569	4.784	4.997	5.206	5.413	5.618	5.820
9	0.585	0.991	1.348	1.678	1.988	2.283	2.567	2.841	3.108	3.367	3.619	3.867	4.109	4.348	4.582	4.812	5.039	5.263	5.483	5.701	5.917	6.130
10	0.613	1.038	1.412	1.757	2.082	2.392	2.689	2.976	3.255	3.526	3.791	4.050	4.304	4.554	4.799	5.040	5.278	5.512	5.743	5.972	6.197	6.420
11	0.639	1.082	1.473	1.833	2.171	2.494	2.804	3.104	3.394	3.677	3.954	4.224	4.489	4.749	5.005	5.256	5.504	5.748	5.989	6.228	6.463	6.695
12	0.664	1.124	1.530	1.904	2.256	2.592	2.914	3.225	3.527	3.821	4.108	4.389	4.664	4.934	5.200	5.461	5.719	5.973	6.223	6.471	6.715	6.957
13	0.688	1.165	1.585	1.973	2.337	2.684	3.018	3.340	3.653	3.958	4.255	4.546	4.831	5.111	5.386	5.657	5.924	6.187	6.446	6.703	6.956	7.206
14	0.711	1.203	1.638	2.038	2.415	2.773	3.118	3.451	3.774	4.089	4.396	4.697	4.991	5.281	5.565	5.845	6.120	6.392	6.660	6.925	7.186	7.445
15	0.732	1.240	1.688	2.101	2.489	2.859	3.214	3.558	3.891	4.215	4.532	4.841	5.145	5.443	5.736	6.025	6.309	6.589	6.865	7.138	7.408	7.674
16	0.754	1.276	1.737	2.161	2.561	2.941	3.307	3.660	4.003	4.336	4.662	4.981	5.293	5.600	5.902	6.198	6.490	6.779	7.063	7.344	7.621	7.895
17	0.774	1.311	1.784	2.220	2.630	3.021	3.396	3.759	4.111	4.454	4.788	5.116	5.436	5.751	6.061	6.366	6.666	6.962	7.254	7.542	7.827	8.109
18	0.794	1.344	1.829	2.276	2.697	3.098	3.483	3.855	4.216	4.567	4.910	5.246	5.575	5.898	6.215	6.528	6.836	7.139	7.439	7.734	8.027	8.315
19	0.813	1.376	1.873	2.331	2.762	3.172	3.567	3.947	4.317	4.677	5.028	5.372	5.709	6.040	6.365	6.685	7.000	7.311	7.618	7.921	8.220	8.516
20	0.831	1.408	1.916	2.384	2.825	3.245	3.648	4.038	4.416	4.784	5.143	5.495	5.839	6.178	6.510	6.838	7.160	7.478	7.792	8.101	8.407	8.710
21	0.849	1.438	1.958	2.436	2.886	3.315	3.727	4.125	4.512	4.888	5.255	5.614	5.966	6.312	6.652	6.986	7.315	7.640	7.961	8.277	8.590	8.899
22	0.867	1.468	1.998	2.486	2.946	3.384	3.804	4.211	4.605	4.989	5.363	5.730	6.090	6.442	6.789	7.130	7.467	7.798	8.125	8.448	8.767	9.083
23	0.884	1.497	2.037	2.535	3.004	3.450	3.879	4.294	4.696	5.087	5.469	5.843	6.210	6.570	6.923	7.271	7.614	7.952	8.286	8.615	8.941	9.262
24	0.901	1.525	2.076	2.583	3.061	3.516	3.953	4.375	4.785	5.183	5.573	5.954	6.327	6.694	7.054	7.409	7.758	8.103	8.442	8.778	9.110	9.437
25	0.917	1.553	2.114	2.630	3.116	3.579	4.024	4.454	4.871	5.277	5.674	6.062	6.442	6.815	7.182	7.543	7.899	8.249	8.595	8.937	9.275	9.609
26	0.933	1.580	2.150	2.676	3.170	3.642	4.094	4.532	4.956	5.369	5.773	6.167	6.554	6.934	7.307	7.674	8.036	8.393	8.745	9.093	9.436	9.776
27	0.949	1.607	2.186	2.721	3.224	3.703	4.163	4.608	5.039	5.459	5.869	6.270	6.664	7.050	7.429	7.803	8.171	8.534	8.891	9.245	9.594	9.939
28	0.964	1.633	2.222	2.765	3.276	3.762	4.230	4.682	5.120	5.547	5.964	6.372	6.771	7.164	7.549	7.929	8.303	8.671	9.035	9.394	9.749	10.100
29	0.979	1.658	2.256	2.808	3.327	3.821	4.296	4.755	5.200	5.633	6.057	6.471	6.877	7.275	7.667	8.052	8.432	8.806	9.175	9.540	9.901	10.257
30	0.994	1.683	2.290	2.850	3.377	3.878	4.360	4.826	5.278	5.718	6.148	6.568	6.980	7.384	7.782	8.173	8.558	8.938	9.313	9.684	10.049	10.411

Table A1-3– Current Limits for 1/3 oz copper external traces

For ½ oz copper

Current Limits for External Traces (Amperes)

Trace Width in MILS

ΔT temp rise in Deg C	10	20	30	40	50	60	70	80	90	100	110	120	130	140	150	160	170	180	190	200	210	220
1	0.222	0.377	0.513	0.638	0.756	0.868	0.976	1.081	1.182	1.280	1.377	1.471	1.563	1.653	1.742	1.830	1.916	2.001	2.085	2.168	2.250	2.331
2	0.302	0.511	0.696	0.866	1.026	1.178	1.324	1.466	1.603	1.737	1.867	1.995	2.120	2.243	2.364	2.483	2.600	2.715	2.829	2.941	3.053	3.162
3	0.361	0.611	0.832	1.035	1.226	1.408	1.583	1.752	1.916	2.076	2.232	2.385	2.534	2.681	2.825	2.967	3.107	3.245	3.381	3.516	3.649	3.780
4	0.409	0.693	0.944	1.174	1.391	1.598	1.797	1.989	2.175	2.356	2.533	2.706	2.876	3.043	3.207	3.368	3.527	3.683	3.838	3.990	4.141	4.290
5	0.452	0.765	1.041	1.295	1.535	1.763	1.982	2.194	2.399	2.599	2.795	2.986	3.173	3.357	3.538	3.715	3.891	4.063	4.234	4.402	4.568	4.733
6	0.489	0.829	1.128	1.404	1.663	1.910	2.148	2.377	2.600	2.816	3.028	3.235	3.438	3.637	3.833	4.026	4.216	4.403	4.587	4.770	4.950	5.128
7	0.524	0.887	1.207	1.502	1.780	2.044	2.298	2.544	2.782	3.014	3.241	3.462	3.679	3.892	4.102	4.308	4.511	4.712	4.909	5.104	5.297	5.488
8	0.555	0.941	1.280	1.593	1.888	2.168	2.438	2.698	2.951	3.197	3.437	3.672	3.902	4.128	4.350	4.569	4.784	4.997	5.206	5.413	5.618	5.820
9	0.585	0.991	1.348	1.678	1.988	2.283	2.567	2.841	3.108	3.367	3.619	3.867	4.109	4.348	4.582	4.812	5.039	5.263	5.483	5.701	5.917	6.130
10	0.613	1.038	1.412	1.757	2.082	2.392	2.689	2.976	3.255	3.526	3.791	4.050	4.304	4.554	4.799	5.040	5.278	5.512	5.743	5.972	6.197	6.420
11	0.639	1.082	1.473	1.833	2.171	2.494	2.804	3.104	3.394	3.677	3.954	4.224	4.489	4.749	5.005	5.256	5.504	5.748	5.989	6.228	6.463	6.695
12	0.664	1.124	1.530	1.904	2.256	2.592	2.914	3.225	3.527	3.821	4.108	4.389	4.664	4.934	5.200	5.461	5.719	5.973	6.223	6.471	6.715	6.957
13	0.688	1.165	1.585	1.973	2.337	2.684	3.018	3.340	3.653	3.958	4.255	4.546	4.831	5.111	5.386	5.657	5.924	6.187	6.446	6.703	6.956	7.206
14	0.711	1.203	1.638	2.038	2.415	2.773	3.118	3.451	3.774	4.089	4.396	4.697	4.991	5.281	5.565	5.845	6.120	6.392	6.660	6.925	7.186	7.445
15	0.732	1.240	1.688	2.101	2.489	2.859	3.214	3.558	3.891	4.215	4.532	4.841	5.145	5.443	5.736	6.025	6.309	6.589	6.865	7.138	7.408	7.674
16	0.754	1.276	1.737	2.161	2.561	2.941	3.307	3.660	4.003	4.336	4.662	4.981	5.293	5.600	5.902	6.198	6.490	6.779	7.063	7.344	7.621	7.895
17	0.774	1.311	1.784	2.220	2.630	3.021	3.396	3.759	4.111	4.454	4.788	5.116	5.436	5.751	6.061	6.366	6.666	6.962	7.254	7.542	7.827	8.109
18	0.794	1.344	1.829	2.276	2.697	3.098	3.483	3.855	4.216	4.567	4.910	5.246	5.575	5.898	6.215	6.528	6.836	7.139	7.439	7.734	8.027	8.315
19	0.813	1.376	1.873	2.331	2.762	3.172	3.567	3.947	4.317	4.677	5.028	5.372	5.709	6.040	6.365	6.685	7.000	7.311	7.618	7.921	8.220	8.516
20	0.831	1.408	1.916	2.384	2.825	3.245	3.648	4.038	4.416	4.784	5.143	5.495	5.839	6.178	6.510	6.838	7.160	7.478	7.792	8.101	8.407	8.710
21	0.849	1.438	1.958	2.436	2.886	3.315	3.727	4.125	4.512	4.888	5.255	5.614	5.966	6.312	6.652	6.986	7.315	7.640	7.961	8.277	8.590	8.899
22	0.867	1.468	1.998	2.486	2.946	3.384	3.804	4.211	4.605	4.989	5.363	5.730	6.090	6.442	6.789	7.130	7.467	7.798	8.125	8.448	8.767	9.083
23	0.884	1.497	2.037	2.535	3.004	3.450	3.879	4.294	4.696	5.087	5.469	5.843	6.210	6.570	6.923	7.271	7.614	7.952	8.286	8.615	8.941	9.262
24	0.901	1.525	2.076	2.583	3.061	3.516	3.953	4.375	4.785	5.183	5.573	5.954	6.327	6.694	7.054	7.409	7.758	8.103	8.442	8.778	9.110	9.437
25	0.917	1.553	2.114	2.630	3.116	3.579	4.024	4.454	4.871	5.277	5.674	6.062	6.442	6.815	7.182	7.543	7.899	8.249	8.595	8.937	9.275	9.609
26	0.933	1.580	2.150	2.676	3.170	3.642	4.094	4.532	4.956	5.369	5.773	6.167	6.554	6.934	7.307	7.674	8.036	8.393	8.745	9.093	9.436	9.776
27	0.949	1.607	2.186	2.721	3.224	3.703	4.163	4.608	5.039	5.459	5.869	6.270	6.664	7.050	7.429	7.803	8.171	8.534	8.891	9.245	9.594	9.939
28	0.964	1.633	2.222	2.765	3.276	3.762	4.230	4.682	5.120	5.547	5.964	6.372	6.771	7.164	7.549	7.929	8.303	8.671	9.035	9.394	9.749	10.100
29	0.97[illegible]	1.658	2.256	2.808	3.327	3.821	4.296	4.755	5.200	5.633	6.057	6.471	6.877	7.275	7.667	8.052	8.432	8.806	9.175	9.540	9.901	10.257
30	0.994	1.683	2.290	2.850	3.377	3.878	4.360	4.826	5.278	5.718	6.148	6.568	6.980	7.384	7.782	8.173	8.558	8.938	9.313	9.684	10.049	10.411

Table A1-4– Current Limits for ½ oz copper external traces

For 1oz copper

Current Limits for External Traces (Amperes)

Trace Width in MILS

ΔT temp rise in Deg C	10	20	30	40	50	60	70	80	90	100	110	120	130	140	150	160	170	180	190	200	210	220
1	0.325	0.550	0.749	0.932	1.104	1.268	1.425	1.578	1.725	1.869	2.009	2.147	2.281	2.414	2.544	2.671	2.797	2.922	3.044	3.165	3.285	3.403
2	0.441	0.746	1.016	1.264	1.497	1.720	1.934	2.140	2.340	2.536	2.726	2.912	3.095	3.274	3.451	3.624	3.795	3.964	4.130	4.294	4.456	4.617
3	0.527	0.892	1.214	1.510	1.790	2.056	2.311	2.558	2.798	3.031	3.258	3.481	3.700	3.914	4.125	4.332	4.536	4.738	4.936	5.133	5.326	5.518
4	0.598	1.012	1.378	1.714	2.031	2.333	2.623	2.903	3.175	3.440	3.698	3.951	4.199	4.442	4.681	4.917	5.148	5.377	5.602	5.825	6.045	6.263
5	0.659	1.117	1.520	1.891	2.241	2.574	2.894	3.203	3.503	3.795	4.080	4.359	4.632	4.900	5.164	5.424	5.679	5.932	6.180	6.426	6.669	6.909
6	0.715	1.210	1.647	2.049	2.428	2.789	3.135	3.470	3.795	4.112	4.420	4.723	5.019	5.310	5.595	5.877	6.154	6.427	6.697	6.963	7.226	7.486
7	0.765	1.295	1.762	2.193	2.598	2.984	3.355	3.714	4.062	4.400	4.731	5.054	5.371	5.682	5.988	6.289	6.586	6.878	7.167	7.452	7.733	8.011
8	0.811	1.373	1.869	2.326	2.755	3.165	3.558	3.938	4.307	4.666	5.017	5.360	5.696	6.026	6.351	6.670	6.984	7.294	7.600	7.902	8.201	8.496
9	0.854	1.446	1.968	2.449	2.902	3.333	3.748	4.148	4.536	4.915	5.284	5.645	5.999	6.347	6.688	7.025	7.356	7.682	8.005	8.323	8.637	8.948
10	0.895	1.515	2.062	2.566	3.040	3.492	3.926	4.345	4.752	5.148	5.535	5.913	6.284	6.648	7.006	7.358	7.705	8.047	8.384	8.718	9.047	9.373
11	0.933	1.580	2.150	2.675	3.170	3.641	4.094	4.531	4.955	5.368	5.772	6.166	6.553	6.933	7.306	7.673	8.035	8.392	8.744	9.091	9.435	9.774
12	0.969	1.642	2.234	2.780	3.294	3.783	4.253	4.708	5.149	5.578	5.997	6.407	6.809	7.203	7.591	7.972	8.348	8.719	9.085	9.446	9.803	10.156
13	1.004	1.700	2.314	2.880	3.412	3.919	4.406	4.876	5.333	5.778	6.212	6.636	7.053	7.461	7.863	8.258	8.648	9.032	9.410	9.785	10.154	10.520
14	1.037	1.757	2.391	2.975	3.525	4.049	4.552	5.038	5.510	5.969	6.418	6.856	7.286	7.709	8.124	8.532	8.934	9.331	9.722	10.109	10.491	10.868
15	1.069	1.811	2.464	3.067	3.633	4.173	4.692	5.193	5.680	6.153	6.615	7.068	7.511	7.946	8.374	8.795	9.210	9.619	10.022	10.420	10.814	11.203
16	1.100	1.863	2.535	3.155	3.738	4.294	4.827	5.343	5.843	6.330	6.806	7.271	7.727	8.175	8.615	9.048	9.475	9.896	10.311	10.721	11.126	11.526
17	1.130	1.913	2.604	3.240	3.839	4.410	4.958	5.487	6.001	6.502	6.990	7.468	7.936	8.396	8.848	9.293	9.731	10.163	10.589	11.010	11.426	11.838
18	1.159	1.962	2.670	3.323	3.937	4.522	5.084	5.627	6.154	6.667	7.168	7.658	8.138	8.610	9.073	9.530	9.979	10.422	10.859	11.291	11.717	12.139
19	1.187	2.009	2.735	3.403	4.032	4.631	5.207	5.763	6.302	6.828	7.341	7.842	8.334	8.817	9.292	9.759	10.219	10.673	11.121	11.563	11.999	12.431
20	1.214	2.055	2.797	3.480	4.124	4.737	5.325	5.894	6.446	6.984	7.508	8.021	8.525	9.018	9.504	9.982	10.452	10.916	11.374	11.827	12.273	12.715
21	1.240	2.100	2.858	3.556	4.213	4.839	5.441	6.022	6.586	7.135	7.671	8.196	8.710	9.214	9.710	10.198	10.679	11.153	11.621	12.083	12.540	12.991
22	1.266	2.143	2.917	3.630	4.300	4.939	5.553	6.147	6.722	7.283	7.830	8.365	8.890	9.405	9.911	10.409	10.900	11.384	11.862	12.333	12.799	13.260
23	1.291	2.186	2.974	3.701	4.385	5.037	5.663	6.268	6.855	7.426	7.984	8.530	9.065	9.590	10.107	10.615	11.115	11.609	12.096	12.577	13.052	13.521
24	1.315	2.227	3.031	3.771	4.468	5.132	5.770	6.386	6.985	7.567	8.135	8.691	9.237	9.772	10.298	10.815	11.325	11.828	12.324	12.814	13.298	13.777
25	1.339	2.267	3.086	3.840	4.549	5.225	5.875	6.502	7.111	7.704	8.283	8.849	9.404	9.949	10.484	11.011	11.531	12.043	12.548	13.047	13.539	14.027
26	1.362	2.307	3.139	3.906	4.628	5.316	5.977	6.615	7.235	7.838	8.427	9.003	9.568	10.122	10.667	11.203	11.731	12.252	12.766	13.274	13.775	14.271
27	1.385	2.345	3.192	3.972	4.706	5.405	6.077	6.726	7.356	7.969	8.568	9.154	9.728	10.292	10.846	11.391	11.928	12.457	12.980	13.496	14.006	14.510
28	1.407	2.383	3.243	4.036	4.782	5.492	6.175	6.835	7.475	8.098	8.706	9.301	9.885	10.458	11.020	11.574	12.120	12.658	13.189	13.714	14.232	14.744
29	1.429	2.420	3.294	4.099	4.856	5.578	6.271	6.941	7.591	8.224	8.842	9.446	10.039	10.620	11.192	11.755	12.309	12.855	13.395	13.927	14.453	14.973
30	1.451	2.457	3.343	4.160	4.929	5.662	6.365	7.045	7.705	8.347	8.975	9.588	10.189	10.780	11.360	11.931	12.494	13.049	13.596	14.136	14.670	15.198

Table A1-5– Current Limits for 1 oz copper external traces

For 2oz copper

Current Limits for External Traces (Amperes)

Trace Width in MILS

ΔT temp rise in Deg C	10	20	30	40	50	60	70	80	90	100	110	120	130	140	150	160	170	180	190	200	210	220
1	0.470	0.797	1.084	1.349	1.598	1.836	2.064	2.284	2.498	2.707	2.910	3.109	3.304	3.495	3.684	3.869	4.051	4.231	4.408	4.584	4.757	4.928
2	0.638	1.081	1.471	1.830	2.168	2.490	2.800	3.099	3.389	3.672	3.948	4.218	4.482	4.742	4.997	5.248	5.496	5.740	5.981	6.218	6.453	6.685
3	0.763	1.292	1.758	2.187	2.592	2.977	3.347	3.704	4.051	4.389	4.719	5.041	5.358	5.668	5.973	6.273	6.569	6.861	7.149	7.433	7.714	7.991
4	0.866	1.466	1.995	2.483	2.941	3.379	3.799	4.204	4.598	4.981	5.355	5.722	6.080	6.433	6.779	7.120	7.456	7.787	8.113	8.436	8.754	9.069
5	0.955	1.617	2.201	2.739	3.245	3.727	4.190	4.638	5.072	5.495	5.908	6.312	6.708	7.096	7.478	7.854	8.225	8.590	8.950	9.306	9.658	10.005
6	1.035	1.752	2.385	2.967	3.516	4.038	4.540	5.025	5.496	5.954	6.401	6.839	7.268	7.689	8.103	8.510	8.912	9.307	9.698	10.083	10.464	10.841
7	1.107	1.875	2.552	3.176	3.763	4.322	4.859	5.378	5.882	6.372	6.851	7.319	7.778	8.229	8.672	9.108	9.537	9.961	10.378	10.791	11.199	11.602
8	1.174	1.989	2.706	3.368	3.990	4.583	5.153	5.704	6.238	6.758	7.265	7.762	8.249	8.727	9.197	9.659	10.114	10.563	11.006	11.444	11.876	12.304
9	1.237	2.095	2.850	3.547	4.203	4.827	5.427	6.007	6.569	7.117	7.652	8.175	8.688	9.191	9.686	10.173	10.652	11.125	11.592	12.053	12.508	12.958
10	1.295	2.194	2.986	3.715	4.402	5.056	5.685	6.292	6.881	7.455	8.015	8.563	9.100	9.627	10.145	10.655	11.158	11.653	12.142	12.625	13.101	13.573
11	1.351	2.288	3.114	3.874	4.591	5.273	5.928	6.561	7.176	7.774	8.358	8.929	9.490	10.039	10.580	11.112	11.636	12.152	12.662	13.165	13.663	14.154
12	1.404	2.377	3.235	4.026	4.770	5.479	6.160	6.817	7.456	8.077	8.684	9.278	9.860	10.431	10.993	11.545	12.090	12.626	13.156	13.679	14.196	14.707
13	1.454	2.462	3.351	4.170	4.941	5.675	6.380	7.062	7.723	8.367	8.996	9.611	10.213	10.805	11.387	11.959	12.523	13.079	13.628	14.169	14.705	15.234
14	1.502	2.544	3.462	4.308	5.104	5.863	6.592	7.296	7.979	8.644	9.294	9.929	10.552	11.163	11.764	12.356	12.938	13.513	14.079	14.639	15.192	15.739
15	1.549	2.622	3.569	4.441	5.262	6.044	6.795	7.521	8.225	8.911	9.580	10.235	10.877	11.507	12.127	12.736	13.337	13.929	14.513	15.090	15.660	16.224
16	1.593	2.698	3.672	4.569	5.413	6.218	6.991	7.737	8.462	9.167	9.856	10.530	11.190	11.839	12.476	13.103	13.721	14.330	14.931	15.525	16.111	16.691
17	1.636	2.771	3.771	4.692	5.560	6.386	7.180	7.947	8.691	9.415	10.123	10.815	11.493	12.159	12.813	13.457	14.092	14.718	15.335	15.945	16.547	17.142
18	1.678	2.841	3.867	4.812	5.701	6.549	7.363	8.149	8.912	9.655	10.380	11.090	11.786	12.468	13.140	13.800	14.451	15.092	15.726	16.351	16.968	17.579
19	1.718	2.910	3.960	4.928	5.839	6.706	7.540	8.345	9.127	9.887	10.630	11.357	12.069	12.769	13.456	14.132	14.799	15.456	16.104	16.744	17.377	18.002
20	1.757	2.976	4.050	5.040	5.972	6.859	7.712	8.536	9.335	10.113	10.873	11.616	12.345	13.060	13.763	14.455	15.137	15.809	16.472	17.127	17.774	18.413
21	1.796	3.041	4.138	5.150	6.101	7.008	7.879	8.721	9.538	10.333	11.109	11.868	12.613	13.343	14.062	14.769	15.465	16.152	16.829	17.498	18.159	18.813
22	1.833	3.104	4.224	5.256	6.228	7.153	8.042	8.901	9.735	10.546	11.339	12.114	12.874	13.619	14.353	15.074	15.785	16.486	17.177	17.860	18.535	19.202
23	1.869	3.165	4.307	5.360	6.351	7.294	8.201	9.077	9.927	10.755	11.563	12.353	13.128	13.888	14.636	15.372	16.097	16.811	17.516	18.213	18.901	19.581
24	1.904	3.225	4.389	5.461	6.471	7.432	8.356	9.249	10.115	10.958	11.781	12.586	13.376	14.151	14.913	15.662	16.401	17.129	17.848	18.557	19.258	19.951
25	1.939	3.283	4.468	5.560	6.588	7.567	8.508	9.416	10.298	11.156	11.995	12.815	13.618	14.407	15.183	15.946	16.698	17.440	18.171	18.893	19.607	20.313
26	1.973	3.340	4.546	5.657	6.703	7.699	8.656	9.580	10.477	11.351	12.203	13.038	13.855	14.658	15.447	16.224	16.989	17.743	18.487	19.222	19.948	20.666
27	2.006	3.396	4.622	5.752	6.815	7.828	8.801	9.741	10.653	11.541	12.408	13.256	14.087	14.904	15.706	16.495	17.273	18.040	18.797	19.544	20.282	21.012
28	2.038	3.451	4.697	5.845	6.925	7.954	8.942	9.898	10.825	11.727	12.608	13.470	14.315	15.144	15.959	16.762	17.552	18.331	19.100	19.859	20.610	21.351
29	2.070	3.505	4.770	5.935	7.032	8.078	9.082	10.052	10.993	11.909	12.804	13.679	14.537	15.380	16.208	17.022	17.825	18.616	19.397	20.168	20.930	21.684
30	2.101	3.558	4.841	6.025	7.138	8.199	9.218	10.203	11.158	12.088	12.996	13.885	14.756	15.611	16.451	17.278	18.093	18.896	19.689	20.472	21.245	22.009

Table A1-6– Current Limits for 2 oz copper external traces

For 3oz copper

Current Limits for External Traces (Amperes)

Trace Width in MILS

ΔT temp rise in Deg C	10	20	30	40	50	60	70	80	90	100	110	120	130	140	150	160	170	180	190	200	210	220
1	0.585	0.992	1.349	1.679	1.989	2.285	2.569	2.844	3.110	3.369	3.622	3.870	4.113	4.351	4.585	4.816	5.043	5.267	5.488	5.706	5.921	6.134
2	0.794	1.345	1.831	2.278	2.699	3.100	3.485	3.858	4.219	4.571	4.914	5.250	5.579	5.902	6.220	6.533	6.841	7.145	7.444	7.740	8.033	8.322
3	0.949	1.608	2.188	2.723	3.226	3.706	4.166	4.611	5.043	5.463	5.874	6.275	6.669	7.055	7.435	7.809	8.177	8.540	8.898	9.252	9.602	9.947
4	1.078	1.825	2.483	3.090	3.661	4.206	4.728	5.233	5.723	6.201	6.666	7.122	7.569	8.007	8.438	8.863	9.280	9.693	10.099	10.501	10.897	11.289
5	1.189	2.013	2.740	3.409	4.039	4.639	5.216	5.773	6.314	6.840	7.354	7.857	8.350	8.833	9.309	9.777	10.238	10.692	11.141	11.584	12.021	12.454
6	1.288	2.181	2.968	3.694	4.377	5.027	5.652	6.255	6.841	7.412	7.968	8.513	9.047	9.571	10.086	10.594	11.093	11.586	12.072	12.551	13.026	13.494
7	1.378	2.334	3.177	3.953	4.684	5.380	6.048	6.694	7.321	7.932	8.528	9.111	9.682	10.243	10.794	11.337	11.872	12.399	12.919	13.432	13.940	14.441
8	1.462	2.476	3.369	4.192	4.967	5.705	6.414	7.100	7.764	8.412	9.044	9.662	10.268	10.863	11.448	12.023	12.590	13.149	13.700	14.245	14.783	15.315
9	1.540	2.607	3.548	4.415	5.231	6.009	6.756	7.477	8.177	8.859	9.525	10.176	10.814	11.441	12.056	12.663	13.260	13.848	14.429	15.003	15.570	16.130
10	1.613	2.731	3.717	4.625	5.479	6.294	7.076	7.832	8.565	9.279	9.977	10.659	11.327	11.983	12.629	13.263	13.889	14.505	15.114	15.715	16.308	16.895
11	1.682	2.848	3.876	4.823	5.714	6.563	7.379	8.167	8.932	9.677	10.404	11.115	11.812	12.497	13.169	13.831	14.484	15.127	15.761	16.388	17.007	17.619
12	1.747	2.959	4.027	5.011	5.937	6.820	7.667	8.486	9.281	10.055	10.810	11.549	12.273	12.984	13.683	14.371	15.049	15.717	16.376	17.027	17.671	18.306
13	1.810	3.065	4.171	5.191	6.150	7.064	7.942	8.790	9.614	10.415	11.197	11.963	12.713	13.450	14.174	14.886	15.588	16.280	16.963	17.638	18.304	18.963
14	1.870	3.167	4.310	5.363	6.354	7.298	8.205	9.082	9.932	10.760	11.569	12.359	13.135	13.896	14.644	15.380	16.105	16.820	17.526	18.222	18.911	19.591
15	1.928	3.264	4.442	5.528	6.550	7.523	8.458	9.362	10.238	11.092	11.925	12.740	13.539	14.324	15.095	15.854	16.601	17.338	18.066	18.784	19.494	20.195
16	1.983	3.358	4.570	5.687	6.738	7.740	8.702	9.631	10.533	11.411	12.269	13.107	13.929	14.736	15.530	16.311	17.080	17.838	18.586	19.325	20.055	20.777
17	2.037	3.449	4.694	5.841	6.921	7.949	8.937	9.892	10.818	11.720	12.600	13.462	14.306	15.135	15.950	16.751	17.541	18.320	19.089	19.847	20.597	21.338
18	2.089	3.537	4.813	5.990	7.097	8.152	9.165	10.144	11.093	12.018	12.921	13.805	14.670	15.520	16.356	17.178	17.988	18.787	19.575	20.353	21.122	21.882
19	2.139	3.622	4.929	6.134	7.268	8.348	9.385	10.388	11.361	12.308	13.232	14.137	15.024	15.894	16.750	17.592	18.421	19.239	20.046	20.843	21.630	22.409
20	2.188	3.705	5.042	6.274	7.434	8.538	9.600	10.625	11.620	12.589	13.534	14.460	15.366	16.257	17.132	17.993	18.842	19.678	20.504	21.319	22.124	22.920
21	2.235	3.785	5.151	6.410	7.595	8.724	9.808	10.855	11.872	12.862	13.828	14.773	15.700	16.610	17.504	18.384	19.250	20.105	20.948	21.781	22.604	23.418
22	2.281	3.863	5.258	6.543	7.752	8.904	10.011	11.080	12.118	13.128	14.114	15.079	16.025	16.953	17.866	18.764	19.649	20.521	21.382	22.232	23.072	23.902
23	2.326	3.940	5.362	6.672	7.905	9.080	10.208	11.299	12.357	13.387	14.393	15.377	16.341	17.288	18.219	19.134	20.037	20.926	21.804	22.671	23.527	24.374
24	2.370	4.014	5.463	6.798	8.054	9.251	10.401	11.512	12.590	13.640	14.665	15.667	16.650	17.615	18.563	19.496	20.415	21.322	22.216	23.099	23.972	24.835
25	2.413	4.087	5.562	6.921	8.200	9.419	10.590	11.721	12.819	13.887	14.931	15.951	16.952	17.934	18.899	19.849	20.785	21.708	22.619	23.518	24.406	25.285
26	2.455	4.158	5.659	7.042	8.343	9.583	10.774	11.925	13.042	14.129	15.190	16.229	17.247	18.246	19.228	20.195	21.147	22.086	23.013	23.927	24.831	25.725
27	2.496	4.228	5.754	7.160	8.483	9.744	10.955	12.125	13.260	14.366	15.445	16.501	17.536	18.552	19.550	20.533	21.501	22.456	23.398	24.328	25.247	26.156
28	2.537	4.296	5.846	7.275	8.620	9.901	11.131	12.320	13.474	14.597	15.694	16.767	17.818	18.851	19.866	20.864	21.848	22.818	23.775	24.720	25.654	26.577
29	2.576	4.363	5.937	7.388	8.754	10.055	11.305	12.512	13.684	14.824	15.938	17.028	18.096	19.144	20.175	21.189	22.188	23.173	24.145	25.105	26.053	26.991
30	2.615	4.428	6.027	7.499	8.885	10.206	11.474	12.700	13.889	15.047	16.178	17.284	18.368	19.432	20.478	21.507	22.522	23.521	24.508	25.482	26.445	27.397

Table A1-7– Current Limits for 3 oz copper external traces

For 4oz copper

Current Limits for External Traces (Amperes)

Trace Width in MILS

ΔT temp rise in Deg C	10	20	30	40	50	60	70	80	90	100	110	120	130	140	150	160	170	180	190	200	210	220
1	0.684	1.158	1.576	1.961	2.324	2.669	3.001	3.322	3.633	3.935	4.231	4.520	4.804	5.082	5.356	5.625	5.890	6.152	6.410	6.665	6.916	7.165
2	0.928	1.571	2.138	2.661	3.153	3.621	4.071	4.506	4.928	5.339	5.740	6.132	6.517	6.894	7.266	7.631	7.991	8.345	8.696	9.041	9.383	9.720
3	1.109	1.878	2.556	3.180	3.768	4.328	4.866	5.386	5.890	6.382	6.861	7.330	7.790	8.241	8.685	9.121	9.551	9.975	10.394	10.807	11.215	11.619
4	1.259	2.131	2.901	3.610	4.277	4.912	5.523	6.113	6.685	7.243	7.787	8.319	8.841	9.353	9.857	10.352	10.840	11.321	11.796	12.265	12.729	13.187
5	1.388	2.351	3.200	3.982	4.718	5.419	6.093	6.744	7.375	7.990	8.590	9.177	9.753	10.318	10.873	11.420	11.959	12.489	13.013	13.531	14.042	14.547
6	1.504	2.548	3.467	4.315	5.112	5.872	6.602	7.307	7.991	8.657	9.308	9.944	10.568	11.180	11.782	12.374	12.957	13.533	14.100	14.661	15.215	15.762
7	1.610	2.727	3.711	4.617	5.471	6.284	7.065	7.820	8.552	9.265	9.961	10.642	11.309	11.964	12.608	13.242	13.867	14.482	15.090	15.690	16.282	16.868
8	1.707	2.892	3.935	4.897	5.802	6.664	7.492	8.293	9.069	9.825	10.564	11.286	11.994	12.688	13.371	14.044	14.706	15.359	16.003	16.639	17.268	17.889
9	1.798	3.045	4.144	5.157	6.110	7.019	7.891	8.734	9.552	10.348	11.125	11.886	12.631	13.363	14.083	14.791	15.488	16.176	16.854	17.524	18.186	18.841
10	1.884	3.190	4.341	5.402	6.400	7.352	8.265	9.148	10.005	10.839	11.653	12.450	13.231	13.997	14.751	15.492	16.223	16.943	17.654	18.356	19.049	19.735
11	1.964	3.326	4.527	5.633	6.675	7.667	8.619	9.540	10.433	11.303	12.152	12.983	13.797	14.597	15.383	16.156	16.918	17.669	18.410	19.142	19.865	20.580
12	2.041	3.456	4.704	5.853	6.935	7.966	8.956	9.912	10.841	11.744	12.627	13.490	14.336	15.167	15.983	16.787	17.578	18.358	19.129	19.889	20.640	21.383
13	2.114	3.580	4.872	6.063	7.184	8.251	9.277	10.268	11.229	12.165	13.079	13.973	14.850	15.710	16.556	17.388	18.208	19.017	19.814	20.602	21.380	22.150
14	2.184	3.699	5.034	6.264	7.422	8.525	9.584	10.608	11.601	12.569	13.513	14.437	15.342	16.231	17.105	17.965	18.812	19.647	20.471	21.285	22.089	22.884
15	2.251	3.813	5.189	6.457	7.650	8.787	9.880	10.935	11.959	12.956	13.929	14.882	15.815	16.731	17.632	18.518	19.392	20.252	21.102	21.941	22.770	23.589
16	2.316	3.923	5.338	6.643	7.871	9.041	10.164	11.250	12.303	13.329	14.331	15.310	16.270	17.213	18.140	19.052	19.950	20.836	21.710	22.573	23.426	24.269
17	2.379	4.029	5.483	6.823	8.084	9.285	10.439	11.554	12.636	13.690	14.718	15.724	16.710	17.678	18.630	19.567	20.489	21.399	22.297	23.183	24.059	24.925
18	2.440	4.131	5.622	6.996	8.289	9.521	10.705	11.848	12.958	14.038	15.093	16.125	17.136	18.129	19.105	20.065	21.011	21.944	22.865	23.773	24.672	25.559
19	2.498	4.231	5.758	7.165	8.489	9.751	10.963	12.134	13.270	14.376	15.456	16.513	17.548	18.565	19.565	20.548	21.517	22.472	23.415	24.346	25.266	26.175
20	2.555	4.327	5.889	7.328	8.683	9.973	11.213	12.411	13.573	14.704	15.809	16.890	17.949	18.989	20.011	21.017	22.008	22.985	23.949	24.902	25.842	26.772
21	2.611	4.421	6.017	7.487	8.871	10.190	11.456	12.680	13.867	15.023	16.152	17.256	18.338	19.401	20.445	21.473	22.486	23.484	24.469	25.442	26.403	27.353
22	2.665	4.513	6.141	7.642	9.055	10.400	11.693	12.942	14.154	15.334	16.486	17.613	18.718	19.802	20.868	21.917	22.951	23.970	24.975	25.968	26.949	27.919
23	2.717	4.602	6.263	7.793	9.234	10.606	11.924	13.198	14.434	15.637	16.812	17.961	19.087	20.193	21.280	22.350	23.404	24.443	25.468	26.481	27.481	28.470
24	2.769	4.689	6.381	7.941	9.408	10.806	12.149	13.447	14.706	15.932	17.129	18.300	19.448	20.575	21.683	22.773	23.846	24.905	25.950	26.981	28.001	29.008
25	2.819	4.774	6.497	8.084	9.579	11.002	12.370	13.691	14.973	16.221	17.440	18.632	19.801	20.948	22.076	23.185	24.279	25.357	26.420	27.471	28.508	29.534
26	2.868	4.857	6.610	8.225	9.745	11.194	12.585	13.929	15.234	16.504	17.743	18.956	20.145	21.313	22.460	23.589	24.701	25.798	26.880	27.949	29.004	30.048
27	2.916	4.938	6.721	8.363	9.908	11.381	12.796	14.162	15.489	16.780	18.041	19.274	20.483	21.669	22.836	23.984	25.115	26.230	27.330	28.417	29.490	30.551
28	2.963	5.018	6.829	8.498	10.068	11.565	13.002	14.391	15.739	17.051	18.332	19.585	20.813	22.019	23.204	24.371	25.520	26.653	27.771	28.875	29.966	31.044
29	3.009	5.096	6.935	8.630	10.225	11.745	13.204	14.615	15.983	17.316	18.617	19.889	21.137	22.362	23.565	24.750	25.917	27.068	28.203	29.324	30.432	31.527
30	3.054	5.173	7.039	8.760	10.379	11.921	13.403	14.834	16.224	17.576	18.897	20.188	21.455	22.698	23.920	25.122	26.307	27.475	28.627	29.765	30.889	32.001

Table A1-8 – Current Limits for 4 oz copper external traces

For ¼ oz copper

Current Limits for Internal Traces (Amperes)

Trace Width in MILS

ΔT temp rise in Deg C	10	20	30	40	50	60	70	80	90	100	110	120	130	140	150	160	170	180	190	200	210	220
1	0.077	0.131	0.178	0.221	0.262	0.301	0.338	0.375	0.410	0.444	0.477	0.510	0.542	0.573	0.604	0.634	0.664	0.694	0.723	0.752	0.780	0.808
2	0.105	0.177	0.241	0.300	0.356	0.408	0.459	0.508	0.556	0.602	0.647	0.692	0.735	0.778	0.819	0.861	0.901	0.941	0.981	1.020	1.058	1.096
3	0.125	0.212	0.288	0.359	0.425	0.488	0.549	0.607	0.664	0.720	0.774	0.827	0.878	0.929	0.979	1.029	1.077	1.125	1.172	1.219	1.265	1.310
4	0.142	0.240	0.327	0.407	0.482	0.554	0.623	0.689	0.754	0.817	0.878	0.938	0.997	1.055	1.112	1.167	1.223	1.277	1.330	1.383	1.435	1.487
5	0.157	0.265	0.361	0.449	0.532	0.611	0.687	0.761	0.832	0.901	0.969	1.035	1.100	1.164	1.226	1.288	1.349	1.409	1.468	1.526	1.584	1.641
6	0.170	0.287	0.391	0.487	0.577	0.662	0.745	0.824	0.901	0.976	1.050	1.121	1.192	1.261	1.329	1.395	1.461	1.526	1.590	1.653	1.716	1.778
7	0.182	0.307	0.418	0.521	0.617	0.709	0.797	0.882	0.964	1.045	1.123	1.200	1.275	1.349	1.422	1.493	1.564	1.633	1.702	1.769	1.836	1.902
8	0.193	0.326	0.444	0.552	0.654	0.752	0.845	0.935	1.023	1.108	1.191	1.273	1.353	1.431	1.508	1.584	1.658	1.732	1.805	1.877	1.947	2.017
9	0.203	0.343	0.467	0.582	0.689	0.792	0.890	0.985	1.077	1.167	1.255	1.340	1.425	1.507	1.588	1.668	1.747	1.824	1.901	1.976	2.051	2.125
10	0.212	0.360	0.490	0.609	0.722	0.829	0.932	1.032	1.128	1.222	1.314	1.404	1.492	1.579	1.664	1.747	1.830	1.911	1.991	2.070	2.148	2.226
11	0.222	0.375	0.511	0.635	0.753	0.865	0.972	1.076	1.177	1.275	1.371	1.464	1.556	1.646	1.735	1.822	1.908	1.993	2.076	2.159	2.240	2.321
12	0.230	0.390	0.530	0.660	0.782	0.898	1.010	1.118	1.223	1.324	1.424	1.521	1.617	1.710	1.803	1.893	1.982	2.070	2.157	2.243	2.328	2.412
13	0.238	0.404	0.549	0.684	0.810	0.931	1.046	1.158	1.266	1.372	1.475	1.576	1.675	1.772	1.867	1.961	2.053	2.145	2.235	2.323	2.411	2.498
14	0.246	0.417	0.568	0.706	0.837	0.961	1.081	1.196	1.308	1.417	1.524	1.628	1.730	1.830	1.929	2.026	2.122	2.216	2.309	2.400	2.491	2.581
15	0.254	0.430	0.585	0.728	0.863	0.991	1.114	1.233	1.349	1.461	1.571	1.678	1.784	1.887	1.988	2.088	2.187	2.284	2.380	2.474	2.568	2.660
16	0.261	0.442	0.602	0.749	0.888	1.020	1.146	1.269	1.388	1.503	1.616	1.727	1.835	1.941	2.046	2.149	2.250	2.350	2.448	2.546	2.642	2.737
17	0.268	0.454	0.618	0.769	0.912	1.047	1.177	1.303	1.425	1.544	1.660	1.773	1.885	1.994	2.101	2.207	2.311	2.413	2.515	2.615	2.713	2.811
18	0.275	0.466	0.634	0.789	0.935	1.074	1.207	1.336	1.461	1.583	1.702	1.818	1.933	2.044	2.155	2.263	2.370	2.475	2.579	2.681	2.782	2.883
19	0.282	0.477	0.649	0.808	0.957	1.100	1.236	1.368	1.497	1.621	1.743	1.862	1.979	2.094	2.206	2.317	2.427	2.534	2.641	2.746	2.849	2.952
20	0.288	0.488	0.664	0.826	0.979	1.125	1.265	1.400	1.531	1.658	1.783	1.905	2.024	2.142	2.257	2.370	2.482	2.592	2.701	2.808	2.914	3.019
21	0.294	0.499	0.679	0.844	1.000	1.149	1.292	1.430	1.564	1.694	1.822	1.946	2.068	2.188	2.306	2.422	2.536	2.648	2.760	2.869	2.978	3.085
22	0.301	0.509	0.693	0.862	1.021	1.173	1.319	1.460	1.596	1.729	1.859	1.986	2.111	2.233	2.353	2.472	2.588	2.703	2.817	2.929	3.039	3.149
23	0.306	0.519	0.706	0.879	1.041	1.196	1.345	1.488	1.628	1.763	1.896	2.026	2.153	2.277	2.400	2.521	2.639	2.757	2.872	2.986	3.099	3.211
24	0.312	0.529	0.720	0.896	1.061	1.219	1.370	1.517	1.659	1.797	1.932	2.064	2.193	2.320	2.445	2.568	2.689	2.809	2.927	3.043	3.158	3.271
25	0.318	0.538	0.733	0.912	1.080	1.241	1.395	1.544	1.689	1.829	1.967	2.101	2.233	2.362	2.490	2.615	2.738	2.860	2.980	3.098	3.215	3.331
26	0.323	0.548	0.745	0.928	1.099	1.262	1.419	1.571	1.718	1.861	2.001	2.138	2.272	2.404	2.533	2.660	2.786	2.909	3.031	3.152	3.271	3.389
27	0.329	0.557	0.758	0.943	1.117	1.284	1.443	1.597	1.747	1.892	2.035	2.174	2.310	2.444	2.575	2.705	2.832	2.958	3.082	3.205	3.326	3.445
28	0.334	0.566	0.770	0.958	1.135	1.304	1.466	1.623	1.775	1.923	2.067	2.209	2.347	2.483	2.617	2.748	2.878	3.006	3.132	3.256	3.379	3.501
29	0.339	0.575	0.782	0.973	1.153	1.325	1.489	1.648	1.803	1.953	2.100	2.243	2.384	2.522	2.658	2.791	2.923	3.053	3.181	3.307	3.432	3.556
30	0.344	0.583	0.794	0.988	1.170	1.344	1.512	1.673	1.830	1.982	2.131	2.277	2.420	2.560	2.698	2.833	2.967	3.098	3.228	3.357	3.484	3.609

Table A1-9 – Current Limits for ¼ oz copper internal traces

For $^1/_3$ oz copper

Current Limits for Internal Traces (Amperes)

Trace Width in MILS

ΔT temp rise in Deg C	10	20	30	40	50	60	70	80	90	100	110	120	130	140	150	160	170	180	190	200	210	220
1	0.077	0.131	0.178	0.221	0.262	0.301	0.338	0.375	0.410	0.444	0.477	0.510	0.542	0.573	0.604	0.634	0.664	0.694	0.723	0.752	0.780	0.808
2	0.105	0.177	0.241	0.300	0.356	0.408	0.459	0.508	0.556	0.602	0.647	0.692	0.735	0.778	0.819	0.861	0.901	0.941	0.981	1.020	1.058	1.096
3	0.125	0.212	0.288	0.359	0.425	0.488	0.549	0.607	0.664	0.720	0.774	0.827	0.878	0.929	0.979	1.029	1.077	1.125	1.172	1.219	1.265	1.310
4	0.142	0.240	0.327	0.407	0.482	0.554	0.623	0.689	0.754	0.817	0.878	0.938	0.997	1.055	1.112	1.167	1.223	1.277	1.330	1.383	1.435	1.487
5	0.157	0.265	0.361	0.449	0.532	0.611	0.687	0.761	0.832	0.901	0.969	1.035	1.100	1.164	1.226	1.288	1.349	1.409	1.468	1.526	1.584	1.641
6	0.170	0.287	0.391	0.487	0.577	0.662	0.745	0.824	0.901	0.976	1.050	1.121	1.192	1.261	1.329	1.395	1.461	1.526	1.590	1.653	1.716	1.778
7	0.182	0.307	0.418	0.521	0.617	0.709	0.797	0.882	0.964	1.045	1.123	1.200	1.275	1.349	1.422	1.493	1.564	1.633	1.702	1.769	1.836	1.902
8	0.193	0.326	0.444	0.552	0.654	0.752	0.845	0.935	1.023	1.108	1.191	1.273	1.353	1.431	1.508	1.584	1.658	1.732	1.805	1.877	1.947	2.017
9	0.203	0.343	0.467	0.582	0.689	0.792	0.890	0.985	1.077	1.167	1.255	1.340	1.425	1.507	1.588	1.668	1.747	1.824	1.901	1.976	2.051	2.125
10	0.212	0.360	0.490	0.609	0.722	0.829	0.932	1.032	1.128	1.222	1.314	1.404	1.492	1.579	1.664	1.747	1.830	1.911	1.991	2.070	2.148	2.226
11	0.222	0.375	0.511	0.635	0.753	0.865	0.972	1.076	1.177	1.275	1.371	1.464	1.556	1.646	1.735	1.822	1.908	1.993	2.076	2.159	2.240	2.321
12	0.230	0.390	0.530	0.660	0.782	0.898	1.010	1.118	1.223	1.324	1.424	1.521	1.617	1.710	1.803	1.893	1.982	2.070	2.157	2.243	2.328	2.412
13	0.238	0.404	0.549	0.684	0.810	0.931	1.046	1.158	1.266	1.372	1.475	1.576	1.675	1.772	1.867	1.961	2.053	2.145	2.235	2.323	2.411	2.498
14	0.246	0.417	0.568	0.706	0.837	0.961	1.081	1.196	1.308	1.417	1.524	1.628	1.730	1.830	1.929	2.026	2.122	2.216	2.309	2.400	2.491	2.581
15	0.254	0.430	0.585	0.728	0.863	0.991	1.114	1.233	1.349	1.461	1.571	1.678	1.784	1.887	1.988	2.088	2.187	2.284	2.380	2.474	2.568	2.660
16	0.261	0.442	0.602	0.749	0.888	1.020	1.146	1.269	1.388	1.503	1.616	1.727	1.835	1.941	2.046	2.149	2.250	2.350	2.448	2.546	2.642	2.737
17	0.268	0.454	0.618	0.769	0.912	1.047	1.177	1.303	1.425	1.544	1.660	1.773	1.885	1.994	2.101	2.207	2.311	2.413	2.515	2.615	2.713	2.811
18	0.275	0.466	0.634	0.789	0.935	1.074	1.207	1.336	1.461	1.583	1.702	1.818	1.933	2.044	2.155	2.263	2.370	2.475	2.579	2.681	2.782	2.883
19	0.282	0.477	0.649	0.808	0.957	1.100	1.236	1.368	1.497	1.621	1.743	1.862	1.979	2.094	2.206	2.317	2.427	2.534	2.641	2.746	2.849	2.952
20	0.288	0.488	0.664	0.826	0.979	1.125	1.265	1.400	1.531	1.658	1.783	1.905	2.024	2.142	2.257	2.370	2.482	2.592	2.701	2.808	2.914	3.019
21	0.294	0.499	0.679	0.844	1.000	1.149	1.292	1.430	1.564	1.694	1.822	1.946	2.068	2.188	2.306	2.422	2.536	2.648	2.760	2.869	2.978	3.085
22	0.301	0.509	0.693	0.862	1.021	1.173	1.319	1.460	1.596	1.729	1.859	1.986	2.111	2.233	2.353	2.472	2.588	2.703	2.817	2.929	3.039	3.149
23	0.306	0.519	0.706	0.879	1.041	1.196	1.345	1.488	1.628	1.763	1.896	2.026	2.153	2.277	2.400	2.521	2.639	2.757	2.872	2.986	3.099	3.211
24	0.312	0.529	0.720	0.896	1.061	1.219	1.370	1.517	1.659	1.797	1.932	2.064	2.193	2.320	2.445	2.568	2.689	2.809	2.927	3.043	3.158	3.271
25	0.318	0.538	0.733	0.912	1.080	1.241	1.395	1.544	1.689	1.829	1.967	2.101	2.233	2.362	2.490	2.615	2.738	2.860	2.980	3.098	3.215	3.331
26	0.323	0.548	0.745	0.928	1.099	1.262	1.419	1.571	1.718	1.861	2.001	2.138	2.272	2.404	2.533	2.660	2.786	2.909	3.031	3.152	3.271	3.389
27	0.329	0.557	0.758	0.943	1.117	1.284	1.443	1.597	1.747	1.892	2.035	2.174	2.310	2.444	2.575	2.705	2.832	2.958	3.082	3.205	3.326	3.445
28	0.334	0.566	0.770	0.958	1.135	1.304	1.466	1.623	1.775	1.923	2.067	2.209	2.347	2.483	2.617	2.748	2.878	3.006	3.132	3.256	3.379	3.501
29	0.339	0.575	0.782	0.973	1.153	1.325	1.489	1.648	1.803	1.953	2.100	2.243	2.384	2.522	2.658	2.791	2.923	3.053	3.181	3.307	3.432	3.556
30	0.344	0.583	0.794	0.988	1.170	1.344	1.512	1.673	1.830	1.982	2.131	2.277	2.420	2.560	2.698	2.833	2.967	3.098	3.228	3.357	3.484	3.609

Table A1-10 – Current Limits for 1/3 oz copper internal traces

For ½ oz copper

Current Limits for Internal Traces (Amperes)

ΔT temp rise in Deg C	Trace Width in MILS: 10	20	30	40	50	60	70	80	90	100	110	120	130	140	150	160	170	180	190	200	210	220
1	0.111	0.188	0.256	0.319	0.378	0.434	0.488	0.540	0.591	0.640	0.688	0.735	0.781	0.827	0.871	0.915	0.958	1.001	1.043	1.084	1.125	1.166
2	0.151	0.256	0.348	0.433	0.513	0.589	0.662	0.733	0.802	0.868	0.934	0.998	1.060	1.122	1.182	1.241	1.300	1.358	1.414	1.471	1.526	1.581
3	0.180	0.305	0.416	0.517	0.613	0.704	0.792	0.876	0.958	1.038	1.116	1.192	1.267	1.341	1.413	1.484	1.554	1.623	1.691	1.758	1.824	1.890
4	0.205	0.347	0.472	0.587	0.696	0.799	0.898	0.994	1.087	1.178	1.267	1.353	1.438	1.521	1.603	1.684	1.763	1.842	1.919	1.995	2.071	2.145
5	0.226	0.382	0.521	0.648	0.767	0.882	0.991	1.097	1.200	1.300	1.397	1.493	1.586	1.678	1.769	1.858	1.945	2.032	2.117	2.201	2.284	2.366
6	0.245	0.414	0.564	0.702	0.832	0.955	1.074	1.189	1.300	1.408	1.514	1.618	1.719	1.819	1.916	2.013	2.108	2.201	2.294	2.385	2.475	2.564
7	0.262	0.444	0.604	0.751	0.890	1.022	1.149	1.272	1.391	1.507	1.620	1.731	1.840	1.946	2.051	2.154	2.256	2.356	2.455	2.552	2.649	2.744
8	0.278	0.470	0.640	0.797	0.944	1.084	1.219	1.349	1.475	1.598	1.718	1.836	1.951	2.064	2.175	2.284	2.392	2.498	2.603	2.707	2.809	2.910
9	0.293	0.495	0.674	0.839	0.994	1.142	1.284	1.421	1.554	1.683	1.810	1.933	2.055	2.174	2.291	2.406	2.519	2.631	2.742	2.851	2.958	3.065
10	0.306	0.519	0.706	0.879	1.041	1.196	1.345	1.488	1.627	1.763	1.896	2.025	2.152	2.277	2.400	2.520	2.639	2.756	2.872	2.986	3.099	3.210
11	0.320	0.541	0.736	0.916	1.086	1.247	1.402	1.552	1.697	1.839	1.977	2.112	2.244	2.374	2.502	2.628	2.752	2.874	2.995	3.114	3.231	3.348
12	0.332	0.562	0.765	0.952	1.128	1.296	1.457	1.612	1.763	1.910	2.054	2.194	2.332	2.467	2.600	2.731	2.859	2.986	3.112	3.235	3.358	3.478
13	0.344	0.582	0.793	0.986	1.169	1.342	1.509	1.670	1.827	1.979	2.128	2.273	2.416	2.556	2.693	2.829	2.962	3.093	3.223	3.351	3.478	3.603
14	0.355	0.602	0.819	1.019	1.207	1.387	1.559	1.726	1.887	2.045	2.198	2.348	2.496	2.640	2.782	2.922	3.060	3.196	3.330	3.462	3.593	3.722
15	0.366	0.620	0.844	1.050	1.244	1.429	1.607	1.779	1.945	2.108	2.266	2.421	2.573	2.722	2.868	3.012	3.154	3.294	3.433	3.569	3.704	3.837
16	0.377	0.638	0.868	1.081	1.280	1.471	1.653	1.830	2.001	2.168	2.331	2.490	2.647	2.800	2.951	3.099	3.245	3.389	3.531	3.672	3.811	3.948
17	0.387	0.655	0.892	1.110	1.315	1.510	1.698	1.879	2.055	2.227	2.394	2.558	2.718	2.876	3.031	3.183	3.333	3.481	3.627	3.771	3.914	4.054
18	0.397	0.672	0.915	1.138	1.348	1.549	1.741	1.927	2.108	2.284	2.455	2.623	2.787	2.949	3.108	3.264	3.418	3.570	3.719	3.867	4.013	4.158
19	0.406	0.688	0.937	1.165	1.381	1.586	1.783	1.974	2.159	2.339	2.514	2.686	2.855	3.020	3.183	3.343	3.500	3.656	3.809	3.960	4.110	4.258
20	0.416	0.704	0.958	1.192	1.412	1.622	1.824	2.019	2.208	2.392	2.572	2.747	2.920	3.089	3.255	3.419	3.580	3.739	3.896	4.051	4.204	4.355
21	0.425	0.719	0.979	1.218	1.443	1.658	1.864	2.063	2.256	2.444	2.627	2.807	2.983	3.156	3.326	3.493	3.658	3.820	3.980	4.139	4.295	4.449
22	0.433	0.734	0.999	1.243	1.473	1.692	1.902	2.105	2.302	2.494	2.682	2.865	3.045	3.221	3.395	3.565	3.733	3.899	4.063	4.224	4.384	4.541
23	0.442	0.749	1.019	1.268	1.502	1.725	1.940	2.147	2.348	2.544	2.735	2.922	3.105	3.285	3.462	3.636	3.807	3.976	4.143	4.308	4.470	4.631
24	0.450	0.763	1.038	1.292	1.530	1.758	1.976	2.187	2.392	2.592	2.786	2.977	3.164	3.347	3.527	3.704	3.879	4.051	4.221	4.389	4.555	4.719
25	0.459	0.777	1.057	1.315	1.558	1.790	2.012	2.227	2.436	2.639	2.837	3.031	3.221	3.408	3.591	3.772	3.949	4.125	4.298	4.469	4.637	4.804
26	0.467	0.790	1.075	1.338	1.585	1.821	2.047	2.266	2.478	2.685	2.886	3.084	3.277	3.467	3.654	3.837	4.018	4.196	4.373	4.546	4.718	4.888
27	0.474	0.803	1.093	1.360	1.612	1.851	2.081	2.304	2.520	2.730	2.935	3.135	3.332	3.525	3.715	3.901	4.085	4.267	4.446	4.622	4.797	4.970
28	0.482	0.816	1.111	1.382	1.638	1.881	2.115	2.341	2.560	2.774	2.982	3.186	3.386	3.582	3.775	3.964	4.151	4.336	4.517	4.697	4.874	5.050
29	0.489	0.829	1.128	1.404	1.663	1.910	2.148	2.377	2.600	2.817	3.028	3.235	3.438	3.638	3.833	4.026	4.216	4.403	4.588	4.770	4.950	5.128
30	0.497	0.841	1.145	1.425	1.688	1.939	2.180	2.413	2.639	2.859	3.074	3.284	3.490	3.692	3.891	4.087	4.279	4.469	4.657	4.842	5.025	5.206

Table A1-11 – Current Limits for ½ oz copper internal traces

For 1oz copper

Current Limits for Internal Traces (Amperes)

Trace Width in MILS

ΔT temp rise in Deg C	10	20	30	40	50	60	70	80	90	100	110	120	130	140	150	160	170	180	190	200	210	220
1	0.162	0.275	0.374	0.466	0.552	0.634	0.713	0.789	0.863	0.935	1.005	1.073	1.141	1.207	1.272	1.336	1.399	1.461	1.522	1.583	1.642	1.702
2	0.220	0.373	0.508	0.632	0.749	0.860	0.967	1.070	1.170	1.268	1.363	1.456	1.548	1.637	1.725	1.812	1.898	1.982	2.065	2.147	2.228	2.308
3	0.263	0.446	0.607	0.755	0.895	1.028	1.156	1.279	1.399	1.515	1.629	1.741	1.850	1.957	2.062	2.166	2.268	2.369	2.468	2.566	2.663	2.759
4	0.299	0.506	0.689	0.857	1.016	1.167	1.312	1.452	1.588	1.720	1.849	1.975	2.099	2.221	2.341	2.458	2.574	2.688	2.801	2.913	3.023	3.131
5	0.330	0.558	0.760	0.946	1.120	1.287	1.447	1.601	1.751	1.897	2.040	2.179	2.316	2.450	2.582	2.712	2.840	2.966	3.090	3.213	3.334	3.454
6	0.357	0.605	0.823	1.025	1.214	1.394	1.568	1.735	1.898	2.056	2.210	2.361	2.509	2.655	2.798	2.938	3.077	3.214	3.348	3.481	3.613	3.743
7	0.382	0.647	0.881	1.096	1.299	1.492	1.678	1.857	2.031	2.200	2.365	2.527	2.686	2.841	2.994	3.145	3.293	3.439	3.583	3.726	3.867	4.006
8	0.405	0.687	0.934	1.163	1.378	1.583	1.779	1.969	2.154	2.333	2.508	2.680	2.848	3.013	3.175	3.335	3.492	3.647	3.800	3.951	4.101	4.248
9	0.427	0.723	0.984	1.225	1.451	1.667	1.874	2.074	2.268	2.457	2.642	2.823	3.000	3.173	3.344	3.512	3.678	3.841	4.002	4.161	4.319	4.474
10	0.447	0.757	1.031	1.283	1.520	1.746	1.963	2.172	2.376	2.574	2.767	2.956	3.142	3.324	3.503	3.679	3.852	4.023	4.192	4.359	4.524	4.686
11	0.466	0.790	1.075	1.338	1.585	1.821	2.047	2.265	2.478	2.684	2.886	3.083	3.276	3.466	3.653	3.837	4.017	4.196	4.372	4.546	4.717	4.887
12	0.485	0.821	1.117	1.390	1.647	1.892	2.127	2.354	2.574	2.789	2.998	3.203	3.404	3.602	3.795	3.986	4.174	4.360	4.542	4.723	4.901	5.078
13	0.502	0.850	1.157	1.440	1.706	1.959	2.203	2.438	2.667	2.889	3.106	3.318	3.526	3.731	3.931	4.129	4.324	4.516	4.705	4.892	5.077	5.260
14	0.519	0.878	1.195	1.487	1.762	2.024	2.276	2.519	2.755	2.985	3.209	3.428	3.643	3.854	4.062	4.266	4.467	4.665	4.861	5.054	5.245	5.434
15	0.535	0.905	1.232	1.533	1.817	2.087	2.346	2.597	2.840	3.077	3.308	3.534	3.756	3.973	4.187	4.397	4.605	4.809	5.011	5.210	5.407	5.602
16	0.550	0.932	1.268	1.578	1.869	2.147	2.414	2.671	2.922	3.165	3.403	3.636	3.864	4.088	4.308	4.524	4.737	4.948	5.155	5.360	5.563	5.763
17	0.565	0.957	1.302	1.620	1.920	2.205	2.479	2.744	3.001	3.251	3.495	3.734	3.968	4.198	4.424	4.646	4.866	5.082	5.295	5.505	5.713	5.919
18	0.579	0.981	1.335	1.661	1.968	2.261	2.542	2.814	3.077	3.334	3.584	3.829	4.069	4.305	4.537	4.765	4.989	5.211	5.430	5.645	5.859	6.069
19	0.593	1.005	1.367	1.701	2.016	2.315	2.603	2.881	3.151	3.414	3.670	3.921	4.167	4.409	4.646	4.879	5.110	5.336	5.560	5.781	6.000	6.216
20	0.607	1.028	1.398	1.740	2.062	2.368	2.663	2.947	3.223	3.492	3.754	4.011	4.262	4.509	4.752	4.991	5.226	5.458	5.687	5.913	6.137	6.357
21	0.620	1.050	1.429	1.778	2.107	2.420	2.720	3.011	3.293	3.568	3.836	4.098	4.355	4.607	4.855	5.099	5.340	5.577	5.811	6.042	6.270	6.495
22	0.633	1.072	1.458	1.815	2.150	2.470	2.777	3.073	3.361	3.641	3.915	4.182	4.445	4.702	4.955	5.205	5.450	5.692	5.931	6.167	6.399	6.630
23	0.645	1.093	1.487	1.851	2.193	2.519	2.832	3.134	3.427	3.713	3.992	4.265	4.533	4.795	5.053	5.307	5.558	5.804	6.048	6.288	6.526	6.761
24	0.657	1.113	1.515	1.886	2.234	2.566	2.885	3.193	3.492	3.783	4.068	4.346	4.618	4.886	5.149	5.408	5.663	5.914	6.162	6.407	6.649	6.889
25	0.669	1.134	1.543	1.920	2.275	2.613	2.937	3.251	3.556	3.852	4.141	4.424	4.702	4.974	5.242	5.506	5.765	6.021	6.274	6.523	6.770	7.013
26	0.681	1.153	1.570	1.953	2.314	2.658	2.989	3.308	3.617	3.919	4.213	4.502	4.784	5.061	5.333	5.602	5.866	6.126	6.383	6.637	6.888	7.135
27	0.692	1.173	1.596	1.986	2.353	2.703	3.039	3.363	3.678	3.985	4.284	4.577	4.864	5.146	5.423	5.695	5.964	6.229	6.490	6.748	7.003	7.255
28	0.704	1.192	1.622	2.018	2.391	2.746	3.088	3.417	3.737	4.049	4.353	4.651	4.942	5.229	5.510	5.787	6.060	6.329	6.595	6.857	7.116	7.372
29	0.715	1.210	1.647	2.049	2.428	2.789	3.136	3.471	3.796	4.112	4.421	4.723	5.019	5.310	5.596	5.877	6.154	6.428	6.697	6.964	7.227	7.487
30	0.725	1.228	1.672	2.080	2.465	2.831	3.183	3.523	3.853	4.174	4.487	4.794	5.095	5.390	5.680	5.966	6.247	6.524	6.798	7.068	7.335	7.599

Table A1-12 – Current Limits for 1 oz copper internal traces

For 2oz copper

Current Limits for Internal Traces (Amperes)

Trace Width in MILS

ΔT temp rise in Deg C	10	20	30	40	50	60	70	80	90	100	110	120	130	140	150	160	170	180	190	200	210	220
1	0.235	0.398	0.542	0.674	0.799	0.918	1.032	1.142	1.249	1.353	1.455	1.554	1.652	1.748	1.842	1.934	2.026	2.115	2.204	2.292	2.378	2.464
2	0.319	0.540	0.735	0.915	1.084	1.245	1.400	1.550	1.695	1.836	1.974	2.109	2.241	2.371	2.499	2.624	2.748	2.870	2.990	3.109	3.227	3.343
3	0.381	0.646	0.879	1.094	1.296	1.488	1.673	1.852	2.026	2.195	2.359	2.521	2.679	2.834	2.987	3.137	3.285	3.430	3.574	3.716	3.857	3.996
4	0.433	0.733	0.998	1.241	1.471	1.689	1.899	2.102	2.299	2.491	2.678	2.861	3.040	3.216	3.390	3.560	3.728	3.893	4.057	4.218	4.377	4.535
5	0.477	0.809	1.100	1.369	1.622	1.864	2.095	2.319	2.536	2.748	2.954	3.156	3.354	3.548	3.739	3.927	4.112	4.295	4.475	4.653	4.829	5.003
6	0.517	0.876	1.192	1.484	1.758	2.019	2.270	2.513	2.748	2.977	3.201	3.420	3.634	3.845	4.052	4.255	4.456	4.654	4.849	5.042	5.232	5.420
7	0.554	0.938	1.276	1.588	1.881	2.161	2.430	2.689	2.941	3.186	3.425	3.660	3.889	4.114	4.336	4.554	4.769	4.980	5.189	5.395	5.599	5.801
8	0.587	0.994	1.353	1.684	1.995	2.292	2.577	2.852	3.119	3.379	3.633	3.881	4.124	4.363	4.598	4.829	5.057	5.282	5.503	5.722	5.938	6.152
9	0.618	1.047	1.425	1.774	2.101	2.414	2.714	3.003	3.285	3.559	3.826	4.087	4.344	4.595	4.843	5.086	5.326	5.563	5.796	6.026	6.254	6.479
10	0.648	1.097	1.493	1.858	2.201	2.528	2.842	3.146	3.441	3.727	4.007	4.281	4.550	4.814	5.073	5.328	5.579	5.827	6.071	6.312	6.551	6.786
11	0.675	1.144	1.557	1.937	2.295	2.636	2.964	3.281	3.588	3.887	4.179	4.465	4.745	5.020	5.290	5.556	5.818	6.076	6.331	6.583	6.831	7.077
12	0.702	1.189	1.618	2.013	2.385	2.739	3.080	3.409	3.728	4.039	4.342	4.639	4.930	5.216	5.496	5.773	6.045	6.313	6.578	6.840	7.098	7.353
13	0.727	1.231	1.676	2.085	2.470	2.837	3.190	3.531	3.862	4.183	4.498	4.805	5.107	5.403	5.693	5.980	6.262	6.540	6.814	7.085	7.352	7.617
14	0.751	1.272	1.731	2.154	2.552	2.932	3.296	3.648	3.990	4.322	4.647	4.965	5.276	5.582	5.882	6.178	6.469	6.756	7.040	7.320	7.596	7.869
15	0.774	1.311	1.784	2.220	2.631	3.022	3.397	3.760	4.113	4.455	4.790	5.118	5.439	5.754	6.063	6.368	6.668	6.965	7.257	7.545	7.830	8.112
16	0.797	1.349	1.836	2.284	2.707	3.109	3.495	3.869	4.231	4.584	4.928	5.265	5.595	5.919	6.238	6.552	6.861	7.165	7.466	7.762	8.056	8.346
17	0.818	1.385	1.885	2.346	2.780	3.193	3.590	3.973	4.345	4.708	5.061	5.407	5.746	6.079	6.407	6.729	7.046	7.359	7.668	7.972	8.273	8.571
18	0.839	1.421	1.933	2.406	2.851	3.274	3.681	4.074	4.456	4.828	5.190	5.545	5.893	6.234	6.570	6.900	7.225	7.546	7.863	8.175	8.484	8.790
19	0.859	1.455	1.980	2.464	2.919	3.353	3.770	4.173	4.563	4.944	5.315	5.678	6.035	6.384	6.728	7.066	7.399	7.728	8.052	8.372	8.688	9.001
20	0.879	1.488	2.025	2.520	2.986	3.430	3.856	4.268	4.667	5.057	5.436	5.808	6.172	6.530	6.882	7.228	7.568	7.904	8.236	8.563	8.887	9.207
21	0.898	1.520	2.069	2.575	3.051	3.504	3.940	4.360	4.769	5.166	5.554	5.934	6.306	6.672	7.031	7.384	7.733	8.076	8.415	8.749	9.080	9.406
22	0.916	1.552	2.112	2.628	3.114	3.577	4.021	4.451	4.867	5.273	5.669	6.057	6.437	6.810	7.176	7.537	7.892	8.243	8.589	8.930	9.267	9.601
23	0.934	1.583	2.154	2.680	3.175	3.647	4.101	4.539	4.964	5.377	5.781	6.176	6.564	6.944	7.318	7.686	8.048	8.406	8.758	9.106	9.450	9.791
24	0.952	1.612	2.194	2.731	3.235	3.716	4.178	4.624	5.057	5.479	5.891	6.293	6.688	7.075	7.456	7.831	8.200	8.565	8.924	9.279	9.629	9.976
25	0.969	1.642	2.234	2.780	3.294	3.783	4.254	4.708	5.149	5.578	5.997	6.407	6.809	7.204	7.591	7.973	8.349	8.720	9.086	9.447	9.804	10.156
26	0.986	1.670	2.273	2.829	3.351	3.849	4.328	4.790	5.239	5.675	6.102	6.519	6.928	7.329	7.724	8.112	8.494	8.872	9.244	9.611	9.974	10.333
27	1.003	1.698	2.311	2.876	3.407	3.914	4.400	4.870	5.326	5.770	6.204	6.628	7.044	7.452	7.853	8.248	8.637	9.020	9.398	9.772	10.141	10.506
28	1.019	1.726	2.348	2.922	3.462	3.977	4.471	4.949	5.412	5.863	6.304	6.735	7.157	7.572	7.980	8.381	8.776	9.166	9.550	9.930	10.305	10.676
29	1.035	1.752	2.385	2.968	3.516	4.039	4.541	5.026	5.496	5.955	6.402	6.840	7.269	7.690	8.104	8.511	8.913	9.308	9.699	10.084	10.465	10.842
30	1.050	1.779	2.421	3.012	3.569	4.100	4.609	5.101	5.579	6.044	6.498	6.942	7.378	7.805	8.226	8.639	9.046	9.448	9.844	10.236	10.622	11.005

Table A1-13 – Current Limits for 2 oz copper internal traces

For 3oz copper

Current Limits for Internal Traces (Amperes)

Trace Width in MILS

ΔT temp rise in Deg C	10	20	30	40	50	60	70	80	90	100	110	120	130	140	150	160	170	180	190	200	210	220
1	0.293	0.496	0.675	0.840	0.995	1.143	1.285	1.422	1.555	1.685	1.811	1.935	2.056	2.175	2.293	2.408	2.521	2.633	2.744	2.853	2.961	3.067
2	0.397	0.673	0.915	1.139	1.349	1.550	1.743	1.929	2.109	2.285	2.457	2.625	2.790	2.951	3.110	3.266	3.420	3.572	3.722	3.870	4.016	4.161
3	0.475	0.804	1.094	1.361	1.613	1.853	2.083	2.306	2.521	2.732	2.937	3.138	3.334	3.528	3.718	3.904	4.089	4.270	4.449	4.626	4.801	4.974
4	0.539	0.912	1.242	1.545	1.831	2.103	2.364	2.617	2.862	3.100	3.333	3.561	3.784	4.004	4.219	4.431	4.640	4.846	5.050	5.250	5.449	5.645
5	0.594	1.007	1.370	1.705	2.020	2.320	2.608	2.887	3.157	3.420	3.677	3.928	4.175	4.417	4.654	4.888	5.119	5.346	5.570	5.792	6.011	6.227
6	0.644	1.091	1.484	1.847	2.188	2.513	2.826	3.128	3.421	3.706	3.984	4.257	4.524	4.786	5.043	5.297	5.547	5.793	6.036	6.276	6.513	6.747
7	0.689	1.167	1.588	1.977	2.342	2.690	3.024	3.347	3.661	3.966	4.264	4.555	4.841	5.121	5.397	5.668	5.936	6.199	6.459	6.716	6.970	7.221
8	0.731	1.238	1.684	2.096	2.484	2.853	3.207	3.550	3.882	4.206	4.522	4.831	5.134	5.431	5.724	6.012	6.295	6.574	6.850	7.123	7.392	7.658
9	0.770	1.304	1.774	2.208	2.616	3.004	3.378	3.739	4.089	4.430	4.762	5.088	5.407	5.720	6.028	6.331	6.630	6.924	7.215	7.501	7.785	8.065
10	0.806	1.365	1.858	2.312	2.740	3.147	3.538	3.916	4.283	4.640	4.988	5.329	5.664	5.992	6.314	6.632	6.944	7.253	7.557	7.857	8.154	8.448
11	0.841	1.424	1.938	2.411	2.857	3.282	3.690	4.084	4.466	4.838	5.202	5.558	5.906	6.248	6.585	6.916	7.242	7.563	7.881	8.194	8.503	8.809
12	0.874	1.480	2.013	2.506	2.969	3.410	3.834	4.243	4.640	5.027	5.405	5.774	6.137	6.492	6.842	7.186	7.524	7.859	8.188	8.514	8.835	9.153
13	0.905	1.533	2.086	2.595	3.075	3.532	3.971	4.395	4.807	5.207	5.599	5.981	6.357	6.725	7.087	7.443	7.794	8.140	8.482	8.819	9.152	9.481
14	0.935	1.583	2.155	2.681	3.177	3.649	4.103	4.541	4.966	5.380	5.784	6.180	6.567	6.948	7.322	7.690	8.053	8.410	8.763	9.111	9.455	9.796
15	0.964	1.632	2.221	2.764	3.275	3.762	4.229	4.681	5.119	5.546	5.963	6.370	6.770	7.162	7.547	7.927	8.301	8.669	9.033	9.392	9.747	10.098
16	0.992	1.679	2.285	2.844	3.369	3.870	4.351	4.816	5.267	5.706	6.134	6.554	6.965	7.368	7.765	8.155	8.540	8.919	9.293	9.662	10.028	10.388
17	1.018	1.725	2.347	2.920	3.460	3.975	4.469	4.946	5.409	5.860	6.300	6.731	7.153	7.567	7.975	8.376	8.771	9.160	9.544	9.924	10.299	10.669
18	1.044	1.768	2.407	2.995	3.548	4.076	4.582	5.072	5.547	6.009	6.461	6.902	7.335	7.760	8.178	8.589	8.994	9.393	9.787	10.176	10.561	10.941
19	1.069	1.811	2.465	3.067	3.634	4.174	4.693	5.194	5.680	6.154	6.616	7.068	7.512	7.947	8.375	8.796	9.211	9.619	10.023	10.421	10.815	11.204
20	1.094	1.852	2.521	3.137	3.717	4.269	4.800	5.312	5.810	6.294	6.767	7.230	7.683	8.128	8.566	8.997	9.421	9.839	10.252	10.659	11.062	11.460
21	1.118	1.893	2.576	3.205	3.797	4.362	4.904	5.428	5.936	6.431	6.914	7.387	7.850	8.305	8.752	9.192	9.625	10.053	10.474	10.891	11.302	11.709
22	1.141	1.932	2.629	3.271	3.876	4.452	5.005	5.540	6.059	6.564	7.057	7.539	8.012	8.477	8.933	9.382	9.824	10.260	10.691	11.116	11.536	11.951
23	1.163	1.970	2.681	3.336	3.952	4.540	5.104	5.649	6.178	6.694	7.196	7.688	8.171	8.644	9.109	9.567	10.018	10.463	10.902	11.335	11.764	12.187
24	1.185	2.007	2.731	3.399	4.027	4.626	5.201	5.756	6.295	6.820	7.332	7.834	8.325	8.807	9.281	9.748	10.208	10.661	11.108	11.550	11.986	12.417
25	1.207	2.043	2.781	3.461	4.100	4.710	5.295	5.861	6.409	6.944	7.465	7.976	8.476	8.967	9.450	9.925	10.393	10.854	11.309	11.759	12.203	12.642
26	1.228	2.079	2.829	3.521	4.172	4.792	5.387	5.963	6.521	7.065	7.595	8.114	8.623	9.123	9.614	10.097	10.574	11.043	11.506	11.964	12.416	12.862
27	1.248	2.114	2.877	3.580	4.241	4.872	5.477	6.062	6.630	7.183	7.722	8.250	8.768	9.276	9.775	10.267	10.751	11.228	11.699	12.164	12.624	13.078
28	1.268	2.148	2.923	3.638	4.310	4.950	5.566	6.160	6.737	7.299	7.847	8.383	8.909	9.425	9.933	10.432	10.924	11.409	11.888	12.360	12.827	13.289
29	1.288	2.181	2.969	3.694	4.377	5.027	5.652	6.256	6.842	7.412	7.969	8.514	9.048	9.572	10.087	10.594	11.094	11.587	12.073	12.553	13.027	13.496
30	1.307	2.214	3.013	3.750	4.443	5.103	5.737	6.350	6.945	7.524	8.089	8.642	9.184	9.716	10.239	10.754	11.261	11.761	12.254	12.741	13.222	13.698

Table A1-14 – Current Limits for 3 oz copper internal traces

For 4oz copper

Current Limits for Internal Traces (Amperes)

Trace Width in MILS

ΔT temp rise in Deg C	10	20	30	40	50	60	70	80	90	100	110	120	130	140	150	160	170	180	190	200	210	220
1	0.342	0.579	0.788	0.981	1.162	1.335	1.500	1.661	1.816	1.968	2.116	2.260	2.402	2.541	2.678	2.812	2.945	3.076	3.205	3.332	3.458	3.583
2	0.464	0.786	1.069	1.330	1.576	1.811	2.036	2.253	2.464	2.669	2.870	3.066	3.258	3.447	3.633	3.815	3.995	4.173	4.348	4.521	4.691	4.860
3	0.554	0.939	1.278	1.590	1.884	2.164	2.433	2.693	2.945	3.191	3.430	3.665	3.895	4.121	4.342	4.561	4.776	4.988	5.197	5.404	5.608	5.809
4	0.629	1.066	1.450	1.805	2.138	2.456	2.761	3.056	3.343	3.621	3.893	4.160	4.420	4.677	4.928	5.176	5.420	5.661	5.898	6.133	6.364	6.593
5	0.694	1.176	1.600	1.991	2.359	2.710	3.046	3.372	3.687	3.995	4.295	4.589	4.876	5.159	5.437	5.710	5.979	6.245	6.507	6.765	7.021	7.274
6	0.752	1.274	1.734	2.157	2.556	2.936	3.301	3.653	3.995	4.329	4.654	4.972	5.284	5.590	5.891	6.187	6.479	6.766	7.050	7.330	7.607	7.881
7	0.805	1.363	1.855	2.309	2.735	3.142	3.532	3.910	4.276	4.632	4.980	5.321	5.655	5.982	6.304	6.621	6.933	7.241	7.545	7.845	8.141	8.434
8	0.854	1.446	1.968	2.448	2.901	3.332	3.746	4.146	4.535	4.913	5.282	5.643	5.997	6.344	6.686	7.022	7.353	7.679	8.002	8.320	8.634	8.945
9	0.899	1.523	2.072	2.579	3.055	3.509	3.945	4.367	4.776	5.174	5.563	5.943	6.316	6.682	7.041	7.395	7.744	8.088	8.427	8.762	9.093	9.420
10	0.942	1.595	2.171	2.701	3.200	3.676	4.133	4.574	5.002	5.420	5.827	6.225	6.615	6.999	7.375	7.746	8.112	8.472	8.827	9.178	9.525	9.867
11	0.982	1.663	2.264	2.817	3.337	3.833	4.310	4.770	5.217	5.652	6.076	6.492	6.899	7.298	7.691	8.078	8.459	8.834	9.205	9.571	9.933	10.290
12	1.020	1.728	2.352	2.927	3.468	3.983	4.478	4.956	5.420	5.872	6.313	6.745	7.168	7.583	7.992	8.393	8.789	9.179	9.564	9.944	10.320	10.692
13	1.057	1.790	2.436	3.032	3.592	4.126	4.638	5.134	5.615	6.083	6.540	6.987	7.425	7.855	8.278	8.694	9.104	9.508	9.907	10.301	10.690	11.075
14	1.092	1.849	2.517	3.132	3.711	4.262	4.792	5.304	5.801	6.284	6.756	7.218	7.671	8.115	8.552	8.982	9.406	9.823	10.236	10.642	11.044	11.442
15	1.126	1.906	2.594	3.229	3.825	4.394	4.940	5.467	5.979	6.478	6.965	7.441	7.907	8.366	8.816	9.259	9.696	10.126	10.551	10.970	11.385	11.795
16	1.158	1.961	2.669	3.322	3.935	4.520	5.082	5.625	6.152	6.665	7.165	7.655	8.135	8.607	9.070	9.526	9.975	10.418	10.855	11.286	11.713	12.134
17	1.189	2.014	2.741	3.411	4.042	4.643	5.220	5.777	6.318	6.845	7.359	7.862	8.355	8.839	9.315	9.783	10.245	10.700	11.148	11.592	12.029	12.462
18	1.220	2.066	2.811	3.498	4.145	4.761	5.352	5.924	6.479	7.019	7.546	8.062	8.568	9.064	9.552	10.033	10.506	10.972	11.432	11.887	12.336	12.780
19	1.249	2.115	2.879	3.582	4.245	4.875	5.481	6.067	6.635	7.188	7.728	8.256	8.774	9.283	9.782	10.274	10.759	11.236	11.708	12.173	12.633	13.087
20	1.278	2.164	2.945	3.664	4.341	4.987	5.606	6.205	6.786	7.352	7.904	8.445	8.975	9.494	10.006	10.509	11.004	11.493	11.975	12.451	12.921	13.386
21	1.305	2.211	3.008	3.744	4.436	5.095	5.728	6.340	6.934	7.512	8.076	8.628	9.169	9.700	10.223	10.737	11.243	11.742	12.235	12.721	13.202	13.677
22	1.332	2.256	3.071	3.821	4.527	5.200	5.847	6.471	7.077	7.667	8.243	8.807	9.359	9.901	10.434	10.959	11.475	11.985	12.488	12.984	13.475	13.959
23	1.359	2.301	3.131	3.897	4.617	5.303	5.962	6.599	7.217	7.818	8.406	8.980	9.544	10.097	10.640	11.175	11.702	12.222	12.734	13.240	13.741	14.235
24	1.384	2.344	3.191	3.970	4.704	5.403	6.075	6.724	7.353	7.966	8.565	9.150	9.724	10.288	10.841	11.386	11.923	12.453	12.975	13.491	14.000	14.504
25	1.409	2.387	3.248	4.042	4.789	5.501	6.185	6.845	7.486	8.111	8.720	9.316	9.900	10.474	11.038	11.593	12.139	12.678	13.210	13.735	14.254	14.767
26	1.434	2.428	3.305	4.113	4.873	5.597	6.292	6.965	7.617	8.252	8.872	9.478	10.073	10.656	11.230	11.795	12.351	12.899	13.440	13.974	14.502	15.024
27	1.458	2.469	3.360	4.181	4.954	5.691	6.398	7.081	7.744	8.390	9.020	9.637	10.241	10.835	11.418	11.992	12.557	13.115	13.665	14.208	14.745	15.276
28	1.482	2.509	3.414	4.249	5.034	5.782	6.501	7.195	7.869	8.525	9.166	9.792	10.407	11.009	11.602	12.185	12.760	13.327	13.886	14.438	14.983	15.522
29	1.505	2.548	3.468	4.315	5.112	5.872	6.602	7.307	7.992	8.658	9.308	9.945	10.568	11.181	11.783	12.375	12.959	13.534	14.102	14.662	15.216	15.764
30	1.527	2.586	3.520	4.380	5.189	5.961	6.701	7.417	8.112	8.788	9.448	10.094	10.727	11.349	11.960	12.561	13.153	13.737	14.314	14.883	15.445	16.001

Table A1-15 – Current Limits for 4 oz copper internal traces

Lead and Hole sizes

The size of holes to be drilled in the PCB will depend on a number of factors, namely; the lead size of the component to be accommodated (if applicable), and the tolerance of the drilling and hole plating process of the fabrication house.

Most components are mounted by soldering each pin into a hole (a 'through hole'). Accordingly, most component manufacturers usually specify 'footprint' for their device, including the location and size of each lead and the corresponding holes required.

The reader may use the following guidelines in arriving at the appropriate hole sizes.

Step 1 – Calculate the Nominal Lead Hole Size

The following tables show some common component lead dimensions for different lead cross sections.

LEAD SIZE (Diameter) (mm) mils
(0.46) 18
(0.51) 20
(0.60) 24
(0.64) 25
(0.76) 30
(0.89) 35
(1.14) 45
(1.32) 52

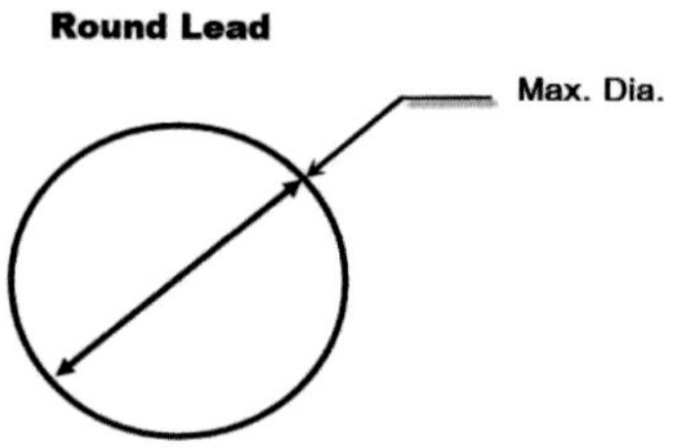

Table A1-16 — Common lead dimensions for round leads

LEAD SIZE (square x section) (mm) mils
(0.30) 12
(0.41) 16
(0.46) 18
(0.51) 20
(0.64) 25
(1.14) 45

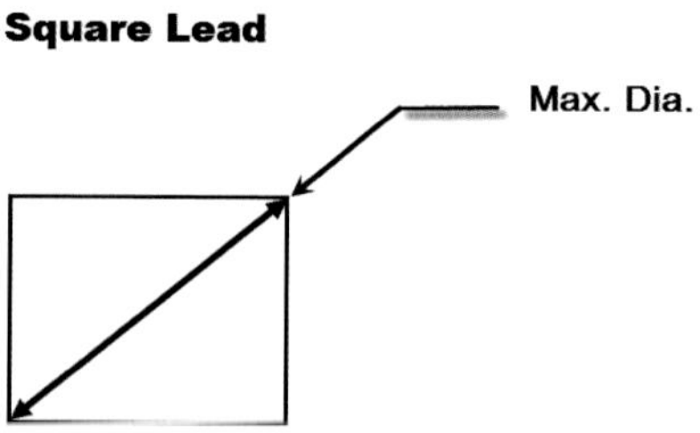

Table A1-17 — Common lead dimensions for square cross-section leads

LEAD SIZE (rectangular x section) (mm) mils
(0.13) 05 x (0.41) 16
(0.20) 08 x (0.71) 28
(0.25) 10 x (0.36) 14
(0.25) 10 x (0.51) 20
(0.41) 16 x (0.51) 20
(0.41) 16 x (0.61) 24
(0.41) 16 x (0.79) 31

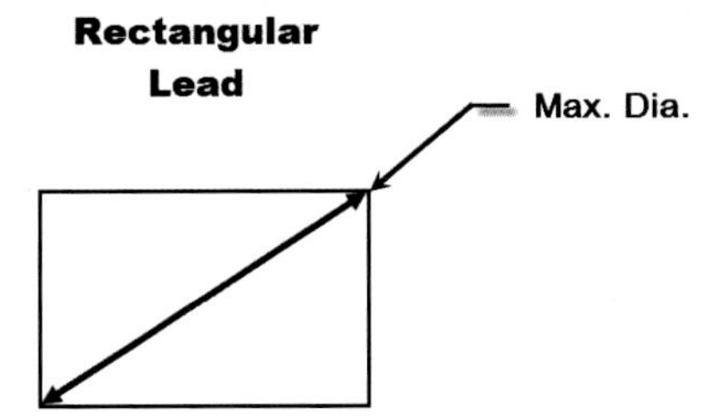

Table 8-18 — Common lead dimensions for rectangular cross-section leads

For rectangular and square leads calculate the diagonal (using $\sqrt{x^2 + y^2}$) to find the maximum lead size (or diameter) for any hole to accommodate it.

Step 2 – Calculate the Minimum Lead Hole Size

After determining the maximum lead size for a particular lead, the reader may now calculate the minimum hole over lead size for that same lead. The IPC standard offers some guidance as follows:

	Level A	Level B	Level C
Min. Hole Diameter addition	≥ 0.25	≥ 0.20	≥ 0.15

Derived from IPC-2222

Where the 'Levels' are defined in IC-2221 as 'design producibility levels of features, tolerances, measurements, assembly, testing of completion or verification of the manufacturing process that reflect progressive increases in .... fabrication cost' These are:

Level A General Design Producibility – Preferred
Level B Moderate Design Producibility – Standard
Level C High Design Producibility – Reduced

By way of example, for a lead of 0.5mm the minimum hole required may be calculated as follows:

Minimum Hole = Maximum Lead Diameter + addition (at appropriate Level)
i.e. = 0.5mm + 0.25 (at Level A) = 0.75mm

In any case, the reader should refer to tolerance guidelines given by their fabrication house when specifying the actual hole sizes for PTHs (Plated-Through Holes), NPTHs (Non Plated-Through Holes) and VIAs.

Step 3 – Calculate the Minimum Annular Ring& Pad Size

Traces on a circuit board may terminate on a pad in order to connect to another layer (through a via); or to connect to a component mounting hole/pad. An **annular ring** is the area on the pad that surrounds the via or hole i.e. the circumferential copper ring around a plated contact. The parameters of these are illustrated in **Figures 8-1 and 8-2** for external and internal PTHs.

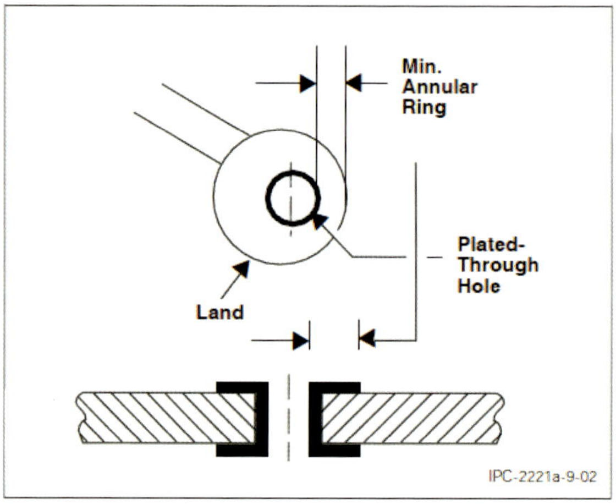

Source IPC-2221A

Figure A1-1 External Annular Ring

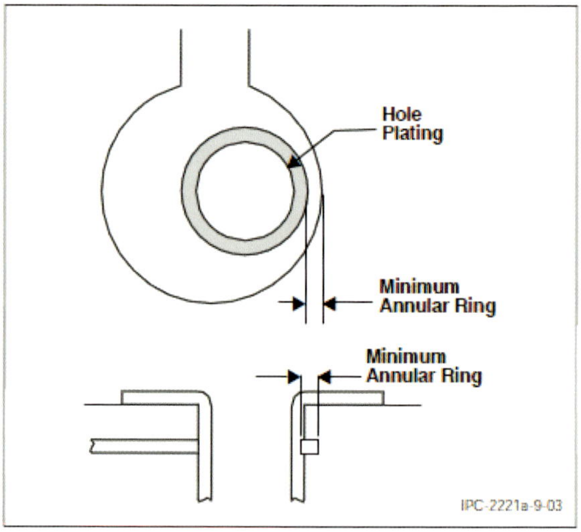

Source IPC-2221A

Figure A1-2 Internal Annular Ring

Of necessity, the annular ring requires certain excess limits arising from drilling and other tolerances.

IPC-221A gives guidance for the determination of the minimum annular ring dimension for both external and internal layers. It states:

> *'The minimum annular ring on external layers is the minimum amount of copper (at the narrowest point) between the edge of the hole and the edge of the land after plating of the finished hole.' See Figure 8-1.*

and

> *'The minimum annular ring on internal layers is the minimum amount of copper (at the narrowest point) between the edge of the drilled hole and the edge of the land after plating of the finished hole.' See Figure 8-1.*

The actual allowances recommended by IPC are given in Table A1-19.

Annular Ring	Class 1, 2 and 3
Internal Supported	0.025 mm (0.00098 in)
External Supported	0.050 mm (0.00197 in)
External Unsupported	0.150 mm (0.005906 in)

Source IPC-2221A

Table A1-19 – Minimum Annular Rings

Where IPC-221A defines the different Classes of equipment as:

Class 1 General Electronic Products – Includes consumer products, some computer and computer peripherals, and hardware suitable for applications where the major requirement is function of the completed assembly.

Class 2 Dedicated Service Electronic – Products Includes communications equipment, sophisticated business machines, and instruments where high performance and extended life is required, and for which uninterrupted service is desired but not mandatory. Typically the end-use environment would not cause failures.

Class 3 High Reliability Electronic Products – Includes all equipment where continued performance or performance-on-demand is mandatory. Equipment downtime cannot be tolerated, end-use environment may be uncommonly harsh, and the equipment must function when required, such as life support systems and other critical systems.

Step 4 – Calculate the Minimum Pad Size

The final step is to calculate the minimum pad diameter allowance for a given hole. This is given in IPC-2221A as follows:

Level A	Level B	Level C
0.4 mm (0.016 in)	0.25 mm (0.00984 in)	0.2 mm (0.0079 in)

Source IPC-2221A

Table A1-20 – Minimum Fabrication Allowance

So, the required Pad Diameter may be calculated as follows:

Pad Diameter = Maximum Lead + Hole over Lead + Minimum Annular Ring x2 + Minimum Fabrication Allowance

Metric to Imperial Conversion

The PCB fabrication industry uses both the imperial measure of inches and the SI metric of (milli)meters. The actual requirement depends entirely on the specifications accepted by the fabrication house and designers should be guided by them.

By definition:

- One millimeter, in the metric system, is equivalent to $\frac{1}{100}$ (one thousandth) of a meter i.e. 1 mm = m.
- One mil in the imperial system, is equivalent to $\frac{1}{100}$ (one thousandth) of an inch i.e. 1 mil = in. (the mil is also referred to as 'thou').

In order to convert between these metrics a simple formula may be used:

$$L_{mils} = L_{mm} \times \frac{5000}{127}$$

Or conversely:

$$L_{mm} = L_{mils} \times \frac{127}{5000}$$

Where:

L_{mm} is the length in millimeters

L_{mils} is the length in mils.

The closest unit to the mil in the metric system is the micrometer, or micron, where one mil is equivalent to 25.4 μm (microns).

Electrical Conductor Spacing

The spacing of traces and other electrical connections are essential to the successful execution of any design in a PCB – especially when electrical safety requirements are considered. Table 8-21 gives the IPC specifications for conductor spacing on PCBs under various conditions.

Voltage Between Conductors (DC or AC Peaks)	Minimum Spacing						
	Bare Board				Assembly		
	B1	B2	B3	B4	A5	A6	A7
0-15	0.05 mm	0.1 mm	0.1 mm	0.05 mm	0.13 mm	0.13 mm	0.13 mm
16-30	0.05 mm	0.1 mm	0.1 mm	0.05 mm	0.13 mm	0.25 mm	0.13 mm
31-50	0.1 mm	0.6 mm	0.6 mm	0.13 mm	0.13 mm	0.4 mm	0.13 mm
51-100	0.1 mm	0.6 mm	1.5 mm	0.13 mm	0.13 mm	0.5 mm	0.13 mm
101-150	0.2 mm	0.6 mm	3.2 mm	0.4 mm	0.4 mm	0.8 mm	0.4 mm
151-170	0.2 mm	1.25 mm	3.2 mm	0.4 mm	0.4 mm	0.8 mm	0.4 mm
171-250	0.2 mm	1.25 mm	6.4 mm	0.4 mm	0.4 mm	0.8 mm	0.4 mm
251-300	0.2 mm	1.25 mm	12.5 mm	0.4 mm	0.4 mm	0.8 mm	0.8 mm
301-500	0.25 mm	2.5 mm	12.5 mm	0.8 mm	0.8 mm	1.5 mm	0.8 mm
> 500 See para. 6.3 for calc.	0.0025 mm /volt	0.005 mm /volt	0.025 mm /volt	0.00305 mm /volt	0.00305 mm /volt	0.00305 mm /volt	0.00305 mm /volt

Source IPC-2221A

Table A1-21 – Minimum conductor spacings

B1-Internal Conductors
B2-External Conductors, uncoated, sea level to 3050m
B3-External Conductors, uncoated, over 3050m
B4-External Conductors, with permanent polymer coating (any elevation)
A5-External Conductors, with conformal coating over assembly (any elevation)
A6-External Component lead/termination, uncoated
A7-External Component lead termination, with conformal coating (any elevation)

The newer IPC-9592 standard for power conversion circuits originally provided linear functional spacing requirements given by the formula:

$$D = 0.6 + V_{peak} \times 0.005$$

Where:

D = trace/conductor spacing in mm
V_{peak} = peak voltage between traces

The above formula results in higher spacings than necessary and a conservatively designed circuit board.

Later revisions of this same document provide a step function and relaxed requirements at the low voltage end of requirements. The result is given in Table 8-22

Voltage Range	Spacing (mm)
<15V	0.13
15V≤V<30V	0.25
30V≤V<100V	0.1+V×0.01

Table A1-22 – Peak voltages for conductor spacings

Appendix 2 • Common Component Packaging Specifications

This appendix is intended to provide guidance to parameter packaging and dimensions of some of the more commonly available components. The contents is by no means exhaustive; rather it is simply illustrative of the extent and variety of global component stock, which exceeds many tens of thousands, and grows daily.

The specifications cited in this appendix give an indication of the dimensions of common components. Whenever the exact size needs to be known, the user should always check the manufacturer's datasheet. All measurements are in millimeters, except where otherwise stated.

SMD Resistor and Capacitor Packages

Small surface mounted resistors and capacitors share, at some level, a common set of packaging specifications. These have been defined by the Electronic Industries Alliance (EIA) and have been adopted widely in industry. Figure A2-1 provides a comparison of the sizes of these respective packages.

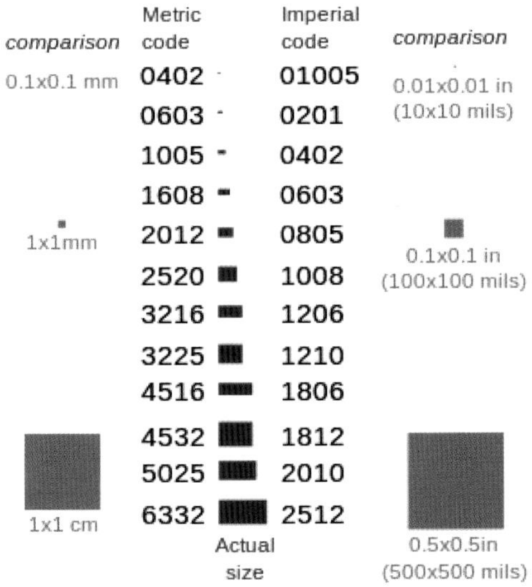

Source: Wikipedia

Figure A2-1 Comparison of Case Dimensions of common EIA SMD packages

The nominal packaging dimensions and the Land Pattern for EAGLE for these devices, are given in Table A3-1.

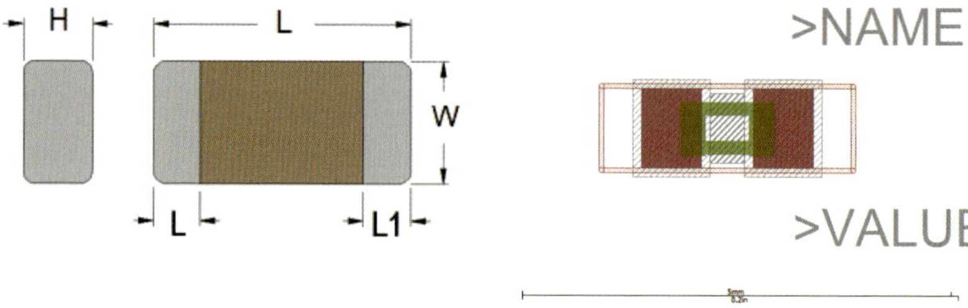

Source PCB Libraries, CadSoftComputer GmbH

Figure A2-2 Dimensions & EAGLE Land Pattern for EIA SMD packages

Case Designator		Length (L)		Width (W)		Height (H)	
Imperial	**Metric**	**inch**	**mm**	**inch**	**mm**	**inch**	**mm**
0201	0603	0.024	0.6	0.012	0.3	0.01	0.25
0402	1005	0.04	1.0	0.02	0.5	0.014	0.35
0603	1608	0.06	1.55	0.03	0.85	0.018	0.45
0805	2012	0.08	2.0	0.05	1.2	0.018	0.45
1206	3216	0.12	3.2	0.06	1.6	0.022	0.55
1210	3225	0.12	3.2	0.10	2.5	0.022	0.55
1218	3246	0.12	3.2	0.18	4.6	0.022	0.55
2010	5025	0.20	5.0	0.10	2.5	0.024	0.6
2512	6332	0.25	6.3	0.12	3.2	0.024	0.6

Table A2-1 – Case dimensions for some common EIA SMD packages

Through–hole axial resistor packages

The dimension of through-hole axial resistors is standardized as are SMD resistors packages. As a result their specifications differ with each manufacturer, power rating and type of resistor (i.e. carbon composition, wirewound, carbon or metal film).

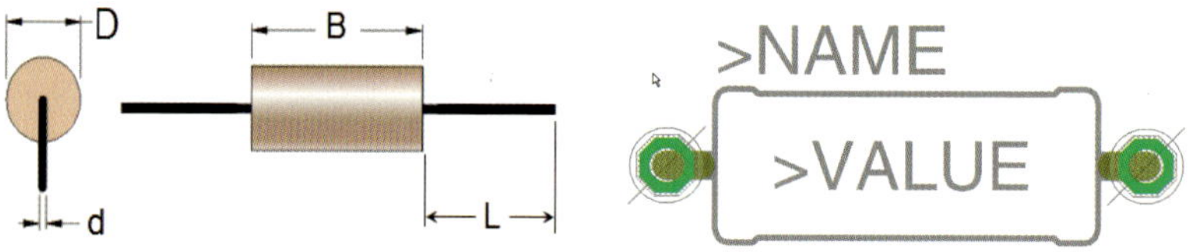

Source: PCB Libraries Inc, CADSoft Computer GmbH

Power rating Watts	Body length (B) mm	Body diameter (D) mm	Lead length (L) mm	Lead diameter (d) mm
1/8 (0.125)	3.0 ± 0.3	1.8 ± 0.3	28 ± 3	0.45 ± 0.05
¼ (0.25)	6.5 ± 0.5	2.5 ± 0.3	28 ± 3	0.6 ± 0.05
½ (0.5)	8.5 ± 0.5	3.2 ± 0.3	28 ± 3	0.6 ± 0.05
1	11 ± 1	5 ± 0.5	28 ± 3	0.8 ± 0.05

Table A2-2 – Case dimensions for some common through –hole axial resistor packages

Inductor Package Outlines

Chip Inductors

The packaging for inductors in surface mounted chip configurations is very similar to that of resistors. Therefore the reader should refer to the section above: 'SMD Resistor and Capacitor Packages'.

Molded Inductors

The packaging for inductors in molded, surface-mounted chip configuration is very similar to that of semiconductors, but varies significantly between manufacturers. Therefore the reader should refer to the section above: 'SMA' for diodes and to the manufacturers' specifications. An example of one type of surface-mounted, molded inductor package appears in Figure A2-3.

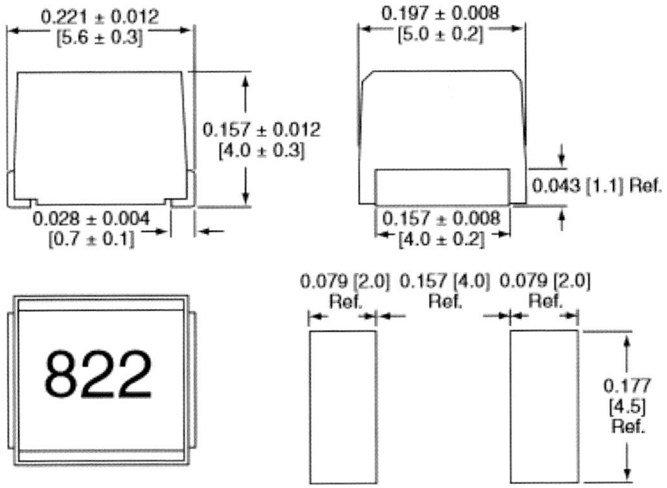

Datasheet extract courtesy of Vishay Intertechnology, Inc.

Figure A2-3 Example of surface mounted, molded inductor packaging

Standard Package Diode Outlines

Diodes come packaged in both axial, through-hole and surface mount forms. Some of the more common specifications are given here.

DO-15 (DO-204AC) –Diode Axial Lead

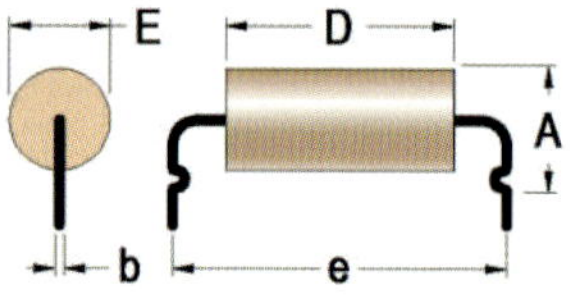

Dimensions (mm)		
	Min	Max
D	5.85	7.62
E	2.65	3.55
b	0.69	0.88

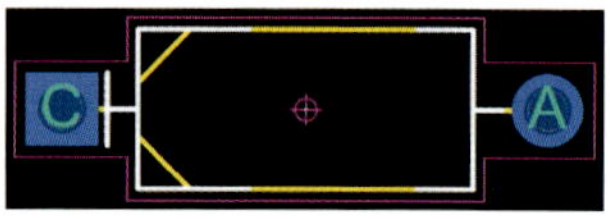

Source: PCB Libraries Inc.

DO-35 (DO-204AH) –Diode Axial Lead

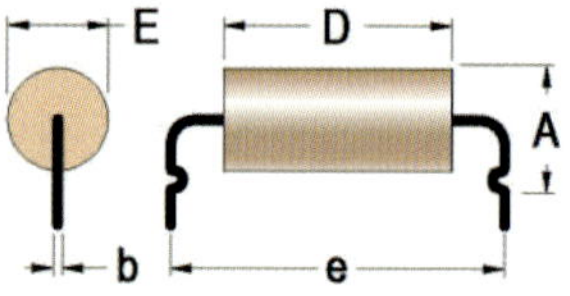

Dimensions (mm)		
	Min	Max
D	3.05	5.08
E	1.53	2.28
b	0.46	0.55

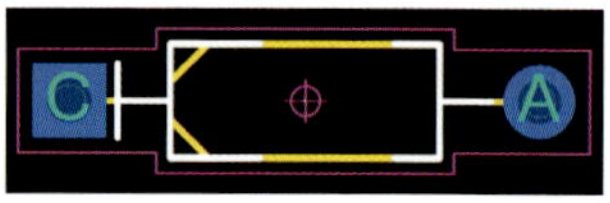

Source: PCB Libraries Inc.

DO-41 (DO-204AL) –Diode Axial Lead

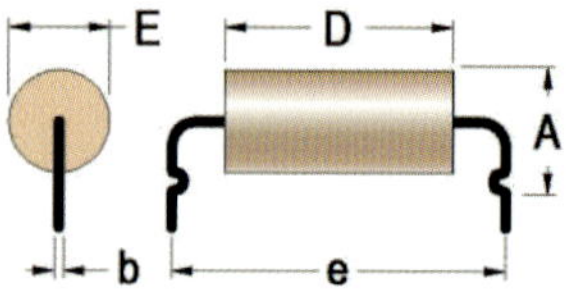

Dimensions (mm)		
	Min	Max
D	4.07	5.20
E	2.04	2.71
b	0.72	0.86

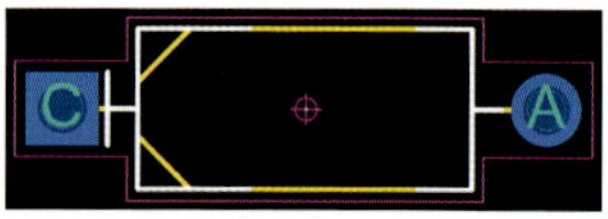

Source: PCB Libraries Inc.

SODFL – Small Outline Diode Flat Lead

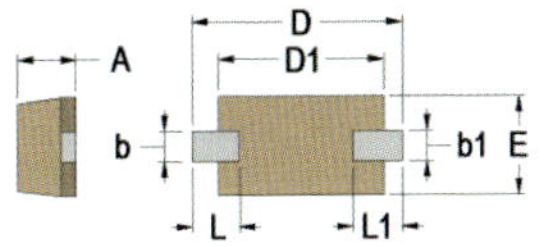

Ref.	Nom	- Tol	+ Tol	Min	Max
A					0.70
b	0.30	-0.05	0.05	0.25	0.35
b1					
D	1.60	-0.10	0.10	1.50	1.70
D1	1.20	-0.10	0.10	1.10	1.30
E	0.80	-0.10	0.10	0.70	0.90
L	0.20	-0.05	0.05	0.15	0.25
L1					

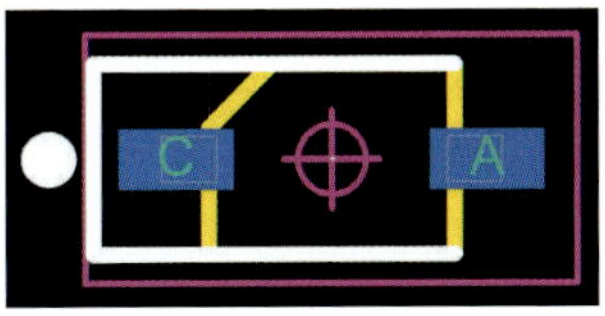

Source: PCB Libraries Inc.

SOD – Small Outline Diode 'gullwing' Leads

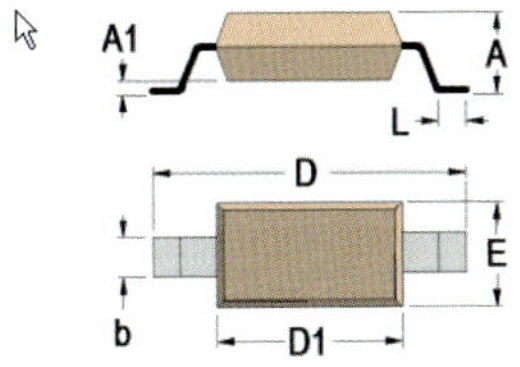

Ref.	Nom	- Tol	+ Tol	Min	Max
A					1.27
A1				0.01	
b	0.65	-0.10	0.10	0.55	0.75
D	3.75	-0.15	0.15	3.60	3.90
D1	2.70	-0.15	0.15	2.55	2.85
E	1.60	-0.20	0.20	1.40	1.80
L	0.285	-0.035	0.035	0.25	0.32

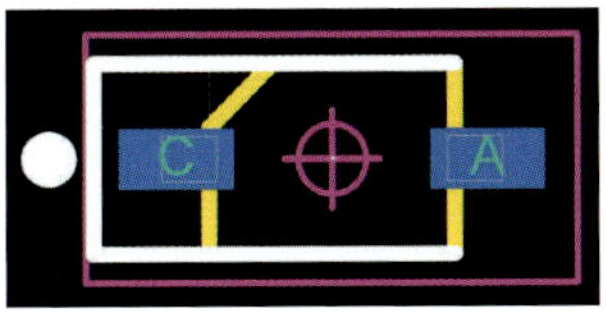

Source: PCB Libraries Inc.

MELF – Metal Electrode Face (DO-213 Var. AA)

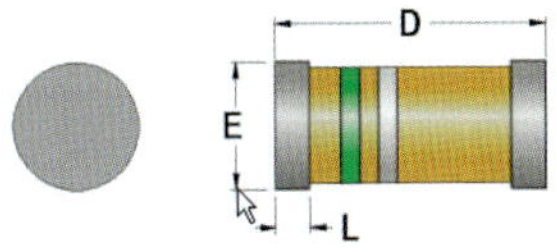

Ref.	Nom	- Tol	+ Tol	Min	Max
D	3.50	-0.20	0.20	3.30	3.70
E	1.525	-0.075	0.075	1.45	1.60
L	0.425	-0.075	0.075	0.35	0.50

Source: PCB Libraries Inc.

SMA – Diode Molded Body (DO-214-D Var.AC)

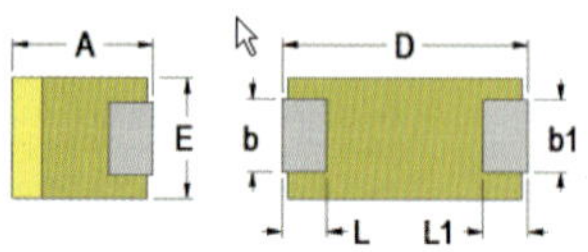

Ref.	Nom	- Tol	+ Tol	Min	Max
A					2.70
b	1.425	-0.225	0.225	1.20	1.65
b1					
D	5.20	-0.40	0.40	4.80	5.60
E	2.725	-0.225	0.225	2.50	2.95
L	1.135	-0.385	0.385	0.75	1.52
L1					

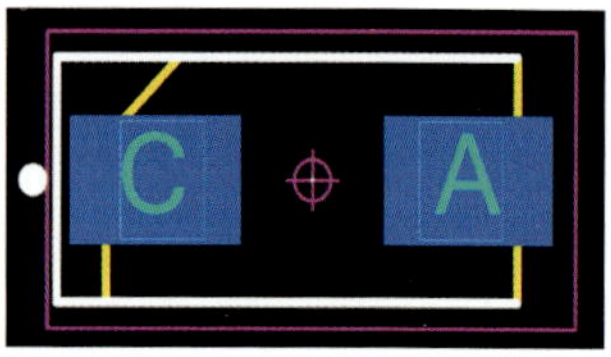

Source: PCB Libraries Inc.

SMA – Diode Molded Body (DO-214-D Var. AA)

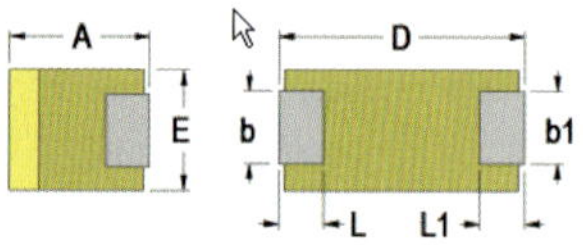

Ref.	Nom	- Tol	+ Tol	Min	Max
A					2.65
b	2.055	-0.145	0.145	1.91	2.20
b1					
D	5.34	-0.26	0.26	5.08	5.60
E	3.625	-0.325	0.325	3.30	3.95
L	1.175	-0.425	0.425	0.75	1.60
L1					

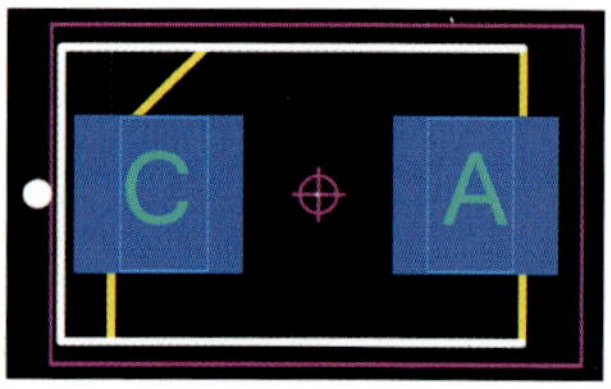

Source: PCB Libraries Inc.

SMA – Diode Molded Body (DO-214-D Var. AB)

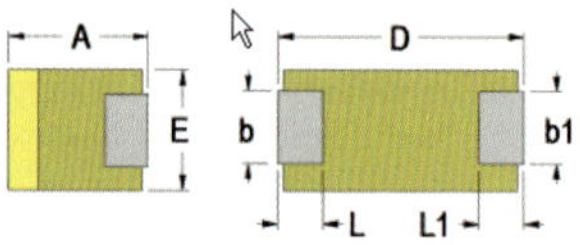

Ref.	Nom	- Tol	+ Tol	Min	Max
A					2.65
b	3.01	-0.26	0.26	2.75	3.27
b1					
D	7.95	-0.20	0.20	7.75	8.15
E	5.90	-0.35	0.35	5.55	6.25
L	1.175	-0.425	0.425	0.75	1.60
L1					

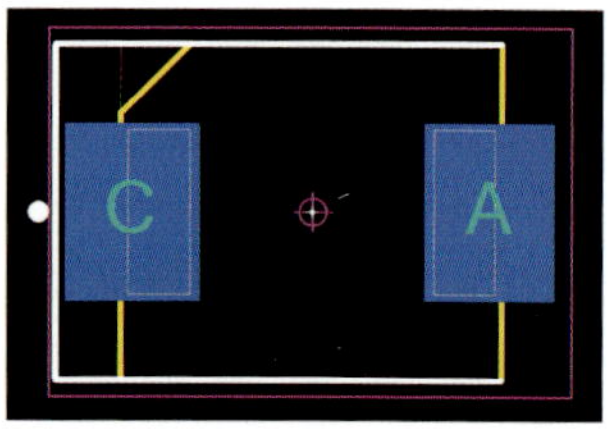

Source: PCB Libraries Inc.

Standard Package Microelectronic Outlines

Microelectronic devices are packaged in a large number of forms, with the variations growing as the need of the designers change. Figure A2-4 gives a perspective of the evolution, and overall types of packaging used in industry today.

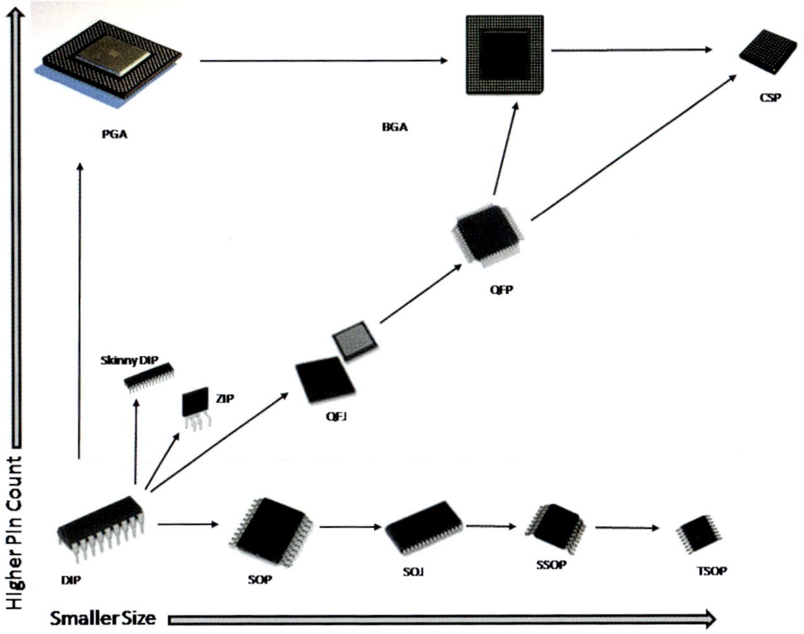

Source: Rohm Semiconductor

Figure A2-4 – Types of microelectronic packaging

One of the earliest and most popular forms of microelectronic packaging is the dual in-line package (DIP or DIL). It comprises a rectangular form factor and two parallel rows of electrical connecting pins. It is usually through-hole mounted to a printed circuit board. Table A3-2 gives the most common types of DIP packages.

Package Name	Characteristics
Dual In-line Package	Standard DIP packages are most widely used. The lead pitch is 2.54 mm (100 mil), and the spacing between terminal rows is 300, 400, or 600 mil.
Skinny Dual In-line Package	Skinny DIP packages are standard DIPs with spacing between terminal rows of 7.62 mm (300 mil) and with 20 or more pins.
Shrink Dual In-line Package	Shrink DIP packages are standard DIPs with a lead pitch reduced to 1.778 mm (70 mil). They are smaller in external size than standard DIPs and suited to compact electronic equipment using high-pin-density IC packages.

Table A2-3 – Types of DIP packages

	Basic DIP Package Types		
Nominal Size	300mil	400mil	600mil
Lead Pitch	100mil (2.54mm)	100mil (2.54mm)	100mil (2.54mm)
Sample Image			
Pin count	8 - 18	20,22	22 - 48

Source: Farnell PLC

The DIP packaging evolved into a form suitable for surface mounting of the components. This 'family' of devices is known as the 'Small Outline Package' (SOP). A selection of their packaging specifications is given in the following diagrams.

SSOP Narrow Body (14, 16, 18, 20, 24, 28 pin)

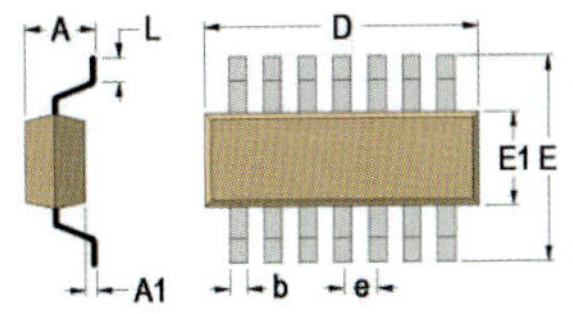

Ref.	Nom	- Tol	+ Tol	Min	Max
A					* 1.10
A1				* 0.05	
b	0.245	-0.055	0.055	* 0.19	* 0.30
D	6.50	-0.10	0.10	* 6.40	* 6.60
E	6.40	-0.20	0.20	* 6.20	* 6.60
E1	4.40	-0.10	0.10	* 4.30	* 4.50
L	0.625	-0.125	0.125	* 0.50	* 0.75

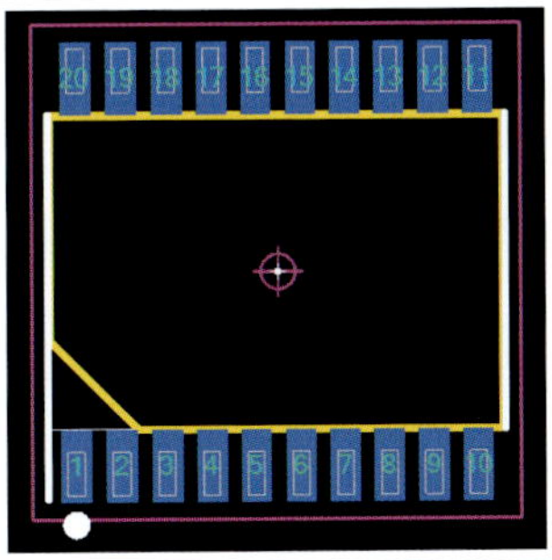

Source: PCB Libraries Inc.

SSOP Wide Body (28, 48, 56, 64 pin)

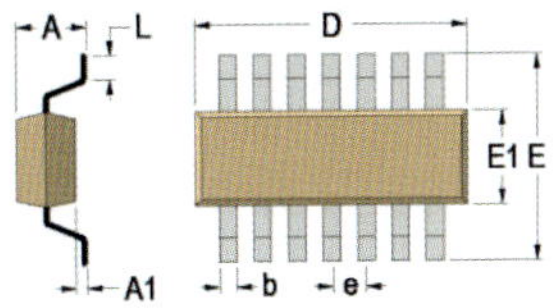

Ref.	Nom	- Tol	+ Tol	Min	Max
A					* 2.00
A1				* 0.05	
b	0.30	-0.08	0.08	* 0.22	* 0.38
D	10.20	-0.30	0.30	* 9.90	* 10.50
E	7.80	-0.40	0.40	* 7.40	* 8.20
E1	5.30	-0.30	0.30	* 5.00	* 5.60
L	0.75	-0.20	0.20	* 0.55	* 0.95

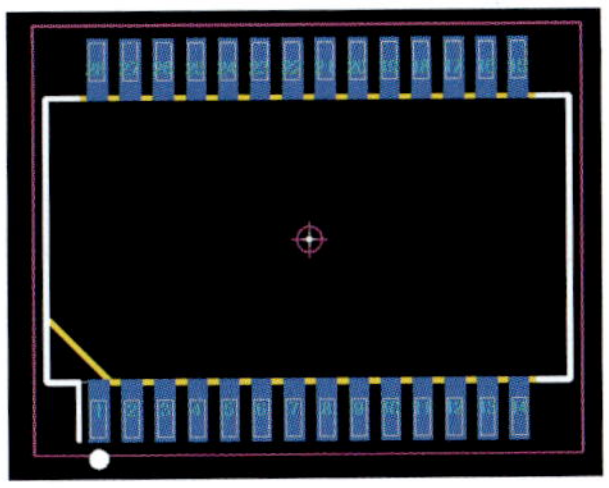

Source: PCB Libraries Inc.

SOP Various package configurations (44 - 90 pin)

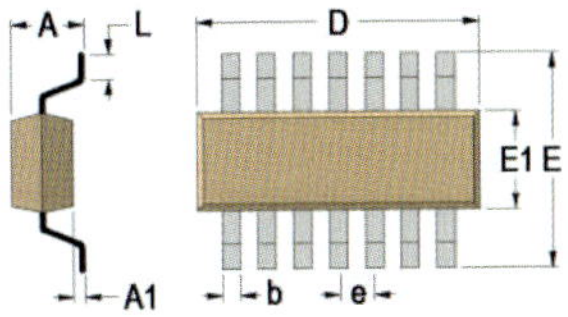

Pitch (e)	0.50	
	Pkg	Count
Pins	44	44

Set tab stops for: ○ Nom/Tol ◉ Min/Max

Ref.	Nom	- Tol	+ Tol	Min	Max
A					* 1.20
A1				* 0.05	
b	0.22	-0.05	0.05	* 0.17	* 0.27
D	11.00	-0.10	0.10	* 10.90	* 11.10
E	6.40	-0.20	0.20	* 6.20	* 6.60
E1	4.40	-0.10	0.10	* 4.30	* 4.50
L	0.60	-0.15	0.15	* 0.45	* 0.75

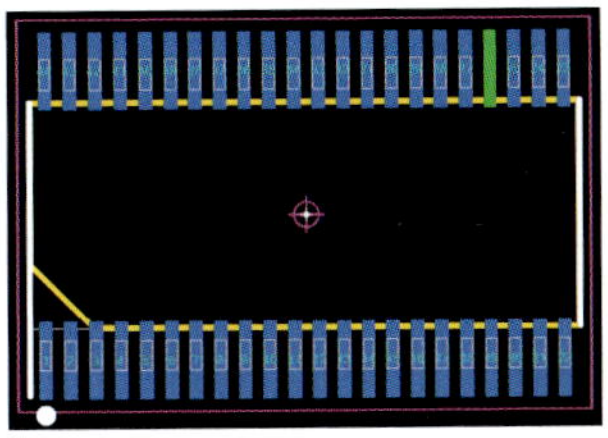

Source: PCB Libraries Inc.

MSOP Various package configurations (8-pin)

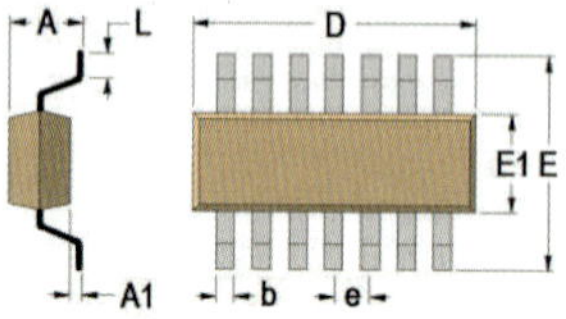

Pitch (e)	0.65				
	Pkg	Count			
Pins	8	8			
Set tab stops for:	○ Nom/Tol		⦿ Min/Max		
Ref.	Nom	- Tol	+ Tol	Min	Max
A					* 1.10
A1				* 0.05	
b	0.30	-0.07	0.07	* 0.23	* 0.37
D	3.00	-0.10	0.10	* 2.90	* 3.10
E	4.90	-0.20	0.20	* 4.70	* 5.10
E1	3.00	-0.10	0.10	* 2.90	* 3.10
L	0.55	-0.15	0.15	* 0.40	* 0.70

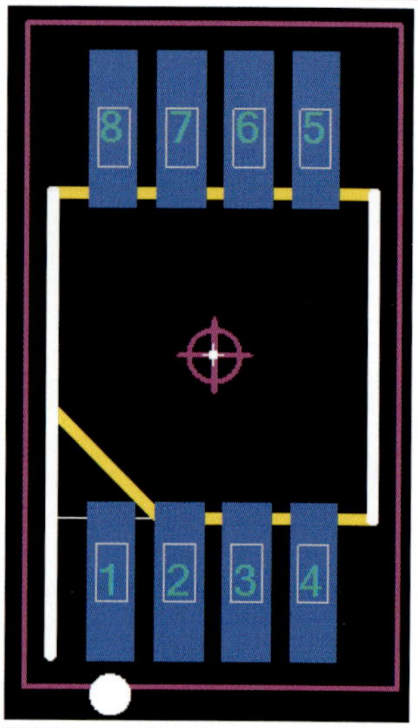

Source: PCB Libraries Inc.

MSOP Various package configurations (10-pin)

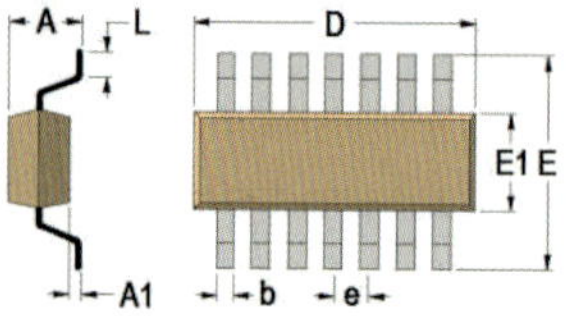

Pitch (e)	0.50				
	Pkg	Count			
Pins	10	10			
Set tab stops for:	○ Nom/Tol		⦿ Min/Max		
Ref.	Nom	- Tol	+ Tol	Min	Max
A					* 1.10
A1				* 0.00	
b	0.25	-0.08	0.08	* 0.17	* 0.33
D	3.00	-0.10	0.10	* 2.90	* 3.10
E	4.90	-0.25	0.25	* 4.65	* 5.15
E1	3.00	-0.10	0.10	* 2.90	* 3.10
L	0.60	-0.20	0.20	* 0.40	* 0.80

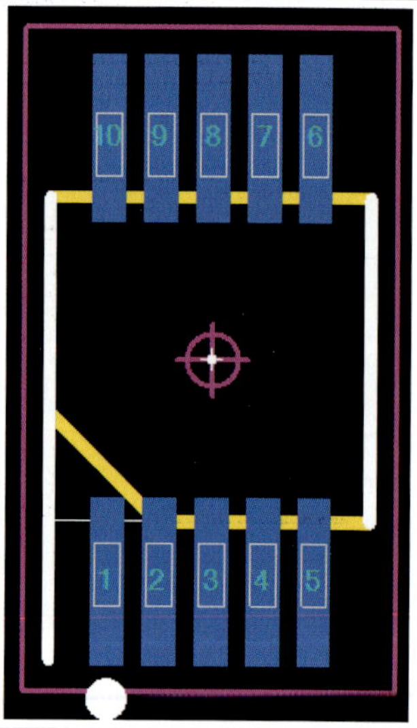

Source: PCB Libraries Inc.

SOIC Narrow Body (8-, 14-, 16-pin)

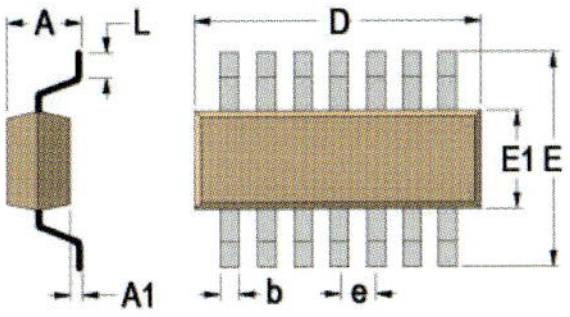

Pitch (e)	1.27	
	Pkg	Count
Pins	8	8

Set tab stops for: ○ Nom/Tol ◉ Min/Max

Ref.	Nom	- Tol	+ Tol	Min	Max
A					1.75
A1				0.10	
b	0.41	-0.10	0.10	0.31	0.51
D	4.90	-0.10	0.10	4.80	5.00
E	6.00	-0.20	0.20	5.80	6.20
E1	3.90	-0.10	0.10	3.80	4.00
L	0.835	-0.435	0.435	0.40	1.27

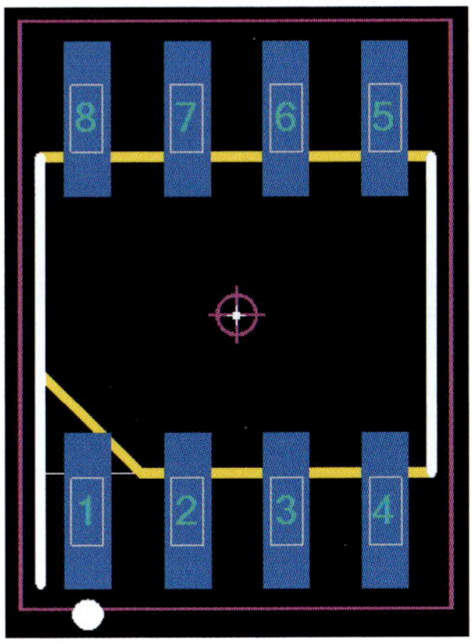

Source: PCB Libraries Inc.

SOIC Wide Body (14,- 16-, 18-, 20-, 24-, 28-pin)

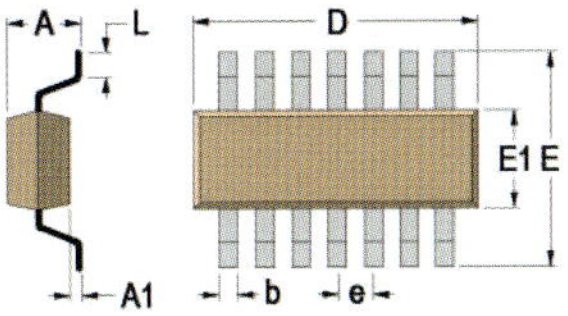

Pitch (e)	1.27	
	Pkg	Count
Pins	16	16

Set tab stops for: ○ Nom/Tol ◉ Min/Max

Ref.	Nom	- Tol	+ Tol	Min	Max
A					2.65
A1				0.10	
b	0.41	-0.10	0.10	0.31	0.51
D	10.30	-0.20	0.20	10.10	10.50
E	10.30	-0.33	0.33	9.97	10.63
E1	7.50	-0.10	0.10	7.40	7.60
L	0.835	-0.435	0.435	0.40	1.27

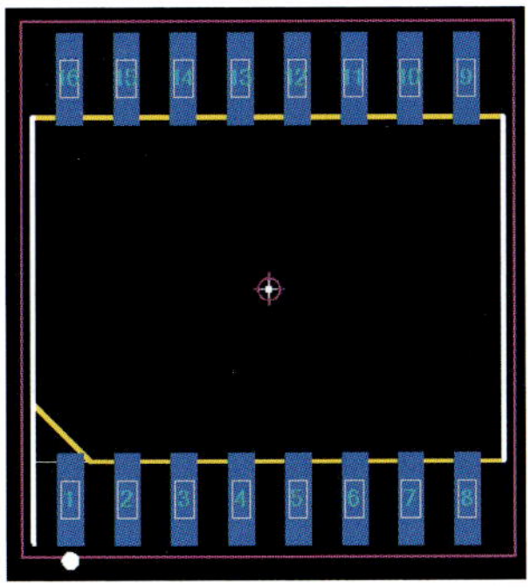

Source: PCB Libraries Inc.

Selection of Small Outline Transistor Packages

Discrete transistors are manufactured in a variety of package types. Some of these are illustrated here. These through-hole package types are also used for other devices. Note: Specific manufacturer package dimensions may not apply to all devices bearing the same package designation.

TO-220 Transistor Outline

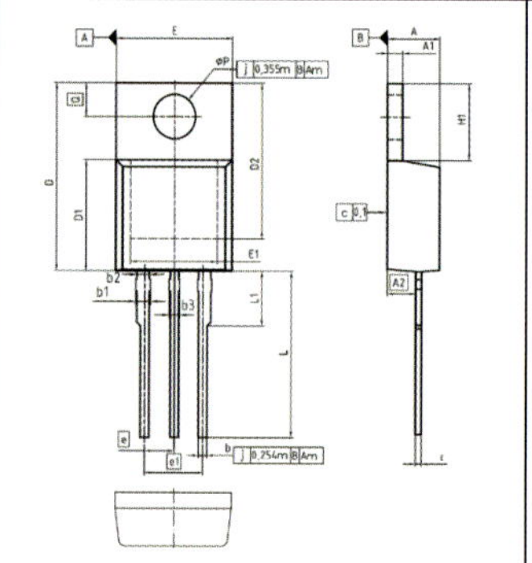

DIM	MILLIMETERS	
	MIN	MAX
A	4.30	4.57
A1	1.17	1.40
A2	2.15	2.72
b	0.65	0.86
b1	0.95	1.40
b2	0.95	1.15
b3	0.65	1.15
c	0.33	0.60
D	14.81	15.95
D1	8.51	9.45
D2	12.19	13.10
E	9.70	10.36
E1	6.50	8.60
e	2.54	
e1	5.08	
N	3	
H1	5.90	6.90
L	13.00	14.00
L1	-	4.80
øP	3.60	3.89
Q	2.60	3.00

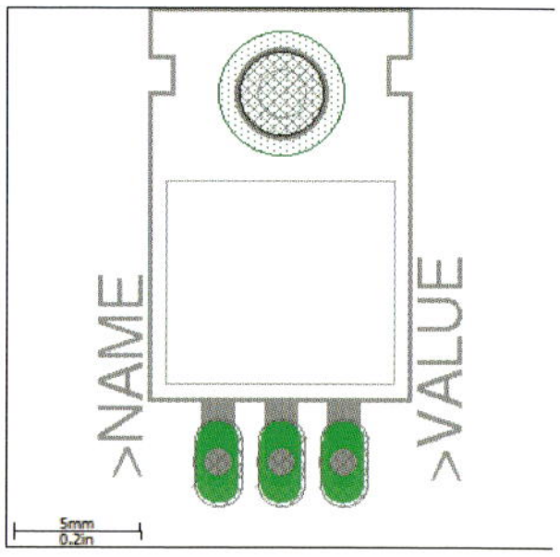

Source: Infineon Technologies AG, CadSoftComputer GmbH

TO-247 Transistor Outline

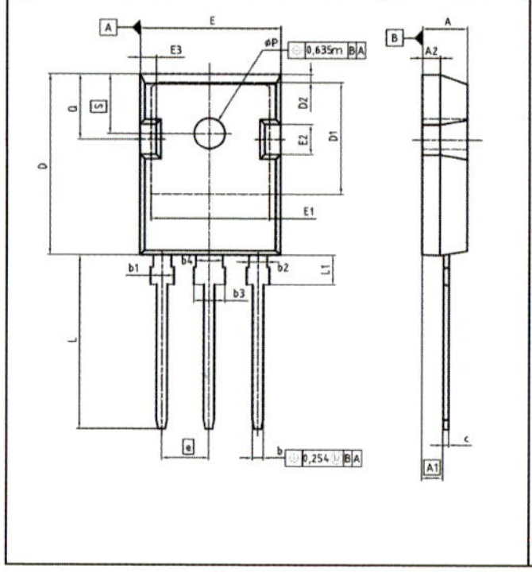

DIM	MILLIMETERS	
	MIN	MAX
A	4.83	5.21
A1	2.27	2.54
A2	1.85	2.16
b	1.07	1.33
b1	1.90	2.41
b2	1.90	2.16
b3	2.87	3.38
b4	2.87	3.13
c	0.55	0.68
D	20.80	21.10
D1	16.25	17.65
D2	0.95	1.35
E	15.70	16.13
E1	13.10	14.15
E2	3.68	5.10
E3	1.00	2.60
e	5.44	
N	3	
L	19.80	20.32
L1	4.10	4.47
øP	3.50	3.70
Q	5.49	6.00
S	6.04	6.30

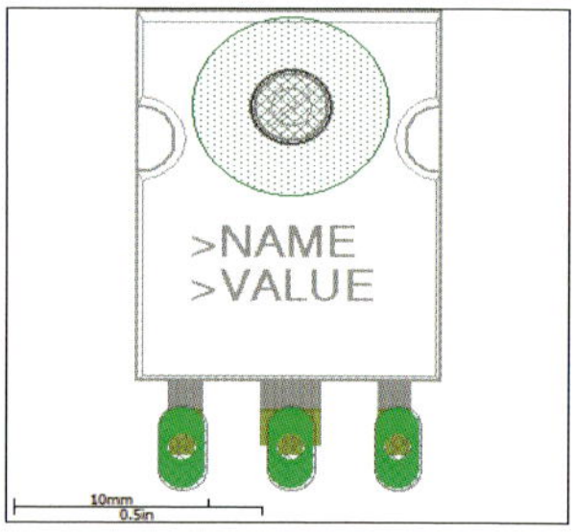

Source: Infineon Technologies AG, CadSoftComputer GmbH

TO-262 Transistor Outline

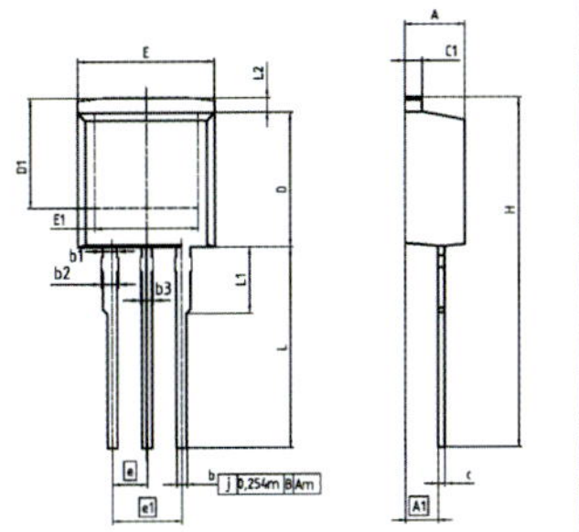

DIM	MILLIMETERS	
	MIN	MAX
A	4.300	4.572
A1	2.150	2.718
b	0.650	0.864
b1	0.950	1.093
b2	0.950	1.400
b3	0.650	1.118
c	0.330	0.600
c1	1.170	1.400
D	8.509	9.450
D1	6.900	-
E	9.700	10.363
E1	6.500	8.600
e	2.540	
e1	5.080	
N	3	
L	13.000	14.000
L1	-	4.800
L2	-	1.727

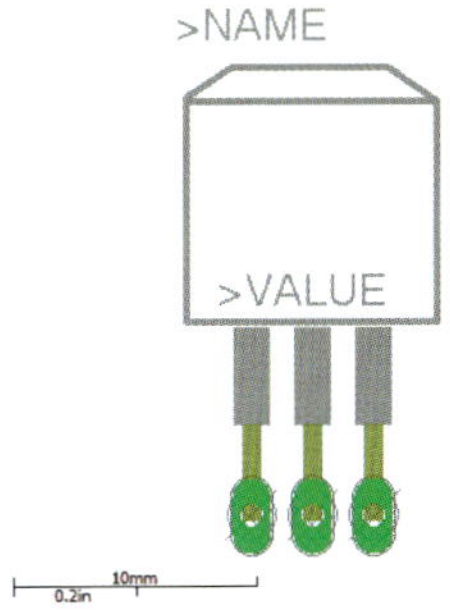

Source: Infineon Technologies AG, CadSoftComputer GmbH

TO-263 Transistor Outline

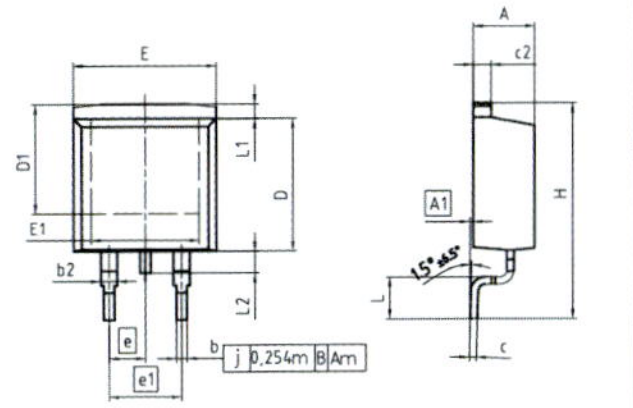

DIM	MILLIMETERS	
	MIN	MAX
A	4.30	4.57
A1	0.00	0.25
b	0.65	0.85
b2	0.95	1.15
c	0.33	0.65
c2	1.17	1.40
D	8.51	9.45
D1	7.10	7.90
E	9.80	10.31
E1	6.50	8.60
e	2.54	
e1	5.08	
N	2	
H	14.61	15.88
L	2.29	3.00
L1	0.70	1.60

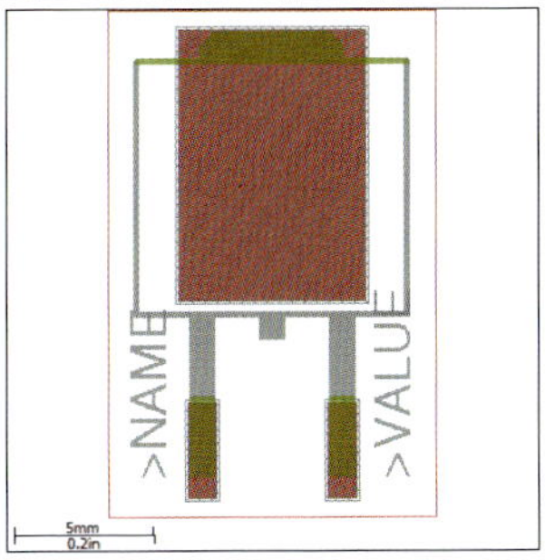

Source: Infineon Technologies AG, CadSoftComputer GmbH

TO-251 Transistor Outline

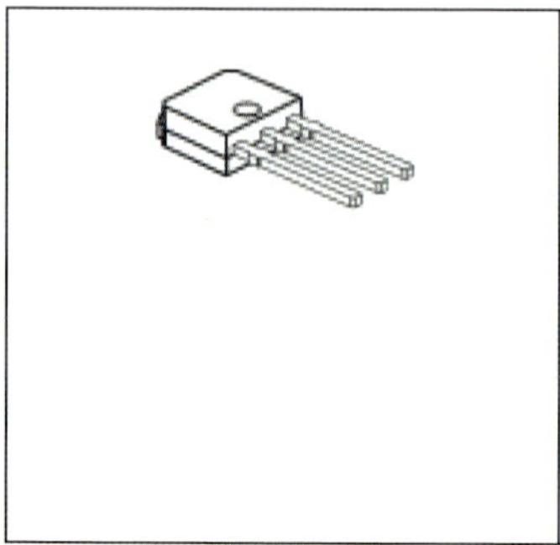

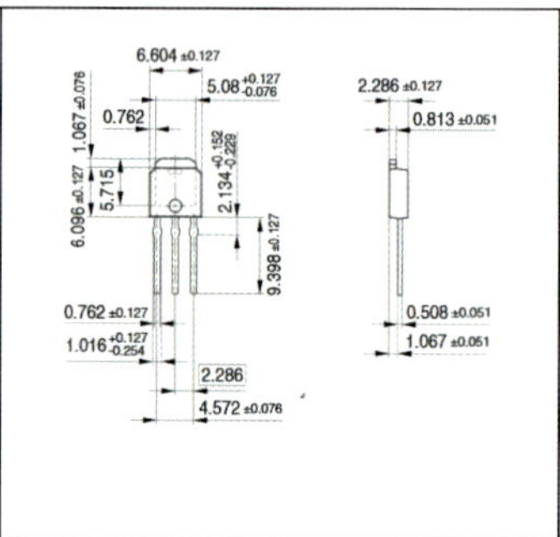

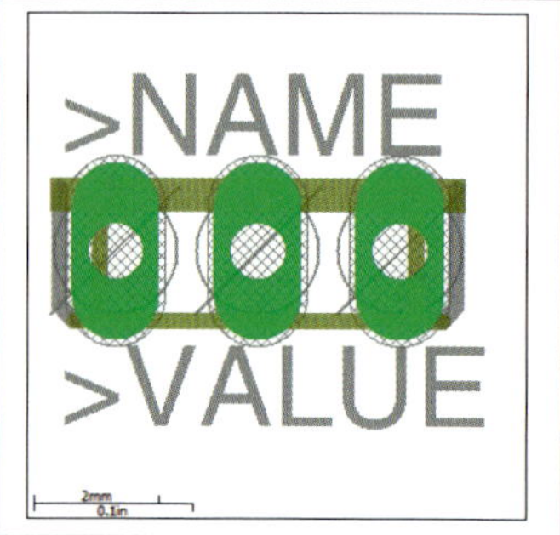

Source: Infineon Technologies AG, CadSoftComputer GmbH

TO-92 Transistor Outline

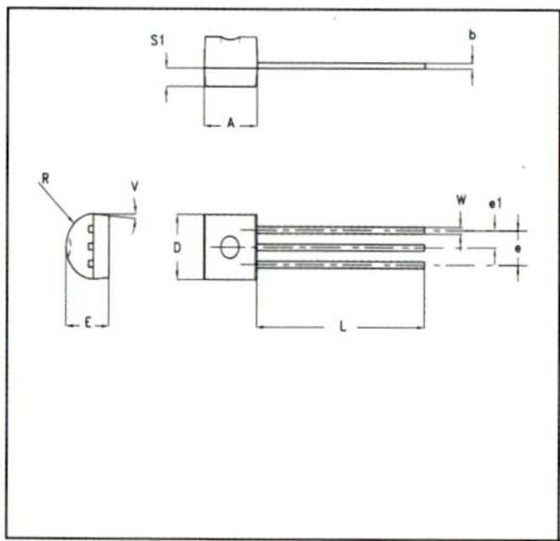

Dim.	mm		
	Min.	Typ.	Max.
A	4.32		4.95
b	0.36		0.51
D	4.45		4.95
E	3.30		3.94
e	2.41		2.67
e1	1.14		1.40
L	12.70		15.49
R	2.16		2.41
S1	0.92		1.52
W	0.41		0.56
V		5°	

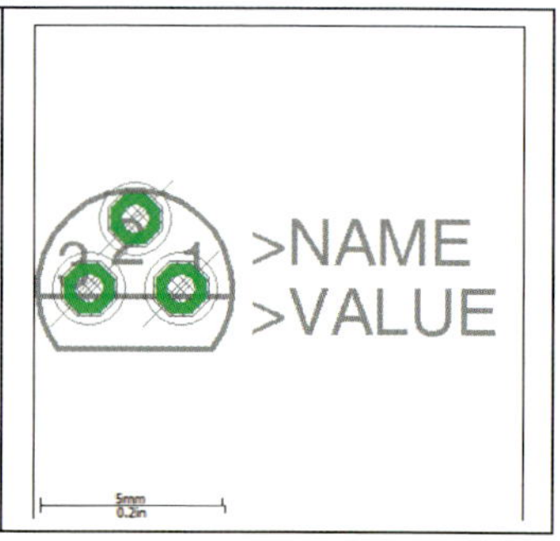

Source: Infineon Technologies AG, CadSoftComputer GmbH

TO-264 Transistor Outline

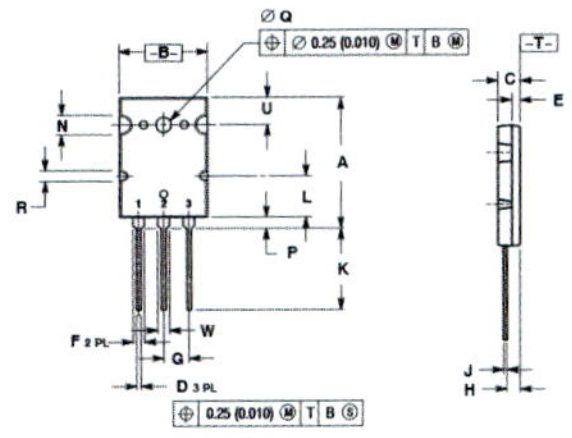

DIM	MILLIMETERS MIN	MILLIMETERS MAX
A	28.0	29.0
B	19.3	20.3
C	4.7	5.3
D	0.93	1.48
E	1.9	2.1
F	2.2	2.4
G	5.45 BSC	
H	2.6	3.0
J	0.43	0.78
K	17.6	18.8
L	11.2 REF	
N	4.35 REF	
P	2.2	2.6
Q	3.1	3.5
R	2.25 REF	
U	6.3 REF	
W	2.8	3.2

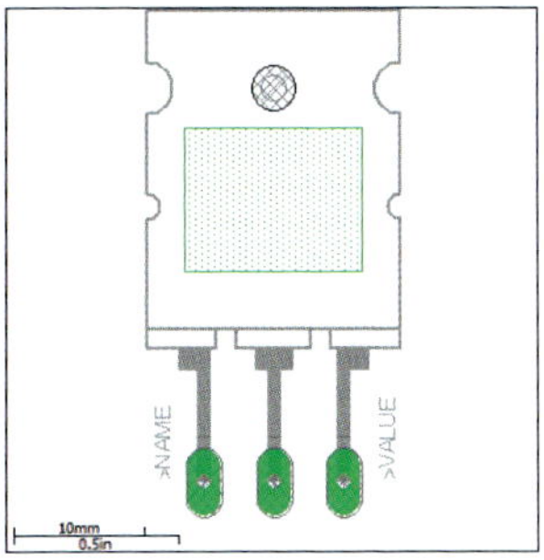

Source: Infineon Technologies AG, CadSoftComputer GmbH

TO-218 Transistor Outline

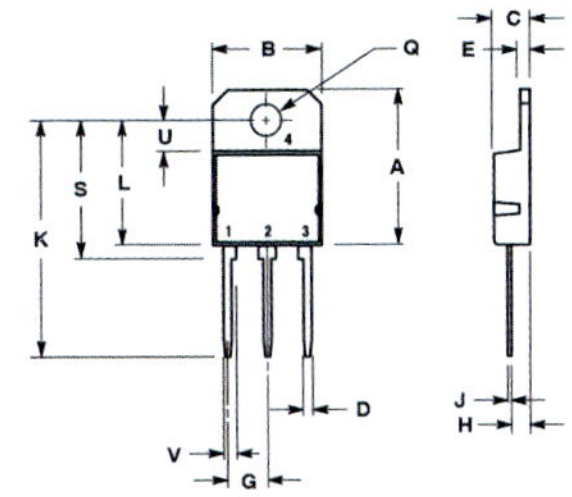

DIM	MILLIMETERS MIN	MILLIMETERS MAX
A	---	20.35
B	14.70	15.20
C	4.70	4.90
D	1.10	1.30
E	1.17	1.37
G	5.40	5.55
H	2.00	3.00
J	0.50	0.78
K	31.00 REF	
L	---	16.20
Q	4.00	4.10
S	17.80	18.20
U	4.00 REF	
V	1.75 REF	

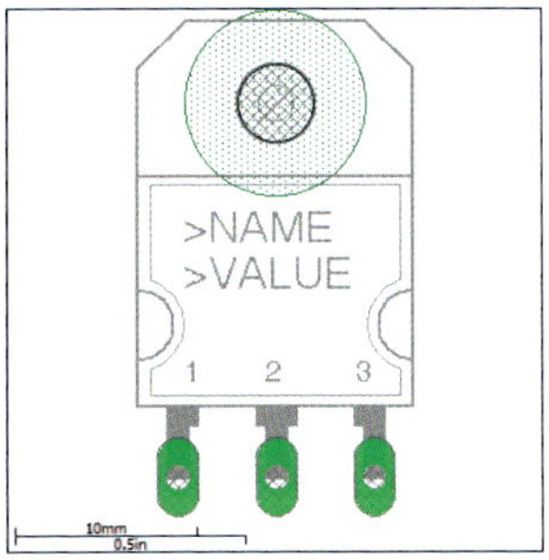

Source: Infineon Technologies AG, CadSoftComputer GmbH

SOT23 3 PIN Transistor Outline

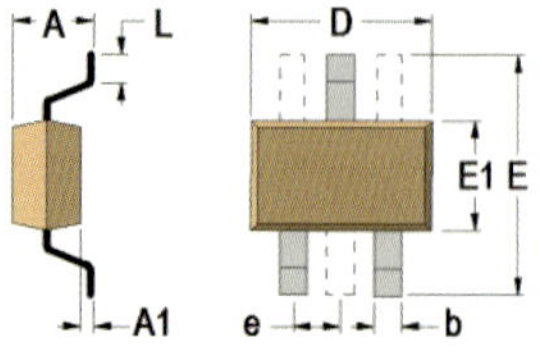

Pitch (e): 0.95
Pins: 3
Set tab stops for: ○ Nom/Tol ◉ Min/Max

Ref.	Nom	- Tol	+ Tol	Min	Max
A					* 1.11
A1				* 0.01	
b	0.435	-0.065	0.065	* 0.37	* 0.50
D	2.92	-0.12	0.12	* 2.80	* 3.04
E	2.37	-0.27	0.27	* 2.10	* 2.64
E1	1.30	-0.10	0.10	* 1.20	* 1.40
L	0.20	-0.10	0.10	* 0.10	* 0.30

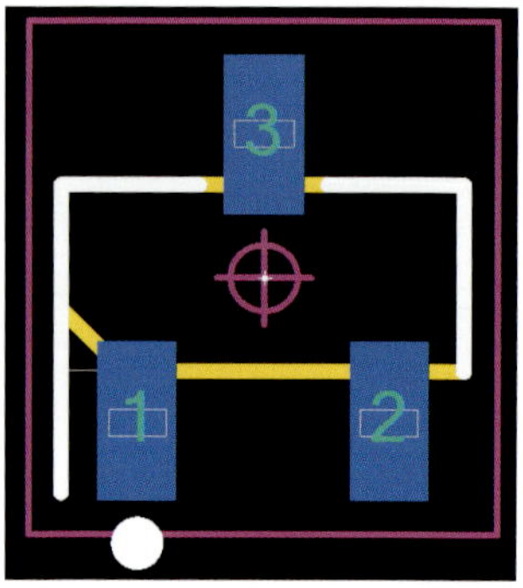

Source: PCB Libraries Inc.

SOT23 6 PIN Transistor Outline

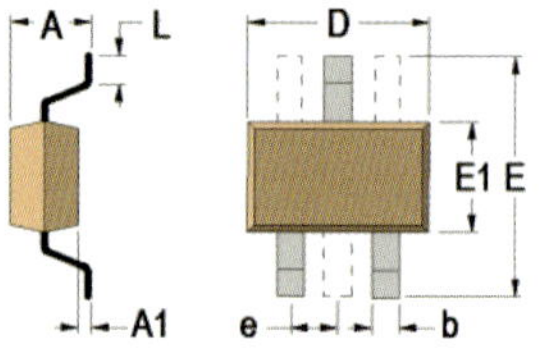

Pitch (e): 0.95
Pins: 6
Set tab stops for: ○ Nom/Tol ◉ Min/Max

Ref.	Nom	- Tol	+ Tol	Min	Max
A					* 1.45
A1				* 0.05	
b	0.40	-0.10	0.10	* 0.30	* 0.50
D	2.90	-0.10	0.10	* 2.80	* 3.00
E	2.80	-0.20	0.20	* 2.60	* 3.00
E1	1.60	-0.10	0.10	* 1.50	* 1.70
L	0.45	-0.10	0.10	* 0.35	* 0.55

Source: PCB Libraries Inc.

SOT23 8 PIN Transistor Outline

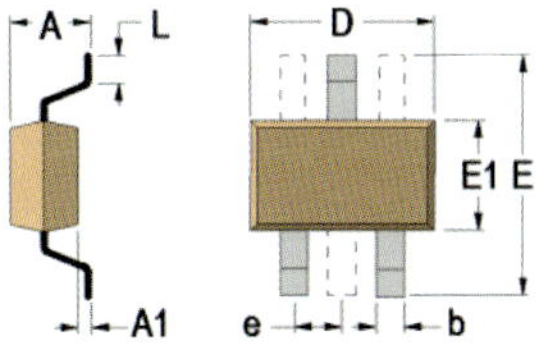

Pitch (e)	0.65
Pins	8

Set tab stops for: Nom/Tol ● Min/Max

Ref.	Nom	- Tol	+ Tol	Min	Max
A					1.00
A1				0.05	
b	0.30	-0.08	0.08	0.22	0.38
D	2.90	-0.10	0.10	2.80	3.00
E	2.80	-0.20	0.20	2.60	3.00
E1	1.60	-0.10	0.10	1.50	1.70
L	0.45	-0.15	0.15	0.30	0.60

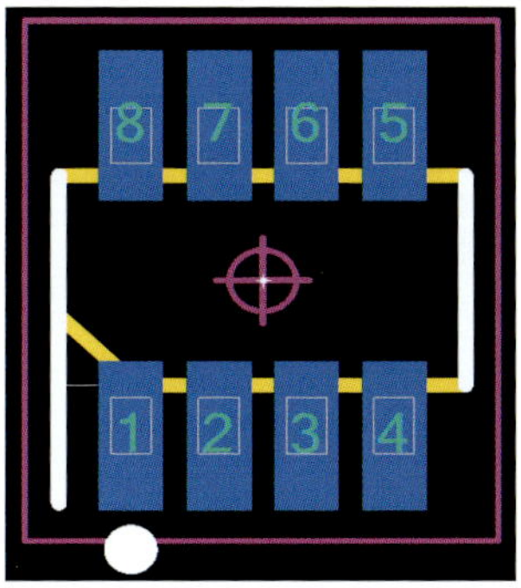

Source: PCB Libraries Inc.

SOT223 4 PIN Transistor Outline

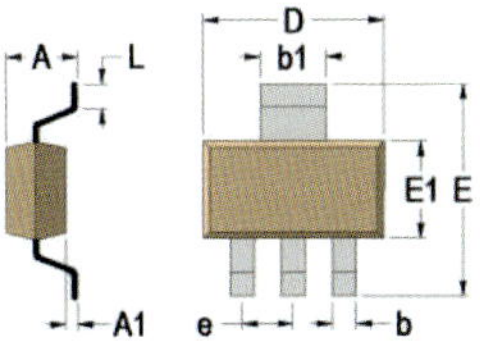

Pitch (e)	2.30
Pins	4

Set tab stops for: Nom/Tol ● Min/Max

Ref.	Nom	- Tol	+ Tol	Min	Max
A					1.80
A1				0.02	
b	0.74	-0.14	0.14	0.60	0.88
b1	3.04	-0.14	0.14	2.90	3.18
D	6.50	-0.20	0.20	6.30	6.70
E	7.00	-0.30	0.30	6.70	7.30
E1	3.50	-0.20	0.20	3.30	3.70
L	1.10	-0.20	0.20	0.90	1.30

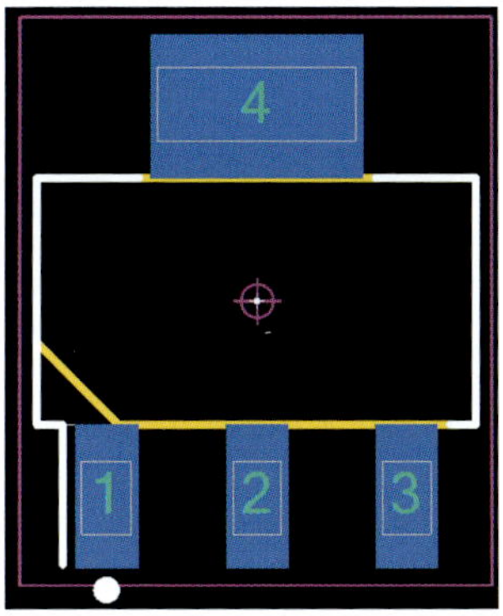

Source: PCB Libraries Inc.

SOT223 5 PIN Transistor Outline

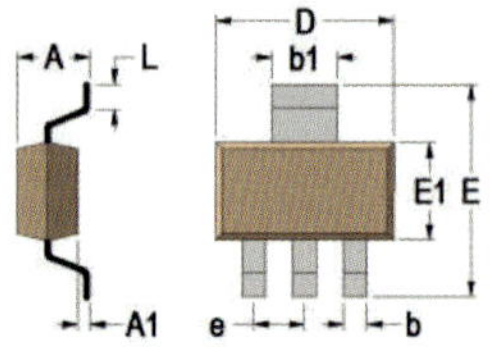

Pitch (e)	2.30				
Pins	4				
Set tab stops for: ○ Nom/Tol			⦿ Min/Max		
Ref.	Nom	- Tol	+ Tol	Min	Max
A					* 1.80
A1				* 0.02	
b	0.74	-0.14	0.14	* 0.60	* 0.88
b1	3.04	-0.14	0.14	* 2.90	* 3.18
D	6.50	-0.20	0.20	* 6.30	* 6.70
E	7.00	-0.30	0.30	* 6.70	* 7.30
E1	3.50	-0.20	0.20	* 3.30	* 3.70
L	1.10	-0.20	0.20	* 0.90	* 1.30

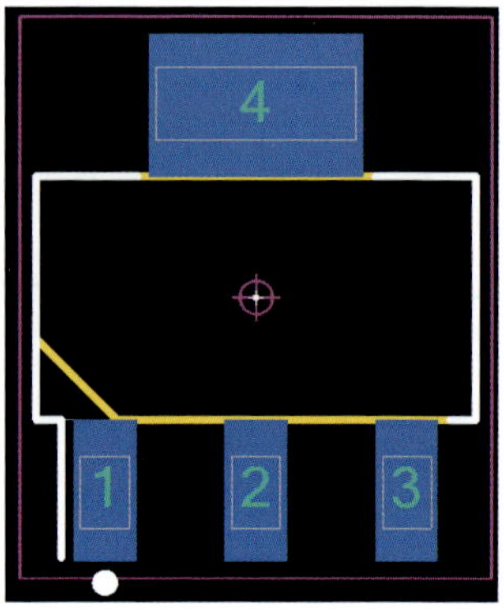

Source: PCB Libraries Inc.

SOT89 4 PIN Transistor Outline

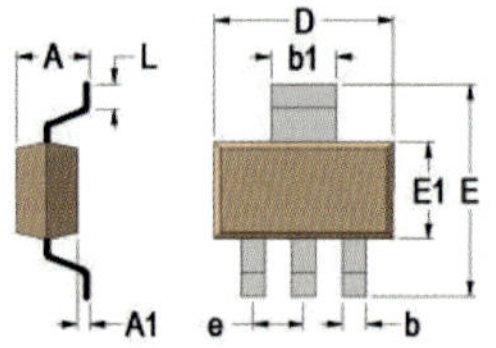

Pitch (e)	1.50				
Pins	4				
Set tab stops for: ○ Nom/Tol			⦿ Min/Max		
Ref.	Nom	- Tol	+ Tol	Min	Max
A					* 1.30
A1				* 0.02	
b	0.40	-0.10	0.10	* 0.30	* 0.50
b1	1.70	-0.10	0.10	* 1.60	* 1.80
D	4.55	-0.05	0.05	* 4.50	* 4.60
E	4.00	-0.30	0.30	* 3.70	* 4.30
E1	2.55	-0.05	0.05	* 2.50	* 2.60
L	0.35	-0.10	0.10	* 0.25	* 0.45

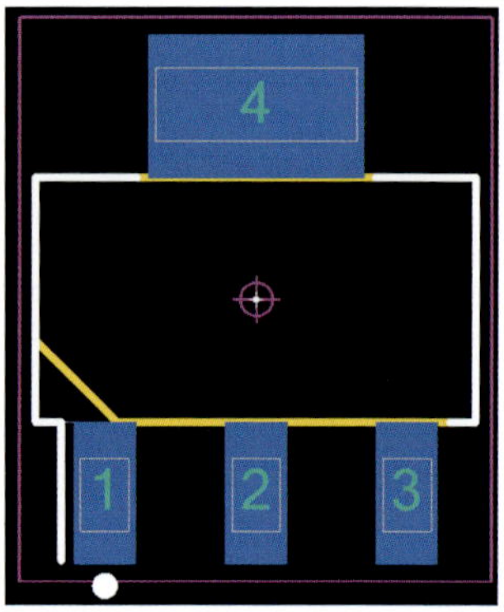

Source: PCB Libraries Inc.

SOT143 4 PIN Transistor Outline

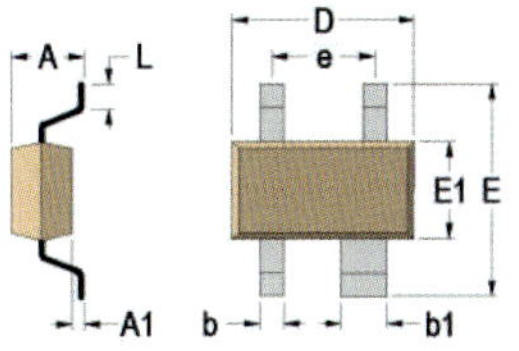

Pitch (e): 1.92

Set tab stops for: Nom/Tol ● Min/Max

Ref.	Nom	- Tol	+ Tol	Min	Max
A					1.22
A1				0.01	
b	0.425	-0.075	0.075	0.35	0.50
b1	0.825	-0.065	0.065	0.76	0.89
D	2.92	-0.12	0.12	2.80	3.04
E	2.37	-0.27	0.27	2.10	2.64
E1	1.30	-0.10	0.10	1.20	1.40
L	0.50	-0.10	0.10	0.40	0.60

Source: PCB Libraries Inc.

SOT353 5 PIN Transistor Outline

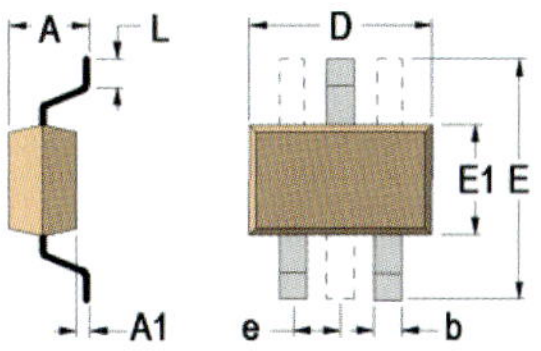

Pitch (e): 0.65

Pins: 5

Set tab stops for: Nom/Tol ● Min/Max

Ref.	Nom	- Tol	+ Tol	Min	Max
A					1.10
A1				0.00	
b	0.225	-0.075	0.075	0.15	0.30
D	2.05	-0.20	0.20	1.85	2.25
E	2.125	-0.125	0.125	2.00	2.25
E1	1.25	-0.10	0.10	1.15	1.35
L	0.335	-0.125	0.125	0.21	0.46

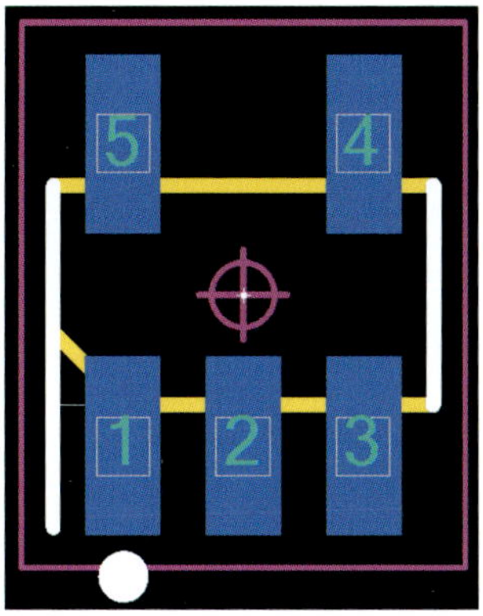

Source: PCB Libraries Inc.

Appendix 3 • EAGLE User Language Reference Manual

Author's Note: Material in this appendix is taken directly from EAGLE documentation sources. This has been done in order present this information in a more convenient, accessible and integrated form.

The author acknowledges that full ownership and rights of this material reside with CadSoftComputer GmbH.

EAGLE

EASILY APPLICABLE GRAPHICAL LAYOUT EDITOR

User Language

Version 7.2.0

Table of Contents

EAGLE Help Version 7.2.0

User Language

The EAGLE User Language can be used to access the EAGLE data structures and to create a wide variety of output files.

To use this feature you have to write a User Language Program (ULP), and then execute it.

The following sections describe the EAGLE User Language in detail:

Syntax	lists the rules a ULP file has to follow
Data Types	defines the basic data types
Object Types	defines the EAGLE objects
Definitions	shows how to write a definition
Operators	lists the valid operators
Expressions	shows how to write expressions
Statements	defines the valid statements
Builtins	lists the builtin constants, functions etc.
Dialogs	shows how to implement a graphical frontent to a ULP

Writing a ULP

A User Language Program is a plain text file which is written in a C-like syntax. User Language Programs use the extension `.ulp`. You can create a ULP file with any text editor (provided it does not insert any additional control characters into the file) or you can use the builtin text editor.

A User Language Program consists of two major items, definitions and statements.

Definitions are used to define constants, variables and functions to be used by statements.

A simple ULP could look like this:

```
#usage "Add the characters in the word 'Hello'\n"
       "Usage: RUN sample.ulp"
// Definitions:
string hello = "Hello";
int count(string s)
{
  int c = 0;
  for (int i = 0; s[i]; ++i)
      c += s[i];
  return c;
}
// Statements:
output("sample") {
  printf("Count is: %d\n", count(hello));
  }
```

If the `#usage` directive is present, its value will be used in the Control Panel to display a description of the program.

If the result of the ULP shall be a specific command that shall be executed in the editor window, the `exit()` function can be used to send that command to the editor window.

Executing a ULP

User Language Programs are executed by the RUN command from an editor window's command line.

A ULP can return information on whether it has run successfully or not. You can use the `exit()` function to terminate the program and set the return value.

A return value of `0` means the ULP has ended "normally" (i.e. successfully), while any other value is considered as an abnormal program termination.

The default return value of any ULP is `0`.

When the RUN command is executed as part of a script file, the script is terminated if the ULP has exited with a return value other than `0`.

A special variant of the `exit()` function can be used to send a command to the editor window as a result of the ULP.

Syntax

The basic building blocks of a User Language Program are

- Whitespace
- Comments
- Directives
- Keywords
- Identifiers
- Constants
- Punctuators

All of these have to follow certain syntactical rules, which are described in their respective sections.

Whitespace

Before a User Language Program can be executed, it has to be read in from a file. During this read in process, the file contents is *parsed* into tokens and *whitespace*.

14

Any spaces (blanks), tabs, newline characters and comments are considered *whitespace* and are discarded.

The only place where ASCII characters representing *whitespace* are not discarded is within literal strings, like in

```
string s = "Hello World";
```

where the blank character between `'o'` and `'W'` remains part of the string.

If the final newline character of a line is preceded by a backslash (\), the backslash and newline character are both discarded, and the two lines are treated as one line:

```
"Hello \
World"
```

is parsed as `"Hello World"`

Comments

When writing a User Language Program it is good practice to add some descriptive text, giving the reader an idea about what this particular ULP does. You might also want to add your name (and, if available, your email address) to the ULP file, so that other people who use your program could contact you in case they have a problem or would like to suggest an improvement.

There are two ways to define a comment. The first one uses the syntax

```
/* some comment text */
```

which marks any characters between (and including) the opening `/*` and the closing `*/` as comment. Such comments may expand over more than one lines, as in

```
/* This is a
   multi line comment
*/
```

but they do not nest. The first `*/` that follows any `/*` will end the comment.

The second way to define a comment uses the syntax

```
int i; // some comment text
```

which marks any characters after (and including) the `//` and up to (but not including) the newline character at the end of the line as comment.

Directives

The following *directives* are available:

#include

A User Language Program can reuse code in other ULP files through the `#include` directive. The syntax is

```
#include "filename"
```

The file `filename` is first looked for in the same directory as the current source file (that is the file that contains the `#include` directive). If it is not found there, it is searched for in the directories contained in the ULP directory path.

The maximum include depth is 10.

Each `#include` directive is processed only **once**. This makes sure that there are no multiple definitions of the same variables or functions, which would cause errors.

Portability note

If *filename* contains a directory path, it is best to always use the **forward slash** as directory separator (even under Windows!). Windows drive letters should be avoided. This way a User Language Program will run on all platforms.

#require

Over time it may happen that newer versions of EAGLE implement new or modified User Language features, which can cause error messages when such a ULP is run from an older version of EAGLE. In order to give the user a dedicated message that this ULP requires at least a certain version of EAGLE, a ULP can contain the `#require` directive. The syntax is

```
#require version
```

The *version* must be given as a real constant of the form

```
V.RRrr
```

where V is the version number, RR is the release number and `rr` is the (optional) revision number (both padded with leading zeros if they are less than 10). For example, if a ULP requires at least EAGLE version 4.11r06 (which is the beta version that first implemented the `#require` directive), it could use

```
#require 4.1106
```

The proper directive for version 5.1.2 would be

```
#require 5.0102
```

#usage

Every User Language Program should contain information about its function, how to use it and maybe who wrote it.
The directive

```
#usage text [, text...]
```

implements a standard way to make this information available.

If the `#usage` directive is present, its `text` (which has to be a string constant) will be used in the Control Panel to display a description of the program.

In case the ULP needs to use this information in, for example, a dlgMessageBox(), the `text` is available to the program through the builtin constant `usage`.

Only the `#usage` directive of the main program file (that is the one started with the RUN command) will take effect. Therefore pure include files can (and should!) also have `#usage` directives of their own.

It is best to have the `#usage` directive at the beginning of the file, so that the Control Panel doesn't have to parse all the rest of the text when looking for the information to display.

If the usage information shall be made available in several langauges, the texts of the individual languages have to be separated by commas. Each of these texts has to start with the two letter code of the respective language (as delivered by the language() function), followed by a colon and any number of blanks. If no suitable text is found for the language used on the actual system, the first given text will be used (this one should generally be English in order to make the program accessible to the largest number of users).

Example

```
#usage "en: A sample ULP\n"
           "Implements an example that shows how to use the EAGLE User
Language\n"
           "Usage: RUN sample.ulp\n"
           "Author: john@home.org",
       "de: Beispiel eines ULPs\n"
           "Implementiert ein Beispiel das zeigt, wie man die EAGLE User
Language benutzt\n"
           "Aufruf: RUN sample.ulp\n"
           "Author: john@home.org"
```

Keywords

The following *keywords* are reserved for special purposes and must not be used as normal identifier names:

break
case
char
continue
default
do
else
enum
for
if
int
numeric
real
return
string
switch
void
while

In addition, the names of builtins and object types are also reserved and must not be used as identifier names.

Identifiers

An *identifier* is a name that is used to introduce a user defined constant, variable or function.

Identifiers consist of a sequence of letters (`a b c`..., `A B C`...), digits (`1 2 3`...) and underscores (_). The first character of an identifier **must** be a letter or an underscore.

Identifiers are case-sensitive, which means that

```
int Number, number;
```

would define two **different** integer variables.

The maximum length of an identifier is 100 characters, and all of these are significant.

Constants

Constants are literal data items written into a User Language Program. According to the different data types, there are also different types of constants.

- Character constants
- Integer constants

- Real constants
- String constants

Character Constants

A *character constant* consists of a single character or an escape sequence enclosed in single quotes, like

```
'a'
'='
'\n'
```

The type of a character constant is `char`.

Integer Constants

Depending on the first (and possibly the second) character, an *integer constant* is assumed to be expressed in different base values:

first	second	constant interpreted as
`0`	`1-7`	octal (base 8)
`0`	`x,X`	hexadecimal (base 16)
`1-9`		decimal (base 10)

The type of an integer constant is `int`.

Examples

`16`	decimal
`020`	octal
`0x10`	hexadecimal

Real Constants

A *real constant* follows the general pattern

`[-]`*`int`*`.`*`frac`*`[e|E[±]`*`exp`*`]`

which stands for

- optional sign
- decimal integer
- decimal point
- decimal fraction
- `e` or `E` and a signed integer exponent

You can omit either the decimal integer or the decimal fraction (but not both). You can omit either the decimal point or the letter `e` or `E` and the signed integer exponent (but not both).

The type of an real constant is `real`.

Examples

Constant	Value
`23.45e6`	23.45 x 10^6
`.0`	0.0
`0.`	0.0
`1.`	1.0
`-1.23`	-1.23
`2e-5`	2.0 x 10^-5
`3E+10`	3.0 x 10^10
`.09E34`	0.09 x 10^34

String Constants

A *string constant* consists of a sequence of characters or escape sequences enclosed in double quotes, like

```
"Hello world\n"
```

The type of a string constant is `string`.

String constants can be of any length (provided there is enough free memory available).

String constants can be concatenated by simply writing them next to each other to form larger strings:

```
string s = "Hello" " world\n";
```

It is also possible to extend a string constant over more than one line by escaping the newline character with a backslash (\):

```
string s = "Hello \
world\n";
```

Escape Sequences

An *escape sequence* consists of a backslash (\), followed by one or more special characters:

Sequence	Value
`\a`	audible bell
`\b`	backspace
`\f`	form feed

\n	new line
\r	carriage return
\t	horizontal tab
\v	vertical tab
\\	backslash
\'	single quote
\"	double quote
\O	O = up to 3 octal digits
\xH	H = up to 2 hex digits

Any character following the initial backslash that is not mentioned in this list will be treated as that character (without the backslash).

Escape sequences can be used in character constants and string constants.

Examples

```
'\n'
"A tab\tinside a text\n"
"Ring the bell\a\n"
```

Punctuators

The *punctuators* used in a User Language Program are

[]	Brackets
()	Parentheses
{}	Braces
,	Comma
;	Semicolon
:	Colon
=	Equal sign

Other special characters are used as operators in a ULP.

Brackets

Brackets are used in array definitions

```
int ai[];
```

in array subscripts

```
n = ai[2];
```

and in string subscripts to access the individual characters of a string

```
string s = "Hello world";
```

```
char c = s[2];
```

Parentheses

Parentheses group expressions (possibly altering normal operator precedence), isolate conditional expressions, and indicate function calls and function parameters:

```
d = c * (a + b);
if (d == z) ++x;
func();
void func2(int n) { ... }
```

Braces

Braces indicate the start and end of a compound statement:

```
if (d == z) {
   ++x;
   func();
   }
```

and are also used to group the values of an array initializer:

```
int ai[] = { 1, 2, 3 };
```

Comma

The *comma* separates the elements of a function argument list or the parameters of a function call:

```
int func(int n, real r, string s) { ... }
int i = func(1, 3.14, "abc");
```

It also delimits the values of an array initializer:

```
int ai[] = { 1, 2, 3 };
```

and it separates the elements of a variable definition:

```
int i, j, k;
```

Semicolon

The *semicolon* terminates a statement, as in

```
i = a + b;
```

and it also delimits the init, test and increment expressions of a for statement:

```
for (int n = 0; n < 3; ++n) {
    func(n);
    }
```

Colon

The *colon* indicates the end of a label in a switch statement:

```
switch (c) {
  case 'a': printf("It was an 'a'\n"); break;
  case 'b': printf("It was a  'b'\n"); break;
  default:  printf("none of them\n");
  }
```

Equal Sign

The *equal sign* separates variable definitions from initialization lists:

```
int i = 10;
char c[] = { 'a', 'b', 'c' };
```

It is also used as an assignment operator.

Data Types

A User Language Program can define variables of different types, representing the different kinds of information available in the EAGLE data structures.

The four basic data types are

`char`	for single characters
`int`	for integral values
`real`	for floating point values
`string`	for textual information

Besides these basic data types there are also high level Object Types, which represent the data structures stored in the EAGLE data files.

The special data type `void` is used only as a return type of a function, indicating that this function does **not** return any value.

char

The data type `char` is used to store single characters, like the letters of the alphabet, or small unsigned numbers.

A variable of type `char` has a size of 8 bit (one byte), and can store any value in the range `0..255`.

See also Operators, Character Constants

int

The data type `int` is used to store signed integral values, like the coordinates of an object.

A variable of type `int` has a size of 32 bit (four byte), and can store any value in the range `-2147483648..2147483647`.

See also Integer Constants

real

The data type `real` is used to store signed floating point values, like the grid distance.

A variable of type `real` has a size of 64 bit (eight byte), and can store any value in the range `±2.2e-308..±1.7e+308` with a precision of 15 digits.

See also Real Constants

string

The data type `string` is used to store textual information, like the name of a part or net.

A variable of type `string` is not limited in it's size (provided there is enough memory available).

Variables of type `string` are defined without an explicit *size*. They grow automatically as necessary during program execution.

The elements of a `string` variable are of type `int` and can be accessed individually by using `[index]`. The first character of a `string` has the index `0`:

```
string s = "Layout";
printf("Third char is: %c\n", s[2]);
```

This would print the character `'y'`. Note that `s[2]` returns the **third** character of `s`!

A lossless conversion to `char` is possible for standard ASCII strings:

```
string s = "Layout";
char c = s[2];
```

See also Operators, Builtin Functions, String Constants

Implementation details

The data type `string` is actually implemented like native C-type zero terminated strings. Looking at the following variable definition

```
string s = "abcde";
```

`s[4]` is the character `'e'`, and `s[5]` is the character `'\0'`, or the integer value `0x00`. This fact may be used to determine the end of a string without using the `strlen()` function, as in

```
for (int i = 0; s[i]; ++i) {
    // do something with s[i]
    }
```

It is also perfectly ok to "cut off" part of a string by "punching" a zero character into it:

```
string s = "abcde";
s[3] = 0;
```

This will result in `s` having the value `"abc"`. Note that everything following the zero character will actually be gone, and it won't come back by restoring the original character. The same applies to any other operation that sets a character to 0, for instance --s[3].

Type Conversions

The result type of an arithmetic expression, such as `a + b`, where `a` and `b` are different arithmetic types, is equal to the "larger" of the two operand types.

Arithmetic types are `char`, `int` and `real` (in that order). So if, e.g. `a` is of type `int` and `b` is of type `real`, the result of the expression `a + b` would be `real`.

See also Typecast

Typecast

The result type of an arithmetic expression can be explicitly converted to a different arithmetic type by applying a *typecast* to it.

The general syntax of a typecast is

```
type(expression)
```

where `type` is one of `char`, `int` or `real`, and `expression` is any arithmetic expression.

When typecasting a `real` expression to `int`, the fractional part of the value is truncated!

See also Type Conversions

Object Types

The EAGLE data structures are stored in XML files:

- Library (*.lbr)
- Schematic (*.sch)
- Board (*.brd)

These data files contain a hierarchy of objects. In a User Language Program you can access these hierarchies through their respective builtin access statements:

```
library(L) { ... }
schematic(S) { ... }
board(B) { ... }
```

These access statements set up a context within which you can access all of the objects contained in the library, schematic or board.

The properties of these objects can be accessed through *members*.

There are two kinds of members:

- Data members
- Loop members

Data members immediately return the requested data from an object. For example, in

```
board(B) {
  printf("%s\n", B.name);
  }
```

the data member *name* of the board object *B* returns the board's name.
Data members can also return other objects, as in

```
board(B) {
  printf("%f\n", B.grid.size);
  }
```

where the board's *grid* data member returns a grid object, of which the *size* data member then returns the grid's size.

Loop members are used to access multiple objects of the same kind, which are contained in a higher level object:

```
board(B) {
  B.elements(E) {
    printf("%-8s %-8s\n", E.name, E.value);
    }
  }
```

This example uses the board's *elements()* loop member function to set up a loop through all of the board's elements. The block following the `B.elements(E)` statement is executed in turn for each element, and the current element can be referenced inside the block through the name `E`.

Loop members process objects in alpha-numerical order, provided they have a name.

A loop member function creates a variable of the type necessary to hold the requested objects. You are free to use any valid name for such a variable, so the above example might also be written as

```
board(MyBoard) {
  MyBoard.elements(TheCurrentElement) {
    printf("%-8s %-8s\n", TheCurrentElement.name, TheCurrentElement.value);
    }
  }
```

and would do the exact same thing. The scope of the variable created by a loop member function is limited to the statement (or block) immediately following the loop function call.

Object hierarchy of a Library:

```
LIBRARY
  GRID
  LAYER
  DEVICESET
    DEVICE
    GATE
  PACKAGE
    CONTACT
      PAD
      SMD
    CIRCLE
    HOLE
    RECTANGLE
    FRAME
    DIMENSION
    TEXT
    WIRE
    POLYGON
      WIRE
  SYMBOL
    PIN
    CIRCLE
    RECTANGLE
    FRAME
    DIMENSION
    TEXT
    WIRE
    POLYGON
      WIRE
```

Object hierarchy of a Schematic:

```
SCHEMATIC
  GRID
  LAYER
```

```
  LIBRARY
  ATTRIBUTE
  VARIANTDEF
  PART
    ATTRIBUTE
    VARIANT
  SHEET
    CIRCLE
    RECTANGLE
    FRAME
    DIMENSION
    TEXT
    WIRE
    POLYGON
      WIRE
    INSTANCE
      ATTRIBUTE
    MODULEINST
    BUS
      SEGMENT
        LABEL
          TEXT
          WIRE
        WIRE
    NET
      SEGMENT
        JUNCTION
        PINREF
        PORTREF
        TEXT
        WIRE
  MODULE
    PORT
    PART
    SHEET
      (same as above)
```

Change note from version 5 to version 6, compatibility

- Since version 6 the instance is in the hierarchy no longer below the part but below the sheet.
- The part is no longer below the sheet, but below the schematic.

For compatibility reasons the access by the according member functions is further supported, but the behaviour of the Object Functions reflects the new hierarchy.

Object hierarchy of a Board:

```
BOARD
  GRID
  LAYER
  LIBRARY
  ATTRIBUTE
  VARIANTDEF
  CIRCLE
  HOLE
```

28

```
RECTANGLE
FRAME
DIMENSION
TEXT
WIRE
POLYGON
  WIRE
ELEMENT
  ATTRIBUTE
  VARIANT
SIGNAL
  CONTACTREF
  POLYGON
    WIRE
  VIA
  WIRE
```

UL_ARC

Data members

`angle1`	real (start angle, `0.0`...`359.9`)
`angle2`	real (end angle, `0.0`...`719.9`)
`cap`	int (`CAP_...`)
`layer`	int
`radius`	int
`width`	int
`x1, y1`	int (starting point)
`x2, y2`	int (end point)
`xc, yc`	int (center point)

See also UL_WIRE

Constants

`CAP_FLAT`	flat arc ends
`CAP_ROUND`	round arc ends

Note

Start and end angles are defined mathematically positive (i.e. counterclockwise), with `angle1` < `angle2`. In order to assure this condition, the start and end point of an UL_ARC may be exchanged with respect to the UL_WIRE the arc has been derived from.

Example

```
board(B) {
  B.wires(W) {
    if (W.arc)
       printf("Arc: (%f %f), (%f %f), (%f %f)\n",
```

```
          u2mm(W.arc.x1), u2mm(W.arc.y1), u2mm(W.arc.x2), u2mm(W.arc.y2),
u2mm(W.arc.xc), u2mm(W.arc.yc));
    }
  }
```

UL_AREA

Data members

`x1, y1`	int (lower left corner)
`x2, y2`	int (upper right corner)

See also UL_BOARD, UL_DEVICE, UL_PACKAGE, UL_SHEET, UL_SYMBOL

A UL_AREA is an abstract object which gives information about the area covered by an object. For a UL_PACKAGE or UL_SYMBOL in a UL_ELEMENT or UL_INSTANCE context, respectively, the area is given in absolute drawing coordinates, including the offset of the element or instance and including the area of moved texts after SMASH.

Example

```
board(B) {
  printf("Area: (%f %f), (%f %f)\n",
         u2mm(B.area.x1), u2mm(B.area.y1), u2mm(B.area.x2), u2mm(B.area.y2));
  }
```

UL_ATTRIBUTE

Data members

`constant`	int (0=variable, i.e. allows overwriting, 1=constant - see note)
`defaultvalue`	string (see note)
`display`	int (`ATTRIBUTE_DISPLAY_FLAG_...`)
`name`	string
`text`	UL_TEXT (see note)
`value`	string

See also UL_DEVICE, UL_PART, UL_INSTANCE, UL_ELEMENT

Constants

`ATTRIBUTE_DISPLAY_FLAG_OFF`	nothing is displayed
`ATTRIBUTE_DISPLAY_FLAG_VALUE`	value is displayed
`ATTRIBUTE_DISPLAY_FLAG_NAME`	name is displayed

A UL_ATTRIBUTE can be used to access the *attributes* that have been defined in the library for a device, or assigned to a part in the schematic or board.

30

Note

`display` contains a bitwise or'ed value consisting of `ATTRIBUTE_DISPLAY_FLAG_...` and defines which parts of the attribute are actually drawn. This value is only valid if `display` is used in a UL_INSTANCE or UL_ELEMENT context.

In a UL_ELEMENT context `constant` only returns an actual value if f/b annotation is active, otherwise it returns 0.

The `defaultvalue` member returns the value as defined in the library (if different from the actual value, otherwise the same as `value`). In a UL_ELEMENT context `defaultvalue` only returns an actual value if f/b annotation is active, otherwise an empty string is returned.

The `text` member is only available in a UL_INSTANCE or UL_ELEMENT context and returns a UL_TEXT object that contains all the text parameters. The value of this text object is the string as it will be displayed according to the UL_ATTRIBUTE's 'display' parameter. If called from a different context, the data of the returned UL_TEXT object is undefined.

For global attributes only `name` and `value` are defined.

Example

```
schematic(SCH) {
  SCH.parts(P) {
    P.attributes(A) {
      printf("%s = %s\n", A.name, A.value);
      }
    }
  }
schematic(SCH) {
  SCH.attributes(A) { // global attributes
    printf("%s = %s\n", A.name, A.value);
    }
  }
```

UL_BOARD

Data members

`alwaysvectorfont`	int (`ALWAYS_VECTOR_FONT_..., see note`)
`area`	UL_AREA
`checked`	int (see note)
`description`	string
`grid`	UL_GRID
`headline`	string
`name`	string (see note)
`verticaltext`	int (`VERTICAL_TEXT_...`)

Loop members

`attributes()`	UL_ATTRIBUTE (see note)
`circles()`	UL_CIRCLE
`classes()`	UL_CLASS
`dimensions()`	UL_DIMENSION
`elements()`	UL_ELEMENT
`errors()`	UL_ERROR
`frames()`	UL_FRAME
`holes()`	UL_HOLE
`layers()`	UL_LAYER
`libraries()`	UL_LIBRARY
`polygons()`	UL_POLYGON
`rectangles()`	UL_RECTANGLE
`signals()`	UL_SIGNAL
`texts()`	UL_TEXT
`variantdefs()`	UL_VARIANTDEF
`wires()`	UL_WIRE

See also UL_LIBRARY, UL_SCHEMATIC

Constants

ALWAYS_VECTOR_FONT_GUI	alwaysvectorfont is set in the user interface dialog
ALWAYS_VECTOR_FONT_PERSISTENT	alwaysvectorfont is set persistent in this board
VERTICAL_TEXT_UP	reading direction for vertical texts: up
VERTICAL_TEXT_DOWN	reading direction for vertical texts: down

Note

The value returned by `alwaysvectorfont` can be used in boolean context or can be masked with the `ALWAYS_VECTOR_FONT_...` constants to determine the source of this setting, as in

```
if (B.alwaysvectorfont) {
   // alwaysvectorfont is set in general
   }
if (B.alwaysvectorfont & ALWAYS_VECTOR_FONT_GUI) {
   // alwaysvectorfont is set in the user interface
   }
```

The value returned by `checked` can be used in boolean context and is set only after a recent 'Design Rule Check' (DRC).

The `name` member returns the full file name, including the directory.

The `attributes()` loop member loops through the *global* attributes.

Example

```
board(B) {
  B.elements(E) printf("Element: %s\n", E.name);
  B.signals(S)  printf("Signal: %s\n", S.name);
  }
```

UL_BUS

Data members

`name`	string (BUS_NAME_LENGTH)

Loop members

`segments()`	UL_SEGMENT

See also UL_SHEET

Constants

BUS_NAME_LENGTH	max. length of a bus name (obsolete - as from version 4 bus names can have any length)

Example

```
schematic(SCH) {
  SCH.sheets(SH) {
    SH.busses(B) printf("Bus: %s\n", B.name);
    }
  }
```

UL_CIRCLE

Data members

`layer`	int
`radius`	int
`width`	int
`x, y`	int (center point)

See also UL_BOARD, UL_PACKAGE, UL_SHEET, UL_SYMBOL

Example

```
board(B) {
  B.circles(C) {
    printf("Circle: (%f %f), r=%d, w=%d\n",
           u2mm(C.x), u2mm(C.y), u2mm(C.radius), u2mm(C.width));
    }
  }
```

33

UL_CLASS

Data members

clearance[number]	int (see note)
drill	int
name	string (see note)
number	int
width	int

See also Design Rules, UL_NET, UL_SIGNAL, UL_SCHEMATIC, UL_BOARD

Note

The clearance member returns the clearance value between this net class and the net class with the given number. If the number (and the square brackets) is ommitted, the net class's own clearance value is returned. If a number is given, it must be between 0 and the number of this net class.

If the name member returns an empty string, the net class is not defined and therefore not in use by any signal or net.

Example

```
board(B) {
  B.signals(S) {
    printf("%-10s %d %s\n", S.name, S.class.number, S.class.name);
    }
  }
```

UL_CONTACT

Data members

name	string (CONTACT_NAME_LENGTH)
pad	UL_PAD
signal	string
smd	UL_SMD
x, y	int (center point, see note)

Loop members

polygons()	UL_POLYGON (of arbitrary pad shapes)
wires()	UL_WIRE (of arbitrary pad shapes)

See also UL_PACKAGE, UL_PAD, UL_SMD, UL_CONTACTREF, UL_PINREF

Constants

CONTACT_NAME_LENGT max. recommended length of a contact name (used in formatted

34

H output only)

Note

The `signal` data member returns the signal this contact is connected to (only available in a board context).

The coordinates (`x, y`) of the contact depend on the context in which it is called:

- if the contact is derived from a UL_LIBRARY context, the coordinates of the contact will be the same as defined in the package drawing
- in all other cases, they will have the actual values from the board

Example

```
library(L) {
  L.packages(PAC) {
    PAC.contacts(C) {
      printf("Contact: '%s', (%f %f)\n",
             C.name, u2mm(C.x), u2mm(C.y));
      }
    }
  }
```

UL_CONTACTREF

Data members

`contact`	UL_CONTACT
`element`	UL_ELEMENT
`route`	int (`CONTACT_ROUTE_...`)
`routetag`	string (see note)

See also UL_SIGNAL, UL_PINREF

Constants

`CONTACT_ROUTE_ALL`	must explicitly route to all contacts
`CONTACT_ROUTE_ANY`	may route to any contact

Note

If `route` has the value `CONTACT_ROUTE_ANY`, the `routetag` data member returns an additional tag which describes a group of `contactref`s belonging to the same pin.

Example

```
board(B) {
```

```
B.signals(S) {
  printf("Signal '%s'\n", S.name);
  S.contactrefs(C) {
    printf("\t%s, %s\n", C.element.name, C.contact.name);
    }
  }
}
```

UL_DEVICE

Data members

`activetechnology`	string (see note)
`area`	UL_AREA
`description`	string
`headline`	string
`library`	string
`name`	string (DEVICE_NAME_LENGTH)
`package`	UL_PACKAGE (see note)
`prefix`	string (DEVICE_PREFIX_LENGTH)
`technologies`	string (see note)
`value`	string ("On" or "Off")

Loop members

`attributes()`	UL_ATTRIBUTE (see note)
`gates()`	UL_GATE

See also UL_DEVICESET, UL_LIBRARY, UL_PART

Constants

DEVICE_NAME_LENGTH	max. recommended length of a device name (used in formatted output only)
DEVICE_PREFIX_LENGTH	max. recommended length of a device prefix (used in formatted output only)

All members of UL_DEVICE, except for `name` and `technologies`, return the same values as the respective members of the UL_DEVICESET in which the UL_DEVICE has been defined. The `name` member returns the name of the package variant this device has been created for using the PACKAGE command. When using the `description` text keep in mind that it may contain newline characters (`'\n'`).

Note

The value returned by the `activetechnology` member depends on the context in which it is called:

- if the device is derived from the deviceset that is currently edited in the library editor

36

window, the active technology, set by the TECHNOLOGY command, will be returned
- if the device is derived from a UL_PART, the actual technology used by the part will be returned
- otherwise an empty string will be returned.

The `package` data member returns the package that has been assigned to the device through a PACKAGE command. It can be used as a boolean function to check whether a package has been assigned to a device (see example below).

The value returned by the `technologies` member depends on the context in which it is called:

- if the device is derived from a UL_DEVICESET, `technologies` will return a string containing all of the device's technologies, separated by blanks
- if the device is derived from a UL_PART, only the actual technology used by the part will be returned.

The `attributes()` loop member takes an additional parameter that specifies for which technology the attributes shall be delivered (see the second example below).

Examples

```
library(L) {
  L.devicesets(S) {
    S.devices(D) {
      if (D.package)
         printf("Device: %s, Package: %s\n", D.name, D.package.name);
      D.gates(G) {
        printf("\t%s\n", G.name);
        }
      }
    }
  }

library(L) {
  L.devicesets(DS) {
    DS.devices(D) {
      string t[];
      int n = strsplit(t, D.technologies, ' ');
      for (int i = 0; i < n; i++) {
          D.attributes(A, t[i]) {
            printf("%s = %s\n", A.name, A.value);
            }
          }
      }
    }
  }
```

UL_DEVICESET

Data members

37

`activedevice`	UL_DEVICE (see note)
`area`	UL_AREA
`description`	string
`headline`	string (see note)
`library`	string
`name`	string (`DEVICE_NAME_LENGTH`)
`prefix`	string (`DEVICE_PREFIX_LENGTH`)
`value`	string ("On" or "Off")

Loop members

`devices()`	UL_DEVICE
`gates()`	UL_GATE

See also UL_DEVICE, UL_LIBRARY, UL_PART

Constants

`DEVICE_NAME_LENGTH`	max. recommended length of a device name (used in formatted output only)
`DEVICE_PREFIX_LENGTH`	max. recommended length of a device prefix (used in formatted output only)

Note

If a deviceset is currently edited in a library editor window, the `activedevice` member returns the active device, selected by a PACKAGE command. It can be used as a boolean function to check the availability of such an `activedevice` (see example below).

The `description` member returns the complete descriptive text as defined with the DESCRIPTION command, while the `headline` member returns only the first line of the description, without any HTML tags. When using the `description` text keep in mind that it may contain newline characters (`'\n'`).

Example

```
library(L) {
  L.devicesets(D) {
    printf("Device set: %s, Description: %s\n", D.name, D.description);
    D.gates(G) {
      printf("\t%s\n", G.name);
      }
    }
  }

if (deviceset)
   deviceset(DS) {
     if (DS.activedevice)
        printf("Active Device: %s\n", DS.activedevice.name);
     }
```

UL_DIMENSION

Data members

dtype	int (DIMENSION_...)
layer	int
extlength	int
extoffset	int
extwidth	int
precision	int
ratio	int
size	int
unit	int (GRID_UNIT_...)
visible	int (unit, 0=off, 1=on)
width	int
x1, y1	int (first reference point)
x2, y2	int (second reference point)
x3, y3	int (alignment reference point)

Loop members

texts()	UL_TEXT
wires()	UL_WIRE

See also UL_BOARD, UL_GRID, UL_PACKAGE, UL_SHEET, UL_SYMBOL

Constants

DIMENSION_PARALLEL	linear dimension with parallel measurement line
DIMENSION_HORIZONTAL	linear dimension with horizontal measurement line
DIMENSION_VERTICAL	linear dimension with vertical measurement line
DIMENSION_RADIUS	radial dimension
DIMENSION_DIAMETER	diameter dimension
DIMENSION_ANGLE	angle dimension
DIMENSION_LEADER	an arbitrary pointer

Note

The `texts()` and `wires()` loop members loop through all the texts and wires the dimension consists of.

Example

```
board(B) {
  B.dimensions(D) {
    printf("Dimension: (%f %f), (%f %f), (%f %f)\n",
```

39

```
            u2mm(D.x1), u2mm(D.y1), u2mm(D.x2), u2mm(D.y2), u2mm(D.x3),
u2mm(D.y3));
        }
    }
```

UL_ELEMENT

Data members

`angle`	real (0.0...359.9)
`attribute[]`	string (see note)
`column`	string (see note)
`locked`	int
`mirror`	int
`name`	string (ELEMENT_NAME_LENGTH)
`package`	UL_PACKAGE
`populate`	int (0=do not populate, 1=populate)
`row`	string (see note)
`smashed`	int (see note)
`spin`	int
`value`	string (ELEMENT_VALUE_LENGTH)
`x, y`	int (origin point)

Loop members

`attributes()`	UL_ATTRIBUTE
`texts()`	UL_TEXT (see note)

See also UL_BOARD, UL_CONTACTREF

Constants

ELEMENT_NAME_LENGTH	max. recommended length of an element name (used in formatted output only)
ELEMENT_VALUE_LENGTH	max. recommended length of an element value (used in formatted output only)

Note

The `attribute[]` member can be used to query a UL_ELEMENT for the value of a given attribute (see the second example below). The returned string is empty if there is no attribute by the given name, or if this attribute is explicitly empty.

The `texts()` member only loops through those texts of the element that have been detached using **SMASH**, and through the visible texts of any attributes assigned to this element. To process all texts of an element (e.g. when drawing it), you have to loop through the element's own `texts()` member as well as the `texts()` member of the element's package.

`angle` defines how many degrees the element is rotated counterclockwise around its origin.

The `column` and `row` members return the column and row location within the frame in the board drawing. If there is no frame in the drawing, or the element is placed outside the frame, a `'?'` (question mark) is returned.

The `smashed` member tells whether the element is smashed. This function can also be used to find out whether there is a detached text parameter by giving the name of that parameter in square brackets, as in `smashed["VALUE"]`. This is useful in case you want to select such a text with the MOVE command by doing `MOVE R5>VALUE`. Valid parameter names are "NAME" and "VALUE", as well as the names of any user defined attributes. They are treated case insensitive, and they may be preceded by a `'>'` character.

Examples

```
board(B) {
  B.elements(E) {
    printf("Element: %s, (%f %f), Package=%s\n",
           E.name, u2mm(E.x), u2mm(E.y), E.package.name);
    }
  }

board(B) {
  B.elements(E) {
    if (E.attribute["REMARK"])
       printf("%s: %s\n", E.name, E.attribute["REMARK"]);
    }
  }
```

UL_ERROR

Data members

`area`	UL_AREA
`area2`	UL_AREA (see note)
`code`	int (identification number)
`description`	string
`layer`	int
`modulename`	string
`s1`	string (see note)
`s2`	string
`s3`	string
`s4`	string
`s5`	string
`s6`	string
`sheet`	int (sheet number)
`signature`	string (signature string)
`state`	int (ERROR_STATE_...)
`type`	int (ERROR_TYPE_...)

41

x, y	int (center point)

Loop members

contours()	UL_WIRE (see note)

See also UL_BOARD, UL_SCHEMATIC

Constants

ERROR_STATE_ACTIVE	error has not yet been approved or processed
ERROR_STATE_APPROVED	error has been approved
ERROR_STATE_PROCESSED	error has been processed
ERROR_TYPE_NONE	no error
ERROR_TYPE_WARNING	warning
ERROR_TYPE_ERROR	error
ERROR_TYPE_CONSISTENCY	consistency error

Note

A UL_ERROR is an abstract object which gives informations about ERC/DRC errors.

The members `layer` and `contours()` are only available in UL_BOARD context and the members `area2`, `modulename`, `s1..s6` and `sheet` are only available in UL_SCHEMATIC context.

The member `area2` is a second area, only available on some ERC errors and refers to the corresponding area in the board. The members `s1..s6` are string values, which contain for ERC errors specific informations like names.

The `contours()` loop member loops through the contour wires of the DRC error polygon.

Example

```
string s1;
string ErrLst[];
int ErrCnt = 0;
string ErrLstHeader;
if (board) board(B) {
   ErrLstHeader = "Code\tState\tDescription\tLayer\tSignature";
   if (B.checked) {
      B.errors(ER) {
         if (ER.state == ERROR_STATE_ACTIVE) {
            sprintf(s1, "%d\t%d\t%s\t%d\t%s", ER.code, ER.state, ER.description,
ER.layer, ER.signature);
            ErrLst[ErrCnt++] = s1;
         }
      }
   }
}
if (schematic) schematic(SCH) {
```

```
   ErrLstHeader =
"Code\tState\tDescription\tSheet\tModule\ts1\ts2\ts3\ts4\ts5\ts6";
   if (SCH.checked) {
      SCH.errors(ER) {
         if (ER.state == ERROR_STATE_ACTIVE) {
            sprintf(s1, "%d\t%d\t%s\t%d\t%s\t%s\t%s\t%s\t%s\t%s\t%s", ER.code,
ER.state, ER.description, ER.sheet, ER.modulename, ER.s1, ER.s2, ER.s3, ER.s4,
ER.s5, ER.s6);
            ErrLst[ErrCnt++] = s1;
         }
      }
   }
}
dlgDialog("Errors") {
   int sel = -1;
   dlgListView(ErrLstHeader, ErrLst, sel);
   dlgPushButton("+OK") dlgAccept();
};
```

UL_FRAME

Data members

`columns`	int (-127...127)
`rows`	int (-26...26)
`border`	int (FRAME_BORDER_...)
`layer`	int
`x1, y1`	int (lower left corner)
`x2, y2`	int (upper right corner)

Loop members

`texts()`	UL_TEXT
`wires()`	UL_WIRE

See also UL_BOARD, UL_PACKAGE, UL_SHEET, UL_SYMBOL

Constants

FRAME_BORDER_BOTTOM	bottom border is drawn
FRAME_BORDER_RIGHT	right border is drawn
FRAME_BORDER_TOP	top border is drawn
FRAME_BORDER_LEFT	left border is drawn

Note

`border` contains a bitwise or'ed value consisting of `FRAME_BORDER_...` and defines which of the four borders are actually drawn.

The `texts()` and `wires()` loop members loop through all the texts and wires the frame consists

43

of.

Example

```
board(B) {
  B.frames(F) {
    printf("Frame: (%f %f), (%f %f)\n",
           u2mm(F.x1), u2mm(F.y1), u2mm(F.x2), u2mm(F.y2));
    }
  }
```

UL_GATE

Data members

addlevel	int (GATE_ADDLEVEL_...)
name	string (GATE_NAME_LENGTH)
swaplevel	int
symbol	UL_SYMBOL
x, y	int (origin point, see note)

See also UL_DEVICE

Constants

GATE_ADDLEVEL_MUST	must
GATE_ADDLEVEL_CAN	can
GATE_ADDLEVEL_NEXT	next
GATE_ADDLEVEL_REQUEST	request
GATE_ADDLEVEL_ALWAYS	always
GATE_NAME_LENGTH	max. recommended length of a gate name (used in formatted output only)

Note

The coordinates of the origin point (x, y) are always those of the gate's position within the device, even if the UL_GATE has been derived from a UL_INSTANCE.

Example

```
library(L) {
  L.devices(D) {
    printf("Device: %s, Package: %s\n", D.name, D.package.name);
    D.gates(G) {
      printf("\t%s, swaplevel=%d, symbol=%s\n",
             G.name, G.swaplevel, G.symbol.name);
      }
    }
  }
```

UL_GRID

Data members

`distance`	real
`dots`	int (0=lines, 1=dots)
`multiple`	int
`on`	int (0=off, 1=on)
`unit`	int (`GRID_UNIT_...`)
`unitdist`	int (`GRID_UNIT_...`)

See also UL_BOARD, UL_LIBRARY, UL_SCHEMATIC, Unit Conversions

Constants

`GRID_UNIT_MIC`	microns
`GRID_UNIT_MM`	millimeter
`GRID_UNIT_MIL`	mil
`GRID_UNIT_INCH`	inch

Note

`unitdist` returns the grid unit that was set to define the actual grid size (returned by `distance`), while `unit` returns the grid unit that is used to display values or interpret user input.

Example

```
board(B) {
  printf("Gridsize=%f\n", B.grid.distance);
  }
```

UL_HOLE

Data members

`diameter[layer]`	int (see note)
`drill`	int
`drillsymbol`	int
`x, y`	int (center point)

See also UL_BOARD, UL_PACKAGE

Note

`diameter[]` is only defined vor layers `LAYER_TSTOP` and `LAYER_BSTOP` and returns the diameter of the solder stop mask in the given layer.

`drillsymbol` returns the number of the drill symbol that has been assigned to this drill diameter

45

(see the manual for a list of defined drill symbols). A value of 0 means that no symbol has been assigned to this drill diameter.

Example

```
board(B) {
  B.holes(H) {
    printf("Hole: (%f %f), drill=%f\n",
           u2mm(H.x), u2mm(H.y), u2mm(H.drill));
    }
  }
```

UL_INSTANCE

Data members

angle	real (0, 90, 180 and 270)
column	string (see note)
gate	UL_GATE
mirror	int
name	string (INSTANCE_NAME_LENGTH)
part	UL_PART
row	string (see note)
sheet	int (0=unused, >0=sheet number)
smashed	int (see note)
value	string (PART_VALUE_LENGTH)
x, y	int (origin point)

Loop members

attributes()	UL_ATTRIBUTE (see note)
texts()	UL_TEXT (see note)
xrefs()	UL_GATE (see note)

See also UL_PINREF

Constants

INSTANCE_NAME_LENGTH	max. recommended length of an instance name (used in formatted output only)
PART_VALUE_LENGTH	max. recommended length of a part value (instances do not have a value of their own!)

Note

The attributes() member only loops through those attributes that have been explicitly assigned to this instance (including *smashed* attributes).

The texts() member only loops through those texts of the instance that have been detached using **SMASH**, and through the visible texts of any attributes assigned to this instance. To process all texts of an instance, you have to loop through the instance's own `texts()` member as well as the `texts()` member of the instance's gate's symbol. If attributes have been assigned to an instance, `texts()` delivers their texts in the form as they are currently visible.

The `column` and `row` members return the column and row location within the frame on the sheet on which this instance is invoked. If there is no frame on that sheet, or the instance is placed outside the frame, a `'?'` (question mark) is returned. These members can only be used in a sheet context.

The `smashed` member tells whether the instance is smashed. This function can also be used to find out whether there is a detached text parameter by giving the name of that parameter in square brackets, as in `smashed["VALUE"]`. This is useful in case you want to select such a text with the MOVE command by doing `MOVE R5>VALUE`. Valid parameter names are "NAME", "VALUE", "PART" and "GATE", as well as the names of any user defined attributes. They are treated case insensitive, and they may be preceded by a `'>'` character.

The `xrefs()` member loops through the contact cross-reference gates of this instance. These are only of importance if the ULP is going to create a drawing of some sort (for instance a DXF file).

Example

```
schematic(S) {
  S.parts(P) {
    printf("Part: %s\n", P.name);
    P.instances(I) {
      if (I.sheet != 0)
         printf("\t%s used on sheet %d\n", I.name, I.sheet);
      }
    }
  }
```

UL_JUNCTION

Data members

`diameter`	int
`x, y`	int (center point)

See also UL_SEGMENT

Example

```
schematic(SCH) {
  SCH.sheets(SH) {
    SH.nets(N) {
      N.segments(SEG) {
        SEG.junctions(J) {
          printf("Junction: (%f %f)\n", u2mm(J.x), u2mm(J.y));
```

47

```
          }
        }
      }
    }
  }
```

UL_LABEL

Data members

`angle`	real (`0.0`...`359.9`)
`layer`	int
`mirror`	int
`spin`	int
`text`	UL_TEXT
`x, y`	int (origin point)
`xref`	int (0=plain, 1=cross-reference)

Loop members

`wires()`	UL_WIRE (see note)

See also UL_SEGMENT

Note

If `xref` returns a non-zero value, the `wires()` loop member loops through the wires that form the flag of a cross-reference label. Otherwise it is an empty loop.

The `angle`, `layer`, `mirror` and `spin` members always return the same values as those of the UL_TEXT object returned by the `text` member. The `x` and `y` members of the text return slightly offset values for cross-reference labels (non-zero `xref`), otherwise they also return the same values as the UL_LABEL.

`xref` is only meaningful for net labels. For bus labels it always returns 0.

Example

```
sheet(SH) {
  SH.nets(N) {
    N.segments(S) {
      S.labels(L) {
        printf("Label: (%f %f) '%s'", u2mm(L.x), u2mm(L.y), L.text.value);
        }
      }
    }
  }
```

UL_LAYER

Data members

`color`	int
`fill`	int
`name`	string (`LAYER_NAME_LENGTH`)
`number`	int
`used`	int (0=unused, 1=used)
`visible`	int (0=off, 1=on)

See also UL_BOARD, UL_LIBRARY, UL_SCHEMATIC

Constants

`LAYER_NAME_LENGTH`	max. recommended length of a layer name (used in formatted output only)
`LAYER_TOP`	layer numbers
`LAYER_BOTTOM`	
`LAYER_PADS`	
`LAYER_VIAS`	
`LAYER_UNROUTED`	
`LAYER_DIMENSION`	
`LAYER_TPLACE`	
`LAYER_BPLACE`	
`LAYER_TORIGINS`	
`LAYER_BORIGINS`	
`LAYER_TNAMES`	
`LAYER_BNAMES`	
`LAYER_TVALUES`	
`LAYER_BVALUES`	
`LAYER_TSTOP`	
`LAYER_BSTOP`	
`LAYER_TCREAM`	
`LAYER_BCREAM`	
`LAYER_TFINISH`	
`LAYER_BFINISH`	
`LAYER_TGLUE`	
`LAYER_BGLUE`	
`LAYER_TTEST`	
`LAYER_BTEST`	
`LAYER_TKEEPOUT`	
`LAYER_BKEEPOUT`	
`LAYER_TRESTRICT`	
`LAYER_BRESTRICT`	
`LAYER_VRESTRICT`	
`LAYER_DRILLS`	

LAYER_HOLES	
LAYER_MILLING	
LAYER_MEASURES	
LAYER_DOCUMENT	
LAYER_REFERENCE	
LAYER_TDOCU	
LAYER_BDOCU	
LAYER_NETS	
LAYER_BUSSES	
LAYER_PINS	
LAYER_SYMBOLS	
LAYER_NAMES	
LAYER_VALUES	
LAYER_INFO	
LAYER_GUIDE	
LAYER_USER	lowest number for user defined layers (100)

Example

```
board(B) {
  B.layers(L) printf("Layer %3d %s\n", L.number, L.name);
  }
```

UL_LIBRARY

Data members

description	string (see note)
grid	UL_GRID
headline	string
name	string (LIBRARY_NAME_LENGTH, see note)

Loop members

devices()	UL_DEVICE
devicesets()	UL_DEVICESET
layers()	UL_LAYER
packages()	UL_PACKAGE
symbols()	UL_SYMBOL

See also UL_BOARD, UL_SCHEMATIC

Constants

LIBRARY_NAME_LENGTH	max. recommended length of a library name (used in formatted output only)

The devices() member loops through all the package variants and technologies of all

UL_DEVICESETs in the library, thus resulting in all the actual device variations available. The `devicesets()` member only loops through the UL_DEVICESETs, which in turn can be queried for their UL_DEVICE members.

Note

The `description` member returns the complete descriptive text as defined with the DESCRIPTION command, while the `headline` member returns only the first line of the description, without any HTML tags. When using the `description` text keep in mind that it may contain newline characters (`'\n'`). The `description` and `headline` information is only available within a library drawing, not if the library is derived form a UL_BOARD or UL_SCHEMATIC context.

If the library is derived form a UL_BOARD or UL_SCHEMATIC context, `name` returns the pure library name (without path or extension). Otherwise it returns the full library file name.

Example

```
library(L) {
  L.devices(D)      printf("Dev: %s\n", D.name);
  L.devicesets(D)   printf("Dev: %s\n", D.name);
  L.packages(P)     printf("Pac: %s\n", P.name);
  L.symbols(S)      printf("Sym: %s\n", S.name);
  }
schematic(S) {
  S.libraries(L) printf("Library: %s\n", L.name);
  }
```

UL_MODULE

Data members

`dx, dy`	int (size)
`description`	string
`headline`	string
`name`	string
`prefix`	string

Loop members

`parts()`	UL_PART
`ports()`	UL_PORT
`sheets()`	UL_SHEET
`variantdefs()`	UL_VARIANTDEF

See also UL_PORT, UL_SCHEMATIC

51

Example

```
schematic(SCH) {
  SCH.modules(M) {
    M.parts(P) printf("Part: %s\n", P.name);
    }
  }
```

UL_MODULEINST

Data members

angle	real (0, 90, 180 and 270)
column	string (see note)
mirror	int
module	UL_MODULE
modulevariant	string (selected variantdef of module)
name	string (INSTANCE_NAME_LENGTH)
offset	int
row	string (see note)
sheet	int (sheet number)
smashed	int (see note)
x, y	int (origin point)

Loop members

texts()	UL_TEXT (see note)
wires()	UL_WIRE

See also UL_PORTREF, UL_VARIANTDEF

Constants

INSTANCE_NAME_LENGTH	max. recommended length of an instance name (used in formatted output only)

Note

The `texts()` member loops through all texts of the module instance, no matter if `smashed` or not.

The `column` and `row` members return the column and row location within the frame on the sheet on which this instance is invoked. If there is no frame on that sheet, or the instance is placed outside the frame, a `'?'` (question mark) is returned. These members can only be used in a sheet context.

The `smashed` member tells whether the instance is smashed. This function can also be used to find out whether there is a detached text parameter by giving the name of that parameter in square brackets, as in `smashed["NAME"]`. This is useful in case you want to select such a text with the MOVE command by doing `MOVE MOD1>NAME`.

Example

```
schematic(SCH) {
  SCH.sheets(SH) {
    SH.moduleinsts(MI) {
      printf("Module instance %s is located on sheet %d\n", MI.name, MI.sheet);
      }
    }
  }
```

UL_NET

Data members

class	UL_CLASS
column	string (see note)
name	string (NET_NAME_LENGTH)
row	string (see note)

Loop members

portrefs()	UL_PORTREF
pinrefs()	UL_PINREF (see note)
segments()	UL_SEGMENT (see note)

See also UL_SHEET, UL_SCHEMATIC

Constants

NET_NAME_LENGTH	max. recommended length of a net name (used in formatted output only)

Note

The `pinrefs()` loop member can only be used if the net is in a schematic context.

The `segments()` loop member can only be used if the net is in a sheet context.

The `column` and `row` members return the column and row locations within the frame on the sheet on which this net is drawn. Since a net can extend over a certain area, each of these functions returns two values, separated by a blank. In case of `column` these are the left- and rightmost columns touched by the net, and in case of `row` it's the top- and bottommost row.

When determining the column and row of a net on a sheet, first the column and then the row within that column is taken into account. Here XREF labels take precedence over normal labels, which again take precedence over net wires.

If there is no frame on that sheet, `"? ?"` (two question marks) is returned. If any part of the net is placed outside the frame, either of the values may be `'?'` (question mark). These members can only be used in a sheet context.

Example

```
schematic(S) {
  S.nets(N) {
    printf("Net: %s\n", N.name);
    // N.segments(SEG) will NOT work here!
    }
  }
schematic(S) {
  S.sheets(SH) {
    SH.nets(N) {
      printf("Net: %s\n", N.name);
      N.segments(SEG) {
        SEG.wires(W) {
          printf("\tWire: (%f %f) (%f %f)\n",
                 u2mm(W.x1), u2mm(W.y1), u2mm(W.x2), u2mm(W.y2));
          }
        }
      }
    }
  }
```

UL_PACKAGE

Data members

area	UL_AREA
description	string
headline	string
library	string
name	string (PACKAGE_NAME_LENGTH)

Loop members

circles()	UL_CIRCLE
contacts()	UL_CONTACT
dimensions()	UL_DIMENSION
frames()	UL_FRAME
holes()	UL_HOLE
polygons()	UL_POLYGON (see note)
rectangles()	UL_RECTANGLE
texts()	UL_TEXT (see note)
wires()	UL_WIRE (see note)

See also UL_DEVICE, UL_ELEMENT, UL_LIBRARY

Constants

PACKAGE_NAME_LENGTH	max. recommended length of a package name (used in formatted output only)

54

Note

The `description` member returns the complete descriptive text as defined with the DESCRIPTION command, while the `headline` member returns only the first line of the description, without any HTML tags. When using the `description` text keep in mind that it may contain newline characters (`'\n'`).

If the UL_PACKAGE is derived from a UL_ELEMENT, the `texts()` member only loops through the non-detached texts of that element.

If the UL_PACKAGE is derived from a UL_ELEMENT, polygons and wires belonging to contacts with arbitrary pad shapes are available through the loop members `polygons()` and `wires()` of this contact.

Example

```
library(L) {
  L.packages(PAC) {
    printf("Package: %s\n", PAC.name);
    PAC.contacts(C) {
      if (C.pad)
         printf("\tPad: %s, (%f %f)\n",
                C.name, u2mm(C.pad.x), u2mm(C.pad.y));
      else if (C.smd)
         printf("\tSmd: %s, (%f %f)\n",
                C.name, u2mm(C.smd.x), u2mm(C.smd.y));
      }
    }
  }
board(B) {
  B.elements(E) {
    printf("Element: %s, Package: %s\n", E.name, E.package.name);
    }
  }
```

UL_PAD

Data members

`angle`	real (`0.0...359.9`)
`diameter[layer]`	int
`drill`	int
`drillsymbol`	int
`elongation`	int
`flags`	int (`PAD_FLAG_...`)
`name`	string (`PAD_NAME_LENGTH`)
`shape[layer]`	int (`PAD_SHAPE_...`)
`signal`	string
`x, y`	int (center point, see note)

See also UL_PACKAGE, UL_CONTACT, UL_SMD

Constants

PAD_FLAG_STOP	generate stop mask
PAD_FLAG_THERMALS	generate thermals
PAD_FLAG_FIRST	use special "first pad" shape
PAD_SHAPE_SQUARE	square
PAD_SHAPE_ROUND	round
PAD_SHAPE_OCTAGON	octagon
PAD_SHAPE_LONG	long
PAD_SHAPE_OFFSET	offset
PAD_NAME_LENGTH	max. recommended length of a pad name (same as CONTACT_NAME_LENGTH)

Note

The parameters of the pad depend on the context in which it is accessed:

- if the pad is derived from a UL_LIBRARY context, the coordinates (`x, y`) and `angle` will be the same as defined in the package drawing
- in all other cases, they will have the actual values from the board

The diameter and shape of the pad depend on the layer for which they shall be retrieved, because they may be different in each layer depending on the Design Rules. If one of the layers LAYER_TOP...LAYER_BOTTOM, LAYER_TSTOP or LAYER_BSTOP is given as the index to the diameter or shape data member, the resulting value will be calculated according to the Design Rules. If LAYER_PADS is given, the raw value as defined in the library will be returned.

`drillsymbol` returns the number of the drill symbol that has been assigned to this drill diameter (see the manual for a list of defined drill symbols). A value of `0` means that no symbol has been assigned to this drill diameter.

`angle` defines how many degrees the pad is rotated counterclockwise around its center.

`elongation` is only valid for shapes PAD_SHAPE_LONG and PAD_SHAPE_OFFSET and defines how many percent the long side of such a pad is longer than its small side. This member returns 0 for any other pad shapes.

The value returned by `flags` must be masked with the `PAD_FLAG_...` constants to determine the individual flag settings, as in

```
if (pad.flags & PAD_FLAG_STOP) {
   ...
   }
```

56

Note that if your ULP just wants to draw the objects, you don't need to check these flags explicitly. The `diameter[]` and `shape[]` members will return the proper data; for instance, if `PAD_FLAG_STOP` is set, `diameter[LAYER_TSTOP]` will return `0`, which should result in nothing being drawn in that layer. The `flags` member is mainly for ULPs that want to create script files that create library objects.

Example

```
library(L) {
  L.packages(PAC) {
    PAC.contacts(C) {
      if (C.pad)
         printf("Pad: '%s', (%f %f), d=%f\n",
                C.name, u2mm(C.pad.x), u2mm(C.pad.y),
u2mm(C.pad.diameter[LAYER_BOTTOM]));
      }
    }
  }
```

UL_PART

Data members

`attribute[]`	string (see note)
`device`	UL_DEVICE
`deviceset`	UL_DEVICESET
`module`	UL_MODULE (see note)
`modulepart`	UL_PART (see note)
`modulepath`	string (see note)
`name`	string (`PART_NAME_LENGTH`)
`populate`	int (0=do not populate, 1=populate)
`value`	string (`PART_VALUE_LENGTH`)

Loop members

`attributes()`	UL_ATTRIBUTE (see note)
`instances()`	UL_INSTANCE (see note)
`variants()`	UL_VARIANT

See also UL_SCHEMATIC, UL_SHEET

Constants

`PART_NAME_LENGTH`	max. recommended length of a part name (used in formatted output only)
`PART_VALUE_LENGTH`	max. recommended length of a part value (used in formatted output only)

Note

The `attribute[]` member can be used to query a UL_PART for the value of a given attribute (see the second example below). The returned string is empty if there is no attribute by the given name, or if this attribute is explicitly empty.

When looping through the `attributes()` of a UL_PART, only the `name`, `value`, `defaultvalue` and `constant` members of the resulting UL_ATTRIBUTE objects are valid.

If the part is in a sheet context, the `instances()` loop member loops only through those instances that are actually used on that sheet. If the part is in a schematic or module context, all instances are looped through.

If the part is a *virtual part* (virtual parts can be retrieved with `UL_SCHEMATIC.allparts()`, see UL_SCHEMATIC) the `instances()` loop is empty.

If the part is from a module or is a virtual part, `module` refers to this. If not (part in main schematic), `module` is null.

If the part is virtual, `modulepart` is the (real) part from the source module `module`. If it's a part in main schematic or if it's a module part itself `modulepart` is null.

If the part is virtual, `modulepath` is a string with the sequence of names of the module instances that point to the module containing the part being used. These names are separated by ':'. In other cases this string is empty.
For example, a virtual part with name 'MI1:R1' has `modulepath` 'MI1'.
'R101' coming from a module instance 'MX' with offset notation, delivers `modulepath` 'MX'.
'MAIN:SUB1:SUBSUB1:C5' has `modulepath` 'MAIN:SUB1:SUBSUB1'.

Examples

```
schematic(S) {
  S.parts(P) printf("Part: %s\n", P.name);
}

schematic(S) {
  S.allparts(P) {
    if (P.attribute["REMARK"])
       printf("%s: %s\n", P.name, P.attribute["REMARK"]);
    if (P.modulepart) {
       P.modulepart.instances(I)
         printf("%s is a virtual part from %s in module %s with part instance on
sheet %d\n",
                P.name, P.modulepart.name, P.module.name, I.sheet);
    }
    else {
       P.instances(I)
         printf("%s is a part on main schematic with instance on sheet %d\n",
                P.name, I.sheet);
```

58

```
      }
    }
  }

schematic(S) {
  S.allparts(P) {
    if (P.modulepart) {
       string miNames[];
       int nr = strsplit(miNames, P.modulepath, ':');
       if (nr == 1)
          printf("%s is a virtual part created by module instance %s in main
schematic.\n",
                 P.name, miNames[0]);
       else {
          printf("%s is a virtual part in a multiple hierarchy created by this
path of module instances:\n", P.name);
          for (int i = 0; i < nr; ++i)
              printf("%s\n", miNames[i]);
       }
    }
  }
}
```

UL_PIN

Data members

`angle`	real (`0`, `90`, `180` and `270`)
`contact`	UL_CONTACT (deprecated, see note)
`direction`	int (`PIN_DIRECTION_...`)
`function`	int (`PIN_FUNCTION_FLAG_...`)
`length`	int (`PIN_LENGTH_...`)
`name`	string (`PIN_NAME_LENGTH`)
`net`	string (see note)
`route`	int (`CONTACT_ROUTE_...`)
`swaplevel`	int
`visible`	int (`PIN_VISIBLE_FLAG_...`)
`x, y`	int (connection point)

Loop members

`circles()`	UL_CIRCLE
`contacts()`	UL_CONTACT (see note)
`texts()`	UL_TEXT
`wires()`	UL_WIRE

See also UL_SYMBOL, UL_PINREF, UL_CONTACTREF

Constants

`PIN_DIRECTION_NC`	not connected

PIN_DIRECTION_IN	input
PIN_DIRECTION_OUT	output (totem-pole)
PIN_DIRECTION_IO	in/output (bidirectional)
PIN_DIRECTION_OC	open collector
PIN_DIRECTION_PWR	power input pin
PIN_DIRECTION_PAS	passive
PIN_DIRECTION_HIZ	high impedance output
PIN_DIRECTION_SUP	supply pin
PIN_FUNCTION_FLAG_NONE	no symbol
PIN_FUNCTION_FLAG_DOT	inverter symbol
PIN_FUNCTION_FLAG_CLK	clock symbol
PIN_LENGTH_POINT	no wire
PIN_LENGTH_SHORT	0.1 inch wire
PIN_LENGTH_MIDDLE	0.2 inch wire
PIN_LENGTH_LONG	0.3 inch wire
PIN_NAME_LENGTH	max. recommended length of a pin name (used in formatted output only)
PIN_VISIBLE_FLAG_OFF	no name drawn
PIN_VISIBLE_FLAG_PAD	pad name drawn
PIN_VISIBLE_FLAG_PIN	pin name drawn
CONTACT_ROUTE_ALL	must explicitly route to all contacts
CONTACT_ROUTE_ANY	may route to any contact

Note

The `contacts()` loop member loops through the contacts that have been assigned to the pin through a CONNECT command. This is the case in a UL_DEVICE context or coming via UL_PINREF, but not via UL_LIBRARY.symbols(). If this is not the case the list is empty.

The `contact` data member returns the contact that has been assigned to the pin through a CONNECT command. ***This member is deprecated! It will work for backwards compatibility and as long as only one pad has been connected to the pin, but will cause a runtime error when used with a pin that is connected to more than one pad.***

The `route` member also only makes sense if there's a relation to contacts the pin is connected to. Otherwise the value is set to 0.

The coordinates (and layer, in case of an SMD) of the contact returned by the `contact` data member depend on the context in which it is called:

60

- if the pin is derived from a UL_PART that is used on a sheet, and if there is a corresponding element on the board, the resulting contact will have the coordinates as used on the board
- in all other cases, the coordinates of the contact will be the same as defined in the package drawing

The `name` data member always returns the name of the pin as it was defined in the library, with any `'@'` character for pins with the same name left intact (see the PIN command for details).
The `texts` loop member, on the other hand, returns the pin name (if it is visible) in the same way as it is displayed in the current drawing type.

The `net` data member returns the name of the net to which this pin is connected to (only available in a UL_SCHEMATIC context).

Example

```
library(L) {
  L.symbols(S) {
    printf("Symbol: %s\n", S.name);
    S.pins(P) {
      printf("\tPin: %s, (%f %f)", P.name, u2mm(P.x), u2mm(P.y));
      if (P.direction == PIN_DIRECTION_IN)
         printf(" input");
      if ((P.function & PIN_FUNCTION_FLAG_DOT) != 0)
         printf(" inverted");
      printf("\n");
      }
    }
  }
```

UL_PINREF

Data members

`instance`	UL_INSTANCE
`part`	UL_PART
`pin`	UL_PIN

See also UL_SEGMENT, UL_CONTACTREF

Example

```
schematic(SCH) {
  SCH.sheets(SH) {
    printf("Sheet: %d\n", SH.number);
    SH.nets(N) {
      printf("\tNet: %s\n", N.name);
      N.segments(SEG) {
        SEG.pinrefs(P) {
          printf("connected to: %s, %s, %s\n",
                 P.part.name, P.instance.name, P.pin.name);
          }
```

```
         }
      }
   }
}
```

UL_POLYGON

Data members

isolate	int
layer	int
orphans	int (0=off, 1=on)
pour	int (POLYGON_POUR_...)
rank	int
spacing	int
thermals	int (0=off, 1=on)
width	int

Loop members

contours()	UL_WIRE (see note)
fillings()	UL_WIRE
wires()	UL_WIRE

See also UL_BOARD, UL_PACKAGE, UL_SHEET, UL_SIGNAL, UL_SYMBOL

Constants

POLYGON_POUR_SOLID	solid
POLYGON_POUR_HATCH	hatch
POLYGON_POUR_CUTOUT	cutout

Note

The `contours()` and `fillings()` loop members loop through the wires that are used to draw the calculated polygon if it is part of a signal and the polygon has been calculated by the RATSNEST command. The `wires()` loop member always loops through the polygon wires as they were drawn by the user. For an uncalculated signal polygon `contours()` does the same as `wires()`, and `fillings()` does nothing.

If the `contours()` loop member is called without a second parameter, it loops through all of the contour wires, regardless whether they belong to a positive or a negative polygon. If you are interested in getting the positive and negative contour wires separately, you can call `contours()` with an additional integer parameter (see the second example below). The sign of that parameter determines whether a positive or a negative polygon will be handled, and the value indicates the index of that polygon. If there is no polygon with the given index, the statement will not be executed. Another advantage of this method is that you don't need to determine the beginning and end of a particular polygon yourself (by comparing coordinates). For any given index, the statement will be executed for all the wires of that polygon. With the second parameter `0` the behavior is the same as without a second parameter.

Polygon width

When using the `fillings()` loop member to get the fill wires of a solid polygon, make sure the *width* of the polygon is not zero (actually it should be quite a bit larger than zero, for example at least the hardware resolution of the output device you are going to draw on). **Filling a polygon with zero width may result in enormous amounts of data, since it will be calculated with the smallest editor resolution of 1/320000mm!**

Partial polygons

A calculated signal polygon may consist of several distinct parts (called *positive* polygons), each of which can contain extrusions (*negative* polygons) resulting from other objects being subtracted from the polygon. Negative polygons can again contain other positive polygons and so on.

The wires looped through by `contours()` always start with a positive polygon. To find out where one partial polygon ends and the next one begins, simply store the (x1,y1) coordinates of the first wire and check them against (x2,y2) of every following wire. As soon as these are equal, the last wire of a partial polygon has been found. It is also guaranteed that the second point (x2,y2) of one wire is identical to the first point (x1,y1) of the next wire in that partial polygon.

To find out where the "inside" and the "outside" of the polygon lays, take any contour wire and imagine looking from its point (x1,y1) to (x2,y2). The "inside" of the polygon is always on the right side of the wire. Note that if you simply want to draw the polygon you won't need all these details.

Example

```
board(B) {
  B.signals(S) {
    S.polygons(P) {
      int x0, y0, first = 1;
      P.contours(W) {
        if (first) {
           // a new partial polygon is starting
           x0 = W.x1;
           y0 = W.y1;
           }
        // ...
        // do something with the wire
        // ...
        if (first)
           first = 0;
        else if (W.x2 == x0 && W.y2 == y0) {
           // this was the last wire of the partial polygon,
           // so the next wire (if any) will be the first wire
```

```
            // of the next partial polygon
            first = 1;
            }
         }
       }
     }
  }

board(B) {
  B.signals(S) {
    S.polygons(P) {
      // handle only the "positive" polygons:
      int i = 1;
      int active;
      do {
         active = 0;
         P.contours(W, i) {
           active = 1;
           // do something with the wire
           }
         i++;
         } while (active);
      }
    }
  }
```

UL_PORT

Data members

border	int (MODULE_BORDER_...)
bus	string (see note)
direction	int (PIN_DIRECTION_... (see note))
name	string (PORT_NAME_LENGTH)
net	string (see note)
x, y	int (connection point)

Loop members

nets()	UL_NET (see note)
texts()	UL_TEXT
wires()	UL_WIRE

See also UL_MODULE, UL_MODULEINST, UL_PORTREF

Constants

MODULE_BORDER_BOTTOM	at bottom border of module
MODULE_BORDER_RIGHT	at right border of module
MODULE_BORDER_TOP	at top border of module
MODULE_BORDER_LEFT	at left border of module
PORT_NAME_LENGTH	max. recommended length of a port name (used in formatted output

64

only)

Note

The direction values are identical to the PIN_DIRECTION_... values (without PIN_DIRECTION_SUP).

The `bus` and the `net` data members return the name of the bus or net to which this port is connected to (only available in a UL_MODULEINST context). Additionally the `nets` loop member loops through all available nets of this connection.

Example

```
schematic(SCH) {
  SCH.modules(M) {
    M.ports(P) printf("Port: %s\n", P.name);
    }
  }
```

UL_PORTREF

Data members

`moduleinst`	UL_MODULEINST
`port`	UL_PORT

See also UL_SEGMENT

Example

```
schematic(SCH) {
  SCH.sheets(SH) {
    printf("Sheet: %d\n", SH.number);
    SH.nets(N) {
      printf("\tNet: %s\n", N.name);
      N.segments(SEG) {
        SEG.portrefs(P) {
          printf("\tconnected to: %s, %s\n",
                 P.moduleinst.name, P.port.name);
          }
        }
      }
    }
  }
```

UL_RECTANGLE

Data members

`angle`	real (`0.0`...`359.9`)
`layer`	int

x1, y1	int (lower left corner)
x2, y2	int (upper right corner)

See also UL_BOARD, UL_PACKAGE, UL_SHEET, UL_SYMBOL

The coordinates (x1 y1) and (x2 y2) are always referring to the initial orientation of the rectangle regardless of the `angle`.

`angle` defines how many degrees the rectangle is rotated counterclockwise around its center. The center coordinates are given by `(x1+x2)/2` and `(y1+y2)/2`.

Example

```
board(B) {
  B.rectangles(R) {
    printf("Rectangle: (%f %f), (%f %f)\n",
           u2mm(R.x1), u2mm(R.y1), u2mm(R.x2), u2mm(R.y2));
    }
  }
```

UL_SCHEMATIC

Data members

alwaysvectorfont	int (ALWAYS_VECTOR_FONT_..., see note)
checked	int (see note)
description	string
grid	UL_GRID
headline	string
name	string (see note)
verticaltext	int (VERTICAL_TEXT_...)
xreflabel	string
xrefpart	string

Loop members

allparts()	UL_PART (see note)
attributes()	UL_ATTRIBUTE (see note)
classes()	UL_CLASS
errors()	UL_ERROR
layers()	UL_LAYER
libraries()	UL_LIBRARY
modules()	UL_MODULE
nets()	UL_NET
parts()	UL_PART
sheets()	UL_SHEET
variantdefs()	UL_VARIANTDEF

See also UL_BOARD, UL_LIBRARY

66

Constants

`ALWAYS_VECTOR_FONT_GUI`	alwaysvectorfont is set in the user interface dialog
`ALWAYS_VECTOR_FONT_PERSISTENT`	alwaysvectorfont is set persistent in this schematic
`VERTICAL_TEXT_UP`	reading direction for vertical texts: up
`VERTICAL_TEXT_DOWN`	reading direction for vertical texts: down

Note

The value returned by `alwaysvectorfont` can be used in boolean context or can be masked with the `ALWAYS_VECTOR_FONT_...` constants to determine the source of this setting, as in

```
if (sch.alwaysvectorfont) {
   // alwaysvectorfont is set in general
   }
if (sch.alwaysvectorfont & ALWAYS_VECTOR_FONT_GUI) {
   // alwaysvectorfont is set in the user interface
   }
```

The value returned by `checked` can be used in boolean context and is set only after a recent 'Electrical Rule Check' (ERC).

The `name` member returns the full file name, including the directory.

The `xreflabel` and `xrefpart` members return the format strings used to display cross-reference labels and part cross-references.

The `attributes()` loop member loops through the *global* attributes.

Virtual parts, `allparts()` loop

Hierarchical parts are generated by module instances and actually do not exist in the schematic, only corresponding parts in the modules. For this we sometimes call them 'Virtual parts'. One module part can be used by several virtual parts via several module instances. As each virtual part corresponds to a (real existing) element in the board, the User Language supplies those parts as well, e.g. for BOM generation.
The `allparts()` loop member loops through the `parts()` of the schematic itself and through all the virtual parts.

Example

```
schematic(S) {
  S.parts(P) printf("Part: %s\n", P.name);
  }
```

UL_SEGMENT

Loop members

`junctions()`	UL_JUNCTION (see note)
`labels()`	UL_LABEL
`pinrefs()`	UL_PINREF (see note)
`portrefs()`	UL_PORTREF
`texts()`	UL_TEXT (deprecated, see note)
`wires()`	UL_WIRE

See also UL_BUS, UL_NET

Note

The `junctions()` and `pinrefs()` loop members are only available for net segments.

The `texts()` loop member was used in older EAGLE versions to loop through the labels of a segment, and is only present for compatibility. It will not deliver the text of cross-reference labels at the correct position. Use the `labels()` loop member to access a segment's labels.

Example

```
schematic(SCH) {
  SCH.sheets(SH) {
    printf("Sheet: %d\n", SH.number);
    SH.nets(N) {
      printf("\tNet: %s\n", N.name);
      N.segments(SEG) {
        SEG.pinrefs(P) {
          printf("connected to: %s, %s, %s\n",
                 P.part.name, P.instance.name, P.pin.name);
          }
        }
      }
    }
  }
```

UL_SHEET

Data members

`area`	UL_AREA
`description`	string
`headline`	string
`number`	int

Loop members

`busses()`	UL_BUS

68

`circles()`	UL_CIRCLE
`dimensions()`	UL_DIMENSION
`frames()`	UL_FRAME
`instances()`	UL_INSTANCE
`moduleinsts()`	UL_MODULEINST
`nets()`	UL_NET
`polygons()`	UL_POLYGON
`rectangles()`	UL_RECTANGLE
`texts()`	UL_TEXT
`wires()`	UL_WIRE

See also UL_SCHEMATIC

Example

```
schematic(SCH) {
  SCH.sheets(S) {
    printf("Sheet: %d\n", S.number);
    }
  }
```

UL_SIGNAL

Data members

`airwireshidden`	int
`class`	UL_CLASS
`name`	string (`SIGNAL_NAME_LENGTH`)

Loop members

`contactrefs()`	UL_CONTACTREF
`polygons()`	UL_POLYGON
`vias()`	UL_VIA
`wires()`	UL_WIRE

See also UL_BOARD

Constants

`SIGNAL_NAME_LENGTH`	max. recommended length of a signal name (used in formatted output only)

Example

```
board(B) {
  B.signals(S) printf("Signal: %s\n", S.name);
  }
```

UL_SMD

Data members

angle	real (0.0...359.9)
dx[layer], dy[layer]	int (size)
flags	int (SMD_FLAG_...)
layer	int (see note)
name	string (SMD_NAME_LENGTH)
roundness	int (see note)
signal	string
x, y	int (center point, see note)

See also UL_PACKAGE, UL_CONTACT, UL_PAD

Constants

SMD_FLAG_STOP	generate stop mask
SMD_FLAG_THERMALS	generate thermals
SMD_FLAG_CREAM	generate cream mask
SMD_NAME_LENGTH	max. recommended length of an smd name (same as CONTACT_NAME_LENGTH)

Note

The parameters of the smd depend on the context in which it is accessed:

- if the smd is derived from a UL_LIBRARY context, the coordinates (x, y), angle, layer and roundness of the smd will be the same as defined in the package drawing
- in all other cases, they will have the actual values from the board

If the dx and dy data members are called with an optional layer index, the data for that layer is returned according to the Design Rules. Valid layers are LAYER_TOP, LAYER_TSTOP and LAYER_TCREAM for an smd in the Top layer, and LAYER_BOTTOM, LAYER_BSTOP and LAYER_BCREAM for an smd in the Bottom layer, respectively.

angle defines how many degrees the smd is rotated counterclockwise around its center.

The value returned by flags must be masked with the SMD_FLAG_... constants to determine the individual flag settings, as in

```
if (smd.flags & SMD_FLAG_STOP) {
   ...
   }
```

Note that if your ULP just wants to draw the objects, you don't need to check these flags explicitly. The dx[] and dy[] members will return the proper data; for instance, if SMD_FLAG_STOP is set, dx[LAYER_TSTOP] will return 0, which should result in nothing being drawn in that layer. The `flags` member is mainly for ULPs that want to create script files that create library objects.

Example

```
library(L) {
  L.packages(PAC) {
    PAC.contacts(C) {
      if (C.smd)
         printf("Smd: '%s', (%f %f), dx=%f, dy=%f\n",
                C.name, u2mm(C.smd.x), u2mm(C.smd.y), u2mm(C.smd.dx),
u2mm(C.smd.dy));
      }
    }
  }
```

UL_SYMBOL

Data members

`area`	UL_AREA
`description`	string
`headline`	string
`library`	string
`name`	string (SYMBOL_NAME_LENGTH)

Loop members

`circles()`	UL_CIRCLE
`dimensions()`	UL_DIMENSION
`frames()`	UL_FRAME
`rectangles()`	UL_RECTANGLE
`pins()`	UL_PIN
`polygons()`	UL_POLYGON
`texts()`	UL_TEXT (see note)
`wires()`	UL_WIRE

See also UL_GATE, UL_LIBRARY

Constants

`SYMBOL_NAME_LENGTH`	max. recommended length of a symbol name (used in formatted output only)

Note

If the UL_SYMBOL is derived from a UL_INSTANCE, the `texts()` member only loops through the non-detached texts of that instance.

Example

```
library(L) {
  L.symbols(S) printf("Sym: %s\n", S.name);
  }
```

UL_TEXT

Data members

`align`	int (`ALIGN_...`)
`angle`	real (`0.0`...`359.9`)
`font`	int (`FONT_...`)
`layer`	int
`linedistance`	int
`mirror`	int
`ratio`	int
`size`	int
`spin`	int
`value`	string
`x, y`	int (origin point)

Loop members

`wires()`	UL_WIRE (see note)

See also UL_BOARD, UL_PACKAGE, UL_SHEET, UL_SYMBOL

Constants

`FONT_VECTOR`	vector font
`FONT_PROPORTIONAL`	proportional font
`FONT_FIXED`	fixed font
`ALIGN_BOTTOM_LEFT`	bottom/left aligned
`ALIGN_BOTTOM_CENTER`	bottom/center aligned
`ALIGN_BOTTOM_RIGHT`	bottom/right aligned
`ALIGN_CENTER_LEFT`	center/left aligned
`ALIGN_CENTER`	centered
`ALIGN_CENTER_RIGHT`	center/right aligned
`ALIGN_TOP_LEFT`	top/left aligned
`ALIGN_TOP_CENTER`	top/center aligned
`ALIGN_TOP_RIGHT`	top/right aligned

Note

The `wires()` loop member always accesses the individual wires the text is composed of when using the vector font, even if the actual font is not `FONT_VECTOR`.

If the UL_TEXT is derived from a UL_ELEMENT or UL_INSTANCE context, the member values will be those of the actual text as located in the board or sheet drawing.

Example

```
board(B) {
  B.texts(T) {
    printf("Text: %s\n", T.value);
    }
  }
```

UL_VARIANTDEF

Data members

`name`	string

See also UL_VARIANT, UL_SCHEMATIC, UL_BOARD

Example

```
schematic(SCH) {
  SCH.variantdefs(VD) {
    printf("Variant: '%s'\n", VD.name);
    }
  }
```

UL_VARIANT

Data members

`populate`	int (0=do not populate, 1=populate)
`value`	string
`technology`	string
`variantdef`	UL_VARIANTDEF

See also UL_VARIANTDEF, UL_PART

Example

```
schematic(SCH) {
  SCH.parts(P) {
    P.variants(V) {
      printf("%s: %spopulate\n", V.variantdef.name, V.populate ? "" : "do not
");
      }
    }
  }
```

73

UL_VIA

Data members

diameter[layer]	int
drill	int
drillsymbol	int
end	int
flags	int (VIA_FLAG_...)
shape[layer]	int (VIA_SHAPE_...)
start	int
x, y	int (center point)

See also UL_SIGNAL

Constants

VIA_FLAG_STOP	always generate stop mask
VIA_SHAPE_SQUARE	square
VIA_SHAPE_ROUND	round
VIA_SHAPE_OCTAGON	octagon

Note

The diameter and shape of the via depend on the layer for which they shall be retrieved, because they may be different in each layer depending on the Design Rules. If one of the layers LAYER_TOP...LAYER_BOTTOM, LAYER_TSTOP or LAYER_BSTOP is given as the index to the diameter or shape data member, the resulting value will be calculated according to the Design Rules. If LAYER_VIAS is given, the raw value as defined in the via will be returned.

Note that `diameter` and `shape` will always return the diameter or shape that a via would have in the given layer, even if that particular via doesn't cover that layer (or if that layer isn't used in the layer setup at all).

`start` and `end` return the layer numbers in which that via starts and ends. The value of `start` will always be less than that of `end`.

`drillsymbol` returns the number of the drill symbol that has been assigned to this drill diameter (see the manual for a list of defined drill symbols). A value of `0` means that no symbol has been assigned to this drill diameter.

Example

```
board(B) {
  B.signals(S) {
    S.vias(V) {
      printf("Via: (%f %f)\n", u2mm(V.x), u2mm(V.y));
```

74

```
      }
    }
  }
```

UL_WIRE

Data members

`arc`	UL_ARC
`cap`	int (`CAP_...`)
`curve`	real
`layer`	int
`style`	int (`WIRE_STYLE_...`)
`width`	int
`x1, y1`	int (starting point)
`x2, y2`	int (end point)

Loop members

`pieces()`	UL_WIRE (see note)

See also UL_BOARD, UL_PACKAGE, UL_SEGMENT, UL_SHEET, UL_SIGNAL, UL_SYMBOL, UL_ARC

Constants

`CAP_FLAT`	flat arc ends
`CAP_ROUND`	round arc ends
`WIRE_STYLE_CONTINUOUS`	continuous
`WIRE_STYLE_LONGDASH`	long dash
`WIRE_STYLE_SHORTDASH`	short dash
`WIRE_STYLE_DASHDOT`	dash dot

Wire Style

A UL_WIRE that has a *style* other than `WIRE_STYLE_CONTINUOUS` can use the `pieces()` loop member to access the individual segments that constitute for example a dashed wire. If `pieces()` is called for a UL_WIRE with `WIRE_STYLE_CONTINUOUS`, a single segment will be accessible which is just the same as the original UL_WIRE. The `pieces()` loop member can't be called from a UL_WIRE that itself has been returned by a call to `pieces()` (this would cause an infinite recursion).

Arcs at Wire level

Arcs are basically wires, with a few additional properties. At the first level arcs are treated exactly the same as wires, meaning they have a start and an end point, a width, layer and wire style. In addition to these an arc, at the wire level, has a *cap* and a *curve* parameter. *cap* defines whether the arc endings are round or flat, and *curve* defines the "curvature" of the arc. The valid range for *curve* is -360..+360, and its value means what part of a full circle the arc consists of. A value of 90, for instance, would result in a 90° arc, while 180 would give you a semicircle. The maximum value of 360 can only be reached theoretically, since this would mean that the arc consists of a full circle, which, because the start and end points have to lie on the circle, would have to have an infinitely large diameter. Positive values for *curve* mean that the arc is drawn in a mathematically positive sense (i.e. counterclockwise). If *curve* is 0, the arc is a straight line ("no curvature"), which is actually a wire.

The *cap* parameter only has a meaning for actual arcs, and will always return CAP_ROUND for a straight wire.

Whether or not an UL_WIRE is an arc can be determined by checking the boolean return value of the arc data member. If it returns 0, we have a straight wire, otherwise an arc. If arc returns a non-zero value it may be further dereferenced to access the UL_ARC specific parameters start and end angle, radius and center point. Note that you may only need these additional parameters if you are going to draw the arc or process it in other ways where the actual shape is important.

Example

```
board(B) {
  B.wires(W) {
    printf("Wire: (%f %f) (%f %f)\n",
           u2mm(W.x1), u2mm(W.y1), u2mm(W.x2), u2mm(W.y2));
    }
  }
```

Definitions

The data items to be used in a User Language Program must be defined before they can be used.

There are three kinds of definitions:

- Constant Definitions
- Variable Definitions
- Function Definitions

The scope of a *constant* or *variable* definition goes from the line in which it has been defined to the end of the current block, or to the end of the User Language Program, if the definition appeared outside any block.

The scope of a *function* definition goes from the closing brace (}) of the function body to the end of the User Language Program.

Constant Definitions

Constants are defined using the keyword `enum`, as in

```
enum { a, b, c };
```

which would define the three constants `a`, `b` and `c`, giving them the values `0`, `1` and `2`, respectively.

Constants may also be initialized to specific values, like

```
enum { a, b = 5, c };
```

where `a` would be `0`, `b` would be `5` and `c` would be `6`.

Variable Definitions

The general syntax of a *variable definition* is

```
[numeric] type identifier [= initializer][, ...];
```

where `type` is one of the data or object types, `identifier` is the name of the variable, and `initializer` is a optional initial value.

Multiple variable definitions of the same `type` are separated by commas (`,`).

If `identifier` is followed by a pair of brackets (`[]`), this defines an array of variables of the given `type`. The size of an array is automatically adjusted at runtime.

The optional keyword `numeric` can be used with string arrays to have them sorted alphanumerically by the sort() function.

By default (if no `initializer` is present), data variables are set to `0` (or `""`, in case of a string), and object variables are "invalid".

Examples

`int i;`	defines an int variable named `i`
`string s = "Hello";`	defines a string variable named `s` and initializes it to `"Hello"`
`real a, b = 1.0, c;`	defines three real variables named `a`, `b` and `c`, initializing `b` to the value `1.0`
`int n[] = { 1, 2, 3 };`	defines an array of int, initializing the first three elements to `1`, `2` and `3`
`numeric string names[];`	defines a string array that can be sorted alphanumerically
`UL_WIRE w;`	defines a UL_WIRE object named `w`

The members of array elements of object types can't be accessed directly:

```
UL_SIGNAL signals[];
...
UL_SIGNAL s = signals[0];
printf("%s", s.name);
```

Function Definitions

You can write your own User Language functions and call them just like the Builtin Functions.

The general syntax of a *function definition* is

```
type identifier(parameters)
{
  statements
}
```

where `type` is one of the data or object types, `identifier` is the name of the function, `parameters` is a list of comma separated parameter definitions, and `statements` is a sequence of statements.

Functions that do not return a value have the type `void`.

A function must be defined **before** it can be called, and function calls can not be recursive (a function cannot call itself).

The statements in the function body may modify the values of the parameters, but this will not have any effect on the arguments of the function call.

Execution of a function can be terminated by the `return` statement. Without any `return` statement the function body is executed until it's closing brace (`}`).

A call to the `exit()` function will terminate the entire User Language Program.

The special function `main()`

If your User Language Program contains a function called `main()`, that function will be explicitly called as the main function, and it's return value will be the return value of the program.

Command line arguments are available to the program through the global Builtin Variables `argc` and `argv`.

Example

```
int CountDots(string s)
{
  int dots = 0;
  for (int i = 0; s[i]; ++i)
      if (s[i] == '.')
         ++dots;
```

```
  return dots;
}
string dotted = "This.has.dots...";
output("test") {
  printf("Number of dots: %d\n",
                 CountDots(dotted));
  }
```

Operators

The following table lists all of the User Language operators, in order of their precedence (*Unary* having the highest precedence, *Comma* the lowest):

<table>
<tr><td>Unary</td><td>! ~ + - ++ --</td></tr>
<tr><td>Multiplicative</td><td>* / %</td></tr>
<tr><td>Additive</td><td>+ -</td></tr>
<tr><td>Shift</td><td><< >></td></tr>
<tr><td>Relational</td><td>< <= > >=</td></tr>
<tr><td>Equality</td><td>== !=</td></tr>
<tr><td>Bitwise AND</td><td>&</td></tr>
<tr><td>Bitwise XOR</td><td>^</td></tr>
<tr><td>Bitwise OR</td><td>|</td></tr>
<tr><td>Logical AND</td><td>&&</td></tr>
<tr><td>Logical OR</td><td>||</td></tr>
<tr><td>Conditional</td><td>?:</td></tr>
<tr><td>Assignment</td><td>= *= /= %= += -= &= ^= |= <<= >>=</td></tr>
<tr><td>Comma</td><td>,</td></tr>
</table>

Associativity is **left to right** for all operators, except for *Unary*, *Conditional* and *Assignment*, which are **right to left** associative.

The normal operator precedence can be altered by the use of parentheses.

Bitwise Operators

Bitwise operators work only with data types `char` and `int`.

<table>
<tr><td>Unary</td><td></td></tr>
<tr><td>~</td><td>Bitwise (1's) complement</td></tr>
<tr><td>Binary</td><td></td></tr>
<tr><td><<</td><td>Shift left</td></tr>
<tr><td>>></td><td>Shift right</td></tr>
<tr><td>&</td><td>Bitwise AND</td></tr>
<tr><td>^</td><td>Bitwise XOR</td></tr>
<tr><td>|</td><td>Bitwise OR</td></tr>
<tr><td>Assignment</td><td></td></tr>
<tr><td>&=</td><td>Assign bitwise AND</td></tr>
</table>

^=	Assign bitwise XOR
|=	Assign bitwise OR
<<=	Assign left shift
>>=	Assign right shift

Logical Operators

Logical operators work with expressions of any data type.

Unary

!	Logical NOT

Binary

&&	Logical AND
||	Logical OR

Using a `string` expression with a logical operator checks whether the string is empty.

Using an Object Type with a logical operator checks whether that object contains valid data.

Comparison Operators

Comparison operators work with expressions of any data type, except Object Types.

<	Less than
<=	Less than or equal to
>	Greater than
>=	Greater than or equal to
==	Equal to
!=	Not equal to

Evaluation Operators

Evaluation operators are used to evaluate expressions based on a condition, or to group a sequence of expressions and have them evaluated as one expression.

?:	Conditional
,	Comma

The *Conditional* operator is used to make a decision within an expression, as in

```
int a;
// ...code that calculates 'a'
string s = a ? "True" : "False";
```

which is basically the same as

```
int a;
string s;
// ...code that calculates 'a'
```

80

```
if (a)
   s = "True";
else
   s = "False";
```

but the advantage of the conditional operator is that it can be used in an expression.

The *Comma* operator is used to evaluate a sequence of expressions from left to right, using the type and value of the right operand as the result.

Note that arguments in a function call as well as multiple variable declarations also use commas as delimiters, but in that case this is **not** a comma operator!

Arithmetic Operators

Arithmetic operators work with data types `char`, `int` and `real` (except for `++`, `--`, `%` and `%=`).

Unary	
`+`	Unary plus
`-`	Unary minus
`++`	Pre- or postincrement
`--`	Pre- or postdecrement
Binary	
`*`	Multiply
`/`	Divide
`%`	Remainder (modulus)
`+`	Binary plus
`-`	Binary minus
Assignment	
`=`	Simple assignment
`*=`	Assign product
`/=`	Assign quotient
`%=`	Assign remainder (modulus)
`+=`	Assign sum
`-=`	Assign difference

See also String Operators

String Operators

String operators work with data types `char`, `int` and `string`. The left operand must always be of type `string`.

Binary	
`+`	Concatenation
Assignment	

=	Simple assignment
+=	Append to string

The + operator concatenates two strings, or adds a character to the end of a string and returns the resulting string.

The += operator appends a string or a character to the end of a given string.

See also Arithmetic Operators

Expressions

An *expression* can be one of the following:

- Arithmetic Expression
- Assignment Expression
- String Expression
- Comma Expression
- Conditional Expression
- Function Call

Expressions can be grouped using parentheses, and may be recursive, meaning that an expression can consist of subexpressions.

Arithmetic Expression

An *arithmetic expression* is any combination of numeric operands and an arithmetic operator or a bitwise operator.

Examples

```
a + b
c++
m << 1
```

Assignment Expression

An *assignment expression* consists of a variable on the left side of an assignment operator, and an expression on the right side.

Examples

```
a = x + 42
b += c
```

```
s = "Hello"
```

String Expression

A *string expression* is any combination of string and char operands and a string operator.

Examples

```
s + ".brd"
t + 'x'
```

Comma Expression

A *comma expression* is a sequence of expressions, delimited by the comma operator

Comma expressions are evaluated left to right, and the result of a comma expression is the type and value of the rightmost expression.

Example

```
i++, j++, k++
```

Conditional Expression

A *conditional expression* uses the conditional operator to make a decision within an expression.

Example

```
int a;
// ...code that calculates 'a'
string s = a ? "True" : "False";
```

Function Call

A *function call* transfers the program flow to a user defined function or a builtin function. The formal parameters defined in the function definition are replaced with the values of the expressions used as the actual arguments of the function call.

Example

```
int p = strchr(s, 'b');
```

Statements

A *statement* can be one of the following:

- Compound Statement
- Control Statement
- Expression Statement
- Builtin Statement
- Constant Definition
- Variable Definition

Statements specify the flow of control as a User Language Program executes. In absence of specific control statements, statements are executed sequentially in the order of appearance in the ULP file.

Compound Statement

A *compound statement* (also known as *block*) is a list (possibly empty) of statements enclosed in matching braces ({}). Syntactically, a block can be considered to be a single statement, but it also controls the scoping of identifiers. An identifier declared within a block has a scope starting at the point of declaration and ending at the closing brace.

Compound statements can be nested to any depth.

Expression Statement

An *expression statement* is any expression followed by a semicolon.

An expression statement is executed by evaluating the expression. All side effects of this evaluation are completed before the next statement is executed. Most expression statements are assignments or function calls.

A special case is the *empty statement*, consisting of only a semicolon. An empty statement does nothing, but it may be useful in situations where the ULP syntax expects a statement but your program does not need one.

Control Statements

Control statements are used to control the program flow.

Iteration statements are

```
do...while
for
while
```

84

Selection statements are

if...else
switch

Jump statements are

break
continue
return

break

The *break* statement has the general syntax

```
break;
```

and immediately terminates the **nearest** enclosing do...while, for, switch or while statement. This also applies to *loop members* of object types.

Since all of these statements can be intermixed and nested to any depth, take care to ensure that your `break` exits from the correct statement.

continue

The *continue* statement has the general syntax

```
continue;
```

and immediately transfers control to the test condition of the **nearest** enclosing do...while, while, or for statement, or to the increment expression of the **nearest** enclosing for statement.

Since all of these statements can be intermixed and nested to any depth, take care to ensure that your `continue` affects the correct statement.

do...while

The *do...while* statement has the general syntax

```
do statement while (condition);
```

and executes the `statement` until the `condition` expression becomes zero.

The `condition` is tested **after** the first execution of `statement`, which means that the statement is always executed at least one time.

If there is no `break` or `return` inside the `statement`, the `statement` must affect the value of the `condition`, or `condition` itself must change during evaluation in order to avoid an endless loop.

Example

```
string s = "Trust no one!";
int i = -1;
do {
   ++i;
   } while (s[i]);
```

for

The *for* statement has the general syntax

```
for ([init]; [test]; [inc]) statement
```

and performs the following steps:

1. If an initializing expression `init` is present, it is executed.
2. If a `test` expression is present, it is executed. If the result is nonzero (or if there is no `test` expression at all), the `statement` is executed.
3. If an `inc` expression is present, it is executed.
4. Finally control returns to step 2.

If there is no `break` or `return` inside the `statement`, the `inc` expression (or the `statement`) must affect the value of the `test` expression, or `test` itself must change during evaluation in order to avoid an endless loop.

The initializing expression `init` normally initializes one or more loop counters. It may also define a new variable as a loop counter. The scope of such a variable is valid until the end of the active block.

Example

```
string s = "Trust no one!";
int sum = 0;
for (int i = 0; s[i]; ++i)
    sum += s[i]; // sums up the characters in s
```

if...else

The *if...else* statement has the general syntax

```
if (expression)
   t_statement
```

```
[else
   f_statement]
```

The conditional `expression` is evaluated, and if its value is nonzero the `t_statement` is executed. Otherwise the `f_statement` is executed in case there is an `else` clause.

An `else` clause is always matched to the last encountered `if` without an `else`. If this is not what you want, you need to use braces to group the statements, as in

```
if (a == 1) {
   if (b == 1)
      printf("a == 1 and b == 1\n");
   }
else
   printf("a != 1\n");
```

return

A function with a return type other than `void` must contain at least one *return* statement with the syntax

```
return expression;
```

where `expression` must evaluate to a type that is compatible with the function's return type. The value of `expression` is the value returned by the function.

If the function is of type `void`, a `return` statement without an `expression` can be used to return from the function call.

switch

The *switch* statement has the general syntax

```
switch (sw_exp) {
  case case_exp: case_statement
  ...
  [default: def_statement]
  }
```

and allows for the transfer of control to one of several `case`-labeled statements, depending on the value of `sw_exp` (which must be of integral type).

Any `case_statement` can be labeled by one or more `case` labels. The `case_exp` of each `case` label must evaluate to a constant integer which is unique within it's enclosing `switch` statement.

There can also be at most one `default` label.

After evaluating sw_exp, the case_exp are checked for a match. If a match is found, control passes to the case_statement with the matching case label.

If no match is found and there is a default label, control passes to def_statement. Otherwise none of the statements in the switch is executed.

Program execution is not affected when case and default labels are encountered. Control simply passes through the labels to the following statement.

To stop execution at the end of a group of statements for a particular case, use the break statement.

Example

```
string s = "Hello World";
int vowels = 0, others = 0;
for (int i = 0; s[i]; ++i)
    switch (toupper(s[i])) {
      case 'A':
      case 'E':
      case 'I':
      case 'O':
      case 'U': ++vowels;
                break;
      default: ++others;
      }
printf("There are %d vowels in '%s'\n", vowels, s);
```

while

The *while* statement has the general syntax

```
while (condition) statement
```

and executes the statement as long as the condition expression is not zero.

The condition is tested **before** the first possible execution of statement, which means that the statement may never be executed if condition is initially zero.

If there is no break or return inside the statement, the statement must affect the value of the condition, or condition itself must change during evaluation in order to avoid an endless loop.

Example

```
string s = "Trust no one!";
int i = 0;
while (s[i])
      ++i;
```

Builtins

Builtins are *Constants, Variables, Functions* and *Statements* that provide additional information and allow for data manipulations.

- Builtin Constants
- Builtin Variables
- Builtin Functions
- Builtin Statements

Builtin Constants

Builtin constants are used to provide information about object parameters, such as maximum recommended name length, flags etc.

Many of the object types have their own **Constants** section which lists the builtin constants for that particular object (see e.g. UL_PIN).

The following builtin constants are defined in addition to the ones listed for the various object types:

`EAGLE_VERSION`	EAGLE program version number (int)
`EAGLE_RELEASE`	EAGLE program release number (int)
`EAGLE_SIGNATURE`	a string containing EAGLE program name, version and copyright information
`EAGLE_PATH`	a string containing the complete path of the EAGLE executable
`EAGLE_DIR`	a string containing the directory of the EAGLE installation (`$EAGLEDIR`)
`EAGLE_HOME`	a string containing the user's home directory when starting EAGLE (`$HOME`)
`OS_SIGNATURE`	a string containing a signature of the operating system (e.g. Mac..., Windows... or Linux)
`REAL_EPSILON`	the minimum positive real number such that `1.0 + REAL_EPSILON != 1.0`
`REAL_MAX`	the largest possible real value
`REAL_MIN`	the smallest possible (positive!) real value the smallest representable number is `-REAL_MAX`
`INT_MAX`	the largest possible int value
`INT_MIN`	the smallest possible int value
`PI`	the value of "pi" (3.14..., real)
`usage`	a string containing the text from the `#usage` directive

These builtin constants contain the directory paths defined in the directories dialog, with any of the special variables (`$HOME` and `$EAGLEDIR`) replaced by their actual values. Since each path can consist of several directories, these constants are string arrays with an individual directory in each member. The first empty member marks the end of the path:

`path_lbr[]`	Libraries
`path_dru[]`	Design Rules
`path_ulp[]`	User Language Programs
`path_scr[]`	Scripts
`path_cam[]`	CAM Jobs
`path_epf[]`	Projects

When using these constants to build a full file name, you need to use a directory separator, as in

```
string s = path_lbr[0] + '/' + "mylib.lbr";
```

The libraries that are currently in use through the USE command:

```
used_libraries[]
```

Builtin Variables

Builtin variables are used to provide information at runtime.

`int argc`	number of arguments given to the RUN command
`string argv[]`	arguments given to the RUN command (`argv[0]` is the full ULP file name)

Builtin Functions

Builtin functions are used to perform specific tasks, like printing formatted strings, sorting data arrays or the like.

You may also write your own functions and use them to structure your User Language Program.

The builtin functions are grouped into the following categories:

- Character Functions
- File Handling Functions
- Mathematical Functions
- Miscellaneous Functions
- Network Functions
- Printing Functions
- String Functions
- Time Functions
- Object Functions
- XML Functions

Alphabetical reference of all builtin functions:

- abs()

90

- acos()
- asin()
- atan()
- ceil()
- cfgget()
- cfgset()
- clrgroup()
- country()
- cos()
- exit()
- exp()
- fdlsignature()
- filedir()
- fileerror()
- fileext()
- fileglob()
- filename()
- fileread()
- filesetext()
- filesize()
- filetime()
- floor()
- frac()
- inch2u()
- ingroup()
- isalnum()
- isalpha()
- iscntrl()
- isdigit()
- isgraph()
- islower()
- isprint()
- ispunct()
- isspace()
- isupper()
- isxdigit()
- language()

- log()
- log10()
- lookup()
- max()
- mic2u()
- mil2u()
- min()
- mm2u()
- neterror()
- netget()
- netpost()
- palette()
- pow()
- printf()
- round()
- setgroup()
- setvariant()
- sin()
- sleep()
- sort()
- sprintf()
- sqrt()
- status()
- strchr()
- strjoin()
- strlen()
- strlwr()
- strrchr()
- strrstr()
- strsplit()
- strstr()
- strsub()
- strtod()
- strtol()
- strupr()
- strxstr()
- system()

92

- t2day()
- t2dayofweek()
- t2hour()
- t2minute()
- t2month()
- t2second()
- t2string()
- t2year()
- tan()
- time()
- tolower()
- toupper()
- trunc()
- u2inch()
- u2mic()
- u2mil()
- u2mm()
- variant()
- xmlattribute()
- xmlattributes()
- xmlelement()
- xmlelements()
- xmltags()
- xmltext()

Character Functions

Character functions are used to manipulate single characters.

The following character functions are available:

- isalnum()
- isalpha()
- iscntrl()
- isdigit()
- isgraph()
- islower()
- isprint()
- ispunct()

- isspace()
- isupper()
- isxdigit()
- tolower()
- toupper()

is...()

Function

Check whether a character falls into a given category.

Syntax

```
int isalnum(char c);
int isalpha(char c);
int iscntrl(char c);
int isdigit(char c);
int isgraph(char c);
int islower(char c);
int isprint(char c);
int ispunct(char c);
int isspace(char c);
int isupper(char c);
int isxdigit(char c);
```

Returns

The `is...` functions return nonzero if the given character falls into the category, zero otherwise.

Character categories

`isalnum`	letters (A to Z or a to z) or digits (0 to 9)
`isalpha`	letters (A to Z or a to z)
`iscntrl`	delete characters or ordinary control characters (0x7F or 0x00 to 0x1F)
`isdigit`	digits (0 to 9)
`isgraph`	printing characters (except space)
`islower`	lowercase letters (a to z)
`isprint`	printing characters (0x20 to 0x7E)
`ispunct`	punctuation characters (`iscntrl` or `isspace`)
`isspace`	space, tab, carriage return, new line, vertical tab, or formfeed (0x09 to 0x0D, 0x20)
`isupper`	uppercase letters (A to Z)
`isxdigit`	hex digits (0 to 9, A to F, a to f)

Example

```
char c = 'A';
if (isxdigit(c))
```

94

```
   printf("%c is hex\n", c);
else
   printf("%c is not hex\n", c);
```

to...()

Function

Convert a character to upper- or lowercase.

Syntax

```
char tolower(char c);
char toupper(char c);
```

Returns

The `tolower` function returns the converted character if `c` is uppercase. All other characters are returned unchanged.

The `toupper` function returns the converted character if `c` is lowercase. All other characters are returned unchanged.

See also strupr, strlwr

File Handling Functions

Filename handling functions are used to work with file names, sizes and timestamps.

The following file handling functions are available:

- fileerror()
- fileglob()
- filedir()
- fileext()
- filename()
- fileread()
- filesetext()
- filesize()
- filetime()

See output() for information about how to write into a file.

fileerror()

Function

Returns the status of I/O operations.

Syntax

```
int fileerror();
```

Returns

The `fileerror` function returns `0` if everything is ok.

See also output, printf, fileread

`fileerror` checks the status of any I/O operations that have been performed since the last call to this function and returns `0` if everything was ok. If any of the I/O operations has caused an error, a value other than `0` will be returned.

You should call `fileerror` before any I/O operations to reset any previous error state, and call it again after the I/O operations to see if they were successful.

When `fileerror` returns a value other than `0` (thus indicating an error) a proper error message has already been given to the user.

Example

```
fileerror();
output("file.txt", "wt") {
  printf("Test\n");
  }
if (fileerror())
   exit(1);
```

fileglob()

Function

Perform a directory search.

Syntax

`int fileglob(string &array[], string pattern);`

Returns

The `fileglob` function returns the number of entries copied into `array`.

See also dlgFileOpen(), dlgFileSave()

`fileglob` performs a directory search using `pattern`.

`pattern` may contain `'*'` and `'?'` as wildcard characters. If `pattern` ends with a `'/'`, the contents of the given directory will be returned.

Names in the resulting `array` that end with a `'/'` are directory names.

The `array` is sorted alphabetically, with the directories coming first.

The special entries `'.'` and `'..'` (for the current and parent directories) are never returned in the `array`.

If `pattern` doesn't match, or if you don't have permission to search the given directory, the resulting `array` will be empty.

Note for Windows users

The directory delimiter in the `array` is always a **forward slash**. This makes sure User Language Programs will work platform independently. In the `pattern` the **backslash** ('\') is also treated as a directory delimiter.

Sorting filenames under Windows is done case insensitively.

Example

```
string a[];
int n = fileglob(a, "*.brd");
```

Filename Functions

Function

Split a filename into its separate parts.

Syntax

```
string filedir(string file);
string fileext(string file);
string filename(string file);
string filesetext(string file, string newext);
```

Returns

`filedir` returns the directory of `file` (including the drive letter under Windows).
`fileext` returns the extension of `file`.
`filename` returns the file name of `file` (including the extension).
`filesetext` returns `file` with the extension set to `newext`.

See also Filedata Functions

Example

```
if (board) board(B) {
  output(filesetext(B.name, ".out")) {
    ...
    }
  }
```

Filedata Functions

Function

Gets the timestamp and size of a file.

Syntax

```
int filesize(string filename);
int filetime(string filename);
```

Returns

`filesize` returns the size (in byte) of the given file.
`filetime` returns the timestamp of the given file in a format to be used with the time functions.

See also time, Filename Functions

Example

```
board(B)
  printf("Board: %s\nSize: %d\nTime: %s\n",
         B.name, filesize(B.name),
         t2string(filetime(B.name)));
```

File Input Functions

File input functions are used to read data from files.

The following file input is available:

- fileread()

See output() for information about how to write into a file.

fileread()

Function
Reads data from a file.
Syntax
`int fileread(`*`dest`*`, string file);`
Returns
`fileread` returns the number of objects read from the file.
The actual meaning of the return value depends on the type of `dest`.

See also lookup, strsplit, fileerror

If `dest` is a character array, the file will be read as raw binary data and the return value reflects the number of bytes read into the character array (which is equal to the file size).

If `dest` is a string array, the file will be read as a text file (one line per array member) and the return value will be the number of lines read into the string array. Newline characters will be stripped.

If `dest` is a string, the entire file will be read into that string and the return value will be the length of that string (which is not necessarily equal to the file size, if the operating system stores text files with "cr/lf" instead of a "newline" character).

Example

```
char b[];
int nBytes = fileread(b, "data.bin");
string lines[];
int nLines = fileread(lines, "data.txt");
string text;
int nChars = fileread(text, "data.txt");
```

Mathematical Functions

Mathematical functions are used to perform mathematical operations.

The following mathematical functions are available:

- abs()
- acos()
- asin()
- atan()
- ceil()
- cos()
- exp()
- floor()
- frac()
- log()
- log10()
- max()
- min()
- pow()
- round()
- sin()
- sqrt()
- trunc()
- tan()

Error Messages

If the arguments of a mathematical function call lead to an error, the error message will show the actual values of the arguments. Thus the statements

```
real x = -1.0;
real r = sqrt(2 * x);
```

will lead to the error message

```
Invalid argument in call to 'sqrt(-2)'
```

Absolute, Maximum and Minimum Functions

Function

Absolute, maximum and minimum functions.

Syntax

```
type abs(type x);
type max(type x, type y);
type min(type x, type y);
```

Returns

`abs` returns the absolute value of `x`.
`max` returns the maximum of `x` and `y`.
`min` returns the minimum of `x` and `y`.

The return type of these functions is the same as the (larger) type of the arguments. `type` must be one of `char`, `int` or `real`.

Example

```
real x = 2.567, y = 3.14;
printf("The maximum is %f\n", max(x, y));
```

Rounding Functions

Function

Rounding functions.

Syntax

```
real ceil(real x);
real floor(real x);
real frac(real x);
real round(real x);
real trunc(real x);
```

Returns

`ceil` returns the smallest integer not less than `x`.
`floor` returns the largest integer not greater than `x`.
`frac` returns the fractional part of `x`.
`round` returns `x` rounded to the nearest integer.
`trunc` returns the integer part of `x`.

Example

```
real x = 2.567;
printf("The rounded value of %f is %f\n", x, round(x));
```

Trigonometric Functions

Function

Trigonometric functions.

Syntax

```
real acos(real x);
real asin(real x);
real atan(real x);
real cos(real x);
real sin(real x);
real tan(real x);
```

Returns

`acos` returns the arc cosine of `x`.
`asin` returns the arc sine of `x`.
`atan` returns the arc tangent of `x`.
`cos` returns the cosine of `x`.
`sin` returns the sine of `x`.
`tan` returns the tangent of `x`.

Constants

`PI`	the value of "pi" (3.14...)

Note

Angles are given in radian.

Example

```
real x = PI / 2;
printf("The sine of %f is %f\n", x, sin(x));
```

Exponential Functions

Function

Exponential Functions.

Syntax

```
real exp(real x);
real log(real x);
```

```
real log10(real x);
real pow(real x, real y);
real sqrt(real x);
```

Returns

`exp` returns the exponential *e* to the power of `x`.
`log` returns the natural logarithm of `x`.
`log10` returns the base 10 logarithm of `x`.
`pow` returns the value of `x` to the power of `y`.
`sqrt` returns the square root of `x`.

Example

```
real x = 2.1;
printf("The square root of %f is %f\n", x, sqrt(x));
printf("The 3rd root of %f is %f\n", x, pow(x, 1.0/3));
```

Miscellaneous Functions

Miscellaneous functions are used to perform various tasks.

The following miscellaneous functions are available:

- country()
- exit()
- fdlsignature()
- language()
- lookup()
- palette()
- sort()
- status()
- system()
- Configuration Parameters
- Unit Conversions

Configuration Parameters

Function

Store and retrieve configuration parameters.

Syntax

```
string cfgget(string name[, string default]);
void cfgset(string name, string value);
```

Returns

`cfgget` returns the value of the parameter stored under the given `name`. If no such parameter has been stored, yet, the value of the optional `default` is returned (or an empty string, if no `default` is given).

The `cfgget` function retrieves values that have previously been stored with a call to `cfgset()`.

The `cfgset` function sets the parameter with the given `name` to the given `value`.

The valid characters for `name` are `'A'-'Z'`, `'a'-'z'`, `'0'-'9'`, `'.'` and `'_'`.
Parameter names are case sensitive.

The parameters are stored in the user's eaglerc file. To ensure that different User Language Programs don't overwrite each other's parameters in case they use the same parameter names, it is recommended to put the name of the ULP at the beginning of the parameter name. For example, a ULP named `mytool.ulp` that uses a parameter named `MyParam` could store that parameter under the name

```
mytool.MyParam
```

Because the configuration parameters are stored in the eaglerc file, which also contains all of EAGLE's other user specific parameters, it is also possible to access the EAGLE parameters with `cfgget()` and `cfgset()`. In order to make sure no ULP parameters collide with any EAGLE parameters, the EAGLE parameters must be prefixed with `"EAGLE:"`, as in

```
EAGLE:Option.XrefLabelFormat
```

Note that there is no documentation of all of EAGLE's internal parameters and how they are stored in the eaglerc file. Also, be very careful when changing any of these parameters! As with the eaglerc file itself, you should only manipulate these parameters if you know what you are doing! Some EAGLE parameters may require a restart of EAGLE for changes to take effect.

In the eaglerc file the User Language parameters are stored with the prefix `"ULP:"`. Therefore this prefix may be optionally put in front of User Language parameter names, as in

```
ULP:mytool.MyParam
```

Example

```
string MyParam = cfgget("mytool.MyParam", "SomeDefault");
MyParam = "OtherValue";
cfgset("mytool.MyParam", MyParam);
```

country()

Function

Returns the country code of the system in use.

Syntax

103

```
string country();
```

Returns

`country` returns a string consisting of two uppercase characters that identifies the country used on the current system. If no such country setting can be determined, the default "US" will be returned.

See also language

Example

```
dlgMessageBox("Your country code is: " + country());
```

exit()

Function

Exits from a User Language Program.

Syntax

```
void exit(int result);
void exit(string command);
```

See also RUN

The `exit` function terminates execution of a User Language Program.

If an integer `result` is given it will be used as the return value of the program.

If a string `command` is given, that command will be executed as if it were entered into the command line immediately after the RUN command. In that case the return value of the ULP is set to `EXIT_SUCCESS`.

Constants

`EXIT_SUCCESS`	return value for successful program execution (value `0`)
`EXIT_FAILURE`	return value for failed program execution (value `-1`)

fdlsignature()

Function

Calculates a digital signature for Premier Farnell's *Design Link*.

Syntax

```
string fdlsignature(string s, string key);
```

The `fdlsignature` function is used to calculate a digital signature when accessing Premier Farnell's *Design Link* interface.

language()

Function

Returns the language code of the system in use.

Syntax

```
string language();
```

Returns

`language` returns a string consisting of two lowercase characters that identifies the language used on the current system. If no such language setting can be determined, the default "en" will be returned.

See also country

The `language` function can be used to make a ULP use different message string, depending on which language the current system is using.

In the example below all the strings used in the ULP are listed in the string array `I18N[]`, preceeded by a string containing the various language codes supported by this ULP. Note the `vtab` characters used to separate the individual parts of each string (they are important for the `lookup` function) and the use of the commas to separate the strings. The actual work is done in the function `tr()`, which returns the translated version of the given string. If the original string can't be found in the `I18N` array, or there is no translation for the current language, the original string will be used untranslated.

The first language defined in the `I18N` array must be the one in which the strings used throughout the ULP are written, and should generally be English in order to make the program accessible to the largest number of users.

Example

```
string I18N[] = {
  "en\v"
  "de\v"
  "it\v"
  ,
  "I18N Demo\v"
  "Beispiel für Internationalisierung\v"
  "Esempio per internazionalizzazione\v"
  ,
  "Hello world!\v"
  "Hallo Welt!\v"
  "Ciao mondo!\v"
  ,
  "+Ok\v"
  "+Ok\v"
  "+Approvazione\v"
  ,
  "-Cancel\v"
  "-Abbrechen\v"
```

```
  "-Annullamento\v"
  };
int Language = strstr(I18N[0], language()) / 3;
string tr(string s)
{
  string t = lookup(I18N, s, Language, '\v');
  return t ? t : s;
}
dlgDialog(tr("I18N Demo")) {
  dlgHBoxLayout dlgSpacing(350);
  dlgLabel(tr("Hello world!"));
  dlgHBoxLayout {
    dlgPushButton(tr("+Ok")) dlgAccept();
    dlgPushButton(tr("-Cancel")) dlgReject();
    }
  };
```

lookup()

Function

Looks up data in a string array.

Syntax

`string lookup(string array[], string key, int field_index[, char separator]);`

`string lookup(string array[], string key, string field_name[, char separator]);`

Returns

`lookup` returns the value of the field identified by `field_index` or `field_name`.
If the field doesn't exist, or no string matching `key` is found, an empty string is returned.

See also filereAD, strsplit

An `array` that can be used with `lookup()` consists of strings of text, each string representing one data record.

Each data record contains an arbitrary number of fields, which are separated by the character `separator` (default is `'\t'`, the tabulator). The first field in a record is used as the `key` and is numbered `0`.

All records must have unique `key` fields and none of the `key` fields may be empty - otherwise it is undefined which record will be found.

If the first string in the `array` contains a "Header" record (i.e. a record where each field describes its contents), using `lookup` with a `field_name` string automatically determines the index of that field. This allows using the `lookup` function without exactly knowing which field index contains the desired data.
It is up to the user to make sure that the first record actually contains header information.

If the `key` parameter in the call to `lookup()` is an empty string, the first string of the `array` will

106

be used. This allows a program to determine whether there is a header record with the required field names.

If a field contains the `separator` character, that field must be enclosed in double quotes (as in `"abc;def"`, assuming the semicolon (`';'`) is used as separator). The same applies if the field contains double quotes (`"`), in which case the double quotes inside the field have to be doubled (as in `"abc;""def"";ghi"`, which would be `abc;"def";ghi`).
It is best to use the default "tab" separator, which doesn't have these problems (no field can contain a tabulator).

Here's an example data file (`';'` has been used as separator for better readability):

```
Name;Manufacturer;Code;Price
7400;Intel;I-01-234-97;$0.10
68HC12;Motorola;M68HC1201234;$3.50
```

Example

```
string OrderCodes[];
if (fileread(OrderCodes, "ordercodes") > 0) {
   if (lookup(OrderCodes, "", "Code", ';')) {
      schematic(SCH) {
        SCH.parts(P) {
          string OrderCode;
          // both following statements do exactly the same:
          OrderCode = lookup(OrderCodes, P.device.name, "Code", ';');
          OrderCode = lookup(OrderCodes, P.device.name, 2, ';');
          }
        }
      }
   else
      dlgMessageBox("Missing 'Code' field in file 'ordercodes');
   }
```

palette()

Function

Returns color palette information.

Syntax

`int palette(int index[, int type]);`

Returns

The `palette` function returns an integer ARGB value in the form 0xaarrggbb, or the type of the currently used palette (depending on the value of `index`).

The `palette` function returns the ARGB value of the color with the given `index` (which may be in the range 0..PALETTE_ENTRIES-1). If `type` is not given (or is `-1`) the palette assigned to the current editor window will be used. Otherwise `type` specifies which color palette to use (PALETTE_BLACK, PALETTE_WHITE or PALETTE_COLORED).

The special value `-1` for `index` makes the function return the type of the palette that is currently in use by the editor window.

If either `index` or `type` is out of range, an error message will be given and the ULP will be terminated.

Constants

PALETTE_TYPES	the number of palette types (3)
PALETTE_BLACK	the black background palette (0)
PALETTE_WHITE	the white background palette (1)
PALETTE_COLORED	the colored background palette (2)
PALETTE_ENTRIES	the number of colors per palette (64)

sleep()

Function

Sleeps number of `seconds`.

Syntax

```
void sleep(int seconds);
```

See also time()

The `sleep` function delays the execution of an ULP program for number of `seconds`.

sort()

Function

Sorts an array or a set of arrays.

Syntax

```
void sort(int number, array1[, array2,...]);
```

The `sort` function either directly sorts a given `array1`, or it sorts a set of arrays (starting with `array2`), in which case `array1` is supposed to be an array of **int**, which will be used as a pointer array.

In any case, the `number` argument defines the number of items in the array(s).

Sorting a single array

If the `sort` function is called with one single array, that array will be sorted directly, as in the following example:

```
string A[];
int n = 0;
```

```
A[n++] = "World";
A[n++] = "Hello";
A[n++] = "The truth is out there...";
sort(n, A);
for (int i = 0; i < n; ++i)
    printf(A[i]);
```

Sorting a set of arrays

If the `sort` function is called with more than one array, the first array must be an array of **int**, while all of the other arrays may be of any array type and hold the data to be sorted. The following example illustrates how the first array will be used as a pointer:

```
numeric string Nets[], Parts[], Instances[], Pins[];
int n = 0;
int index[];
schematic(S) {
  S.nets(N) N.pinrefs(P) {
    Nets[n] = N.name;
    Parts[n] = P.part.name;
    Instances[n] = P.instance.name;
    Pins[n] = P.pin.name;
    ++n;
    }
  sort(n, index, Nets, Parts, Instances, Pins);
  for (int i = 0; i < n; ++i)
      printf("%-8s %-8s %-8s %-8s\n",
             Nets[index[i]], Parts[index[i]],
             Instances[index[i]], Pins[index[i]]);
  }
```

The idea behind this is that one net can have several pins connected to it, and in a netlist you might want to have the net names sorted, and within one net you also want the part names sorted and so on.

Note the use of the keyword `numeric` in the string arrays. This causes the strings to be sorted in a way that takes into account a numeric part at the end of the strings, which leads to IC1, IC2,... IC9, IC10 instead of the alphabetical order IC1, IC10, IC2,...IC9.

When sorting a set of arrays, the first (index) array must be of type `int` and need not be initialized. Any contents the index array might have before calling the `sort` function will be overwritten by the resulting index values.

status()

Function

Displays a status message in the status bar.

Syntax

```
void status(string message);
```

See also dlgMessageBox()

The `status` function displays the given `message` in the status bar of the editor window in which the ULP is running.

system()

Function

Executes an external program.

Syntax

```
int system(string command);
```

Returns

The `system` function returns the exit status of the command. This is typically `0` if everything was ok, and non-zero in case of an error.

The `system` function executes the external program given by the `command` string, and waits until the program ends.

Input/Output redirection

If the external program shall read its standard input from (or write its standard output to) a particular file, input/output needs to be redirected.

On **Linux** and **Mac OS X** this is done by simply adding a `'<'` or `'>'` to the command line, followed by the desired file name, as in

```
system("program < infile > outfile");
```

which runs `program` and makes it read from `infile` and write to `outfile`.

On **Windows** you have to explicitly run a command processor to do this, as in

```
system("cmd.exe /c program < infile > outfile");
```

(on DOS based Windows systems use `command.com` instead of `cmd.exe`).

Background execution

The `system` function waits until the given program has ended. This is useful for programs that only run for a few seconds, or completely take over the user's attention.

If an external program runs for a longer time, and you want the system call to return immediately, without waiting for the program to end, you can simply add an `'&'` to the command string under **Linux** and **Mac OS X**, as in

```
system("program &");
```

Under Windows you need to explicitly run a command processor to do this, as in

```
system("cmd.exe /c start program");
```

(on DOS based Windows systems use `command.com` instead of `cmd.exe`).

Example

```
int result = system("simulate -f filename");
```

This would call a simulation program, giving it a file which the ULP has just created. Note that `simulate` here is just an example, it is not part of the EAGLE package!

If you want to have control over what system commands are actually executed, you can write a wrapper function that prompts the user for confirmation before executing the command, like

```
int MySystem(string command)
{
  if (dlgMessageBox("!Ok to execute the following command?<p><tt>" + command +
"</tt>", "&Yes", "&No") == 0)
     return system(command);
  return -1;
}
int result = MySystem("simulate -f filename");
```

Unit Conversions

Function

Converts internal units.

Syntax

```
real u2inch(int n);
real u2mic(int n);
real u2mil(int n);
real u2mm(int n);
int inch2u(real n);
int mic2u(real n);
int mil2u(real n);
int mm2u(real n);
```

Returns

`u2inch` returns the value of `n` in *inch*.
`u2mic` returns the value of `n` in *microns* (1/1000mm).
`u2mil` returns the value of `n` in *mil* (1/1000inch).
`u2mm` returns the value of `n` in *millimeters*.
`inch2u` returns the value of `n` (which is in *inch*) as internal units.
`mic2u` returns the value of `n` (which is in *microns*) as internal units.
`mil2u` returns the value of `n` (which is in *mil*) as internal units.
`mm2u` returns the value of `n` (which is in *millimeters*) as internal units.

See also UL_GRID

EAGLE stores all coordinate and size values as `int` values with a resolution of 1/320000mm (0.003125µ). The above unit conversion functions can be used to convert these internal units to the desired measurement units, and vice versa.

Example

```
board(B) {
  B.elements(E) {
    printf("%s at (%f, %f)\n", E.name,
           u2mm(E.x), u2mm(E.y));
    }
  }
```

Network Functions

Network functions are used to access remote sites on the Internet.

The following network functions are available:

- neterror()
- netget()
- netpost()

neterror()

Function

Returns the error message of the most recent network function call.

Syntax

`string neterror(void);`

Returns

`neterror` returns a textual message describing the error that occurred in the most recent call to a network function.
If no error has occurred, the return value is an empty string.

See also netget, netpost

The `neterror` function should be called after any of the other network functions has returned a negative value, indicating that an error has occurred. The return value of `neterror` is a textual string that can be presented to the user.

For errors related to SSL connections (HTTPS) also consider the note in netget.

Example

```
string Result;
if (netget(Result, "http://www.cadsoft.de/cgi-bin/http-test?see=me&hear=them")
>= 0) {
   // process Result
   }
else
   dlgMessageBox(neterror());
```

netget()

Function

Performs a GET request on the network.

Syntax

`int netget(`*`dest`*`, string url[, int timeout]);`

Returns

`netget` returns the number of objects read from the network.

The actual meaning of the return value depends on the type of `dest`.

In case of an error, a negative value is returned and neterror() may be called to display an error message to the user.

See also netpost, neterror, fileread

The `netget` function sends the given `url` to the network and stores the result in the `dest` variable.

If no network activity has occurred for `timeout` seconds, the connection will be terminated. The default timeout is 20 seconds.

The `url` must contain the protocol to use (HTTP, HTTPS or FTP) and can contain name=value pairs of parameters, as in

```
http://www.cadsoft.de/cgi-bin/http-test?see=me&hear=them
ftp://ftp.cadsoft.de/eagle/userfiles/README
```

If a user id and password is required to access a remote site, these can be given as

```
https://userid:password@www.secret-site.com/...
```

If `dest` is a character array, the result will be treated as raw binary data and the return value reflects the number of bytes stored in the character array.

If `dest` is a string array, the result will be treated as text data (one line per array member) and the return value will be the number of lines stored in the string array. Newline characters will be stripped.

If `dest` is a string, the result will be stored in that string and the return value will be the length of the string. Note that in case of binary data the result is truncated at the first occurrence of a byte with the value 0x00.

If you need to use a proxy to access the Internet with HTTP or HTTPS, you can set that up in the "Configure" dialog under "Help/Check for Update" in the Control Panel.

SSL Connections

For SSL connections (request per HTTPS) certificates are necessary, which may miss or be expired on some systems. The connection fails then with according error message that you can query with `neterror()`.
With this error message it should be possible to install missing or update expired certificates and make the connection work this way. It depends on your system how to do this (in Windows e.g. via Control Panel/Internet Options etc.).

Example

```
string Result;
if (netget(Result, "http://www.cadsoft.de/cgi-bin/http-test?see=me&hear=them")
>= 0) {
   // process Result
   }
else
   dlgMessageBox(neterror());
```

netpost()

Function

Performs a POST request on the network.

Syntax

`int netpost(`*`dest`*`, string url, string data[, int timeout[, string content_type] ]);`

Returns

`netpost` returns the number of objects read from the network.
The actual meaning of the return value depends on the type of `dest`.
In case of an error, a negative value is returned and neterror() may be called to display an error message to the user.

See also netget, neterror, fileread

The `netpost` function sends the given `data` to the given `url` on the network and stores the result in the `dest` variable.
If no network activity has occurred for `timeout` seconds, the connection will be terminated. The default timeout is 20 seconds.
If `content_type` is given, it overwrites the default content type of `"text/html; charset=utf-8"`.

114

The `url` must contain the protocol to use (HTTP or HTTPS).

If a user id and password is required to access a remote site, these can be given as

`https://userid:password@www.secret-site.com/...`

If `dest` is a character array, the result will be treated as raw binary data and the return value reflects the number of bytes stored in the character array.

If `dest` is a string array, the result will be treated as text data (one line per array member) and the return value will be the number of lines stored in the string array. Newline characters will be stripped.

If `dest` is a string, the result will be stored in that string and the return value will be the length of the string. Note that in case of binary data the result is truncated at the first occurrence of a byte with the value 0x00.

If you need to use a proxy to access the Internet with HTTP or HTTPS, you can set that up in the "Configure" dialog under "Help/Check for Update" in the Control Panel.

If you should face problems related to SSL connections (HTTPS) consider the note in netget.

Example

```
string Data = "see=me\nhear=them";
string Result;
if (netpost(Result, "http://www.cadsoft.de/cgi-bin/http-test", Data) >= 0) {
   // process Result
   }
else
   dlgMessageBox(neterror());
```

Printing Functions

Printing functions are used to print formatted strings.

The following printing functions are available:

- printf()
- sprintf()

printf()

Function

Writes formatted output to a file.

Syntax

```
int printf(string format[, argument, ...]);
```

Returns

The `printf` function returns the number of characters written to the file that has been opened by the most recent output statement.

In case of an error, `printf` returns `-1`.

See also sprintf, output, fileerror

Format string

The format string controls how the arguments will be converted, formatted and printed. There must be exactly as many arguments as necessary for the format. The number and type of arguments will be checked against the format, and any mismatch will lead to an error message.

The format string contains two types of objects - *plain characters* and *format specifiers*:

- Plain characters are simply copied verbatim to the output
- Format specifiers fetch arguments from the argument list and apply formatting to them

Format specifiers

A format specifier has the following form:

```
% [flags] [width] [.prec] type
```

Each format specification begins with the percent character (%). After the % comes the following, in this order:

- an optional sequence of flag characters, `[flags]`
- an optional width specifier, `[width]`
- an optional precision specifier, `[.prec]`
- the conversion type character, `type`

Conversion type characters

d	**signed** decimal **int**
o	**unsigned** octal **int**
u	**unsigned** decimal **int**
x	**unsigned** hexadecimal **int** (with **a**, **b**,...)
X	**unsigned** hexadecimal **int** (with **A**, **B**,...)
f	**signed real** value of the form `[-]dddd.dddd`
e	**signed real** value of the form `[-]d.dddde[±]ddd`
E	same as `e`, but with **E** for exponent
g	**signed real** value in either `e` or `f` form, based on given value and precision
G	same as `g`, but with **E** for exponent if `e` format used

116

c single character
s character string
% the % character is printed

Flag characters

The following flag characters can appear in any order and combination.

"-" the formatted item is left-justified within the field; normally, items are right-justified
"+" a signed, positive item will always start with a plus character (+); normally, only negative items begin with a sign
" " a signed, positive item will always start with a space character; if both "+" and " " are specified, "+" overrides " "

Width specifiers

The width specifier sets the minimum field width for an output value.

Width is specified either directly, through a decimal digit string, or indirectly, through an asterisk (*). If you use an asterisk for the width specifier, the preceding argument (which must be an `int`) to the one being formatted (with this format specifier) determines the minimum output field width.

In no case does a nonexistent or small field width cause truncation of a field. If the result of a conversion is wider than the field width, the field is simply expanded to contain the conversion result.

n At least *n* characters are printed. If the output value has less than *n* characters, the output is padded with blanks (right-padded if "-" flag given, left-padded otherwise).
0*n* At least *n* characters are printed. If the output value has less than *n* characters, it is filled on the left with zeros.
* The argument list supplies the width specifier, which must precede the actual argument being formatted.

Precision specifiers

A precision specifier always begins with a period (.) to separate it from any preceding width specifier. Then, like width, precision is specified either directly through a decimal digit string, or indirectly, through an asterisk (*). If you use an asterisk for the precision specifier, the preceding argument (which must be an `int`) to the one being formatted (with this format specifier) determines the precision.

none Precision set to default.
.0 For `int` types, precision is set to default; for `real` types, no decimal point is printed.
.*n* *n* characters or *n* decimal places are printed. If the output value has more than *n* characters the output might be truncated or rounded (depending on the type character).
* The argument list supplies the precision specifier, which must precede the actual argument being formatted.

Default precision values

`douxX`	1
`eEf`	6
`gG`	all significant digits
`c`	no effect
`s`	print entire string

How precision specification (`.n`) affects conversion

`douxX`	.*n* specifies that at least *n* characters are printed. If the input argument has less than *n* digits, the output value is left-padded with zeros. If the input argument has more than *n* digits, the output value is **not** truncated.
`eEf`	.*n* specifies that *n* characters are printed after the decimal point, and the last digit printed is rounded.
`gG`	.*n* specifies that at most *n* significant digits are printed.
`c`	.*n* has no effect on the output.
`s`	.*n* specifies that no more than *n* characters are printed.

Binary zero characters

Unlike sprintf, the `printf` function can print binary zero characters (0x00).

```
char c = 0x00;
printf("%c", c);
```

Example

```
int i = 42;
real r = 3.14;
char c = 'A';
string s = "Hello";
printf("Integer: %8d\n", i);
printf("Hex:     %8X\n", i);
printf("Real:    %8f\n", r);
printf("Char:    %-8c\n", c);
printf("String:  %-8s\n", s);
```

sprintf()

Function

Writes formatted output into a string.

Syntax

`int sprintf(string result, string format[, argument, ...]);`

Returns

The `sprintf` function returns the number of characters written into the `result` string.

In case of an error, `sprintf` returns `-1`.

See also printf

Format string

See printf.

Binary zero characters

Note that `sprintf` can not return strings with embedded binary zero characters (0x00). If the resulting string contains a binary zero character, any characters following that zero character will be dropped. Use printf if you need to output binary data.

Example

```
string result;
int number = 42;
sprintf(result, "The number is %d", number);
```

String Functions

String functions are used to manipulate character strings.

The following string functions are available:

- strchr()
- strjoin()
- strlen()
- strlwr()
- strrchr()
- strrstr()
- strsplit()
- strstr()
- strsub()
- strtod()
- strtol()
- strupr()
- strxstr()

strchr()

Function

Scans a string for the first occurrence of a given character.

Syntax

`int strchr(string s, char c[, int index]);`

Returns

The `strchr` function returns the integer offset of the character in the string, or `-1` if the character does not occur in the string.

See also strrchr, strstr

If `index` is given, the search starts at that position. Negative values are counted from the end of the string.

Example

```
string s = "This is a string";
char c = 'a';
int pos = strchr(s, c);
if (pos >= 0)
   printf("The character %c is at position %d\n", c, pos);
else
   printf("The character was not found\n");
```

strjoin()

Function

Joins a string array to form a single string.

Syntax

`string strjoin(string array[], char separator);`

Returns

The `strjoin` function returns the combined entries of `array`.

See also strsplit, lookup, fileread

`strjoin` joins all entries in `array`, delimited by the given `separator` and returns the resulting string.

If `separator` is the newline character (`'\n'`) the resulting string will be terminated with a newline character. This is done to have a text file that consists of N lines (each of which is terminated with a newline) and is read in with the fileread() function and split into an array of N strings to be joined to the original string as read from the file.

Example

```
string a[] = { "Field 1", "Field 2", "Field 3" };
string s = strjoin(a, ':');
```

strlen()

Function

Calculates the length of a string.

Syntax

`int strlen(string s);`

Returns

The `strlen` function returns the number of characters in the string.

Example

```
string s = "This is a string";
int l = strlen(s);
printf("The string is %d characters long\n", l);
```

strlwr()

Function

Converts uppercase letters in a string to lowercase.

Syntax

`string strlwr(string s);`

Returns

The `strlwr` function returns the modified string. The original string (given as parameter) is not changed.

See also strupr, tolower

Example

```
string s = "This Is A String";
string r = strlwr(s);
printf("Prior to strlwr: %s - after strlwr: %s\n", s, r);
```

strrchr()

Function

Scans a string for the last occurrence of a given character.

Syntax

`int strrchr(string s, char c[, int index]);`

Returns

The `strrchr` function returns the integer offset of the character in the string, or `-1` if the character does not occur in the string.

See also strchr, strrstr

If `index` is given, the search starts at that position. Negative values are counted from the end of the string.

Example

```
string s = "This is a string";
char c = 'a';
int pos = strrchr(s, c);
if (pos >= 0)
   printf("The character %c is at position %d\n", c, pos);
else
   printf("The character was not found\n");
```

strrstr()

Function

Scans a string for the last occurrence of a given substring.

Syntax

`int strrstr(string s1, string s2[, int index]);`

Returns

The `strrstr` function returns the integer offset of the first character of s2 in s1, or `-1` if the substring does not occur in the string.

See also strstr, strrchr

If `index` is given, the search starts at that position. Negative values are counted from the end of the string.

Example

```
string s1 = "This is a string", s2 = "is a";
int pos = strrstr(s1, s2);
if (pos >= 0)
   printf("The substring starts at %d\n", pos);
else
   printf("The substring was not found\n");
```

strsplit()

Function

Splits a string into separate fields.

Syntax

`int strsplit(string &array[], string s, char separator);`

Returns

The `strsplit` function returns the number of entries copied into `array`.

See also strjoin, lookup, fileread

`strsplit` splits the string `s` at the given `separator` and stores the resulting fields in the `array`.

If `separator` is the newline character (`'\n'`) the last field will be silently dropped if it is empty. This is done to have a text file that consists of N lines (each of which is terminated with a newline) and is read in with the fileread() function to be split into an array of N strings. With any other `separator` an empty field at the end of the string will count, so `"a:b:c:"` will result in 4 fields, the last of which is empty.

Example

```
string a[];
int n = strsplit(a, "Field 1:Field 2:Field 3", ':');
```

strstr()

Function

Scans a string for the first occurrence of a given substring.

Syntax

`int strstr(string s1, string s2[, int index]);`

Returns

The `strstr` function returns the integer offset of the first character of s2 in s1, or `-1` if the substring does not occur in the string.

See also strrstr, strchr, strxstr

If `index` is given, the search starts at that position. Negative values are counted from the end of the string.

Example

```
string s1 = "This is a string", s2 = "is a";
int pos = strstr(s1, s2);
if (pos >= 0)
   printf("The substring starts at %d\n", pos);
else
   printf("The substring was not found\n");
```

strsub()

Function

Extracts a substring from a string.

Syntax

```
string strsub(string s, int start[, int length]);
```

Returns

The `strsub` function returns the substring indicated by the `start` and `length` value.

The value for `length` must be positive, otherwise an empty string will be returned. If `length` is ommitted, the rest of the string (beginning at `start`) is returned.

If `start` points to a position outside the string, an empty string is returned.

Example

```
string s = "This is a string";
string t = strsub(s, 4, 7);
printf("The extracted substring is: %s\n", t);
```

strtod()

Function

Converts a string to a real value.

Syntax

```
real strtod(string s);
```

Returns

The `strtod` function returns the numerical representation of the given string as a `real` value. Conversion ends at the first character that does not fit into the format of a real constant. If an error occurs during conversion of the string `0.0` will be returned.

See also strtol

Example

```
string s = "3.1415";
real r = strtod(s);
printf("The value is %f\n", r);
```

strtol()

Function

Converts a string to an integer value.

Syntax

```
int strtol(string s);
```

Returns

The `strtol` function returns the numerical representation of the given string as an `int` value. Conversion ends at the first character that does not fit into the format of an integer constant. If an error occurs during conversion of the string `0` will be returned.

See also strtod

Example

```
string s = "1234";
int i = strtol(s);
printf("The value is %d\n", i);
```

strupr()

Function

Converts lowercase letters in a string to uppercase.

Syntax

```
string strupr(string s);
```

Returns

The `strupr` function returns the modified string. The original string (given as parameter) is not changed.

See also strlwr, toupper

Example

```
string s = "This Is A String";
string r = strupr(s);
printf("Prior to strupr: %s - after strupr: %s\n", s, r);
```

strxstr()

Function

Scans a string for the first occurrence of a given regular expression.

Syntax

```
int strxstr(string s1, string s2[, int index[, int &length]]);
```

Returns

The `strxstr` function returns the integer offset of the substring in s1 that matches the regular expression in s2, or `-1` if the regular expression does not match in the string.

See also strstr, strchr, strrstr

If `index` is given, the search starts at that position. Negative values are counted from the end of the string.

If `length` is given, the actual length of the matching substring is returned in that variable.

Regular expressions allow you to find a pattern within a text string. For instance, the regular expression "i.*a" would find a sequence of characters that starts with an 'i', followed by any character ('.') any number of times ('*'), and ends with an 'a'. It would match on "is a" as well as "is this a" or "ia".
Details on regular expressions can be found, for instance, in the book *Mastering Regular Expressions* by Jeffrey E. F. Friedl.

Example

```
string s1 = "This is a string", s2 = "i.*a";
int len = 0;
int pos = strxstr(s1, s2, 0, len);
if (pos >= 0)
   printf("The substring starts at %d and is %d charcaters long\n", pos, len);
else
   printf("The substring was not found\n");
```

Time Functions

Time functions are used to get and process time and date information.

The following time functions are available:

- sleep()
- t2day()
- t2dayofweek()
- t2hour()
- t2minute()
- t2month()
- t2second()
- t2string()
- t2year()
- time()
- timems()

time()

Function

Gets the current system time.

Syntax

```
int time(void);
```

Returns

The `time` function returns the current system time as the number of seconds elapsed since a system dependent reference date.

See also Time Conversions, filetime, timems()

Example

```
int CurrentTime = time();
```

timems()

Function

Gets the number of milliseconds since the start of the ULP.

Syntax

```
int timems(void);
```

Returns

The `timems` function returns the number of milliseconds since the start of the ULP.

After 86400000 milliseconds (i.e. every 24 hours), the value starts at 0 again.

See also time

Example

```
int elapsed = timems();
```

Time Conversions

Function

Convert a time value to day, month, year etc.

Syntax

```
int t2day(int t);
int t2dayofweek(int t);
int t2hour(int t);
int t2minute(int t);
int t2month(int t);
int t2second(int t);
int t2year(int t);

string t2string(int t[, string format]);
```

Returns

`t2day` returns the day of the month (`1`..`31`)

`t2dayofweek` returns the day of the week (`0`=sunday..`6`)

`t2hour` returns the hour (`0`..`23`)
`t2minute` returns the minute (`0`..`59`)
`t2month` returns the month (`0`..`11`)
`t2second` returns the second (`0`..`59`)
`t2year` returns the year (including century!)
`t2string` returns a formatted string containing date and time

See also time

The `t2string` function without the optional `format` parameter converts the given time `t` into a country specific string in local time.

If `t2string` is called with a `format` string, that format is used to determine what the result should look like.

The following expressions can be used in a `format` string:

d	the day as a number without a leading zero (1 to 31)
dd	the day as a number with a leading zero (01 to 31)
ddd	the abbreviated localized day name (e.g. "Mon" to "Sun")
dddd	the long localized day name (e.g. "Monday" to "Sunday")
M	the month as a number without a leading zero (1-12)
MM	the month as a number with a leading zero (01-12)
MMM	the abbreviated localized month name (e.g. "Jan" to "Dec")
MMMM	the long localized month name (e.g. "January" to "December")
yy	the year as a two digit number (00-99)
yyyy	the year as a four digit number
h	the hour without a leading zero (0 to 23 or 1 to 12 if AM/PM display)
hh	the hour with a leading zero (00 to 23 or 01 to 12 if AM/PM display)
m	the minute without a leading zero (0 to 59)
mm	the minute with a leading zero (00 to 59)
s	the second without a leading zero (0 to 59)
ss	the second with a leading zero (00 to 59)
z	the milliseconds without leading zeros (always 0, since the given time only has a one second resolution)
zzz	the milliseconds with leading zeros (always 000, since the given time only has a one second resolution)
AP	use AM/PM display (*AP* will be replaced by either "AM" or "PM")
ap	use am/pm display (*ap* will be replaced by either "am" or "pm")
U	display the given time as UTC (must be the first character; default is local time)

All other characters will be copied "as is". Any sequence of characters that are enclosed in singlequotes will be treated as text and not be used as an expression. Two consecutive single quotes ('') are replaced by a single quote in the output.

Example

```
int t = time();
printf("It is now %02d:%02d:%02d\n",
```

128

```
       t2hour(t), t2minute(t), t2second(t));
printf("ISO time is %s\n", t2string(t, "Uyyyy-MM-dd hh:mm:ss"));
```

Object Functions

Object functions are used to access common information about objects.

The following object functions are available:

- clrgroup()
- ingroup()
- setgroup()
- setvariant()
- variant()

clrgroup()

Function
Clears the group flags of an object.
Syntax
```
void clrgroup(object);
```

See also ingroup(), setgroup(), GROUP command

The `clrgroup()` function clears the group flags of the given object, so that it is no longer part of the previously defined group.

When applied to an object that contains other objects (like a UL_BOARD or UL_NET) the group flags of all contained objects are cleared recursively, but with analogous limitations like for setgroup().

Example

```
board(B) {
  B.elements(E)
    clrgroup(E);
  }
```

ingroup()

Function
Checks whether an object is in the group.
Syntax
```
int ingroup(object);
```

Returns

The `ingroup` function returns a non-zero value if the given object is in the group.

See also clrgroup(), setgroup(), GROUP command

If a group has been defined in the editor, the `ingroup()` function can be used to check whether a particular object is part of the group.

Objects with a single coordinate that are individually selectable in the current drawing (like UL_TEXT, UL_VIA, UL_CIRCLE etc.) return a non-zero value in a call to `ingroup()` if that coordinate is within the defined group.

A UL_WIRE returns 0, 1, 2 or 3, depending on whether none, the first, the second or both of its end points are in the group.

A UL_RECTANGLE and UL_FRAME returns a non-zero value if one or more of its corners are in the group. The value has bit 0 set for the upper right corner, bit 1 for the upper left, bit 2 for the bottom left, and bit 3 for the bottom right corner.

Higher ranking objects that have no coordinates (UL_NET, UL_SEGMENT, UL_SIGNAL, UL_POLYGON) or that are actually not available as drawing objects (UL_SHEET, UL_DEVICESET, UL_SYMBOL, UL_PACKAGE), return a non-zero value if one or more of the objects within them are in the group. For details on the object hierarchies see Object Types.
UL_CONTACTREF and UL_PINREF, though not having coordinates of their own, return a non-zero value if the referenced UL_CONTACT or UL_PIN, respectively, is within the group.
For other not selectable objects like UL_GRID, UL_VARIANT or wires of a UL_TEXT or UL_FRAME object, the behaviour of `ingroup()` is undefined and therefore should not be used.

Identifying the context menu object

If the ULP is started from a context menu the selected object can be accessed by the group mechansim. A one element group is made from the selected object. So it can be identified with `ingroup()`. (see also SET and RUN).

Example

```
output("group.txt") {
  board(B) {
    B.elements(E) {
      if (ingroup(E))
         printf("Element %s is in the group\n", E.name);
      }
    }
  }
```

setgroup()

Function

Sets the group flags of an object.

Syntax

```
void setgroup(object[, int flags]);
```

See also clrgroup(), ingroup(), GROUP command

The `setgroup()` function sets the group flags of the given object, so that it becomes part of the group.

If no `flags` are given, the object is added to the group as a whole (i.e. all of its selection points, in case it has more than one).

If `flags` has a non-zero value, only the group flags of the given points of the object are set. For a UL_WIRE this means that `'1'` sets the group flag of the first point, `'2'` that of the second point, and `'3'` sets both. Any previously set group flags remain unchanged by a call to `setgroup()`.

When applied to an object that contains other objects (like a UL_BOARD or UL_NET) the group flags of all contained objects are set recursively with following limitations:
It's not the case for UL_LIBRARY and UL_SCHEMATIC. Subordinate objects that are not selectable or not inidividually selectable are not flagged (e.g. UL_GRID or UL_VARIANT objects or wires of UL_TEXT or UL_FRAME objects).
For details on the object hierarchies see Object Types.

Example

```
board(B) {
  B.elements(E)
    setgroup(E);
  }
```

setvariant()

Function

Sets the current assembly variant.

Syntax

```
int setvariant(string name);
```

See also variant(), UL_VARIANTDEF, VARIANT command

The `setvariant()` function sets the current assembly variant to the one given by `name`. This can be used to loop through all of the parts and "see" their data exactly as defined in the given variant.

`name` must reference a valid assembly variant that is contained in the current drawing.

This function returns a non-zero value if the given assembly variant exists, zero otherwise.

The assembly variant that has been set by a call to `setvariant()` is only active until the User Language Program returns. After that, the variant in the drawing will be the same as before the start of the ULP.

Setting the assembly variant in a board is only possible if the consistent schematic is loaded.

Example

```
if (setvariant("My variant")) {
   // do something ...
else
   // error: unknown variant
```

variant()

Function

Query the current assembly variant.

Syntax

```
string variant(void);
```

See also setvariant(), UL_VARIANTDEF, VARIANT command

The `variant()` function returns the name of the current assembly variant. If no variant is currently selected, the empty string (`''`) is returned.

Example

```
string CurrentVariant = variant();
```

XML Functions

XML functions are used to process XML (*Extensible Markup Language*) data.

The following XML functions are available:

- xmlattribute()
- xmlattributes()
- xmlelement()
- xmlelements()
- xmltags()
- xmltext()

xmlattribute(), xmlattributes()

Function

Extract the attributes of an XML tag.

Syntax

```
string xmlattribute(string xml, string tag, string attribute);
int xmlattributes(string &array[], string xml, string tag);
```

See also xmlelement(), xmltags(), xmltext()

The `xmlattribute` function returns the value of the given `attribute` from the given `tag` within the given `xml` code. If an attribute appears more than once in the same tag, the value of its last occurrence is taken.

The `xmlattributes` function stores the names of all attributes from the given `tag` within the given `xml` code in the `array` and returns the number of attributes found. The order is not necessarily the same like in the given `xml` code. If an attribute appears more than once in the same tag, its name appears only once in the `array`.

The `tag` is given in the form of a *path*.

If the given `xml` code contains an error, the result of any XML function is empty, and a warning dialog is presented to the user, giving information about where in the ULP and XML code the error occurred. Note that the line and column number within the XML code refers to the actual string given to this function as the `xml` parameter.

Example

```
// XML contains the following data:
<root>
  <body abc="def" xyz="123">
    ...
  </body>
</root>
//
string s[];
int n = xmlattributes(s, XML, "root/body");
Result: { "abc", "xyz" }
string s = xmlattribute(XML, "root/body", "xyz");
Result: "123"
```

xmlelement(), xmlelements()

Function

Extract elements from an XML code.

Syntax

```
string xmlelement(string xml, string tag);
```

```
int xmlelements(string &array[], string xml, string tag);
```

See also xmltags(), xmlattribute(), xmltext()

The `xmlelement` function returns the complete XML element of the given `tag` within the given `xml` code. The result still contains the element's outer XML tag, and can thus be used for further processing with the other XML functions. Any whitespace within plain text parts of the element is retained. The overall formatting of the XML tags within the element and the order of element attributes may be different than the original `xml` code, though.
If there is more than one occurrence of `tag` within `xml`, the first one will be returned. Use `xmlelements` if you want to get all occurrences.

The `xmlelements` function works just like `xmlelement`, but returns all occurrences of elements with the given `tag`. The return value is the number of elements stored in the `array`.

The `tag` is given in the form of a *path*.

If the given `xml` code contains an error, the result of any XML function is empty, and a warning dialog is presented to the user, giving information about where in the ULP and XML code the error occurred. Note that the line and column number within the XML code refers to the actual string given to this function as the `xml` parameter.

Example

```
// XML contains the following data:
<root>
  <body>
    <contents>
      <string>Some text 1</string>
      <any>anything 1</any>
    </contents>
    <contents>
      <string>Some text 2</string>
      <any>anything 2</any>
    </contents>
    <appendix>
      <string>Some text 3</string>
    </appendix>
  </body>
</root>
//
string s = xmlelement(XML, "root/body/appendix");
Result: " <appendix>\n  <string>Some text 3</string>\n </appendix>\n"
string s[];
int n = xmlelements(s, XML, "root/body/contents");
Result: { " <contents>\n  <string>Some text 1</string>\n  <any>anything
1</any>\n </contents>\n",
          " <contents>\n  <string>Some text 2</string>\n  <any>anything
2</any>\n </contents>\n"
        }
```

xmltags()

Function

Extract the list of tag names within an XML code.

Syntax

```
int xmltags(string &array[], string xml, string tag);
```

See also xmlelement(), xmlattribute(), xmltext()

The `xmltags` function returns the names of all the tags on the top level of the given `tag` within the given `xml` code. The return value is the number of tag names stored in the `array`.

Each tag name is returned only once, even if it appears several times in the XML code.

The `tag` is given in the form of a *path*.

If the given `xml` code contains an error, the result of any XML function is empty, and a warning dialog is presented to the user, giving information about where in the ULP and XML code the error occurred. Note that the line and column number within the XML code refers to the actual string given to this function as the `xml` parameter.

Example

```
// XML contains the following data:
<root>
  <body>
    <contents>
      <string>Some text 1</string>
      <any>anything 1</any>
    </contents>
    <contents>
      <string>Some text 2</string>
      <any>anything 2</any>
    </contents>
    <appendix>
      <string>Some text 3</string>
    </appendix>
  </body>
</root>
//
string s[];
int n = xmltags(s, XML, "root/body");
Result: { "contents", "appendix" }
int n = xmltags(s, XML, "");
Result: "root"
```

xmltext()

Function

Extract the textual data of an XML element.

Syntax

```
string xmltext(string xml, string tag);
```

See also xmlelement(), xmlattribute(), xmltags()

The `xmltext` function returns the textual data from the given `tag` within the given `xml` code.

Any tags within the text are stripped, whitespace (including newline characters) is retained.

The `tag` is given in the form of a *path*.

If the given `xml` code contains an error, the result of any XML function is empty, and a warning dialog is presented to the user, giving information about where in the ULP and XML code the error occurred. Note that the line and column number within the XML code refers to the actual string given to this function as the `xml` parameter.

Example

```
// XML contains the following data:
<root>
  <body>
    Some <b>text</b>.
  </body>
</root>
//
string s = xmltext(XML, "root/body");
Result: "\n    Some text.\n  "
```

Builtin Statements

Builtin statements are generally used to open a certain context in which data structures or files can be accessed.

The general syntax of a builtin statement is

```
name(parameters) statement
```

where `name` is the name of the builtin statement, `parameters` stands for one or more parameters, and `statement` is the code that will be executed inside the context opened by the builtin statement.

Note that `statement` can be a compound statement, as in

```
board(B) {
  B.elements(E) printf("Element: %s\n", E.name);
  B.Signals(S)  printf("Signal: %s\n", S.name);
  }
```

The following builtin statements are available:

136

- board()
- deviceset()
- library()
- module()
- output()
- package()
- schematic()
- sheet()
- symbol()

board()

Function

Opens a board context.

Syntax

```
board(identifier) statement
```

See also schematic, library

The `board` statement opens a board context if the current editor window contains a board drawing. A variable of type UL_BOARD is created and is given the name indicated by `identifier`.

Once the board context is successfully opened and a board variable has been created, the `statement` is executed. Within the scope of the `statement` the board variable can be accessed to retrieve further data from the board.

If the current editor window does not contain a board drawing, an error message is given and the ULP is terminated.

Check if there is a board

By using the `board` statement without an argument you can check if the current editor window contains a board drawing. In that case, `board` behaves like an integer constant, returning `1` if there is a board drawing in the current editor window, and `0` otherwise.

Accessing board from a schematic

If the current editor window contains a schematic drawing, you can still access that schematic's board by preceding the `board` statement with the prefix `project`, as in

```
project.board(B) { ... }
```

This will open a board context regardless whether the current editor window contains a board or a schematic drawing. However, there must be an editor window containing that board somewhere on the desktop!

Example

```
if (board)
   board(B) {
     B.elements(E)
       printf("Element: %s\n", E.name);
     }
```

deviceset()

Function

Opens a device set context.

Syntax

`deviceset(identifier) statement`

See also package, symbol, library

The `deviceset` statement opens a device set context if the current editor window contains a device drawing. A variable of type UL_DEVICESET is created and is given the name indicated by `identifier`.

Once the device set context is successfully opened and a device set variable has been created, the `statement` is executed. Within the scope of the `statement` the device set variable can be accessed to retrieve further data from the device set.

If the current editor window does not contain a device drawing, an error message is given and the ULP is terminated.

Check if there is a device set

By using the `deviceset` statement without an argument you can check if the current editor window contains a device drawing. In that case, `deviceset` behaves like an integer constant, returning `1` if there is a device drawing in the current editor window, and `0` otherwise.

Example

```
if (deviceset)
   deviceset(D) {
     D.gates(G)
       printf("Gate: %s\n", G.name);
     }
```

library()

Function

Opens a library context.

Syntax

`library(identifier) statement`

See also board, schematic, deviceset, package, symbol

The `library` statement opens a library context if the current editor window contains a library drawing. A variable of type UL_LIBRARY is created and is given the name indicated by `identifier`.

Once the library context is successfully opened and a library variable has been created, the `statement` is executed. Within the scope of the `statement` the library variable can be accessed to retrieve further data from the library.

If the current editor window does not contain a library drawing, an error message is given and the ULP is terminated.

Check if there is a library

By using the `library` statement without an argument you can check if the current editor window contains a library drawing. In that case, `library` behaves like an integer constant, returning `1` if there is a library drawing in the current editor window, and `0` otherwise.

Example

```
if (library)
   library(L) {
     L.devices(D)
       printf("Device: %s\n", D.name);
     }
```

module()

Function

Opens a module context.

Syntax

`module(identifier) statement`

See also board, library, schematic, sheet

#The `module` statement opens a module context if the current editor# #window contains a module drawing. A variable of type# The `module` statement opens a module context if in the editor window currently a module drawing is edited. A variable of type UL_MODULE is created and is given the name indicated by `identifier`.

Once the module context is successfully opened and a module variable has been created, the `statement` is executed. Within the scope of the `statement` the module variable can be accessed to retrieve further data from the module.

#If the current editor window does not contain a module drawing, an error# #message is given and the ULP is terminated.# If in the editor window currently no module drawing is edited, an error message is given and the ULP is terminated.

Check if there is a module

By using the `module` statement without an argument you can check #if the current editor window contains a module drawing. In that case,# if in the editor window currently a module drawing is edited. In that case, `module` behaves like an integer constant, returning `1` if there is a module drawing in the current editor window, and `0` otherwise.

Example

```
if (module)
   module(M) {
     printf("Module: %s\n", M.name);
     }
```

output()

Function

Opens an output file for subsequent printf() calls.

Syntax

`output(string filename[, string mode]) statement`

See also printf, fileerror

The `output` statement opens a file with the given `filename` and `mode` for output through subsequent printf() calls. If the file has been successfully opened, the `statement` is executed, and after that the file is closed.

If the file cannot be opened, an error message is given and execution of the ULP is terminated.

By default the output file is written into the **Project** directory.

File Modes

The `mode` parameter defines how the output file is to be opened. If no `mode` parameter is given, the default is "wt".

a append to an existing file, or create a new file if it does not exist
w create a new file (overwriting an existing file)
t open file in text mode
b open file in binary mode
D delete this file when ending the EAGLE session (only works together with w)
F force using this file name (normally *.brd, *.sch and *.lbr are rejected)

Mode characters may appear in any order and combination. However, only the last one of a and w or t and b, respectively, is significant. For example a mode of "abtw" would open a file for textual write, which would be the same as "wt".

Nested Output statements

output statements can be nested, as long as there are enough file handles available, and provided that no two active output statements access the **same** file.

Example

```
void PrintText(string s)
{
  printf("This also goes into the file: %s\n", s);
}
output("file.txt", "wt") {
  printf("Directly printed\n");
  PrintText("via function call");
  }
```

package()

Function

Opens a package context.

Syntax

```
package(identifier) statement
```

See also library, deviceset, symbol

The package statement opens a package context if the current editor window contains a package drawing. A variable of type UL_PACKAGE is created and is given the name indicated by identifier.

Once the package context is successfully opened and a package variable has been created, the statement is executed. Within the scope of the statement the package variable can be accessed to retrieve further data from the package.

If the current editor window does not contain a package drawing, an error message is given and the ULP is terminated.

Check if there is a package

By using the `package` statement without an argument you can check if the current editor window contains a package drawing. In that case, `package` behaves like an integer constant, returning `1` if there is a package drawing in the current editor window, and `0` otherwise.

Example

```
if (package)
   package(P) {
     P.contacts(C)
       printf("Contact: %s\n", C.name);
     }
```

schematic()

Function

Opens a schematic context.

Syntax

`schematic(identifier) statement`

See also board, library, module, sheet

The `schematic` statement opens a schematic context if the current editor window contains a schematic drawing. A variable of type UL_SCHEMATIC is created and is given the name indicated by `identifier`.

Once the schematic context is successfully opened and a schematic variable has been created, the `statement` is executed. Within the scope of the `statement` the schematic variable can be accessed to retrieve further data from the schematic.

If the current editor window does not contain a schematic drawing, an error message is given and the ULP is terminated.

Check if there is a schematic

By using the `schematic` statement without an argument you can check if the current editor window contains a schematic drawing. In that case, `schematic` behaves like an integer constant, returning `1` if there is a schematic drawing in the current editor window, and `0` otherwise.

Accessing schematic from a board

If the current editor window contains a board drawing, you can still access that board's schematic by preceding the `schematic` statement with the prefix `project`, as in

```
project.schematic(S) { ... }
```

This will open a schematic context regardless whether the current editor window contains a schematic or a board drawing. However, there must be an editor window containing that schematic somewhere on the desktop!

Access the current Sheet

Use the `sheet` statement to directly access the currently loaded sheet.

Access the current Module

Use the `module` statement to directly access the currently edited module.

Example

```
if (schematic)
   schematic(S) {
     S.parts(P)
       printf("Part: %s\n", P.name);
     }
```

sheet()

Function

Opens a sheet context.

Syntax

```
sheet(identifier) statement
```

See also schematic

The `sheet` statement opens a sheet context if the current editor window contains a sheet drawing. A variable of type UL_SHEET is created and is given the name indicated by `identifier`.

Once the sheet context is successfully opened and a sheet variable has been created, the `statement` is executed. Within the scope of the `statement` the sheet variable can be accessed to retrieve further data from the sheet.

If the current editor window does not contain a sheet drawing, an error message is given and the ULP is terminated.

Check if there is a sheet

By using the `sheet` statement without an argument you can check if the current editor window contains a sheet drawing. In that case, `sheet` behaves like an integer constant, returning `1` if there is a sheet drawing in the current editor window, and `0` otherwise.

Example

```
if (sheet)
   sheet(S) {
     S.instances(I)
       printf("Instance: %s\n", I.name);
     }
```

symbol()

Function

Opens a symbol context.

Syntax

`symbol(identifier) statement`

See also library, deviceset, package

The `symbol` statement opens a symbol context if the current editor window contains a symbol drawing. A variable of type UL_SYMBOL is created and is given the name indicated by `identifier`.

Once the symbol context is successfully opened and a symbol variable has been created, the `statement` is executed. Within the scope of the `statement` the symbol variable can be accessed to retrieve further data from the symbol.

If the current editor window does not contain a symbol drawing, an error message is given and the ULP is terminated.

Check if there is a symbol

By using the `symbol` statement without an argument you can check if the current editor window contains a symbol drawing. In that case, `symbol` behaves like an integer constant, returning `1` if there is a symbol drawing in the current editor window, and `0` otherwise.

Example

```
if (symbol)
   symbol(S) {
     S.pins(P)
       printf("Pin: %s\n", P.name);
```

```
}
```

Dialogs

User Language Dialogs allow you to define your own frontend to a User Language Program.

The following sections describe User Language Dialogs in detail:

Predefined Dialogs	describes the ready to use standard dialogs
Dialog Objects	defines the objects that can be used in a dialog
Layout Information	explains how to define the location of objects within a dialog
Dialog Functions	describes special functions for use with dialogs
A Complete Example	shows a complete ULP with a data entry dialog

Predefined Dialogs

Predefined Dialogs implement the typical standard dialogs that are frequently used for selecting file names or issuing error messages.

The following predefined dialogs are available:

- dlgDirectory()
- dlgFileOpen()
- dlgFileSave()
- dlgMessageBox()

See Dialog Objects for information on how to define your own complex user dialogs.

dlgDirectory()

Function

Displays a directory dialog.

Syntax

`string dlgDirectory(string Title[, string Start])`

Returns

The `dlgDirectory` function returns the full pathname of the selected directory.
If the user has canceled the dialog, the result will be an empty string.

See also dlgFileOpen

The `dlgDirectory` function displays a directory dialog from which the user can select a directory.

`Title` will be used as the dialog's title.

If `Start` is not empty, it will be used as the starting point for the `dlgDirectory`.

Example

```
string dirName;
dirName = dlgDirectory("Select a directory", "");
```

dlgFileOpen(), dlgFileSave()

Function

Displays a file dialog.

Syntax

```
string dlgFileOpen(string Title[, string Start[, string
Filter]])
string dlgFileSave(string Title[, string Start[, string
Filter]])
```

Returns

The `dlgFileOpen` and `dlgFileSave` functions return the full pathname of the selected file.
If the user has canceled the dialog, the result will be an empty string.

See also dlgDirectory

The `dlgFileOpen` and `dlgFileSave` functions display a file dialog from which the user can select a file.

`Title` will be used as the dialog's title.

If `Start` is not empty, it will be used as the starting point for the file dialog. Otherwise the current directory will be used.

Only files matching `Filter` will be displayed. If `Filter` is empty, all files will be displayed.

`Filter` can be either a simple wildcard (as in `"*.brd"`), a list of wildcards (as in `"*.bmp *.jpg"`) or may even contain descriptive text, as in `"Bitmap files (*.bmp)"`. If the "File type" combo box of the file dialog shall contain several entries, they have to be separated by double semicolons, as in
`"Bitmap files (*.bmp);;Other images (*.jpg *.png)"`.

Example

```
string fileName;
fileName = dlgFileOpen("Select a file", "", "*.brd");
```

dlgMessageBox()

Function

Displays a message box.

Syntax

`int dlgMessageBox(string Message[, *button_list*])`

Returns

The `dlgMessageBox` function returns the index of the button the user has selected. The first button in `button_list` has index `0`.

See also status()

The `dlgMessageBox` function displays the given `Message` in a modal dialog and waits until the user selects one of the buttons defined in `button_list`.

If `Message` contains any HTML tags, the characters '<', '>' and '&' must be given as "<", ">" and "&", respectively, if they shall be displayed as such.

`button_list` is an optional list of comma separated strings, which defines the set of buttons that will be displayed at the bottom of the message box.
A maximum of three buttons can be defined. If no `button_list` is given, it defaults to `"OK"`.

The first button in `button_list` will become the default button (which will be selected if the user hits ENTER), and the last button in the list will become the "cancel button", which is selected if the user hits ESCape or closes the message box. You can make a different button the default button by starting its name with a `'+'`, and you can make a different button the cancel button by starting its name with a `'-'`. To start a button text with an actual `'+'` or `'-'` it has to be escaped.

If a button text contains an `'&'`, the character following the ampersand will become a hotkey, and when the user hits the corresponding key, that button will be selected. To have an actual `'&'` character in the text it has to be escaped.

The message box can be given an icon by setting the first character of `Message` to

- `';'` - for an *Information*
- `'!'` - for a *Warning*
- `':'` - for an *Error*

If, however, the `Message` shall begin with one of these characters, it has to be escaped.

On **Mac OS X** only the character `':'` will actually result in showing an icon. All others are ignored.

Example

```
if (dlgMessageBox("!Are you sure?", "&Yes", "&No") == 0) {
   // let's do it!
   }
```

Dialog Objects

A User Language Dialog is built from the following *Dialog Objects*:

dlgCell	a grid cell context
dlgCheckBox	a checkbox
dlgComboBox	a combo box selection field
dlgDialog	the basic container of any dialog
dlgGridLayout	a grid based layout context
dlgGroup	a group field
dlgHBoxLayout	a horizontal box layout context
dlgIntEdit	an integer entry field
dlgLabel	a text label
dlgListBox	a list box
dlgListView	a list view
dlgPushButton	a push button
dlgRadioButton	a radio button
dlgRealEdit	a real entry field
dlgSpacing	a layout spacing object
dlgSpinBox	a spin box selection field
dlgStretch	a layout stretch object
dlgStringEdit	a string entry field
dlgTabPage	a tab page
dlgTabWidget	a tab page container
dlgTextEdit	a text entry field
dlgTextView	a text viewer field
dlgVBoxLayout	a vertical box layout context

dlgCell

Function

Defines a cell location within a grid layout context.

Syntax

```
dlgCell(int row, int column[, int row2, int column2])
statement
```

See also dlgGridLayout, dlgHBoxLayout, dlgVBoxLayout, Layout Information, A Complete Example

The `dlgCell` statement defines the location of a cell within a grid layout context.

The row and column indexes start at 0, so the upper left cell has the index (0, 0).

With two parameters the dialog object defined by `statement` will be placed in the single cell addresses by `row` and `column`. With four parameters the dialog object will span over all cells from `row`/`column` to `row2`/`column2`.

148

By default a `dlgCell` contains a dlgHBoxLayout, so if the cell contains more than one dialog object, they will be placed next to each other horizontally.

Example

```
string Text;
dlgGridLayout {
  dlgCell(0, 0) dlgLabel("Cell 0,0");
  dlgCell(1, 2, 4, 7) dlgTextEdit(Text);
  }
```

dlgCheckBox

Function

Defines a checkbox.

Syntax

`dlgCheckBox(string Text, int &Checked) [ statement ]`

See also dlgRadioButton, dlgGroup, Layout Information, A Complete Example

The `dlgCheckBox` statement defines a check box with the given `Text`.

If `Text` contains an `'&'`, the character following the ampersand will become a hotkey, and when the user hits `Alt+hotkey`, the checkbox will be toggled. To have an actual `'&'` character in the text it has to be escaped.

`dlgCheckBox` is mainly used within a dlgGroup, but can also be used otherwise.
All check boxes within the same dialog must have **different** `Checked` variables!

If the user checks a `dlgCheckBox`, the associated `Checked` variable is set to `1`, otherwise it is set to `0`. The initial value of `Checked` defines whether a checkbox is initially checked. If `Checked` is not equal to `0`, the checkbox is initially checked.

The optional `statement` is executed every time the `dlgCheckBox` is toggled.

Example

```
int mirror = 0;
int rotate = 1;
int flip   = 0;
dlgGroup("Orientation") {
  dlgCheckBox("&Mirror", mirror);
  dlgCheckBox("&Rotate", rotate);
  dlgCheckBox("&Flip", flip);
  }
```

dlgComboBox

Function

Defines a combo box selection field.

Syntax

`dlgComboBox(string array[], int &Selected) [ statement ]`

See also dlgListBox, dlgLabel, Layout Information, A Complete Example

The `dlgComboBox` statement defines a combo box selection field with the contents of the given `array`.

`Selected` reflects the index of the selected combo box entry. The first entry has index `0`.

Each element of `array` defines the contents of one entry in the combo box. None of the strings in `array` may be empty (if there is an empty string, all strings after and including that one will be dropped).

The optional `statement` is executed whenever the selection in the `dlgComboBox` changes. Before the `statement` is executed, all variables that have been used with dialog objects are updated to their current values, and any changes made to these variables inside the `statement` will be reflected in the dialog when the statement returns.

If the initial value of `Selected` is outside the range of the `array` indexes, it is set to `0`.

Example

```
string Colors[] = { "red", "green", "blue", "yellow" };
int Selected = 2; // initially selects "blue"
dlgComboBox(Colors, Selected) dlgMessageBox("You have selected " +
Colors[Selected]);
```

dlgDialog

Function

Executes a User Language Dialog.

Syntax

`int dlgDialog(string Title) block ;`

Returns

The `dlgDialog` function returns an integer value that can be given a user defined meaning through a call to the `dlgAccept()` function.
If the dialog is simply closed, the return value will be `-1`.

See also dlgGridLayout, dlgHBoxLayout, dlgVBoxLayout, dlgAccept, dlgReset, dlgReject, A Complete Example

The `dlgDialog` function executes the dialog defined by `block`. This is the only dialog object that actually is a User Language builtin function. Therefore it can be used anywhere where a function call is allowed.

The `block` normally contains only other dialog objects, but it is also possible to use other User Language statements, for example to conditionally add objects to the dialog (see the second example below).

By default a `dlgDialog` contains a dlgVBoxLayout, so a simple dialog doesn't have to worry about the layout.

A `dlgDialog` should at some point contain a call to the `dlgAccept()` function in order to allow the user to close the dialog and accept its contents.

If all you need is a simple message box or file dialog you might want to use one of the Predefined Dialogs instead.

Examples

```
int Result = dlgDialog("Hello") {
  dlgLabel("Hello world");
  dlgPushButton("+OK") dlgAccept();
  };
int haveButton = 1;
dlgDialog("Test") {
  dlgLabel("Start");
  if (haveButton)
     dlgPushButton("Here") dlgAccept();
  };
```

dlgGridLayout

Function

Opens a grid layout context.

Syntax

`dlgGridLayout` *`statement`*

See also dlgCell, dlgHBoxLayout, dlgVBoxLayout, Layout Information, A Complete Example

The `dlgGridLayout` statement opens a grid layout context.

The only dialog object that can be used directly in `statement` is dlgCell, which defines the location of a particular dialog object within the grid layout.

The row and column indexes start at 0, so the upper left cell has the index (0, 0).
The number of rows and columns is automatically extended according to the location of dialog objects that are defined within the grid layout context, so you don't have to explicitly define the number of rows and columns.

Example

```
dlgGridLayout {
  dlgCell(0, 0) dlgLabel("Row 0/Col 0");
  dlgCell(1, 0) dlgLabel("Row 1/Col 0");
  dlgCell(0, 1) dlgLabel("Row 0/Col 1");
  dlgCell(1, 1) dlgLabel("Row 1/Col 1");
  }
```

dlgGroup

Function

Defines a group field.

Syntax

`dlgGroup(string Title)` *`statement`*

See also dlgCheckBox, dlgRadioButton, Layout Information, A Complete Example

The `dlgGroup` statement defines a group with the given `Title`.

By default a `dlgGroup` contains a dlgVBoxLayout, so a simple group doesn't have to worry about the layout.

`dlgGroup` is mainly used to contain a set of radio buttons or check boxes, but may as well contain any other objects in its `statement`.
Radio buttons within a `dlgGroup` are numbered starting with `0`.

Example

```
int align = 1;
dlgGroup("Alignment") {
  dlgRadioButton("&Top", align);
  dlgRadioButton("&Center", align);
  dlgRadioButton("&Bottom", align);
  }
```

dlgHBoxLayout

Function

Opens a horizontal box layout context.

Syntax

`dlgHBoxLayout` *`statement`*

See also dlgGridLayout, dlgVBoxLayout, Layout Information, A Complete Example

The `dlgHBoxLayout` statement opens a horizontal box layout context for the given `statement`.

Example

```
dlgHBoxLayout {
  dlgLabel("Box 1");
  dlgLabel("Box 2");
  dlgLabel("Box 3");
  }
```

dlgIntEdit

Function

Defines an integer entry field.

Syntax

```
dlgIntEdit(int &Value, int Min, int Max)
```

See also dlgRealEdit, dlgStringEdit, dlgLabel, Layout Information, A Complete Example

The `dlgIntEdit` statement defines an integer entry field with the given `Value`.

If `Value` is initially outside the range defined by `Min` and `Max` it will be limited to these values.

Example

```
int Value = 42;
dlgHBoxLayout {
  dlgLabel("Enter a &Number between 0 and 99");
  dlgIntEdit(Value, 0, 99);
  }
```

dlgLabel

Function

Defines a text label.

Syntax

```
dlgLabel(string Text [, int Update])
```

See also Layout Information, A Complete Example, dlgRedisplay()

The `dlgLabel` statement defines a label with the given `Text`.

`Text` can be either a string literal, as in `"Hello"`, or a string variable.

If `Text` contains any HTML tags, the characters '<', '>' and '&' must be given as "<", ">" and "&", respectively, if they shall be displayed as such.

External hyperlinks in the `Text` will be opened with the appropriate application program.

If the `Update` parameter is not `0` and `Text` is a string variable, its contents can be modified in the statement of, e.g., a dlgPushButton, and the label will be automatically updated. This, of course, is only useful if Text is a dedicated string variable (not, e.g., the loop variable of a for statement).

If Text contains an '&', and the object following the label can have the keyboard focus, the character following the ampersand will become a hotkey, and when the user hits Alt+hotkey, the focus will go to the object that was defined immediately following the dlgLabel. To have an actual '&' character in the text it has to be escaped.

Example

```
string OS = "Windows";
dlgHBoxLayout {
  dlgLabel(OS, 1);
  dlgPushButton("&Change OS") { OS = "Linux"; }
  }
```

dlgListBox

Function

Defines a list box selection field.

Syntax

dlgListBox(string array[], int &Selected) [*statement*]

See also dlgComboBox, dlgListView, dlgSelectionChanged, dlgLabel, Layout Information, A Complete Example

The dlgListBox statement defines a list box selection field with the contents of the given array.

Selected reflects the index of the selected list box entry. The first entry has index 0.

Each element of array defines the contents of one line in the list box. None of the strings in array may be empty (if there is an empty string, all strings after and including that one will be dropped).

The optional statement is executed whenever the user double clicks on an entry of the dlgListBox (see dlgSelectionChanged for information on how to have the statement called when only the selection in the list changes).
Before the statement is executed, all variables that have been used with dialog objects are updated to their current values, and any changes made to these variables inside the statement will be reflected in the dialog when the statement returns.

If the initial value of Selected is outside the range of the array indexes, no entry will be selected.

Example

```
string Colors[] = { "red", "green", "blue", "yellow" };
int Selected = 2; // initially selects "blue"
dlgListBox(Colors, Selected) dlgMessageBox("You have selected " +
Colors[Selected]);
```

dlgListView

Function

Defines a multi column list view selection field.

Syntax

```
dlgListView(string Headers, string array[], int &Selected[,
int &Sort]) [ statement ]
```

See also dlgListBox, dlgSelectionChanged, dlgLabel, Layout Information, A Complete Example

The `dlgListView` statement defines a multi column list view selection field with the contents of the given `array`.

`Headers` is the tab separated list of column headers.

`Selected` reflects the index of the selected list view entry in the `array` (the sequence in which the entries are actually displayed may be different, because the contents of a `dlgListView` can be sorted by the various columns). The first entry has index `0`.
If no particular entry shall be initially selected, `Selected` should be initialized to `-1`. If it is set to `-2`, the first item according to the current sort column is made current.

`Sort` defines which column should be used to sort the list view. The leftmost column is numbered `1`. The sign of this parameter defines the direction in which to sort (positive values sort in ascending order). If `Sort` is `0` or outside the valid number of columns, no sorting will be done. The returned value of `Sort` reflects the column and sort mode selected by the user by clicking on the list column headers. By default `dlgListView` sorts by the first column, in ascending order.

Each element of `array` defines the contents of one line in the list view, and must contain tab separated values. If there are fewer values in an element of `array` than there are entries in the `Headers` string the remaining fields will be empty. If there are more values in an element of `array` than there are entries in the `Headers` string the superfluous elements will be silently dropped. None of the strings in `array` may be empty (if there is an empty string, all strings after and including that one will be dropped).

A list entry that contains line feeds (`'\n'`) will be displayed in several lines accordingly.

The optional `statement` is executed whenever the user double clicks on an entry of the `dlgListView` (see dlgSelectionChanged for information on how to have the `statement` called

when only the selection in the list changes).
Before the `statement` is executed, all variables that have been used with dialog objects are updated to their current values, and any changes made to these variables inside the `statement` will be reflected in the dialog when the statement returns.

If the initial value of `Selected` is outside the range of the `array` indexes, no entry will be selected.

If `Headers` is an empty string, the first element of the `array` is used as the header string. Consequently the index of the first entry is then `1`.

The contents of a `dlgListView` can be sorted by any column by clicking on that column's header. Columns can also be swapped by "click&dragging" a column header. Note that none of these changes will have any effect on the contents of the `array`. If the contents shall be sorted alphanumerically a `numeric string[]` array can be used.

Example

```
string Colors[] = { "red\tThe color RED", "green\tThe color GREEN", "blue\tThe
color BLUE" };
int Selected = 0; // initially selects "red"
dlgListView("Name\tDescription", Colors, Selected) dlgMessageBox("You have
selected " + Colors[Selected]);
```

dlgPushButton

Function

Defines a push button.

Syntax

`dlgPushButton(string Text)` *`statement`*

See also Layout Information, Dialog Functions, A Complete Example

The `dlgPushButton` statement defines a push button with the given `Text`.

If `Text` contains an `'&'`, the character following the ampersand will become a hotkey, and when the user hits `Alt+hotkey`, the button will be selected. To have an actual `'&'` character in the text it has to be escaped.

If `Text` starts with a `'+'` character, this button will become the default button, which will be selected if the user hits ENTER.
If `Text` starts with a `'-'` character, this button will become the cancel button, which will be selected if the user closes the dialog.
CAUTION: Make sure that the `statement` of such a marked cancel button contains a call to dlgReject()! Otherwise the user may be unable to close the dialog at all!

To have an actual `'+'` or `'-'` character as the first character of the text it has to be escaped.

If the user selects a `dlgPushButton`, the given `statement` is executed.
Before the `statement` is executed, all variables that have been used with dialog objects are updated to their current values, and any changes made to these variables inside the `statement` will be reflected in the dialog when the statement returns.

Example

```
int defaultWidth = 10;
int defaultHeight = 20;
int width = 5;
int height = 7;
dlgPushButton("&Reset defaults") {
  width = defaultWidth;
  height = defaultHeight;
  }
dlgPushButton("+&Accept") dlgAccept();
dlgPushButton("-Cancel") { if (dlgMessageBox("Are you sure?", "Yes", "No") == 0)
dlgReject(); }
```

dlgRadioButton

Function

Defines a radio button.

Syntax

`dlgRadioButton(string Text, int &Selected) [ statement ]`

See also dlgCheckBox, dlgGroup, Layout Information, A Complete Example

The `dlgRadioButton` statement defines a radio button with the given `Text`.

If `Text` contains an `'&'`, the character following the ampersand will become a hotkey, and when the user hits `Alt+hotkey`, the button will be selected. To have an actual `'&'` character in the text it has to be escaped.

`dlgRadioButton` can only be used within a dlgGroup.
All radio buttons within the same group must use the **same** `Selected` variable!

If the user selects a `dlgRadioButton`, the index of that button within the `dlgGroup` is stored in the `Selected` variable.
The initial value of `Selected` defines which radio button is initially selected. If `Selected` is outside the valid range for this group, no radio button will be selected. In order to get the correct radio button selection, `Selected` must be set **before** the first `dlgRadioButton` is defined, and must not be modified between adding subsequent radio buttons. Otherwise it is undefined which (if any) radio button will be selected.

The optional `statement` is executed every time the `dlgRadioButton` is selected.

Example

```
int align = 1;
dlgGroup("Alignment") {
  dlgRadioButton("&Top", align);
  dlgRadioButton("&Center", align);
  dlgRadioButton("&Bottom", align);
  }
```

dlgRealEdit

Function

Defines a real entry field.

Syntax

`dlgRealEdit(real &Value, real Min, real Max)`

See also dlgIntEdit, dlgStringEdit, dlgLabel, Layout Information, A Complete Example

The `dlgRealEdit` statement defines a real entry field with the given `Value`.

If `Value` is initially outside the range defined by `Min` and `Max` it will be limited to these values.

Example

```
real Value = 1.4142;
dlgHBoxLayout {
  dlgLabel("Enter a &Number between 0 and 99");
  dlgRealEdit(Value, 0.0, 99.0);
  }
```

dlgSpacing

Function

Defines additional space in a box layout context.

Syntax

`dlgSpacing(int Size)`

See also dlgHBoxLayout, dlgVBoxLayout, dlgStretch, Layout Information, A Complete Example

The `dlgSpacing` statement defines additional space in a vertical or horizontal box layout context.

`Size` defines the number of pixels of the additional space.

Example

```
dlgVBoxLayout {
  dlgLabel("Label 1");
  dlgSpacing(40);
  dlgLabel("Label 2");
  }
```

dlgSpinBox

Function

Defines a spin box selection field.

Syntax

```
dlgSpinBox(int &Value, int Min, int Max)
```

See also dlgIntEdit, dlgLabel, Layout Information, A Complete Example

The `dlgSpinBox` statement defines a spin box entry field with the given `Value`.

If `Value` is initially outside the range defined by `Min` and `Max` it will be limited to these values.

Example

```
int Value = 42;
dlgHBoxLayout {
  dlgLabel("&Select value");
  dlgSpinBox(Value, 0, 99);
  }
```

dlgStretch

Function

Defines an empty stretchable space in a box layout context.

Syntax

```
dlgStretch(int Factor)
```

See also dlgHBoxLayout, dlgVBoxLayout, dlgSpacing, Layout Information, A Complete Example

The `dlgStretch` statement defines an empty stretchable space in a vertical or horizontal box layout context.

`Factor` defines the stretch factor of the space.

Example

```
dlgHBoxLayout {
  dlgStretch(1);
  dlgPushButton("+OK")    { dlgAccept(); };
```

```
  dlgPushButton("Cancel") { dlgReject(); };
  }
```

dlgStringEdit

Function

Defines a string entry field.

Syntax

`dlgStringEdit(string &Text[, string &History[][, int Size]])`

See also dlgRealEdit, dlgIntEdit, dlgTextEdit, dlgLabel, Layout Information, A Complete Example

The `dlgStringEdit` statement defines a one line text entry field with the given `Text`.

If `History` is given, the strings the user has entered over time are stored in that string array. The entry field then has a button that allows the user to select from previously entered strings. If a `Size` greater than zero is given, only at most that number of strings are stored in the array. If `History` contains data when the dialog is newly opened, that data will be used to initialize the history. The most recently entered user input is stored at index 0.
None of the strings in `History` may be empty (if there is an empty string, all strings after and including that one will be dropped).

Example

```
string Name = "Linus";
dlgHBoxLayout {
  dlgLabel("Enter &Name");
  dlgStringEdit(Name);
  }
```

dlgTabPage

Function

Defines a tab page.

Syntax

`dlgTabPage(string Title)` *`statement`*

See also dlgTabWidget, Layout Information, A Complete Example

The `dlgTabPage` statement defines a tab page with the given `Title` containing the given `statement`.

If `Title` contains an `'&'`, the character following the ampersand will become a hotkey, and when the user hits `Alt+hotkey`, this tab page will be opened. To have an actual `'&'` character in the text it has to be escaped.

160

Tab pages can only be used within a dlgTabWidget.

By default a `dlgTabPage` contains a dlgVBoxLayout, so a simple tab page doesn't have to worry about the layout.

Example

```
dlgTabWidget {
  dlgTabPage("Tab &1") {
    dlgLabel("This is page 1");
    }
  dlgTabPage("Tab &2") {
    dlgLabel("This is page 2");
    }
  }
```

dlgTabWidget

Function

Defines a container for tab pages.

Syntax

`dlgTabWidget` *`statement`*

See also dlgTabPage, Layout Information, A Complete Example

The `dlgTabWidget` statement defines a container for a set of tab pages.

`statement` must be a sequence of one or more dlgTabPage objects. There must be no other dialog objects in this sequence.

Example

```
dlgTabWidget {
  dlgTabPage("Tab &1") {
    dlgLabel("This is page 1");
    }
  dlgTabPage("Tab &2") {
    dlgLabel("This is page 2");
    }
  }
```

dlgTextEdit

Function

Defines a multiline text entry field.

Syntax

`dlgTextEdit(string &Text)`

See also dlgStringEdit, dlgTextView, dlgLabel, Layout Information, A Complete Example

The `dlgTextEdit` statement defines a multiline text entry field with the given `Text`.

The lines in the `Text` have to be delimited by a newline character (`'\n'`). Any whitespace characters at the end of the lines contained in `Text` will be removed, and upon return there will be no whitespace characters at the end of the lines. Empty lines at the end of the text will be removed entirely.

Example

```
string Text = "This is some text.\nLine 2\nLine 3";
dlgVBoxLayout {
  dlgLabel("&Edit the text");
  dlgTextEdit(Text);
  }
```

dlgTextView

Function

Defines a multiline text viewer field.

Syntax

```
dlgTextView(string Text)
dlgTextView(string Text, string &Link) statement
```

See also dlgTextEdit, dlgLabel, Layout Information, A Complete Example

The `dlgTextView` statement defines a multiline text viewer field with the given `Text`.

The `Text` may contain HTML tags.

External hyperlinks in the `Text` will be opened with the appropriate application program.

If `Link` is given and the `Text` contains hyperlinks, `statement` will be executed every time the user clicks on a hyperlink, with the value of `Link` set to whatever the `<a href=...>` tag defines as the value of *href*. If, after the execution of `statement`, the `Link` variable is not empty, the default handling of hyperlinks will take place. This is also the case if `Link` contains some text before dlgTextView is opened, which allows for an initial scrolling to a given position. If a `Link` is given, external hyperlinks will not be opened.

Example

```
string Text = "This is some text.\nLine 2\nLine 3";
dlgVBoxLayout {
  dlgLabel("&View the text");
  dlgTextView(Text);
  }
```

dlgVBoxLayout

Function

Opens a vertical box layout context.

Syntax

`dlgVBoxLayout` *`statement`*

See also dlgGridLayout, dlgHBoxLayout, Layout Information, A Complete Example

The `dlgVBoxLayout` statement opens a vertical box layout context for the given `statement`.

By default a dlgDialog contains a `dlgVBoxLayout`, so a simple dialog doesn't have to worry about the layout.

Example

```
dlgVBoxLayout {
  dlgLabel("Box 1");
  dlgLabel("Box 2");
  dlgLabel("Box 3");
  }
```

Layout Information

All objects within a User Language Dialog a placed inside a *layout context.*

Layout contexts can be either grid, horizontal or vertical.

Grid Layout Context

Objects in a grid layout context must specify the grid coordinates of the cell or cells into which they shall be placed. To place a text label at row 5, column 2, you would write

```
dlgGridLayout {
  dlgCell(5, 2) dlgLabel("Text");
  }
```

If the object shall span over more than one cell you need to specify the coordinates of the starting cell and the ending cell. To place a group that extends from row 1, column 2 up to row 3, column 5, you would write

```
dlgGridLayout {
  dlgCell(1, 2, 3, 5) dlgGroup("Title") {
    //...
    }
  }
```

Horizontal Layout Context

Objects in a horizontal layout context are placed left to right.

The special objects dlgStretch and dlgSpacing can be used to further refine the distribution of the available space.

To define two buttons that are pushed all the way to the right edge of the dialog, you would write

```
dlgHBoxLayout {
  dlgStretch(1);
  dlgPushButton("+OK")    dlgAccept();
  dlgPushButton("Cancel") dlgReject();
  }
```

Vertical Layout Context

Objects in a vertical layout context follow the same rules as those in a horizontal layout context, except that they are placed top to bottom.

Mixing Layout Contexts

Vertical, horizontal and grid layout contexts can be mixed to create the desired layout structure of a dialog. See the Complete Example for a demonstration of this.

Dialog Functions

The following functions can be used with User Language Dialogs:

dlgAccept()	closes the dialog and accepts its contents
dlgRedisplay()	immediately redisplays the dialog after changes to any values
dlgReset()	resets all dialog objects to their initial values
dlgReject()	closes the dialog and rejects its contents
dlgSelectionChanged()	tells whether the current selection in a dlgListView or dlgListBox has changed

dlgAccept()

Function

Closes the dialog and accepts its contents.

Syntax

```
void dlgAccept([ int Result ]);
```

See also dlgReject, dlgDialog, A Complete Example

The `dlgAccept` function causes the dlgDialog to be closed and return after the current statement sequence has been completed.

164

Any changes the user has made to the dialog values will be accepted and are copied into the variables that have been given when the dialog objects were defined.

The optional `Result` is the value that will be returned by the dialog. Typically this should be a positive integer value. If no value is given, it defaults to `1`.

Note that `dlgAccept()` does return to the normal program execution, so in a sequence like

```
dlgPushButton("OK") {
  dlgAccept();
  dlgMessageBox("Accepting!");
  }
```

the statement after `dlgAccept()` will still be executed!

Example

```
int Result = dlgDialog("Test") {
               dlgPushButton("+OK")    dlgAccept(42);
               dlgPushButton("Cancel") dlgReject();
               };
```

dlgRedisplay()

Function

Redisplays the dialog after changing values.

Syntax

`void dlgRedisplay(void);`

See also dlgReset, dlgDialog, A Complete Example

The `dlgRedisplay` function can be called to immediately refresh the dlgDialog after changes have been made to the variables used when defining the dialog objects.

You only need to call `dlgRedisplay()` if you want the dialog to be refreshed while still executing program code. In the example below the status is changed to "Running..." and `dlgRedisplay()` has to be called to make this change take effect before the "program action" is performed. After the final status change to "Finished." there is no need to call `dlgRedisplay()`, since all dialog objects are automatically updated after leaving the statement.

Example

```
string Status = "Idle";
int Result = dlgDialog("Test") {
               dlgLabel(Status, 1); // note the '1' to tell the label to be
updated!
               dlgPushButton("+OK")    dlgAccept(42);
               dlgPushButton("Cancel") dlgReject();
```

```
        dlgPushButton("Run") {
          Status = "Running...";
          dlgRedisplay();
          // some program action here...
          Status = "Finished.";
          }
        };
```

dlgReset()

Function

Resets all dialog objects to their initial values.

Syntax

`void dlgReset(void);`

See also dlgReject, dlgDialog, A Complete Example

The `dlgReset` function copies the initial values back into all dialog objects of the current dlgDialog.

Any changes the user has made to the dialog values will be discarded.

Calling `dlgReject()` implies a call to `dlgReset()`.

Example

```
int Number = 1;
int Result = dlgDialog("Test") {
               dlgIntEdit(Number);
               dlgPushButton("+OK")    dlgAccept(42);
               dlgPushButton("Cancel") dlgReject();
               dlgPushButton("Reset")  dlgReset();
               };
```

dlgReject()

Function

Closes the dialog and rejects its contents.

Syntax

`void dlgReject([ int Result ]);`

See also dlgAccept, dlgReset, dlgDialog, A Complete Example

The `dlgReject` function causes the dlgDialog to be closed and return after the current statement sequence has been completed.

Any changes the user has made to the dialog values will be discarded. The variables that have been given when the dialog objects were defined will be reset to their original values when the dialog returns.

The optional `Result` is the value that will be returned by the dialog. Typically this should be `0` or a negative integer value. If no value is given, it defaults to `0`.

Note that `dlgReject()` does return to the normal program execution, so in a sequence like

```
dlgPushButton("Cancel") {
  dlgReject();
  dlgMessageBox("Rejecting!");
  }
```

the statement after `dlgReject()` will still be executed!

Calling `dlgReject()` implies a call to `dlgReset()`.

Example

```
int Result = dlgDialog("Test") {
               dlgPushButton("+OK")    dlgAccept(42);
               dlgPushButton("Cancel") dlgReject();
               };
```

dlgSelectionChanged()

Function

Tells whether the current selection in a dlgListView or dlgListBox has changed.

Syntax

`int dlgSelectionChanged(void);`

Returns

The `dlgSelectionChanged` function returns a nonzero value if only the selection in the list has changed.

See also dlgListView, dlgListBox

The `dlgSelectionChanged` function can be used in a list context to determine whether the statement of the `dlgListView` or `dlgListBox` was called because the user double clicked on an item, or whether only the current selection in the list has changed.

If the statement of a `dlgListView` or `dlgListBox` doesn't contain any call to `dlgSelectionChanged`, that statement is only executed when the user double clicks on an item in the list. However, if a ULP needs to react on changes to the current selection in the list, it can call `dlgSelectionChanged` within the list's statement. This causes the statement to also be called if the current selection in the list changes.

If a list item is initially selected when the dialog is opened and the list's statement contains a call to `dlgSelectionChanged`, the statement is executed with `dlgSelectionChanged` returning true in order to indicate the initial change from "no selection" to an actual selection. Any later programmatical changes to the strings or the selection of the list will not trigger an automatic execution of the list's statement. This is important to remember in case the current list item controls another dialog object, for instance a `dlgTextView` that shows an extended representation of the currently selected item.

Example

```
string Colors[] = { "red\tThe color RED", "green\tThe color GREEN", "blue\tThe
color BLUE" };
int Selected = 0; // initially selects "red"
string MyColor;
dlgLabel(MyColor, 1);
dlgListView("Name\tDescription", Colors, Selected) {
  if (dlgSelectionChanged())
     MyColor = Colors[Selected];
  else
     dlgMessageBox("You have chosen " + Colors[Selected]);
  }
```

Escape Character

Some characters have special meanings in button or label texts, so they need to be *escaped* if they shall appear literally.

To do this you need to prepend the character with a *backslash*, as in

```
dlgLabel("Miller \\& Co.");
```

This will result in "Miller & Co." displayed in the dialog.

Note that there are actually **two** backslash characters here, since this line will first go through the User Language parser, which will strip the first backslash.

A Complete Example

Here's a complete example of a User Language Dialog.

```
int hor = 1;
int ver = 1;
string fileName;
int Result = dlgDialog("Enter Parameters") {
  dlgHBoxLayout {
    dlgStretch(1);
    dlgLabel("This is a simple dialog");
    dlgStretch(1);
    }
  dlgHBoxLayout {
    dlgGroup("Horizontal") {
      dlgRadioButton("&Top", hor);
```

```
      dlgRadioButton("&Center", hor);
      dlgRadioButton("&Bottom", hor);
      }
    dlgGroup("Vertical") {
      dlgRadioButton("&Left", ver);
      dlgRadioButton("C&enter", ver);
      dlgRadioButton("&Right", ver);
      }
    }
  dlgHBoxLayout {
    dlgLabel("File &name:");
    dlgStringEdit(fileName);
    dlgPushButton("Bro&wse") {
      fileName = dlgFileOpen("Select a file", fileName);
      }
    }
  dlgGridLayout {
    dlgCell(0, 0) dlgLabel("Row 0/Col 0");
    dlgCell(1, 0) dlgLabel("Row 1/Col 0");
    dlgCell(0, 1) dlgLabel("Row 0/Col 1");
    dlgCell(1, 1) dlgLabel("Row 1/Col 1");
    }
  dlgSpacing(10);
  dlgHBoxLayout {
    dlgStretch(1);
    dlgPushButton("+OK")    dlgAccept();
    dlgPushButton("Cancel") dlgReject();
    }
  };
```

Supported HTML tags

EAGLE supports a subset of the tags used to format HTML pages. This can be used to format the text of several User Language Dialog objects, in the `#usage` directive or in the description of library objects.

Text is considered to be HTML if the first line contains a tag. If this is not the case, and you want the text to be formatted, you need to enclose the entire text in the `<html>...</html>` tag.

The following table lists all supported HTML tags and their available attributes:

Tag	Description
<html>...</html>	An HTML document.
<html>...</html>	The body of an HTML document. It understands the following attribute • `bgcolor` - The background color, for example `bgcolor="yellow"` or `bgcolor="#0000FF"`. This attribute works only within a dlgTextView.
<h1>...</h1>	A top-level heading.
<h2>...</h2>	A sub-level heading.
<h3>...</h3>	A sub-sub-level heading.

<p>...</p>	A left-aligned paragraph. Adjust the alignment with the `align` attribute. Possible values are `left`, `right` and `center`.
<center>...</center>	A centered paragraph.
<blockquote>...</blockquote>	An indented paragraph, useful for quotes.
<ul>...</ul>	An un-ordered list. You can also pass a type argument to define the bullet style. The default is `type=disc`, other types are `circle` and `square`.
<ol>...</ol>	An ordered list. You can also pass a type argument to define the enumeration label style. The default is `type="1"`, other types are `"a"` and `"A"`.
<li>...</li>	A list item. This tag can only be used within the context of `ol` or `ul`.
<pre>...</pre>	For larger chunks of code. Whitespaces in the contents are preserved. For small bits of code, use the inline-style `code`.
<a>...</a>	An anchor or link. It understands the following attributes: • `href` - The reference target as in `<a href="target.html">...</a>`. You can also specify an additional anchor within the specified target document, for example `<a href="target.html#123">...</a>`. If you want to link to a local file that has a blank in its name, you need to prepend the file name with `file:`, as in `<a href="file:/path with blanks/target.html">...</a>`. • `name` - The anchor name, as in `<a name="123">...</a>`.
<em>...</em>	Emphasized (same as `<i>...</i>`).
<strong>...</strong>	Strong (same as `<b>...</b>`).
<i>...</i>	Italic font style.
<b>...</b>	Bold font style.
<u>...</u>	Underlined font style.
<big>...</big>	A larger font size.
<small>...</small>	A smaller font size.
<code>...</code>	Indicates Code. (same as `<tt>...</tt>`. For larger chunks of code, use the block-tag `pre`.
<tt>...</tt>	Typewriter font style.
<font>...</font>	Customizes the font size, family and text color. The tag understands the following attributes: • `color` - The text color, for example `color="red"` or `color="#FF0000"`. • `size` - The logical size of the font. Logical sizes 1 to 7 are supported. The value may either be absolute, for example `size=3`, or relative like `size=-2`. In the latter case, the sizes are simply added. • `face` - The family of the font, for example `face=times`.
<img...>	An image. This tag understands the following attributes:

- `src` - The image name, for example `<img src="image.png">`. The URL of the image may be external, as in `<img src="http://www.cadsoft.de/cslogo.gif">`.
- `width` - The width of the image. If the image does not fit to the specified size, it will be scaled automatically.
- `height` - The height of the image.
- `align` - Determines where the image is placed. Per default, an image is placed inline, just like a normal character. Specify `left` or `right` to place the image at the respective side.

<hr> A horizonal line.

 A line break.

<nobr>...</nobr> No break. Prevents word wrap.

<table>...</table> A table definition. The default table is frameless. Specify the boolean attribute `border` in order to get a frame. Other attributes are:

- `bgcolor` - The background color.
- `width` - The table width. This is either absolute in pixels or relative in percent of the column width, for example `width=80%`.
- `border` - The width of the table border. The default is 0 (= no border).
- `cellspacing` - Additional space around the table cells. The default is 2.
- `cellpadding` - Additional space around the contents of table cells. Default is 1.

<tr>...</tr> A table row. Can only be used within `table`. Understands the attribute

- `bgcolor` - The background color.

<td>...</td> A table data cell. Can only be used within `tr`. Understands the attributes

- `bgcolor` - The background color.
- `width` - The cell width. This is either absolute in pixels or relative in percent of the entire table width, for example `width=50%`.
- `colspan` - Defines how many columns this cell spans. The default is 1.
- `rowspan` - Defines how many rows this cell spans. The default is 1.
- `align` - Alignment, possible values are `left`, `right` and `center`. The default is left-aligned.

<th>...</th> A table header cell. Like `td` but defaults to center-alignment and a bold font.

<author>...</author> Marks the author of this text.

<dl>...</dl> A definition list.

<dt>...</dt> A definition tag. Can only be used within `dl`.

<dd>...</dd>	Definition data. Can only be used within `dl`.

Tag	**Meaning**
<	<
>	>
&	&
	non-breaking space
ä	ä
ö	ö
ü	ü
Ä	Ä
Ö	Ö
Ü	Ü
ß	ß
©	©
°	°
µ	µ
±	±
"	"

Index of Figures and Illustrations

Index of Tables

Alphabetical Index